In 1311, at the council of Vienne, William Durant the Younger (c. 1266–1330), the French bishop and count, demanded that general councils ought to meet every ten years in order to place effective limits on the papal plenitude of power because 'what touches all must be approved by all'.

This is the first systematic interpretation of William Durant's remarkable project to transfer supreme legislative authority from the papacy to general councils. It suggests that the conciliar theory has a more ambivalent complexion than is sometimes recognized. It confirms, on the one hand, that constitutional ideas were deeply embedded in the tradition of the church which enabled Durant to anticipate the council of Constance by more than a hundred years. On the other hand, Durant attributed an authority to ancient laws that overrode his republican ideas, sapped their vitality, and launched him on a pursuit of the true meaning of the law that could end only in his transformation into an historian and a reluctant champion of monarchy. William Durant the Younger's ideas thus help us to understand the origins of the conciliar theory and the transition from late medieval reform movements to early modern humanism and princely sovereignty.

*Cambridge studies in medieval life and thought*

# COUNCIL AND HIERARCHY

*Cambridge studies in medieval life and thought*
*Fourth series*

General Editor:
D. E. LUSCOMBE
*Professor of Medieval History, University of Sheffield*

Advisory Editors:
R. B. DOBSON
*Professor of Medieval History, University of Cambridge, and Fellow of Christ's College*

ROSAMOND MCKITTERICK
*Lecturer in History, University of Cambridge, and Fellow of Newnham College*

The series Cambridge Studies in Medieval Life and Thought was inaugurated by G. G. Coulton in 1921. Professor D. E. Luscombe now acts as General Editor of the Fourth Series, with Professor R. B. Dobson and Dr Rosamond McKitterick as Advisory Editors. The series brings together outstanding work by medieval scholars over a wide range of human endeavour extending from political economy to the history of ideas.

For a list of titles in the series, see end of book.

# COUNCIL AND HIERARCHY

## The Political Thought of William Durant the Younger

### CONSTANTIN FASOLT

*Associate Professor of History, University of Chicago*

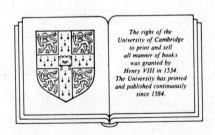

The right of the
University of Cambridge
to print and sell
all manner of books
was granted by
Henry VIII in 1534.
The University has printed
and published continuously
since 1584.

## CAMBRIDGE UNIVERSITY PRESS

CAMBRIDGE
NEW YORK    PORT CHESTER
MELBOURNE    SYDNEY

Published by the Press Syndicate of the University of Cambridge
The Pitt Building, Trumpington Street, Cambridge CB2 IRP
40 West 20th Street, New York, NY 10011, USA
10 Stamford Road, Oakleigh, Melbourne 3166, Australia

First published 1991

Printed in Great Britain at the University Press, Cambridge

*British Library cataloguing in publication data*
Fasolt, Constantin
Council and hierarchy: the political thought of William
Durant the Younger.
1. Christian church. Ecumenical councils, history
I. Title
262.5

*Library of Congress cataloguing in publication data*
Fasolt, Constantin, 1951–
Council and hierarchy: the political thought of William Durant
the Younger / Constantin Fasolt.
p.   cm. – (Cambridge studies in medieval life and thought:
4th ser.)
Revision of the author's thesis – Columbia University, 1981.
Includes bibliographical references.
ISBN 0 521 39285 3
1. Church and state – History.   2. Popes – Temporal power.
3. Durant, William, d. 1330   Contributions in political science.
I. Title.   II. Series.
JC513.F37   1991
322′.1′09 – dc20   90-1665   CIP

ISBN 0 521 39285 3 hardback

*To Svetlana*

Unser Ausgangspunkt ist der vom einzigen bleibenden und für uns möglichen Zentrum, vom duldenden, strebenden und handelnden Menschen, wie er ist und immer war und sein wird; daher unsere Betrachtung gewissermassen pathologisch sein wird.

Jacob Burckhardt

# CONTENTS

# Contents

# Contents

# FIGURES

# ACKNOWLEDGMENTS

The beginnings of this book go back to a paper written in the autumn of 1976 in John Mundy's seminar at Columbia University. It is a pleasure to acknowledge my gratitude to him. He suggested the topic; by correcting my Germanic meanderings with a mixture of painstaking impatience and sarcastic wit he taught me how to write passable English prose; he gave me a unique perspective on medieval history; and most of all he never hesitated to let me benefit from his acute intolerance for shallowness. If I have managed to commit myself in this book to less than the usual number of inanities it is in no small part thanks to him.

For taking a personal interest in my work and for the many kindnesses they have shown me over the years I am grateful to Paul Oskar Kristeller, Jürgen Miethke, and especially to my colleagues Julius Kirshner and Robert Bartlett, whose confidence sustained me at a critical time. Hubert Jedin passed away before this book was even half finished, but since he favoured me with his scholarship and his humanity, and since his enthusiasm was one of the reasons that persuaded me to go ahead with this book, I would like to acknowledge my indebtedness to him.

Malcolm Bean, Louis Pascoe, Eugene Rice, and Robert Somerville gave me their generous advice during the time when I was writing the dissertation out of which this book has grown. Robert Benson, Elizabeth Brown, Reinhard Elze, Marc Fumaroli, Stephan Kuttner, Domenico Maffei, Gert Melville, Quentin Skinner, Johannes Straub, and Joseph Strayer furnished me with specific bits and pieces of sometimes crucial information that I would otherwise have ignored. Marie-Thérèse d'Alverny, Sigmund Benker, F. Bernier, Martin Bertram, F. Bibolet, Bernhard Bischoff, Denise Bloch, Monique-Cécile Garand, Pierre Gasnault, Jean Glénisson, Hermann Goldbrunner, Neil Ker, Hélène Loyau, Adriana Marucchi, M. Morelli, Gilbert Ouy, A. Schönherr, the members of the

Institut de Recherche et d'Histoire des Textes, and the hundreds of librarians who responded to my request to check the unpublished inventories of their holdings helped me to obtain valuable information about the manuscripts of Durant's treatise. The Bibliothèque Nationale and the Bibliothèque Mazarine in Paris, the municipal libraries of Tours and Troyes, the Bayerische Staatsbibliothek in Munich, the library of the St. Nikolaus Hospital in Kues, the Zentralbibliothek in Zurich, the Biblioteca Nazionale Centrale in Rome, the Vatican Library, Butler Library of Columbia University, Widener Library of Harvard University, the Regenstein Library of the University of Chicago, and the Newberry Library in Chicago gave me access to their collections, answered my requests for information, and supplied me with microfilms of books and manuscripts. To all of these I am grateful for their help, without which it would have been impossible to write this book.

From 1981 to 1983 the Society of Fellows in the Humanities at Columbia University, under the guidance of William Theodore de Bary and the care of Loretta Nassar, gave me time to pursue my research in an academic setting animated by an incomparable blend of curiosity, hospitality, and liberality. My thanks for that go to all of its members and fellows. In 1986 the Institut für Europäische Geschichte in Mainz and its director Karl Otmar Freiherr von Aretin not only gave me a place to read and write in quiet, but also showed uncommon magnanimity in allowing me to pursue my interests at my own pace. Since 1983 the University of Chicago has supported my research both by granting me a leave of absence on very generous terms and by furnishing an exceptionally challenging intellectual environment. To all of these institutions and to the individuals of which they really consist I am grateful for their confidence in my work and for the assistance they have lent to its completion.

For helping me to refine the substance and the presentation of my argument I would like to thank the two anonymous readers who encouraged me to sharpen points of contention, Mary Van Steenbergh, who spent countless hours poring over my prose and suggested many improvements, cuts, and clarifications, David Reis, who checked the bibliography, and Brian Urbaszewski, who drew a beautiful map of the Gévaudan.

Finally, I am indebted to David Luscombe and Rosamond McKitterick for their close and thoughtful reading of my manu-

## Acknowledgments

script, to Jean Field for her thorough copy-editing, and to William Davies for his expeditious management of the publishing process.

# ABBREVIATIONS

| | |
|---|---|
| a. | *ante*; for Gratian's commentary preceding a canon |
| C. | *Causa*; subsection of Gratian's *Decretum*, part 2 |
| c. | *capitulum* or *canon* |
| C.I.Can. | *Corpus Iuris Canonici* |
| C.I.Civ. | *Corpus Iuris Civilis*. Eds. T. Mommsen, P. Krüger, and R. Scholl. 3 vols. (Berlin, 1872–95) |
| Clem. | Clement V, *Clementinae* |
| Cod. | *Codex Iustinianus* |
| COD | *Conciliorum Oecumenicorum Decreta* |
| D. | *Distinctio*; subsection of Gratian's *Decretum*, part 1 |
| DDC | *Dictionnaire de droit canonique* |
| De cons. | *De consecratione*; Gratian's *Decretum*, part 3 |
| De pen. | *De penitentia*; C.33 q.3 of Gratian's *Decretum* |
| DHGE | *Dictionnaire d'histoire et de géographie ecclésiastiques* |
| Dig. | *Digesta Iustiniani* |
| GC | *Gallia Christiana* |
| Ins. | *Institutiones* |
| LC | John XXII, *Lettres communes* |
| LS | John XXII, *Lettres secrètes* |
| MGH | *Monumenta Germaniae Historica* |
| Nov. | *Novellae* |
| Ordonnances | *Ordonnances des roys de France de la troisième race* |
| p. | *post*; for Gratian's commentary following a canon |
| PL | *Patrologia Latina* |
| q. | *quaestio*; subsection of the *causae* in Gratian's *Decretum*, part 2 |

xvii

| | |
|---|---|
| R–S | J. Roucaute and M. Saché, eds., *Lettres de Philippe-le-Bel relatives au pays de Gévaudan* |
| S. d. L. | Société d'Agriculture, Industrie, Sciences et Arts du Département de la Lozère. Also: Société des Lettres, Sciences et Arts du Département de la Lozère |
| *TMA* | William Durant the Younger, *Tractatus Maior* |
| *TMI* | William Durant the Younger, *Tractatus Minor* |
| Viollet | P. Viollet, 'Guillaume Durant le Jeune' |
| VI. | Boniface VIII, *Liber Sextus* |
| X. | Gregory IX, *Liber Extra* |

# MANUSCRIPT SIGLA

B      Vatican City, Biblioteca Apostolica Vaticana, ms. Barb. lat. 1487, fols. 313r–362r

C      Kues, St. Nikolaus Hospital, ms. 168, fols. 1r–95v

M      Munich, Bayerische Staatsbibliothek, clm. 6605, fols. 1r–69v

Ma      Paris, Bibliothèque Mazarine, ms. 1687, fols. 1r–82r

O      Vatican City, Biblioteca Apostolica Vaticana, ms. Ottob. lat. 823, fols. 23r–53r

P      Paris, Bibliothèque Nationale, ms. lat. 1443

R      Rome, Biblioteca Nazionale Centrale, Fondo Varia, ms. 1, fols. 85r–196v

Tr      Troyes, Bibliothèque Municipale, ms. 786, fols. 1r–179r

Tu      Tours, Bibliothèque Municipale, ms. 237

Z      Zurich, Zentralbibliothek, ms. S 2040, fols. 129r–141r

# INTRODUCTION

I have no doubt that there are some who will be irritated by my having at
such length and with such enthusiasm advanced an argument which in
reality may be not that important, not that indispensable, and even of no
use to life at all.                                                    Hermann Conring[1]

In 1311, at the council of Vienne, William Durant the Younger,
bishop of Mende and count of Gévaudan, demanded a reform of
the church 'in head and members' – a phrase that would reverberate throughout the later middle ages and which he was among the
first to introduce into public debate.[2] The centre-piece of this

---

[1] 'Non dubito, fore qui aegre laturi sint, ea prolixitate, atque illo studio actum esse de
argumento fortasse ponderis reapse non adeo magni, nec adeo necessarii, imo nullius
singularis ad vitam usus.' Hermann Conring, *De civili prudentia, Opera*, 3:281.

[2] 'Videretur deliberandum, si posset, per quam utile fore et necessarium quod ante omnia
corrigerentur et reformarentur illa que sunt in ecclesia dei corrigenda et reformanda tam
in capite quam in membris.' *TMA* 1.1, fol. 4rb. The opinion that William Durant the
Younger was actually the first to coin the phrase 'reform in head and members' is
expressed by McNeill, 'Emergence', pp. 298f.; Lecler, *Vienne*, p. 40; Lecler, *Le Pape ou le
concile?*, p. 49. But although Durant certainly helped to give it greater currency, Neiske,
'Reform oder Kodifizierung?', p. 74 n. 18, has discovered the same formula as early as
1289 in the letters of Nicholas IV, no. 1556 (5.IX.1289) and especially no. 1772
(10.XII.1289): 'Ad statum pacificum et tranquillum Cluniacensis ordinis paternis studiis
intendentes, quamplura statuta pro reformatione ipsius tam in capite quam in membris
edidimus.' It is surely noteworthy that the earliest known use of 'reform in head and
members' should be found in papal letters regarding a monastic order as intimately
linked to the rise of the medieval papacy as Cluny. The notion of reform in the middle
ages has been thoroughly investigated; Burdach, *Reformation, Renaissance, Humanismus*,
Ladner, *The Idea of Reform*, and Panofsky, *Renaissance and Renascences* are three basic,
classic, and complementary statements. More recent are Ladner, 'Terms and Ideas of
Renewal'; Constable, 'Renewal and Reform'; Benson, 'Political Renovatio'; and
Morrison, *The Mimetic Tradition of Reform*. On the vicissitudes of ecclesiastical reform in
the later middle ages Haller, *Papsttum und Kirchenreform* is still the single best study, to be
accompanied by works like Barraclough, *Papal Provisions*; Leff, *The Dissolution of the
Medieval Outlook*; Pascoe, *Jean Gerson*; Stump, 'Reform in Head and Members'; and
Stockmeier, 'Causa reformationis'. For an understanding of the objects of reform the
following four are especially useful: Murray, *Reason and Society*; Schwer, *Stand und
Ständeordnung*; Stutz, *Die Eigenkirche*; Schulte, *Der Adel und die deutsche Kirche*. A
perspective on the assimilation of reform by the laity is furnished by Strayer, 'The
Laicization of French and English Society' and Lagarde, *La Naissance de l'esprit laïque*.

reform was to consist of the transferral of the responsibility for the law of the church from the papacy to general councils, which would meet at ten-year intervals: 'Henceforth the church of Rome ought to enact no general laws unless a general council has been convoked, and such a council ought to be convoked every ten years.'[3] Lest anyone should think that the papacy would still be free to change existing laws by granting dispensations, Durant declared explicitly that the papacy was not to 'issue any dispensations, privileges, or exemptions contrary to the provident conciliar constitutions of the holy fathers unless a general council has been called.'[4] In support of these demands he invoked the famous principle that 'what touches all must, according to the rule of both canon law and civil law, be approved by all in common'.[5] Finally, in what was perhaps his most farsighted proposition, he suggested a kind of budgetary process that would have made the finances of the papacy dependent on its compliance with 'whatever may seem reasonable to the council'.[6] In sum, Durant wished to endow general councils with sufficient power to control the government of the church.

As far as we know, never before had anyone proposed such radical ideas. Of course, Durant's *démarche* was not entirely unprecedented. During the two centuries preceding the council of Vienne, canonists had already gone to considerable lengths in attempting to place effective limits on papal government. They had declared that the church had an immutable constitution, a 'state of the church' that no one, not even the pope, could change or abrogate, and they insisted that this state of the church was by no means limited to the faith but extended to the organization and government of the church as well – although its precise definition

---

[3] 'Item quod [Romana ecclesia] nulla iura generalia deinceps conderet nisi vocato concilio generali, quod de decennio in decennium vocaretur.' *TMA* 2.96 (3.27), fol. 59rb.

[4] '[Presidentes monarchie non] sine generali concilio *agant* [P] contra ea que sunt in conciliis a sanctis patribus provide constituta in dispensationibus, privilegiis, et exemptionibus, et aliis exercendis.' *TMA* 1.4, fol. 7ra.

[5] 'Illud quod omnes tangit secundum iuris utriusque regulam ab omnibus debeat communiter approbari.' *TMA* 1.4, fol. 7rb. Cf. VI.5.12 De reg. iuris 29.

[6] 'Item quod de bonis ecclesiasticarum personarum superabundantibus talis provisio fieret supradicte Romane ecclesie quod absque omni taxationis nota et infamia posset communiter et divisim honorabiliter vivere *et* [M] onera incumbentia supportare, proviso tamen quod ultra et contra predicta et alia que concilio rationabilia viderentur contra divinas et humanas leges non posset absque generali concilio habenas extendere plenitudinis potestatis.' *TMA* 2.96 (3.27) fol. 59rb.

was much in dispute.[7] They had discussed how a pope who violated the state of the church, especially by falling into heresy or by committing outrageous and notorious crimes, was to be judged and deposed, and most of them agreed that the responsibility for such action rested with general councils.[8] General councils thus played a crucial role in contemporary theories about the government and structure of the church. Attempts were sometimes made to turn these theories into practice: in the mid thirteenth century Emperor Frederick II had appealed to a general council against Pope Innocent IV, and King Philip IV had very recently lodged a similar appeal against Pope Boniface VIII.[9] Moreover, even apart from the crises associated with attacks on papal government by temporal rulers, councils had played a regular and important part in the government of the church. During the 200 years preceding the council of Vienne, six general councils met at an average of one council every thirty years – more frequently than in any comparable length of time before or after – and this activity was more than equalled by councils on the local level.[10] Indeed, in the 1280s the church of France had mounted a flurry of provincial and national councils designed to overturn the privileges that the papacy had granted to the mendicant orders, which the prelates of France regarded as a direct violation of their rights and which provoked them into clear statements both of their understanding of the state of the church and of their willingness to organize resistance to the papacy 'for the common good'.[11] Even without considering the councils convened by royal and urban governments, and even omitting Magna Carta, there can be little doubt that during the twelfth and thirteenth centuries conciliar activity intensified in both theory and practice to a degree unmatched either before or since. As Brian Tierney has put it, 'the roots of the conciliar

---

[7] On the concept of the 'state of the church' see the precisely focused investigations of Hackett, 'State of the Church', Congar, 'Status ecclesiae', and Post, 'Copyists' Errors', as well as more broadly conceived works like Tierney, *Foundations*, Tierney, *Origins of Papal Infallibility*, Pennington, *Pope and Bishops*, and Buisson, *Potestas und Caritas*.

[8] Tierney, *Foundations*; Tierney, 'Pope and Council'.

[9] See Kempf, 'Die Absetzung Friedrichs II.', Arquillière, 'L'Appel au concile', and now Becker, *Die Appellation vom Papst an ein Allgemeines Konzil*.

[10] It has been estimated, for example, that over one hundred councils met in France during the thirteenth century; Gaudemet, 'Aspects'.

[11] See Schleyer, *Anfänge des Gallikanismus*, Glorieux, 'Prélats français', Lagarde, 'La Philosophie sociale'.

tradition lie deeper in the past than has usually been supposed'.[12]

And yet William Durant the Younger's idea was radically new. If in the middle of a learned commentary on Gratian's *Decretum* a canonist reflected on the potential applications of a canon demanding that popes who fell into heresy be judged – that was one thing; it was quite different for a bishop to appear at a general council that had been convoked explicitly for the reform of the church and to ask the council publicly henceforth to prevent all popes, heretical or otherwise, from making law without convoking general councils. It was one thing for thirteenth-century canonists to analyse the relationship between a bishop and his cathedral chapter in terms of Roman legal theories of corporation; but it was quite different for Durant to subject the papal plenitude of power to the discretion of a general council. General councils had frequently met before, and in practice they had often served as channels to communicate resistance to papal government. But they had always met at the bidding of the papacy and with the proviso that their decisions were invalid unless they received the approval of the pope. Requiring the pope to obtain the approval of a general council for all new legislation was a complete reversal; substituting a period of ten years for a period at the pope's discretion was an emancipation of the council from papal government; and combining both proposals was a restriction on the papal plenitude of power that amounted to a prodigious innovation in the constitution of the church.[13]

The radical quality of Durant's ideas was immediately recognized, and it immediately got him into trouble with the pope. When he convoked the council of Vienne Clement V had expressly asked for written suggestions on reforming the church, but clearly this was not what he expected. Alerted to the displeasure of the pope, Durant thought it wise to reconsider: while the council of Vienne was in session, he composed a more modest treatise (*Tractatus Minor*) that retained many of the ideas he had developed in his earlier work (*Tractatus Maior*) and that in many ways foreshadowed the reforms later enacted at the council of Trent, but

---

[12] Tierney, *Foundations*, p. 245. On conciliar action by the laity see the excellent study by Reynolds, *Kingdoms and Communities*.

[13] Sieben, *Konzilsidee des lateinischen Mittelalters*, p. 257, even speaks of 'revolution': 'Während die Verbindung von Konzils- und Reformidee, die uns im Werk des Durandus zum ersten Mal entgegentritt, für die Ebene der *membra* eine Wiederherstellung des altkirchlichen Konzilswesen besagt, bedeutete sie auf der Ebene des *caput*, würde sie in die Tat umgesetzt, eine Revolution.'

that made no mention whatsoever of reform by means of general councils. When he died in 1330 it may therefore have seemed as though his revolutionary plans had been forever laid to rest. But they were not forgotten: some seventy years after the council of Vienne, under the extraordinary circumstances of the great schism that divided the church from 1378 to 1417, they came into their own. Just over one hundred years after Durant's apparent defeat, the council of Constance wrote his ideas into law with the decrees *Haec sancta* and *Frequens*.[14]

There is of course a certain difference between demanding, as Durant had done, that the pope should not be allowed to issue general laws or to dispense from such laws without the assistance of a general council, and declaring, as *Haec sancta* did, that the pope was subject to councils in the three specific matters of faith, schism, and reform. Constance was both more radical in subjecting the pope explicitly to conciliar authority and more moderate in limiting the scope of that authority to three specific subjects. But it is hard to imagine any activity by the pope that would not have affected matters construed as broadly as faith, schism, and reform. If the formulation differed, the thrust of Durant's proposal was nonetheless preserved – not to mention that Constance followed him precisely in joining its enactment of conciliar authority to a 'reform in head and members' and in adopting the same decennial period for conciliar assemblies.

In the two centuries following the council of Constance William Durant the Younger's treatise enjoyed considerable popularity. To be sure, no more than ten manuscripts have been preserved, of which three are quite fragmentary while only two include both the *Tractatus Maior* and the *Tractatus Minor*, and there are only six printed editions.[15] Those numbers do not compare favourably

---

[14] *COD*, pp. 409f., 438–42. For the transmission of Durant's ideas see Fasolt, 'Die Rezeption der Traktate Wilhelm Durantis d. J.'.

[15] P and M are the two 'best' manuscripts and the only ones to contain both the *Tractatus Maior* and the *Tractatus Minor*. C, R, B, Ma, and Tr, which contain the *Tractatus Maior* in its entirety, but not the *Tractatus Minor*, are more derivative. Tu contains the *Tractatus Maior* up to chapter 2.71. O and Z are each conflated from at least two different sources and contain only a fragment of the *Tractatus Maior* extending barely beyond the end of the first part. The printed editions are Lyons 1531 (reprinted with a different frontispiece in 1534), Paris 1545 (two printings), Lyons 1549 in the second volume of a large collection of *Tractatus ex variis iuris interpretibus*, Venice 1562, Venice 1584 in volume 13 of the *Tractatus universi iuris*, and Paris 1671. For more details see Fasolt, 'Manuscripts and Editions', Fasolt, 'A New View', and Fasolt, 'William Durant the Younger's "Tractatus"', pp. 18–157.

with, for example, the massive number of manuscripts and editions of the *Speculum iudiciale* or the *Rationale divinorum officiorum* by his more famous uncle and predecessor as bishop of Mende, William Durant the Elder, commonly known as the Speculator.[16] It seems that the respect with which the younger Durant was received after the council of Constance was that accorded to a precursor whose central ideas had now been realized and whom his followers were pleased to invoke to lend respectability to their own endeavours or to reflect on their own origins, but who did not dominate public debate. Indeed, the man who edited his treatise in 1531 expressed some mild embarrassment about what he considered the quaint antiquity of Durant's detailed proposals.[17] But this is not surprising. What is surprising is that the *Tractatus Maior* was copied, read, and printed without noticeable interruption from the council of Constance down to the late seventeenth century – indeed, printed more frequently than Nicholas of Cusa's *De concordantia catholica*, a book that is sometimes regarded as the outstanding achievement in the history of the conciliar theory and thus perhaps allows for a more instructive comparison than standard works of reference like the *Speculum iudiciale* or the *Rationale divinorum officiorum*.[18] It is striking as well that both manuscripts and editions appear with great regularity in the proximity of dominant figures and pivotal events in the history of the conciliar theory. The readers of the *Tractatus Maior* are thought to have included Pierre d'Ailly (certainly) and Jean Gerson (probably) at the beginning of the period and Etienne Baluze (probably) toward the end.[19] Among the owners of the manuscripts were Pope Benedict XIII, who cherished it sufficiently to place it in the *Biblioteca minor* accompanying him on his wide-ranging travels through Europe in the first decade of the fourteenth century;[20] Nicholas of Cusa, who did not

[16] See below, p. 67, no. 45.
[17] 'Nonnulla fortasse ab huius aetatis institutionibus videbuntur aliena.' Jean Crespin, *TMA*, fol. 2ra.
[18] Kallen, ed. Nicholas of Cusa, *Concordantia catholica*, pp. xiii–xxix, lists eighteen complete and five fragmentary manuscripts of the *Concordantia*, but only four editions from 1514 to 1609.
[19] On d'Ailly and Gerson see Viollet, pp. 123–6. Since Baluze, *Miscellanea*, 3:301–50, used Ma for his edition of Jordan Brice's treatise against cardinal Capranica, and since he acquired P for the library of Colbert in 1682, it is not unlikely that he read the *Tractatus Maior* as well.
[20] Maier, 'Die "Bibliotheca Minor" Benedikts XIII.', p. 37, no. 312. This manuscript appears to have been lost. The catalogue of the papal library, which Franz Ehrle believed

like his copy because it was full of mistakes but clearly read it with attention, placed annotations in its margins, and put it into the library of the hospital that he built in his home-town on the Moselle, where it can still be read today;[21] Peter Nümagen, humanist, secretary to Andrea Zamometic during the ill-fated attempt to revive the council of Basle in 1482, and notary at the Grossmünster in Zurich where he died in 1517 shortly before Zwingli reorganized the church on Protestant principles;[22] Louis Pinelle, who served as rector of the college of Navarre from 1497, as chancellor of the university of Paris thereafter, and from 1511 until his death in 1516 as bishop of Meaux, where he set the stage for the well-known attempt to reform the church of France by his successor in the bishopric, Guillaume Briçonnet, and Briçonnet's ally Jacques Lefèvre d'Etaples, who edited the works of Nicholas of Cusa;[23] Guglielmo Sirleto, scriptor of the Vatican Library and cardinal, well known for his contribution to the council of Trent;[24] Pierre Pithou (1539–1596), lawyer, humanist, editor of classical texts, and author of *Les Libertés de l'église gallicane*, a famous work in the history of Gallicanism and 'the classical text for parliamentarians, especially in the eighteenth century';[25] and finally Colbert.[26]

The editions tell a similar story. Although the Jean Crespin who produced the first edition in Lyons in 1531 is not to be confused with the more famous Genevan martyrologist of the same name, it seems more than likely that his decision to publish Durant's ideas was inspired by the desire for reform that was current in France,

---

was composed in 1375 for Gregory XI, but which Anneliese Maier has shown was prepared for Benedict XIII at the very beginning of his pontificate in 1394, includes a work entitled *Consilia generalia et institutiones domini Guillelmi episcopi Mimatensis*. But it is impossible to decide whether this refers to the *Tractatus Maior* or, perhaps, to the older Durant's *Instructiones et constitutiones*; see Ehrle, *Historia*, p. 527, no. 1,201; Maier, 'Die "Bibliotheca Minor" Benedikts XIII.', pp. 1–6; and Fasolt, 'The Manuscripts', pp. 304–6.

[21] On the first folio of C Nicholas commented: 'Liber iste corrupte multum scriptus est.' In C, fol. 95r, he annotated the beginning of Durant's long quotation of D.21 c.2 and C.24 q.1 c.18 with the words 'Petri eminentia'. Gerhard Kallen, in his edition of the *Concordantia catholica*, p. 150 n. 8, was therefore certainly right to trace Nicholas' use of these canons to Durant's treatise.    [22] Nümagen owned Z.

[23] Pinelle owned Ma.    [24] Sirleto owned O.

[25] 'Le texte classique où puisèrent les parlementaires, notamment au XVIIIᵉ siècle.' Carreyre, 'Pithou', p. 2,237. Pithou owned Tr.

[26] Colbert owned P. For more information about the various owners of the manuscripts of Durant's treatise and detailed bibliographical references see Fasolt, 'The Manuscripts', and Fasolt, 'William Durant the Younger's "Tractatus"', pp. 18–53.

particularly in Lyons, in the 1530s.[27] Philippe le Preux or Philippus Probus, jurist of Bourges, published his edition of Paris 1545 on the occasion of the opening of the council of Trent and introduced it with a fulsome dedication to Pope Paul III, in which he expressed the hope that Durant's ideas might help to combat the 'heretical depravity' of the Protestants.[28] In 1549 the treatise was included in a collection of legal treatises known as the *Tractatus ex variis iuris interpretibus* that surely helped to make Durant's ideas more accessible;[29] in 1562, when the council of Trent reconvened for the third and last time, Michele Tramezino reprinted the edition which Philippus Probus had published on the occasion of the council's beginning;[30] in 1584, in the aftermath of the council of Trent and the reorganization of the law of the church that it engendered, the treatise was incorporated in the massive collection of legal wisdom that was published at the request of Pope Gregory XIII under the title of *Tractatus universi iuris*, which has perhaps done more than any other publication to introduce Durant's ideas to a wide audience.[31] And as late as the second half of the seventeenth century Louis XIV's sharp disagreements with the papacy made the printers become active again: in 1668 César du Boulay decided to include in his history of the university of Paris a crucial chapter from the *Tractatus Maior* in which Durant had sought to demonstrate that exemptions from episcopal authority violated the state of the church;[32] and in 1671 François Clousier published the

[27] Jean Crespin was active in Lyons from about 1525 to 1543; his widow and heirs continued his business down to 1570: Muller, *Dictionnaire*, p. 32. His publications are well documented by Baudrier, *Bibliographie lyonnaise*. On his more famous colleague and namesake from Arras who converted to Protestantism and enjoyed such remarkable success in Geneva in the third quarter of the sixteenth century see Gilmont, *Jean Crespin*.

[28] In his preface, *Tractatus de modo generalis concilii celebrandi* (Paris, 1545), sig. a iiv, Philippus Probus described Durant's treatise as a 'dignum certe opus, quod omnium teratur manibus, quodque ob oculos omnium versetur, ob multiiugam conditionem, et in quo contineantur omnia, quae in conciliis universalibus proponenda sint et tractanda, et in his praesertim fidei tractatur negotium, quibusque mediis infandissimum haereticae pravitatis crimen e Christianorum animis eradendum sit: quod prohdolor multis iam retroactis annis, non sine gravi animarum iactura, impune toto orbe grassatur.' There were two separate printings by Poncet le Preux and Galliot du Pré, on whom see Renouard, *Répertoire*, pp. 131f., 268f. On Philippus Probus see Izbicki, '"Clericis Laicos"', p. 190.

[29] *Secundum volumen tractatuum ex variis iuris interpretibus collectorum* (Lyons, 1549), fols. 88v–117v. The entire collection comprises 18 volumes.

[30] *Tractatus de modo generalis concilii celebrandi*. Ed. Michele Tramezino (Venice, 1562).

[31] *Tractatus universi iuris, duce et auspice Gregorio XIII in unum congesti*, 22 vols. (Venice, 1584–86), here vol. 13, part I: *De potestate ecclesiastica* (Venice, 1584), fols. 154–182v.

[32] *TMA* 1.4 De exemptionibus, fols. 8rb–13rb, in Du Boulay, *Historia*, 4:130–8. Parts of the same chapter were also included in P. de Marca, *De concordia sacerdotii et imperii* (Paris, 1704), pp. 445f., 467, a work first published in 1641.

8

entire treatise and dedicated it to Achille du Harlay, count of Beaumont and a protagonist of the Gallican cause.[33] No new editions were to be produced thereafter, but it seems not unlikely that Durant's ideas continued to be studied. Indeed, one of the later occasions on which they were invoked may well have been one of the most dramatic: in 1682 Bossuet relied on the bishop of Mende for support in his defence of the famous declaration of Gallican liberties promulgated by the bishops of France that confirmed the validity of the decrees of Constance concerning the superiority of the council over the pope.[34] In short, throughout the late medieval and early modern period Durant caught the attention of a group of intellectuals – theologians, lawyers, humanists, philosophers, and administrators – many of whom were not inconspicuous and some of whom may be counted among the greatest minds of the age.

Considering the forbiddingly technical nature of the *Tractatus Maior* this was a remarkable success. In part it was probably due to the fact that some of the manuscripts and all of the editions confused William Durant the Younger with his uncle and predecessor William Durant the Elder, a confusion that is commonly perpetuated by library catalogues today – understandably, as both were distinguished canonists and both were bishops of Mende.[35] If one knows the obvious pleasure with which Bossuet invoked 'the greatest man of his age, a light not only of France but of the Catholic Church, whom the interpreters of papal law prefer the most' in his support of the Gallican position, one cannot but conclude that the *Tractatus Maior* must have benefited from the

---

[33] *Tractatus de modo generalis concilii celebrandi*. Ed. F. Clousier (Paris, 1671). In the early 1960s, perhaps 1963, this edition was photographically reproduced by the Gregg Press in London.

[34] See Bossuet, *Oeuvres*, 31:115–20; and Viollet, p. 3 n. 3. It may be worth noting that it was precisely at this time that Colbert, through the services of his librarian Baluze, acquired P.

[35] M, P, and O merely name the author; Tu, C, R, Ma, Tr, and Z explicitly identify the author with the Speculator; only B, fol. 313r, explicitly distinguishes the author from the Speculator. Jean Crespin made the confusion canonical by introducing his edition, fol. 3, with an 'authoris vita ex Antonio Columbano Lugdunensi utriusque Censure professore' that actually described the life of William Durant the Elder, but extended it down to the council of Vienne and credited him with having written the treatise of the younger Durant. This account was reproduced in the editions of Paris 1545, Venice 1562, and Paris 1671. Antonius Columbanus may be identical with Antoine de Lyon (d. 1560), on whom see *Dictionnaire de biographie française*, 3:45. For a typical example of the muddled details found in some early modern biographical reference works see Panzirolus, *De claris legum interpretibus*, pp. 330–2. The *National Union Catalog, Pre-1956 Imprints*, 152:596f., and many library catalogues following in its wake still attribute the *Tractatus de modo generalis concilii celebrandi* to William Durant the Elder.

enormous prestige accorded to the Speculator.[36] But in much greater part the success of the *Tractatus Maior* must be attributed to the inherent merit of ideas that anticipated by more than a hundred years the most important decrees of the council of Constance and that could still be quoted effectively in ecclesiastical debates as late as 1682.

One might have thought that the works of a man who clearly played a major role in the history of the conciliar theory would have received much attention from historians, but such is not the case. To be sure, Durant's demand for decennial councils is regularly cited in general histories of medieval political thought and in a broad array of studies that touch on the development of the conciliar theory from a variety of perspectives.[37] There are also about a dozen articles and chapters in books that deal directly with Durant and that have been appearing with some regularity since Döllinger first drew attention to his radical critique of papal government on the occasion of the First Vatican Council.[38] Valuable though many of these studies are, however, they have not succeeded in securing for Durant a place proportionate to his significance.

One reason why Durant's ideas have not received as much attention as they deserve is that the text of the *Tractatus Maior* has gravely suffered from an accident in its transmission. All of the printed editions obliterate the distinction between the *Tractatus Maior* and the *Tractatus Minor*: they seem to contain a single book with the spurious title *Tractatus de modo generalis concilii celebrandi*.[39]

---

[36] 'Haec scripsit ille Durandus Mimatensis Episcopus, sui aevi vir maximus, neque tantum Galliae, sed etiam Catholicae Ecclesiae lumen, quem juris pontificii interpretes potissimum sequuntur; qui Romanis Pontificibus gratissimus vixit, ac de Concilii oecumenici habendi ratione a Clemente V jussus, haec scripsit, viamque celebrando Viennensi Concilio, cujus ipse pars fuit maxima, praeparavit.' Bossuet, *Oeuvres*, 31:119.

[37] See, for example, Carlyle, *History*, 6:24; Dempf, *Sacrum Imperium*, p. 421; McIlwain, *Growth*, pp. 249, 256; Martin, *Origines*, 1:92, 357, 2:31; Caillet, *La Papauté*, pp. 380–5; Merzbacher, 'Wandlungen', pp. 305f.; Jedin, *Geschichte*, 1:5–7; Oakley, *Council over Pope?*, p. 62; Lecler, *Le Pape*, pp. 48f.; Alberigo, *Chiesa conciliare*, p. 299; Hofmann, *Repräsentation*, pp. 253–5; Stieber, *Pope Eugenius IV*, p. 67 n. 12. The younger Durant is strikingly, but not uncharacteristically, absent from Ullmann, *History*, and the *Cambridge History of Medieval Political Thought*.

[38] Döllinger, *Der Papst und das Concil*, pp. 241–3; Heber, *Gutachten*, pp. 40–56, 64–74; Scholz, *Die Publizistik*, pp. 208–23; Haller, *Papsttum und Kirchenreform*, pp. 58–66, 70; Viollet; Posch, 'Die Reformvorschläge des Wilhelm Durandus'; Rivière, *Le Problème*, pp. 363–9; Müller, *Konzil von Vienne*, pp. 587f., 591–610; Torquebiau, 'Le Gallicanisme'; Tierney, *Foundations*, pp. 190–9; Lecler, *Vienne*, pp. 38–50; Bellone, 'Cultura e studi'; Vereecke, 'La Réforme de l'église'; Sieben, *Konzilsidee des lateinischen Mittelalters*, pp. 317–21, 351–7.

[39] For details see Fasolt, 'A New View', *passim*. See also the Note on Texts and Citations and figure 2 below, pp. 321–5.

Introduction

Since the *Tractatus Maior* was written while Durant was still
hopeful of reform whereas the *Tractatus Minor* exhibited the effects
of his encounter with the papacy, the result is somewhat comparable to including Paul's letter to the Romans among the five books
of Moses. Small wonder that historians have charged Durant with
inexplicable contradictions, unmotivated repetitions, and a griev-
ous lack of organization overall.[40] Small wonder, too, that they
have not been able to discern the underlying patterns that shaped
Durant's proposals into a systematic programme of reform.
Indeed, several scholars, perhaps sharing Jean Crespin's embarrassment about Durant's firm attachment to the time-bound particulars of practice, have not been able to persuade themselves that he
had any theory at all.[41]

But it must also be confessed that even in its original condition
Durant's *Tractatus Maior* is exceptionally difficult to understand.
This is because Durant self-consciously refrained from articulating
the theory that he did have. He was content to offer a vast array of
specific proposals for reform and to support each of them by direct
quotations from canon and civil laws. Not even the systematic
argument for general councils that forms the substance of the first
part of the *Tractatus Maior* can qualify as theory in any straightforward sense. As far as he was able – and his ability was great – Durant
disguised his personal point of view in the conventional language
of the laws. That is emphatically not to say that he possessed no
authorial identity, much less that he expressed nothing deserving of
the name of theory. Quite the contrary – the analytical power of his
intellect allowed him to cut straight to the heart of the consti-

---

40  Typical is Rivière, *Le Problème*, p. 363: 'Il y déploie un très grand luxe d'érudition
canonique, mais une absence totale de composition.' Similarly Viollet, p. 82: 'Précedé
d'un avertissement très sobre, [le *Tractatus de modo generalis concilii celebrandi*] est divisé en
trois parties, et chaque partie est subdivisée en titres, divisions et subdivisions qui
s'adressent à l'œil plus qu'à l'intelligence, car, dans son ensemble, l'œuvre est confuse et
hâtive; ce sont, pourrait-on dire, des notes jetées comme en courant.' For more
complaints about Durant's lack of organization see Posch, 'Reformvorschläge', p. 289;
Müller, *Konzil von Vienne*, pp. 609f.; Torquebiau, 'Le Gallicanisme', pp. 275f.; McNeill,
'Emergence', pp. 298f.; Tierney, *Foundations*, pp. 190f.; and especially Viollet, pp. 80, 85,
87, 101, 110, 117. For a counter-argument see Fasolt, 'At the Crossroads'.
41  Heber, *Gutachten*, p. 73: 'Da er kein Theoretiker, sondern ein Mann der Praxis war, der
keine systematische Abhandlung über die Verfassungsfragen der Kirche schreiben
wollte, so begnügte er sich, diese Forderung [for general councils] aufzustellen, das Ziel
zu dem man kommen musste und auch kam, anzugeben.' Haller, *Papsttum und
Kirchenreform*, p. 65: 'Alles dies zwar ohne systematische Grundlegung, bloss in einzelnen
praktischen Forderungen formuliert, aber darum nicht weniger deutlich.' Oakley,
*Council over Pope?*, p. 62: 'He produced no systematic ecclesiology and it would certainly
be improper to regard him as a proponent of the strict Conciliar theory.'

tutional problems that confronted the church in his time and to divine where they would lead in the distant future. But for the sake of enhancing the authority of his ideas he effectively blurred the line between the law and his interpretation of it. At first sight there is therefore no theory at all in the *Tractatus Maior* but only an interminable sequence of quotations shot through by sometimes surprisingly radical suggestions for reform; and even at a second glance it is exceptionally difficult to penetrate the thicket of legal verbiage in order to arrive at Durant's own meaning.

This is hardly the stuff to capture the imagination of historians who are often more interested in determining the origins of the conciliar theory than in determining Durant's intentions. Thus it has happened that the body of scholarship devoted to Durant, small though it is, exhibits considerable interpretative uncertainties. Historians who have dealt with the *Tractatus Maior* agree that Durant planned to reform the church 'in head and members' – but that is the extent of their agreement. Even on such a basic question as whether he meant to impose strict limits on the papal plenitude of power, opinions are sharply divided. Döllinger was sure that Durant was a staunch antipapalist whose reforms were 'basically directed against the entire papal system as it had developed during the previous 200 years'.[42] To one or another degree his view was adopted by Max Heber,[43] Richard Scholz,[44] Johannes Haller,[45]

---

[42] Döllinger, *Der Papst und das Concil*, pp. 241–3: 'Er zählt nun die nothwendigsten Reformen auf, ohne welche die Kirche immer mehr in Corruption versinken müsse; aber sie sind im Grunde gegen das ganze päpstliche System, wie es seit 200 Jahren geworden war, gerichtet, und so ist denn von seinem Buche, obgleich es der Papst begehrt hatte und es als Denkschrift für das Concil von Vienne dienen sollte, keine irgend nennenswerte Wirkung ausgegangen.'

[43] Heber, *Gutachten*, p. 73: 'Duranti will einen konstitutionellen Souverän haben.'

[44] Scholz, *Die Publizistik*, p. 220: 'Für Duranti [ist] das Ideal eine aristokratische, vom Episkopat unter dem Vorsitz des Papstes, nach einer festen Verfassung geleitete Kirche, deren souveräne Autorität nicht im Papste, sondern im Generalkonzil liegt.'

[45] Haller, *Papsttum und Kirchenreform*, p. 65: 'Wer die Lage des Episkopats ... kennt, ... der wird über die Kühnheit einer Phantasie nur staunen können, die unter solchen Umständen nichts Geringeres als die Wiederherstellung einer ideal gedachten ursprünglichen Kirchenverfassung auf Grundlage des Episkopalismus und Konziliarismus zu predigen wagte und die gesamte Entwicklung, die das Papsttum seit mehr als einem Jahrhundert genommen, schlechtweg austilgen wollte, um das Oberhaupt der Kirche, das bisher des unangefochtenen Besitzes unbegrenzter Alleinherrschaft sich erfreut hatte, in eine von den Beschlüssen der ihm untergeordneten Organe abhängige Beamtenstellung herabzudrücken.' However, in his review of Scholz, *Die Publizistik*, Haller dissented sharply with Scholz's conception of Durant as representing the party of aristocratic reaction to papal government.

Brian Tierney,[46] and Antonio Marongiu,[47] all of whom agree that Durant was a radical reformer who wished to turn the pope into something of a constitutional monarch, subject to the authority of general councils. The opposite point of view was first enunciated by Paul Viollet, who declared that Durant may have criticized papal abuses but that he 'does not deny the power of the sovereign pontiff. To abuse those powers and to lack them completely are two different things.'[48] This opinion, too, had followers, such as Pierre Torquebiau,[49] Louis Vereecke,[50] and above all Hubert Jedin, who insisted that 'by reform of the head Durant meant proper use of papal power. He did not think of constitutional limitations upon papal power.'[51] And naturally there is a third group of scholars, consisting mainly of Jean Rivière,[52] Andreas

---

[46] Tierney, *Foundations*, pp. 192, 195f.: 'Durantis . . . condemned the whole system of centralized administration . . . Guilielmus Durantis seems to have overstepped the bounds of Decretist thought in thus applying the *Quod omnes tangit* principle to the general legislative authority of the Papacy, for Joannes Teutonicus had maintained in a quite contrary sense that to deny the Roman See's right of establishing law for the whole Church was heresy . . . Durantis . . . wished to assign to the Council a regular constitutional role in the government of the Church, to make it the necessary channel for taxation and all important legislation . . . Indeed, this sprawling ill-designed work . . . strikes for the first time the authentic note of the Conciliar Movement properly so called.'

[47] Marongiu, 'The Theory of Democracy', p. 406: 'In his hands the principle [that what touches all must be approved by all] became exceptionally important; it became the justification and foundation of conciliar theory in its broadest sense. The supreme power in the field of Christian doctrine and Church discipline would be entrusted to an ecumenical council, superior to the Pope, kings, and princes . . . Such a clear statement of the democratic principle was truly exceptional.'

[48] Viollet, p. 119: 'Nous ne voyons pas qu'il nie l'existence des pouvoirs du souverain pontife; mésuser de ses pouvoirs et manquer absolument de pouvoirs sont deux choses différentes.'

[49] Torquebiau, 'Gallicanisme', pp. 279, 289: 'Durand ne dit pas que le Pontife romain n'a pas le droit d'édicter des lois universelles sans le Concile général; simplement il souhaite qu'il ne le fasse pas sans lui. Durand ne conteste donc pas le pouvoir du chef suprême de l'Eglise; il se borne à souhaiter, et si l'on veut, à demander que l'exercice de ce pouvoir soit entouré de sérieuses garanties . . . Le neveu et successeur sur le siège de Mende de Guillaume Durand, dit le *Speculator*, qui saluait le Pape des titres les plus magnifiques, reconnaissait en lui le dépositaire de tous les pouvoirs religieux dans l'Eglise du Christ et la source du pouvoir de tous les prélats inférieurs, ne pouvait être, ne fut pas un ennemi déclaré du système papal ni un gallican qui s'ignore.'

[50] Vereecke, 'La Réforme', p. 288: 'Ne voyons pas en Durand un conciliariste ou un gallican avant la lettre, car il affirme bien haut la primauté du Pape.'

[51] Jedin, *Geschichte*, 1:5: 'Für Duranti besteht die "Reform des Hauptes" im richtigen Gebrauch der päpstlichen Gewalt; an eine konstitutionelle Beschränkung derselben denkt er nicht.'

[52] Rivière, *Le Problème*, pp. 367f.: 'Sans doute Guillaume se garde de dire que le concile soit l'autorité suprême dans l'Eglise – et c'est par là que sa pensée se distingue des théories

Posch,[53] Ewald Müller,[54] Joseph Lecler,[55] and more recently Francis Oakley[56] and Hermann Josef Sieben,[57] who attempt in different ways to find some common ground between the two opposing camps. But no one has been able to offer a convincing explanation of how it was possible for Durant to provoke the displeasure of the papacy in Vienne and nevertheless to cooperate with it both before and after, while Heber is virtually alone in

conciliaires que fit éclater le grand schisme. Quelles que soient les similitudes apparentes, on ne doit pas perdre de vue que, pour lui, le pape et les évêques sont faits pour collaborer. Mais, par son culte des canons, par l'ardeur qu'il manifeste à maintenir la responsabilité de l'épiscopat, par l'essai qu'il tente de lui faire reconnaître un droit régulier de contrôle, l'évêque de Mende se révèle, à n'en pas douter, comme un adversaire du pouvoir absolu dans l'Eglise et mérite de compter devant l'histoire parmi les tenants de ces tendances particularistes qui furent désignées dans la suite sous le nom de gallicanisme.'

[53] Posch, 'Reformvorschläge', p. 303: 'Fehlt bei ihm auch die gründliche Fundierung seines Standpunktes, wie sie Marsilius und Okam, ausgehend von naturrechtlichen Postulaten, später boten, erscheint der Konzilsgedanke bei ihm auch keineswegs in seine letzten Konsequenzen ausgebaut, so ist er doch der erste, der das Konzil als ständige Einrichtung, als konstitutionellen Faktor in der Kirche fordert und demselben die Legislative überweist.'

[54] Müller, *Konzil von Vienne*, pp. 596, 593 n. 27: 'Diese bereits nach der konziliaristischen Seite hinüberneigenden Ideen führt Duranti weiter aus, indem er für die Regierung der Welt den Gedanken einer konstitutionellen Monarchie . . . vorschlägt . . . Duranti hat aber an anderer Stelle wieder ganz klar den Primat bekannt.'

[55] Lecler, *Le Pape*, p. 49: 'Sans nier le pouvoir suprême du pape, il est d'avis que le concil des cardinaux et le concile général peuvent fort opportunément en tempérer l'exercice.'

[56] Oakley, 'Conciliar Theory', p. 518: '[Durant] must have realized that he was introducing something of a novelty when he went on to urge that general councils should be assembled regularly at ten-year intervals. We would be ill-advised to take for granted this association of the demand for reform in head and members with the call to establish the general council as a regularly functioning constitutional mechanism within the structure of church government . . . Still less should we take for granted the further combination of those two notions with the claims advanced on behalf of the council's authority by those who subscribed to the strict conciliar theory. Of that theory there is nothing in Durand's tract – no more, indeed, than there is about reform in John of Paris' *Tractatus de potestate regia et papali*.'

[57] Sieben, *Konzilsidee des lateinischen Mittelalters*, pp. 347f.: 'Im Vergleich zu Johannes Quidort stellt Wilhelm Durandus' Beitrag zur Konzeption des Konzils als *repraesentatio ecclesiae* eher einen Rückschritt dar. Er ist eben kein Anhänger der Volkssouveränitäts-idee, sondern ein episkopaler Konstitutionalist . . . Einschlussweise ist freilich auch bei Durandus der Gedanke der Volkssouveränitätsidee und Repräsentation vorhanden, nämlich da, wo er auf die Konzilien als Grenze der päpstlichen Macht hinweist und dabei das Prinzip *Quod omnes tangit, secundum iuris utriusque regulam ab omnibus debeat communiter approbari* anführt. Zu Ende gedacht, führt dieser Satz des Römischen Rechts freilich notwendig zur Konzeption des Konzils als *repraesentatio populi*.' Ibid., p. 357: 'Durandus leugnet zwar nicht den päpstlichen Primat, aber der Papst darf nach ihm kein absoluter, sondern nur noch ein konstitutioneller Monarch sein. Mit dieser Konzeption des Verhältnisses Papst/Konzil geht Durandus beträchtlich über die alte kanonistische Lehre hinaus.'

wondering with disarming honesty about the strange harmony between the radical conciliarist and the papacy.[58]

There is a corresponding difference of opinion about the sincerity of Durant's intentions. Some of the historians who have dealt with Durant are so terse or maintain such balance in their judgment that their sentiments have to remain a matter of conjecture.[59] The sympathies of others, however, are plain to see. Döllinger clearly regarded Durant as an upright critic of moral corruption in the church, a kind of prophet in the wilderness who deserved respect for his courageous attack on papal absolutism. Haller improved on Döllinger by portraying Durant as an innocent victim of Pope John XXII.[60] Paul Viollet, on the contrary, suspected Durant of moral duplicity and charged him with cynical disregard for the laws.[61] Brian Tierney has similarly found that Durant 'was perhaps not wholly uninfluenced by personal considerations in his denunciations of ecclesiastical abuses'.[62] Ewald Müller, on the other hand, saw scarcely any trace of selfishness but rather 'childlike reverence' toward the papacy, and Torquebiau saw nothing but a youthful prelate's exaggerated eagerness to defend his prerogatives.[63]

There are, in other words, two sets of opposing views. Histor-

---

[58] Heber, *Gutachten*, pp. 72f.     [59] E.g. Rivière, Posch, and Jedin.

[60] 'Aus den Worten des Papstes [Johannes XXII.] spricht deutlich die Erbitterung. Man errät, dass die formelle Anklage, die gegen Durand erhoben war, nur einen Vorwand bildete, und dass es sich in Wirklichkeit um einen Racheprozess handelte.' Haller, *Papsttum und Kirchenreform*, p. 59. On the details see below, pp. 309–12.

[61] 'Ils sont l'un et l'autre [Durant and Pope John XXII] cuirassés de fer. Mais, sous ce fer, que de mollesse, que de souplesse, parfois que de duplicité! A qui la lit tout entière, la bulle *Exsecrabilis* elle-même trahit déjà cette faiblesse de caractère. Quant à l'auteur du *De modo celebrandi concilii*, ce pur chrétien des premiers siècles et des grands conciles oecuméniques, il oublie trop facilement certains préceptes de morale chrétienne et même de morale naturelle ... Si notre évêque n'entend pas se laisser vaincre par la coutume, il ne sera non plus l'esclave des documents qu'il a colligés; et, au sujet de ces sources (conciles et textes divers), il reproduit, sous couvert d'une prétendue citation de saint Ambroise, une maxime heureuse, qui fait bien augurer de ce qui va suivre.' Viollet, pp. 39, 86. Viollet was wrong in charging Durant with misquoting Ambrose; see below, p. 119 n. 11.

[62] Tierney, *Foundations*, p. 192. For similar statements see Posch, 'Reformvorschläge', p. 298; Scholz, *Publizistik*, pp. 209, 213.

[63] Müller, *Konzil von Vienne*, p. 593 n. 30: 'Vgl. die durchaus korrekte Art, ja kindliche Ehrfurcht in seinen Ausdrücken über die römische Kirche.' Torquebiau, 'Le Gallicanisme', p. 273: 'Mais si l'on observe les nuances parfois très délicates de la pensée de l'auteur, si l'on considère avec soin l'ensemble du traité, si l'on tient compte du tempérament de ce jeune prélat, Guillaume Durant apparaît ... comme un prélat qui est jaloux à l'excès des prérogatives réelles ou supposées de sa charge.' When this 'young prelate' wrote the *Tractatus Maior*, he was well over forty years old.

ians are divided first as to whether Durant was radical or not, and second as to whether he was sincere or not. Moreover, these sets overlap. If Döllinger treats Durant as a sincere radical, Tierney treats him as an insincere radical; if Müller regards him as a sincere moderate, Viollet regards him as an insincere moderate. Some of the more fanciful assertions about his character can be dismissed as prejudiced and untinged by any sense that self-interestedness can go quite well with righteousness, especially since Christian laws sometimes turn out to be blissfully supportive of one's own advantage. But even more balanced judgments are far too closely linked to contemporary ecclesiastical debates to be well suited to describe Durant's intentions.[64] Döllinger, one of the spiritual fathers of Old Catholicism, was clearly pleased to enlist Durant in his search for ammunition against the imminent declaration of papal infallibility at the First Vatican Council. Heber, Scholz, and Haller were German Protestants who relished Durant's attacks upon the medieval papacy but were less than enthusiastic about his infatuation with canon law. Viollet, a devoted French Catholic who was at the same time deeply embroiled in the defence of Dreyfus, suffered a stinging rebuke from the papacy for his attempt to mediate between the extremes that clashed during the Modernism crisis, which helps to explain his disparagement of both Durant and John XXII as a reflection of his bitter disenchantment with both the contemporary papacy and its opponents. Rivière and Posch were Catholic moderates attempting to restore civility to the debates provoked by the ultramontane view of papal monarchy while Torquebiau and Müller were members of religious orders who do not seem to have been greatly troubled by the ultramontane view. And Jedin, Tierney, and Oakley are dedicated Catholics who have helped to shift the boundaries of Catholic debate since World War II in favour of *aggiornamento* and general councils.

The different assessments of William Durant the Younger's place in the history of conciliar theory are, of course, no more than miniature reflections of disagreements about the conciliar theory overall. For, in spite of the great progress that has been made in this century, historians continue to be deeply divided over the fundamental issues. Brian Tierney is convinced that medieval canonists

---

[64] For details about the following statements and further bibliographical references see Fasolt, 'Die Erforschung'.

laid the foundations of early modern political thought, and he insists that they elaborated a theory of representation in the full sense of the word.[65] Indeed, from his perspective the jurists of the twelfth and thirteenth centuries have world-historical significance: their work marks the real turning point in the history of European political thought, the point at which the West began to develop its unique tradition of representative government by consent.[66] Francis Oakley does not quite share Tierney's willingness to place the turning point as early as the twelfth century.[67] He also tends to suggest that the conciliar theory was fundamentally about the nature of the church and only secondarily about government by consent, and he is therefore concerned to distinguish conciliarists who were primarily dedicated to the reform of the church from conciliarists of the 'strict' variety.[68] But he emphatically agrees that the conciliarists

succeeded in formulating the theoretical principles underlying medieval constitutionalism in general with such clarity and universality that their formulations reverberated right down to the mid-seventeenth century, generating explicit echoes especially among the Protestant resistance theorists of the sixteenth century (English, French, Scottish) and among the Parliamentary opponents of Charles I of England during the civil war.[69]

Walter Ullmann, on the other hand, disputes both the sincerity and the success of the conciliarists: 'Conciliarism was a resuscitation of the old episcopalist theory; under the cover of a progressive

---

[65] Tierney, 'Hierarchy, Consent, and the "Western Tradition"', p. 647: 'The massive work of the medieval jurists . . . provided the real foundations for medieval and early modern theories of government.' Tierney, *Foundations*, p. 4: 'To the conciliar thinkers the idea of representation came to mean something more than mere personification. It implied also an actual bestowal of authority upon the representative by those whom he was to represent, with the corollary that such authority could be withdrawn in case of abuse.'

[66] Tierney, 'Hierarchy, Consent, and the "Western Tradition"', pp. 650f.: 'The distinctive feature of medieval thought was not that it preserved the old notion of hierarchy but that it introduced a radical innovation by using the egalitarian concept as a foundation for new legal and philosophical theories of government by consent.'

[67] Oakley, 'Conciliar Theory', p. 510: 'Although some of its roots are engaged in scriptural soil and in the corporate and conciliar history of the early Christian church, [the conciliar theory] did not grow to maturity until the thirteenth and fourteenth centuries, flowering in the years after the beginning of the Great Schism in 1378 and winning widespread acceptance in the ensuing "conciliar epoch".'

[68] 'Conciliar theory, a term often used interchangeably with conciliarism, is a doctrine concerning the nature of the church's unity and the locus of the supreme jurisdictional authority within it.' Oakley, 'Conciliar Theory', p. 510.

[69] Oakley, 'Legitimation by Consent', p. 321.

movement an old theme was presented in a new cloak.'[70] Far from providing the foundations of modern constitutional thought, the conciliar movement was therefore followed by the 'religious and political cataclysm' of the Reformation, a calamity for which the conciliarists themselves bore much responsibility:

They had not the courage of their conviction to transplant their own theories into reality. It was the amorphous multitude which first frightened them and then made them abandon their own position, only to retreat into the old papal-monarchic framework. Indeed, it was fear of the multitude – of the laity – which made the conciliarists join the 'Establishment' in which they found a secure bulwark against the rising tide of popular forces.[71]

And it could hardly have been otherwise because in Ullmann's view the medieval church was essentially identified with a 'descending' theory of government in which 'original power was located in a supreme being which, because of the prevailing Christian ideas, came to be seen as divinity itself'.[72] To be sure, Francis Oakley has subjected Ullmann's interpretation of ecclesiastical history to withering criticism.[73] But that should not obscure the fact that a considerable number of distinguished scholars have reached conclusions about the conciliar theory that are quite similar to Ullmann's – sometimes because they are persuaded by his interpretation, sometimes on independent grounds.[74] Conversely,

---

[70] Ullmann, *History*, p. 223.      [71] Ibid., p. 224.

[72] Ibid., p. 13. The classic exposition of Ullmann's fundamental assumptions is to be found in Ullmann, *The Relevance of Medieval Ecclesiastical History*, and Ullmann, *History*, pp. 11–18.

[73] Oakley, 'Figgis', and especially Oakley, 'Celestial Hierarchies'. See also Stickler, 'Concerning the Political Theories of the Medieval Canonists', and Kempf, 'Die päpstliche Gewalt in der mittelalterlichen Welt', both fierce attacks on Ullmann's ideas, as well as Zuckerman, 'The Relationship of Theories of Universals to Theories of Church Government', an attack on Ullmann's student Wilks and his book on *The Problem of Sovereignty*.

[74] For a sampling of the broad support that Ullmann's view enjoys see Lagarde, *La Naissance*, 4:118: 'Jamais le moyen âge n'a lié l'idée de représentation à celle d'une délégation populaire.' Hofmann, *Repräsentation*, pp. 274f.: 'Von einer demokratischen "Mandatstheorie" der Konziliaristen kann nach alledem im Ernst noch nicht die Rede sein.' Gaines Post, 'A Romano-Canonical Maxim', p. 251, maintains that the principle of 'what touches all must be approved by all' was 'simply an embodiment of a constant medieval theory of consent, without constitutional and political implications', and that the kind of consent it demanded was never really that of a free and sovereign people, but 'compulsory, procedural, judicial consent'. John Morrall, *Political Thought*, p. 128, agrees that the whole conciliar position 'was still inseparably wedded to the orthodox hierarchical conception of authority as coming from above rather than below'. Michael Wilks, *The Problem of Sovereignty*, has argued that the subsumption of all members of

# Introduction

substantial criticisms have been mounted against Tierney's and Oakley's reconstructions.[75] Quite recently, in a book whose conciliatory tone masks an outright assault on the central element in Tierney's thesis, Hermann Josef Sieben has tried to cut the 'foundations' of the conciliar theory down to size by showing that the decretists and the decretalists of the twelfth and thirteenth centuries overwhelmingly considered general councils to be subordinate to papal authority, so that their thought could hardly have been the immediate source of the conciliar theory.[76] And Giuseppe

---

society under the leadership of the pope was a natural consequence of the philosophical underpinning of medieval thought in the Platonic 'realism' of ideas. J. P. Canning, 'Introduction: Politics, Institutions and Ideas', p. 366, has recently stated that, 'although conciliarism was a theory of representation based upon the ultimate authority of the Christian people, it was clearly in no sense a genuine expression of the idea of government by the people: there was no delegation of power by that people to the fathers of Constance or Basel'. And Antony Black, 'The Conciliar Movement', p. 586, agrees that 'the conciliar movement succeeded in reuniting the Western Church in 1417, but failed in its reformist and constitutionalist aims. These could only be achieved through lay support, and most conciliarists remained committed clericalists.'

[75] Seidlmayer, Review of B. Tierney, pp. 156–73, and Bäumer, 'Die Erforschung', pp. 29–34, stressed the degree to which Tierney's emphasis on the canonists had been anticipated by Bliemetzrieder and suggested that his interpretation of Hostiensis amounts to 'Überinterpretation'. Similarly Walther, *Imperiales Königtum*, p. 187. Sieben, *Konzilsidee des lateinischen Mittelalters*, p. 255, criticizing Tierney, *Foundations*, and Watt, 'The Early Medieval Canonists', points out that both 'berufen sich für ihre These, dass der spätere Konziliarismus zumindest ansatzweise schon bei unseren Kanonisten vorkomme, ausschliesslich auf deren Denkmodelle für Ausnahmesituationen, sehen aber völlig davon ab, zunächst den grundsätzlichen Standpunkt unserer Kanonisten zu analysieren. Wie verhalten sich Konzil und Papst normalerweise zueinander, das heisst, wenn es beides gibt, einen rechtmässigen Papst und ein Konzil?' In fairness to Tierney it should be stressed, as it is by Seidlmayer, Review, p. 160, that in the opening words of his book, *Foundations*, p. ix, he limited himself explicitly to emphasizing a major current of the canonistic tradition that had not been sufficiently credited for its contribution to the conciliar movement; he neither meant to argue that canonistic conciliarism was the only foundation of the conciliar theory nor that it was the only variety of canonistic thought. But since his case for the significance of canonistic conciliarism was stated so persuasively and has in the meantime grown to the size of a major interpretative account of the place of Western political thought in world history, the limits of the original argument are easily, and to some extent justifiably, forgotten.

[76] Sieben, *Konzilsidee des lateinischen Mittelalters*, pp. 232–76. Sieben divides his account of the canonistic treatment of general councils into three stages: the first *summae* on Gratian's *Decretum* showed relatively little interest in general councils; thereafter their interest in general councils began to increase; but after culminating with Huguccio it plummeted with the decretalists, who paid hardly any attention to general councils at all. Concerning the basic relationship between councils and popes Sieben arrives at a conclusion diametrically opposed to Tierney's, p. 255: 'Über dieses grundsätzliche Verhältnis zueinander geben unsere Definitionen [that is, the definitions of the decretists and the decretalists] eine Auskunft, wie sie klarer nicht sein kann: das Generalkonzil gibt es schlechterdings nicht ohne den Papst, wohl aber den Papst ohne das Generalkonzil! Wenn die päpstliche Erlaubnis konstitutiv ist für die

## Introduction

Alberigo has done something similar for the late medieval flowering of the conciliar theory by declaring that

in fact conciliarism was nothing like a complete and organized doctrine
that anyone could have applied, with more or less intransigence, to the
schism in the Western church, but a movement that was gradually
formed and drew on the traditional doctrinal patrimony for the sake of
responding to a state of crisis and necessity that had appeared in the very
heart of Christianity.[77]

The differences of opinion about William Durant the Younger's
treatise must therefore not be seen in isolation. They are a
microcosmic reflection of differences of opinion about the history
of the conciliar theory in general.[78] This makes the interpretation
of the *Tractatus Maior* an especially challenging, but also an
especially rewarding task. Durant's intentions are so effectively
cloaked in the traditional language of the law that they cannot be
made to fit the categorical distinctions between papalists and
conciliarists in which the secondary literature abounds. On the
contrary, the interpretation of his thought requires us to grapple
directly with assumptions that were shared by papalists and

Definition eines Generalkonzils, dann ist das Generalkonzil dem Papst von seinem
Wesen her untergeordnet. Wenn das Generalkonzil ohne päpstliche *licentia nullius
momenti* ist (Huguccio), dann ist der Papst wesentlich dem Konzil übergeordnet, freilich
immer vorausgesetzt, dass es überhaupt einen Papst gibt.' The concluding concession to
Tierney does little to mitigate the central thrust of this statement.

77 Alberigo, *Chiesa conciliare*, p. 345: 'Infatti il conciliarismo non è una dottrina compiuta e
organizzata che qualcuno, con intransigenza maggiore o minore, avrebbe applicato allo
scisma d'occidente, ma è un movimento che si forma gradualmente, attingendo al
patrimonio dottrinale tradizionale allo scopo di rispondere a uno stato di crisi e di
necessità apertosi nel cuore stesso della cristianità.' As a consequence Alberigo, *Chiesa
conciliare*, p. 345, sharply contests Oakley's thesis that three different strands of the
conciliar theory must be distinguished from each other if they are not to be misunderstood: 'Mi sembra sempre più chiaro che le distinzioni tra un conciliarismo moderato,
uno equilibrato, e uno estremista obbediscono più al tentativo ideologico di salvare
almeno qualcosa dall'accusa globale di estremismo formulata dalla polemica curiale, che
non a differenziazioni dottrinali effettive. Si tratta piuttosto di un elemento di confusione
che non di uno strumento di comprensione.'

78 Since I have taken the liberty of criticizing what appear to me to be real biases in existing
scholarship, including that of some eminent historians who are still actively publishing,
and since I am uncomfortably aware of the Germanico-Protestant features of my own
interpretation, I hope it will not be considered immodest but an expression of my desire
to facilitate the task of those who wish to advance the cause of scholarship by identifying
my own biases if I make it explicit that I am a naturalized American citizen of mixed
German, Russian, and English background who has been baptized in the Russian
Orthodox faith and grew up in post-war West Germany in an intellectual environment
determined to roughly equal degrees by Lutheranism, humanism, idealism, and
agnosticism.

conciliarists alike, assumptions that defined the ground on which they were debating against each other. That is difficult to do and has so far prevented an adequate account of his role in the history of medieval political thought. But it also transforms the *Tractatus Maior* into something of a test case for any interpretation of the history of the conciliar thought. If the difficulty can be solved, it promises not only to lead to a better understanding of the *Tractatus Maior* but also to shed new light on the fundamental issues by which historians of the conciliar theory continue to be divided.

This may help to explain why I have paid relatively little attention to the by now considerable body of secondary literature on twelfth- and thirteenth-century canon law, especially as it affects the history of political thought. I have done so deliberately, and for two reasons. First, Durant himself paid little attention to the development of canon law in the preceding two centuries, not because he was ignorant of it, but because he was critical of it. He wished to go back directly to the old law of the church as he found it in the Pseudo-Isidorean collection and as it had been digested in Gratian's *Decretum*. Second, I have found the secondary literature less of a help than a burden in explicating what is distinctive and important about Durant because so much of it proceeds on the assumption that medieval canonists can be divided into those who favoured papal authority and those who favoured conciliar authority. This distinction may be useful as a heuristic device for those who are concerned to impose some logical order on comparable passages that have been collected from a large number of canonical works that are widely separated in time, place, and intention. At the time of the great schism it may even have acquired a considerable measure of historical force. But at bottom it remains a logical construct that is as likely to reveal some aspects of medieval thought as it is to conceal others and that in many ways says more about modern debates between liberals and conservatives, and modern ways of distinguishing between theory and practice, than it does about the issues that confronted William Durant the Younger. Thus, just as canonistic writings of the twelfth and thirteenth centuries furnished the subtext of Durant's return to the old law, so the recent investigations of those writings form the subtext of the present book; just as Durant's studied silence with regard to the achievements of thirteenth-century canon lawyers may be read as evidence for his scepticism about their ability to preserve the order of the church, so mine about the historians of those lawyers may be read as evidence for my scepticism about the categories by which existing scholarship is informed. This is no slight on the admirable results that have been gained by publishing hitherto unknown sources, elucidating their meaning, and integrating them into the history of medieval political thought, but it is a reminder that there remain things to be said about conciliar thought that have so far escaped attention.

In order to avoid prejudging the issue by agreeing to widely held but nonetheless questionable assumptions about the history of medieval political and legal thought, I am therefore going to refrain from surveying Durant's relations to the canonistic literature of the preceding two centuries in any greater detail than is necessary to clarify his dissent from it. Instead, I shall try to establish the context of his intentions from the ground up, as it were, by concentrating on a piece of evidence that is far more directly rooted in politics than is usually the case with, or can be ascertained of, canonical treatises. For we are fortunate indeed to have a document at our disposal that tells us a great deal about Durant's intentions from an entirely different point of view than that of legal theory and therefore stands in a particularly illuminating relationship to the *Tractatus Maior*. This is the so-called *paréage* of Mende. The *paréage* of Mende was the settlement by which Philip the Fair and William Durant the Younger concluded a celebrated dispute between the bishops of Mende and the kings of France over their respective powers in the Gévaudan, the territory in the south of France where Durant was count and bishop. The roots of this dispute extended back to the middle of the twelfth century when one of Durant's predecessors, Aldebert de Tournel, entered into an alliance with Louis VII in order to obtain support against the local nobility. The terms of this alliance were codified in the so-called golden bull of Mende of 1161: Bishop Aldebert accepted his subordination to the king of France in exchange for the king's confirmation of his complete liberty from any interference with the government of the Gévaudan. But the golden bull did not determine precisely how Aldebert's subordination was to be reconciled with his liberty. When in the aftermath of the Albigensian wars the kings of France extended their control over the south of France, Aldebert's successors therefore clashed frequently and sometimes violently with the king and his officers; in 1269, bereft of all other means of resistance, they brought a suit in Parlement that was still pending when Durant ascended to the bishopric in

1296. This was the suit which in 1307 Philip and Durant brought to an amicable end: they agreed to exercise most of the responsibility for governing the Gévaudan conjointly and not to molest each other on lands under their separate control. At the same time Durant agreed to accept the ultimate 'superiority' of the king of France in three specific matters: appeals, taxation for the defence of the realm, and crimes against the king. In spite of the violent opposition of the local nobility this understanding furnished a basis for local government that remained virtually unchanged until the end of the *ancien régime* in the French Revolution.

The *paréage* of Mende and the *Tractatus Maior* are obviously two very different kinds of documents: one is a public act of government, the other a private legal treatise; one is a pact between a local lord and his king, the other an admonition by a bishop to the pope on how to reform the church; one is shaped by practical negotiations on the basis of power as it was actually distributed in the Gévaudan, the other by theoretical reflections on the ways in which power ought to be reconciled with reason; one has local, the other, universal significance; and, most important, one accepts the 'superiority' of the king whereas the other aims to place constitutional limits on the papal plenitude of power. In other words, the *paréage* of Mende and the *Tractatus Maior* are worlds apart in terms of substance, origin, and form. And yet they are closely related to each other in historical reality. Both were completed at almost the same time under the same conditions and both had William Durant the Younger as their author: if one represented what he wished in theory, the other represented what he was willing to accept in practice. Precisely the differences between these documents are therefore of the greatest value for our enterprise. If it were possible to construct a single interpretative framework that successfully accounts for both of them, we could be reasonably sure that we have really understood the issues with which Durant was faced and the solutions he devised in writing the *Tractatus Maior*.

These considerations dictate the sequence of the following exposition. The first part contains an account of the factors that went into the making of the *paréage*. Beginning with a look at the diocese of Mende, it describes the lasting rivalry between the bishop and the local nobility, the changing relationship between the bishop and the king of France, the growth of central government in church and state, the alternation of cooperation and hostility between the king of France and the pope, and above all the different expectations and methods of government that were brought to bear on the Gévaudan by local noblemen like the de Peyre and the Mercoeur who held the bishopric until the latter part of the thirteenth century, on the one hand, and commoners like the Durant, on the other, who supplanted the nobility towards the end of the thirteenth century because they were distinguished by jurisprudential expertise and administrative skills that made them the favourites of papal and royal government. Part I concludes with an analysis of the ways in which the *paréage* of Mende managed to reconcile these factors.

The second part contains an analysis of the *Tractatus Maior*. Chapter 4 furnishes essential information about the overall design of the treatise and a description of its first part that stays close to Durant's own presentation. It is meant to inform the reader about how Durant himself justified his conciliar proposal. Chapters 5 and 6 serve two purposes: on the one hand, they contain a reasonably full description of the most telling elements in the vast programme of reform that Durant unfolded in the second part of the treatise; on the other hand, they offer an analysis of that programme on the assumption that it was informed by two competing models of political thought, one that was hierarchical and another that was republican. The seventh and final chapter in this second part attempts to clarify how these models were related to each other both in Durant's intention and in fact. Part II concludes with a summary of the results of this analysis and a few words about their implications for the received view of the conciliar theory.

The third and briefest part deals with Durant's fate from the council of Vienne until his death. Chapter 8 considers the defeat of his plan for constitutional reform at the council of Vienne and specifies the ways in which he reformulated his ideas in the *Tractatus Minor*. Chapter 9 portrays his rise to prominence under Philip V until his clash with Pope John XXII, his slow decline in his old age, and his demise in Cyprus on his return from a fruitless attempt to revive the crusade.

Lest this procedure should be misunderstood I should like to state explicitly what this book is not: although it constantly refers to ideas, it is not the history of an idea; although it contains much information about the life and thought of William Durant the Younger, it is not a biography, intellectual or otherwise; and although it deals in detail with the events that transformed the Gévaudan in the high middle ages it is most certainly not a history of the Gévaudan. It is an attempt to identify the meaning of the conciliar proposal made by Durant in the *Tractatus Maior*. More broadly, since the *Tractatus Maior* played a central role in the history of the conciliar theory, it is an attempt as well to identify the fundamental factors that would eventually shape the meaning of the decrees of Constance and Basle. It may surprise and possibly irritate the reader to discover how closely I have juxtaposed specific empirical details concerning, for example, the distribution of fiefs in the Gévaudan during the Albigensian wars or the benefices bestowed by the papacy on Durant's relatives with highly abstract speculations about hierarchy, commonwealth, history, and sovereignty. Unusual though this may be, it is a function of my attempt to understand William Durant the Younger's ideas about reform in their historical, not just their canonical, setting. Such an attempt necessitates an approach that is in some ways more specific and in others more abstract than histories of an idea, a person, or a territory.[79] Perhaps a sympathetic reader will discern the single narrative that moves from the twelfth-century Gévaudan through the life of William Durant the Younger and into his book, then back out of his book and past his encounter with the pope at the council of Vienne to conclude with his decline in later years – a narrative, in other words, that moves freely across the boundaries by which the subjects of historical investigation (ideas, persons, politics) are conventionally separated from each other. The subject of this narrative may be described as the web of memories, ideas, and interests that shaped the exercise of power in medieval Europe, a web that is hard to identify except in the writings of the literate and in the actions of the powerful – the bishops, the nobility, the king, the pope, the officers of central government – but whose effects reached everyone who had experience of domination and lasted well beyond the middle ages. The title of my book fails to name this subject properly; perhaps it has no name. Yet the title does reflect that this web was suspended between two poles by which its unity was regularly threatened and sometimes violently torn asunder: council and hierarchy.

[79] I agree with Skinner's observation in 'Meaning and Understanding', p. 64, that 'once the appropriate focus of the study is seen in this way to be essentially linguistic and the appropriate methodology is seen in consequence to be concerned in this way with the recovery of intentions, the study of all the facts about the social context of the given text can then take its place as a part of this linguistic enterprise'.

# PART I

## THE FORMATION OF INTEREST

Bit by bit, like a flood, temporal lords are bringing everything under their control. As a wolf bit by bit devours a lamb, they devour bit by bit the jurisdiction of the church.　　　　　William Durant, *Tractatus Maior* 2.70

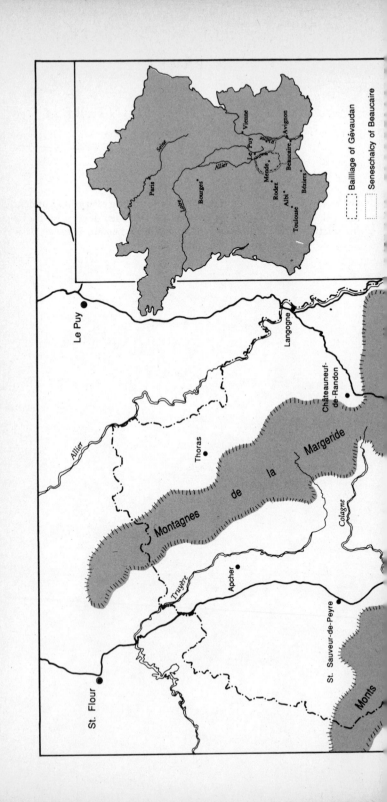

Bailliage of Gévaudan

Seneschalcy of Beaucaire

Le Puy

Langogne

Châteauneuf-de-Randon

Thoras

Montagnes    de    la    Margeride

Allier

Colagne

Truyère

Apcher

St. Sauveur-de-Peyre

St. Flour

Monts

Paris

Seine

Loire

Allier

Bourges

Le Puy

Vienne

Rhône

Avignon

Mende

Beaucaire

Rodez

Albi

Béziers

Toulouse

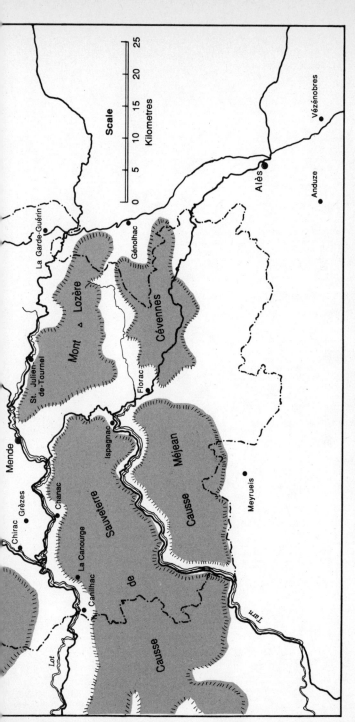

Figure 1 The Gévaudan in about 1300. Conception of map: Constantin Fasolt; cartography by Brian Urbaszewski, The University of Chicago

## Chapter 1

# THE BISHOPS OF MENDE

Let it be known to everyone present and future that we grant the entire bishopric of Gévaudan, including the regalian rights of our crown, to the glorious church of the martyr Privatus and to every bishop who succeeds canonically to our venerable friend Aldebert.          Louis VII[1]

Mende was the capital of a large and ancient diocese in the southern parts of the Massif Central that coincided with the county of Gévaudan.[2] Situated on the river Lot, about ten miles to the west of

---

[1] 'Notum facimus universis praesentibus et futuris, quod ecclesiae gloriosi martyris Privati, et episcopis omnibus, venerabili amico nostro Aldeberto canonice succedentibus, totum Gaballorum episcopatum cum regalibus ad nostram coronam pertinentibus, ex integro concedimus.' From the golden bull of Mende, *Ordonnances*, 16:255.

[2] For a brief introduction to the geography of the Languedoc see Nelli, *Histoire du Languedoc*, pp. 7–11. Besides the familiar historical atlases, such as Longnon, *Atlas historique de la France*, plates 7, 13, see Dubois, 'La Carte des diocèses de France', pp. 686ff.; Michel, *L'Administration royale*, p. 499; Roucaute, *La Formation territoriale*; and Wolff, ed., *Histoire du Languedoc*, p. 441, all of which contain useful but in some respects contradictory maps. The roadmaps published by Michelin are detailed and very useful. For the administrative and ecclesiastical geography of the Gévaudan, Molinier, 'Sur la géographie de . . . Languedoc', pp. 130–355, here especially pp. 169f., 219f., 237–9, 248f., 256, 288f., 338–46, 353, is superb. For the distribution of fiefs and demesnes between the king, the bishop, and the barons, see Porée, 'Les Evêques-comtes', pp. 369–409; Porée, 'La Domination Aragonaise', pp. 195–266; and Roucaute, *La Formation territoriale*. For the ecclesiastical geography Besse, *Abbayes et prieurés*, 4:53–71, is still useful. A concise *mise-en-scène* for the relationships between the Gévaudan and the Languedoc can be found in Lot and Fawtier, *Histoire des institutions françaises*, 1:71–99.

The most important sources for the history of the Gévaudan during our period are available in Burdin, ed., *Documents historiques*; Brunel, ed., *Les Miracles de Saint Privat*; Roucaute and Saché, eds., *Lettres de Philippe-le-Bel*; and the *Mémoire relatif au paréage de 1307*, ed. A. Maisonobe. Additional information can be gleaned from *Gallia Christiana*, especially vol. 1; *Ordonnances des roys de France*, especially vols. 1, 5, 11, and 16; and from the papal registers, especially those of Clement V and John XXII. For unpublished sources on Mende and the Gévaudan see André, *Inventaire sommaire des archives communales*; André et al., *Inventaire sommaire des archives départementales*; and Barroux et al., *Archives départementales de la Lozère*. Somewhat dated but still by far the best studies of the medieval Gévaudan come from the pen of Charles Porée, archivist of the Département de la Lozère; see his *Le Consulat et l'administration municipale de Mende*, and especially his rich *Etudes historiques sur le Gévaudan*. Michel, *L'Administration royale*, is good, but neither as precise nor as reliable. Bisson, *Assemblies and Representation in*

its springs and ten miles to the northwest of Mont Lozère – at well over 5,500 feet the highest elevation between the Rhône and the Atlantic coast – it dominated the easternmost extension of a long and tortuous valley that slowly descends in a western direction until it opens onto the plains of Aquitaine where, a few miles to the west of Agen, the Lot merges into the Garonne. Roughly speaking, the county has the shape of an oval with a radius varying from about twenty to thirty miles that is cut in half by the Lot and has its centre in Mende itself. The northern half is composed of two mountainous plateaus joined in the middle by a ridge that is formed by the Monts d'Aubrac in the northwest and the Montagnes de la Margeride in the north and northeast. The county's southern half,

*Languedoc*, pp. 111–24, 186–228, in spite of its special perspective, is the most satisfactory recent account. For histories of Mende other than Porée's, see Martin, *Notice historique sur la ville de Mende*; and Balmelle and Pouget, *Histoire de Mende*. For histories of Marvéjols, see Bosse, 'Notes pour servir à l'histoire de Marvéjols'; Denisy, 'Notice historique sur la ville de Marvéjols'; and Denisy, *Notice topographique et historique sur le canton de Marvéjols*. There are a few good studies of local families: Boudet, *Les Derniers Mercoeurs*; Prunières, 'L'Ancienne Baronnie de Peyre'; Philippe, *La Baronnie du Tournel*; and Chazaud, 'L'Evêque de Mende et les seigneurs du Tournel'. The following are excellent and more recent studies of special subjects in the history of the Gévaudan: Brunel, 'Les Juges de la paix en Gévaudan'; Castaing-Sicard, *Monnaies féodales et circulation monétaire en Languedoc*; Strayer, 'La Noblesse du Gévaudan'; and Rogozinski, 'The Counsellors of the Seneschal of Beaucaire and Nîmes'. See also Balmelle, *Bibliographie du Gévaudan*; and Dollinger and Wolff, eds., *Bibliographie de l'histoire des villes de France, s.v.* Mende and Marvéjols, which lists fifty-two pertinent items.

As a result of its location the Gévaudan fits few of the established moulds of historical investigation. On the one hand, it does not really belong to the feudal world of northern France. The counts of Auvergne tried, but in the long run failed, to annex it to their holdings; in spite of many property and family ties to the Auvergne, the Gévaudan was too close to the south for that: Molinier, 'Sur la géographie de . . . Languedoc', pp. 237–9; Dunbabin, *France in the Making*, pp. 104, 300; and Lot and Fawtier, *Histoire des institutions françaises*, 1:73–75. On the other hand, it does not really belong to the south either. It is generally considered to be part of the Languedoc, but studies of Languedocian history generally treat it as marginal territory, like the Vivarais and the Velay, and some will pointedly exclude it from consideration altogether: see Nelli, *Histoire du Languedoc*, pp. 8f.; Lot and Fawtier, *Histoire des institutions françaises*, 1:71; Friedlander, 'Les sergents royaux du Languedoc', p. 242. Devic and Vaissete, *Histoire générale de Languedoc*, contains much information, but not connected history. Shorter and more recent histories like Le Roy Ladurie, *Histoire du Languedoc*, and the excellent *Cahiers de Fanjeaux* contain very little information relating specifically to the Gévaudan. Wolff, ed., *Histoire du Languedoc*, is a welcome exception. The general historical literature has neglected the Gévaudan almost completely. For example, the index of Dunbabin, *France in the Making*, p. 436, *s.v.* Gévaudan, offers four entries, two of which really concern the Rouergue, as compared with twenty-seven for the Auvergne and more than sixty for Normandy. Similar observations can be made about older works like Langlois, *Saint Louis*, or more recent ones like Jordan, *Louis IX*; Richard, *Saint Louis*; Sivéry, *Saint Louis*; and Strayer, *Reign of Philip the Fair*. Not even the history of Catharism has attracted attention to the Gévaudan; see Wakefield, *Heresy, Crusade, and Inquisition*.

composed of mountains, hills, and dry highlands interspersed with irregularly shaped valleys sloping south and west from Mende, is less forbidding – hence the cultural and economic proximity of the Gévaudan to Languedoc.

Two general points are worth remembering about the geography of the Gévaudan. The first is that it was part of Languedoc – that is, part of a borderland halfway between France and Italy, between the lordships of the north and the self-governing towns of the south, and, perhaps most important, between the two greatest medieval monarchies: the spiritual monarchy of Rome and the 'most Christian' temporal monarchy of Paris.[3] This is nicely symbolized by its bi-partite geography of mountainous plateaus in the north and river valleys in the south. It was an area where different cultures intersected, an area given to extremes and ambivalence. While Languedoc is best known for having fostered heresy in the twelfth century, during the fourteenth century it furnished every single one of the seven popes who took up residence in Avignon.[4] Much time and bitter fighting were required to establish the control of the Capetian monarchy there, but thereafter Languedoc appealed to Parlement more frequently than any other region of France except Paris itself.[5] Developments in the Gévaudan mirrored those in the region at large. Until the end of the thirteenth century it was something of an ecclesiastical backwater whose bishops appeared but rarely in the papal records. But in the fourteenth century it furnished the church with two masters general of the Hospitallers, eight bishops, five cardinals, and a pope, Guillaume de Grimoard, who rose from the priory of Chirac to become Urban V in 1362.[6] In addition, the Gévaudan was one of the last areas in Languedoc to come within the orbit of the Capetian monarchy, but when it did Philip IV and his council were closely involved in its affairs.[7]

The second point is that, unlike the rest of Languedoc, the Gévaudan was difficult of access from without and difficult to travel within. It was a separate little world up there in the

---

[3] On the close contact between Languedoc, Provence, and Italy, see e.g., Le Roy Ladurie, *Histoire*, pp. 26–9; Michel, *L'Administration royale*, pp. 195–9.

[4] It also furnished 96 out of a total of 134 cardinals and almost half the curial officials: Oakley, *Western Church*, p. 42; cf. Wolff, ed., *Histoire du Languedoc*, pp. 258f.

[5] Strayer, *Reign of Philip the Fair*, pp. 200, 260–9. Local justice was good, so that first suits went more rarely to Paris.

[6] André, 'Evêques de Mende', pp. 29 n. 1, 40f.; Mollat, *Les Papes*, pp. 119f.

[7] See the collection of Philip IV's letters regarding the Gévaudan, R-S, *passim*.

mountains, with a peculiarly distinct character. Because of its isolation it preserved the localism of the early middle ages longer than did the plains below, and therefore the methods of centralized government were not introduced to Mende until they had already been developed to a high degree of technical perfection. This heightened their conflict with memories of local independence.

Combine both points and you obtain a kind of Languedocian Brittany, a region where conflicts that are familiar from other parts of the medieval world unfolded with greater clarity and deeper intensity. As late as the 1330s, when a native of the region, Albert de Lordet, was once again occupying the bishop's chair, the men of Mende greeted royal officers entering the city with shouts expressing local patriotism and defiance: 'We have no king in Gévaudan except the bishop! Let's kill those bandits; don't let them get away!'[8] Of course, these sentiments were dated at the time. There was in fact a king besides the bishop, and he was capable of exercising more than a little power. Not only did the charge of banditry fail to stick, therefore – it could have been reversed. But even so the men of Mende persisted in seeing themselves as citizens of Gévaudan, not France. Such matters may be worth remembering in order to explain why it was the debates over the autonomy of the Gévaudan that led William of Plaisians to formulate what is regarded as one of the most lucid statements of the medieval French theory of sovereignty, and why a treatise as illuminating for the later middle ages as William Durant the Younger's *Tractatus Maior* was written by a bishop of Mende.[9]

### THE BISHOP AND THE NOBILITY

The story that we need to tell in order to understand William Durant the Younger's rebellion against central government begins (insofar as anything in history can be said to begin) when the

[8] 'Nos non habemus regem in Gaballitano nisi episcopum Mimatensem. Moriantur isti ribaudi et non evadant manus nostras!' Porée, *Le Consulat*, p. xx n. 1; cf. André, 'Evêques de Mende', p. 36. The occasion was an attempt by the *bailli* to levy a tax on episcopal territory.

[9] William of Plaisians declared that 'omnia que sunt infra fines regni sui sint domini regis, saltim quoad protectionem et altam jurisdictionem et dominationem et etiam quantum ad proprietatem omnium singularum rerum mobilium et immobilium regni sui, quas idem dominus rex donare, recipere et consumere potest, ex causa publice utilitatis et deffensionis regni sui'. Strayer, 'La Noblesse du Gévaudan', p. 66 and n. 2, with reference to the *Mémoire relatif au paréage de 1307*, p. 521. Strayer has repeatedly used the case of the Gévaudan and this passage in particular to illustrate the claims of Philip IV; see the essays collected in his *Medieval Statecraft*, pp. 259 n. 9, 261 n. 16, 298, 301 n. 2, 345.

political structures that the Germanic invaders of Europe had once inherited from antiquity were finally disassembled into their smallest constituent parts, and when the localism that had reached its peak with the disintegration of the Carolingian empire was just about to be reversed.[10] In the Gévaudan this occurred around the beginning of the twelfth century.

From the tenth century to the beginning of the twelfth, the Gévaudan was ruled by a family of viscounts who are also known as the viscounts of Grèzes, after the chief castle in their lands.[11] They can just as well be said to have maintained the last vestiges of Carolingian officialdom as to have abolished them by turning control of the region into a heritable property. In 1112 their line died out and the viscounty was inherited by the counts of Barcelona, and when they in turn died out in 1172, the viscounty passed into the hands of the kings of Aragon.[12] But neither Barcelona nor Aragon were close enough to the Gévaudan to allow the exercise of any real control. At the beginning of the twelfth century the question of who would govern the Gévaudan was thus thrown wide open.

In later centuries it may have been believed that the Gévaudan had always been ruled by the bishop. In fact, nothing could have been further from the truth. The bishops had only moved their see from Javols, the ancient *civitas Gabalorum*, to Mende in the tenth century.[13] By the middle of the twelfth century they may have received the right to exercise some form of control over the city of Mende, but their situation was still far from promising.[14] On all

---

[10] Cf. Sullivan, 'The Carolingian Age'.

[11] On the history of the Gévaudan during this period see Porée, 'Les Evêques-comtes de Gévaudan', pp. 348–53; Porée, 'La Domination Aragonaise', pp. 195–201; Molinier, 'Sur la géographie de . . . Languedoc', pp. 237–9, 248f., 288f.; Devic and Vaissete, *Histoire générale*, 4:133–8; Lot and Fawtier, *Histoire des institutions*, 1:73–8; and Dunbabin, *France in the Making*, pp. 104, 300. For a brief period the Gévaudan was controlled by Raimond IV of Saint-Gilles before it passed into the hands of the counts of Barcelona. It should be noted that the viscounty initially included the entire Gévaudan but became increasingly limited to the lands under the immediate control of the viscounts near their capital, Marvéjols (where they shared control with the de Peyre), and their main castle, Grèzes. Both were located in the western parts of the diocese. Porée, 'La Domination Aragonaise', pp. 198f.; Porée, 'Les Evêques-comtes', pp. 412f. Hence the viscounty is just as often called 'of Grèzes' as 'of Gévaudan'.

[12] At the time of William Durant the Younger the connection to Aragon was still alive; see Valls-Taberner, 'Une Lettre de Guillaume Durand'.

[13] Molinier, 'Sur la géographie de . . . Languedoc', pp. 169f. 'Gévaudan' derives from *Gabali*. Hence the inhabitants of the Gévaudan will be referred to as Gabalitans.

[14] Porée, 'Les Evêques-comtes', pp. 357–9. It took until 1269 for the bishops to complete their acquisition of all lordly rights over the city of Mende; ibid., pp. 369f.

four sides their cathedral was surrounded by the fortified residences of noble Gabalitans. The same state of affairs obtained in the diocese at large. The bishops' demesne was small, their vassals were few, and they were surrounded on all sides by large estates of powerful local lords.[15] The Tournel controlled the lands to the east, the Randon those to the near north, the Mercoeur and the Apcher those to the far north, the de Peyre those to the northwest, the Canilhac and the successors of the viscounts those to the west, and the Anduze the mountains and valleys of the Cévennes to the southeast – not to mention any of the minor castles that were spread over the Causse de Sauveterre and along the course of the Tarn in the south. The bishop, far from ruling, was effectively held hostage by the noble barons of the Gévaudan.[16]

Under these circumstances the barons found it easy to control the church. On the reasonable grounds that they alone were able to provide the church with protection, they shared its revenues, enjoyed the right of spoils upon a bishop's death, and placed their members in the church's offices.[17] Through the entire period of church reform from Pope Leo IX's famous synod of 1049 down to the Fourth Lateran Council we know of not a single bishop who did not belong to the local nobility.[18] As late as 1219, the bishop, the provost, and the archdeacon of Mende were all members of the de Peyre family.[19] In short, the church of Mende exhibited all the

---

[15] On the episcopal demesne and the lands of the barons see Porée, 'Les Evêques-comtes', pp. 369–409; Philippe, *La Baronnie du Tournel*, pp. i–xlvi; Prunières, 'L'Ancienne Baronnie de Peyre', pp. 169–219.

[16] For a general characterization of the rough manner of life in the Gabalitan mountains see Michel, *L'Administration royale*, pp. 109–14.

[17] Porée, 'Les Evêques-comtes', p. 358.

[18] Seven bishops are known during the 171 years from 1052 to 1223. For two of them we cannot ascertain the family name: William II (*c.* 1095), and Robert (*c.* 1098). The other five, who appear to have ruled for a combined total of more than 150 years, belonged to the local nobility: Aldebert I de Peyre (*c.* 1052–92), Aldebert II de Peyre (*c.* 1098–1109), William III de Peyre (*c.* 1109–51), Aldebert III de Tournel (1151–87), and William IV de Peyre (1187–1222). The chronology of the bishops before 1151 is uncertain; see Porée, 'Les Evêques-comtes', p. 360 n. 1; *GC*, 1:89–91; Gams, *Series episcoporum*, 1:577 (who gives 1062 as the year of Aldebert I's death, is blank for the years 1063–94, 1096–7, 1099–1108, and 1110–22, and gives 1123–50 as the years of William III without identifying him as a de Peyre); and Devic and Vaissete, *Histoire générale*, 4:392 (who suggest that Aldebert II ruled from 1098 to 1109). I have preferred the chronology of Porée and Devic and Vaissete, who are more reliable than Gams or the *Gallia Christiana*.

[19] Chazaud, 'L'Evêque de Mende', pp. 311f. Devic and Vaissete, *Histoire générale*, 4:392, were as wrong to date the evidence to 1223 as Chazaud was to date it to 1209. Nor does it seem likely that they were right in believing that the occasion for the event was Bishop William de Peyre's departure for the Holy Land; see Porée, 'La Domination Aragonaise', pp. 212f.

characteristics of what has been called the proprietary church of early medieval Europe.[20]

Two factors helped the bishops to extricate themselves from this state of affairs. One was that the local families were relatively evenly matched. To be sure, in the abstract the difference between a family like, say, the Mostuéjols and the Mercoeur, easily the most powerful lords in the Gévaudan, was comparable to that between David and Goliath.[21] But the Mercoeur were far removed from Mende, and none of those who were closer were powerful enough to eliminate their rivals. The bishop's name was thus always that of a local family during the period under consideration, but it changed first from de Peyre to Tournel, then back to de Peyre, and finally to Mercoeur. Such shifts helped the episcopal office to avoid being utterly appropriated by any one of the baronial families and perhaps enabled the bishop to play upon their rivalries in order to attain a measure of independence.

The second factor that enabled the bishops to maintain a precarious freedom from the rule of the nobility was the movement for peace and reform that swept through Europe in the eleventh and twelfth centuries. At first it was by no means obvious that reform would serve the bishops' cause. Signs of reform had been seen in the Gévaudan since the tenth century, but they invariably originated with the nobility itself. It was the nobility that built priories;[22] it was the Mercoeur who supplied the monastery of Cluny with one of its most famous abbots;[23] and there can be little doubt that the canons of the church of Mende

---

[20] See the classic work of Stutz, *Die Eigenkirche*. It may be worth pointing out that the viscounts of the Gévaudan were no less closely associated with the counts of Barcelona than were the viscounts of Narbonne, whom Richard Southern has immortalized as shining examples of simony as a noble way of life; see his *The Making of the Middle Ages*, pp. 118f., 122. Even Bishop William Durant the Younger was still close to the viscounts of Narbonne, long after the viscounts of the Gévaudan had passed away and the king had taken their place; see Viollet, pp. 29, 57.

[21] On the Mercoeur see Boudet, *Les Derniers Mercoeurs, passim*, and Porée, 'La Domination Aragonaise', p. 224; Viollet, pp. 39–44; Strayer, 'La Noblesse du Gévaudan', p. 68; and R-S, pp. 94, 151, 161, 203, 210, 211f.

[22] In 998 a priory was established at Langogne. In 1060 Bishop Aldebert I de Peyre gave his church at La Canourge to the monastery of St Victor in Marseille. In 1062 he and his brother Astorg founded a monastery at Chirac that was also tied to St Victor and appears to have been consecrated by Pope Urban II; see Devic and Vaissete, *Histoire générale*, 3:335, 4:134–6, 392; *GC*, 1:89; cf. Nicholas III, no. 503 (27.iv.1279); Nicholas IV, no. 527 (12.ii.1289). The documents for 1060 and 1062 are printed in *GC*, 1:Instrumenta:23f.

[23] Namely Odilo of Cluny (994–1049), the friend of Emperor Henry II; see Devic and Vaissete, *Histoire générale*, 3:243.

who joined the movement for reform in 1123 by adopting the rule of Augustine in return for a major privilege from Pope Calixtus II were noble, too.[24] Noble control proved to be durable. In spite of Pope Calixtus' rules the canons were still in the habit of transferring their benefices to their relatives in 1233.[25] Two generations later, William Durant the Younger still thought a special effort was needed to limit the nobles' access to the canonries.[26] And even though in the early fourteenth century many priors were appointed by the papacy, the great majority still came from local families.[27]

Reform, in other words, was not identical with the bishop's freedom from lay control. Yet it did furnish at least two means to further his independence. One was his right to raise a so-called peace compensation, *compensum pacis*, from all the inhabitants of the Gévaudan. That provided him with an independent source of considerable income. It also enabled him to pay for a little army of commoners that was known as 'the peace', *pax*, because the bishop used it to enforce the peace (with the curious result that he could be seen leading the peace into war).[28] Second, and ultimately more important, the movement for reform established contacts between the little world of the Gévaudan and the larger medieval world of state and church. It breached local borders and put the bishop in touch with distant sources of power that were beyond the reach of

---

[24] Devic and Vaissete, *Histoire générale*, 3:584f. The privilege is printed in Calixtus II, *Bullaire*, no. 355, pp. 126–9. *GC*, 1:90, reports that Bishop William III installed canons in seventeen of the churches in his diocese. On the nobility's contribution to church reform in general see Howe, 'The Nobility's Reform'. Plique, 'Etude sur le chapitre cathédral de Mende', is not particularly useful for our purposes because it deals almost exclusively with the later middle ages.

[25] We are informed about the prevalence of this *pessima consuetudo* by the criticism of Gregory IX, no. 1,615 (11.XII.1233).

[26] See below, p. 76 n. 17.

[27] The leniency with which Boniface VIII treated the fourteen-year-old prior of Langogne, Heracle de Tournel, in 1298 is particularly noteworthy: Boniface VIII, no. 2,864 (29.XI.1298). See also Clement V, nos. 4,708 (6.XI.1309), 4,762 (6.XI.1309), 9,659 (20.IV.1313), 9,661 (8.VIII.1313), 9,682 (13.IX.1313). In one instance Clement V did not appoint a nobleman: Clement V, no. 6,970 (14.IV.1311). In another he deposed the prior of Ispagnac, Aldebert de Peyre, because of his violent rebellion against Durant and entrusted the priory to Etienne de Suisy; see below, p. 96. Given Durant's firm stand on episcopal control over all ecclesiastical establishments in his diocese, he cannot have been altogether happy that his influence over the priories was so limited; see *TMA*, 1.4 De exemptionibus, fols. 8rb–13rb.

[28] On the *compensum pacis* and 'the peace' see Brunel, 'Les Juges de la paix', *passim*; Bisson, *Assemblies*, pp. 111–24; Porée, 'Les Evêques-comtes', pp. 352–4, 363f., 415f.

local noblemen and could be used to overturn the local equilibrium of power.

## THE GOLDEN BULL OF MENDE: ALDEBERT DE TOURNEL
## (1151–87)

The first to realize the opportunities presented by these circumstances was Bishop Aldebert de Tournel, a forceful and aggressive ruler who seems to have been active in the field of church reform.[29] He was in touch with Stephen of Tournai, one of the more notable canonists of the age, from whom he may have learned how to use law for the advantage of his church.[30] He raised the charge of simony against the nobles' stranglehold over the church of Mende, recovered the rights to ecclesiastical income that had been alienated to the nobility, and restored them to his church.[31] He purchased the buildings that surrounded his cathedral and fortified the city. He levied a new tax on all the silver that was mined in Gévaudan, which yielded forty marks each year.[32] He was the first bishop to obtain homage from the castles – not the lands – of Randon, Cénaret, and de Peyre. But above all he forged an alliance with King Louis VII. That was his masterstroke, a step so novel and far-reaching that it warrants closer examination.

The alliance of the bishop with the king was completed on the occasion of Aldebert's attendance at a royal assembly in Paris in 1161. It consisted essentially of two mutual concessions that were confirmed in a famous document known as the golden bull of Mende.[33] First came that of Aldebert:

Recognizing conscientiously that the justice of the material sword pertains to the sceptre of the kingdom, Bishop Aldebert approached our

---

[29] On Aldebert de Tournel, see Porée, 'Les Evêques-comtes', pp. 355–63; *Chronicon breve de gestis Aldeberti* in Brunel, ed., *Les Miracles de Saint Privat*, pp. 124–34; cf. Daunou, 'Adelbert de Tournel'.

[30] See Stephen's letter to Aldebert in *PL* 211:317.

[31] Porée, 'Les Evêques-comtes', pp. 358f.

[32] Ibid., p. 361.

[33] Porée, 'Les Evêques-comtes', pp. 359–61; Michel, *L'Administration royale*, p. 117; Devic and Vaissete, *Histoire générale*, 3:816f. Richard, *Saint Louis*, p. 21, suggests that Louis VII chose to seal the document in gold to emphasize his equality with Frederick Barbarossa, who had similarly sealed a grant to Lyons in gold. The golden bull of Mende was confirmed by Louis IX in 1257, 1262, and 1265, by Charles V in 1373, and by Louis XI in 1464; see *Ordonnances*, 5:603–5 and 16:255, 261; Porée, 'Les Evêques-comtes', p. 465. Louis VII is well known for the alliances he forged with ecclesiastical lords by confirming their liberty from other princes; see Mundy, *Europe*, pp. 387f.

Serenity in Paris where, in the presence of all our barons, he acknowledged his bishopric to be [held] of the crown of our kingdom. He
subordinated himself to us and, having solemnly touched the sacred
Gospel, swore an oath of fealty to ourselves and to the kingdom.[34]

The king reciprocated for this sweeping acceptance of his claims
to ultimate lordship over the Gévaudan as follows:

We grant the entire bishopric of Gévaudan, including the regalian rights
of our crown, to the glorious church of the martyr Privatus and to every
bishop who succeeds canonically to our venerable friend Aldebert. We
confirm this grant by our royal authority so that they may possess the
bishopric in freedom and in quiet forever. And providing out of our royal
kindness for its peace and quiet we grant it freedom and immunity from
all exactions, so that none of our successors may attempt hereafter to
molest or violate this church in any way.[35]

In order to appreciate the significance of these clauses, we must
distinguish between two levels of meaning, both with their own
validity: one was going to predominate in the long run, the other
predominated in the short run. On the former, the most important
aspect of the golden bull was its distinction between possession and
overlordship. The bishop would possess the bishopric in peace and
quiet, but he would also be subordinated to the overlordship of the
king. If only very faintly, this distinction adumbrated the modern
one between private rights of property and public rights of
jurisdiction.

The meaning that predominated in the short run was altogether
different. According to that reading, the bishop obtained complete
control over the bishopric, including the regalia, free and immune
from all exactions. This gave him as much sovereignty as was
perhaps conceivable in medieval times; and the bishops, therefore,

[34] 'Vir autem illustris jam dictus Aldebertus episcopus, religiose cogitans materiales gladii
justicias ad virgam regni pertinere, nostram serenitatem Parisius adiit, et ibidem in
presencia tocius Baronie nostre cognovit episcopatum suum de corona regni nostri esse,
et se nobis subdens, nobis et regno, celebriter tacto Evangelio sacro, fidelitatem fecit.'
*Ordonnances*, 16:255. The golden bull is also printed in Burdin, *Documents historiques*,
1:355f.; and *GC*, 1:Instrumenta:24f.

[35] 'Ecclesie gloriose martyris Privati et episcopis omnibus venerabili amico nostro Aldeberto canonice succedentibus, totum Gabalitanorum episcopatum, cum regalibus ad
nostram coronam pertinentibus, ex integro concedimus, et ut libere et quiete in
perpetuum possideant, auctoritate regia confirmamus. Ne autem de cetero aliquis
successorum nostrorum molestiam vel violenciam aliquo modo inferre conetur, paci et
quieti predicte ecclesie regia benignitate providentes, ipsam liberam et ab omni
exactionem immunem esse concedimus.' *Ordonnances*, 16:255. Cf. Devic and Vaissete,
*Histoire générale*, 3:816f. St Privatus was the patron saint of the cathedral of Mende.

could, and later sometimes did, declare their status to be equivalent to that of kings.[36] That was the basis on which they asked and obtained oaths of fealty, not merely from their vassals but also from all the inhabitants of the Gévaudan.[37] There are good reasons to doubt the soundness of this interpretation. Sovereignty is something absolute and unconditional. As William of Plaisians would point out, therefore, how could the bishop have been sovereign to begin with if he required confirmation of his sovereignty from Louis VII? And if he was not sovereign, how could Louis have made him so?[38] Nevertheless, it seemed to make good sense because the golden bull did treat the bishopric as an indivisible whole that ought in its entirety to be in the control of the bishop 'in peace and quiet, free and immune from all exactions'. In that sense it appeared to confirm the bishop in something like sovereignty.

It should be obvious that this conception of an undivided power over the whole bishopric was utterly incompatible with the distinction between possession and overlordship. The bishop could not possibly have undivided control and at the same time be subordinated to the king. The golden bull gave in one clause what it denied in the next. This ambivalence was to fuel a protracted struggle over which interpretation would prevail – that which benefited the king or that which benefited the bishop. It lasted until the time of William Durant the Younger and ended only when both protagonists admitted that the golden bull was, strictly speaking, incomprehensible.[39]

All this, however, lay in the distant future. For the present the conceptual illogic of the golden bull seems not to have been recognized, or at least not to have troubled either the bishop or the king. Louis VII, whose court possessed no recollection of any previous contacts between Paris and Mende, believed that 'the

---

[36] The royal inquests of the 1270s made it apparent that in the inhabitants' minds *major dominatio* was closely associated with *jus regale* and that both were interpreted as rights of ultimate lordship over the Gévaudan. Armand de Rouffiac, sacristan of Mende, for example, 'interrogatus quid vocat majorem dominationem, dixit quod, quando dominus cognoscit solus inter barones et alius non, vocat illud pertinere ad majorem dominationem. Dixit etiam quod dicti domini episcopi sunt usi juribus regalibus in Guaballitano. Et dixit esse jura regalia quia usus fuerat episcopus sicut rex utitur in regno suo. Et in signum regalium portatur quedam virga sive sceptrum argentea.' Porée, 'Les Evêques-comtes', p. 464 n. 3.

[37] Porée, 'Les Evêques-comtes', pp. 381–3, 440; Bisson, *Assemblies*, pp. 117f.

[38] See below, p. 87.

[39] More precisely, Plaisians regarded it as incomprehensible, whereas Durant regarded it as incompatible with episcopal sovereignty; see below, p. 87 n. 45.

entire territory, which is difficult to reach and mountainous, has always been in the power of the bishops, regarding not only ecclesiastical censures but also judgment by the sword'.[40] That may have been excusable, but it was wrong. In point of law, the Gévaudan still belonged to the counts of Barcelona. In point of fact, it was neither the bishop nor the king nor the counts, but rather the local nobility who really controlled the Gévaudan. The golden bull flew in the face of reality.[41] Thus, while the clash between episcopal and royal claims to lordship may have been significant in principle, that principle was still illusory, and therefore there was no reason for them to question the logical validity of the golden bull.

The only ones who did perceive quite clearly what had happened were those who were no party to the bargain: the local noblemen. They recognized that with the help of a Capetian ally from the distant north the bishop had usurped a power that was not his; that he had paid for this by selling the freedom of the Gévaudan, and that he threatened to overturn their own privileges, which they considered to be at least as ancient as the bishop's rights. They mounted a rebellion against the bishop that took him seven years to overcome.[42] Under the leadership of Aldebert's illegitimate brother, who had an axe of his own to grind, they repeatedly besieged the city and ultimately forced concessions from Aldebert, among them the surrender of the castle of Chapieu, which he himself had built on family estates to increase his power. Aldebert seems to have been spared worse only because of his fortunate discovery in 1170 of certain bones which he promptly declared to be those of St Privatus, protector of Mende. That commanded

---

[40] 'Longe est a memoria omnium mortalium nostri temporis, quod aliquis episcoporum Gaballorum ad curiam antecessorum nostrorum Francorum regum venerit, et eorum subditionem noverit, sive fidelitatem eis fecerit, quamvis tota terra illa difficilius aditu et montuosa, in potestate episcoporum semper extiterit, non tantum ad faciendum ecclesiasticam censuram, sed ad judicandum in gladio super eos quos culpa sua monstrabat sic redarguendos.' *Ordonnances*, 16:255. More likely this was Louis VII's excuse for what was in effect an attack on the rights of the legitimate lords of the Gévaudan, the counts of Barcelona.

[41] Porée, 'Les Evêques-comtes', pp. 359–61.

[42] Ibid., pp. 359–62; *Chronicon breve de gestis Aldeberti*, pp. 124–34. Cf. Aldebert's letter asking Louis VII for help in Duchesne, *Historiae*, 4:651f. No credence ought to be given to the legend, however, that Aldebert de Tournel died in the prison of his brother: Brunel, *Les Miracles*, p. xxxviii. This story is reported in *GC*, 1:90 n. a), and repeated by Devic and Vaissete, *Histoire générale*, 4:392.

enough respect from the nobility to end their uprising. Thus the cult of saints had proved more effective than the help of the Capetians. Clearly the golden bull had promised more than it could deliver and the bishop's power was still precarious.[43]

## THE BISHOP IN CHARGE: WILLIAM DE PEYRE (1187–1222)

Matters changed under Aldebert's successor, William de Peyre.[44] He was no less energetic in his defence of episcopal rights than Aldebert had been, and he expanded the demesne aggressively by purchasing the ever smaller shares of land into which noble estates were being divided under laws of equal inheritance.[45] Moreover, he frequently led 'the peace' into campaigns against the barons, and he ruled Mende with such a heavy hand that its citizens, incited by noblemen and canons, rebelled. That earned them a charter guaranteeing moderate liberties in 1194, but they still had no town government and no effective means of countering the bishop's arbitrary will.[46] Compared to Aldebert, William really ruled the Gévaudan. His task was vastly facilitated by two great strokes of luck. The first of these occurred when, in 1204, the kings of Aragon pledged the viscounty of Gévaudan to the counts of Toulouse for a large amount of money.[47] That proved to be a source of endless confusion over the right to govern the viscounty. The second was that both of the claimants, the counts of Toulouse and the kings of Aragon, were deeply compromised by their part in the Albigensian wars.

There is no need for us to relate the details of William's policies.[48] The main events of his tenure were these: in 1209, fearing that the count of Toulouse might not be able to protect the Gévaudan from the crusade against the Cathars, the king of

---

[43] See the judgment of Porée, 'Les Evêques-comtes', pp. 362f., and especially p. 464: 'De la souveraineté, les évêques de Mende n'avaient en réalité qu'une faible image, une vaine apparence.'    [44] Porée, 'Les Evêques-comtes', pp. 363–8.

[45] On the episcopal demesne, see Porée, 'Les Evêques-comtes', pp. 369–85.

[46] Porée, *Le Consulat*, p. vii: 'Contre son arbitraire ils n'ont, en somme, d'autre garantie que ses promesses et d'autre arme que la révolte.'

[47] Porée, 'La Domination Aragonaise', pp. 201–4. The pledge included the viscounty of Millau as well.

[48] They have been expertly described by Porée, 'La Domination Aragonaise', pp. 205–20, who clarifies several errors of Devic and Vaissete, *Histoire générale*, as well as Roucaute, *La Formation*.

Aragon rescinded his pledge to Toulouse and placed the viscounty in the bishop's care. In 1214 the king was killed in battle, his possessions were confiscated by the church of Rome, and the viscounty was once again entrusted to the bishop, this time as part of the estate of a deceased heretic. In 1219 the lords of Tournel, Florac, and Randon, all of whom were concerned to receive orthodox protection and to distance themselves from Toulouse, did homage to the bishop. William de Peyre thus adroitly took advantage of every opportunity afforded by the embarrassment of his opponents under the onslaught of the crusaders. If Aldebert had masterminded a plan to ascend to power, William put it into effect.

Old age forced William to resign from his episcopate in 1222, but it took no longer than three years for his successor, Stephen of Brioude, to see his plans through to completion.[49] In 1225 the king of Aragon, convinced that he could no longer protect his rights over the Gévaudan, surrendered the viscounty to the bishop for good, declared himself to be the bishop's vassal, and did homage. In the next year the bishop, encouraged by the papal legate, preached a crusade, captured Grèzes, and expelled the last remnant of Toulousan forces from the Gévaudan.[50]

Thus the situation had been totally reversed since the middle of the eleventh century. The bishop was no longer subject to a viscount or struggling to assert control over any part of the Gévaudan. Now he himself was viscount, lord of the previous viscount, and consequently lord of all the former viscount's vassals, including not only those who had already done homage to him but also the de Peyre, the Mercoeur, the Apcher, and even the counts of Rodez. He presided over jurisdiction, controlled the roads, and minted coins. Each year he received a penny from the inhabitants of the Gévaudan in recognition of their submission to the church of St Privatus.[51] And in his processions he had a sceptre carried before

---

[49] Devic and Vaissete's dating of William de Peyre's resignation to 1223, *Histoire générale*, 4:392, is uncertain. Honorius III, no. 3540 (22.IX.1221) orders the papal legate in southern France to receive William's resignation. Porée, 'La Domination Aragonaise', pp. 220f., thus seems right in dating the beginning of Stephen of Brioude's episcopate to 1222.

[50] Porée, 'La Domination Aragonaise', pp. 220–3; Porée, 'Les Evêques-comtes', pp. 367f.; *GC*, 1:Instrumenta:25.

[51] The 'Penny of St Privatus', which was levied down to the fourteenth century 'ratione servitutis quam suberant homines beato Privato', is not to be confused with the *compensum pacis*; Bisson, *Assemblies*, p. 111 n. 34.

him in evidence of his temporal power. He had achieved the goal that had been promised by the golden bull.[52]

## AMBIVALENCE: STEPHEN OF BRIOUDE (1222–47)

The bishop's success, however, was shortlived. Now that his rights of possession had been realized, his duties of submission were beginning to be realized as well. So far he had benefited from the threat posed to his rivals by the papacy and the monarchy of France. Now those rivals had been defeated – but the papacy and the monarchy had set up camp in southern France and neither had any plans to leave. Now a real price was going to be asked for benefits that the bishop had so far obtained free.

William de Peyre had already received the first indication that such might be the future course of events;[53] but it was his successor, Stephen of Brioude, who for the first time felt the full weight of central government. Stephen's very person marked a new phase in the history of the bishopric. He did not belong to the Gabalitan nobility, and he had not even, as he put it, been taken 'from the bosom of the church of Mende'.[54] Stephen came from Brioude, not far to the north of the Gévaudan, where he had served as *magister scholarum*.[55] He was something of an outsider in the circles from which the bishops of Mende had been drawn so far, a man who owed his promotion to his merits as a scholar, not to his birth. Indeed, his birth was illegitimate, so that he needed a special dispensation from the pope in order to be elevated to the bishopric.[56]

---

[52] Michel, *L'Administration royale*, pp. 116f. Actually he controlled only the county's eastern parts, and even those not nearly as effectively as the king later did; Porée, 'Les Evêques-comtes', pp. 384f., 432. For a survey of the bishop's powers in the thirteenth century see Porée, 'Les Evêques-comtes', pp. 453–64.

[53] In 1214 William not only taken charge of the viscounty of Gévaudan, but also the viscounty of Millau, which had been included in the Aragonese pledge to Toulouse. But at the request of Honorius III he had to restore the viscounty of Millau to the Aragonese in 1217, while the profits which he had derived from it in the meantime were reserved for the crusade; Honorius III, no. 612 (6.VI.1217); Barbiche, ed. *Actes pontificaux*, 1:46, no. 108 (2.IV.1215).

[54] 'Assumtus non fuerat de gremio ecclesiae Mimatensis.' *GC*, 1:Instrumenta:25.

[55] It is worth noting that at King Louis VII's request Aldebert de Tournel had intervened against simony in Brioude, which prompted the dean of Brioude to appeal to the pope; see Aldebert's letter to Louis in Duchesne, *Historiae*, 4:656.

[56] Honorius III, nos. 4836 (2.III.1224), 4841 (7.III.1224), 4851 (11.III.1224); Eubel, *Hierarchia catholica*, 1:357 n. 1.

From one point of view Stephen's accession evidenced the progress of reform. It seems quite fitting that the first bishop of Mende to be appointed after the Fourth Lateran Council excelled in knowledge and broke forever the stranglehold by which the de Peyre and the Tournel had so far held the bishop's office.[57] From another point of view, however, Stephen's appointment signalled a quantum leap in the degree to which state and church were able to interfere in the affairs of a diocese that had so far lain securely beyond their reach.

Stephen's vulnerability was manifested first in his relations with the church. The pope and his legates took an active hand in his appointment (which may indeed have been decisive in persuading the chapter to accept his candidacy) and in resolving the obstacles raised by the archbishop of Bourges, who feared that this manner of appointment infringed upon his rights as metropolitan. Stephen was the first bishop of Mende to be consecrated in Rome.[58] He had to reckon more frequently than any of his predecessors with the interference of papal legates, who were sent with full authority to combat heresy.[59] He was also the first to experience the papacy's growing inclination to draw upon Gabalitan revenues in order to settle debts that he had not incurred.[60]

[57] With the exception of a single bishop who ruled for just two years (Aldebert de Peyre, 1441–3), no de Peyre and no Tournel would ever again occupy the see of St Privatus.

[58] William de Peyre had resigned the bishopric into the hands of the papal legate, who had ordered the chapter of Mende to proceed to elect a successor. Their choice of Stephen required confirmation by Honorius III because Innocent III, dispensing Stephen from his illegitimate birth on the occasion of his ordination to the priesthood, had prohibited him from accepting an election to the episcopate without a further special permission from the pope. Since the archbishop of Bourges had not yet received the pallium, Stephen was consecrated by the bishop of Chartres: *GC*, 1:91, *GC*, 1:Instrumenta:25, Eubel, *Hierarchia catholica*, 1:357 n. 2. The document in *GC* is dated to 1223, but given the dates in Honorius III, nos. 4836 (2.III.1224), 4841 (7.III.1224), that must be according to the Old Style.

[59] For the inclusion of Mende in the competency of papal legates in 1233 and later, see Gregory IX, nos. 1,472 (27.VII.1233), 1,474 and 1,477 (28.VII.1233), 4,347 (23.VIII.1238), and Innocent IV, no. 31 (19.VII.1243).

[60] During the seven years from 1232 to 1239 Gregory IX requested three contributions from the dioceses of southern France, including Mende, to help settle the sizeable debts incurred by the counts of Montfort, the church of Le Puy, and the church of Valence with moneylenders in Cahors and Sens. We have no direct information about the amounts requested from Mende in the first two instances, but since it had to pay only 80 lbs. out of a total of 10,000 lbs. (*tournois* money) for the church of Valence, they were probably moderate. That may explain why Mende does not figure among the dioceses that appealed against the collection of the subsidy for Valence. On the debts of Le Puy see Gregory IX, nos. 902–6 (9.X.1232). On Valence, Gregory IX, nos. 4,857 (17.V.1239), 4,859 (25.V.1239). On the Montforts, Gregory IX, nos. 3,926 (31.X.1237), 5,282 (1.VIII.1240), 5,310 (16.XI.1240), and Innocent IV, no. 361 (2.I.1244).

In the temporal realm the same vulnerability manifested itself far more dramatically. The Gévaudan may have been too poor and mountainous to form a central target of Capetian expansion, but its roads, which were more secure from the threat of the Empire than those in the Rhône valley, formed an important geographic link between Paris and the Mediterranean coast. Hence the region had to be kept under control.[61] Only a few months after Stephen had taken charge of the viscounty, King Louis VIII declared that the claims of Toulouse, to which he had succeeded, were still valid, and he appointed Béraud de Mercoeur as viscount. In 1229 the treaty of Paris confirmed his point of view.[62] 'That was the time when the Frenchmen began to control Grèzes' was how it was later remembered, and there is no doubt that 'the Frenchmen' were resented as alien intruders.[63] But there was nothing that Stephen could do to stop the Capetians. On the contrary, with his treasury depleted by costly campaigns, lacking the vassals on whom a de Peyre might have relied, and embroiled in a conflict with the Tournel, he was forced to call for royal help. In 1233 he invited the seneschal of Beaucaire to supply him with military assistance for the following three years.[64] In return he promised him half the *compensum pacis* and half of the profits from any campaigns to preserve the peace. It was the first breach in the exemption from taxation that had been promised by the golden bull. After some hesitation the seneschal (whose anxiety that the king might not wish him to interfere in the Gévaudan was speedily removed by an encouraging letter from Paris) appeared in the Gévaudan with forces that made a great enough impression on the nobility to obtain their consent to the new arrangement.[65] Immediately thereafter the seneschal embarked on a campaign to make a quick example of the rebellious

---

[61] Michel, *L'Administration royale*, pp. 163–5.

[62] Porée, 'La Domination Aragonaise', pp. 223–5; Porée, 'Les Evêques-comtes', pp. 411–15; cf. Devic and Vaissete, *Histoire générale*, 4:137f. Porée, 'Les Evêques-comtes', pp. 410–32, contains the best account of the relationship between bishop and king during Stephen's reign. For a more general description of the expansion of royal power in the Gévaudan see Michel, *L'Administration royale*, pp. 117f., 146–53, 162–5, 175–81.

[63] 'Et tunc Gallici inceperunt possidere Gredonam.' Cited by Michel, *L'Administration royale*, p. 117 n. 7. In 1341, on the eve of the hundred years war Bishop Albert de Lordet declared in no uncertain terms that he would rather be a subject of the English than the French: 'Si Deus me adjuvet, melius esset nobis et toti patrie isti quod venissent Anglici ad partes istas quam vos et non dubito quod ipsi minus nocerent nobis quam vos faciatis.' Porée, *Le Consulat*, p. xx n. 2.

[64] On the circumstances see Porée, 'Les Evêques-comtes', pp. 416–19.

[65] Only the lord of Tournel, who seems to have noticed which way the wind was blowing, was firmly opposed; Porée, 'Les Evêques-comtes', pp. 419f.

lords of Servissac. On leaving the Gévaudan he installed a knight named Mercadier as the first royal *bailli* in Marvéjols.[66]

Mercadier and his successors campaigned repeatedly and forcefully against the de Peyre, Apcher, Anduze, Randon, and Tournel, seizing their castles, holding assizes, and imposing truces on their feuds. They also confiscated property and summoned Gabalitan barons to campaign against Toulouse. In short, they were irresistible: they kept the peace far more effectively than the bishop had ever done. Gabalitans who were later asked to assess the impact of the royal forces were unanimous in their opinion that 'after the lord king arrived in these lands, there was greater peace than ever before', for 'the bishop did not and could not keep the peace. Peace in the land was not established by the bishop, but by the king', for 'out of fear of him no one dared to make war'.[67]

This was no easy lesson for the bishop to swallow. For a while he flattered himself that the king's *bailli* did everything at his request, under a temporary agreement that he was at liberty not to renew and that expressly preserved his rights from any prejudice. But the reality was different. By 1236, when the agreement was about to expire for the first time, the local nobility were outright opposed to a renewal. Raymond Anduze exclaimed that 'we are of great blood. It is not good that we are being sold like pork or mutton.'[68] Stephen himself had serious doubts. The seneschal, however, knew how to remind him of the value of royal protection: he encouraged the lord of Canilhac to start a small rebellion against the bishop.[69] Lacking the support of his nobles and with nowhere else to turn, Stephen renewed the agreement in 1237, in 1239, and in 1241, despite his misgivings. But matters kept getting worse.[70] Stephen

---

66 Ibid., pp. 421f.
67 'Postquam dominus rex fuit in terris istis, fuit major pax quam nunquam fuit.' 'Episcopus non tenebat nec poterat tenere pacem, nec per ipsum episcopum erat pax in terra, sed per dominum regem.' 'Postquam dominus rex dominatus fuit in terris istis, dominus rex custodivit pacem ita quod, ejus timore, nullus fuit ausus facere guerram.' Porée, 'Les Evêques-comtes', p. 432 n. 2.
68 'Nos sumus de magno sanguine et non est bonum quod vendamur sicut porcus vel muto.' Porée, 'Les Evêques-comtes', p. 425 n. 3.
69 According to Porée, 'Les Evêques-comtes', pp. 425f., few Gabalitan lords were more firmly associated with the viscounts than those of Canilhac.
70 Guillaume de Pian, Mercadier's successor since 1242, campaigned against the Tournel, whose cattle he captured and returned for 10,000 shillings. He also conquered Château-neuf, where he kept assizes, and Apcher, which he returned for 53,000 shillings to the Apcher; Porée, 'Les Evêques-comtes', pp. 426–30.

began to take an active stand against the royal officers, and in 1243, when Louis IX appointed Hugues de la Tour, bishop of Clermont, as viscount of Gévaudan, he finally refused to renew the agreement.[71] But when he tried to levy the *compensum pacis* for himself he found it was too late. The bishop of Clermont simply abolished the *compensum pacis* on the grounds that peace was now being kept by the king, and he sent knights against both Mende and the bishop's lands.[72] That was the end of Stephen's reign. Unable to defend Mende, he was expelled by the citizens and was forced to seek asylum with the noble family that was now vindicated for having resisted the introduction of royal forces from the beginning: the Tournel. In 1246 he died, defeated and humiliated.

The effect of Stephen's reign thus was to end the splendid isolation of the Gévaudan and to reveal the ambivalence of the golden bull. If his reign had begun with a stunning justification of Aldebert's policies, it ended with an equally stunning revelation of their cost. Control over the bishopric came at the price of subjection to the king. If the king once seemed the bishop's most reliable ally, now he had been revealed as a far more dangerous rival than the local barons had ever been.

REACTION: ODILO DE MERCOEUR (1247–74)

In the aftermath of Stephen's reign local policies underwent a reversal. If the bishop had previously relied on the help of the king in order to increase his power over the nobility, he now fell back on the assistance of the nobility in order to combat royal encroachments. If the barons had previously attacked him as a rival, they now rallied around him as a champion of their freedoms. This had already been implicit in Stephen's final turn to the Tournel for help. It became quite evident as soon as the chapter of Mende began to deliberate on a successor to Stephen. The canons were split between two candidates, but they were united in their preference

---

[71] He once arrested Mercadier, he defended the lordship of Florac against a campaign led by the seneschal, and he made sure that the standard of St Privatus took precedence over that of the king; Porée, 'Les Evêques-comtes', p. 431; Michel, *L'Administration royale*, pp. 149–52.

[72] Since the late 1220s some of the barons had protested against the *compensum pacis*. Unhappy as they were about royal interventions, they were happy enough to be relieved of this tax; Porée, 'Les Evêques-comtes', pp. 416, 433f.

for members of powerful noble houses of the Gévaudan who could count on vassals for support.[73]

The man who eventually won the election belonged to the most powerful house of all: Odilo de Mercoeur.[74] He could make do without the *pax* that Hugues de la Tour had suppressed; from the beginning of his episcopate he relied on fealty and homage to re-establish episcopal control over the Gévaudan. As a great noble he also enjoyed a form of access to King Louis IX that may well have been beyond Stephen's possibilities. And he seems to have recognized that the assistance of the pope could be of use against the encroachments of the king.[75]

Such resources endowed his episcopate with some success. He repressed attempts at rebellion by the Tournel and the Randon soon after his election, and he not only renewed the homages that had been given in the past but also managed to procure homages from the Apcher and the first homage ever from the de Peyre in 1261.[76] No doubt he was helped by the conviction that royal attacks on local liberties could only be repulsed if the barons acted in unison: sentiments of local patriotism were growing stronger under the centralizing pressure from abroad.[77] Nevertheless, these were major victories that extended the bishop's power for the first time to the northwest of the diocese. Odilo made further progress when in 1257 he persuaded Louis IX to confirm the golden bull.[78]

---

[73] The two candidates were Arnaud de Peyre, canon of Mende, and Bernard d'Apcher, dean of Le Puy; Devic and Vaissete, *Histoire générale*, 4:393.

[74] In 1247 Bernard d'Apcher and Arnaud de Peyre renounced their claims before Innocent IV in Lyons, whereupon he exercised his plenitude of power to appoint Odilo de Mercoeur, dean at the cathedral of Bourges, as procurator, 'sibi liberam administrationem ipsius ecclesiae in spiritualibus et temporalibus committentes'. Martène and Durand, *Thesaurus novus*, 1:1,029. As late as 1255 Odilo had not yet been consecrated; *GC*, 1:92f.; Innocent IV, no. 2,333 (23.XII.1246); Eubel, *Hierarchia catholica*, 1:357 n. 2.

[75] On the character of Odilo's power see Porée, 'Les Evêques-comtes', pp. 437. On his relations with the papacy, see below, pp. 51, 52f.

[76] Porée, 'Les Evêques-comtes', pp. 435f., 437–41; Chazaud, 'L'Evêque de Mende', pp. 309–21; Devic and Vaissete, *Histoire générale*, 4:393. The Apcher had given their first homage to Stephen in the year before he died, but they resisted Odilo, in part because Bernard d'Apcher had competed with Odilo for the episcopal office. They attempted to form an alliance with the counts of Rodez but had to surrender to Odilo in 1262; Porée, 'Les Evêques-comtes', pp. 383f., 438; Devic and Vaissete, *Histoire générale*, 8:1,447–9.

[77] Thus, before leaving for Paris in order to negotiate with Louis IX in 1263, Odilo assembled the barons at St Chély d'Apcher and persuaded them to send two delegates to Paris to assist him; Porée, 'Les Evêques-comtes', p. 448.

[78] Odilo obtained two further confirmations in 1262 and 1265: Porée, 'Les Evêques-comtes', pp. 445, 447, 451, 465; Michel, *L'Administration royale*, p. 179; Devic and

In 1262 he defeated a rebellion by the citizens of Mende, who failed once again to create a communal government.[79] With Louis IX's support he suppressed the actions of a particularly aggressive seneschal and may even have instigated his removal from office.[80] Finally, he enlisted the help of Innocent IV to support his claims on the viscounty.[81]

All this was quite impressive – but it was not enough and did not last. In 1258 the treaty of Corbeil sealed the Capetian claims to the rights of Aragon. At that moment the bishop's hopes of recovering the viscounty of Gévaudan, which had long since been dashed in practice, were dashed in theory as well.[82] Odilo managed to get the most out of a hopeless situation. Agreeing to surrender what he could not keep, and hoping that it might be enough to satisfy the royal appetite, he formally relinquished all of his rights to the viscounty and recognized the conquests of Louis in the southeast of the Gévaudan. In return he obtained an annual rent and some lands and castles in the Cévennes, along with another solemn guarantee that the golden bull would be respected.[83] That was a reasonable compromise, but it proved to be ephemeral. For a few years the settlement with Louis IX kept the seneschals at bay, but in 1268

Vaissete, *Histoire générale*, 4:138, 8:1,550–2. To avoid misleading impressions it ought to be pointed out that the confirmations of the golden bull were not isolated events but fit into the pattern of Louis IX's attempts in the 1250s to bring the upheavals of the Albigensian wars to a peaceful conclusion; see Jordan, *Louis IX*, pp. 136f. Note also that Louis did not confirm the golden bull without adding the clause 'salvo in omnibus jure nostro et eciam alieno'. *Ordonnances*, 16:261.

[79] The citizens had established syndics, but Odilo refused to recognize them, and the rebellion ended with the citizens' complete surrender; Porée, *Le Consulat*, pp. viii–xiii, 1–49. The town only managed to establish syndics during the initial phases of the hundred years' war; Porée, *Le Consulat*, pp. xxif.

[80] The seneschal, Guy de Rochefort, had endorsed the rebellion of Mende against Odilo, punished barons who refused to assist him, and ravaged the episcopal lands in the west of the diocese. In 1264 he was replaced by Arnoul de Courfraud: Porée, 'Les Evêques-comtes', pp. 446–9.

[81] In 1250, Innocent IV asked Queen Blanche of Castile, who legally controlled the former Aragonese fiefs in the Gévaudan, to put an end to usurpations by royal officials and to allow the bishop to reassert control over the town of Marvéjols; Porée, 'Les Evêques-comtes', pp. 449f.; Michel, *L'Administration royale*, pp. 178f. and n. 7.

[82] Devic and Vaissete, *Histoire générale*, 4:138.

[83] Michel, *L'Administration royale*, pp. 179f.; Porée, 'Les Evêques-comtes', pp. 450f.; Devic and Vaissete, *Histoire générale*, 4:138. The documents are printed in Devic and Vaissete, *Histoire générale*, 8:1,550–2, and Burdin, *Documents historiques*, 1:358. Cf. R-S, no. 2 (18.X.1291), pp. 3–5, no. 23 (3.II.1307), pp. 47–50, no. 62 (*melius* no. 67; 7.IV.1311), pp. 128–30, and appendix 11, pp. 213–16.

they vigorously resumed their former course of action.[84] Indeed, now they were more convinced than ever that 'the whole Gabalitan bishopric, insofar as temporal jurisdiction is concerned, is under the king of the French and belongs to him in full right'.[85] In 1269 Odilo saw no other choice than to seek justice from the very king whose officers were troubling him. He appealed to Parlement.[86]

Nor did matters take a more promising turn in church affairs. Pope Innocent IV, who is well known for his extension of centralization in the church through reservations and provisions, introduced the practice of provisions to the Gévaudan as well.[87] Moreover, Odilo was repeatedly requested to execute papal business.[88] And last, but hardly least, the mendicants entered the Gévaudan.[89] Not that each and every sign of growing centralization provoked Odilo's displeasure – Pope Innocent's provisions were granted at his own request and benefited his own favourites.[90] As for the mendicants, there is no indication that he resisted

---

[84] Porée, 'Les Evêques-comtes', pp. 465f. Even before 1268 the seneschals had prohibited the circulation of episcopal coins, an issue that had not been settled by the compromise of 1265. They also requested service from Gabalitan barons and called them before their courts. By that time the entire region south of the Tarn was already firmly under their control. Porée, 'Les Evêques-comtes', pp. 442–9, 465f.; Michel, *L'Administration royale*, pp. 175–81.

[85] 'Quod totus episcopatus Gaballitanus quantum ad temporalem jurisdictionem subest et pertinet ad dominum regem Francorum pleno jure, quoad majorem jurisdictionem et districtum seu cohertionem temporalem.' Cited by Michel, *L'Administration royale*, p. 181 n. 2.

[86] Porée, 'Les Evêques-comtes', pp. 466f. On the proceedings that unfolded during Odilo's episcopate see Porée, 'Le Procès', pp. 282–7.

[87] Innocent IV, nos. 6,948 (19.VIII.1253), 6,959 (25.VIII.1253). Judging from the published papal records, these are the first papal provisions in the history of Mende. On Innocent's role in general see, e.g., Ganzer, *Papsttum*, pp. 44–6, 50, 68f., 70–2, 90f.

[88] Alexander IV charged Odilo, among others, with investigating the 'excesses' of his neighbour, the bishop of Rodez. The mission failed over understandable resistance from Rodez. Urban IV sent him back to Rodez in 1262. The bishop of Rodez refused to appear before the papal emissary and had Odilo excommunicated. The conflict seems to have caused no negligible danger to Odilo's person: Urban IV, nos. 2,886 (7.II.1262), 2,970 (14.X.1263). An order to execute a papal mandate was given to a sacristan of Mende in 1263: Urban IV, no. 884 (31.X.1263).

[89] On several occasions in the late 1240s Pope Innocent IV sent Dominicans as inquisitors to Mende; Barbiche, ed. *Actes pontificaux*, no. 521 (21.IV.1245); Innocent IV, nos. 3,421 (12.XI.1247), 3,423 (12.XI.1247), 3,424 (19.XI.1247). In 1278, with the support of the Canilhac, the Dominicans established a house in Marvéjols: *GC*, 1:93; cf. Bernard Gui, *De fundatione*, p. 267. Franciscans can first reliably be documented to have entered Mende in 1263, but after 1273 they, too, are regularly found in Marvéjols: Emery, *Friars*, p. 87, and Vicaire, 'Le Developpement', pp. 58, 68, 73. The dates given by Besse, *Abbayes et prieurés*, 4:59 (1220 for the Franciscans in Mende, and 1254 for the Carmelites) seem unreliable.

[90] Both of the dispensations from pluralism that Innocent IV had sent to Mende in 1253

their arrival. On the contrary, in keeping with the habits of his noble peers, he may have welcomed them to Mende.[91] Yet whatever gains he may have foreseen from such developments were turned into losses no less easily than those Aldebert had expected from his alliance with the king. Provisions, once become a habit, could be exercised against the bishop's wishes, and the mendicants, once installed, could raise a serious threat to his spiritual authority.[92] Indeed, it soon became evident how quickly papal interference could turn from a boon into a burden. Odilo seems to have relied on Innocent IV to wrest the priory of Ispagnac from the de Peyre, but the de Peyre soon returned the favour, appealing to Innocent's successors until Urban IV re-established their right.[93]

When Odilo de Mercoeur died in 1274, the reversal of local

were granted at Odilo's request. One was destined to support a certain master Durandus Radulfus, canon of Mende and *commensalis* of Odilo: Innocent IV, no. 6,948 (19.VIII.1253). The other was granted to Pierre de Montaigu, canon of Brioude, explicitly in order to honour his noble relatives, Odilo and Béraud de Mercoeur: Innocent IV, no. 6,959 (25.VIII.1253). Besides, Odilo himself had become bishop as a result of Innocent's intervention and was allowed to keep his benefices; *GC*, 1:93.

[91] On the favourable relationship between mendicant orders and the southern French nobility see Dossat, 'Opposition', pp. 273–8. But note that toward the end of Odilo's life the Franciscans seem to have preferred Marvéjols, the capital of the de Peyre, over Mende and that the Dominicans established their house in Marvéjols to begin with.

[92] Indeed, the provisions that were issued by Innocent's successors do not seem to have been granted to Odilo's favourites: see Urban IV, no. 1,340 (12.II.1264); Clement IV, no. 600 (28.IX.1267); Martin IV, no. 342 (21.VI.1283). Odilo's relationship with Innocent IV, an Italian pope who had imperial aspirations, seems to have been better than his relationship with French popes like Clement IV and especially Urban IV, who were inclined to cooperate with the French monarchy and were therefore less supportive of the French church.

[93] The details are worth mentioning because they afford an excellent illustration of the effects of papal justice on local church government. Some time before 1264 the abbot of the Benedictine monastery of Aurillac in the diocese of Clermont appointed Aldebert de Peyre as prior of Ispagnac. On the grounds of a letter obtained from Innocent IV, Odilo protested that the prior of Ispagnac was to be chosen by himself. Aldebert appealed to Urban IV, who committed the matter to Cardinal Richardus de Annibaldis, vicar of Rome and himself a member of the Benedictine order. Cardinal Richard in turn committed the matter to the noted canonist Bernard of Spain the Younger, who called the parties to testify. Aldebert appeared, but since the bishop's procurator appealed to be heard directly by the pope, Bernard refused to confirm Aldebert's right to the priory. Acting on a report by two papal chaplains who had questioned the bishop's procurator and Aldebert de Peyre on the proceedings that had taken place so far, Urban thereupon commanded the bishop of Béziers to assure himself that Aldebert's rights were legitimate and to let him enter into possession of the priory. All of the evidence is contained in Urban IV, no. 2,493 (13.II.1264). This was no minor defeat for Odilo. More important for our purposes is the fact that later on Ispagnac turned into a focal point of violent resistance to William Durant the Younger; see below, pp. 95f.

policies had turned out to be ineffective.[94] To fall back on lordship and personal connections was an expedient that could delay but not prevent the extension of centralized control. The ambivalence of the golden bull had been recognized and the bishop had run out of ideas. That left the church of Mende in an impasse.[95]

[94] *GC*, 1:93, and Eubel, *Hierarchia catholica*, 1:357 n. 2, are wrong in giving 1273 as the year of Odilo's death. 1274 is supported by Porée, 'Les Evêques-comtes', pp. 287f. and Devic and Vaissete, *Histoire générale*, 4:393. *GC*, 1:92f., moreover, is totally confused in believing that Odilo de Mercoeur was followed by an Odilo de Tournel, who is supposed to have been responsible for the settlement of 1265.

[95] Odilo's successor was another Stephen; see Eubel, *Hierarchia catholica*, 1:358. *GC*, 1:93, Gams, *Series episcoporum*, p. 577, and Falletti, 'Guillaume Durand', col. 1,025, are wrong in dating the death of Stephen to 1278. As late as November 1283 he is reported to have purchased certain lands from the Tournel; see Philippe, *La Baronnie*, lxxxv. But their error is excusable since his episcopate is devoid of any major initiatives. The registers of Gregory X, John XXI, and Martin IV contain not a single reference to his activities. A solitary trace of his role consists of an order by Pope Nicholas III in 1278 to join the bishop of Rodez and the abbot of Tulle in examining the chapter of Albi, whose regular canons were to be turned into secular ones: Nicholas III, no. 192 (8.XII.1278). We also know that he granted a new charter to the citizens of Mende (Porée, *Le Consulat*, pp. xivf., 52–7), participated in a council in Orléans in 1278 (*GC*, 1:93), and became involved in a disagreement with the Hospitaller Grand Prior of St Gilles in 1278, to whom the Tournel had rendered unprecedented homages. The disagreement was arbitrated by the archbishop of Arles; Philippe, *La Baronnie*, pp. lxxxii–lxxxv.

## Chapter 2

# THE STATE OF THE CHURCH

What God has joined together let no man put asunder. These words were said about the first parents, Adam and Eve, but they apply just as well to the church of Rome and the kingdom and kings of the French, whom God has joined forever.                                                    Boniface VIII[1]

So far we have considered the diocese of Mende from a local perspective. But ever since the beginning of Stephen's reign the control over the diocese had been passing out of local hands. During the years after the death of Odilo de Mercoeur, it finally passed into the hands of the spiritual and the temporal monarchies. We therefore need to shift our attention toward the growth of central government.

This matter is so broad and has received so much attention that it is neither possible nor necessary for us to deal with it in much detail.[2] We do, however, need to identify two of its basic features. One was that the demise of the Hohenstaufen freed the papacy from the long-standing burden of war with the emperor and thus enabled it to resume vigorous leadership of the Christian commonwealth. The other was that in so doing it entered into an ever closer partnership with the most Christian king of France. It was the

---

[1] 'Quos Deus coniunxit homo non separet. Licet haec verba dicta sint de primis parentibus Eva et Adam, tamen convenienter applicantur ad ecclesiam istam et regnum et reges Francorum, quos coniunxit semper.' Dupuy, *Histoire*, p. 77.

[2] The pertinent studies are too abundant to be listed here in any detail. For the papacy an outstanding general account has just been published by Morris, *The Papal Monarchy*, to be supplemented by Southern, *Western Society and the Church*, Oakley, *The Western Church in the Later Middle Ages*, and Mollat, *Les Papes d'Avignon*. For the state there are the survey of Mitteis, *Der Staat des hohen Mittelalters*, Strayer's incisive essay *On the Medieval Origins of the Modern State*, and Strayer's superlative history of the *Reign of Philip the Fair*. These may be accompanied by Haller, *Papsttum und Kirchenreform*, Barraclough, *Papal Provisions*, Hashagen, *Staat und Kirche vor der Reformation*, Partner, *The Lands of St. Peter*, and Moore, *The Formation of a Persecuting Society*.

French whom the papacy called upon to pacify the lands of the Hohenstaufen in southern Italy; Frenchmen ascended to the papal throne; and general councils met in France.[3]

The benefits for both parties were undeniable. The papacy took charge of southern Italy, restrained its unruly subjects, and played a more active part in the ecclesiastical affairs of France. At the second council of Lyons negotiations with the Greeks conducted on the basis of this new security almost bore fruit. The monarchy of France, in turn, was able to draw on the tenths that were levied on the revenues of the French church in no less than twenty-one of the thirty years from 1247 to 1277.[4] After the Aragonese had wrested Sicily from Anjou in the Vespers of 1282 this symbiotic relationship grew still stronger.[5] Hence Pope Boniface VIII could remind Philip IV during their later strife that 'during the times of the great Philip [Augustus], the income of the king of France from allocated revenues did not exceed eighteen thousand pounds. Today, however, because of the encouragements, graces, and dispensations of the church of Rome, he gets forty thousand pounds and more.'[6] What was created in this way was a joint spiritual–temporal monarchy, a 'state of the church' in which the universal papal government in Rome entered into a happy union with the government of France.

[3] It has therefore by now become a commonplace that Clement V's decision to reside in France did not amount to a break from previous patterns but rather was the natural extension of a process that had begun at least two generations earlier, and perhaps as far back as the eleventh and twelfth centuries, when Popes Urban II and Alexander III had found refuge from imperial troops in France. See, for example, Mollat, *Les Papes d'Avignon*, pp. 9–13; Oakley, *The Western Church*, pp. 32–4. The same point was forcefully made from a broader perspective by Haller, *Das Papsttum*, 5:223–7, but Haller, of course, deplored the cooperation of the papacy with France as a central cause of the decline of the medieval church.

[4] See Hashagen, *Staat und Kirche*, pp. 129–33, for the tenths and Partner, *Papal State*, pp. 269–75, as well as Strayer, *Reign of Philip the Fair*, pp. 245, 254, for French support of the papal cause in Italy. For English parallels in the collection of tenths see, e.g., Gibbs and Lang, *Bishops*, p. 132. Full of excellent insights and precise detail, Hashagen, *Staat und Kirche*, esp. pp. 81–299, is still one of the most illuminating accounts of the motives that led the papacy and the French monarchy to cooperate in the formation of national or territorial churches.

[5] Pope Nicholas IV thus instructed the bishops who were to collect the tenth of 1289 for the war against Aragon that they should think of nothing but 'solum Deum et justiciam ac predicti negocii a predicto rege Francorum suscepti necessitatem.' Boutaric, 'Notices', pp. 91–102, here p. 102.

[6] 'Scimus quod aliquando temporibus Magni Philippi rex Franciae non habebat de situatis redditibus decem octo mill. libr. et hodie per fomenta, gratias, et dispensationes istius ecclesiae habet quadraginta mill. lib. et plus.' Dupuy, *Histoire*, p. 77.

## THE BISHOPS BETWEEN KING AND POPE

Among the first to feel the power of this 'state' were, naturally, the French bishops.[7] Throughout the thirteenth century they experienced increasing pressure both from the papacy and from the king of France. As long as the two centralizing powers had not combined their efforts the bishops had held their own. They frustrated the papacy's attempts to organize a system of ecclesiastical taxation;[8] they submitted bitter *gravamina* against Pope Innocent IV in 1247;[9] and even when they went along with requests for taxation they insisted on making their independence public.[10] But in the 1280s the fortunes of the bishops changed for the worse. In spite of a concerted effort they were defeated in two causes that were particularly dear to them: their battle against the mendicants and their attempts to restrain the extension of royal jurisdiction over ecclesiastical affairs. A closer look at their defeat will illuminate the effects of cooperation between the pope and the king of France on episcopal autonomy.

The bishops' conflict with the mendicants had been brewing ever since the Franciscans and the Dominicans had been established as independent orders early in the thirteenth century.[11] Indeed, it

[7] On the impact of centralization on the local church in general Schulte, *Der Adel und die deutsche Kirche*, is an old but unsurpassed classic. Murray, *Reason and Society*, is equally good, but from a very different perspective. For circumstances in France see Gaudemet, *La Société ecclésiastique*; Gaudemet, *Eglise et société*; Guenée, *Entre l'église et l'état*; and *Les Evêques, les clercs, et le roi, 1250–1300*. The impact of centralization on the local church has been much more intensively investigated for England than for France. Even though conditions differed from country to country, English studies are therefore essential for an understanding of the situation in France as well; see, for example, Cheney, *From Becket to Langton*, Gibbs and Lang, *Bishops and Reform, 1215–1272*, Edwards, *English Secular Cathedrals*, Pantin, *The English Church in the Fourteenth Century*, and Southern, *Robert Grosseteste*.

[8] Emperor Henry VI seems to have been the first who thought of a general tax on the clergy, but Pope Honorius III was the first who tried it – and he failed decisively at the council of Bourges in 1225; Congar, 'Quod omnes tangit', p. 218; Hall, 'Henry III', p. 128; Kay, 'An Eye-Witness Account'; Matthew Paris, *Chronica*, 3:107; Mansi, *Collectio*, 22:1,216–20.

[9] Campbell, 'The Protest of Saint Louis'; Jones, 'Relations'; Jones, 'Bishops'.

[10] The council of Béziers thus declared in 1255 that it assisted the king, 'non ex mandato vel rogatu dicti senescalci sed potius ex gratia et honore dicti regis', and the council of Paris in 1263 first refused a papal request for a hundredth and then went on to grant it 'ex ipsorum praelatorum mera gratia, non ex vi litterae super subventione Terrae Sanctae a Domino papa impetrata, non aliqua coactione, sed sponte'. Gaudemet, 'Aspects', pp. 324f.

[11] On this topic, too, there is a considerable body of literature. The most instructive general study remains Schleyer, *Anfänge des Gallikanismus*, to be supplemented by Douie, *The*

had been more than brewing. Bishops and parish priests resented the degree to which the friars, equipped with papal letters of exemption from episcopal authority, moved through their dioceses at will, preached sermons, heard confessions, absolved and buried the flock, usurped revenues, and acted on behalf of the papacy in matters of ecclesiastical taxation and jurisdiction. In the 1250s a major conflict had disrupted the university of Paris, and on the occasion of the second council of Lyons there had been acrimonious exchanges. Bishop Bruno of Olmütz had complained that 'we can no longer be called pastors' because the friars had so completely usurped the care of souls, while Friar Gilbert of Tournai pointed out that prelates were 'no colleagues of Peter but of Simon, no disciples of Christ but of Nero'.[12] In short, there was no dearth of skirmishes – but there had never been a war.

That changed in 1281, when Martin IV published the bull *Ad fructus uberes*.[13] The meaning of this bull is still a subject of debate, but fortunately we can skirt what Gilbert of Tournai called the 'libidinous prostitutions of the human intellect' to which the interpretation of *Ad fructus uberes* can all too easily give rise.[14] The point that matters is a simple one: the bishops thought *Ad fructus uberes* amounted to a horrible attack on their own authority. They were afraid that if the friars were to get the powers it promised them, 'the people would say, as in fact they are saying, "what do we care about our bishop? Surely nothing at all, for a friar will absolve us just as well as he from all our sins, and even better, because he has the power of the pope."'[15] The result would be 'a

---

*Conflict between the Seculars and the Mendicants*, and Paulus, *Welt- und Ordensklerus*. On the growth of the mendicant orders in general see: Brooke, *The Coming of the Friars*, Moorman, *A History of the Franciscan Order*, Gratien, *Histoire de la fondation et de l'évolution de l'ordre des frères mineurs*. For France see the excellent study by Emery, *The Friars in Medieval France*, and for the south of France *Les Mendiants en pays d'Oc*.

[12] 'Pastores ammodo dici non debeamus.' Bruno of Olmütz, *Relatio*, p. 592. '[Praelati sunt] non collegae Petri sed Simonis, non Christi discipuli sed Neronis.' Gilbert of Tournai, *Collectio*, p. 40. For the events at the university of Paris in the 1250s see *Auseinandersetzungen an der Pariser Universität*, Dufeil, *Guillaume de Saint-Amour*, Miethke, 'Papst, Ortsbischof und Universität', and Michaud–Quantin, 'Le Droit universitaire'.

[13] On *Ad fructus uberes* and everything that followed see Glorieux, 'Prélats'; Schleyer, *Anfänge*, pp. 44–76; Marrone, 'Ecclesiology', pp. 120–45; Gratien, 'Ordres mendiants et clergé séculier'; Gratien, *Histoire*, pp. 339–54.

[14] 'Fateor quod arguendae sunt in casu nimiae subtilitates, quae sunt intellectus humani libidinosae prostitutiones.' Gilbert of Tournai, *Collectio*, p. 48. This was written before *Ad fructus uberes* was published, but it referred to the same issues.

[15] 'Nunc autem si fratres possunt absolvere in casibus illis [reservatis] – ut dicunt – minus timerent homines peccare, quia et minus erubescent confitendo fratribus, qui faciles

great rebellion against the prelates and the rectors of our churches'.[16]

The bishops quickly organized their forces in order to forestall such a revolution.[17] In 1282 the archbishop of Rouen demanded that a full-blown system of corporate representation be established in order to bring victory to the common cause:

Every archbishop . . . ought to convoke a provincial council and invite not only the bishops but also the chapters of cathedrals and other churches, abbots with and without exemptions, as well as rural deans and other clerics who fear God and who can read. This affair concerns everyone. A common and useful way of meeting these dangers ought therefore to be chosen with the advice of all, and the burden of defending our cause ought to be borne by all.[18]

His advice was heeded. The bishops and their clergy met repeatedly in provincial and national councils where they resolved upon a common course of action. Sermons were preached in order to disseminate their point of view. Committees were appointed to represent their demands. Embassies were sent to Rome in order to persuade the papacy to stand back from favouring the mendicants. The documents of law and history were searched. The universities of Paris and of Orléans were called upon for expert help. Scholars, Henry of Ghent foremost among them, helped to elaborate a theory of order in which there was no room for general exemptions from episcopal jurisdiction. The wrath of God was systematically invoked in order to pressure the faithful into avoiding the friars. In short, the bishops organized themselves on an unprecedented scale in order to protect their view of the church and overturn the papacy's support of the mendicants.[19]

sunt ad veniam et de facili habentur. Et dicerent populares et dicunt: Quid curamus de episcopo nostro? Certe nihil, quia frater unus absolvet aeque nos de omnibus sicut ipse et melius, quia habet potestatem papae.' *Tractatus de usurpata potestate fratrum*, pp. 172f.

16 Thomas of Pontoise on the prelates' embassy to Pope Nicholas IV in late 1288: 'Rebellione magna namque contra praelatos et ecclesiarum rectores insurgunt iura episcoporum absorbere et sibi applicare volentes.' Schleyer, *Anfänge*, pp. 70f.

17 Schleyer, *Anfänge*, pp. 44–76.

18 'Quod quilibet metropolitanus infra festum S. Remigii suum provinciale convocet concilium, non solum de episcopis, verum etiam de capitulis cathedralium et aliarum ecclesiarum, abbatibus exemptis et non exemptis, necnon de decanis ruralibus et aliis ecclesiasticis viris Deum timentibus et peritiam habentibus litterarum; ut communi omnium consilio, cum dictum negotium omnes tangat, via communis et utilis eligatur ad obviandum periculis memoratis, et onus prosequendi negotium praedictum ab omnibus supportetur.' Bessin, *Concilia Rotomagensis provinciae*, p. 155.

19 The best general studies of the ecclesiological differences provoked by the quarrel over the mendicants are Congar, 'Aspects ecclésiologiques de la querelle entre mendiants et

Whether they would succeed was still uncertain when they were challenged on the temporal front as well. In 1285 Philip IV became the king of France, and from the beginning of his reign he left no doubt that he was not as willing to follow the church's leadership as his father and grandfather had been.[20] Soon thereafter, in 1288, he went on the offensive by claiming jurisdiction over the churches of Chartres and Poitiers in matters from which the monarchy had been traditionally excluded.[21] Both conflicts were of limited extent, but they were understood to involve matters of principle. They have therefore properly been termed 'the first great controversy with the Church in Philip's reign'.[22]

As long as the bishops were able to move freely between their opponents, matters remained undecided on both fronts. The bishops relied on the king to support their case in Rome against the mendicants and in return supported his plan to canonize Louis IX.[23] Simultaneously they asked the pope for help against royal usurpations of ecclesiastical jurisdiction.[24] Under Pope Honorius IV it even seemed as though they might succeed in overturning *Ad fructus uberes*.[25] But in 1287, just as success seemed within reach, Honorius passed away and a former minister general of the Franciscans, Nicholas IV, was chosen as his successor. That dealt a death blow to the bishops' aspirations. Nicholas IV was determined

séculiers', and Marrone, 'The Ecclesiology of the Parisian Secular Masters'. See also *Soziale Ordnungen* and Michaud-Quantin, *Universitas*. For the secular point of view in particular see the superb article by Lagarde, 'La Philosophie sociale d'Henri de Gand et Godefroid de Fontaines', and his treatment of the same thinkers in *La Naissance de l'esprit laïque*, 2:161–213, as well as Marrone, 'The Absolute and the Ordained Powers of the Pope'; Koch, 'Der Prozess gegen den Magister Johannes de Polliaco'; Sikes, 'John de Pouilli and Peter de la Palu'. Schwer, *Stand und Ständeordnung*, is good for a broader perspective on the secular views. For the mendicant point of view see Miethke, 'Die Rolle der Bettelorden im Umbruch der politischen Theorie'; Ratzinger, 'Der Einfluss des Bettelordensstreites'; Tierney, *Origins of Papal Infallibility*; and Zuckerman, 'Dominican Theories of the Papal Primacy'.     [20] Strayer, *Reign of Philip the Fair*, pp. 11f.
[21] Ibid., pp. 242–5.     [22] Ibid., p. 242.
[23] In 1283 a royal emissary to Rome, Peter of Mornay, took up the secular cause; Schleyer, *Anfänge*, p. 55. Thomas of Pontoise on his embassy to Rome combined attacks on the mendicants with demands for the canonization of Louis IX; Glorieux, 'Prélats', pp. 328–30.
[24] In response to the complaints from Chartres and Poitiers, Nicholas IV ordered two investigations in 1289 and gave the investigators wide powers that angered Philip considerably; Strayer, *Reign of Philip the Fair*, p. 243.
[25] Honorius had initially supported the mendicants, but in response to the secular embassy of 1286 to Rome he appeared to be willing to revoke *Ad fructus uberes*. Salimbene, at any rate, lamented Honorius' plans and regarded his sudden death as a miracle; Schleyer, *Anfänge*, pp. 60–9.

not only to support the friars but also to obtain the help of France in the war against Aragon. In 1289 he granted Philip IV a tenth, and in 1290 he sent a pair of legates to France, one of whom was Benedict Gaetani, the future Boniface VIII, in order to negotiate an *entente cordiale*.[26]

The result was the immediate collapse of the episcopal strategy. The issue of royal jurisdiction was settled first. With the legates' agreement King Philip assembled the prelates and announced an ordinance that fixed the limits of his jurisdiction over the church for the remainder of his reign:

All prelates could be judged by Parlement, and appeals from their temporal courts were to go to the Parlement whether or not they held their lands from the king. Their goods could be seized, by order of the king, to compel obedience; in fact, if delay caused danger, goods could be seized by royal officials acting on their own initiative. The claim that there were enclaves in the realm that were exempt from ordinary secular justice had been disallowed.[27]

The king had won a signal victory for his sovereignty by unifying and extending his jurisdiction over the entire clergy of the realm.

Immediately thereafter the legates put an end to the debate about *Ad fructus uberes*. In an assembly at Ste Geneviève Gaetani announced their decision in favour of the mendicants.[28] When Henry of Ghent still refused to yield and the masters of the university of Paris defended his point of view, Gaetani addressed them in language that deserves to be quoted:

You masters of Paris are teaching stupidities that throw the entire world into turmoil and you would not do so if you really understood the state of the universal church. You sit in your chairs and you believe that Christ is governed by your reasons ... I have seen your reasons, and they are true, but they can be answered like this: We command you by virtue of obedience and on penalty of being deposed from office and benefice henceforth not to preach about, dispute, or interpret *Ad fructus uberes*, whether secretly or manifestly. The privilege of the friars is to remain in force and whoever has any doubts about its meaning shall request the proper interpretation from the highest pontiff. I shall let you know that the Roman curia will rather confound the university of Paris than take

[26] Haller, *Das Papsttum*, 5:61–3; Schleyer, *Anfänge*, pp. 70–76; Strayer, *Reign of Philip the Fair*, pp. 244f.    [27] Strayer, *Reign of Philip the Fair*, p. 245.
[28] Glorieux, 'Prélats', pp. 491–5; Marrone, 'Ecclesiology', pp. 173–83.

this privilege from the friars, for we have not been called to excel by knowledge or to gain glory, but to save our souls.[29]

These words are a characteristic display not only of Gaetani's ruthlessness but also of his genius for the essential. They express a conflict between two conceptions of order that will preoccupy us a great deal in our analysis of William Durant the Younger's treatise.[30] On the one hand, there was the 'state of the church' as the bishops and the masters of Paris understood it. That state consisted of the various ranks and orders of the church, it was founded on reason (as Gaetani himself allowed, albeit ironically), and it placed eternal, immutable, inviolable limits on the exercise of power. On the other hand, there was Gaetani's own, very different view of the 'state of the church'. That state, too, was founded on reason – but on the reason of Christ, not that of the masters. Its essence was not the different ranks and orders of the church but the distinction between the pope, who had the plenitude of power, and his subjects, who did not. Its function was not to obtain knowledge or glory but 'to save souls'. In Gaetani's view power, the power of Christ's reason, exceeded the understanding of the masters of Paris and perhaps even all human understanding, but it was expressed intelligibly enough through the commands of the supreme pontiff. The conflict between these two conceptions of order thus coincided with a stark opposition between 'reasons' whose feebleness Gaetani denounced and a 'solution' that consisted of a sheer command. It would be wrong to infer that Gaetani's conception therefore rested on a power that was purely arbitrary; but he did express the conviction that power and reason are incommensurable. He thus implicitly endorsed the famous distinction between

[29] 'Vos, magistri Parysienses, stultam fecistis et facitis doctrinam sciencie vestre, turbantes orbem terrarum, quod nullo modo faceretis, si sciretis statum universalis ecclesie. Sedetis in cathedris et putatis, quod vestris racionibus regatur Christus . . . Vidi raciones vestras et vere sunt, set raciones solubiles. Set hec sit solucio: Precipimus in virtute obediencie sub pena privacionis officii et beneficii, ne aliquis magistrorum de cetero de dicto privilegio predicet, disputet vel determinet occulte vel manifeste. Set privilegium fratrum in suo robore stet. Et qui de dicto privilegio dubitet vel dubitaverit, interpretacionem a summo pontifice querat. Vere dico vobis, antequam curia Romana a dictis fratribus hoc privilegium ammoveret, pocius studium Parysiense confunderet. Non enim vocati sumus propter scire vel gloriose apparere, set propter nostras salvare animas.' Finke, *Aus den Tagen Bonifaz VIII.*, pp. vi–vii. Giles of Rome was asked to tell Henry that he was suspended from his teaching duties; Glorieux, 'Prélats', p. 493.

[30] For the principles at issue there is no better starting point than Oakley's *Omnipotence, Covenant and Order*, to be accompanied by Buisson, *Potestas und Caritas*, Ullmann, *The Growth of Papal Government*, Tierney, *Origins of Papal Infallibility*, and Gagnér, *Studien zur Ideengeschichte der Gesetzgebung*.

ordained power and absolute power and firmly sided with the latter. If the masters believed in the power of order, Gaetani believed in an order of power.

The events of the year 1290 thus afford more than a striking example of cooperation between Paris and Rome. They also illustrate how easy such cooperation made it for the rulers of the spiritual–temporal monarchy to overcome the resistance of an unusually well organized and powerful ecclesiastical estate.[31] In addition, they furnished the occasion for a remarkably lucid formulation of what was at stake: the imposition of a novel kind of order whose essence was the right to command unconditional obedience. In short, at least as far as the French episcopate was concerned, they mark a turning point on the road toward the suppression of middling powers and the development of sovereignty.

Mende suffered just as much of a reverse from the events of 1290 as did the other bishoprics of France. Indeed, it may have suffered more. Concerning the battle with the mendicants, it had played a more prominent part than might have been expected, given its relative isolation and the uncertainty into which its disagreements with the monarchy had thrown its affairs.[32] There is no comparable information about any stand it might have taken regarding Philip's ordinance of 1290, but there can be no doubt that the ordinance seriously compromised the bishop's chances of protecting his autonomy. The golden bull had amounted to a concordat between the bishop and the king that was intended to suppress the independence of the local noblemen. The settlement of 1290, by contrast, amounted to a concordat between the king and the pope that was designed to suppress the independence of the bishop as

---

[31] Strayer, *Reign of Philip the Fair*, pp. 399f., stresses that because of their superior organization in provincial and national councils the clergy fared better than either the bourgeoisie or the nobility in resisting Philip IV's impositions of fines for amortizations and *nouveaux acquêts*. Douie, *Conflict*, p. 12, stresses the superiority of the propaganda of the secular clergy. Gaudemet, 'Aspects', pp. 320f., counts more than a hundred French councils in the thirteenth century, and Gaudemet, 'Recherches', p. 149, points to an important reason for the relative strength of the French episcopate: many bishops had long and stable careers.

[32] Two clerics of the church of Mende are mentioned in the records as having played a major part in the attacks upon the friars. One was Paul Banciani of Rodez, vicar general of the bishop of Mende, who appeared at the provincial council of Bourges in September 1286. The other was Peter of Rodez, provost of Mende, who played an equally visible role in the embassy sent by the French clergy to Pope Honorius IV in the same year; Glorieux, 'Prélats', pp. 324–30.

well. That shows how far the social and political organization of Europe had advanced: an alliance that had once been formed between a monarch and a local lord was now paralleled by another on a national and even a European scale. But this very progress created a new source of conflict, for the golden bull demanded what the ordinance denied. In the end, either the ordinance would have to prevail over the golden bull or the golden bull over the ordinance; either king-and-pope or king-and-bishop would govern the Gévaudan – and there was little doubt who was the stronger. A point had thus been reached at which the strategy that the bishops had been following since the twelfth century became obsolete.

## WILLIAM DURANT THE ELDER (1285–96)

The advance of centralization over the autonomy of the Gévaudan took concrete shape in the person of William Durant the Elder, who was elected bishop of Mende in 1285. We know little about his background.[33] He was born around 1230 in Puimisson, a small community not far from Béziers on the Mediterranean coast. According to some early biographers he was a nobleman, but his career provides reasons to doubt that, if he was noble at all, his nobility shaped his attitude toward government in any significant way.[34] What we do know is that he was a servant of central government.

A sketch of his career may serve to clarify his relationship with central government. There is a story that as a young man he was much attracted to philosophy.

---

[33] As is typically the case with thirteenth-century French bishops: Gaudemet, 'Recherches', pp. 144–6. Unless otherwise noted, all of the information about William Durant the Elder is taken from Falletti's excellent article 'Guillaume Durand', *DDC*, 5:1,014–75, with full bibliography. Le Clerc, 'Guillaume Duranti', pp. 411–97, and Schulte, *Quellen*, 2:144–56, are still well worth consulting. More recent publications include Guizard, *L'Œuvre canonique*; Chevailler, 'Observations'; Dykmans, 'Notes autobiographiques'; Dykmans, 'A propos de synodes languedociens'. See also Dykmans, *Cérémonial papal*.

[34] Schulte, *Geschichte*, 2:144 n. 2, accepts Durant's nobility; Falletti, 'Guillaume Durand', col. 1,017, doubts it. Gaudemet, 'Recherches', p. 141, estimates that roughly half of the French episcopate was made up of commoners and that by far the majority of the other half came from the lowest sectors of the nobility. Bishops who rose to office in the province of Narbonne during the years from 1249 to 1317, relatively close in time and space to William Durant the Elder, stemmed mostly from families of small Languedocian nobility, although the number of greater nobles seems to have grown after 1270; see Guillemain, 'Les Elections épiscopales', and Guillemain, 'Origines sociales', pp. 91–106, here p. 104.

But at that time his friends, who wished to see him honoured, prevailed upon him with considerable effort not to let such interests lead him too far astray from the pursuit of honour, but to study only the law of Caesar and the pope. For they affirmed that by the study of that art he would quickly attain honours and the greatest glory.[35]

While the details are almost certainly apocryphal, the gist of the story is true: he went to Bologna to study law.[36] There he sat at the feet of Bernard of Parma; there he obtained his doctorate; and there he began to teach law himself. 'And thus his mind, which is reported to have absorbed the highest kinds of learning with ease and extraordinary eagerness, was cultivated by great diligence and unimaginable study.'[37] Sometime in the mid 1260s he was called to Rome and employed in the papal court of appeals known as the *audientia causarum sacri palatii*. That brought him in touch with perhaps the greatest canonist of the time, Henry of Segusio, cardinal bishop of Ostia, better known as Hostiensis; thereafter Durant consistently referred to him as 'my lord'. In the 1270s he published the first edition of his *Speculum iudiciale*, an amazingly comprehensive 'systematization of doctrine, a veritable sum of romano-canonical procedure in which every judicial and administrative problem of the time was treated', and which earned its author the sobriquet *Speculator*.[38] It was presumably his merits as a

[35] 'Amici qui eum honoratum videre cupiebant, ne talium rerum studium eum longius ab honorum petitione abduceret, magnopere illi authores fuere ne aliud sibi eo tempore preter ius cesareum ac pontificium discendum proponeret. Ex eius enim artis studio affirmabant fore ut celeriter ad honores et summam gloriam perveniret.' *TMA* authoris vita, fol. 3ra–b. Cf. Falletti, 'Guillaume Durand', col. 1,017.

[36] Durant seems to have studied in southern France before he went to Bologna, but where he did so is unknown. It seems unlikely that he went to Toulouse, whose canonists did not amount to much until after 1280 or even 1300, when popes who hailed from southern France helped to promote its fortunes; see Meijers, 'Première époque', *Etudes*, 3:170f., 174, 182f. Avignon, Montpellier, and Béziers, among others, are places where he may have studied; see Falletti, 'Guillaume Durand', col. 1,017; Rashdall, *Universities*, 2:174; Meijers, 'Première époque', *Etudes*, 3:172f.; Kuttner, 'Wer war der Dekretalist "Abbas antiquus"?', p. 485; Gouron, 'Training', p. 222; Gilles, 'Enseignement du droit', pp. 214f. Meijers considers the school of Béziers to have been a flourishing enterprise, whereas Kuttner describes it more disparagingly as a mere episode in the career of Abbas Antiquus. At any rate, Bologna was still the Mecca of medieval lawyers and, in spite of growing competition from French universities, continued to attract a great number of students from the Midi until 1270 and beyond; Gouron, 'Training', p. 220.

[37] 'Itaque illius ingenium (quod facile et avidissimum fuisse traditur in capiendis optimis disciplinis) magna diligentia et incredibili studio excultum est.' *TMA*, fol. 3ra.

[38] '"Systématisation doctrinale", véritable somme de la procédure romano-canonique, où sont traités tous les problèmes judiciaires et administratifs du temps.' Le Bras *et al.*, *L'Age classique*, p. 320. Cf. Stickler, 'Ordines judiciarii', cols. 1,138f. On the popularization of its contents see especially Seckel, *Beiträge*.

canonist and the patronage of Hostiensis that drew the papacy's attention to his qualifications, and that in turn started him on the road to high office. In 1274 he participated in the second council of Lyons, on whose legislation he would later publish a commentary. In 1276 he assisted Cardinal Simon, the future Pope Martin IV, at a legatine council in Bourges. In 1280 he became *rector et capitaneus generalis* of the patrimony of St Peter where he took homage and fealty for his papal lord. In the same year he was asked to move into northern Italy and devote himself to the provinces that had just been acquired from Rudolf of Habsburg and that were going to frustrate all efforts at assuring the smooth functioning of papal government for many decades to come. For most of the following years he stayed in those regions in the midst of incessant local divisions and served there as *vicarius in spiritualibus* – which did not, however, prevent him from hiring armies, buying weapons, and supervising the campaign against the Ghibelline chief Guido da Montefeltre.[39] His prestige seems to have reached its highest point in 1284 when he became *rector provinciae Romaniolae in temporalibus* and founded a *Castrum Durantis* that was later turned into a bishopric and renamed Urbania under Urban VIII.

Besides serving the papacy in deed, William Durant the Elder put his considerable talents to magnifying its role in theory as well. He exalted the role of the papal curia.[40] He insisted on the right of the papacy to dispose of benefices that had not yet been vacated, even though it went against a conciliar decree to do so.[41] He confirmed the exemption of the papacy from human judgment, with the traditional exception of heresy.[42] He declared that

[39] See Martin IV, nos. 266 (26.III.1282), 267 (28.III.1282), 472jj (22.VI.1283).
[40] Le Bras *et al.*, *L'Age classique*, p. 320.
[41] For the sake of comparison with the views of William Durant the Younger it may be useful to offer a few quotations: 'Promissio autem facta a legato de conferendo alicui beneficio primo vacaturo non valet, quia hoc esset contra Lateranense concilium quod prohibet donationem vel promissionem beneficii priusquam vacet, extra de conces. preben. c. ii., contra quod concilium legatus nil potest. Papa autem bene potest.' *Speculum iudiciale* 1.1, De legato 5.2, fol. 17r. Cf. X.3.8.2. Similarly the following passage: 'Et facit tamen [papa] hoc quando vult, ut in c. constitutus, quia ipse conciliis non ligatur, imo contra illa facere potest, ut extra de elec. significasti, et de rescri. nonnulli, licet difficile hoc faciat, ut extra de renun. post translat. prope fi. iure legationis.' *Speculum iudiciale* 1.1, De legato 5.10, fol. 17v. Cf. X.1.3.19, X.1.6.4, X.1.3.28, X.1.9.11.
[42] 'Papa etiam tantum de haeresi accusatur, xl. di. si papa, et tunc vel a synodo vel a principe, ut xxiii. q. v. principes, et xcvi. di. sicut quis et c. nos ad fidem, vel a corpore fidelium, e. di. ubinam, vel si submittat se alicuius iudicio, ii. q. vii. nos si, ff. de iu. om. iu. est receptum; alias nunquam accusatur, ut in pre. c. nunc autem.' *Speculum iudiciale* 1.3, De accusatore 2.3, fol. 78r. Cf. D.40 c.6, C.23 q.5 c.20, D.96 c.15, D.96 c.2, D.96 c.4, C.2 q.7 c.41, Dig.2.1.14, D.21 c.7.

everyone had a right to appeal to the papacy directly, without going through intermediate instances, and supported his point of view with the principle that the pope is the ordinary judge of all.[43] And in often-quoted passages he summed up the papal plenitude of power by declaring that 'so long as he does not go against the faith the pope can do and say whatever he pleases. He can even deprive someone of his rights, for there is no one who may ask him: "Why are you doing this?" . . . His will stands in the place of reason, and whatever pleases him has the force of law.'[44] To be sure, most if not all of what Durant had to say about the pope had been said before. But by compiling the most far-reaching statements of the preceding century or so in a manual that superseded all of its predecessors, influenced all of its successors, and was destined to remain a bestseller into early modern times, he surely increased their impact.[45] In sum, he adopted, perfected, and defended his papal masters' principles both in practice and in theory.

His efforts were well rewarded. He had already been endowed with canonries at Beauvais and Narbonne when in 1279 he obtained the deanery of Chartres as well, a benefice that yielded the substantial sum of 1,000 lbs. (*tournois* money) per year and was accompanied with dispensations from pluralism and absenteeism.[46]

---

[43] 'Excipitur tamen dominus Papa ad quem potest omissis mediis appellari, ut ii. q. vi. ad Romanam, et c. precedenti et c. quotiens, et c. ideo, et extra de appellationibus, si duobus, et c. solicitudinem, extra de privil. antiqua. Et est ratio quia ipse est ordinarius singulorum, ut extra de elec. cum nobis olim.' *Speculum iudiciale* 2.3, De appellationibus 4.1, fol. 188r. Cf. C.2 q.6 c.8, C.2 q.6 c.7, C.2 q.6 c.26, C.2 q.6 c.17, X.2.28.7, X.2.28.54, X.5.33.23, X.1.6.19.

[44] 'Habet etiam papa plenitudinem potestatis ad quam vocatus est, alii vero in partem solicitudinis sunt vocati, ut extra de usu pal. ad honorem, ii. q. vi. decreto, et c. qui se scit, et dummodo contra fidem non veniat in omnibus et per omnia potest facere et dicere quicquid placet, auferendo etiam ius suum cui vult, quia non est qui ei dicat: cur ita facis, xix. di. in memoria, de pe. di. iii. §. ex persona huius, in c. quamvis? Nam et apud eum est pro ratione voluntas: et quod ei placet, legis habet vigorem, insti. de iur. nat. §. sed quod princi., potest etiam omne ius tollere et de iure supra ius dispensare.' *Speculum iudiciale* 1.1, De legato 6.52, fol. 21r. Cf. X.1.8.4, C.2 q.6 c.11–12, D.19 c.3, De pen. D.3 a.c.22, Ins.1.2.6. Even at this early point in our analysis it deserves to be pointed out that the context of such statements does a great deal to limit their significance; see Oakley, *Western Church*, pp. 165–8, for general observations, and Post, 'Vincentius Hispanus', for a detailed analysis.

[45] The *Speculum iudiciale* figured prominently on the stationers' list of books sold at the university of Bologna in the early fourteenth century; see Denifle, 'Statuten', p. 298. According to my own rapid survey, close to a hundred manuscripts and more than fifty early modern printed editions are extant; references to them are most conveniently, but not completely, listed by Le Clerc, 'Guillaume Duranti', pp. 449–56, and in the notes of Schulte, *Quellen*, 2:144–56. On the later influence of the *Speculum iudiciale* see also Le Bras et al., *L'Age classique*, pp. 319f.; Stickler, 'Ordines iudiciarii', cols. 1,138f.; Seckel, *Beiträge*, vol. 1; Chevailler, 'Observations'.     [46] Martin IV, no. 10 (13.V.1281).

Indeed, if Joannes Andreae's anecdote has it right, it was only Ottobuono Fieschi's untimely death in 1276, less than two months after his elevation to the papal dignity as Hadrian V, that prevented Durant's career from being crowned with a cardinal's hat.[47]

The basis on which William Durant the Elder rose from the obscurity of Puimisson to a position of wealth and power thus had nothing to do with ties of lineage. Rather, his elevation rested on a combination of two other factors. The first was that he 'had the mind of a Frenchman, that is, perspicacious and ready to grasp anything', as his admiring biographer put it.[48] The second was the papacy's willingness to put a premium on a well-trained legal mind and a qualified administrator. Durant was the opposite of an Odilo de Mercoeur, more of an outsider in the Gévaudan than even Stephen of Brioude had been. His supervision of the Italian territories had taught him to value efficiency, consistency, and regularity in applying law and force. His main allegiance was to the papacy, which may have been more efficient than any other medieval institution.[49] But that certainly did not prevent him from taking the side of the king of France with an outspoken defence of royal sovereignty that would have been hard to reconcile with the golden bull of Mende.[50] Indeed, such a defence was fitting for a man whose best-known book dealt with romano-canonical procedure – that is, with an area of law where the spiritual had been particularly closely fused to the temporal, where the medieval lawyer's nightmare of contending with two conflicting sets of law had been almost dispelled and his dream of a universe governed by a single set of reasonable principles seemed to be coming true.[51] The beauty of that dream is perhaps the overriding

---

[47] Falletti, 'Guillaume Durand', col. 1,020.

[48] 'Guillelmo Durando fuisse ingenium fateor Gallicum: hoc est perspicax et ad omnia factum.' *TMA*, fol. 3ra.

[49] Hence he is usually treated as a papalist, as for example by Carlyle, *History*, 5:335–7; McIlwain, *Growth*, p. 237; Lagarde, *La Naissance*, 1:63, 66.

[50] 'Homines ipsorum baronum non sunt homines ipsius regis. Bene tamen omnes homines qui sunt in regno Francie sunt sub potestate et principatu regis Francie et in eos habet imperium generalis jurisdictionis et potestatis.' Quoted by Lot and Fawtier, *Histoire*, 2:220 n. 1. 'Rex Franciae princeps est in regno suo.' Quoted by Rivière, *Problème*, p. 425. This was accompanied by incipient expressions of dedication to the national good: 'Rex, qui habet administrationem regni, vocat eos [tenentes] pro communi bono, scilicet pro defensione patriae et coronae. Unde sibi iure gentium obedire tenentur.' Quoted by Kantorowicz, *The King's Two Bodies*, p. 251 n. 180.

[51] Stickler, 'Ordines iudiciarii', cols. 1,113–35.

lesson to be gathered from the writings of the older Durant.[52] In
short, he was a man of neither temporal nor spiritual government
but simply a man of government. He defended sovereignty, not
local autonomy; he was concerned with order, not with freedom.
He could be loyal to the king of France as well as to the pope
because they shared the same ideals.

We do not know what prompted the canons of Mende to elect
this man to be their bishop.[53] We do know that his episcopate
marked a new stage in the history of the diocese. As it turned out,
Honorius IV had no objections to his election but was unwilling to
do without his services in northern Italy for a while. Not until 1291
was Durant finally allowed to take up residence in his new
diocese.[54] That was a fitting beginning for a bishop whose career
had been spent in the service of central government; it meant that
he placed his duties as bishop second to his duties as a curial official.
It also meant that he appeared in Mende just after the king of France
and the pope had successfully joined hands to suppress the French
episcopate.

[52] These writings may not display the originality of a Huguccio or a Hostiensis, and in that
limited sense the charge of plagiarism is perhaps justified; Le Bras *et al.*, *L'Age classique*,
pp. 319f. Cf. Stickler, 'Ordines iudiciarii', cols. 1,138f. But it would be highly misleading
to overlook the creative vigour with which the Speculator facilitated the application of
existing doctrines to the exigencies of practice.

[53] On 10 April 1285 Archbishop Simon of Bourges wrote an exasperated letter chastising
the canons of Mende for their failure to end the vacancy, underlining the risks to which
their inaction exposed their church and suggesting that the right of provision might
already have devolved upon him; *GC*, 1:Instrumenta:25; cf. Falletti, 'Guillaume
Durand', cols. 1,025f. His urgency may have been related to the battle against the
mendicants. Simon of Bourges was one of the chief strategists for the episcopal cause and
at the time, immediately after the death of Martin IV and the election of Honorius IV, he
may have wished to be able to count on the support of one of his more important
suffragans. Mende's contributions to the episcopal cause were indeed made in the next
year. The canons had previously offered the see to a cleric of Narbonne, who declined.
They responded to Simon's prodding by saying that they had already elected Durant 'by
way of compromise', a standard method of election, to be sure, but also one hinting at
disagreements in the electoral body; *GC*, 1:Instrumenta:25f. The nature of those
disagreements is unclear, but the choice of a papal favourite with Durant's stature is
surely indicative of the change that had occurred since the middle of the century. On the
various stages of Durant's appointment see Honorius IV, nos. 181 (5.XI.1285), 285
(4.II.1286), 511 (1.VI.1286). Honorius' letter of 4.II.1286, written to the archbishop of
Bourges to calm his fears that his metropolitan rights had been slighted, is printed in *GC*,
1:Instrumenta:26.

[54] The earliest evidence for any actions taken by Durant in Mende comes in the form of a
permission from Honorius IV to override the customs of Mende by appointing a canon
without the chapter's consent; Honorius IV, no. 734 (9.II.1287). In 1289 Durant obtained

## The formation of interest

It should be no surprise that William Durant the Elder did little to emulate Odilo de Mercoeur in reviving the cause of local liberty. His episcopate was marked by peace, not conflict. Indeed, one suspects that he regarded it as something of a welcome opportunity to retire from the frustrations by which he was burdened in battle-torn Italy. He was now close to sixty years old, and we are told that he was sufficiently concerned about the scarcity of wine in the 'frigid regions' of the Gévaudan to request a parish 'in whose territory wine can grow' for the uses of his table.[55] He took advantage of the leisure that the Gévaudan afforded him to write a number of his major works: a commentary on the constitutions of Gregory X, a pontifical that served as the basis for the Roman pontifical of Innocent VIII in 1484, *Instructiones et constitutiones* for the clerics of his diocese, and especially the *Rationale divinorum officiorum*, an exhaustive interpretation of the symbolism of ecclesiastical liturgy and architecture that turned out to be no less successful than the *Speculum iudiciale*.[56] These were not the occupations of an episcopal activist.

William Durant the Elder's personal predispositions and the political climate in general thus coincided neatly to weight the

permission from Nicholas IV to appoint a notary; Nicholas IV, no. 1,855 (18.XII.1289). In the same year Nicholas IV confirmed the ancient privilege of Calixtus II to the priory of Chirac: Nicholas IV, no. 527 (12.II.1289). Durant can be documented to have remained in Italy until at least 1290: Nicholas IV, nos. 716 (7.III.1289), 1,406 (31.VIII.1289), 2,871 (10.VII.1290). The first indication that he was about to go to Mende comes from the end of 1290 and the beginning of 1291: Nicholas IV, nos. 3,435 (11.X.1290), 4,022 (18.I.1291). By May 1291, when Nicholas IV dispensed a favourite of Durant from pluralism, Durant was probably already residing in Mende; Nicholas IV, no. 5,024 (1.V.1291). In February 1292 he took homage from Odilo de Tournel in Mende; Philippe, *La Baronnie*, pp. xci, 42f. All of Philip IV's letters relating to the older Durant date from October 1291; R-S, nos. 1–5 (18.X.1291), pp. 1–9. R-S, p. 2 n. 2, nevertheless gives 1292 as the year of his arrival in Mende.

55 'Cum igitur, sicut nobis exponere curavisti, ecclesia Mimatensis, sita in frigida regione, vini defectum non modicum patiatur, nos, tuis supplicationibus inclinati, volentes tibi gratiam facere specialem, ut unam ecclesiam parrochialem tue diocesis, ad collationem tuam libere pertinentem, in cujus territorio vinum crescat, cedente vel decedente ipsius ecclesie rectore, usibus mense tue, cum omnibus redditibus, proventibus, juribus ac pertinentiis suis, applicare et in tuos usus proprios convertere valeas, tibi auctoritate presentium duximus concedendum.' Nicholas IV, no. 1,473 (21.IX.1289).

56 See Falletti, 'Guillaume Durand', cols. 1,032f.; Andrieu, *Pontifical Romain*, 3:v–ix, 10, 19. Like the *Speculum*, the *Rationale* ranges at the top of the stationers' book list at Bologna, and I have counted about a hundred early modern printed editions; cf. Denifle, 'Statuten', p. 298. On the *Rationale* see Sauer, *Symbolik*. The second edition of the *Speculum* and the *Repertorium aureum* seem to have been completed before Durant went to Mende.

balance against local liberty. This does not mean that he was negligent about the rights of his church: he procured several assurances from Philip IV that afforded him a measure of protection from the seneschal's continuing usurpations, and he seems to have tried to speed up the proceedings connected with the ongoing suit about the golden bull.[57] But it does mean that he changed course from confrontation to cooperation. He trusted Philip and was content to let the machinery of central government produce regularity and order. Philip rewarded him with expressions of confidence in 'our beloved and faithful bishop of Mende [who], whenever he was asked, has offered to serve us, to increase our honour, and to expedite our affairs to the best of his abilities', and with an order to the seneschal 'to commend the bishop, his church, and his men to your care and to treat them favourably'.[58] He even granted him a rather 'special grace' in the form of an exemption from the jurisdiction of precisely those lower royal officials who were most closely related to the local nobility and most likely to be inimical to the bishop.[59] But in spite of his good feelings for Durant he never surrendered any rights that mattered to his

---

[57] Philip commanded the seneschal not to subvert episcopal jurisdiction by preventing episcopal subjects from gaining access to the episcopal court in personal actions, by prohibiting notaries from drawing up contracts that included oaths, and by seizing episcopal fiefs in order to force the bishop to revoke interdicts and excommunications; R-S, no. 1 (18.x.1291), pp. 1–3. The seneschal was to levy no new imposts, revoke the ones he had already been receiving, appoint no sergeants on the bishop's lands, and call no subjects of the bishop before his courts; R-S, no. 4 (18.x.1291), pp. 6–8. And he was not to continue with the proceedings that he had instituted against the bishop when episcopal officers had tried to prevent a 'show of arms' from taking place in Mende. The evidence was to be sent to Paris so that it could be acted on from there; R-S, no. 5 (18.x.1291), pp. 8–9. The borders of the Pompidou, which had been uncertain ever since Odilo de Mercoeur had acquired it in return for the viscounty of Grèzes, were now to be defined precisely; R-S, no. 2 (18.x.1291), pp. 3–5. The seneschal was asked to conclude his investigation into the royal rights over the Gévaudan and to send the evidence to Paris so that a decision could be made; R-S, no. 4 (18.x.1291), pp. 6–8.

[58] 'Cum dilectus et fidelis noster episcopus Mimatensis se quam plurimum offerat ad servicium et honorem nostrum et ad nostra negotia quotiens ipse per vos vel gentes nostras inde fuerit requisitus, mandamus vobis quatinus eundem episcopum, ecclesiam et gentes suas recomendatos habentes favorabiliter eosdem prosequamini.' R-S, no. 5 (18.x.1291), p. 9.

[59] 'Scire vos volumus quod de speciali gratia placet nobis ad presens quod idem episcopus et ejus officiales coram vobis, senescallo predicto solum modo, et non coram predictis vicariis [Anduzie et Ucecie] et bajulis [Marologii et Mayrosii] respondere teneantur presentis gratie beneficio quamdiu nobis placuit tantummodo duraturo.' R-S, no. 3 (18.x.1291), pp. 5–6. On the difficulties with these local officials cf. R-S, p. ix, and Strayer, *Reign of Philip the Fair*, pp. 139–41.

sovereignty in principle. Instead he kept encouraging the seneschal not to let the bishop undermine his jurisdiction.[60]

William Durant the Elder's episcopate thus marked a turning point no less important than the episcopate of Stephen of Brioude. If Stephen had revealed the ambiguity of the golden bull, Durant restored the certainty that Aldebert had felt. If Stephen had turned against the royal forces, Durant restored the original alliance with the king. In many ways he closed a circle that began with Aldebert – except that now the king had secured a large share of precisely that control over the diocese which Aldebert had coveted for the bishop. Durant thus abandoned the ground on which his predecessors had fought for local independence and accepted royal sovereignty as a *fait accompli*. That was a surrender to which the inhabitants of the Gévaudan may well have found it harder to resign themselves than he did. But it may well have been inevitable, too, and it relieved the Gévaudan of the political paralysis with which it had been threatened before. Of course the bishop of Mende now found himself enclosed within the circle of government, and of course his recognition of the king's superior position conflicted with a venerable tradition of local independence. But for that very reason further gains in subjecting the local nobility to episcopal control would be all the more impressive.

---

[60] 'Caveatis tamen quod idem episcopus vel gentes sue nostra jura vel jurisdictionem nostram injuste non occupent vel usurpent. Ad hoc si forsitan contingat inter dictum episcopum et suos vassallos seu feodatorios questiones oriri, vocatis partibus super hiis, prout ad vos pertinere noveritis, faciatis justicie complementum.' R-S, no. 1 (18.x.1291), pp. 2f. Cf. the clause 'salvo tamen jure nostro et alieno' in R-S, no. 5 (18.x.1291), p. 9. The exemption from *viguiers* and *bayles* was to last only as long as Philip pleased. Whenever Philip asked the seneschal to restrain himself, he added qualifying clauses: the men of the bishop were not to be subjected to vexations 'indebite'; R-S, no. 5 (18.x.1291), p. 9. New imposts were to be revoked, except 'prout rationabile fuerit'. No sergeants were to be appointed on episcopal fiefs, except 'in casibus ad vos spectantes de consuetudine vel de jure'. The bishop's subjects were not to be called before the seneschal's court, except 'in casibus quorum cognitio ad vos spectat'; R-S, no. 4 (18.x.1291), p. 8. And so on.

*Chapter 3*

# THE TWILIGHT OF AUTONOMY

Desiring to provide for the peace and quiet of the bishop and his church as well as for the utility and security of the subjects of the land, we have finally concluded a general transaction, a concord, a composition, and an association with our beloved and faithful William.        Philip the Fair[1]

If William Durant the Elder ever entertained any plans to play an active role in Gabalitan politics, in the event he never had a chance. After only four years his stay in Mende was cut short by an order from Boniface VIII to return to Italy and resume his previous duties in the papal states for which, it seems, his experience was invaluable.[2] Shortly thereafter, on 1 November 1296, he died without having returned to Mende and was buried in Sta Maria sopra Minerva in Rome.[3] A few weeks later, on 17 December 1296, Boniface VIII appointed his nephew, William Durant the Younger, to succeed him.[4]

### WILLIAM DURANT THE YOUNGER (1296–1330)

What we know about William Durant the Younger's early years is similar to what we know about his uncle, and just as scanty.[5] He, too, was born in Puimisson, probably not long after 1266.[6] He,

---

[1] 'Tandem nos quieti et paci dicti episcopi et ecclesie, ac utilitati et securitati subditorum patrie providere volentes . . . transactionem generalem, concordiam et compositionem ac associationem cum dilecto et fideli nostro Guillelmo . . . fecimus.' *Ordonnances*, 11:397.

[2] Falletti, 'Guillaume Durand', cols. 1,028f.

[3] Sta Maria sopra Minerva is a Dominican church, but there is no evidence to confirm the suspicion that Durant was a Dominican.

[4] Boniface VIII, no. 1,492 (17.XII.1296).

[5] The best biographical account is still that of Viollet. See also Göller, 'Zur Geschichte'; Haller, *Papsttum und Kirchenreform*, pp. 58–66, 70; Davidsohn, 'Bericht der päpstlichen Legaten'; Schütte, *Vatikanische Aktenstücke*.

[6] In appointing Durant to the bishopric Boniface VIII granted him dispensation from 'defectum quem in ordinibus patereris, et etiam, ut asseritur, in aetate'. *GC*, 1:Instrumenta:26. If Boniface was correctly informed, Durant would thus have been younger, but probably not much younger, than thirty.

too, must have studied law, but the circumstances of this are unclear. Probably he learned something from his uncle and perhaps he attended one of the centres of legal training in southern France.[7] He may have gone on to a major university, but it is impossible to tell which one. His condemnation of glosses as a source of confusion and ignorance, a cause of contempt for 'the original texts', and a stultifying waste of time and money makes it rather unlikely that he studied in Bologna, where respect for glosses continued to be strong.[8] A French university with an Aristotelian dialectical bent, such as Orléans, appears more likely.[9] But wher-

---

[7] The number of those centres was growing in the latter part of the thirteenth century. We mentioned Béziers, Avignon, and Montpellier as possibilities for the older Durant. Orange, Lyons, and Alès deserve to be added for the younger Durant; see Gouron, 'Training', pp. 223f.; Gilles, 'Enseignement', pp. 214f. Wherever he may have received his first introduction to legal thought, he was surely familiar with the Speculator's writings. He made additions to the *Instructiones et constitutiones* and occasionally turned a phrase that has parallels in the *Speculum iudiciale*; Viollet, pp. 75–9, 81. But Viollet's confidence in tracing William Durant the Younger's citations to the works of the Speculator even when they can just as easily be traced to familiar sources of canon law deserves to be questioned; see below, p. 130 n. 27. I have not found a single unquestionable citation of the older Durant's works in the *Tractatus Maior* or the *Tractatus Minor*.

[8] There is no evidence that he had been to Italy before he surfaced in Mende in 1291. On his attitude toward glosses, see below, pp. 126f., 194.

[9] Because of the prohibition of civil law at the university of Paris, Orléans had become the premier centre of French studies in canon and civil law. It attracted an increasing number of students from the south of France, including the future popes Clement V and John XXII: Meijers, 'Université d'Orléans', *Etudes*, 3:3–148, esp. pp. 6, 24; Meijers, 'Première époque', *Etudes*, 3:174; Fournier, *Science du droit*, 3:1–133, esp. pp. 121f.; Rashdall, *Universities*, 2:139–51, esp. p. 143; Gouron, 'Training', p. 220; Strayer, *Reign of Philip the Fair*, pp. 282f. Students in Orléans, unlike Bologna, were required to demonstrate their familiarity with Aristotelian doctrine by obtaining a degree in arts before being admitted to the faculty of law, which fostered a 'rational' or 'dialectical' approach to law: Meijers, 'Université d'Orléans', *Etudes*, 3:112–14. They were also asked to pay particular attention to Gratian's *Decretum*: Fournier, *Science du droit*, 3:104f. And in the 1280s the university of Orléans supported the secular clergy against the mendicants: *Chartularium Universitatis Parisiensis*, 1:14–16, no. 543; Marrone, 'Ecclesiology', pp. 140f. All of these characteristics (the 'rational' approach to law, close attention to the *Decretum*, and opposition to the mendicants) are important points of contact between Orléans and William Durant the Younger. Since the university of Toulouse did not share these characteristics, it is a less likely place for Durant to have visited as a student. Moreover, Toulouse suffered a protracted slump in the middle of the thirteenth century and would only be launched on the period of its glory by the support of Clement V and John XXII in the early fourteenth century: Meijers, 'Première époque', *Etudes*, 3:167–208, esp. 174, 183; Fournier, *Science du droit*, 3:209–340, esp. pp. 222f., 294; Gouron, 'Training', p. 221; Rashdall, *Universities*, 2:160–73. A *decretorum doctor et rector* by the name of William Durant is reported to have taught at Toulouse from 1290 to 1300: Fournier, *Science du droit*, 3:330. But the credibility of this evidence is weakened by the fact that Durant was rector of a parish in Mende before 1291, ordinary of the same parish since 1291, and bishop after 1296; see Nicholas IV, nos. 4,560–1 (7.III.1291). If the evidence is correct, it must have referred to another William Durant.

ever he may have studied, and whoever his teachers may have been, he proved worthy of his uncle. He 'displayed a familiarity with Decretist literature exceeding that of any contemporary except Guido de Baysio, and an ingenuity in marshalling the Decretist texts in support of his own views that was quite unparalleled'.[10] There can be little doubt that his knowledge of the decretalists and his familiarity with Roman law did not lag far behind.[11]

Unlike his uncle, however, the younger Durant did not have to rely on his talents alone in order to make his way in the world. He had family connections to help him, namely those with his uncle, whose promotion to the bishopric of Mende gave him open access to ecclesiastical patronage. Even before the older Durant had taken up residence in Mende the younger Durant was made rector of the parish of St Médard, exercised control over the chapel of St Michel de Garde, and received an annual pension from the church of Buxo. In 1291 he became the ordinary of St Médard.[12] By 1296 he had added another prebend, a canonry, and the archdeaconry of Mende to the benefices in his possession.[13] Next to the bishop himself he was the single most powerful cleric in the diocese.

The beginning of William Durant the Younger's career thus suggested that he would follow the pattern laid down by his uncle. If anything he might have been expected to follow it even more assiduously. Each of the records shedding light on his first years in Mende involves a papal favour. Indeed, he was the first bishop of Mende who owed his promotion to a papal reservation.[14] Seeing how thoroughly his rise depended on applications of the papal

---

[10] Tierney, *Foundations*, p. 191.

[11] Rogozinski, *Power, Caste, and Law*, p. 110 n. 85, calls him 'an esteemed legist'. Durant made it a practice to cite neither decretists nor decretalists in his *Tractatus Maior*, but the few exceptions are enough to show that he was familiar with the works of the two greatest decretalists, Innocent IV and Hostiensis; see below, p. 127 n. 23. He used Roman law much less frequently in the *Tractatus Maior* than he did canon law, but his abundant use of Roman law in the *Mémoire relatif au paréage de 1307*, especially in the second and third *particulae*, pp. 22–194, leaves no doubt about his mastery in that respect as well.

[12] Nicholas IV, nos. 4,560–1 (7.III.1291).

[13] This can be inferred from the list of positions that Durant had to vacate upon his assumption of the episcopacy; see Boniface VIII, no. 1,762 (2.IV.1297). Cf. Viollet, p. 5.

[14] Since Hugues d'Aiguesvives had died *in curia*, the grant of St Médard was based on Clement IV's famous reservation *Licet ecclesiarum* of 1265; see Ganzer, *Papsttum*, p. 34; Clement IV, no. 319 (11.VI.1266); VI.3.4.2. William Durant the Elder's death *in curia* gave the papacy another opportunity to apply *Licet ecclesiarum* in his nephew's favour; see GC, 1:Instrumenta:26; Boniface VIII, no. 1,492 (17.XII.1296); cf. Barbiche, ed. *Actes pontificaux*, no. 2,026 (17.XII.1296).

plenitude of power, Boniface VIII was surely justified in believing that this 'provident man, well versed in letters, of upright morals, and endowed with other gifts of virtue' would 'follow in the footsteps of Bishop William, his predecessor, and govern the church of Mende with success'.[15] There was also sufficient local opposition to his appointment to remind him of the bishop's continued dependence on the support of central government. It took until about 1300 for him to establish himself as the new lord of the Gévaudan over the resistance of the local nobility.[16] In addition, his relations with his chapter appear to have been strained,[17] and his finances were weak.[18] Under those circum-

[15] 'Considerantes, quod tanquam vir providus, litterarum scientia praeditus, morum honestate decorus, et aliis circumamictus donis virtutum, praefati Guillelmi episcopi inhaerens vestigiis, ecclesiam ipsam feliciter gubernabis . . .' *GC*, 1:Instrumenta:26.

[16] Soon after his election a number of Gabalitan nobles occupied his lands, usurped his rights, and resisted their duty to do homage; R–S, no. 8 (18.IV.1298), p. 13, orders the seneschal to investigate the matter and return to the bishop goods and rights that had been occupied *irrationabiliter*. The Tournel accepted Durant's lordship in 1299; Philippe, *La Baronnie*, pp. 50–52. Cénaret did, too; Viollet, p. 7. Florac posed a special problem. It was in royal wardship and even though William Nogaret, with whom Durant seems to have had a good relationship, supported its transfer to the bishop, the *viguier* of Anduze and his wards continued to resist until 1299, when an uneasy peace was established only after Durant threatened to refuse a Christian burial to Lady Isabel of Florac, the mother of the heirs: Viollet, pp. 7f.

[17] In 1297 and in 1300 Durant engaged the canons in a formal exchange of promises to 'respect the liberties, customs, and statutes of the church of Mende'. See Viollet, p. 6. In order to increase his control over the chapter he also issued a statute prohibiting anyone who had violated the rights of the church of Mende or who was related to such a person within the third degree from becoming a canon there. This was directed against the local nobility. Durant may have gotten the idea from his uncle, who had participated in the legatine council of Bourges of 1276 where a similar measure had been enacted: Falletti, 'Guillaume Durand', col. 1,220. He had his statute confirmed by Boniface VIII, no. 4,985 (25.XII.1302), and successfully recommended it to the council of Vienne; see below, pp. 239, 303f. We do not know the degree to which it eliminated noble control over his chapter, but it may be worth mentioning that within three years of his appointment two noble canons of Mende were promoted to the bishoprics of Viviers and Rodez respectively; André, 'Evêques de Mende', p. 29.

[18] In November 1297 Durant asked his chapter for a subsidy to pay for defending the rights of Mende. The chapter granted sixty shillings (*tournois* money) payable annually by every beneficed cleric with sufficient income and granted annates from all vacant benefices for six years. It continued with six-year grants of annates in 1309 and 1315; Viollet, pp. 9, 136f. The twelve-year interval between 1297 and 1309 makes it probable that another six-year grant was issued in 1303. In 1315 Durant claimed that he had spent 20,000 gold florins of his own money on defending the rights of Mende. That may have been exaggerated, but there can be no doubt that the suit over the golden bull alone involved considerable costs. In 1297 Durant also owed the papacy 'common services' to the amount of 4,000 florins: Hoberg, *Taxae*, p. 79; cf. Oakley, *Western Church*, p. 50; Barraclough, *Medieval Papacy*, pp. 120–3. That was the third-largest sum recorded for the province of Bourges, barely less than the 5,000 florins that Hoberg used as the limit

stances he had little choice but to cooperate with central government. Meanwhile, what we have called the spiritual–temporal monarchy continued to strengthen its grasp on the Gévaudan. There was a small peak in the number of papal provisions and dispensations from pluralism,[19] and there was a measurable increase in the degree to which the king drew on the revenues of the Gévaudan.[20] There also is some evidence that the mendicants were making headway in expanding their association with the local nobility.[21] In short, the circumstances were hardly favourable to a basic change of course.

Nevertheless, from the beginning there were reasons to doubt that the younger Durant's relationship with the monarchs would be as harmonious as that of his uncle had been. His character appears to have been different. He was not only younger when he acceded to the see but also more energetic and ambitious. There seems to be an element of ruthless vindictiveness in his treatment of his enemies and one of single-minded perseverance in his pursuit of pet issues.[22] His conduct is in many ways more reminiscent of

for what he forthrightly called *taxae maximae*; Hoberg, *Taxae*, p. 374. For the sake of comparison, Clermont-Ferrand paid 5,000 fls. in 1302; Bourges, 4,400 fls. in 1295; Le Puy, 2,000 fls. in 1296; and St Flour, 900 fls. in 1318. In order to raise sufficient cash Durant had to obtain permission from Boniface VIII to raise a loan in the amount of 3,000 lbs. (*tournois* money); Boniface VIII, no. 1,958 (24.VI.1297).

19 Boniface VIII, nos. 1,762 (2.IV.1297), 2,205 (19.XI.1297), 1,719 (30.I.1297).

20 This was the time when the war in Aquitaine and Flanders was just beginning to strain Philip IV's finances to the breaking point. In 1297 his request for subsidies provided 'several nobles' with an opportunity to collect money on the bishop's lands. Durant protested. His right to exercise control over the collection of subsidies on his lands was quickly reaffirmed, but the subsidies did of course have to be paid: R-S, nos. 6 (12.II.1298) and 7 (28.V.1298), pp. 10–12. Durant was less successful in his attempt to prevent the seneschal from levying a fine for amortization on lands sold by William Randon of Châteauneuf without his consent to the Benedictine abbey of Chaise-Dieu. The king merely asked the seneschal to investigate and to refer the results to Parlement; R-S, no. 10 (1.XII.1298), pp. 15f.; Viollet, p. 11. On amortizations, which seem to have annoyed the clergy a great deal and which had recently been increased beyond the usual level in the Beaucaire, see Strayer, *Reign of Philip the Fair*, pp. 238f., 256–8, 397–9 and n. 65.

21 An interesting specific case involved William Randon, one of the lords of Génolhac just to the east of the Gévaudan in the diocese of Uzès, and one of William Durant the Younger's certified opponents. He enjoyed a good relationship with the Dominicans in Marvéjols, granted lands and money for a convent to the Dominicans in Génolhac around 1298, and received papal authorization to establish the convent in 1300. The bishop of Uzès refused to go along, which delayed the project temporarily. But in 1304 Pope Benedict XI decided to overrule the bishop. The convent was established in 1305; see Benedict XI, no. 1,153 (8.I.1304); Dossat, 'Opposition', pp. 270–2, 276.

22 For his vindictiveness see his oath of October 1304, below, pp. 95f. For his perseverance, see the doggedness with which he pushed his statute to exclude inimical noblemen from canonries; above, p. 76 n. 17, and below, pp. 239, 303f.

Boniface VIII's imperiousness than of the Speculator's equanimity.
He somehow seems to have been at odds with the world.

By themselves, however, those traits (if they did exist, which our
slender evidence does not permit us to assert with certainty) are
insufficient to explain why he was to become a champion of local
autonomy and a bitter critic of the papacy. The older Durant
himself, after all, was nothing if not ambitious and his pronouncements on the papal plenitude of power were not quite as unambiguous as is sometimes thought. Ambition had prompted him to
study law, and had been rewarded with a bishopric.[23] Sometimes
he interspersed his support of papal supremacy with pointed
attacks on papal policy that would be resumed by his nephew.[24]
And if he had amassed canonical doctrines that were designed to
support the plenitude of power, he did the same for those that
supported canonical constitutionalism.[25] His support of the

[23] See the anecdote about Durant's decision to study law, above, pp. 64f. Revealing
evidence for the role of ambition in the older Durant's life comes from the circumstances
surrounding his elevation to the bishopric. When he had received the offer from Mende
he consulted with Honorius IV, who reported that he 'ne, si absque nostra conscientia
petitioni dictorum capituli annuisset in hac parte, per hoc a praedictorum obsequiorum
prosecutione forte non sine ambitionis nota se velle subducere videretur, quid super hoc
sibi esset agendum a nobis cum reverentia postulavit, et tandem eidem electioni de se
factae recepto apostolico responso consensit.' *GC*, 1:Instrumenta:26. Precisely because
the episcopacy gave him greater independence from the papacy, it raised the suspicion of
ambition particularly clearly.
[24] See his dissatisfaction with the canonical right to appeal directly to the pope: 'Benedictus
tamen sit imperator qui, licet dominus mundi sit, ut ff. ad l. Rho. de iact. deprecatio, . . .
non tamen patitur in preiudicium inferiorum ordinariorum et in damnum et laborem
inestimabilem litigatorum ad se omissis mediis appellari.' *Speculum iudiciale* 2.3, De
appellationibus 4.1, fol. 188r. Cf. Dig.14.2.9. See also Stickler, 'Ordines iudiciarii', cols.
1,133–5; Ganzer, *Papsttum*, pp. 31, 40f.; VI.1.6.4, VI.1.6.10. Regarding procurations he
declared that 'apostolica sedes pro magna parte per sua privilegia divites a praestatione
procurationum exemit, cum potius pauperes eximere debuisset'. *Speculum iudiciale* 1.1,
De legato 4.27, fol. 15r. His charge in *Speculum iudiciale* 1.1, De dispensationibus 5.7, fol.
30v, that 'ecclesia tamen Romana . . . tanquam domina omnia ad se trahit', was repeated
by the younger Durant: 'Ad se que ad minores et medios pertinent trahere volunt, ut in
eis verificetur illud: "Cum exaltatus fuero a terra omnia traham ad meipsum."' *TMI* 8
(3.31), fol. 62ra. The source is John 12:32.
[25] See especially his definition of limits on dispensations: 'Hec autem sunt in quibus papa
dispensare non potest: primo contra apostolum ut bigamus fiat diaconus vel sacerdos vel
episcopus, ut xxxi. di. acutius, et c. una tamen, et c. deinde, xxv. q. i. sunt quidam, extra
de biga. c. iii., ar. tamen contra xxiiii. di. lector, vel ut quis simul plures possit habere
uxores, ut extra de biga. super eo, et c. de bigamis, et c. nuper. Jo. notat in preallegato c.
sunt quidam quod bene potest dispensare contra apostolum, non tamen in his que
pertinent ad articulos fidei. Secundo contra decem precepta decalogi, ut xiii. di. sicut,
quia, etsi non sint articuli, sunt tamen articularia fidei, id est ita annexa articulis fidei,
quod sine eis salutem prestare non possunt, secundum Jo. de Deo, ut in pre. c. sunt
quidam, et vi. di. §. fi., lxxxvi. di. non satis ad fi. Tertio contra evangelium, ut in c. sunt
quidam, et xxvi. di. deinde, et xiiii. di. sicut, et ar. extra de cle. miss. cum marte. Contra

papacy, in other words, was never a foregone conclusion. It just so happened that the circumstances of his life inclined him not to act upon whatever doubts he may have had about the conduct of the papacy and, if the circumstances had remained the same, William Durant the Younger might have been just so inclined as well. But circumstances changed. If William Durant the Elder had gone to Rome before he went to Mende, William Durant the Younger bypassed Rome and went to Mende directly. Thus he lacked his uncle's experience of how intimately his success was tied to the success of his papal lord, and was not taught how to accommodate his wishes to the requirements of a slow-moving government as his uncle had been during long years of service to the papacy. His obligations to the papacy were just as strong, but his experience with it was indirect and limited. Hence his loyalty to Rome was less substantial than that of the Speculator, and his impatience with Roman vices was greater.

The most important circumstance which changed the episcopate of William Durant the Younger, however, had nothing to do with his personal career. It did not even have anything to do with Mende; rather, it concerned the relation of Rome to Paris. William Durant the Elder entered Mende just after Benedict Gaetani and

enim ius naturale dispensatio locum non habet, ut xiii. di. c. i, extra de transac. c. fi. Ius autem naturale est quod in lege et in evangelio continetur, i. di. humanum, ix. di. circa finem. Quarto contra quatuor concilia principalia tollendo ea, ut supra in pre. c. sunt quidam. Quinto cum homicida voluntary ut post quantancumque poenitentiam ministret in officio altaris, extra de tempo. or. c. fi., l. di. miror, i. q. vii. si quis omnem, extra de excess. prela. ex literis, extra de accu. inquisitionis, extra de temp. or. c. fi., extra de ho. c. i.' *Speculum iudiciale* 1.1, De dispensationibus 7.2, fol. 33v. Cf. D.26 c.2, D.26 c.4, D.26 c.3, C.25 q.1 c.6, X.1.21.3, D.34 c.18, X.1.21.2–4, D.14 c.2, C.25 q.1 c.6, D.6 p.c.3, D.86 c.14, C.25 q.1 c.6, D.26 c.3, D.14 c.2, X.3.41.6, D.13 c.1, X.1.36.11, D.1 a.c.1, D.9 p.c.11, C.25 q.1 c.6, X.1.11.17, D.50 c.4, C.1 q.7 c.2, X.5.31.10, X.5.1.21, X.1.11.17, X.5.12.1. Note the repeated references to *Sunt quidam*, C.25 q.1 c.6, and *Sicut*, D.14 c.2, both crucial canons in the arsenal of canonical constitutionalism, and both prominently used in the *Tractatus Maior*. Like the younger Durant the Speculator similarly required the pope to abide by general law according to the well-known principle of Roman law that 'licet enim princeps omnia possit et legibus non adstringatur, tamen vivere debet secundum leges, ut extra de concess. preben. proposuit, et C. de legi. digna, et xxv. q. i. §. si ergo, in princip., alias in §. his ita. Tunc enim iura sua servantur, quando eis ipse reverentiam exhibet, ut ix. di. iustum.' *Speculum iudiciale* 2.3, De appellationibus 4.1, fol. 188r. Cf. X.3.8.4, Cod.1.14.4, C.25 q.1 p.c.16, D.9 c.2. The last three references to *Digna vox* (Cod.1.14.4), Gratian's account of papal supereminence over the law (C.25 q.1 p.c.16), and *Iustum* (D.9 c.2), were crucial to the younger Durant as well. But it is worth pointing to the care with which the Speculator noted that in the body of his *dictum* C.25 q.1 p.c.16 §. *his ita*, Gratian allotted a rather more exalted role to the papal legislative power than he did at the beginning, §. *si ergo*. The younger Durant was going to proceed rather differently; see below, pp. 151–3.

Philip IV had reached their settlement – thus his episcopate was shaped by their cooperation. William Durant the Younger, in contrast, entered Mende just after the first clash between Boniface VIII and Philip IV; hence his episcopate was shaped by their dissension.

## CRISIS

Two equally basic but contrasting facts concerning the conflict between Boniface VIII and Philip IV ought to be kept in mind.[26] First, dramatic as the conflict between the spiritual and the temporal monarchies undoubtedly was, it did not destroy their underlying agreement. This is all too easily forgotten in the excitement surrounding the spectacle of a king who ordered the seemingly sacrilegious and effectively murderous attack of Anagni on the vicar of Christ. But the drama did not change any of the reasons that had brought the alliance between the papacy and the French monarchy into existence, and, as we have observed previously, those reasons were excellent. What therefore needs to be remembered is not the violence of Anagni, but the observation that 'in actual fact, Philip was on good terms with the papacy during all but 5 of the 29 years that he was king'.[27]

Across the great divide of 1303 there was real continuity in the cooperation between king and pope. However, the continuity was accompanied by a profound discontinuity on the symbolic level of ideas about the proper order of the world, which is the second fact to be borne in mind. Although the alliance between pope and king weathered the storm, the idea of a Christian commonwealth, of a single body politic, universal in its aspirations, governed by Christ and by his Roman vicar, united by a single faith, obedient to a Christian law, administered by spiritual and temporal rulers who were at peace with each other, in concord with their mother church, and dedicated to driving infidels out of the birthland of

[26] It should not be necessary here to deal with this conflict in detail, as it has been studied exhaustively elsewhere: Strayer, *Reign of Philip the Fair*, pp. 249–81, is a superb recent summary. See also Digard, *Philippe le Bel*; Boase, *Boniface VIII*; Bautier, 'Le Jubilé de 1300'; Poquet du Haut-Jussé, 'Le Second Différend'; Marrone and Zuckerman, 'Cardinal Simon of Beaulieu'; Ruiz, 'Reaction to Anagni'. On the publicistic literature: Scholz, *Die Publizistik*; Rivière, *Le Problème*; Miethke, 'Die Traktate "De potestate papae"'. On the role of councils in this conflict: Kay, 'Ad nostram praesentiam'; Arquillière, 'L'Appel au concile'; Arquillière, 'L'Origine des théories conciliaires'; Dondaine, 'L'Appel au concile'. [27] Strayer, *Reign of Philip the Fair*, pp. 237ff.

their saviour – the idea of such a Christian commonwealth became doomed in 1303. Boniface VIII and Philip IV came to blows because they were competing for men and money to carry out their dreams of empire. But there were neither enough men nor enough money to realize such dreams – hence the universal projects inspired by memories of ancient Rome and by 'political Augustinianism' collapsed.[28]

The period from the outbreak of hostilities between Boniface VIII and Philip IV to the restoration of friendly relations at the council of Vienne – and, in a wider sense, the later middle ages as a whole – thus bears the marks of crisis. Crisis is a term with many meanings.[29] But all of them revolve around one main idea: crisis denotes the emergence of a conflict between opposing elements in what had previously appeared to be a single whole. Its basic meaning, as is suggested by its etymology, is 'distinction', 'separation'. What was distinguished in the present case, not just by abstract speculation but by the course of historical events itself, were the real power of the king and the ideal power of the pope. What underwent a crisis was that conception of a single Christian commonwealth which Boniface VIII had just resoundingly reaffirmed in *Unam sanctam*.[30]

As a result the experience of time was divided into two different and conflicting kinds. One of them was measured beneath the surface of events, where pope and king continued to cooperate for the sake of governmental centralization, with only a slight interruption in their common progress on the road toward a national mode of politics on which they had been moving all along. But a different kind of temporal experience governed the surface of events where discontinuity, disruption, and disorder appeared more dominant. The crisis in ideas about the proper order of the world seemed to drive a real wedge between the temporal and spiritual monarchies and thereby to reverse the course of previous

[28] The term was given prominence by Arquillière, *L'Augustinisme politique.*
[29] For an excellent introduction to the manifold issues raised by this term see the article 'Krise' in *Geschichtliche Grundbegriffe,* 3:617–50.
[30] The cynicism, anger, and, indeed, the terror which the distinction between real and ideal could provoke from men habituated to accept their fundamental unity was put into bold relief in the brief exchange between Peter Flote and Boniface reported by Walsingham: 'De cujus audacia Papa exasperatus, dicto Petro respondit; – "Nos habemus", inquit, "utramque potestatem." Et mox Petrus, pro domino suo, respondit; – "Utique, Domine, sed vestra est verbalis, nostra autem realis." Qua responsione, tantum excanduit ira Papae, ut diceret se movere contra eum coelum et terram.' *Chronica Monasterii S. Albani,* 2:197f.

history. That, on the one hand, threatened the Christian common-wealth with schism, but on the other hand it benefited the victims of centralization, the 'middling powers', to whom it restored an open space in which they could try to reclaim a place of honour for local autonomy and for what they may have thought was Christian decency in politics.

Hence, for a while, all sorts of plans were entertained about the most profitable manner of reorganizing the world, some of them remarkably old fashioned and conventional, others quite extra-ordinary, even a little crazy, some destined to end up in the dustbin of history, others so full of premonitions of the future as to remain in fashion for centuries. One thinks of Raymond Lull, of Dante, of Pierre Dubois, perhaps of Marsiglio, and, of course, of William Durant the Younger. Their writings all share a similar quality of unreality. Not that they were without effect, or that they were all alike. Some borrowed their effectiveness not from a strength that was their own but from a weakness that was someone else's. It was the weakness of the papacy that made Dante dream of universal monarchy and that provoked Pierre Dubois to put his projects of French imperialism into writing. Marsiglio, in contrast, borrowed his strength from visions of a future that was not to be realized until much later, and never on his terms. But none of them perceived that the integration of the temporal with the spiritual power continued unabated; hence all of them were in a certain sense thrown out of time, or more precisely, unable to keep their concentration focused on both of the conflicting tendencies by which their present was divided. All were afflicted by a political and moral double vision. Soon, therefore, it would be manifest that the appearances that seemed to lend such strength to their ideas of universal renewal were quite deceptive; soon local autonomy would be kept at bay by central, local states which invested their bureaucracies with spiritual authority and which, indeed, almost succeeded in establishing local papacies.

From hindsight one can do no better than to respect the speed and possibly the courage with which the papacy abandoned its own dreams, seized on the realities of political life, and completed the inevitable transition to the latter, as is more than symbolized by its move from Rome to Avignon. Compared to the single-minded determination with which Dante and Pierre Dubois, and later the Emperors Sigismund and Charles V and even King Louis XIV, held fast to universal aspirations, the willingness to lower their ambitions to a smaller scale exhibited by Clement V and John XXII, Eugenius IV and Alexander VI, may strike impartial observers as wholesomely pragmatic. By 1312, when the council of Vienne came to an end, the *factum Bonifacianum* had been laid to rest, friendly relations with Philip IV had been restored, and the papacy had recovered its balance.

That such would be the outcome of the great clash of 1303, however, and that it would take less than ten years to bring about, was hardly obvious at the beginning. Even when an agreement was reached it seems to have been welcomed with less than enthusiasm by most contemporaries – including, one suspects, some of the central participants, who may have preferred to think that they were acting under the constraints of necessity rather than the guidance of the Holy Spirit. If only for a while, and only on the surface, the clash thus seemed to have permanently altered the balance of power between central governments and middling powers.

POLITICAL MANOEUVRES

Under these circumstances the circle that seemed to have been closed by William Durant the Elder was opened once again. The quarrel between Philip and Boniface turned out to be a stroke of luck for the bishops. To be sure, the basic parameters that had been established for the relationship between the king and the bishops in 1290 were not removed. On the contrary, the clash between the central rulers provoked at least one observer, the author of the famous *Disputation of a Cleric with a Knight*, to highlight the dependence of the bishops on royal protection from local noblemen more forthrightly than had been done before.[31] And the price of that protection was higher than ever: in almost every single year from 1295 until 1304 the bishops had to pay a tenth to Philip, and in some years they paid twice. Meanwhile, Pope Boniface VIII

---

[31] 'Ne perstrepite sed pacienter audite. Considerate vicinos vestros suis egentes et ad vestra respicientes. Si deficeret regia potestas, qualis esset requies vestra? Nonne nobiles egeni et prodigi, si consumpsissent sua, converterentur ad vestra? Ergo regia manus est munus vestra, pax regis pax vestra, salus regis salus vestra, que si deessct aut forsitan esset subtracta, vel peccatis vestris exigentibus a vobis discederet . . . cogeremini omnibus servire.' *Disputatio inter clericum et militem*, ed. Erickson, p. 298.

published the *Liber Sextus* and had more extensive recourse to papal reservations than any pope before. This is hardly evidence for a resurgence of the middling powers. But even though the bishops hesitated to take full advantage of the freedom that the disagreements of their rulers gave to them, they recovered a degree of political mobility permitting them to extract more significant concessions in return for their support than had seemed possible during the previous decade.[32]

The same political mobility was visible in Mende. For a while it may have seemed as though the ancient association of the bishop with the king was going to be modified by new alliances between the bishop and the pope and between the king and the local nobility.[33] But soon the traditional pattern was resoundingly affirmed. Durant was quite successful in playing both sides of the dispute: he went to Paris in 1302 and actively participated in helping Philip out of the dire fiscal straits in which the defeat of Courtrai had placed him,[34] but he also heeded Pope Boniface

[32] The bishops probably secured their most important gains in Boniface VIII's *Super cathedram* of 1300 (Clem.3.7.2), which asserted the bishops' right to a quarter of the income of the friars, and in Philip IV's great reform ordinance of 1303; see *Ordonnances*, 1:354–67, to be compared with Philip's ordinance in favour of the churches of Languedoc of 1302, *Ordonnances*, 1:340–4. Strayer, *Reign of Philip the Fair*, pp. 247f., 256f., concludes that royal ordinances in favour of the church peaked in the period 1299–1304.

[33] In 1298 Aldebert de Peyre, prior of Ispagnac, concluded a *paréage* that established his and the king's joint rulership over Ispagnac; R-S, appendix 12, pp. 216–21. The lords of Canilhac and of Chirac entered into comparable settlements; Strayer, 'La Noblesse du Gévaudan', p. 67. The de Peyre traditionally shared control over the town and court of Marvéjols with Philip. William Durant, meanwhile, appealed to Pope Benedict XI for protection against the local nobility in 1303, but the bull for which he asked was never issued; Viollet, p. 15.

[34] On 19 April 1302, Durant witnessed an assembly of prelates and barons in Paris at which the archbishop of Bordeaux, the future Pope Clement V, tried to explain to Peter Flote the complicated course of action that he was trying to steer between king and pope; *GC*, 2:300f., no. 42. Viollet, pp. 14f. n. 5, must have slipped in dating this event to 1303 since Peter Flote died in the summer of 1302. Probably the reason why Durant was in Paris at the time was that he had obeyed Philip's request to attend an assembly of the estates, which has coincidentally been published in the version that was sent to the seneschal of Beaucaire; Picot, ed., *Documents*, pp. 1–5. But there is no positive evidence that Durant actually participated in the assembly that met on 10 April 1302. In the summer of 1303 Durant joined the French clergy in granting a tenth and a half to Philip IV, and in March 1304, as one of only two bishops attending the provincial council of Bourges, he was instrumental in the grant of another tenth, which he, too, made dependent on conditions, such as that the pope would enter no objections and that the king would enact clearly specified reforms; R-S, no. 17 (26.VIII.1303), pp. 29–33; Viollet, pp. 15f.

VIII's command to attend the Roman synod in November 1302, where he must have listened to the publication of that uncompromising restatement of papal claims on ruling the world in general and France in particular that is *Unam sanctam*.[35] Thus he maintained his favour with the papacy while at the same time benefiting from Philip IV's good will.[36]

Durant's greatest success during those years was that he persuaded Philip to settle the issue of the golden bull by means of a *paréage*.[37] As late as 1300 William of Plaisians had argued that the bishop's pretended rights over the Gévaudan were unfounded and that all of the proceedings that had taken place since 1269 ought to have been suppressed in Philip's favour.[38] It was precisely in response to this threat that Durant composed the so-called *Mémoire relatif au paréage de 1307*, a major treatise in which he set forth the rights of his office and tried to refute the arguments of Plaisians in

[35] Dupuy, *Histoire*, p. 86; Viollet, p. 14. It was on this occasion that Durant obtained Boniface's confirmation of his statute for the chapter; see above, p. 76 n. 17. Durant's presence in Rome at that time was no negligible matter. Philip IV had explicitly prohibited the clergy from going to Rome. They begged the pope to excuse them and most of them did not in fact attend. William Durant the Younger thus joined the relatively small number of thirty-three French bishops (out of a total of seventy-nine) who were willing to defy the king's command (six bishops were already in Rome for unrelated reasons; Strayer, *Reign of Philip the Fair*, pp. 272f.) It has been remarked, however, that thirty-three bishops were not enough to represent the French church as a whole, especially since most came from the south of France, like Durant, while very few came from the old royal domain. That confused an already complicated issue, which could only help the case of a king who had every intention of frustrating the pope's proceedings. Hence it has even been suggested that the bishops who did go to Rome went with Philip's tacit approval; Strayer, *Reign of Philip the Fair*, pp. 272f.

[36] As early as February 1300 Durant had received a major privilege from Philip IV that was renewed in 1302 and confirmed by Louis X in 1315; R-S, no. 11 (24.II.1300), pp. 17–21; Viollet, p. 11. Among other things it abolished royal levies on clerics, even married ones provided they 'lived clerically without fraud'. This was one of Durant's pet issues. On borderline clerics in general see Gilles, 'Clergé méridional'; Strayer, *Reign of Philip the Fair*, pp. 193f., 198, 243f. In August of 1303 and June of 1304, expressly in return for his willingness to contribute to the king's financial needs, Durant received further grants which, among other things, gave him the right to keep the royal lands he had acquired in the past, promised to restore good money, and assured him that he would not have to pay concurrent tenths to the pope and the king; R-S, nos. 17 (26.VIII.1303), pp. 29–33, 20 (15.VI.1304), pp. 37–41, the latter also in *Ordonnances*, 1:412. The privilege of 1304 should be compared with the grant made to the church of Narbonne in *Ordonnances*, 1:402–5. In general see the command to the seneschal of Beaucaire to treat the bishop of Mende with favour in R-S, no. 19 (10.III.1304), p. 36.

[37] That is, by an agreement to share power as equals (*pares, pairs, peers*) rather than to allot power to one or the other of the conflicting parties.

[38] Porée, 'Le Procès', pp. 290f.

# The formation of interest

detail.[39] And he succeeded. Philip saw no virtue in prolonging a dispute with someone whose support he needed. He intervened to take the case out of the hands of Parlement and instead placed it before his royal council, where it was speedily resolved under the leadership of Gaucelin de la Garde, the bishop of Maguelonne, who until shortly before had been a canon of the church of Mende.[40] By 1304 the basic outlines of an agreement seem to have been clear, and in 1307 it was complete.[41]

## THE 'PARÉAGE' OF MENDE

The *paréage* of Mende is a document of such importance for an understanding of the changes that had taken place in the Gévaudan since the twelfth century, of the redistribution of powers that followed the crisis in royal–papal relations, and of the circumstances under which Durant composed the *Tractatus Maior*, that we must look at it in some detail.[42] Given its length – more than

[39] Durant declared that the *Mémoire* was composed 'ad deffendendum processum in causa ista habitum et ad ostendendum quod pars regia non debet de novo admitti ad probandum at quod pro ipso episcopo sententia sit ferenda.' *Mémoire*, p. 1. His reasons why the proceedings were to be considered valid are detailed in the second *pars principalis* of the *Mémoire*, pp. 482–556. See Porée, 'Les Evêques-comtes', pp. 467f.; Porée, 'Le Procès', pp. 325f. Porée, 'Les Evêques-comtes', pp. 468–75, contains a good analysis of the *paréage*.

[40] The other members of the council who helped to formulate the *paréage* were Peter Flote, Pierre de la Chapelle, Pierre de Belleperche, and of course William of Plaisians himself. It ought to be noted that the papal legates in France agreed; Porée, 'Le Procès', pp. 291–3. The decision to entrust the formulation of a compromise to Gaucelin de la Garde seems to have been taken no earlier than 1299, but apparently before Plaisians tried to attack the validity of past proceedings in 1300 or 1301; Porée, 'Le Procès', pp. 325f.; cf. Porée, 'Les Evêques-comtes', p. 478f. In 1301 the chapter of Mende authorized Durant to settle with the king; Viollet, pp. 11–13.

[41] Gaucelin de la Garde died on 12 March 1304. Thereafter the royal council introduced only minor changes in favour of the king; Porée, 'Le Procès', pp. 292f. In 1305 and 1306 Durant was abroad. In order to avoid the misleading impression that Durant's success was unique, it ought to be stressed that in 1307, the year in which the *paréage* of Mende was signed, Philip IV concluded *paréages* with four other ecclesiastical lords in southern France, namely the bishops of Cahors, Le Puy, Limoges, and Viviers; Strayer, *Reign of Philip the Fair*, pp. 202, 248. Boutaric, *France*, p. 9 n. 3, lists a total of nineteen *paréages* that were concluded by Philip IV, only two of them with lay lords. Neither the *paréage* of Mende nor the *Mémoire* have ever received the detailed analysis that they deserve, but there is a good study of the *paréage* of Le Puy by Delcambre, 'Paréage du Puy'.

[42] I have used the edition in *Ordonnances*, 11:396–403. The *paréage* is also printed by Burdin, *Documents historiques*, 1:359–76. The edition in R-S, appendix 1, pp. 173–95, is seriously marred by misprints and omissions. A French summary can be found in Devic and Vaissete, *Histoire générale*, 9:294–6. It should be noted that the *paréage* is written from the perspective of the king, so that personal pronouns such as 'we', 'our', etc. refer to the king, not Durant.

twenty pages of elaborately detailed legalese – its structure was surprisingly simple. It began with a straightforward admission that both the bishop and the king claimed virtually complete rights to the Gévaudan, and it continued with a statement of their positions that differed in only two respects from the description of their rights in the golden bull of 1161.[43] The first was the much more elaborate detail in which their rights were defined, which is good evidence for the increase in legal sophistication that is so familiar an aspect of high medieval history. The second was that the contradiction between the rights of the king and those of the bishop now formed the focus of attention: the logical inconsistency that had been implicit in the golden bull was at last explicitly recognized.[44]

Given this inconsistency, the golden bull was obviously ill suited to serve as the foundation for a compromise. Indeed, William of Plaisians and William Durant the Younger had already decided not to rest their argument on that venerable charter, although for different reasons.[45] Their willingness to forsake legal proceedings

---

[43] The bishop insisted that 'totus episcopatus Gaballitanus tam ex privilegiis antiquis regum Francie quam ex consuetudine antiqua et usu longissimo pleno jure pertinebat ad ipsos [episcopos] nomine dicte ecclesie Mimatensi, et suberat eidem episcopo et ecclesie Mimatensi et subesse debebat et consueverat quantum ad majorem jurisdictionem episcopalem et altiorem potestatem et dominationem majorem cum jure regalium'. *Ordonnances*, 11:396f. The bishop allowed only two exceptions. One consisted of the lands that the king held in full ownership or as feudal lord, in part as a result of the settlement with Odilo de Mercoeur of 1265. The other consisted of the bishop's obligation to swear an oath of fealty to the king. The king declared exactly the opposite, namely that 'totus episcopatus predictus, tam de jure communi quam de antiqua et approbata consuetudine et usu longissimo quantum ad temporalem jurisdictionem nobis subest, et ad nos pertinet pleno jure quoad majorem jurisdictionem et cohertionem et districtum temporalem.' *Ordonnances*, 11:397.

[44] 'In quibus juribus dicebat [episcopus] se turbari et inquietari indebite et ea usurpari per dictum senescallum, et per dictas gentes nostras dicte senescallie Bellicadri, et ea petebat cum instantia revocari, gentibus nostris predictis hec omnia negantibus et ex adverso ad defensionem juris nostri contraria facta proponentibus.' *Ordonnances*, 11:397.

[45] See Porée, 'Les Evêques-comtes', pp. 347f., 472–4; cf. *Mémoire*, pp. 520–33, on the nullity of the golden bull *in materia*. Although the debate is far too extensive to be considered in detail, the central arguments on either side are worth quoting. In typical dialectical fashion William of Plaisians constructed a dichotomy to demonstrate the nullity of the golden bull: 'Pro eo quod dominus Aldebertus episcopus suggessit inclite recordationis domino Ludovico regi, proavo beati Ludovici, quod totus episcopatus Gaballitani semper extiterit in potestate episcoporum ad judicandum in gladio materiali et quod subditionem regis Francie non cognoverant episcopi nec fidelitatem fecerant eidem, unde, cum non sit dare medium, quin illud quod suggessit episcopus fuerit verum vel falsum, utroque casu constare videtur dictum indultum regium esse nullum. Nam, si fuerit verum, concessio regia non valuit, quia quod erat episcopi, ut episcopus asserebat, rex sibi dare non potuit et, si hoc fecit, donatio nulla fuit. Et ideo, si episcopus erat prius dominus, ex illa concessione iterum dominus effici non potuit, cum res propria non possit donari alicui sicut etiam nec legari. Secundum etiam hoc, si episcopus erat dominus, rex

---

based on existing documents was clearly stated in the introduction of the *paréage* itself:

Many witnesses and very many instruments, registers, acts, and other muniments have been produced, and the suit has already lasted thirty-five years and more, and yet for many reasons it cannot be conveniently judged, especially because the seneschal and other men of ours who desired to be heard in order to prove certain points said that the matter had not yet been decided and that the outcome of the suit was doubtful.[46]

non poterat sibi dare quod non habebat et quod suum non erat, nec episcopus debebat impetrare quod de jure communi competebat eidem, cum hoc superfluum reputetur. Ad hec, si falsum erat quod suggessit episcopus, scilicet quod non esset dominus temporalis Gaballitani et quod non esset subditus regis Francie nec fidelis, talis falsitas fuit suggesta et talis veritas tacita quod indultum reddidit ipso jure nullum, sive etiam suggessit falsum sive etiam tacuerit verum; et ideo unde penam meruit non potuit premium reportare.' *Mémoire*, pp. 519f. In order to combat the formidable weapons of this dialectic William Durant argued that 'quicquid igitur opposuit circa istam materiam dictus advocatus regius de finibus regni et de falsi suggestione et de veri suppressione, et quod episcopus haberet probare induci continentiam esse veram, ex ista sola ratione solvitur, quia in dicto privilegio non determinatur si ante ipsum privilegium episcopatus erat de regno et si episcopus erat fidelis regis et subditus, vel non, set dicitur quod non erat memoria. Et hoc rex et sui qui aderant bene sciebant, quia aliquis episcopus hoc recognovisset. Unde superfluum est an falsum suggestum fuerit per episcopum vel verum suppressum fuerit in dicto privilegio disputare, cum privilegium non determinet nec dicat et ideo reprehendi et reprobari ex eo, quod in ipso privilegio non determinatur, non potest . . . Et eodem modo quo potest poni duos esse imperatores temporales in uno mundo, eodem modo habet necesse ponere duos reges esse posse in regno uno, licet episcopus non dicat se esse regem.' *Mémoire*, pp. 530f. His own interpretation of the golden bull was subtle, not to say specious: 'Cum dicitur: si episcopus erat dominus, non igitur rex, et ita quod non habebat rex dare non potuit, respondetur quod non dicitur in dicto privilegio quod rex dederit, sed quod concessit et confirmavit, ut est dictum. Quorum verborum est sensus et interpretatio juris quod, si rex aliquid in dicto episcopatu habebat de facto, vel de jure habere debebat, vel de novo acquirebat propter illa que episcopus de novo faciebat, vel quod, posito quod olim episcopatus fuisset de regno, illud jus dictus rex episcopo et ecclesie concedebat, id est dabat. Si vero nichil juris dictus rex ab antiquo in dicto episcopatu habuerat, nec de novo propter illa que faciebat episcopus adquirebat, concedebat dictus rex predicto episcopo ut, infra regnum suum nunc existendo, predicta haberet libere sicut prius habebat, se de regno non esse profitendo. Et sic dicta concessio erat quodammodo localis potius quam realis.' *Mémoire*, pp. 525f. At the same time it clearly troubled Durant that Aldebert had in fact accepted a grant from Louis VII, even if it was purely 'local' and not 'real'; he was at pains to stress, not only that Louis had issued the grant 'ex suo motu proprio', without any prompting on Aldebert's part, but also that Aldebert had proceeded 'absque sedis apostolice et capituli sui consensu et licentia baronum et nobilium dicte terre'. *Mémoire*, p. 524; cf. *Mémoire*, pp. 3f. Curiously enough Durant thus looked just as critically on the implications of the golden bull as Aldebert's noble opponents had done.

[46] 'Plures testes et instrumenta quam plurima, registra, acta, et alia quam plurima munimenta producta fuissent, et lis ipsa triginta quinque annis durasset et ultra, et non posset commode judicio terminari propter multas causas, et maxime quia dictus senescallus et alie gentes nostre que ad probandum aliquos articulos petebant se admitti dicebant quod non erat adhuc in causa conclusum, et esset dubius ipsius litis eventus.' *Ordonnances*, 11:397.

Doubtful indeed it had to be, in spite of documentation amounting to seventy-one registers and nineteen rolls submitted by the seneschal and thirty-five volumes and forty-eight rolls submitted by the bishop.[47] As was now clear, none of that documentation helped since no legal analysis could extract much light from the document on which all of the proceedings were founded and which was itself a cause of obscurity: the golden bull of Mende. Meanwhile real damage was being done both to the principals and to the inhabitants of the Gévaudan.[48] New law had to be established to provide for peace and justice.

The opening passages of the *paréage* thus furnished an excellent justification for a fresh beginning. Its central dispositions consisted of two basic steps. The first was to form an association in which the bishop and the king would be equal partners with identical rights:

First of all, by reason of this composition, convention, and general transaction we associate the bishop and his successors as well as the church of Mende to ourselves and our successors in every high and low jurisdiction, mere and mixed *imperium*, and in every domain, temporal power, and resort, as well as the regalian rights and all other rights, domains, and jurisdictions which pertain to us, or are capable of pertaining to us, in any way, in the entire land and county and bishopric of Gévaudan and the entire diocese of Mende, in any place, over any person, noble or common, ecclesiastical or secular, for whichever reason or occasion.[49]

As is so commonly the case with legal texts, the precise meaning of the terms that are here used is subject to much doubt. But the basic point is obvious: there was to be a novel public entity, a single office held by two persons in a kind of hypostatic union that represents a perfect counter-image to the familiar personal unions

[47] R-S, no. 84 (22.III.1314), pp. 157–9.
[48] 'Lis dicto episcopo, ecclesie, et patrie foret ex multis causis damnosa, et etiam sumptuosa, et occasione ipsius litis jura dicte ecclesie a subditis et vicinis, ut audivimus, lederentur, et multa ex ejus occasione remanerent maleficia impunita, – nos etiam in multis juribus nobis competentibus fraudaremur.' *Ordonnances*, 11:397.
[49] 'In primis ex causa hujus compositionis, conventionis, et transactionis generalis nos associamus dictum episcopum et successores suos episcopos et ecclesiam Mimatensem pro nobis et successoribus nostris in omni jurisdictione alta et bassa, mero et mixto imperio et in omni dominatione et potestate temporali et ressorto, et in juribus regalium, et in omnibus aliis juribus, dominationibus, et jurisdictionibus ad nos pertinentibus, vel pertinere valentibus quoquomodo in tota terra et comitatu et episcopatu Gaballitani et tota diocesi Mimatensi in quibuscumque locis et supra quascumque personas, nobiles et ignobiles, ecclesiasticas vel seculares, et quibuscumque causis vel occasionibus.' *Ordonnances*, 11:398. The bishop reciprocated in virtually identical words; ibid.

which united the rulerships of distant territories in a single person. This office under the joint control of king and bishop was to exercise exclusive jurisdiction over all of the lands in the Gévaudan and all of the inhabitants, 'noble or common, ecclesiastical or secular'.[50] It was embodied in a new 'common court of the Gévaudan' and a variety of new officers: a *bailli*, a judge, a judge of appeals, sergeants, notaries (who doubled as receivers for the emoluments of justice), and gaolers. In all respects that might have given undue preponderance to either one of the contracting parties, such as the location of the common court or the choice of officers, strict parity was guarantied by requiring unanimity or by alternating the right to make a decision annually between the bishop and the king, and by alternating the location of the common court annually between Mende and Marvéjols. A common seal bearing the insignia of both the king and the bishop was created to symbolize joint rule. So as to complete the arsenal of justice, new prisons, gallows, and pillories were established as well. Special care was taken to forestall official misconduct. A slew of regulations was added to protect the new officials from interference by officials of the previous dispensation, who were bound to be resentful of the new limits on their power. Lower royal officials, such as the *bayle* and the judge of Marvéjols, were enjoined from 'exercising any form of judgment or coercion over the men of the bishop's own land and the common land'.[51] If for some reason they were found to have violated the bishop's rights without official royal business to excuse them, they would be surrendered to the bishop.[52] The royal *bayle* of Marvéjols was prohibited from using the title *baillivius* and instead had to call himself by the lesser title *bajulus*.[53] The jurisdiction of the *viguiers* of Anduze, Uzès, Meyrueis, and Alès in the Gévaudan was now completely abolished.[54] The priory of Ispagnac, over which Odilo de Mercoeur had quarrelled with the de Peyre, was explicitly included among the

---

[50] *Ordonnances*, 11:399–402, describes the new order in detail.
[51] 'Officiales vero seu ministri nostri proprii non poterunt homines de terra propria dicti episcopi vel de terra dicte communionis, etiamsi se obligarent ad sigillum nostrum proprium alicujus nostre curie proprie in Gaballitano, justitiare vel in aliquo coercere vel facere coerceri, nisi cum reperirentur in locis in quibus esset celebratus contractus. Et idem est intelligendum de ministris terre proprie dicti episcopi, salvo jure ipsi episcopo in sigillo suo et curie spiritualis.' *Ordonnances*, 11:401.
[52] *Ordonnances*, 11:401.    [53] Cf. R-S, appendix 10, pp. 212f.
[54] *Ordonnances*, 11:402f. Cf. the temporary grant of exemption from their jurisdiction which Philip IV had given to the older Durant in 1291, above p. 71.

lands under the jurisdiction of the common court.[55] Appeals were discouraged and the cases in which they were permitted were strictly limited according to civil law.[56] In sum, the *paréage* established a new *bailliage* and a new court with powers over the entire Gévaudan to which all older rights of jurisdiction were firmly subjected, so that no one 'who used to be under our jurisdiction or under the bishop's temporal jurisdiction before the present association may for any reason decline the jurisdiction of the said *bailli* and judge'.[57]

The second step was to exclude three matters from the sway of the new order. One concerned the lands that were in the undisputed control of either the bishop or the king – their *loca propria* as they were to be called.[58] These, unlike the lands held by the Gabalitan nobility, were not to be subjected to the jurisdiction of the common court. The second exclusion related to certain rights that Philip reserved for himself alone; these were rather broadly defined as 'our greater superiority and superior resort (of whatever kind they may be), in which we do not intend to associate the bishop to ourselves, in such a way, however, that this reservation of our greater superiority and superior resort will in no way derogate from the bishop's rights over the areas of shared power'.[59] The

---

55 *Ordonnances*, 11:399.
56 'Nec dicti baillivius et judex tenebuntur a suis processibus desistere, nec recipere appellationes frivolas, seu frustratorias, nec ante definitivam sententiam aliquas, nisi interponantur in casibus in jure civili expressis.' *Ordonnances*, 11:400. Appeals could only be made from a judgment that had already been passed or, prior to judgment, by claiming a 'defect of justice' according to the procedure laid down in royal statutes. Defect of justice could only be claimed if suspicions of judicial bias could be demonstrated by probable and clearly defined causes. In such cases the same judge was to render judgment, but had to be joined by a 'good man above suspicion' specifically chosen for the purpose by the seneschal and the bishop.
57 'Nullus de terra seu locis dicte associationis qui ante presentem associationem esset justitiabilis noster vel episcopi ratione jurisdictionis temporalis, quacumque causa poterit declinare jurisdictionem dictorum ballivii et judicis.' *Ordonnances*, 11:400. Cf. R-S, appendix 6, p. 209.
58 The king excluding the bishop: 'exceptis et retentis nobis et nostris successoribus castris, villis, et eorum territoriis et pertinenciis, hominibus, jurisdictionibus, domanis et aliis rebus et juribus quibuscumque nostris quae nunc ad manum nostram habemus et possidemus, vel habere et possidere modo quolibet possumus et debemus, infra fines dicti episcopatus, . . . in quibus, quecumque et qualiacumque sint, non intendimus associare dictum episcopum'. *Ordonnances*, 11:398. The bishop's parallel statement, ibid.
59 '[exceptis et retentis] nostra majori superioritate ac superiori ressorto in quibus, quecumque et qualiacumque sint, non intendimus associare dictum episcopum, ita tamen quod per hanc retentionem nostre majoris superioritatis et superioris ressorti in nullo derogetur supra communicatis episcopo supradicto'. *Ordonnances*, 11:398.

studied vagueness of this formulation leaves room for endless speculations about which rights precisely were included under 'greater superiority and superior resort'. Fortunately for our purposes those rights were clarified in three particulars. First, royal superiority included the right to tax the Gévaudan 'for the general defence of our realm'.[60] Second, it included the right to judge and punish 'crimes committed against our person or against the crown of our realm'.[61] And third, all appeals from local jurisdiction were destined to end up in royal courts, regardless whether they had originated in a baronial court, an episcopal court, or a royal court.[62] The king thus reserved for himself rights of taxation, of adjudicating treason, and of serving as the final arbiter in all matters of the law – what we may call a nucleus of sovereignty.

The first and second exclusions from the power of the new offices that were established by the *paréage* thus consisted of the proper lands of the bishop or the king and of sovereignty. The third exclusion is slightly more complicated but especially interesting. It affected the fiefs held by vassals of the bishop or the king. These fiefs were to be treated in two separate stages. For the time being, the rights pertaining to these fiefs would be divided into two different kinds: rights of ownership and rights of jurisdiction. Rights that concerned 'the property and the possession of the fief' would be treated like the ownership of lands held directly by the

---

[60] 'Si in terra seu locis vel a personis hujus communionis levaretur compensum seu paciagium erit commune nobis et dicto episcopo, et levari non poterit nisi communi nomine et voluntate utriusque. Nec poterimus de terra seu locis predictis dicte communionis a quibuscumque personis aliquot tallium vel exactionem, subsidium, redemptionem vel emolumentum levare vel habere, *nisi hoc levaremus pro generali defensione regni nostri*, quin omnia sint communia nobis et episcopo predicto.' *Ordonnances*, 11:399. My italics.

[61] 'Cujuscumque criminis, etiam false monete cusse vel expense, lese majestatis in quibuscumque casibus, *preterquam si contra personam nostram committeretur aut contra regni nostri coronam*, fractionis pacis, portationis armorum, seu alterius cujuscumque ordinarii vel extraordinarii, publici vel privati, in terra dicte communionis cognitio, punitio, et commoditas . . . erunt communia deinceps nobis et episcopo supradicto.' *Ordonnances*, 11:400. My italics. But note the extraordinary extent of the new jurisdiction. Not even crimes of *lèse-majesté* as such were excluded from its powers.

[62] The precise route by which they arrived in Parlement varied, however. Appeals from judgments by the common court first went to the new judge of appeals and from there either to the seneschal or to Parlement, depending on the appellant's choice. Appeals from judgments by the courts in the hand of the Gabalitan nobility first went to the common court and from there to the king *in solidum*, bypassing the judge of appeals. Appeals from the bishop's judges went to the bishop himself and from there, again bypassing the judge of appeals, either to the seneschal or to Parlement.

king or bishop: they were not included in the power of the *bailli* and the common court but kept in the undivided control of king or bishop.[63] But jurisdiction over 'all personal actions and any public or private crimes, both capital and non-capital, ordinary and extraordinary, as well as the right of escheat, occupation, publication, vacation, or confiscation of the said fiefs and sub-fiefs . . . along with the execution of such jurisdiction' was to be shared.[64] To put it differently, the indissoluble mixture of property rights with jurisdiction which had been part of the essence of a fief was now cleanly divided into two separate elements: one consisted of rights of ownership over land, which would be held indivisibly like private property; the other consisted of rights of jurisdiction outside ownership, which would be shared and divided between the representatives of public power.

This arrangement, however, was meant to be temporary. Whenever a fief reverted to the king or to the bishop, the land would be evenly divided between them and added to their proper lands.[65] In other words, although it was unclear at what time any particular fief would be so treated, it was to be expected that in the end no fiefs would remain in the Gévaudan; ultimately all of them would be transferred in equal parts into the ownership of king and bishop.

---

[63] 'Nos associamus dictum episcopum . . . exceptis feudis et retrofeudis nostris quoad hoc scilicet quod proprietas et possessio dictorum feudorum, homogia, recognitiones, fidelitates, laudimia, et jura recipiendi vendas, retinendi, vel laudandi et investiendi castrorum et fortalitiorum redditiones et receptiones, et alia deveria, et obsequia nobis pro dictis feudis et retrofeudis retentis debita, et cognitio realium petitionum pro eis nostra propria remaneant absque communione episcopi supradicti.' *Ordonnances*, 11:398. The bishop's parallel declaration, stated in absolutely identical terms, follows ibid.

[64] 'Jus vero cognoscendi de quibuscumque personalibus actionibus, et de quibuscumque criminibus publicis vel privatis, capitalibus vel non capitalibus, ordinariis vel extraordinariis, ac jus commissionis, incursionis, publicationis, vacationis seu confiscationis feudorum et retrofeudorum predictorum, quacumque causa vel ratione ea committi vel confiscari contingeret, ex causis preteritis, presentibus, vel futuris, nobis, de jure vel consuetudine patrie, et explectationem jurisdictionis in predictis feudis et retrofeudis nostris et personis vassalorum et pro personis vassalorum in proxime dictis casibus communicamus dicto episcopo et ecclesie Mimatensi.' *Ordonnances*, 11:398. The bishop's parallel declaration, again in absolutely identical terms, ibid.

[65] 'Ita ut sive causa et occasione cujuslibet felonie commisse vel committende, vel recognitionis non facte, vel homagii non prestiti, vel alia quacumque causa, jure vel consuetudine, dicta feuda committi contingat, ad dictum episcopum et successores suos et ecclesiam Mimatensem dimidia pars pertineat, et ad nos et successores nostros alia dimidia pars.' *Ordonnances*, 11:398. The parallel declaration by the bishop, *Ordonnances*, 11:399.

PRIVATE PROPERTY AND PUBLIC POWER

These, in rough outline, are the terms on which Philip and William agreed. Now let us analyse them to throw some light on their underlying logic. If we compare the *paréage* to the golden bull, one difference is glaring. The golden bull had spoken of the bishopric as an undifferentiated whole, which, as a whole, was to be possessed by the bishop and, again as a whole, was to be subordinated to royal overlordship; the question of how to avoid any conflict between the competing claims of king and bishop was answered by the faith which the bishop was to swear to the king. How different the *paréage*! It distinguished sharply between rights of ownership and rights of jurisdiction and treated them according to different principles. It created a single public power in whose exercise the king and the bishop were to be fused by what we have referred to as a kind of hypostatic union. It recognized as separate their rights of ownership over lands on which they encountered each other as equals. And at least in three respects it defined precisely what it meant to be subject to the king. If the operative principles of the golden bull were wholeness and faith those of the *paréage* are identity, equality, and subjection.

This transformation was achieved by making distinctions in places where the golden bull made none. The *paréage* divided what used to be called 'the whole bishopric' into three different kinds of lands: those that were owned by king or bishop; those that were owned by the local nobility; and fiefs, that is, lands that were owned by no one person, strictly speaking. Where the golden bull had vaguely spoken of two types of right or power, possession and overlordship, the *paréage* sharply distinguished between three: possession, the jurisdiction of the common court, and sovereignty. These rights enter into different combinations on the three types of land to constitute three different regimes of power: lands owned by king or bishop were subject to possession, on the one hand, and sovereignty, on the other; lands in the hands of the local nobility were subject to both of these and also to the jurisdiction of the common court; and fiefs were divided into rights of possession and rights of jurisdiction until they could be fully assimilated to the lands owned by king or bishop.

Clearly the combinations of rights of possession, jurisdiction, and sovereignty that applied to fiefs, royal or episcopal lands, and

94

noble lands are different from each other. The rights of possession in the hands of local nobles, subject both to sovereignty and to the common court, were more private, so to speak, than those in the hands of king and bishop, subject only to sovereignty, with more of the privileges of lordship still intact. But for that there is a simple reason. Neither the bishop nor the king had any interest in distinguishing between public power and private property on lands that were under their own control and which they were unable to wrest one from the other. On those lands they were content to preserve their lordship and limit it by no more than the three narrow rights of sovereignty which the king claimed over all of the lands in the Gévaudan. But it was different with the lands of the local noblemen. There king and bishop shared a common interest in driving a wedge as deeply into lordship as possible in order to divide property from public power and claim the latter for themselves. Hence public power on those lands was most elaborate and property most private. At bottom the *paréage* thus represents the operation of the single distinction between private property and public power at two different stages of development.[66]

## DURANT'S ASCENDANCY

This, then, was the *paréage* of Mende. It was not put into effect without a major effort.[67] The nobility, of course, was furious. As early as 1304, when the outlines of an agreement were becoming visible, a group of local noblemen led by Astorg de Peyre, head of his family, and Aldebert de Peyre, prior of Ispagnac, conspired to kill the bishop in hopes of forestalling the unthinkable.[68] However, their plot was discovered and, in October, Durant assembled the canons in the cathedral of Mende and in a curious display of

---

[66] It may be pointed out that 'private' derives from *privare*, 'to deprive', which by definition denotes not an absolute but a relative condition. Absolutely private property is therefore a contradiction in terms. Private property is rather that residue of lordship which is left over after the state has deprived it of public power. Even the 'private property' of modern society, though far more private than any medieval property, still bears the traces of lordship, as testified, for example, by the expression 'my home is my castle'. On the question of property in general see Coleman, 'The Two Jurisdictions', and Coleman, 'Property and Poverty'.

[67] The complicated ceremonies at which the *paréage* was promulgated and at which Jacques of Plaisians, the brother of William, was installed as *bailli* are fully described in two notarial reports in R-S, appendix 3, pp. 196–202.     [68] Viollet, pp. 15–19.

Christian justice solemnly declared on his own and his successors' behalf that, whatever he might do or say in the future to contradict his present words, he would never forgive Astorg de Peyre, Gui de Cénaret, Hugues de Quintinhac, Richard de Peyre, and Raymond de Meyrières for the harm they had done to him and to his church.[69] He kept his word and the consequences for the de Peyre were severe. The king mobilized the seneschal of Beaucaire and the *baillis* of Rodez, Auvergne, and Velay to seize all of the conspirators and to surrender the laymen to royal justice and the clerics to the bishop.[70] Aldebert de Peyre was deposed from his priory and Durant made sure that no de Peyre would regain possession of Ispagnac: he had the priory transferred to Etienne de Suisy, a close adviser of Philip IV whom Clement V was soon going to promote to the cardinalate.[71] Richard de Peyre was imprisoned and seems never to have regained the bishop's favour, and Astorg and later heads of the senior line of the family remained in trouble with Durant until at least 1326.[72] When the dust finally settled, the de Peyre had lost a good part of their lands and castles, more of their prestige, and most of their former independence.

The conspiracy of the de Peyre was the earliest and most dramatic instance of violent resistance, but it was not by any means the only one. After the *paréage* was signed there were several more incidents, the most serious among them involving the Mercoeur.[73]

---

[69] Viollet, p. 2 n. 1.     [70] R-S, nos. 21 (29.II.1305), pp. 41–3; 22 (24.VI.1305), pp. 43–6.

[71] Etienne de Suisy followed Peter Flote and preceded William of Nogaret as keeper of the royal seal. Viollet, pp. 45f.; Strayer, *Reign of Philip the Fair*, pp. 61, 71, 94f., 285; Clement V, no. 1,049 (12.VI.1306). In order to assure that Ispagnac would not slip from their control, the new officials of the Gévaudan were given a special mandate to hold frequent assizes there: R-S, no. 42 (*melius* 41, 20.III.1309), pp. 80f.

[72] Viollet, pp. 46–55.

[73] R-S, nos. 81 (25.X.1313), pp. 151–4; 86 (15.VIII.1314), pp. 161–2; appendix 9, pp. 211f.; Strayer, 'La Noblesse', p. 68; Viollet, pp. 25f. One colourful incident deserves special mention: Sometime before April 1309 a lieutenant of the *bayle* of Marvéjols by the name of Champlonc led an armed and disguised crowd in a night attack on the *bailli* and his officials. One man was killed, the lieutenant of the *bailli* was wounded in the arm and another man in the head. When the *bailli* and his men tried to retreat into their house, the mob pursued them with taunts and insults and besieged their stronghold 'clamantes et horribiliter vociferantes: "Ad mortem! ad mortem! destruatur domus communis et moriantur officiales communes et illi de regalia qui intus sunt."' For the following four or five days the besieged found themselves unable to escape for fear of their lives – and increasingly hungry, for no one in town was willing to incur the wrath of Champlonc by supplying them with victuals. In April 1309, after an official investigation, the king sentenced Champlonc and his accomplices to imprisonment, stiff fines, and exclusion from public office; R-S, no. 43 (*melius* 42, 7.IV.1309), pp. 81–5.

When the king's superior force defeated their attempts to overturn the *paréage* by violent means, the barons turned to Parlement, where they kept a suit alive for many years to come.[74] Besides these obstacles there were a number of issues that might have put the bishop at odds with the king. The precise extent of the lands covered by the *paréage* remained to be determined.[75] The property of the Jews, whom Philip IV had expelled in 1306, was claimed by William Durant.[76] Royal officers with special mandates and local royal officials exceeded their authority in violation of the bishop's rights.[77] The king had to intervene repeatedly and even had to threaten the seneschal himself with punishment to persuade him to abide by the terms of the *paréage*.[78] But in the end the king's and

[74] Strayer, 'La Noblesse', pp. 61, 68; Strayer, *Reign of Philip the Fair*, pp. 409f.; R-S, no. 33 (21.II.1308), pp. 67–9; and especially R-S, appendix 4, pp. 202–8. The list of nobles opposing the *paréage*, R-S, pp. 203f., includes forty-eight names, among which the most notable are those of Béraud de Mercoeur, Guérin d'Apcher, Gui de Cénaret, the Marquis de Canilhac, Astorg de Peyre, William de Peyre, Raymond de Peyre, Astorg de Peyre jr, the lords of Garde-Guérin, Raymond d'Anduze, William Randon de Châteauneuf, and Hugues de Quintinhac. In 1311 Astorg de Peyre lodged a separate complaint in Parlement that the bishop and the king had interfered with his jurisdiction in the court of Marvéjols; R-S, no. 68 (16.IV.1311), pp. 130–2.

[75] That took more than four years: R-S, nos. 23 (3.II.1307), pp. 47–50, and 27 (11.II.1307), pp. 56–8, contain the initial instructions. R-S, nos. 29 (1307?), p. 61; 34 (22.VI.1308), pp. 69–73; 37 (20.III.1309), p. 76; 41 (*melius* 40, 20.III.1309), pp. 79f.; and 57 (28.III.1310), pp. 114–16, deal with intermediate steps. R-S, no. 61 (*melius* 66, 7.IV.1311), pp. 126–8, settles the matter. R-S, no. 62 (*melius* 67, 7.IV.1311), pp. 128–30, instructs Plaisians and the seneschal to formulate a separate *paréage* for the lands in the Cévennes; cf. R-S, appendix 11, pp. 213–16. In 1313 the duty of supervising the confiscation and forfeiture of fiefs was entrusted to a salaried procurator at the common court of the Gévaudan: R-S, no. 78 (13.VI.1313), pp. 146f.; cf. no. 80 (19.X.1313), pp. 149f.

[76] The king kept two-thirds for himself and gave the bishop the remaining third along with a house on the outskirts of Mende that had been owned by the Jew Ferrier: R-S, nos. 26 (4.II.1307), pp. 53–6; 58 (IV.1310), pp. 116–18; 60 (*melius* 65, 7.XII.1310), pp. 125f.; Viollet, pp. 25f. Durant is reported to have used the synagogue as a residence for the chaplains of a College of All Souls that he established in 1312; *GC*, 1:96; Viollet, p. 30.

[77] R-S, nos. 32 (19.II.1308), pp. 65–7; 35 (30.VII.1308), pp. 74f.; 44 (*melius* 43, 10.IV.1309), pp. 86–8; 47 (4.X.1309), pp. 94–6; 48 (4.X.1309), pp. 96–8; 49 (5.X.1309), pp. 98–100; 51 (4.XII.1309), pp. 102–4; 53 (8.XII.1309), pp. 106f.; 56 (16.III.1310), pp. 111–13; 57 (*melius* 62, 1.IX.1310), pp. 122–3; 73 (3.XI.1312), pp. 137–40; 76 (29.V.1313), pp. 143–4; 77 (30.V.1313), pp. 144–6; 83 (16.III.1314), pp. 155–7; 85 (7.V.1314), pp. 159–61; 87 (9.X.1314), pp. 162f.; 89 (24.X.1314), pp. 164–5; 91 (29.X.1314), pp. 166f.; 92 (30.X.1314), pp. 167f. Cf. R-S, appendix 10, pp. 212f.

[78] Royal letters instructing the seneschal to abide by the provisions of the *paréage* make up the bulkiest category of letters against official misconduct in the Gévaudan: see R-S, nos. 52 (6.XII.1309), pp. 104–5; 69 (28.IV.1311), pp. 132–3; 70 (14.V.1311), pp. 133–4; 79 (14.VII.1313), pp. 147–9; 88 (13.X.1314), pp. 163f. On at least two occasions Philip IV explicitly cautioned the seneschal that he might be liable for damages the bishop suffered from any failure to abide by the terms of the *paréage*, and on one he warned him in no

bishop's determination to prevail turned out to be invincible. The opposition was suppressed, potential disagreements between king and bishop were amicably settled, royal officers were called to order, and special signs of trust were given to the bishop.[79]

Meanwhile, Durant's star was rising in the church as well. In 1305 and 1306 he served as papal legate in northern Italy,[80] and in 1307 he went to England in order to promote the canonization of Thomas Cantilupe.[81] On both occasions the pope rewarded him with major grants.[82] And where the older Durant had managed to provide his nephew with a benefice or two, the younger one was able to give an entire train of relatives access to the church's wealth.[83]

uncertain terms that 'si contra compositionem predictam presumpseritis attemptari in prejudicium episcopi supradicti, ipsum episcopum super hoc dedampnificari et vos puniri prout rationabile fuerit faciemus'. R-S, no. 47 (*melius* 46, 6.VIII.1309), p. 93; cf. no. 54 (13.III.1310), pp. 108f.

[79] Philip's faith in Durant is evident from his decision of March 1314 to deposit all of the documentation for the suit preceding the *paréage* in the treasury of the chapter of Mende; R-S, no. 84 (22.III.1314), pp. 157–9.

[80] Viollet, pp. 64–71; Davidsohn, 'Bericht der päpstlichen Legaten'; Göller, 'Zur Geschichte'; Schütte, *Vatikanische Aktenstücke*. The reasons for Durant's legacy in Italy may have included his desire to be absent from the Gévaudan at a time when a conspiracy against his life had just taken place and when the *paréage* was not yet signed; Viollet, p. 19.

[81] Durant left France after the *paréage* had taken effect in April of 1307; Viollet, pp. 20, 72–5; cf. *Acta Sanctorum*, October, 1:539–99. For two minor tasks with which Clement V entrusted Durant during those years, see Clement V, nos. 759, 760 (25.VI.1306); 3,646 (2.I.1309).

[82] In 1306 Clement added four parishes to the episcopal *mensa*; Clement V, nos. 1,382 (19.VIII.1306), 1,383–4 (19.VIII.1306). In 1308 he did the same with two more parishes; Clement V, no. 3,048 (25.VII.1308).

[83] The extent to which Durant's good standing with the papacy allowed the members of his family to pursue lucrative ecclesiastical careers is worth documenting in some detail. Three of his brothers are mentioned in the papal registers as having received papal favours: William, an Augustinian canon in St Mary of Cassan in Béziers, received three grants from Clement V and two from John XXII: Clement V, nos. 1,347 (19.VIII.1306), 3,046 (25.VII.1308), 3,071 (25.VII.1308); John XXII, *LC* nos. 6,529 (10.III.1318), 6,531 (10.III.1318); Viollet, pp. 3f. Bernard, canon of Mende and Agde, received three letters from John XXII, *LC* nos. 6,525 (10.III.1318), 6,526 (10.III.1318), 6,601 (13.III.1318). Pons canon of Mende and Mirepoix, also received three grants from John XXII, *LC* nos. 6,552 (10.III.1318), 6,613 (15.III.1318), 6,615 (15.III.1318); Viollet, pp. 3f. Pierre, the oldest brother, is the only one who did not make a living as a cleric. He remained in Puimisson to take care of his inheritance and received no papal grants; Viollet, p. 3 and n. 6. Nephew William Durant of Cessone became canon of Mende in 1306 and was entitled to the cure of Esclanèdes. He went on to study law and accompanied his uncle to the council of Vienne in 1311. In the same year Pope Clement V gave him permission to continue his studies of law and dispensed him from the obligation to enter priestly orders. There is no evidence that this William Durant the Youngest ever exercised the care of souls in Mende. He taught Roman and canon law at Toulouse, is mentioned as *rector studii*

The contrast between the beginning of William Durant the Younger's career and the success he had achieved by 1308 is instructive. In 1296 he had been an embattled nepotist of unproven worth who, apart from his own wits, was largely dependent on the support of the king of France and the pope. Confronted by obstreperous local noble families who were not pleased by his succession to the bishopric and placed obstacles in his way wherever possible, both on his lands and in his chapter, he had to struggle for control and was unable to resist the combined demands of king and pope on his revenues.[84] Not much than ten years later, however, through a combination of luck, skill, and determination he had turned himself into a lord who ruled his diocese and county with a firm hand, who enjoyed the confidence of both the pope and the king, and who could act with a measure of independence. He had settled the lawsuit between the crown and the bishopric that had imperilled the bishop's government for almost forty years and he had been formally recognized as count of the Gévaudan. The pope, meanwhile, had just appointed him to join the commission

*Tholosani*, taught law at Lerida in later years, and acted as papal treasurer in Benevent in 1318 and 1320: Clement V, nos, 1,246 (4.III.1306), 7,013 (30.III.1311), 8,719 (23.VI.1312); Meijers, 'Première époque', *Etudes*, 3:198. 'Cousin' William Carrerie of Bassan held a parish in Mende and received a dispensation from Clement to study law in 1308. In the same year the archdeaconry of Armagh was added to his benefices, which may have been a beneficial consequence of Durant's journey to England. For unknown reasons William Carrerie never managed to exercise his office in Armagh. Pope John XXII consoled him with the promise of a benefice in Mende in 1316: Clement V, no. 3,047 (25.VII.1308); John XXII, *LC* no. 1,571 (20.X.1316); Viollet, pp. 4f. The list continues with Raymond André de Bassan, Benedictine monk at St Victor in Marseille: John XXII, *LC* nos. 1,567 (20.X.1316), 6,531 (10.III.1318); Viollet, pp. 4f.; Raymond Blanc: John XXII, *LC* no. 1,568 (20.X.1316); Viollet, p. 4.; Etienne Bedot, canon and vicar general of Mende in 1322: John XXII, *LC* no. 6,524 (10.III.1318); Viollet, pp. 4f.; Guillaume d'Aiguesvives, Benedictine monk at St Tiberius in Agde: John XXII, *LC* no. 6,530 (10.III.1318); and Pierre Rainaud, who held the cure of Chadenet: John XXII, *LC* nos. 6,603 (13.III.1318), 6,612 (15.III.1318); Viollet, pp. 4f. William Durant the Elder had opened the door to clerical success just far enough to let his nephew enter; but William Durant the Younger allowed a whole crowd of relatives to follow in his train.

[84] A particularly instructive event occurred in 1298: the chapter of Mende had granted Durant annates in order to defray the costs of the suit pending in Paris. But four months earlier Boniface VIII had already promised the same annates to Philip IV, as part of the deal that settled their dispute over *Clericis laicos*. William Durant complained and the king yielded a quarter of the sums collected until the matter could be cleared up. But Philip must soon have realized, as he may have suspected right away, that the pope's grant to him preceded, and thus superseded, the chapter's grant to Durant. We do not know what happened thereafter, but in 1300 Philip seems to have collected all of the annates in the Gévaudan; Viollet, pp. 9f.; R-S, nos. 9 (1.VIII.1298), pp. 14f.; 11 (24.II.1300), p. 20; and Boniface VIII, no. 2,367 (8.VIII.1297).

charged with the investigation of the Templars, a task so sensitive that it spoke highly of the confidence which Durant now enjoyed both at the court of the pope and at the court of the king.[85] These circumstances go a long way to explain the confidence which Durant was to show in writing the *Tractatus Maior.*

[85] Viollet, pp. 28f.; Müller, *Konzil von Vienne*, p. 32; Clement V, nos. 3,402, 3,531 (both 12.VIII.1308); R-S, no. 71 (22.VII.1311), pp. 135f. In May 1311 Durant was further charged with supervising the administrators of the Templars' properties: Clement V, no. 6,816 (12.V.1311).

# RESULTS: LIBERTY AND COMPROMISE

The purpose of the preceding chapters has been to define the context in which William Durant the Younger composed the *Tractatus Maior*. Generally speaking, that context consisted of the relation between local government and central government; but it brought together actors of different social origins with varying ideas of social order who added a considerable measure of complexity to the underlying pattern. Over a period of about 200 years the situation in the Gévaudan thus underwent a series of permutations, none of which abolished entirely what had come before but each of which added another layer of motives and memories. Indeed, the changes were so profound that one may wonder if the relationship between Aldebert de Tournel and Louis VII was at all comparable with that between William Durant and Philip IV. It may therefore be useful to summarize these developments and state a few conclusions.

The story we have told involved three main participants – the bishop, the local nobility, and the rulers of church and state – and it unfolded in three phases. During the first phase, the bishop took the lead by introducing reform to the Gévaudan in an attempt to shake off his dependence on the laity and to establish himself as sole lord of 'the entire bishopric of Gévaudan'. Reform began in earnest when in 1161 Aldebert de Tournel decided to enlist the aid of the king of France. It culminated in the brief glory of 1225 when the bishop seemed to have achieved the goals that, on a larger scale, the Gregorian reformers had set for the entire church. If he could have stopped the process he had started, this would have been the time. But reform had a logic of its own, and the process continued to his disadvantage in a second phase that lasted until 1296. At first, growing assertions of central power by the king caused ambivalence and vacillation on the local scene as the bishop wavered between asserting his control over the nobility and defending himself against the king; but by the 1270s all means of keeping central government out of the Gévaudan had been tried in vain. In 1285, with the appointment of William Durant the Elder, government took centre stage, and the bishop stepped back to play a secondary role. Local autonomy was on the wane, central administration on the rise, and liberty about to be replaced by subjection.

Up to this point the history of the Gévaudan can be described as the integration of an independent territory into the larger medieval world of church and state that successfully reversed the early medieval process of dispersion. From the perspective of a detached observer that course was straight, but from the bishop's point of view it went through two major turning points. The first occurred when the bishop seceded from his noble peers and usurped the political initiative; the second, when that initiative passed out of his hands into those of central government. Both were leading to the same result: regardless of whether the agent was the bishop or the king, in either case an order that gave pride of place to liberty and honour was replaced with an order composed of offices and sovereignty. But the bishop's role in this transition was Janus-faced: he was the only one who first promoted, then resisted change. The golden bull reflected this ambivalence implicitly, and the history of the thirteenth century made it explicit. By the final decades of the thirteenth century it seemed clear that the bishop had no choice but to submit to central government.

The third and final phase undid that clarity. It began in 1296 with the succession of William Durant the Younger to the bishopric, and was not yet concluded when he went to the council of Vienne. The process of social integration that had begun in the twelfth century now overreached itself. By 1300 it became apparent that progress was not infinite, and government was forced to reduce its ambitions from universal to territorial proportions. The main effect of this rescaling was that political ideas were severed from political development, as symbolized by the clash of Philip IV with Boniface VIII. From hindsight it is clear that political development was not interrupted. The alliance between local reformers and the universal church that had stood behind reform so far was taken over by territorial states that, as the heirs of local powers, continued reform with ultimately greater efficiency. But most minds, particularly those of secular rulers, continued to be fixed on the church's view of universal order, even while they were struggling to hold their own against the papacy and while real order was manifestly different from the ideals at which the church had aimed since the eleventh century. Hence reform appeared to have lost direction.

The result is not well described as a political vacuum. True, insofar as politics requires a direction (if politics, as Aristotle thought, is the art of realizing a highest good) the temporary lapse in central government's ability to set a clear direction that became manifest in the early fourteenth century gives the appearance of a vacuum. But more important is the fact that it encouraged everyone who had been pushed offstage to make a second entrance and allowed many who had not yet been heard at all to make their debut. This was no vacuum but rather a plethora of actors jostling side by side to assert their particular ideas of the highest good.

As a result the ambivalence which local rulers had felt toward central government, drawn alternately to associate themselves with it and to resist it, too, recurred, but with a crucial difference from the state of affairs in the middle of the thirteenth century. At that time central government had not yet proved its power. By 1300, however, its power was an integral element of manifest political experience – at least of the experience of those with whom we are mainly concerned, the bishops of France, to whom Philip IV and Benedict Gaetani had taught the meaning of central government in 1290. Both the cause of local autonomy and that of central government had thus been articulated clearly. If previously the conflict between local rulers and central government had been like that between a certain past and an uncertain future, now both the future and the past were certain and, what is more, as a result of the crisis of the early fourteenth century, both were collapsed into the present to compete with each other as rivals on equal terms.

The most striking feature of this phase, therefore, is a kind of dimorphism, an oscillation between two poles which signify the past and the future, local and central government, autonomy and sovereignty, and which is reminiscent of those optical illusions which unsettle the observer by encouraging two radically different but equally plausible interpretations of the same image. In a manner of speaking this is the case even with central government itself. Philip IV was both most Christian King and ruthless politician; Clement V was both weak pope and great promoter of reservations and provisions. But it is much more clearly so on the local scene where for some time the bishop had been taking sides with both past and future. Government most certainly did not retreat: judging by any standard William Durant the Younger's episcopate rather marked a quantum leap in centralization. If in 1161 King Louis VII could not remember if any bishop of Mende had ever come to Paris, the bishop now had a manor in Argenteuil and a house in the rue de la Calandre.[1] Royal and papal letters reached Mende with greater frequency than before.[2] More officials of central government took a more active hand in Gabalitan affairs.[3] And the benefices of the church of Mende fell more regularly to the uses of papal patronage.[4] Indeed, even William

---

[1] The golden bull declared that 'longe est a memoria omnium mortalium nostri temporis, quod aliquis episcoporum Gaballorum ad curiam antecessorum nostrorum Francorum regum venerit.' GC, 1:Instrumenta:24. For the manor and the house see Viollet, pp. 8f.; R-S, p. vif.; André, 'Evêques de Mende', p. 33. Cf. R-S, no. 88 (13.X.1314), pp. 163f.

[2] From 1297 to 1314 Philip IV wrote about four letters per year regarding the Gévaudan, compared with a total of five for the period 1285–96, not to mention his predecessors. Similar proportions can be calculated from the papal registers. Only three popes in the thirteenth century wrote more than about one letter annually regarding the Gévaudan: Urban IV (two), Honorius IV (four), and Nicholas IV (five), but all of these were occasioned by special circumstances: Urban IV settled the quarrel between Odilo de Mercoeur and Aldebert de Peyre over Ispagnac; Honorius IV dealt with William Durant the Elder's election to the bishopric; and Nicholas IV inundated the entire church, including the Gévaudan, with a flood of indulgences, usually for a year and forty days, an incitement for pilgrimages to this or that church on specified feast days; see Nicholas IV, nos. 1,422 (21.IX.1289), 1,474 (21.IX.1289), 2,164 (23.XII.1289), 3,586 (4.XI.1290), 4,087 (7.X.1290), 4,871 (20.IV.1291), 5,043 (16.V.1291), 5,158 (15.V.1291), 5,535 (13.VI.1291). Not even Boniface VIII wrote more than about one letter every year. Clement V, however, wrote ten. The sum of his letters written in just a little under ten years almost matches the sum total of papal letters written in the entire previous history of Mende. There is of course a bias in the evidence. Some records were better kept than others, and some have been better published. Nevertheless the evidence speaks clearly for increased centralization, if only because better records make for more effective government control.

[3] We have already mentioned William of Nogaret, William of Plaisians, his brother Jacques of Plaisians, Gaucelin de la Garde, and Etienne de Suisy. We may add Jacques Duèse and his nephew Jacques de la Rue, on whom see below, pp. 309f., as well as seven cardinals: Matthew Orsini: Boniface VIII, no. 2,205 (19.XI.1297); Benedict XI, no. 136 (30.XI.1303); Napoleon Orsini: Clement V, no. 5,328 (13.II.1310); Peter de Capella: Clement V, no. 6,144 (4.IX.1310); Bertrand des Bordes: Clement V, no. 6,490 (8.I.1311); Berengar Frédol the Elder: Clement V, nos. 759–60 (25.VI.1306), 3,183 (30.IX.1308), 8,050 (17.VI.1312); Arnaud de Pellegrue: Clement V, no. 955 (26.II.1306); and Raimond Guilhelm de Farges: Clement V, no. 7,656 (28.XII.1311). The last three were relatives of Clement V. It may also be worth pointing out that the links between Mende, Paris, and Avignon were not unrelated to each other but formed a triangle, as it were. Small facts, such as the occasion in 1308 on which Clement V informed Durant of certain favours he was bestowing upon William of Plaisians, speak loudly and clearly to this effect: R-S, pp. ix, 199; Clement V, nos. 3,146, 3,196–7 (all of 5.VIII.1308).

[4] For the increased number of pluralists with benefices in Mende see Clement V, nos. 955 (26.II.1306), 1,113 (9.II.1305), 1,791 (1307), 3,107 (27.VI.1308), 3,183 (30.IX.1308), 4,223 (6.IV.1309), 5,328 (13.II.1310), 5,990 (13.II.1310), 6,144 (4.IX.1310), 7,656 (28.XII.1311),

Durant the Younger's victories over his local enemies sometimes served only to subject him all the more directly to central government.[5] Yet at the same time the most exalted claims of central government were formally rejected while Durant presided over an energetic expansion of episcopal powers. Only very recently William of Plaisians had stated that 'everything within the limits of the realm belongs to the lord king, at least as far as protection, high jurisdiction, and domination are concerned, even the property of all mobile and immobile goods in his realm, which the king can give, receive, and consume for the sake of public utility and the defence of his realm'.[6] Perhaps those extraordinary words were never meant quite seriously – but they did amount to a serious threat of things to come that must have made the hair of every self-respecting local patriot stand on end. To have such claims suppressed was a successful, if partial, reaffirmation of the old claim of episcopal sovereignty over 'the entire bishopric of Gévaudan'. The rise of William Durant the Younger thus had the curious result that this protegé of a curial official was the first bishop of Mende whose rule as 'count of the Gévaudan' was formally accepted by the king. Here we are beginning to approach what was later called *noblesse de robe*. The *noblesse d'épée* meanwhile suffered a less ambiguous fate than anybody else because they were opposed by the two most powerful lords on the scene: the bishop and the king. But even in their case we can perceive a tenuous renewal of old ideas of noble liberty, for even if the noblemen were unsuccessful in their violent assaults on the bishop and their protracted battle against the *paréage*, the union which they formed in 1308 in order

---

7,962 (30.V.1312), 8,050 (17.VI.1312), 8,703 (31.V.1312). For a particularly interesting case of papal interference, which concerned the benefices of William Durant the Younger's *officialis* Jacques Fouquer and a cleric in the service of cardinal Bertrand des Bordes, see Clement V, nos. 6,490 (8.I.1311), 6,631 (11.III.1311), 7,962 (30.V.1312); cf. John XXII, *LC* no. 1,566 (20.X.1316).

[5] Thus the reader may remember that William Durant the Younger managed to wrest the priory of Ispagnac from the de Peyre by having it transferred to Etienne de Suisy; above p. 96. But since the latter was a high government official who soon became a cardinal, the most important effect of his appointment to Ispagnac may have been that upon his death in 1311 the right to appoint a successor devolved upon Pope Clement V, who chose the Benedictine monk and pluralist Galhardus de Mota; Clement V, no. 7,735 (2.I.1312).

[6] 'Omnia que sunt infra fines regni sui sint domini regis, saltim quoad protectionem et altam jurisdictionem et dominationem et etiam quantum ad proprietatem omnium singularum rerum mobilium et immobilium regni sui, quas idem dominus rex donare, recipere et consumere potest, ex causa publice utilitatis et deffensionis regni sui.' *Mémoire relatif au paréage de 1307*, p. 521.

to oppose the *paréage* foreshadowed the local estates that were soon to appear in the Gévaudan.[7]

The great achievement of the *paréage* was that it arrested the oscillation between autonomy and sovereignty, between a past that was no longer viable and a future that still exceeded the imagination. It did so by establishing new institutions that were capable both of expressing and of containing this dimorphism. It created a stable political space that was bounded by two extremes. At one extreme there were the fiefs, old symbol of the dispersion of central power to local lords. Fiefs would continue to exist for some time to come, but by implication they had already been declared to be incompatible with the logic of government. At the other extreme was the new distinction between private property and sovereignty. This distinction was nowhere fully elaborated. The nobility still exercised rights of jurisdiction on its lands, king and bishop still were lords in an emphatic sense, and sovereignty was still narrowly circumscribed; some properties were more private than others, and some powers were more public than others, but no property was purely private and no power purely public.[8] The cumulative rights of which lordship was composed, in other words, had not yet been fully dissociated. Nevertheless they were already very clearly being pulled in one or other of the two directions that are indicated by the distinction between private property and sovereignty; how long lordship would manage to survive by keeping them united was merely a question of time.

The space between the two extremes was therefore marked by an all-pervasive dualism. This dualism did emphatically not coincide with the dualism of state and church. If anything, it rather

---

[7] On which see Burdin, *Documents*, 1:37–50. Think also of the secular 'conciliar movement' directed against Philip IV in 1314 and the annual general assembly with an annually changed committee of two nobles as executives and a third as arbiter between them that was created by the Burgundian league: Boutaric, 'Notices', pp. 220–5; Artonne, *Le Mouvement de 1314*; Brown, 'Reform and Resistance to Royal Authority', pp. 109–37.

[8] It may be noted that of the two public powers at issue, the 'more' public one (sovereignty) is much less elaborately defined than the 'less' public one (the common court), while private property is not defined at all – except by implication, as whatever was left over after sovereignty, the power of the common court, and the bishop's and king's *loca propria* had been subtracted. That was perhaps the reason which prompted Jean Roucaute and Marc Saché to add an appendix with a definition of the allod in the Gévaudan to their edition of the *paréage*: 'Alodium appellatur in Gaballitano terra libera quam habet aliquis nobilis vel ignobilis in qua vestire et disvestire vel in emphitheosim dare pertinet ad illum cujus est illa terra.' R-S, appendix 7, p. 209.

seems to have encouraged a levelling of the distinction between
clerics and laymen, as well as that between noblemen and commoners.[9] Still less did it coincide in any simple sense with the
opposition between the estates and the ruler, because it affected
both of them equally. Rather, it consisted of two different but in
their own way equally complete ideas of order existing side by side:
one rested on lordship and hierarchy, the other on the distinction
between private property and sovereignty. This dualism manifested itself in several ways. One was that the *paréage*, on the one
hand, consciously made a new beginning by affirming the distinction between rights of ownership and sovereignty while, on the
other hand, at the same time it placed limits on the lengths to which
that new beginning could have been elaborated by letting logic run
full course and turning the bishop into a royal employee and his
lands into private property. Fiefs were to be abolished: in that sense
the state had appeared on the scene; but sovereignty was still strictly
limited and distinguished from the jurisdiction of the common
court, from which the bishop was exempt: in that sense the state's
arrival was delayed. The same dualism found expression, too, in
the distinction between the bishop as 'count of the Gévaudan' and
the bishop as a subject of the king whose title depended on the
king's good graces and who could be taxed, judged, and punished
by royal officers.[10] But it found the most illuminating expression
in the double purpose the king established for the *paréage*:

[9] To the degree that the power of the common court was to be indiscriminately exercised
'supra quascumque personas, nobiles et ignobiles, ecclesiasticas vel seculares', *Ordonnances*, 11:398, it slighted the distinctions between 'noble or common, ecclesiastical or
secular persons' and turned them all into subjects. In that sense it promoted equality. This
was of course not meant to do away with the bishop's spiritual jurisdiction, which was
specifically protected: 'Gentes nostre non impedient dictum episcopum et curiam suam
spiritualem quominus possint cognoscere de realibus et personalibus petitionibus et aliis
casibus de quibus de jure vel consuetudine ad eum et ad dictam suam curiam ante
presentem associationem jurisdictio et cognitio pertinebat. Nec per presentem associationem vel transactionem sue jurisdictioni aut curie spirituali aliquod prejudicium generari
volumus, nec jus novum sibi vel nobis in eadem acquiri.' *Ordonnances*, 11:403. But one
suspects that as a result of the *paréage* the bishop's spiritual jurisdiction had become ever so
slightly more 'spiritual'.

[10] Philip allowed the bishop to retain two other important aspects of lordly power: his coins
were to have currency in the entire Gévaudan, although he was allowed to mint them
only on his own lands, and he was entitled to bear arms in the entire Gévaudan;
*Ordonnances*, 11:402. Theoretically the same distinction applied to the king as an owner of
lands and the king as the sovereign, which made it conceivable in theory to appeal from
the jurisdiction of the king as lord in the Gévaudan to the king as sovereign of France –
one instance of the 'two bodies' made familiar by Kantorowicz, *The King's Two Bodies*.

At last, desiring to provide both for the peace and quiet of the bishop and his church and for the utility and security of the subjects of the land, we have finally concluded a general transaction, a concord, a composition, and an association with our beloved and faithful William, . . . which after mature and considered deliberation we foresaw to be expedient for ourselves, the said church, and the common utility.[11]

'The peace and quiet of the bishop and his church' and 'the utility and security of the subjects of the land' – these were the two kinds of purposes for which the *paréage* was written. The former already existed in the golden bull. It looked back to times of fealty and lordship, when justice was founded on distinctions of order and estate, and when politics was aimed at peace – the kind of peace which Augustine identified as the essence of order. The latter was new. It looked forward to times when politics would be aimed at the common utility of all, without reference to social rank, and when everyone, including bishops, would be equally subjected to the commands of the *patria*.

From an abstractly logical point of view the *paréage* may therefore well have been a monstrosity. Unlike *Unam sanctam*, not only did it not insist on having a single head of government but it even went so far as to insist on having two.[12] Small wonder that it has been given contradictory interpretations. Depending on the perspective it can signify the bishop's conclusive defeat (insofar as the bishop had been used to regarding himself as sole sovereign lord of the Gévaudan) and the bishop's equally conclusive victory (insofar as the bishop had aimed at control over the local nobility).[13] But regarding the very different kind of clarity that is required when history does not keep up with logic, the *paréage* was nothing if not lucid. It foresaw precisely how the conflicts between

---

[11] 'Tandem nos quieti et paci dicti episcopi et ecclesie ac utilitati et securitati subditorum patrie providere volentes, super predictis omnibus et singulis articulis contentiosis et aliis omnibus emergentibus et dependentibus ex eisdem, et aliis que nobis et dicte ecclesie et communi utilitati expedire deliberatione matura et consulta previdimus, transactionem generalem, concordiam et compositionem ac associationem cum dilecto et fideli nostro Guillelmo, nunc Mimatensi episocopo, pro se, suis successoribus, et pro suo capitulo, cujus ad hoc mandatum sufficiens et plenam potestatem habebat transactionem hujusmodi faciendi, cujus personam speciali gratia et favore prosequimur, pro se et suis successoribus amicabilem concordiam pro nobis et successoribus nostris regibus Francie fecimus in hunc modum.' *Ordonnances*, 11:397.

[12] It may be worth linking the ideas about divided sovereignty at the council of Constance that Tierney, '"Divided Sovereignty"', has made familiar to the divided sovereignty actually enshrined in the *paréage*.

king, bishop, and local noblemen could be managed in the future and it furnished the Gévaudan with a framework for political action that remained in effect throughout the later middle ages and early modern times. It was confirmed by Philip VI in 1334, Henry IV in 1595, Louis XV in 1720, and as late as 1769 an anonymous annotator declared, on the occasion of its inclusion in the *Ordonnances des roys de France*, that its provisions, 'especially as far as the administration of justice is concerned, are still being followed today. The only exception is that the judge of appeals has been suppressed. His office has been united with that of the judge presiding over the common court, appeals from which are now brought directly before the seneschal of Beaucaire and Nîmes.'[14] Only at the very end of the *ancien régime* was the work of William Durant the Younger and Philip IV finally undone.[15]

What the *paréage* of Mende thus really signifies is neither the victory nor the defeat of the bishop but the successful integration of several conflicting and inherently unstable elements in a remarkably stable combination of power, interest, and justice. It possessed the kind of double vision without which it was hard in the early fourteenth century to make political realities intelligible. It made room for sovereignty and lordship, for property and fiefs, for liberty and subjection, and for peace and utility. The result was perhaps a curiosity, a heterogeneous amalgam of different strata of political development, a mixture of two different times; it certainly reflected the current balance of powers better than it corresponded to abstract conceptual logic. The protagonists themselves seem to have been aware that logic was more likely to undermine than to confirm their subtle shadings, for they included several provisions specifically designed to prevent that delicate equilibrium from

---

[13] For the former view see, e.g., R–S, p. viii, for the latter Strayer, 'La Noblesse', pp. 66, 68.

[14] 'Les articles qu'elles [the letters of Philip IV] renferment, sur-tout relativement à l'administration de la justice, s'exécutent encore de nos jours: si ce n'est qu'on a supprimé le juge d'appeaux. Son office a été réuni à la cour commune, dont les appellations sont relevées directement devant le sénéchal de Beaucaire et de Nîmes.' *Ordonnances* 11:396 n. a). For confirmations of the *paréage* see Burdin, *Documents historiques*, 1:376–84.

[15] And even then it was not undone completely. When the Constituent Assembly was redrawing the administrative map of France, it decided that the Gévaudan was too small to justify an entire department and proposed dividing it between the departments of Le Puy and Nîmes. But local resistance was so vehement that the plan had to be dropped and the Gévaudan was renamed Département de la Lozère. Hence it is that even nowadays the boundaries of the Département de la Lozère largely coincide with those that were envisioned by Philip IV and William Durant the Younger; *Histoire du Languedoc*, p. 442.

being upset.[16] But in historical reality the sanction which the *paréage* of Mende gave in a single breath to two heterogeneous conceptions of order was the source of the strength that enabled it to remain in effect for close to half a millennium.

The preceding chapters have thus furnished us with a definition of the issue that confronted William Durant the Younger as he wrote the *Tractatus Maior* and a standard by which to assess his ideas about church government. The issue was whether or not he would be willing to compromise with central government. The standard was that he was willing to compromise with the king of France. The question that now posed itself was whether or not he would compromise with the papacy as well. Reasons for such a compromise were excellent. Cooperation with the papacy had allowed him and his family to rise through the ranks of the church, just as cooperation with the king had allowed him to assert his political supremacy over the Gévaudan. Besides, he was not just a local ruler, but also a high official of the church, of whom one might have expected solidarity with the ruler of the church in order to maintain ecclesiastical supremacy over the laity. But there were other and no less compelling reasons that decreased the likelihood of compromise. The church was a universal body politic, and universal rules of order are not as easily transformed as local ones. They make more elevated claims on truth and justice and they are harder to adjust to necessity, utility, and interest. The necessity that compelled the bishop to look for assistance against the local nobility was nothing if not obvious, and consequently the utility of compromising with the king was, too. But in the universal church the case was different: a bishop who remembered Benedict Gaetani's merciless suppression of the French episcopate and who desperately needed the king of France to hold his own in his diocese can surely not be blamed if he believed that Philip IV's attack on Boniface VIII was no attack upon the church or on himself. He

---

[16] Regarding sovereignty, we have already noted the royal promise not to extend it to the bishop's prejudice over the jointly governed lands. We may add that explicit precautions were taken to preserve the present distribution of power forever: jointly governed lands were declared inalienable and, with the exception of escheated fiefs, the king and the bishop were prohibited from adding any lands to their possessions; *Ordonnances*, 11:399. Any violation of the *paréage* by any official for any reason was invalidated by a blanket declaration; any usage, even of long or very long standing, any custom, or any prescription was ruled out as a reason to change the terms of the *paréage*; and none of the officials concerned were to be obeyed by anyone unless they had sworn a sacred oath to observe the terms of the *paréage* to the letter; *Ordonnances*, 11:403.

may have rather welcomed it as an opportunity to place limits on the power of a pope who had tried his patience at least as sorely as the king of France had done, but whose support in the day-to-day affairs of his diocese seemed not so indispensable. Whatever interests might have operated to promote the solidarity of William Durant the Younger with the pope were therefore less effective than interests operating on the local scene to promote his solidarity with the king. Indeed, to the degree that the church was a universal institution, interests were ruled out of order.

That led Durant in the *Tractatus Maior* to argue in terms of principles that made compromise impossible. If the virtue of the *paréage* was that, in the face of compelling interests, it circumnavigated the necessity to choose between alternatives that were threatening to become exclusive, the virtue of the *Tractatus Maior* was that, in the face of overriding principles, it squarely confronted the alternative, made it complete, and thus precipitated the necessity to choose between liberty and sovereignty, honour and subjection, harmonious order and absolute power. The council of Vienne did not produce a compact between the bishop and the pope to parallel the compact between the bishop and the king. To the contrary, it reaffirmed the compact between the king of France and the pope and thus removed the opportunity for a compromise between the pope and the bishops that seemed to have materialized in the aftermath of Pope Boniface VIII's defeat. In the short run, the choice Durant had clarified thus would transform the church into a kind of ecclesiastical state – the system of Avignon – which cost the church the allegiance of the laity and led it to accept a new accommodation with the state in early modern times. In the long run, when the state succeeded to the claims of the church by translating them into terms of national sovereignty, it would prepare the ground for the state to repeat the fate of the church. In either case it would produce those violent disturbances that infallibly accompany radical disjunctures from the past.

# PART II

## THE ASSERTION OF JUSTICE

Law is the art of the good and the equitable – which is why lawyers have been compared to ministers of sacred precepts – and the good and equitable may not be dispensed with unless there is a great necessity or utility, for what is done according to law is done according to justice.
William Durant, *Tractatus Maior* 1.4

*Chapter 4*

# THE THEORY OF REFORM

I read the constitutions for the state of the universal church which the holy fathers, general and provincial councils, and others carefully established once upon a time, which we have abandoned in many ways, and I decided to write down what in my humble view ought to be done by the council that is going to meet in Vienne.                    William Durant[1]

Ever since the Colonna cardinals had turned against Pope Boniface VIII, the call for a general council had been in the air. For years the papacy had successfully stalled. But the arrest of the Templars in 1307 raised the stakes to a point at which the tactics of delay proved ineffective. In August 1308 Pope Clement V convoked a general council in the city of Vienne.[2]

From Clement's point of view, the most important business at hand undoubtedly was to decide the fate of the Templars and to put an end to the damage stemming from the clash between Philip IV and Boniface VIII. But general councils were more than *ad hoc* assemblies convened to deal with specific short-term problems, however urgent: they provided an occasion to promote large-scale reform of the church as well. Hence Clement asked the prelates in his bull of convocation 'carefully to investigate whatever requires honing through correction and reform, either in person or with the help of prudent men who fear God and who are well informed.

---

[1] 'Perlectis dudum cum diligentia a sanctis patribus, conciliis generalibus, provincialibus, et aliis pro statu universalis ecclesie constitutis, a quibus in pluribus est recessum, scribendum duxi ea de quibus iuxta parvitatis mee modulum agendum esse videtur in concilio memorato.' *TMA* prefatio, fol. 4ra–b.

[2] For all matters relating to the council of Vienne, Müller, *Konzil von Vienne*, is the main authority. For a briefer account: Lecler, *Vienne*. For the political context: Lizerand, *Clément V et Philippe IV*; Finke, *Papsttum und Untergang des Templerordens*. Detailed studies: Ehrle, 'Zur Vorgeschichte'; Ehrle, 'Ein Bruchstück'; Ehrle, 'Zur Geschichte'; Göller, 'Die Gravamina'; Mollat, 'Les Doléances'; Heber, *Gutachten und Reformvorschläge*; Lecler, 'La Réforme de l'église'; Vereecke, 'La Réforme'; Bellone, 'Cultura e studi'. On the Colonna appeals: Denifle, 'Denkschriften'; Arquillière, 'L'Appel au concile'.

They should prepare written reports of their findings and bring them to the attention of the council.'[3]

The response to this request was remarkable. Unfortunately most of the evidence has disappeared along with the acts of the council's public sessions, the deliberations of its committees, and the records of the secret negotiations between King Philip and Pope Clement, all of which seem to have been destroyed soon after the council had adjourned in order to spare the papacy embarrassing revelations.[4] But what remains is still enough to discern a veritable flood of gravamina pouring into Vienne.[5] Most of the complaints came from local ecclesiastical bodies, but some were written by individuals who were eager for an occasion to publicize their thoughts about the reform of the church. We know the names of three of them: Bishop William le Maire of Angers, the irrepressible Raymond Lull, and William Durant the Younger.[6]

This was the immediate background for the writing of the *Tractatus Maior*, which therefore must have been completed sometime between August 1308 and October 1311. In his preface William Durant the Younger described it as follows:

Among the canons of the council of Toledo it is written that assisting a good cause with counsel is not only good for this life but will also be eternally rewarded. Hence, when I, William, by divine providence bishop of Mende, received the letter in which the most holy father, our lord by divine providence Pope Clement V, requested all the archbishops and bishops whom he had invited to the projected general council at Vienne to investigate either in person or by representatives what would be useful to uplift the state of the church, the Christian people, and the faith, to prepare written reports of their findings, and to submit them to the council, I remembered that, just as the great have the power to rule and command, so the small must obey; that according to Gregory a written instruction is a command, and a command must be fulfilled, for if it is not fulfilled you will be punished; and that according to the prophet Samuel obedience is better than sacrifice because, as Gregory explains in

---

[3] 'Mandavimus insuper ut iidem archiepiscopi et prelati per se vel alios viros prudentes Deum timentes et habentes pre oculis omnia, que correctionis et reformationis limam exposcunt, inquirentes subtiliter et conscribentes fideliter eadem ad ipsius concilii notitiam deferant.' Clement V, no. 3,626 (12.VIII.1308). For the precedent set by Gregory X see Gregory X, no. 1,160 (17.III.1272); Müller, *Konzil von Vienne*, p. 17.

[4] Ibid., pp. 43–62.

[5] Ehrle, 'Ein Bruchstück', pp. 361–470; Göller, 'Die Gravamina', pp. 195–221; Mollat, 'Les Doléances', pp. 319–26; cf. Müller, *Konzil von Vienne*, pp. 700–3.

[6] Müller, *Konzil von Vienne*, includes detailed analyses of the contributions by all three; they are accessible with the help of his excellent index.

*Moralia* book 25, sacrifice is performed with the flesh of another, whereas obedience is a sacrifice of ourselves. I therefore read the constitutions for the state of the universal church which the holy fathers, general and provincial councils, and others carefully established once upon a time, which we have abandoned in many ways, and I decided to write down what in my humble view ought to be done by the council that is going to meet in Vienne.[7]

These ponderous words may serve as a suitable introduction to William Durant's manner of stating his case. They bear all the marks of an attempt to secure the reader's goodwill in the proper fashion for an opening *captatio benevolentiae*. But Durant's cautious tone should not be allowed to obscure his intention to call the very foundations of church government into question. He informed his readers in no uncertain terms that he was going to deal with the 'state of the universal church'. His use of that term alone is significant, for 'state of the church' embodied the conviction that there existed some form of structure that was essential to the existence of the church and that was neither identical with the articles of the faith nor under anyone's free disposition, not even the pope's.[8] How studiously Clement V had avoided mentioning the term in his call for deliberations on the reform of the church is hardly an accident; and neither is it an accident how prominently

---

[7] 'Scribitur in concilio Toletano quod bone rei dare consilium et presentis vite habetur subsidium et eterne remunerationis expectare cernitur premium, xii. q. ii. bone rei. Unde cum per sanctissimum patrem et dominum nostrum, dominum Clementem divina providentia papam quintum, scriptum fuerit et mandatum omnibus archiepiscopis et episcopis per ipsum ad futurum concilium generale Vienne *convocatis* [P] quod per se et per alios diligenter inquirerent, deliberarent, scriberent, et in scriptis ad dictum concilium deferrent omnia que pro bono statu ecclesie, populi christiani, et exaltatione fidei eis utilia viderentur, idcirco ego, Guillelmus, divina providentia episcopus Mimatensis, qui sum requisitus super hoc et vocatus, considerans quod sicut in maioribus est regendi et iubendi potestas, ita in minoribus est obsequendi necessitas, ut in decretis xxi. di. quamvis §. in his, cum capitulis sequentibus, viii. di. que contra mores, xcvi. di. bene quidem, extra de constitutionibus, ecclesia sancte marie, et de rebus ecclesie non alienandis, cum laicis, et quod secundum Gregorium illud quod precipitur imperatur, et quod imperatur necesse est fieri, et si non fiat, penam habes, xiiii. q. i. quod precipitur, iiii. di. §. hec et si legibus, et quod secundum prophetam Samuelem melior est enim obedientia quam victima, i. Regum xv, quia, sicut Gregorius in moralibus xxv. libro exponit, in obedientia propria, in victima aliena caro mactatur, viii. q. i. sciendum, perlectis dudum cum diligentia a sanctis patribus conciliis generalibus, provincialibus, et aliis pro statu universalis ecclesie constitutis, a quibus in pluribus est recessum, scribendum duxi ea de quibus iuxta parvitatis mee modulum agendum esse videtur in concilio memorato.' *TMA* prefatio, fol. 4ra–b. Cf. C.12 q.2 c.74, D.21 p.c.3 – D.21 c.9, D.8 c.2, D.96 c.1, X.1.2.10, X.3.13.12, C.14 q.1 c.3 §.2, D. 4 p.c.6, 1 Samuel 15:22, *Moralia* 35.13, C.8 q.1 c.10.

[8] Hackett, 'State of the Church'; Congar, 'Status ecclesiae'; and Post, 'Copyists' Errors'.

Durant employed it in the preface to his treatise. He used it to signal his desire to confirm and expand ecclesiastical constitutionalism. More than that, he used it to announce the fundamental insight on which his work was based: he had read the laws concerning the state of the church which had been enacted by the councils of the ancient church, and he had found that they had been abandoned. The present had fallen far behind the ideal conditions of antiquity and it needed urgently to be restored. This was exactly the same charge that had once served the papacy as a battle cry in the Investiture Controversy and to a considerable degree it relied even on the same source, namely, the collection of Pseudo-Isidore – except that now it was directed against the papacy.[9] To call for a return to ancient law at a time when the empire had been defeated and the papacy had risen to the leadership of Europe made for an explosive opening.

## STRUCTURE OF THE 'TRACTATUS MAIOR'

The *Tractatus Maior* was divided into two unequal parts. The first of these developed Durant's argument about the principles of church reform in the abstract. Consisting of a mere four chapters, it was as brief in extent as it was rich in theoretical substance and it will therefore be considered in detail below. The second part, on the other hand, dealt with the many ways in which the good order of the church had been violated in the concrete. It was about five times as long as the first and consisted of no less than one hundred chapters. Ranging from complaints about the lascivious songs that were being sung by the common folk to proposals for radical revisions in the finances of the church and reminders that Emperor Constantine had donated the western half of his empire to the pope, it amounted to a veritable panorama of the concerns of a late medieval reformer.

The way in which Durant presented his argument in the first part of his treatise was rather straightforward: broadly speaking he began with the need for church reform and concluded with his

---

[9] Olsen, 'The Idea of the *Ecclesia Primitiva*'; Ditsche, 'Die ecclesia primitiva'; Fuhrmann, 'Das Reformpapsttum und die Rechtswissenschaft'; Fuhrmann, 'Gregor VII.'; Fuhrmann, *Einfluss und Verbreitung*; Kuttner, 'The Revival of Jurisprudence'. Fuhrmann has clarified that in spite of its prominence Pseudo-Isidore did not furnish the basis of papal reform. That reform was founded on other sources and even required a reinterpretation of Pseudo-Isidore's basic intentions. On this intention see now especially Richter, 'Stufen pseudoisidorischer Verfälschung'.

demand for general councils.[10] But the procedure he chose for the
second part was unusual enough to require an explanation.[11] He
began each chapter by quoting one of the ancient conciliar canons
that was, in his opinion, no longer being observed. These opening
canons established the general theme for each chapter. They were
taken from the so-called *Canones apostolorum*, from general
councils, and from the provincial councils of Greece, Africa, Italy,
Spain, and France which he had read in the Pseudo-Isidorean
collection and which, he took care to stress, had been approved by
the universal church. The body of each chapter then went on to

[10] The first chapter discussed the need for church reform in general terms; the second
insisted on the law as the basis of reform; the third turned to the question of how to assure
the obedience of temporal and spiritual rulers to the law; and the fourth concluded by
requesting a larger role for general councils. In addition, there were three unnumbered
subsections or 'rubrics' dealing with questions that had an important bearing on the main
line of the argument but were separate from it. The first was inserted between the third
and fourth chapters and involved the 'need to limit the power of superiors'. The other
two came at the very end of the first part and dealt with dispensations and exemptions
from the general law of the church.

[11] He explained his rationale in a separate preface: 'Incipit secunda pars istius tractatus in qua
in speciali agitur de his que ab *antiquo fuerunt spiritus sancti instinctu* [P] ab apostolis
constituta, et a sanctis patribus, et a quatuor conciliis, scilicet Niceno, Constantinopoli-
tano, Ephesino, et Calcedonensi, que sicut sancti evangelii quatuor libros sancta ecclesia
veneratur, xv. di. sicut, *et xvi. di. c. ii., iii. et iiii. sequentibus* [P] et ab aliis conciliis in
Grecia primo et postmodum in occidentali ecclesia in diversis provinciis celebratis et a
Romana et universali ecclesia ab antiquo approbatis, que *presentialiter* [P] usquequa-
que non servantur, quorum in presenti tractatu cum paucis concordantiis aliorum iurium
sub *breviloqui* [P] memoria agitur ad hunc finem ut legamus aliqua ne negligantur,
alia ne ignorentur, et alia, non ut teneantur, sed ut repudientur, sicut ait beatus Ambrosius
super Lucam et in decretis, xxxvii. di. legimus. Si aliqua in dicta specificatione casuum
[canonum?] reperiantur utilia et universali ecclesie proficua, quod sacri provisione
concilii super eorum observantia vel revocatione aut *immutatione* [P] vel declaratione
deliberatio, si visum fuerit expediens, habeatur.' *TMA* 2.prefatio, fol. 13rb–va. Cf. D.15
c.2, D.16 c.2–6, D.37 c.9. D.15 c.2 was crucial in discussions of the state of the church; see
Post, 'Copyists' Errors', pp. 378–81; Denifle, 'Denkschriften der Colonna', p. 518. Two
technical points need to be addressed. First, *revocatio* can mean two opposite things: to
repeal and to call back into use. *TMA* 2.4, fol. 16ra, provides an unequivocal example of
*revocare* in the sense of 'repeal': 'Deliberetur si expedit universali ecclesie quod decretalis
Bonifaciana de clericis coniugatis revocetur, cum per eam generalis libertas ecclesie
revocetur quo ad clericos coniugatos.' The context of *TMA* 2.42, fol. 34rb, leaves no
doubt that here the meaning is 'to call back into use': 'videretur pensandum ... si dictum
concilium posset vel expediret revocari'. For an unequivocal example of *revocare* in the
latter sense see R-S, p. 177: 'Ea petebat cum instantia revocari gentibus nostris predictis.'
In the present instance Durant fortunately justified his call for *revocatio* by a quotation
from St Ambrose which used the unambiguous term *repudiare*. The leaves no doubt that
Durant was thinking of 'revocation' in the sense of 'repeal'. Second, Viollet, p. 86 and n.
2, charged Durant with tampering with the text of St Ambrose, because Ambrose's
original reads *ne legantur*, instead of Durant's *ne negligantur*. But *ne negligantur* was the
version on which the ordinary gloss *ad* D.37 c.9 relied, which is why it was still included
in the sixteenth-century Roman edition of the *Corpus Iuris Canonici*.

offer 'concordances to other laws', that is, a more detailed discussion of the topic under consideration with references to related laws, ranging from the most ancient to the most recent civil and canon laws. These were often numerous enough to obscure the basic function of the introductory canon, and they sometimes diverged to deal with topics that were only loosely related to the opening canon. Each chapter normally included a proposal to revoke, modify, or enforce a certain canon or group of canons; thus each chapter may be compared to a legislative bill accompanied by documents intended to determine whether a law that had fallen into disuse still ought to be obeyed.

The opening canons appeared in the same order in which they had been presented by the source from which Durant was quoting them, the Pseudo-Isidorean collection, beginning with the *Canones apostolorum*, continuing with the Greek councils, and concluding with the Latin councils.[12] The second part of the *Tractatus Maior* was thus so closely patterned on the Pseudo-Isidorean collection that it can be regarded as a running commentary on a conciliar nucleus of the Pseudo-Isidorean collection: it bypassed the papal letters which are found in the first section of Pseudo-Isidore, it highlighted a small number of conciliar canons from the second section, presenting them in the same order as Pseudo-Isidore had done, and it added a large body of legal commentary.

Durant thus slighted the ways that had been devised during the previous three centuries to arrange the laws in a systematic fashion so as to make them more easily accessible than they had been in those early medieval collections of which that of Pseudo-Isidore was the most complete and most famous example.[13] His ordering paid no attention to the three parts of Gratian's *Decretum* or to the five books of the *Liber Extra* and the *Liber Sextus*, instead reverting to the chronological order in which the laws had been created. While this caused his treatise to share the very quality that made the older collections so cumbersome to use, it was also a perfect expression of his decision to rely on the 'original texts'.

There are a few exceptions to this arrangement. Some are

---

[12] Durant expressly indicated the point of transition from the Greek councils to the Latin ones between chapters 2.24 and 2.25: 'Expliciunt assumpta ex conciliis Grecis. Incipiunt assumpta ex conciliis Latinis.' *TMA* 2.24, fol. 27rb.

[13] See Fournier and Le Bras, *Histoire des collections*; Fransen, *Les Collections canoniques*; Fransen, *Les Décrétales*.

minor.[14] Others are more significant, such as chapters 2.84–94
(3.15–25), which do have the same basic form as the other chapters,
but whose opening canons were not taken from ancient councils,
most probably because they dealt with contemporary issues, such
as the mendicant orders, *quaestors* from Rome, and the
depreciation of the currency, for which it would have been
difficult to find appropriate canons in antiquity. These chapters are
perhaps best described as a contemporary supplement. But the
most interesting exceptions to the overall arrangement reflect the
tension between Durant's attachment to the chronological structure of his source and his intention to provide a handbook for ready
reference to ancient conciliar law about the state of the church.

He employed three means of resolving that tension. First, he
supplied occasional cross-references.[15] Second, he tried not to
divide the most important topics among separate chapters but
instead to deal with them as completely as possible in individual
chapters, or at least in groups of chapters, even if that meant going
far beyond the point of the introductory canon.[16] And third, in the
five concluding chapters Durant recapitulated and indexed his

[14] *TMA* 2.1, for example, lacks 'concordances' because it consists in its entirety of
quotations from the *Canones Apostolorum*. It serves as a kind of introduction for the entire
second part in which Durant set out the most important issues on his mind. Viollet, p. 87,
correctly recognized that 'ce titre Iᵉʳ, très long, ressemble à un recueil de notes que l'auteur
aurait placé en tête des parties II et III, en manière de table des matières', but he failed to
notice that these 'notes' were quoted from the *Canones apostolorum*; cf. Fasolt, 'A New
View', pp. 303f. *TMA* 2.72 (3.3) and 2.95 (3.26), on the other hand, contain no references
to conciliar canons at all because they consist of brief recommendations to study Giles of
Rome's *De ecclesiastica potestate* for the relation between church and state. Posch,
'Reformvorschläge', pp. 289f., and Müller, *Konzil von Vienne*, p. 596 n. 40, were clearly
mistaken in interpreting this as a reference to Giles of Rome's *De regimine principum*.
[15] *TMA* 2.1, fols. 14rb (*male* 15rb) – 15rb, contains cross-references to chapters 2.7, 2.8,
2.11, 2.20, 2.28, 2.37, 2.38, 2.50, 2.59, 2.93. Other cross-references can be found in *TMA*
2.3, fol. 15vb, *TMA* 2.5, fol. 16rb, *TMA* 2.32, fol. 29vb, *TMA* 2.38, fol. 32vb, *TMA*
2.38, fol. 33rb.
[16] Good examples are the large chapters on the conduct of monks (*TMA* 2.53), abbots
(*TMA* 2.92 (3.23)), the clergy (*TMA* 2.32), and the prelates (*TMA* 2.38). *TMA* 2.52–4
may be considered a cluster of chapters dealing with the clergy's obligation to stay in one
place; the conduct of monks appears in this context because Durant considered their
seclusion in the monasteries and *stabilitas loci* as the most characteristic aspect of their way
of life. *TMA* 2.70–2 is another cluster amounting to quite a substantial treatise on the
relation of church and state, beginning with the fealty owed by clerics to secular rulers,
continuing with abuses of secular power, and concluding with a reference to Giles of
Rome for information about the extent of temporal jurisdiction over clerics and their
goods. In the printed editions this cluster is not recognizable because there the chapters
are dispersed in 2.70–1, 3.30, and 3.1–2, in that order.

most important points according to the hierarchical order of
society that he cherished.[17] Beginning with the church of Rome at
the top and descending via the prelates, the clergy, and the religious
to the laity at the bottom, each of these five chapters ended with an
exhaustive list of cross-references to the main body of the treatise
where the particular order of society that formed the subject of the
chapter had been dealt with in detail, so that together they served as
both a summary and a reasonably efficient index of previously
considered ideas. In addition, however, they also offered a few
proposals that had never been mentioned before: for example, that
after a vacancy of more than three months the right to elect the
pope should devolve from the cardinals to some other body of
men; that the finances of the Roman church ought once and for all
to be based on a permanent source of income; and that ten years
constituted an appropriate interval for general councils.[18] Few
though they are, these are among the most important, most
innovative, and most famous of Durant's suggestions. It may
therefore well be that they were not included in the main body of
the treatise precisely because they were so innovative. They rested
on no other authority than Durant's own opinion about the best
way to achieve reform and they could be expressed in no other
voice than his own – hence he may have considered it inappropriate
to include them in the previous chapters, which were intended to
recall existing law.

## STYLE OF THE 'TRACTATUS MAIOR'

Durant's treatise is written in a style that has baffled and infuriated
many readers. As far as he was able, he let the laws speak for
themselves, either by quoting them directly or by providing
references to the source where they could be looked up. All told,
those references and quotations number more than two thousand.
Roughly half are to Gratian's *Decretum*. The rest, in order of
decreasing bulk, are to the conciliar sections of the Pseudo-
Isidorean collection, the *Liber Extra*, the Bible, Roman law, and the
*Liber Sextus*. There is a handful of occasions on which Durant relies

[17] *TMA* 2.96 (3.27) dealt with the church of Rome, *TMA* 2.97 (3.28) with the prelates,
*TMA* 2.98 (3.29) with the clergy, *TMA* 2.99 (3.30) with the religious orders, and *TMA*
2.100 (2.71–2.72) with the laity. In the printed editions these chapters are dispersed so that
they cannot be recognized as belonging together.
[18] *TMA* 2.96 (3.27), fols. 59rb, 59va.

on other kinds of sources, such as proverbs, anecdotes, or hymns, and in the rubric on the 'need to limit the power of superiors' there is a group of atypical quotations from St Augustine's *De civitate Dei*, Valerius Maximus' *Facta et dicta memorabilia*, Cicero's *De officiis*, and John of Salisbury's *Policraticus* which, though relatively small in size, is of great significance for Durant's argument. But the vast majority of Durant's authorities was supplied by canon and civil law. Sometimes his sentences are terse, but more often they are composed of long chains of subordinate clauses each of which contains the references to the laws supporting a specific point and all of which support the main clause from which they depend: 'Because the laws say such and such, and because they say so and so, and because they say this and that, and for many other reasons that will be considered in due course, we ought to adopt such and such a course of action.' As a result, the treatise has the appearance of an intricate patchwork of direct quotations from the laws, interspersed with statements of opinion or desire in Durant's own words, and bloated by lists of technical references which often grow to the size of veritable compendia of the laws related to a given topic. To read this text is to be bombarded with a relentless staccato of laws in their original wording alternating with ciphers whose meaning has to be sought beyond the limits of the treatise, but only relatively rarely to listen to Durant's own voice.

All of this is more than hard on the reader. Far from permitting him to proceed apace, it slows him down at every point, breaking his discursive line of thought, forcing him to look for implications, and encouraging him to consult other sources. Again and again it unsettles the distinction between text and context and blunts all pre-established tools of interpretation. No wonder that Brian Tierney, echoing a widely felt unease, has spoken of Durant's 'turgid irrelevancies' and opposed them to the 'easy lucidity' of John of Paris.[19] On both counts the point is well taken: Durant's way of writing is turgid indeed and it is separated by a considerable distance from the analytic mode of discourse favoured by scholastic theologians. But it would be thoroughly misleading to regard this lack of systematic clarity as the result of any failure by the author. Rather, the style of the *Maior* reflected an entirely different, but deliberate design.

In part this design expressed a well-known fundamental feature

[19] Tierney, *Foundations*, p. 191.

of medieval thought, especially medieval legal thought: truth was to be sought from the authorities and originality was to be measured, not by the creativity with which an author managed to advance beyond his sources, but by his ability to communicate their meaning fully and faithfully to his audience. Such writing therefore contains no obvious line of demarcation by which to separate the author's personal views from the meaning of his sources. More than that, any attempt to look for such a line seems out of place. Such is the case with Durant. The passages he quoted from the laws were more than illustrations of his argument and more than evidence adduced to substantiate a point: they were the very substance of his case. Enclosing those quotations in quotation marks so as to clarify the difference between Durant's own views and his sources may seem appealing, even necessary, to a particular tradition of source criticism and interpretation. But here it would be thoroughly misleading because, in order to persuade his readers that no such difference did exist, Durant did his best to speak through the laws – and he succeeded to such a remarkable degree that there simply is no way to distinguish clearly between words that are 'his own' and words that are 'quoted'. For the same reason it is often difficult to choose between the several different ways in which a given quotation from the laws might be interpreted. Durant relishes the wealth of latent significations in his legal sources and even cultivates it by providing them with contexts suited to expand, not to constrict, the range of potential interpretations. At every turn the reader is invited, not just to contemplate the text that has just been submitted to his attention, but also to reflect on its relationship to others that were mentioned previously, or that are found side by side with it in the source from which it had been quoted, or that have been placed in the same context by scholarly tradition. Soon he will find himself exploring a seamless universe of meaning where nothing may be considered in isolation and everything has to be viewed at once because each element is linked by a kind of logical simultaneity to every other one in a series of multiple structures of significance which reach to infinity.

Examples occur on every page, but for the sake of illustration take the opening sentence of the preface: 'Among the canons of the council of Toledo it is written that assisting a good cause with counsel is not only good for this life, but will also be eternally rewarded.' This maxim does several things at once. In a literal sense it simply underscores the value of counsel. But it also establishes

Durant's intention to rest his case on ancient authorities and it exemplifies his preference for ancient conciliar canons, especially those of the councils of Toledo. More important, since 'counsel' is precisely what the *Tractatus Maior* offers, it implicitly legitimates Durant's ideas and helps him to prepare the ground for his contention that the papacy ought regularly to obtain the counsel of general councils. And finally the maxim declares that counsel is valued both in this life and in the next, establishing something of a link between the world of time and the world of eternity. This is of special relevance to the treatise because the tension between time and eternity was in a sense the basic issue to which Durant addressed himself and which he hoped to resolve by means of general councils. The opening quotation of the treatise is thus exceptionally well chosen. It is almost as though Durant had tried to make his beginning contain all of his conclusions.

The treatise, in other words, was designed, not as an argument or syllogism, but as an exhibition of the laws; its purpose was not to analyse anything, but to confirm authority; and its style of presentation was coordinated to that purpose. Its method may be likened to a truncated version of the method of Descartes. For, like Descartes, Durant proceeded from the whole to the parts, but unlike Descartes he never went on to analyse the parts in order to reconstitute their relationships. Instead of disassembling for the sake of a different understanding, he disassembled for the sake of a fuller understanding. To make a case, to argue, prove, and strive to convince was all very well, but not unless it agreed with the authorities from which alone in his opinion all proofs derived their strength. Indeed, in the end there was but one authority, and that, of course, was the authority of Him who stood behind all laws: 'The order of the church must neither be slighted nor interdicted because God is its author.'[20] Hence the voice of the law in all of its many modulations had to be magnified. There was no reason for Durant to try to limit his quotations of the law in such a way that they could be interpreted without equivocation. The law was like a natural source of justice. The many different meanings that could be given to his quotations were nothing whatever like equivocation: they rather were so many means to reveal the justice of the universe. If that meant that apparent trivialities ranged side by side

---

[20] 'Non igitur parvipendenda nec interdicenda est dicta ordinatio que Deum habet autorem.' *TMA* 1.4 De exemptionibus, fol. 9va.

with points of principle, so much the better; perhaps that would persuade the reader that there was nothing trivial about the least detail of an order that had God as its author. And if it meant that the voice of the bishop of Mende would be drowned out, so much the better still, for any voice that could not find expression through the law had no right to be heard.

The cumbersome qualities of Durant's style can thus be understood as an expression of his agreement with basic medieval notions of truth, self, and authority – notions which make it difficult and perhaps impossible to use authorial intentionality as the only valid criterion of interpretation, if only because here we are dealing with an author denying his authoriality. In this regard the *Tractatus Maior* was not in the least unusual. Similar qualities mark virtually every medieval text that deals with authorities, particularly legal texts. But in the case of the *Tractatus Maior* there was more to it than that. For even though Durant placed himself squarely on the authority of law, his faith in law was sharply qualified by his conviction that ancient law had fallen out of use. Of course, the insight that ancient and contemporary law conflicted was not new. Precisely the same insight had moved the reformers of the eleventh and twelfth centuries to set out on their project to reshape the world according to the writings of the fathers. The canonistic and civilian efforts to formulate consistent legal doctrines were in great part an attempt to reappropriate a body of laws that had been forgotten. Indeed, at least in part the papal reformers of the eleventh century had founded their case on the same source from which Durant took much of his ammunition: the Pseudo-Isidorean collection. But there was a crucial difference between Durant and his predecessors: they had sought to rid the law of the church from imperfections which had been introduced during the chaos of the early middle ages; Durant, however, looked back on two centuries of sustained reform and therefore found himself confronted with the precarious responsibility of ridding the law from imperfections that seemed to have been introduced by that very progress of reform from which the restoration of the ancient law had been expected. Durant was suspicious both of the uses to which the law had been put by the papacy and of the interpretations to which it had been subjected by the canonists. Indeed, he had nothing but disdain for 'the diversity and the variety of glosses and writings in each of the [university] faculties. They stultify the intelligence of students with multiplicity, prolixity, and similitude. They are a waste of time and money and they produce confusion and ignorance because they lead to contempt for the original texts.'[21] In the same vein he attacked the friars mendicant for their infatuation with the 'phantasms of dialecticians' and the 'curiosities and empty disputations' which they practised in their schools instead of studying 'the Bible and true theology'.[22] In keeping with this point of view he systematically banished the secondary legal literature from the pages of his treatise. This was of course not the result of ignorance. Durant must have been perfectly familiar with the doctrines of decretists and decretalists alike.[23] But neither can it be reduced to the respect which every other canonist, by definition, paid to the law. Durant's dogged faith in the 'original texts' rather bespeaks a radical mistrust of all those glosses, sums, apparatuses, and commentaries which constituted the pride of two centuries of canonistic scholarship.

Durant's treatment of the authorities therefore differed at a fundamental level from that given to it by the decretists and the decretalists, not to mention Pope Gregory VII or Gratian. Where these had still been able to proceed in the hope that their work would unfold the true meaning of the law Durant was sure that they had actually undermined the law. Hence, quite self-consciously and with considerable self-discipline, he refrained as much

---

21 'Quod diversitas glossarum et scriptorum que est in singulis facultatibus, que diversitas et varietas cum multiplicitate et prolixitate ac similitudine dictorum et recitatorum studentium sensus ebetat, tempus et facultates consumit, confusionem et ignorantiam inducit, cum ex hoc textuum et originalium notitia contemnatur, reduceretur per certos magistros in qualibet facultate approbatos et deputatos, resecatis superfluis, similibus, et contrariis, ad compendium veritatis, quod compendium approbaretur per apostolicam sedem.' *TMI* 22 (3.45), fol. 68vb. Cf. *TMA* 2.73 (3.4), fol. 53ra–b, and below, p. 194.

22 'Dicti religiosi, dimisso biblie et vere theologie studio et his que edificare possent ecclesiam Dei, dialecticorum tendiculis et fantasmatibus theologie studium destruentibus, et in sermonibus et predicationibus ad eorum ostentationem frequenter rithmis et quibusdam profunditatibus abutantur, et in generalibus et particularibus studiis curiositatibus et vanis disceptationibus vacent.' *TMA* 2.85 (3.16), fol. 55vb.

23 See the judgment of Tierney, *Foundations*, p. 191, quoted above, p. 75. Concerning civil law, Rogozinski, *Power, Caste, and Law*, p. 110 n. 85, calls him 'an esteemed legist'. The dozen or so occasions on which Durant did after all quote the secondary legal literature demonstrate his familiarity with the ordinary gloss on the *Decretum* and with the opinions of Innocent IV and Hostiensis on specific points of legal doctrine. He quoted the ordinary gloss to the *Decretum* in *TMA* 1.4 De exemptionibus, fol. 9rb; 2.31, fol. 28va; 2.39, fol. 33vb; 2.70, fol. 46vb. Innocent IV is cited in *TMA* 2.70, fol. 49ra. Hostiensis is cited in *TMA* 2.3, fol. 15vb; 2.62, fol. 43rb; and 2.90 (3.21), fol. 56vb. Alberigo, *Chiesa conciliare*, pp. 269f., makes similar observations about Nicholas of Cusa.

as possible from saying anything at all that could not be couched in the words of the laws themselves – an exercise in intellectual asceticism that could not but result in obscurity. His turgidity thus has a systematic quality; it results from a dogmatic preference for the 'original texts' and a decidedly anti-scholastic and anti-interpretative turn of mind. It is in some ways reminiscent of the heady days of reform before scholasticism flourished; in others it foreshadows the renewed attention to the text of the law in the wake of the council of Trent which produced the famous Roman edition of the *Corpus Iuris Canonici*. Indeed, it surely was this very impulse to renew the church by scraping all incrustations off the original texts which in its radical extreme turned into Luther's *sola scriptura*.

Given Durant's mistrust of any exercise of unassisted reason, exclusive attention to the original texts must have appeared to be a plausible means of restoring true authority. But in fact it led him into a deep dilemma by depriving him of any reasons with which to support his case for the ancient laws outside of those laws themselves. But, as his case implied, it was those very laws whose authority was contested. Indeed, the more effectively he quoted ancient laws in order to persuade his readers that those laws ought to be obeyed, the more completely he revealed how little authority they actually possessed. His writing was thus caught in a vicious circle that threatened to turn his argument into pure tautology: the ancient laws must be obeyed because the ancient laws say that they must be obeyed. Tautology was the logical complement of his decision not to speak in his own voice: since he preferred to say only what the laws had said before, he ran the risk of saying nothing whatsoever. In the end it would prove to be impossible to break this vicious circle without speaking on grounds outside of law. Indeed, in the end it was going to be obvious that the case for law could not be stated plausibly without redefining the very nature of authority by reference to reason, utility, and, possibly, sovereignty. This was, to a degree, what Durant himself began to do in the *Tractatus Maior*, and even more so in the *Tractatus Minor*. But on the whole and in principle he remained as firmly attached to law as he was able. The prominence which he gave to the original texts was therefore purchased at the considerable cost of, not just turgidity, but an irremediable ambivalence towards authority that led straight into logical circularity.

### REFORM IN HEAD AND MEMBERS

Durant's theory of reform was designed to conceal a tension that is inherent in the very nature of political thought. As we shall see later on, this can be revealed by closer analysis. But it would be unfair not to give him an opportunity first to present his case on his own terms, especially since it has never been studied in any detail and has often been misunderstood. Before we undertake to dissect its involuted logic, we are therefore going to examine Durant's argument for reform as he himself presented it in the first part of his treatise.

The point of the first chapter is clearly indicated by its heading: 'The ministers of the church should first of all correct whatever is done badly in the church of God in head and members.'[24] This is an early and deservedly famous occurrence of the call for 'reform in head and members' that would reverberate throughout the later middle ages.[25] It should be stressed that this reform was to begin with the church but not to end with it. Durant left no doubt that reform ought to be aimed at both the clergy and the laity. His goal was 'the correction and reformation of the church and of Christendom', or 'the correction and reformation of the church and [the production of] a healthy regime for the human race', or even 'to govern the world and the human race well'.[26] His goal, in other words, was universal. To be sure, he had more to say about the reform of the clergy than about the reform of the laity, but this was not because clerical reform was an end in itself; rather, it was an essential prerequisite for every other kind of reform.

Durant devoted the body of the chapter to an explanation of why reform had to begin with the church. He began with a familiar principle:

First of all, the Lord says in the Gospel of John 8, that he that is without sin among you, let him first cast a stone at her, and in Matthew 7, that he who has a beam in his eye cannot pull out a mote from the eye of his brother. In his *Moralia* Gregory uses this to prove that those who undertake to scold

---

[24] 'De correctione eorum que male aguntur premittenda in Dei ecclesia a ministris ecclesiasticis in capite et in membris.' *TMA* 1.1, fol. 4rb.  [25] See above, p. 1.

[26] 'De modo correctionis et reformationis ecclesie et christianitatis.' *TMA* 1.2, fol. 4vb. 'Correctio et reformatio ecclesie et salubre regimen humani generis.' *TMA* 1.2, fol. 4vb. '. . . mundum et humanum genus salubriter gubernare.' *TMA* 1.3 De limitanda potestate, fol. 7ra.

the sins of others while leaving their own sins unpunished must be reminded of their conscience within so that they will correct their own sins first and then the sins of others. So long, moreover, as someone is weighed down by grave sins of his own, he cannot dissolve the sins of others. And according to Augustine a priest and a wise and perfect doctor must first dissolve his own sins and thereafter wash off and heal the sins of others.[27]

At the heart of these words stood the golden rule of natural law: 'Treat others as you would like them to treat you.'[28] In itself this principle, which has perhaps a better claim on universal acceptance at all times and in all places than any other, was neither particularly medieval nor particularly Christian. But in the present context there was a little more to it. For first of all Durant did not believe that reform could simply begin anywhere; it had to begin with the church. And, second, Saints Gregory and Augustine did not just say that a priest should not dissolve the sins of others unless he had dissolved his own; they said he could not. The priest's relationship to his flock thus rested on more than the reciprocity of natural law: it rested on a real, hierarchical distinction which gave him a responsibility and a power that his flock did not have. For good or ill, his conduct determined the conduct of his flock.

[27] 'Et primo siquidem, cum Dominus dicat in evangelio Joannis c. viii. qui sine peccato est vestrum primus in illam lapidem mittat, et in Matthei vii. c. quod qui trabem gestat in oculo non potest festucam educere de oculo fratris sui, per que probat Gregorius in Moralibus quod qui ad aliena peccata reprehendenda vadunt et sua impunita relinquunt revocari debent intus ad conscientiam ut prius propria corrigant et tunc aliena reprehendant, et in gravibus peccatis quis positus, dum suis premitur, aliena non diluit, iii. q. vii. §. item in evangelio, et c. qui sine, et in c. gravibus, et c. postulatus, et secundum Augustinum *sacerdos et sapiens medicus et perfectus* [M, P] prius debeat sua peccata diluere et postea aliena detergere et sanare, eadem causa et q. sacerdos.' *TMA* 1.1, fol. 4rb. Cf. John 8:7, Matthew 7:3–5, C.3 q.7 a.c.3, C.3 q.7 c.3–6, C.3 q.7 c.7. The reading 'sacerdos et sapiens medicus et perfectus' is surely curious since it likens illness to sin and implies that physicians who are tainted by sin cannot heal the illnesses of others. Friedberg, in fact, reads 'sacerdos ut sapiens medicus et perfectus', and Crespin's edition reads 'sacerdos sapiens ut medicus et perfectus', both of which are easier to understand. Nevertheless the manuscript reading is preferable, not only because it represents the *lectio difficilior*, but also because it agrees well with the quasi-magical view of priestly and medical efficiency that is here implied. Viollet, p. 81, believed that the form of Durant's quotation from Matthew shows the influence of the older Durant's *Instructiones et constitutiones*, ed. Berthelé, p. 10, because both differ from the Biblical version. His suggestion is good, but his reason is not, for uncle and nephew are more likely to have quoted their version of the text independently of each other from C.3 q.7 a.c.3, which differed from the Bible in precisely the same way.

[28] Cf. Matthew 7:12, as quoted by Durant *TMA* 1.2, fol. 4vb.

On this basis Durant proceeded to state his point somewhat more amply:

We are therefore well advised to consider the question, if possible, of how very useful and necessary it would be for us to correct and reform those matters that need to be corrected and reformed in the church of God, both in the head and in the members, before we turn to any other issues.[29]

For otherwise (to explicate the implication) the church cannot improve the ways of laymen. Logically inclined readers may have noticed that the syllogism on which Durant's conclusion rested was incomplete. The major premise that men with beams in their eyes cannot pull out motes from the eyes of others had been stated, but the minor one that in fact the clergy did have beams in their eyes had not. This was no oversight. Durant was not about to leave his opening point dangling by failing to make it plain what he thought of his fellow-clerics, but he preferred to lead into the topic gently, by way of implication, and to delay his charges by announcing them in the form of an apology:

I should like to speak in peace and with permission about this matter and I take obedience as my excuse, lest I should seem to have set my mouth against the heaven. Let me therefore repeat that such reform in head and members conforms with the will of God, and consequently also with the will of man. For, as Jerome said, when he looked through the books of history he could not find that anyone had divided the church of God and led the people away from the house of the Lord except for those whom God had set up to be priests and prophets . . . They follow the road of Balaam of Bozor, who loved the rewards of iniquity and was chastened for his madness by his speechless beast of burden, which spoke to him with a human voice and thus exposed the prophet's folly. This happens nowadays as well, for although the clergy ought to be a light for others and a candle on a candlestick as the Lord said, they inflict so many stupid and immoral acts upon the church of God that they have hardened the minds of Jews and pagans. Even people who are completely ignorant of God detest their madness and are wise enough to prove that their distorted ways are contrary to God. Hence learned men have been compellingly refuted by the unlearned, and clerics by laymen. Augustine says that he who has not understood the reason why he rules nor cleansed away his sins nor corrected the crime of his sons should not be called a bishop but a

---

[29] 'Videretur deliberandum, si posset, per quam utile fore et necessarium quod ante omnia corrigerentur et reformarentur illa que sunt in ecclesia Dei corrigenda et reformanda tam in capite quam in membris.' *TMA* 1.1, fol. 4rb.

filthy dog. The time is therefore come that judgment must begin at the house of God, as Peter said in his first letter . . . For we resist those who are outside the church in vain so long as we are being wounded by those inside.[30]

This marvellous chain of quotations from the canon law speaks for itself. It completed the argument of the first chapter.

### REFORM BY LAW

Having answered the question of where reform ought to begin, the next question clearly was of what it was to consist. Hence the second chapter devoted itself to what Durant called the 'method of correcting and reforming the church and Christendom'.[31] As far as he was concerned there was nothing particularly difficult about the choice of method:

The following short road would surely appear to lead to the correction and reform of the church and to a healthy regime for the human race: for in the beginning of the *Decretum* it is written that the human race is governed by two laws – that is, it ought to be governed by them – namely, natural law and *mores*. Natural law is contained in the Law of the Old Testament and in the Gospel, by which everyone is ordered to do

---

[30] 'Ut tamen cum pace et venia super hoc loquar et ex obedientia excusatus habear, ne os meum videar posuisse in celum, xxi. di. in tantum, xxvi. di. deinde, istud nempe, sicut ex premissis probatum est, plene videretur esse conforme voluntati divine et per consequens humane. Nam sicut Hieronymus ait, xxiiii. q. iii. transferunt, veteres scrutans historias invenire non potuit aliquos alios scidisse ecclesiam Dei, et de domo Domini populum seduxisse, preter eos qui sacerdotes a Deo positi fuerant et prophete, id est speculatores versi in laqueum tortuosum et in omnibus locis ponentes scandalum . . . Nam ut eadem causa et q. sequitur sic in cap. secuti sunt viam Balaam ex Bozor qui mercedem iniquitatis amavit, correctionem vero habuit sue vesanie, nam subiugale mutuum quod hominis voce locutum est prophete insipientiam probavit. Quod etiam hodie accidit, cum tam stulta et dissoluta perpetrentur in ecclesia Dei a dictis personis ecclesiasticis, que deberent esse lumen aliorum et lucerne super candelabrum posite, iuxta id quod Dominus ait. Sensus hebetant Iudeorum et etiam paganorum, et etiam illi qui ratione divine agnitionis omnimodo carent istorum detestantur insaniam et eorum distorta et Deo contraria itinera sanius sapiendo redarguunt. Ex quo secundum eum docti ab indoctis, clerici a laicis necessario redarguuntur, ut ibidem. Et Augustinus ait, qui nec regiminis in se rationem habuit, nec sua delicta detersit, nec filiorum crimen correxit, canis impudicus dicendus est magis quam episcopus, ii. q. vii. nec regiminis. ᴬTempus igitur esse videretur ut iudicium a domo Dei inciperet, sicut ait beatus Petrus in prima sua epistola iiii. c.ᴬ [P] . . . Nam superfluo extra ecclesiam positis resistimus si ab his qui intus sunt vulneramur, xxiiii. q. iii. c. illud sane.' *TMA* 1.1, fol. 4rb–vb. Cf. D.21 c.9, D.26 c.3, C.24 q.3 c.33, Matthew 5:13, Mark 9:49, C.2 q.7 c.28–9, C.2 q.7 c.31, Matthew 5:14–16, C.2 q.7 c.32, 1 Peter 4:17, C.24 q.3 c.34.

[31] 'De modo correctionis et reformationis ecclesie et christianitatis.' *TMA* 1.2, fol. 4rb.

to others what he wants to have done to himself, and prohibited from inflicting on others what he does not want to have done to himself. Hence Christ says in the Gospel of Matthew 7 that all things whatsoever ye would that men should do to you, do ye even so to them, for this is the law and the prophets. All laws and prophets agree on this point and their teachings are summed up by it according to the following verse from the conclusion of Ecclesiastes: Fear God and keep his commandments, for this is the whole duty of man. The human race as such, on the other hand, is governed by *mores*, that is, by human laws, as Isidore attests in book 5 of his *Etymologies*. If, therefore, the two powers that govern the human race as servants of God – that is, ecclesiastical authority and royal power, as Pope Gelasius wrote to Emperor Anastasius – wish to forward this reform and this healthy regime for the human race, they must govern themselves and the human race according to the contents of the Law, the Gospel, the councils approved by the inspiration of the Holy Spirit, and other approved human laws and rights.[32]

On the face of it, this road to reform indeed seems remarkably short, leading no farther than reminding the secular and the spiritual powers that they had a duty to abide by law. However, on closer inspection matters turn out to be more complicated. The laws on which Durant was insisting had, after all, been in existence for a long time, which meant that they had already failed to prevent the clergy from falling into its sinful ways. To point to them now as a cure for every ill was therefore less like answering the question of how to reform the church than like begging the question of how to enforce the laws. Here the tension in Durant's

---

[32] 'Sane videretur ad correctionem et reformationem ecclesie et ad salubre regimen humani generis posse perveniri hac brevi via: scriptum namque est in principio decretorum quod regitur genus humanum duobus, id est, regi debet, videlicet iure naturali *et moribus. Iure naturale* [P] quod in lege et in evangelio continetur, quo quis iubetur alii facere quod sibi vult fieri et prohibetur alii inferre quod sibi non vult fieri. Unde Christus in evangelio Matthei vii. ait, omnia quecunque vultis ut faciant vobis homines, et vos eadem facite illis, hoc enim est lex et prophete, id est omnes leges et prophete in hoc concordant, et in hoc consummantur iuxta illud Ecclesiastici ultimo: Deum time et mandata eius observa, hoc est omnis homo. Moribus vero regitur ipsum genus humanum, id est, humanis legibus, sicut Isidorus in v. libro ethimologiarum attestatur, i. di. omnes leges, et c. sequentibus. Si itaque duo a quibus regitur humanum genus sicut a ministris Dei, videlicet ecclesiastica autoritas et regalis potestas, sicut Gelasius papa scribit Anastasio imperatori, xcvi. di. duo sunt, vellent intendere ad dictam reformationem et salubre regimen humani generis, haberent viam amplecti predictam, ut videlicet seipsos et humanum genus regerent secundum quod in lege et in evangelio et in conciliis spiritus sancti instinctu probatis, ut xvi. di. habeo, et in aliis humanis et comprobatis legibus et iuribus continetur.' *TMA* 1.2, fol. 4vb. Cf. Matthew 7:12, Ecclesiastes 12:13, D.1 a.c.1 ff., D.96 c.10, D.16 c.6.

thought lies close to the surface; but since he did not himself address it we shall postpone considering it until later. For the moment let us simply note that he considered law a sure guide to reform.

Another question to which the answer was not as obvious as the 'short road to reform' implied was that of precisely which laws were to be enforced. On this count Durant himself evidently felt the need to provide some clarification. Having quoted Gratian's famous distinction between two kinds of law and his identification of divine with natural law he expanded on the definition of both kinds and concluded with a brief list of the laws he had in mind: the Law of the Old Testament, the Gospel, conciliar canons, and 'other approved human laws and rights'. But this was not nearly as informative as one might wish. Seeing that the Gospel had superseded at least parts of the Old Testament, which parts of the Old Testament were to be enforced upon Christians? And seeing that conciliar canons were, on the one hand, enacted by a human institution but, on the other hand, inspired by the Holy Spirit, as Durant took care to emphasize, were they to be considered divine immutable law or human mutable law? And seeing that there was a huge variety of human laws, precisely which were the ones he considered to have been 'approved'? We could venture a few suggestions as to how Durant might have answered these questions but, as he never answered them himself, in this respect his views remain uncertain.[33]

An admonition to the rulers to obey the laws was Durant's first – and it remained his basic – definition of a method to reform the church. The remainder of the chapter described the further measures he considered necessary in order to achieve his goal:

If someone other than the spiritual and the temporal rulers should discover any attempts to violate these laws in the rule of the world, that should be corrected and reformed as well as possible. It also ought to be established that no such attempts can be made with impunity; that the

---

[33] As far as the Old Testament was concerned, Durant surely accepted Gratian's distinction between 'moral' prescriptions that corresponded directly to natural law and 'mystical' prescriptions that embodied an immutable 'moral significance' but were not themselves identical with natural law. The former were binding upon Christians, the latter were not; see D.6 p.c.3; cf. Brys, *De dispensatione*, pp. 80–3; Weigand, *Naturrechtslehre*, pp. 375–81. Regarding conciliar canons, see below, pp. 138–44, 225f. Concerning the question of which laws precisely were to be included in the category of 'approved human laws and rights', Durant emphasized that the 'Roman and the universal church' had approved the canons of the ancient Greek and Latin provincial councils; see above, n. 11. That clarified at least one possible uncertainty.

novel circumstances of this life should not lead us to neglect what antiquity once decreed with foresight and deliberation, as that Roman law points out which has been entered into canon law at C.2 q.6 c.28; and finally that all uses – or, rather, abuses – and customs that are to be considered corruptions, and all dispensations, privileges, liberties and exemptions that contradict the above-mentioned divine and human general and approved laws ought to be abolished.[34]

This precisely formulated programme consisted of four distinct elements which constituted an outline of the remainder of the first part of the treatise. First, direct violations of laws that had occurred in the past were to be corrected, even if they were discovered by 'someone other' than the rulers themselves. This topic would be dealt with in the following chapter. Durant does not specify who that 'someone other' might be, but since he insisted that it was necessary to act on such discoveries even if they had not been made by the rulers themselves, he probably suspected that rulers might prefer to conceal such violations rather than act on them if they were left to their own devices.[35] Second, a means would have to be enacted to prevent such attacks from occurring 'with impunity'.[36] Such a means would be suggested in the fourth chapter in the form of general councils. Third, the example of antiquity was to be followed even though times had changed. That referred to Durant's praise for the Roman Republic in the rubric on the 'power of superiors'. And fourth, indirect violations of the laws by surreptitious, unauthorized, or partial deviations were to be abolished. That topic would be treated in the two concluding rubrics on dispensations and exemptions.

## GOVERNMENT BOUND BY LAW

The main difficulty on the road to reform was posed by the rights of government. It was all very well to assert that obedience to the

---

[34] 'Et quicquid per alios invenitur in regimine mundi in contrarium attemptatum corrigeretur et reformaretur prout melius posset, et provideretur ne in contrarium impune attemptaretur, et quod huius vite novitas non negligeret que ab antiquitate fuerant hactenus *consulte* [P] et provide constituta, sicut ait lex illa canonizata, ii. q. vi. anteriorum §. illud, et insuper quod omnes usus, seu verius abusus, consuetudines que censende sunt corruptele, dispensationes, privilegia, libertates, et exemptiones *contrariantes* [P] et contrariantia supradictis divinis et humanis legibus approbatis et generalibus tollerentur.' *TMA* 1.2, fols. 4vb–5ra. Cf. C.2 q.6 c.28, Nov.23.3.
[35] See his use of D.17 p.c.6 and D.21 c.7 below, pp. 152–4.
[36] What precisely *impune* is supposed to mean is another question that is never clearly answered.

laws would assure the success of reform, but laws are passed to address existing circumstances, and circumstances may change.[37] Since popes and princes carried the responsibility for the 'healthy regime of the human race', it was not immediately obvious why they should not be allowed to change the laws in light of changing conditions in order to benefit the human race, especially since they themselves had passed many of the laws at issue.[38] Durant's next order of business therefore was to define the limits of their obligation to the law. In chapter 3 he began to address this issue by recalling a venerable principle:

That the lord pope and kings ought to observe the contents of the Law and the Gospel, [the decrees of] councils, and approved laws is easy to show, for their power stems from God, and what they have ordained is ordained by God, as the Apostle says in Romans 13. Now there can be no better order in their rule than if they conform as much as possible to God, from whom their power proceeds and to whose rule the rule of the world must conform. Above all else, just as Christ, the son of God, true God and true man, true king and true priest, began by doing as well as by teaching, as is written about him in the Gospel of John, chapter 6, so the lord pope and the kings ought first of all to do well and good and compel others by their example to do the same. For, as Seneca says, examples move more strongly than words.[39]

---

[37] Hence a canon taken from Isidore's *Etymologies* declared: 'Erit autem lex honesta, iusta, possibilis, secundum naturam, secundum consuetudinem patriae, loco temporique conveniens, necessaria, utilis, manifesta quoque, ne aliquid per obscuritatem inconveniens contineat, nullo privato commodo, sed pro communi utilitate civium conscripta.' D.4 c.2. Durant referred to this canon on several occasions; see *TMA* 1.4 De exemptionibus, fols. 8rb, 13ra, *TMA* 2.41, fol. 34rb.

[38] Indeed, it was not only not immediately obvious, it was quite impossible to see how changes in the laws could be avoided. Hence it was also impossible to see how the law could furnish an infallible standard against which to measure government. At this point in his argument Durant therefore began to be embroiled in logical difficulties from which he never quite managed to extricate himself.

[39] 'Quod dominus papa et reges debeant servare premissa in lege et in evangelio, conciliis, et iuribus approbatis contenta, de facili potest ostendi. Nam potestas eorum a Deo est et que ab eis ordinata sunt a Deo ordinata existunt sicut ait Apostolus ad Romanos xiii., xi. q. iii. qui resistit, et c. imperatores, x. di. quoniam idem mediator, xcvi. di. cum ad verum, xxiii. q. iiii. quesitum. Ordo autem melior non potest esse in regimine eorundem quam quod in eorum regimine Deo, a quo eorum processit potestas et cuius regimini debet conformari regimen orbis, lxxxix. di. ad hoc, xvi. q. i. ad hoc, inquantum possunt sunt conformes, et in hoc potissime ut, sicut Christus Dei filius, verus deus et verus homo, verus rex et verus pontifex, cepit facere et docere sicut de eo scriptum est, xxvi. di. §. ecce, versi. unde, xxxix. di. §. i., et Ioannis vi. c., sic et predictus dominus papa et reges primo bene et bona facerent et exemplo suo ad idem faciendum alios compellerent cum, prout Seneca ait, plus moveant exempla quam verba.' *TMA* 1.3, fol. 5ra. Cf. C.11 q.3 c.97–8, D.10 c.8, D.96 c.6, C.23 q.4 c.45, D.89 c.7, C.16 q.1 c.63, D.36 p.c.2 §.9, D.39 a.c.1, John

In the final words Durant merely repeated a point he had already made in the first chapter. Just as there he had stressed the impact of the conduct of priests on their flock, so here he stressed the impact of the conduct of rulers on their subjects. It was the responsibility of popes and kings not only to preach but also to practise obedience to the law and to give the same example to their subjects that Christ had given to them, because examples were 'compelling'. But in the present context this point appeared as the consequence of an underlying doctrine about the nature of power: Durant reminded his readers that the power of all rulers stemmed from God and that they were therefore subjected to his order. His evidence came from the famous passage in Romans 13:1 that 'the powers that be are ordained of God' – hence the powers that be had to conduct themselves according to God's commands. It is worth stressing that Paul had actually meant to say almost exactly the opposite. The fact that the powers that be were ordained by God meant to him that it was not up to Christians to question their conduct: 'Wherefore ye must needs be subject, not only for wrath, but also for conscience's sake.'[40] Thus, according to St Paul, temporal government enjoyed an almost unlimited right to exact obedience from its subjects. That interpretation would come into its own during the Reformation, but Durant was quite oblivious to it – perhaps intentionally so. His reading of Romans 13 presupposed the confidence that divine and human power were joined in a single, intelligible order, which

6:11–59. Durant's use of the principle that 'exempla plus movent quam verba' poses interesting questions. He repeated it in a slightly different formulation, but with the same attribution to Seneca, in *TMI* 1 (3.1), fol. 52ra: 'Facta verbis contraria plusquam ipsa verba secundum Senecam moveant.' Nevertheless I have not been able to find it in the writings of the older or the younger Seneca. A close parallel is reported among medieval proverbs, without attribution: 'Exemplo melius quam verbo quisque docetur.' Walther, *Proverbia*, no. 8,420. The closest parallel that I have been able to find occurs in the preface of Humbert of Romans' *Liber de dono timoris*, an influential collection of *exempla* also known as *Tractatus de habundancia exemplorum*, where it is attributed to Pope Gregory I: 'Quoniam plus exempla quam verba movent secundum Gregorium.' Welter, *L'Exemplum*, p. 72; on the *Liber de dono timoris* in general see ibid., pp. 70–4, 224–8; cf. Brémond, Le Goff and Schmitt, *L'Exemplum*; Brett, *Humbert of Romans*. Pope Gregory did indeed often express the same sentiment; see Welter, *L'Exemplum*, pp. 14f. But Gregory, like Seneca, seems never to have used the exact words quoted by Humbert and Durant. Given the close coincidence between Durant's and Humbert's wording, it is conceivable that the *Liber de dono timoris*, a rather influential book surviving in more than forty manuscripts, furnished the source of Durant's quotation. But given the stereotypical nature of the quotation, that can hardly be taken for granted. Besides, it does not answer the far more important question of why Durant attributed this maxim from the medieval literature on *exempla* to one of the chief Stoic philosophers.

[40] Romans 13:5.

made it easy enough to determine whether or not government fulfilled its divinely appointed duty. In his opinion, government that did not obey the law clearly lacked divine support and deserved to be resisted.[41]

The evocation of a divinely ordained order of power furnished Durant with an excellent argument for establishing limits on government. The only step that remained to complete his case was to define what those limits were. It would have been easiest, of course, if they could have been identified with the laws Durant had listed in the previous chapter, and there can be no doubt that this is precisely what he wished to argue. However, there was a major difficulty: rulers were subject to God, but they were also exempt from law. Durant immediately addressed himself to this issue:

If it is objected that they are absolved of the laws, one may reply that they are not absolved of divine laws. For according to Pope Urban, not even the Roman pontiff may issue a new law where the Lord or his apostles and the holy fathers succeeding them have passed definitive judgment, but he must rather enforce those decrees with body and soul. If, God forbid, he should strive to destroy what the apostles and the prophets have taught, he would not issue proper sentences but would rather be convicted of error. Pope Zosimus wrote that not even the authority of the apostolic see can enact decrees or make any changes in conflict with the statutes of the fathers. For, as Zosimus said, the past shall remain alive with us and its roots shall not be torn out, because the fathers decreed that it must be treated with reverence. Pope Gelasius wrote that no see ought to observe and execute conciliar constitutions more readily than the see of Rome. Pope Damasus wrote that those who wilfully violate the canons are judged gravely by the holy fathers and that their condemnation is inspired by the same Holy Spirit by whose gift those canons were pronounced. It therefore seems appropriate to say that anyone who shamelessly infringes upon the holy canons, or who presumes to contradict them, or of his own accord agrees with those who want to contradict them, not because he is compelled by necessity, but wilfully, as has been said before – such a one blasphemes the Holy Spirit. For such presumption is manifestly a kind of blasphemy against the Holy Spirit since it is directed against him at whose command and with whose grace the holy canons were issued, as has been explained. All of which makes it perfectly clear that not only the statutes

---

[41] This confidence distinguished Durant's conception of political order from early modern views of sovereignty while at the same time linking it to early modern theories of resistance. But it should be stressed that at other points his confidence was seriously shaken; see for example below, pp. 154–6.

of divine law but also those issued by the holy fathers in councils and the holy canons must be obeyed.[42]

This was an impressive concatenation of some of the most famous canons that ecclesiastical constitutionalists had employed to limit the power of the papacy – but it concealed an intellectual sleight of hand.[43] Durant's reply to the objection that popes and kings were exempt from the laws was that they were not exempt from divine laws; that was unexceptionable. But his conclusion 'that not only the statutes of divine law, but also those issued by the holy fathers in councils and the holy canons must be obeyed' went further: it appeared to equate conciliar law with divine law. There is no other point at which Durant came so close to making this

---

[42] 'Et si dicatur quod legibus sunt soluti, potest responderi quod non divinis. Nam secundum Urbanum papam etiam Romanus pontifex, ubi Dominus vel eius apostoli et eos sequentes sancti patres sententialiter aliquid diffiniverunt, ibi non legem novam dare sed potius quod predictum est usque ad animam et sanguinem confirmare debet. Si enim quod docuerunt apostoli et prophete destruere, quod absit, niterentur, non sententiam dare sed magis errare convincerentur. Zosimus etiam papa scribit quod contra statuta patrum condere aliquid vel mutare nec huius quidem sedis apostolice potest autoritas. Apud nos enim inconvulsis radicibus, sicut inquit dictus Zosimus, vivat antiquitas, cui decreta patrum censerunt reverentiam exhibendam, xxv. q. i. c. contra, et c. sunt quidam. Gelasius etiam papa scribit, eadem c. et q. confidimus, quod nullam sedem magis oportet servare et exequi a sinodis constituta quam sedem Romanam. Damasus etiam papa scribit quod violatores canonum voluntarie graviter a sanctis patribus iudicantur et a *Sancto Spiritu* [P] instinctu, cuius ac dono dicati sunt, damnantur quoniam blasphemare Spiritum Sanctum non incongrue videntur qui contra eosdem sacros canones, non necessitate compulsi, sed libenter, ut premissum est, aliquid aut proterve agunt, aut loqui presumunt, aut facere volentibus sponte consentiunt. Talis enim presumptio manifeste unum genus est blasphemantium Spiritum Sanctum quoniam, ut iam prelibatum est, contra eum agit cuius nutu et gratia sancti canones editi sunt, eadem c. et q. violatores. Ex quibus liquide constat quod non solum statuta in divinis legibus verum etiam a sanctis patribus in conciliis et sacris canonibus servari debent.' *TMA* 1.3, fol. 5rb–va. Cf. C.25 q.1 c.6–7, C.25 q.1 c.1, C.25 q.1 c.5. The quotations continue with a reference to Pope Leo I, two to Gregory I, and five others, all of which make essentially the same point: C.25 q.1 c.16, C.25 q.2 c.4, D.15 c.1–3, D.16 c.7–8, D.12 c.5. On C.25 q.1 c.6, *Sunt quidam*, which is absolutely crucial for the doctrine of the 'state of the church', see, e.g., Post, 'Copyists' Errors', pp. 378–81, 398–402; Tierney, *Foundations*, p. 81; Schleyer, *Anfänge*, p. 35; Marrone, 'Ecclesiology', pp. 74 n. 75, 148; Gagnér, *Studien*, pp. 180f., and above, p. 78 n. 25. Durant saved the similarly important C.25 q.1 c.3, *Que ad perpetuam*, for a later occasion; see below, p. 166 n. 97.

[43] It also poses serious technical questions about the degree to which terms and phrases such as *ubi sancti patres sententialiter aliquid diffiniverunt, sententia, statuta patrum, decreta patrum, a sinodis constituta, canones, statuta a sanctis patribus in conciliis et sacris canonibus* all refer to the same thing. But here, as on so many other occasions in the *Tractatus Maior*, there is no point in pursuing those questions because Durant displayed no interest in them whatsoever. Whatever the differences between these terms, he was clearly convinced that they were similar enough to lump them together.

equation which would have vastly extended the scope of laws that
government was bound to obey without exception. Yet in reality
the strength of his conclusion was purely rhetorical. Coming right
on the heels of a declaration that violations of conciliar canons
amounted to blasphemy, it fudged the line between divine laws
and conciliar laws. It took advantage of an association of ideas in
order to let some of the immutability of divine law rub off on
conciliar law, but to a critical observer that was scarcely enough to
prove the point. Simon of Beaulieu, in his battle with the
mendicants, had once tried to declare that the contentious canon
*Omnis utriusque* of the Fourth Lateran Council was divine law
because it was directly rooted in Scripture, but he had been
defeated.[44] Conciliar law was not so easily identified with divine
law, and Durant was well aware of that. Indeed, in the *Tractatus
Minor* he roundly included conciliar canons in the category of
human laws.[45] Like his predecessors in the battles of the 1280s, he
surely would have loved to turn them into a part of divine law and
went as far as possible to make his readers think they were, but he
was bound to lose that case and he knew it.[46] The binding force of
conciliar law had to be established on different grounds.

Durant had already tacitly supplied one such argument in the
course of leading his readers to think he was going to demonstrate
the divine nature of conciliar law. For all of the canons he had
quoted had been issued by popes, and all of them expressed the
same conviction: conciliar laws ought to be obeyed by everyone
and above all by the see of Rome itself. If this was so there seemed
to be no need to look for an extraneous source of obligation: the
papacy had obligated itself. In many ways this was much better
than an extraneous source of obligation. It meant that Durant
could circumvent the question of what precisely was divine about

[44] Marrone, 'Ecclesiology', pp. 147–9. Henry of Ghent wisely disagreed, but that did not
spare him from defeat; ibid., p. 154.
[45] '... moribus, hoc est humanis legibus Sancti Spiritus instinctu in canonibus apostolorum,
conciliis, et a Romanis pontificibus et a catholicis principibus prelatis.' *TMI* 8 (3.31), fol.
61vb.
[46] Durant's fudging on the divine nature of conciliar law is highly reminiscent of the case of
Thomas of Bailly. In responding to Benedict XI's bull *Inter cunctas* of 1304, which was a
resounding victory for the mendicant point of view, Thomas, who surely bore the events
of 1290 in mind, went through similar contortions to prove the divinity of *Omnis
utriusque* (X.5.38.12) without actually saying so; Marrone, 'Ecclesiology', pp. 215–21.
John of Pouilly did say so and got into serious trouble as a result; Marrone, 'Ecclesiology',
pp. 249f.

conciliar laws. However, it also raised the question of whether or not the papacy was irrevocably bound by laws that rested on its own authority.

This very question had been debated towards the end of the thirteenth century in the context of the papacy's shifting policies toward the mendicants.[47] More recently Pope Clement V's decision to take several diplomatic steps back from *Unam sanctam* and *Clericis laicos* in order to mollify Philip IV had given further food for thought about the degree to which the papacy was entitled to change positions it had once formally adopted. In the second part of his treatise Durant declared without reservations that 'according to the last canon of the second council of Carthage any prelate or other person should be deposed for going against what they have consented or subscribed to before', and he spoke out sharply against 'the Roman church, where it has sometimes happened that the lord pope revoked not only the favours and concessions granted by his predecessors but even such as he himself had granted, in conflict with ecclesiastical and juridical gravity, authority, and honesty'.[48] At least this once Durant thus found himself agreeing with a mendicant point of view: the papacy must not take back its word.[49] But even though he was surely gratified to be able to quote an ancient canon that defined deposition as the appropriate penalty for clerics who reversed their own considered judgment on important matters, he shied away from any systematic discussion of the principle by which this canon could be countered and over which the mendicants had failed: *par in parem*

---

[47] A point made famous by Tierney, *Origins of Papal Infallibility*.

[48] 'Item cum in ultimo capitulo predicti secundi concilii Carthaginensis fuerit constitutum ut quicunque prelati et alii contra illa in quibus consenserunt vel subscripserunt venerint, deponantur, \*et\* [P] cum non deceat inconstantiam et \*instabilitatem\* [P] in Dei ecclesia reperiri (et in hoc sit conforme concilio Africano, extra de pactis c. i. et aliis iuribus, xx. q. i. puelle in fine, xxii. q. iv. innocens, xviii. q. ii. Eleutherius, ff. de pactis iuris gentium §. pretor ait), et hoc hodie non servetur, hoc videretur honorabile et utile observari, ne paulatim gravitas ecclesiastica deperire videatur, maxime in ecclesia Romana, in qua visum est quod dominus papa revocabat aliquando non solum gratias et alia concessa a predecessoribus suis, verum etiam facta et concessa a seipso contra gravitatem, autoritatem, et honestatem ecclesiasticam et iuridicam, xxv. q. i. et q. ii. quasi per totum, xii. q. ii. hec huius placiti.' *TMA* 2.29, fol. 28ra–b. Cf. II Carthaginense c.13, X.1.35.1, C.20 q.1 c.8, C.22 q.4 c.23, C.18 q.2 c.30, Dig.2.14.7.7, C.25 q.1, C.25 q.2, C.12 q.2 c.38.

[49] Of course, there was a difference: the mendicants tried to prevent the papacy from taking back exemptions once they had been granted, whereas Durant tried to prevent the papacy from granting exemptions against general law in the first place.

*non habet imperium*, which meant that no pope could be obliged to obey decisions by another pope.[50] Presumably Durant recognized that obligations which the papacy imposed upon itself were useful but not sufficient for his purposes. At any rate he left this line of thought implicit and, in the rubric on the 'need to limit the power of superiors', continued on a different route.

Before taking that route, however, Durant extended his conclusion that the papacy was bound to obey conciliar canons in two directions. First, he capped what had been an uninterrupted series of papal pronouncements with a canon that not only had been issued by a council but that also was the very first canon in the entire treatise that had not been included in the *Decretum*. He quoted it directly from the Pseudo-Isidorean collection: 'And the first chapter of the third council of Toledo contains [the rule] that everyone ought to observe and guard the statutes of councils and the decrees of the bishops of Rome.'[51] The source and placement of this canon were hardly accidental. While its substance was not new, merely restating the conclusion that had already been established, citation of this canon served a new purpose: it demonstrated the harmony between papal letters and a Toledan canon that had been omitted from classical canon law, highlighting the fact that the popes were not the only ones who had insisted on the obligation of the church of Rome to abide by conciliar statutes. Councils, even forgotten ones, had done so, too. Because its doctrinal content was identical with that of the preceding papal letters but differed from them in the source of its authority, this canon entered into a kind of circular relationship with them. Its content agreed with their content; hence the papacy appeared to have accepted the authority of this canon; hence its authority was confirmed and could perhaps be used apart or even against that of the papacy. The logic by which Durant introduced the Toledan canon is thus not syllogistic. It draws its power from establishing an identity, in this case the identity of the authority of papal letters with that of a forgotten conciliar canon. It may be called the logic

---

[50] The *locus classicus* is Innocent III in X.1.6.20 as adapted from Dig.4.8.3.4, Dig.4.8.4, and Dig.36.1.13.4. On the details see Tierney, *Origins of Papal Infallibility*; Brys, *De dispensatione*, p. 239; Kuttner, 'Pope Lucius III', pp. 425f.

[51] 'Et in primo capitulo tertii concilii Toletani continetur, quod conciliorum statuta et presulum Romanorum decreta serventur et custodiantur a cunctis.' *TMA* 1.3, fol. 5va–b. According to the indices in Friedberg's edition this canon did not enter into the *Decretum*.

of accretion or amplification, and we shall have more to say about it later on.[52]

Second, Durant extended his argument from the spiritual to the temporal sphere:

Concerning secular rulers there is no doubt at all [that they are subject to the laws] since they themselves profess their wish to live according to their laws. Isidore, moreover, writes in book 3, chapter 52 of his work *On the Highest Good* that it is just for a prince to obey his laws. For he may only believe that his laws must be observed by all if he himself displays his reverence for them. And it is just that princes are bound by their laws and cannot reject as wrong for their own persons what they established as right for their subjects. For the authority of their voice is only just if they do not allow themselves to do what they prohibit their people from doing.[53]

In the secular sphere, in other words, there was no doubt at all that the rulers were bound by their own laws because they themselves had said as much. If Durant had had to leave implicit the argument that the papacy had bound itself to obey conciliar law, at least he could declare expressly that secular rulers had obliged themselves to obey secular laws.

At this stage in his argument Durant had thus established a general obligation of spiritual and temporal government to abide not only by divine but also by certain human laws. But the weight of his documentation should not seduce us into misleading conclusions about its effects. No one had ever believed that any ruler had a right to abandon general laws at will, as though there were no difference between the decrees of the most hallowed institutions of the Christian Republic and a ruler's momentary whims. In this respect Durant's insistence on obedience to the laws was thoroughly uncontroversial. It would have been more to the point, but

---

[52] Durant employed precisely the same tool to lend authority to the principle that 'what touches all must be approved by all'. See below, pp. 281–3.

[53] 'De principibus autem secularibus nequaquam dubium est quin ipsi se velle fateantur vivere secundum leges eorum, C. de legibus, digna vox est, et C. de testamentis, ex imperfecto, et ff. de legatis tertio, ex imperfecto, Inst. quibus modis testamenta infirmentur §. ultimo. Isidorus insuper scribit in tertio libro de summo bono, c. lii., et ponitur pro palea in decretis, ix. di., quod iustum est principem legibus obtemperare suis. Tunc enim iura sua ab omnibus custodienda existimet, quando et ipse illis reverentiam prebet. Principes legibus teneri suis, nec in se posse damnare iura que in subiectis constituunt iustum est. Iusta est enim vocis eorum autoritas si que populis prohibent sibi licere non patiantur.' *TMA* 1.3, fol. 5vb. Cf. Cod.1.14.4, Cod.6.23.3, Dig.32.1.23, Ins.2.17.8, D.9 c.2.

also far more controversial, had he argued that no exceptions from general laws at all were permissible, especially not from conciliar canons. It is clear enough that he would have liked to subscribe to that point of view; some interpreters have even concluded that he did.[54] But we have already noted that, in spite of the rhetoric he used to intimate such a radical extension of conventional doctrine, he stopped short of making it explicit. He insinuated that conciliar laws were divine but never said so in so many words; he implied that the papacy had obliged itself to obey conciliar canons but did not state clearly whether the pope was invariably bound by the decisions of his predecessors. He knew perfectly well, in other words, that conciliar canons were not divine law in the same immutable sense as the Law and the Gospel simply because they had been passed by councils.

These were obstacles that he could not remove, so he did the next best thing: he buried them under a mound of citations calculated to convince by its sheer weight and cleverly constructed to obfuscate the central issue. But that kind of argument could not withstand intensive scrutiny. In the end it did not help him to remove the objection that rulers were exempt from law with regard to precisely those laws that mattered most to his case: conciliar and general human laws. Durant would therefore have to rest his case for limiting the ability of rulers to modify or circumvent human laws on other grounds than he had so far offered.

### GOVERNMENT BOUND BY REASON AND PRECEDENT

Considerations such as these were probably on Durant's mind as he decided to address the 'need to limit the power of superiors' in a separate rubric immediately following the third chapter. Here he shifted his position from law to reason and the precedents furnished

---

[54] E.g. Scholz, *Publizistik*, p. 222: '[Er rechnet] die Konzilsbeschlüsse, weil sie vom heiligen Geist inspiriert sind, zum göttlichen Rechte, während die ohne Konzil erlassenen päpstlichen Dekretalen nur zu den menschlichen Satzungen gehören, die unter Umständen widerrufen werden können'; p. 223: 'Duranti . . . erklärt, dass dem Papste weder gegen (contra ea) noch über das (super his), was die Apostel und Konzilsväter bestimmten, ein Gesetzgebungsrecht zusteht.' This is simply wrong. Tierney, *Foundations*, p. 195, is slightly more cautious: 'Guilielmus Durantis seems to have overstepped the bounds of Decretist thought in thus applying the *Quod omnes tangit* principle to the general legislative authority of the Papacy, for Joannes Teutonicus had maintained in a quite contrary sense that to deny the Roman See's right of establishing law for the whole church was heresy.' With reference to Joannes' gloss *ad* D.19 c.5.

by antiquity – that is, from law to underlying principles of law and to concrete instances of lawfulness. The shift was permanent. From this point on he was no longer going to repeat what he seemed to have said in the third chapter, namely that limits on government were to consist of law and nothing else. Instead he would seek to define limits on government by relying on reason and ancient examples:

For power must be ruled, limited, and restricted by reason, so that reason rules overall, as Pope Gregory wrote to Emperor Maurice in order to prove that constitutions that were instituted and handed on down by superiors and predecessors must be conserved and not despised by inferiors and successors. This agrees with the example given by Christ, who accepted the sacraments of the church in order to sanctify them in his own person before he commanded others to observe them. For injustices must not arise whence rights arise, as Innocent III wrote in X.5.1.17. And he who ought to defend justice on my behalf ought not to attack me, nor may someone do what he must prohibit others from doing. Since therefore the highest good in all things is to cultivate justice and to preserve his rights for each and not to let any subjects usurp the exercise of power but to keep equity intact, as Gregory wrote to Queen Constance of France, this is what the lord pope and all kings ought to thirst for. For as the same Gregory wrote to Romanus, the defender of Sicily, our duty is to protect the order of the church. But if we fail to preserve each bishop in his rights of jurisdiction, what are we doing if not confounding the order of the church? Which is why Augustine says that, if justice is removed, kingdoms and dominions are nothing other than great bands of robbers.[55]

---

[55] 'Regenda igitur atque limitanda et restringenda est sub ratione potestas ut totum ratio regat, sicut Gregorius Mauritio imperatori scribit, xi. q. iii. illa prepositorum, ad hoc ut ab eorum superioribus vel predecessoribus tradita ab eis constituta aliis conservanda, non contemnenda, demonstret, exemplo Christi qui sacramenta ecclesie que observanda mandavit primum in se ipso suscepit ut ea in se ipso sanctificaret, xx. q. i. §. his ita, Luc. ii. c. Non enim debent nasci iniurie unde iura nascuntur, sicut Innocentius iii. scribit, extra de accusationibus, qualiter et quando, primo, C. unde vi, meminerint. Et qui me debet defendere in iustitia non debet me impugnare, nec debet quis facere illud a quo debet alios prohibere, extra de natis ex libero ventre, c. unico, de clericis coniugatis, diversis falatiis, xxvi. di. deinde, xlii. di. §. i., xi. q. i. silvester, ff. si servitus vindicetur, alicuius, ff. de conditione indebiti, frater a fratre, ff. de evictionibus, venditorem, ff. de negotiis gestis, l. si pupilli §. videamus, ff. de administratione tutorum, quoties. Cum itaque summum bonum in rebus sit iustitiam colere atque sua cuique iura servare, et in subditis non sinere quod potestatis est fieri, sed quod equum est custodiri, sicut Gregorius ad Constantiam reginam Francie scribit, xii. q. ii. dum devotissimam, ad hoc debent dominus papa et omnes reges anhelare. Nam sicut idem Gregorius Romano defensori Sicilie *scribit* [P], si qua unicuique episcopo iurisditio non servatur, *quid aliud agitur nisi ut per nos per quos ecclesiasticus ille ordo custodiri debuerat, confundatur* [P], xi. q. i. pervenit. Unde enim ait Augustinus iiii. de civitate Dei, remota iustitia quid sunt regna et dominia nisi

# The assertion of justice

This appeal to underlying principles of law – like reason, equity, the highest good, and justice – raises many questions. Because there are important differences between all of these principles, while each of them has a different relationship to law, they can provide much substance for elaborate investigations of the details of legal doctrine.[56] But even though Durant must have been well aware of such questions, he showed no interest whatsoever in pursuing them. His point was simple. He treated reason, equity, and justice in a single breath because, whatever their differences, they all shared an essential quality: they placed inviolable limits on the power of government. They constituted the immutable, essential core of law from which the constitutions of the past derived their meaning and, as he was quick to emphasize, they furnished the foundation for the order of the church.

Durant thus changed the nature of the argument. So far it had been about the question of whether rulers were exempt from law. Now it was whether rulers were exempt from reason (using 'reason' as a shorthand for all underlying principles of law). In one sense that improved his case, since reason was inviolable and immutable. Now he could say that 'reason should rule overall' without qualification and could advert to St Augustine's fundamental declaration that temporal kingdoms must be founded on justice, that is, true Christian justice, if they are to be better than

magna latrocinia?' *TMA* 1.3 De limitanda potestate, fols. 5vb–6ra. Cf. C.11 q.3 c.67, C.25 q.1 p.c.16 §. *his ita*, Luke 2:22–4, Luke 2:39–40, X.5.1.17, Cod.8.4.6, X.4.10.1, X.3.3.5, D.26 c.3, D.42 a.c.1, C.11 q.1 c.13, Dig.8.5.15, Dig.12.6.38, Dig.21.2.17, Dig.3.5.5.14, Dig.26.7.9, C.12 q.2 c.9, C.11 q.1 c.39, Augustine, *De civitate Dei* 4.4. The language of restricting power *sub ratione* had been prominently used in the French gravamina against Innocent IV of 1247; cf. Matthew Paris, *Chronica* 6:104, 110.
[56] The potential for complexity is vast and the literature is extensive. The topic is best approached through Gagnér, *Studien zur Ideengeschichte*; Buisson, *Potestas und Caritas*; Post, 'Copyists' Errors'; Post, 'Vincentius Hispanus'; Kuttner, 'Pope Lucius III'; Kuttner, 'Urban II'. Brys, *De dispensatione*, remains an extremely useful guide to the doctrines of the decretists and the decretalists on papal legislative activity because it is straightforward, systematic, and faithful to the sources. Cortese, *La norma giuridica*, is the fullest account available. Le Bras *et al.*, *L'Age classique*, pp. 347–557, contains a good summary by Charles Lefebvre, whose only fault is that it occasionally favours systematic clarity over history. Kisch, *Erasmus und die Jurisprudenz*, is excellent on the conflict between ancient, medieval, and modern conceptualizations of equity, but cf. Caron, '"Aequitas et Interpretatio" dans la doctrine canonique'. See also Balon, 'La "ratio" fondement et justification du droit'; Caron, *Aequitas romana*; D'Agostino, *La tradizione dell'epieikeia*; Wohlhaupter, *Aequitas canonica*; Kuttner, 'Sur les origines du terme "droit positif"'; Lefebvre, *Les Pouvoirs du juge*. Meijers, 'Le Conflit entre l'équité et la loi', and Brown, 'Cessante causa', are good for secular law. For Germanic conceptions Kern, 'Recht und Verfassung', is still classic, but should be read in conjunction with Klinkenberg, 'Die Theorie der Veränderbarkeit', and Krause, 'Dauer und Vergänglichkeit'.

bands of criminals. The trouble was, of course, that reason, justice, and equity lacked definitive content: their exact meaning could not be written down or looked up but only thought about, and thought about again. Durant thus found himself in a dilemma. The laws were specific but mutable; reason and justice had immutability to spare but were abstract. By themselves neither the one nor the other provided the sought-after means of making government conform to God's order. But at least they suggested a new way of approaching the problem: the task was no longer to impose the law on rulers but rather to keep law joined to reason.

In the remainder of the rubric Durant turned to specific examples in an attempt to demonstrate that law and reason had been united in the past. At first sight this may seem to reflect nothing more than a moralizer's yearning for better times and places – and to some degree it does. But it has a systematic function, too. Unlike reason, which had to be defined, and laws, which had to be interpreted, examples needed neither definition nor interpretation. They merely needed to be exhibited to plain view for everyone to see what justice really was. Conceptually speaking they fell somewhere in between reason and law, identical with neither, but for that very reason capable of teaching how they were to be combined.

The most important example was obviously that of Christ. On two previous occasions Durant had relied on Christ's example to prove that law must be obeyed – first in the opening lines of chapter 1, where he reminded his readers of Christ's injunction not to remove motes in their brothers' eyes without removing the beams in their own, and then at the beginning of the third chapter, where he used the example of Christ to emphasize to rulers their obligation not merely to teach the law but to practise it as well. This time he drew attention to 'the example of Christ, who first received the sacraments of the church himself in order to sanctify them in his own person before commanding others to observe them'.[57] The reference was to Christ's circumcision and his presentation in the Temple, and its meaning was clear. Could there be any better proof that justice required obedience to the law than that the founder of the Christian faith himself had obeyed the law of the Old Testament? Could there be any better reason to persuade the rulers of today to obey the law of the past?

[57] See above, n. 55.

This was the most important example at Durant's disposal, but he was no longer content to stay within the limits of Christianity. He turned to the history of pagan antiquity in order to convince his readers that obedience to law was no exclusively Christian virtue, since

the ancients who did not even have a notion of divine law observed this very justice [which St Augustine declared essential if kingdoms and dominions were to be anything other than great bands of robbers]. For as Valerius Maximus tells us and proves by many examples, they observed their laws in their own persons, made their people obey them, and even imposed them on others, but they were most concerned to obey them in their own persons. And he says this in order to criticize the powerful who do not observe their own laws but force others to obey them who are weaker than they.[58]

On the following pages Durant offered a brief but nicely constructed anthology of ancient virtues.[59] Some of his stories entered schoolbooks where even today they sometimes continue to fulfil their exemplary function. There is Marcus Regulus, whom the Carthaginians sent to Rome in order to procure the release of their men from captivity and who died a cruel death at the hands of his captors because he preferred the good of Rome to his own and kept the sacred oath that he would return to Carthage.[60] There is Fabricius, who refused the gold that had been offered him because he much preferred to rule the men who had the gold than to have the gold himself.[61] And there is Quintius Cincinnatus, the modest

---

[58] 'Hanc autem iustitiam servasse leguntur veteres qui etiam divine legis notitiam non habebant. Nam que in eorum erant statuta legibus in seipsis, prout narrat Valerius, in suis et in aliis et plusquam in aliis observabant, sicut per multa probat exempla. Quod contra illos potentes qui non observant leges quas condunt, sed alios infirmiores observare compellunt.' *TMA* 1.3 De limitanda potestate, fol. 6ra (*male* 7ra).

[59] Durant mentions the original sources of most of his evidence. They consist of Augustine's *De civitate Dei* 1.15, 4.4, 5.12, 5.18, 18.19; Valerius Maximus' *Facta et dicta memorabilia* 4.3(5–6), 4.4(6), 6.3(3), 7.2(14); and Cicero's *De officiis* 1.13(39), 1.25(85), 3.26(99). The main exception consists of an unacknowledged quotation from John of Salisbury's *Policraticus*, 4.11, on which see below, n. 66. Whether or not Durant relied on any intermediate sources is an important question which I have found impossible to answer with certainty. But given the great fame of his sources, the limited number of chapters from which he borrowed, and the excellent match between his evidence and the uses to which he put it, it seems likely that he did not rely on any intermediate sources but compiled this collection of republican virtues himself. I have pointed out a few important parallels to other writings in the notes.

[60] *TMA* 1.3 De limitanda potestate, fol. 6ra (*male* 7ra); quoted from Augustine, *De civitate Dei* 1.15; Cicero, *De officiis* 1.13(39), 3.26(99).

[61] *TMA* 1.3 De limitanda potestate, fol. 6va (*male* 7va); cf. Valerius Maximus, *Facta et dicta memorabilia* 4.3(6).

farmer who was made dictator and nevertheless returned to his plough and frugal life as soon as he had defeated the enemies of Rome.[62]

These stories and others like them were carefully selected and arranged to illustrate one general principle and two crucial virtues. The general principle was that the ancients had placed the common good of all above the private good of some:

As Tully says in *De officiis*, Plato had two precepts for those who want to govern well and advance the commonwealth, namely, first, to aim only at civic utility and to be oblivious to their private advantage and, second, not to take care of only a part of the commonwealth but to attend to its whole body, lest they should neglect the other parts.[63]

The two virtues were the ancients' abhorrence of greed and their scrupulous avoidance of personal considerations in making appointments to public offices. Concerning money,

they governed the commonwealth salubriously indeed because they had the praiseworthy desire to remain poor in their own homes so that the commonwealth might abound, and they never tried to rule for the sake of material gain or personal honour.[64]

Concerning office, the ancient rulers 'did not want to preside over the commonwealth in any way unless they could be of real help to it'.[65] Even Scipio refused to accept the command in Spain that had

---

[62] *TMA* 1.3 De limitanda potestate, fol. 6va (*male* 7va); cf. Augustine, *De civitate Dei* 5.18.

[63] 'Duo etiam fuerunt precepta Platonis, sicut ait Tullius libro primo de officiis, volentibus rem publicam salubriter gubernare et rei publice prodesse. Unum videlicet ut utilitatem civium sic tuerentur ut quecunque agerent ad eam referrent, obliti commodorum suorum. Alterum ut totum corpus rei publice curarent, ne dum ad partem aliquam attenderent, reliquam desererent.' *TMA* 1.3 De limitanda potestate, fol. 6rb (*male* 7rb). Cf. Cicero, *De officiis* 1.25(85) and Plato, *Republic* 1, 342E, and 4, 420B. This crucial aspect of the classical definition of the body politic was clearly an integral part of the medieval tradition. It occurs in William of Conches' *Moralium dogma philosophorum*, p. 36, and in Brunetto Latini's *Li livres dou tresor*, 2.85.2, but not in John of Salisbury's *Policraticus*. As late as the fifteenth century Aeneas Silvius Piccolomini, *Opera inedita*, p. 579, as cited by Prodi, *Papal Prince*, p. 12, used the same passage to demonstrate 'the possibility of Christian exercise of sovereignty as a ministry of God'.

[64] 'Illud nempe erat laudabile studium rem publicam salubriter gubernantibus ut ipsi in suis domibus pauperes essent et res publica abundaret. Quia dominari propter lucrum et propter honorem nullatenus intendebant.' *TMA* 1.3 De limitanda potestate, fol. 6va (*male* 7va); cf. Augustine, *De civitate Dei* 5.18.

[65] 'De eisdem narrat Valerius libro vi. quod nullo modo rei publice preesse volebant nisi et prodesse valerent. Et ponit exemplum de Cornelio Scipione qui, cum in Hispaniam ut iret forte evenisset, respondit se nolle illuc ire addita causa quod se recte facere nesciret.' *TMA* 1.3 De limitanda potestate, fol. 6va (*male* 7va). Cf. Valerius Maximus, *Facta et dicta memorabilia* 6.3(3).

been offered to him because he was unsure if he could do any good by going there. Still more important,

on top of that these good administrators of the commonwealth did not suffer their sons and other relatives to assist them unless they could be of use to the commonwealth. Hence the following story is reported of Helius Adrianus: when he had been raised from the rank of a senator to that of an emperor, the senate implored him to nominate his son as Augustus Caesar. He replied: It ought to be enough, I say, that I myself shall have ruled against my will. For the principate is not owed to flesh and blood, but to merit. Someone who is born to be a king and does not merit it rules uselessly. Parents who destroy their little ones by imposing insupportable burdens on their shoulders are undoubtedly not moved by parental love. For to promote unworthy relatives in such a way is not to promote them, but to suffocate them. Children must first be trained in virtue. When they have made sufficient progress they must be tried, and among those who have then proved their worth the better ones must be preferred to the rest.[66]

[66] 'Prefati insuper boni administratores rei publice non patiebantur filios et alios propinquos eis adsistere nisi rei publice possent prodesse. Unde narratur in historiis de Helio Adriano, qui cum ex senatoribus esset creatus imperator, obsecrante senatu ut filium suum Augustum Cesarem nominaret, respondit: sufficere, inquam, debet ut ego ipse invitus regnaverim. Principatus enim non carni vel sanguini debetur, sed meritis: Inutiliter regnat, qui rex nascitur, et non meretur. Proculdubio parentum affectum exuit qui parvulos suos importabili mole superiecta extinguit. Hoc enim, scilicet taliter promovere indignos propinquos, est, ut ibi dicitur, non promovere sed suffocare eosdem. Alendi enim sunt primo virtutibus exercendi et, cum in eis profecerint, comprobandi et inter probatos meliores aliis preferendi.' *TMA* 1.3 De limitanda potestate, fol. 6va–b (*male* 7va–b). Without saying so Durant borrowed this interesting story as well as the moralizing comments about its meaning from John of Salisbury, *Policraticus* 4.11, ed. Webb, 1:275f. It is the only example of ancient conduct in the present section which he did not take from Augustine, Cicero, or Valerius Maximus and, as far as I know, the only direct evidence of his familiarity with the *Policraticus*. Professor Johannes Straub has kindly led me to John of Salisbury's source, which Webb had not been able to identify. It has nothing to do with Emperor Hadrian, but consisted of Jerome's description of Helvius Pertinax's accession to power in AD 193: 'Pertinax septuagenario maior, cum praefecturam urbis ageret, ex senatus consulto imperare iussus est . . . Pertinax obsecrante senatu, ut uxorem suam Augustam et filium Caesarem appellaret, contradixit sufficere testatus quod ipse regnaret invitus.' Hieronymus, *Chronik*, p. 210. This was repeated with slight changes by Jordanes: 'Helvius Pertinax maior sexagenario cum praefecturam ageret, ex senatus consulto imperator creatus regnavit m. VI. hic etenim obsecrante senatu, ut uxorem suam Augustam filiumque Caesarem appellaret, "sufficere", inquit, "debet, quod ego ipse invitus regnavi, cum non merer".' Jordanes, *Romana et Getica*, p. 35. Both accounts agree in speaking of a nomination to become Caesar, not Augustus. The confusion between Hadrian and Pertinax, facilitated by the similarity of 'Aelius' with 'Helvius', was probably caused by Hadrian's greater fame and the plausible assumption that the sentiments actually expressed by Pertinax would have been suitable for one of the adoptive emperors.

Thus out of their respect for the common good the ancient pagans had managed to avoid the two vices that, in the opinion of the bishop of Mende and many other late medieval critics, were deeply troubling the contemporary church: avarice and nepotism.

With these observations Durant completed his description of the conduct of the ancient pagans and of the means that were available to make rulers conform to the will of God.[67] Law, reason, and the examples of antiquity, both of Christ and of the pagans, were the three main instruments with which he hoped to achieve the 'correction and reform of the church and a healthy regime for the human race'. It was a powerful combination – but not powerful enough.

As early as the beginning of the rubric on the 'power of superiors' readers familiar with canon law may have suspected that Durant was leading up to a difficulty. That was the point at which he invoked Christ's circumcision to prove that the founder of the Christian religion himself had obeyed the ancient law. But that proof could be turned around: Christ, after all, had come to establish a new dispensation, a New Testament that superseded the Old Testament. Indeed, Durant himself had subtly hinted at Christ's freedom from the law, for the source from which he quoted his example was one of Gratian's more famous *dicta*, and Gratian had interpreted the issue in a very different sense. He had begun his comments harmlessly enough:

If, then, the first see ought to observe the statutes of councils above all others, . . . it is obvious that the Apostolic Father must not grant any privileges contrary to the statutes of the holy canons by which the state of the churches would be confounded or perturbed.[68]

This much was entirely in accord with Durant's argument. But Gratian had continued in a rather different vein:

There is the following response to this: The sacrosanct Roman church imparts justice and authority to the holy canons, but it is not bound by

---

[67] In the heading of the third chapter Durant had already summarized those means: 'Quod predictus modus correctionis et reformationis ecclesie et christianitatis sit conveniens rationi et iuri, maxime quantum ad presidentes spirituali et temporali potestati, et quod non debeant transgredi iura sed se regere et limitare secundum ea et non querere que sua sunt sed que Christi, nec aliorum iura usurpare sed sub ratione se regere. Et additur qualiter ab antiquo res publica gubernabatur.' *TMA* 1.3, fol. 5ra.

[68] 'Si ergo primam sedem statuta conciliorum pre omnibus servare oportet, . . . patet, quod contra statuta sanctorum canonum, quibus status ecclesiarum vel confundantur vel perturbantur, privilegia ab Apostolico concedi non debent.' C.25 q.1 p.c.16 §.*his ita.*

them. For inasmuch as it is the head and the pivot of all churches, from whose rule no one may dissent, it has the right to establish canons. It therefore imparts authority to the canons without subjecting itself to them. Just as Christ, who gave the law, carnally fulfilled the law to sanctify it in his own person with his circumcision on the eighth day and his presentation in the temple with sacrifices on the fortieth, but later healed the leper by his touch against the letter of the law in order to show himself to be the lord of law, . . . so also the pontiffs of the highest see exhibit their reverence to canons which they themselves established, or which others established by their authority, and they protect the canons by humbling themselves before them in order to demonstrate to others the need to observe them. Sometimes, however, they show by commands or definitions or decrees or simply by acting differently that they are the lords and founders of the decrees.[69]

This was one of Gratian's clearest statements of support for papal supremacy over the law, and it was famous for that reason. It left no doubt that Christ had in fact obeyed the law when he was circumcised, but that he had done so only to encourage reverence for laws that were essentially his own – not because he was bound to obey them. He was above the law, and he had demonstrated that as well. 'For the Son of Man is Lord even of the Sabbath day', as Matthew 12:8 had put it. All of this was part of the very same twenty-fifth *causa* from which Durant had taken his quotations of papal decrees to establish the papacy's obligation to obey the law, but it undermined that obligation by declaring that 'the sacrosanct Roman church imparts justice and authority to the holy canons, but is not bound by them'.

We cannot say if Durant's readers appreciated the hint that was implicit in quoting so obviously out of context from a well-known legal source, but if they did not now, they soon would.[70] Even

---

[69] 'His ita respondetur: Sacrosancta Romana ecclesia ius et auctoritatem sacris canonibus inpertit, sed non eis alligatur. Habet enim ius condendi canones, utpote que caput et cardo est omnium ecclesiarum, a cuius regula dissentire nemini licet. Ita ergo canonibus auctoritatem prestat, ut se ipsam non subiciat eis. Sed sicut Christus, qui legem dedit, ipsam legem carnaliter inplevit, octava die circumcisus, quadragesimo die cum hostiis in templo presentatus, ut in se ipso eam sanctificaret, postea vero, ut se dominum legis ostenderet, contra litteram legis leprosum tangendo mundavit . . . sic et summae sedis Pontifices canonibus a se sive ab aliis sua auctoritate conditis reverentiam exhibent, et eis se humiliando ipsos custodiant, ut aliis observandos exhibeant. Nonnunquam vero seu iubendo, seu diffiniendo, seu decernendo, seu aliter agendo se decretorum dominos et conditores esse ostendunt.' C.25 q.1 p.c.16 §.*his ita*. On C.25 q.1 p.c.16 see Brys, *De dispensatione*, pp. 77–9; Congar, 'Status ecclesiae', p. 10.

[70] Like his nephew the Speculator had used the very same passage to establish the papacy's obligation to abide by general law, but unlike his nephew he had been careful to add that

while he was still preoccupied with ancient virtues Durant began to introduce the problem of papal supremacy:

As Cato said, in words reported by St Augustine in *De civitate Dei*, the world is no longer being ruled as it used to be ruled at that time. And he went on: Do not believe that your ancestors turned a little commonwealth into a great one by relying on nothing but arms. If that were so, we would be much better off than they, for we have a much greater abundance of citizens and allies and even horses and arms than they. What made those men great in every respect were other things that we do not have – namely, industry at home, a just empire abroad, and a spirit free to give sound advice and not indebted to the lust for crime. Instead of these, as Cato added, we find luxury, avarice, public poverty, and private opulence in the rulers and administrators of our commonwealth. We praise wealth; we live in sloth; we do not distinguish between good and bad men; and ambition possesses every reward of virtue.[71]

This was an eloquent evocation of true republican virtue and a powerful indictment of the vice that seemed to beset the late medieval church. Its force was strengthened by the fact that it came from the mouth of an ancient pagan. Without losing a beat Durant turned to the rulers of his day:

Painful though it is to say, if such was the conduct of the [ancient] rectors and administrators of the commonwealth, who did not even have a notion of divine law, is it not an incalculable disgrace if modern administrators of the commonwealth, who have been illuminated by faith and who ought to illuminate and correct others, do not conduct

Gratian's commentary on papal authority implied a very different point of view; above pp. 78f. n.25. It thus seems reasonable to believe that anyone familiar with canon law would have noticed the younger Durant's implied disagreement with Gratian.

71 'Sed sicut ait Cato, cuius verba recitat Augustinus v. de civitate Dei xiiii., non sic nunc mundus regitur sicut tunc temporis regebatur. Unde ait ille Cato, nolite, inquit, existimare maiores vestros armis rem publicam ex parva magnam fecisse. Nam si ita esset, multo plura nos quam illi haberemus, quippe civium ac sociorum, preterea equorum armorumque maior copia nobis quam illis est. Sed alia fuere que illos viros magnos ubique fecerunt, que nobis nulla sunt, videlicet domi industria, foris iustum imperium, animus in consulendo liber, neque delictorum libidini obnoxius. Pro his autem, ut ille Cato subiicit, in personas regentium et administrantium rei publice nos habemus luxuriam, avariciam, publicam egestatem, privatam opulentiam, laudamus divitias, sequimur inhertiam, inter bonos et malos discrimen nullum, omnia virtutum premia ambitio possidet.' *TMA* 1.3 De limitanda potestate, fol. 6rb (*male* 7rb); cf. Augustine, *De civitate Dei* 5.12. Next to Cicero's advice on how to govern the commonwealth well, this famous piece of oratory contains the most important direct link between Durant's ideas and Roman republicanism. Like Cicero's advice it also entered into Latini's *Li livres dou tresor*, 3.37.8–9, but unlike Cicero's advice it can also be found in *Policraticus* 8.5.

themselves as well? For we must fear that they are very well aware when they reflect on their conduct in their hearts that they act contrary to law.[72]

It was an incalculable disgrace indeed. But the worst of it was that nothing could be done to stop it. Both of the authorities Durant cited at the end of this exclamation, D.17 p.c.6 and D.21 c.7, required nothing more ·from popes who had been charged with causing such disgrace than to reflect on their conduct in their hearts. Both were decisions of bishops assembled in council to consider the misconduct of a pope – but far from stopping such misconduct, the bishops had refrained even from determining if any misconduct had occurred. 'As far as human beings are concerned', they had said, 'Pope Symmachus, who presides over the apostolic see, although he has been charged, shall be immune and free from any opposition. We reserve his case entirely to the judgment of God.' And to Marcellinus they had said: 'Do not let yourself be heard in our court, but reflect on your conduct in your heart', and they had added as a general principle that 'the first see shall not be judged by anyone'.[73] In this principle Durant's plea for reform had finally encountered a seemingly insurmountable obstacle. How could the pope be made to obey the law if the law left him to his own devices? How could reason be brought to bear on his decisions if he was free to act as he pleased? The plan to base reform on law had thus foundered on the law itself and the 'short road to reform' had led into an abyss.

This time Durant had no answers left. A canon that exempted the pope from human judgment despite the fact that he did not even meet the standards of the ancient pagans made it impossible to join law to reason. There was a gap between the two in which power could assert itself absolutely, without restraint. The gap might be small, but it placed the entire temple of justice in danger of collapse.

---

[72] 'Proh dolor, si premissa servabantur in rectoribus et in administratoribus rei publice qui legis divine notitiam non habebant, nonne est inestimabile dedecus si moderni administratores rei publice, qui fide illuminati sunt et alios illuminare et corrigere debent, in se ipsis talia non observant? Verendum quippe est, si contrarium faciunt, quod et ipsi discernant et in sinu suo colligant causam suam, xvii. di. §. hinc etiam, xxi. di. nunc autem.' *TMA* 1.3 De limitanda potestate, fol. 6vb (*male* 7vb). Cf. D.17 p.c.6, D.21 c.7. On D.21 c.7 see Koeniger, 'Prima sedes', and Martin, 'Comment s'est formée la doctrine de la supériorité', pp. 121–43. John of Paris found D.21 c.7 quite unintelligible; Tierney, *Foundations*, p. 175.

[73] '"Simachus Papa sedis apostolicae presul ab huiusmodi oppositionibus impetitus quantum ad homines respicit, sit immunis et liber, cuius causam totam Dei iudicio reservamus."' D.17 p.c.6. '"Noli audiri in nostro iudicio, sed collige in sinu tuo causam tuam." . . . Et iterum dicunt: "Prima sedes non iudicabitur a quoquam."' D.21 c.7.

Deprived of arguments and confronted with power in the absolute, Durant began to change his tone. He threatened divine wrath:

What is said in Wisdom 6 is becoming true of the administrators of the commonwealth: Hear, O ye kings, and understand; learn, ye that be judges of the ends of the earth; give ear, ye that curb the multitudes and glory in the crowd of nations. For power is given you of the Lord, and virtue from the Highest, who shall try your works and search out your counsels. Because, being ministers of his kingdom, ye have not judged aright, nor kept the law of justice, nor walked after the will of God, horribly and speedily shall he appear to you, for the sharpest judgment shall be on those in high places. For mercy is granted to the mean, but mighty men shall be mightily tormented.[74]

He begged the pope to show respect for law:

I implore him to follow the precept of the fourth council of Carthage not to abide by his pleasure or custom, but by the definitions of the fathers.[75]

He expressed his sympathy for the terrible burdens placed upon the shoulders of rulers:

For as Gregory said in his *Moralia*, whatever is eminent in this world is afflicted with sorrows rather than enjoying honours. And in his *Pastoral Rule* he says that the burdens anyone is forced to bear are equal to those he has commanded to be borne in this world.[76]

And finally he repeated his conviction that reform had to be founded on law, examples, and the common good of Christians:

This much ought to be enough to prove that, if the ecclesiastical and the earthly powers wish to govern the world and the human race salubriously, they ought to conform their deeds and words to divine and

---

[74] 'Quod in eis comprobatur illud quod dicitur Sapientia vi. c.: Audite reges et intelligite, discite iudices finium terre, prebete aures vos qui continetis multitudines et placetis vobis in turbis nationum, quoniam data est a Domino potestas vobis et virtus ab altissimo, qui interrogabit opera vestra et cogitationes scrutabitur, quoniam, cum essetis ministri illius regni, non recte iudicastis neque custodistis legem iustitie neque secundum voluntatem Dei ambulastis, horrende et cito apparebit vobis quoniam iudicium durissimum in his qui presunt fiet. Exiguo enim conceditur misericordia, potentes autem potenter tormenta patientur.' *TMA* 1.3 De limitanda potestate, fols. 6vb–7ra (*male* 7vb–7ra). Cf. Wisdom 6:2–7.

[75] 'Obsecro itaque ut iuxta statuta Carthaginensis concilii quarti non sue delectationi nec suis moribus sed his patrum diffinitionibus acquiescat, xxiii. di. qui episcopi, in fine.' *TMA* 1.3 De limitanda potestate, fol. 7ra. Cf. D.23 c.2 §.3.

[76] 'Nam ut ait Gregorius in Moralibus *parte vi. libro xxxv. c. xiiii.* [P], omne quod hic eminet plus meroribus afficitur quam honoribus gaudeatur, xiii. di. nervi. Et secundum eundem tot unusquisque portare onera cogitur quot in hoc mundo principatur, sicut in pastorali ait.' *TMA* 1.3 De limitanda potestate, fol. 7ra. Cf. D.13 c.2.

human laws, subject themselves to these laws by imitation, give examples of what ought to be done to their followers and subjects, and govern the commonwealth neither for the sake of their presidency nor in order to enrich themselves or their family. For otherwise, according to Pope Leo, if they seek their own advantage rather than that of Christ, they will all too easily digress from the aforesaid laws and doctrines, and if they take greater pleasure in dominating their subjects than in counselling them, their honour will be puffed up with pride and what has been meant to establish concord will rather tend to do harm.[77]

The rhetorical impact of these imprecations, execrations, supplications, admonitions, and entreaties can hardly be denied. But neither can it be denied that there was something wanting in an argument that had been meant to establish limits on the power of the papacy but had ended up by reducing its author to emotions alternating between impotent wrath and the desire to throw himself upon the mercy of his rulers. Simply to warn of divine punishment and ask for obedience to the law, no matter how fine the language, was hardly sufficient when it had just been revealed that ancient pagan rulers excelled above modern Christian rulers and that Christian laws were impotent in the face of the pope's exemption from human judgment. Durant had lost the rational composure with which he had methodically added law on law to build his case, and the case had crumbled. Indeed, the final summary of his ideas itself suggests that in the face of papal supremacy he had forgotten reason. He spoke of divine and human laws, examples, concord, power, honour: but he failed to mention reason, equity, and justice. Had they withdrawn before the papacy's exemption from all human judgment?

## REFORM BY COUNCIL

The conclusion of the rubric on the 'power of superiors' left readers in the midst of a crisis. On the one hand there was the papacy's

[77] 'Que pauca sufficiunt ad probandum quod, si supradicte potestates, scilicet ecclesiastica et terrena, velint mundum et humanum genus salubriter gubernare, quod se et sua facta et dicta deberent divinis et humanis legibus *conformare* [P], et se per imitationem eis subjicere, et exempla eorum que agenda sunt sequentibus et subditis demonstrare, et non ut presint nec ut ipsi vel sui divites efficiantur rem publicam gubernare. Aliter enim, secundum dictum Leonis papae, si querunt que sua sunt, non que Jesu Christi, facile a legibus et doctrinis suprapositis disceditur, et dum dominari magis quam consulere subditis placet, honor inflat in superbiam et quod provisum est ad concordian tendit ad noxam, xlv. di. licet nonnunquam.' *TMA* 1.3 De limitanda potestate, fol. 7ra. Cf. D.45 c.6.

indubitable obligation to abide by law – and if not by law, then by reason and ancient examples. But on the other hand there was the papacy's equally indubitable exemption from judgment. Hence it seemed that there was no reliable way to make the power of government conform to law; justice was crumbling before an arbitrary power that pretended to be accountable to God but was in fact accountable to no one. However, the very clarity with which Durant had formulated the issue suggested a way out. The limits imposed by law on government had proved too uncertain; perhaps they could be specified more clearly. Reason had withdrawn before power; perhaps it could be brought back. The fourth chapter made a fresh beginning:

Fourthly, it is specified how to limit and regulate the exercise of power by those who preside over the monarchy still further by preventing them from acting on their own free will without the counsel of good men and from granting dispensations, privileges, and exemptions, as well as from taking any similar actions against what has been providently constituted in the councils of the holy fathers, without a general council.[78]

In this way Durant introduced a demand for counsel and councils that was to have an illustrious career. His wording suggests that he did not mean to break with the rules and limits that had governed the power of 'the presidents of the monarchy' in the past; rather, he meant to strengthen them by going 'further'. The first words of the chapter explained what qualified councils to serve that function:

In Proverbs 11 it is written: where there are many counsels, there is salvation; and Pope Innocent writes: an answer is more easily found when it is sought from a number of elders (D.20 c.3, X.1.29.21); and Roman law says: the truth is made manifest when several men are consulted (Cod.6.42.32.1, Cod.7.14.3).[79]

---

[78] 'Quarto specificatur amplius de limitando et regulando exercitio potestatis dictorum presidentium monarchie ne in agendis absque *consilio* [P] proborum proprio utantur arbitrio, nec sine generali concilio *agant* [P] contra ea que sunt in conciliis a sanctis patribus provide constituta in dispensationibus, privilegiis, et exemptionibus, et aliis exercendis.' *TMA* 1.4, fol. 7ra. This is the only occasion on which Durant referred to the pope and the kings as 'presidentes monarchie'.

[79] 'Verum cum scribatur Proverbiis xi. quod ibi salus ubi multa consilia, et Innocentius papa scribit quod facilius invenitur illud quod a pluribus senioribus queritur, xx. di. de quibus, extra de off. delegati, prudentiam, in fine primi responsi, et lex dicat quod per ampliores homines manifesta veritas revelatur, de fideicommissis, l. ultima, et C. de ingenuis manumissis, l. iii . . .' *TMA* 1.4, fol. 7rb. Cf. Proverbs 11:14, D.20 c.3, X.1.29.21, Cod.6.42.32.1, Cod.7.14.3. The oldest scriptural source of these convictions is Deutero-

These references were carefully chosen to cover every major type of law: a direct quotation from the Old Testament, an implicit, but important, reference to the New Testament, two papal letters, and two references to Justinian's *Codex*.[80] All of them conveyed the same idea: several men were better qualified to determine the truth than one – hence councils were ideally suited to solve the difficulty Durant had formulated in the preceding chapters.

That was what could be learned from the law. But the law was not the only proof of the value of councils for, as Durant continued,

we also have the example of Moses in the Old Testament, who followed the advice of Jethro, his father-in-law, and betook himself to seventy-two elders, because it was beyond his powers to judge the people by himself; and [we read in the New Testament that] seventy-two disciples were joined in the ministry to the twelve apostles by the command of the Lord, for the harvest was plenteous, but the labourers were few.[81]

---

nomy 19:15: 'Non stabit testis unus contra aliquem quidquid illud peccati, et facinoris fuerit: sed in ore duorum aut trium testium stabit omne verbum.' On Proverbs 11:14 see Congar, 'Quod omnes tangit', p. 228. It may be worth noting that in 1317 Pope John XXII quoted the same passage from Proverbs 11:14 in a letter of appointment for master Arnaldus de Capdenaco, provost of Mende and papal chaplain; John XXII, *LS* no. 443 (5.v.–12.XI.1317); cf. John XXII, *LS* no. 414 (17.X.1317).

[80] The reference to the New Testament is contained in D.20 c.3, which quoted Christ's promise in Matthew 18:19–20 that 'if two or three of you on earth shall gather together in my name, any thing that they shall ask shall be done for them of my father'. D.20 c.3 is indubitably the most important canon in this passage; see Le Bras *et al.*, *L'Age classique*, p. 396–405; Marrone, 'Ecclesiology', p. 99. It is attributed to a Pope Innocent but, as the editors of the Roman Edition of the *Corpus Iuris Canonici* pointed out, is not to be found among the letters of Innocent I and cannot have come from those of Innocent II because it appeared in canonical collections before his time. X.1.29.21 was a more recent decision by Celestine III that dealt, among other things, with the question of whether two judges could render effective judgment in cases where the pope had delegated three, and concluded that, 'sicut sacri canones attestantur, integrum sit iudicium, quod plurimorum sententiis confirmatur'. Cod.6.42.32.1 declared that the reliability of proof by witnesses depended not only on their quality but also on their number, and Cod.7.14.3 instisted on the value of 'tractatus cum peritioribus'. Both laws were cited by Joannes Teutonicus as secular parallels to D.20 c.3, *s.v. pluribus*. There can be little doubt that Durant took them from this source.

[81] '... et exemplum habeamus in veteri testamento de Moyse qui ad consilium Jetro cognati sui lxxii. seniores secum assumpsit quia ultra vires ipsius Moysi erat quod ipse solus populum iudicaret, Exodus xviii., et de mandato Domini xii. apostolis lxxii. discipuli in ministerium sunt adiuncti quia messis multa erat, operarii vero pauci, xxi. di. in novo, Matthei ix. et Ionnis iiii. c.' *TMA* 1.4, fol. 7rb. Cf. Exodus 18:18–25, D.21 c.2, Matthew 9:37, John 4:35. Henry of Ghent, 'Sermo', pp. 142, 149, had already used Exodus for the same purpose.

Thus the Bible supplied two concrete examples to support the teaching of the law. These examples were as carefully chosen as the laws that had just been cited. The first described the constitution that Moses gave to the ancient state of Israel, with its 'heads over the people, rulers of thousands, rulers of hundreds, rulers of fifties, and rulers of tens'.[82] The second described the constitution that Christ had given to the primitive church.[83] This constitution was founded on Peter, with whom

the priestly order began in the New Testament, because he was the first to whom the pontificate was given in the church of Christ when the Lord said to him: 'You are Peter, and upon this rock I will build my church, and the gates of hell shall not prevail against it, and I will give you the keys of the kingdom of Heaven.'

But just as the state of Israel included 'heads over the people', so the primitive church had apostles who 'received honour and power in equal partnership with Peter, although they wanted him to be the first among them'. And just as the state of Israel had rulers of hundreds and fifties beneath the rulers of thousands, so the primitive church had disciples who were added to assist the apostles because 'the harvest was plenteous, but the labourers few'. Moreover, as the same canon pointed out, the constitution of the primitive church lived on in the present church. Bishops had succeeded the apostles, 'in whose place the bishops arose when they passed away', and priests had succeeded the disciples, 'in whose place priests, who were modelled after their image, were later

---

[82] Exodus 18:25.
[83] D.21 c.2, *In novo testamento*, is an excerpt from a Pseudo-Isidorean letter of Pope Anacletus that is among the most frequently cited Pseudo-Isidorean creations of the middle ages: Fuhrmann, *Einfluss und Verbreitung*, 1:569f. Its doctrine that bishops and priests were the modern equivalents of the apostles and disciples to whom they had succeeded was initially developed by Bede, whence it entered Pseudo-Isidore and the *glossa ordinaria* of the Bible: Congar, 'Aspects', pp. 61f. It was the discussion of precisely this canon that led the decretists to distinguish between *potestas iurisdictionis* and *potestas ordinis* in order to increase the papacy's legislative freedom: Tierney, *Foundations*, pp. 30–4, 169f. Hence it played a central role in the secular clergy's defence of their view of order ever since William of St Amour used it for that purpose in the 1250s: Schleyer, *Anfänge*, pp. 80f.; Marrone, 'Ecclesiology', pp. 62–4. Simon of Beaulieu, William of Mâcon, and Henry of Ghent all used it to prove that the power of the prelates was sanctioned directly by God; Marrone, 'Ecclesiology', p. 145; *Chartularium Universitatis Parisiensis*, 1:15; *Tractatus de usurpata potestate fratrum*, pp. 172f. It may be worth adding that the mission of the seventy-two disciples according to Luke 10 was publicly recited in the first session of the council of Vienne; Müller, *Konzil von Vienne*, p. 673.

established in the church'.[84] Whether it was the Old Testament or the New Testament, the state or the church, the past or the present, the message was again the same in every case: heads of government ought not to govern by themselves. They needed the advice of their subordinates.

Having thus carefully prepared his ground with laws and examples, Durant finally presented his answer to the question of how government could be subjected to reason:

It would be advisable for the commonwealth and the administrators of the commonwealth if their power were to be limited by reason (as has been discussed before) in such a way that [first] the lord pope should no longer use the prerogative of his power without the considered advice of the lords cardinals, nor kings and princes the prerogatives of their power without the advice of other good men (as used to be the practice in the commonwealth in the past), especially when they are making concessions contrary to councils and laws approved in common; and [second] that the pope, kings, and princes, can no longer enact any new laws or grant any new concessions contrary to these councils and laws unless a general council has been convoked, for what touches all must, according to the rule of both canon law and civil law, be approved by all in common.[85]

The formulation was complex, but it embodied two straightforward principles. The first was that reason spoke through councils. Hence, in order to assure that power would 'be limited by reason', Durant demanded that government should never again proceed to do anything at all without a council of some kind. The second principle was that there were two fundamentally different types of

---

[84] 'In novo testamento post Christum Dominum a Petro sacerdotalis cepit ordo, quia ipsi primo pontificatus in ecclesia Christi datus est, Domino dicente ad eum: "Tu es, inquit, Petrus, et super hanc petram edificabo ecclesiam meam, et portae inferi non prevalebunt adversus eam: et tibi dabo claves regni celorum." . . . Ceteri vero apostoli cum eodem pari consortio honorem et potestatem acceperunt, ipsumque principem eorum esse voluerunt . . . Ipsis quoque decedentibus in locum eorum surrexerunt episcopi . . . Videntes autem ipsi apostoli messem esse multam et operarios paucos, rogaverunt dominum messis, ut mitteret operarios in messem suam: unde ab eis electi sunt lxxii discipuli, quorum tipum gerunt presbiteri atque in eorum loco sunt constituti in ecclesia.' D.21 c.2.

[85] 'Videretur esse salubre consilium pro re publica et pro dictis administratoribus rei publice quod sic sub ratione, ut premissum est in rubricis proximis, limitaretur potestas eorundem quod absque certo consilio dominorum cardinalium dominus papa, et reges ac principes absque aliorum proborum consilio, sicut hactenus in re publica servabatur, non uterentur prerogativa huiusmodi potestatis, potissime aliquid concedendo contra concilia et contra iura approbata communiter, et quod contra dicta concilia et iura nihil possent de novo statuere vel concedere nisi generali concilio convocato, cum illud quod omnes tangit secundum iuris utriusque regulam ab omnibus debeat communiter approbari.' *TMA* 1.4, fol. 7rb. Cf. VI.5.12 De reg. iuris 29.

governmental actions: to use 'the prerogative of power' and to 'enact new laws'. With due respect for the dangers of anachronism, we can designate the former as the power to execute laws and the latter as the power to institute laws. Since execution left the laws themselves intact, even when it violated their intention, whereas the institution of laws changed the law itself, the latter obviously posed a more basic threat to justice than the former. Hence Durant proposed two different kinds of councils. When popes or kings intended to exercise 'the prerogative of power', they were to consult the cardinals, in the case of the pope, or 'good men' (*probi homines*), in the case of the king, that is, in either case, a kind of standing executive council, a small body of men whose function was to advise their ruler on questions arising about the proper execution of the laws in the everyday affairs of government.[86] But when new general laws were to be instituted, a general council had to be convoked.

This much seems clear; but as one looks more closely some of the clarity begins to fade. Did the demand for general councils apply as equally to popes and kings as Durant's formulation appeared to suggest? Did it mean that kings had to convoke their own 'general councils' when they were planning to institute new laws (more likely), or did it mean that they could not change any general laws without the participation of all of Christianity (less likely)? Again, precisely where was the boundary between the responsibilities of general councils and those of executive councils, between instituting laws and executing them? There is only one kind of measure about which Durant's formulation leaves no doubt at all: new laws that were in conflict with old laws could not be instituted without a general council. But what about new laws that were not in conflict with old laws? Were such laws conceivable? And if so, were popes and kings to be authorized to enact them without general councils? About that he says nothing at all.[87] More important, what about dispensations, exemptions, and other measures which could not

---

[86] On the role of the cardinals cf. Kuttner, 'Cardinalis'; Tierney, *Foundations*; Tierney, 'Hostiensis and Collegiality'; Watt, 'The Constitutional Law'; Watt, 'Hostiensis on "Per Venerabilem"'. Huguccio, among others, had already declared that the pope cannot establish new laws about the state of the church without the participation of the cardinals; Tierney, *Foundations*, p. 81; Congar, 'Status ecclesiae', p. 27.

[87] At least not at this point. Toward the end of the treatise he says unequivocally: 'Item quod [Romana ecclesia] nulla iura generalia deinceps conderet nisi vocato concilio generali.' *TMA* 2.96 (3.27), fol. 59ra. That implies that new laws were not to be passed without the convocation of general councils, regardless of their relationship to old laws.

really be considered legislation in the full sense of the word, but which nevertheless conflicted with general law? About that he says too much. On the one hand, he insists that kings and popes ought 'especially' (*potissime*) to consult their executive councils when they were about to 'make any concessions contrary to the councils and laws approved in common'. Since 'concessions' may be considered as a generic term for dispensations, exemptions, and the like, this means that dispensations were to fall within the responsibility of executive councils. But on the other hand he also said that government should no longer be allowed to 'grant any new concessions contrary to the said councils and laws unless a general council has been convoked'. This means exactly the opposite.

One early modern editor tried to remove the inconsistency by changing the second *concedere* into *condere*.[88] If that were a sound reading, general councils would have had nothing to do with concessions of any kind, but only with the enactment of new legislation. This illustrates how a crucial question of interpretation can on occasion hinge on nothing more than one syllable. It also makes good sense – but it is wrong. All of the manuscripts, as well as the better editions, agree on *concedere*. Moreover, the heading with which Durant prefaced the fourth chapter explicitly states that government should be prevented 'from granting dispensations, privileges, and exemptions, as well as from taking any similar actions against what has been providently constituted in the councils of the holy fathers, without a general council'.[89] This heading is unambiguous: no dispensations from ancient conciliar laws without general councils.

Durant thus seems to have wavered as to whether dispensations from the ancient law of the church should be left in the responsibility of executive councils or general councils, effectively leaving them in both. This outcome is hardly satisfactory, but it is understandable. On the one hand, some dispensations and exemp-

---

[88] Namely the lawyer Philippus Probus from Bourges in his edition of Paris, 1545. His changes were followed by the editions of Venice, 1562, and Paris, 1671. For details see Fasolt, 'A New View', pp. 313f. and n. 97.

[89] Cf. above, p. 157 and n. 78. The heading of the fourth chapter is the only passage in the treatise that leaves no doubt at all about Durant's intention to let general councils have their say about dispensations and exemptions. For reasons that are hard to fathom it was omitted from every edition of the treatise except the *editio princeps*. One is tempted to believe that it was not forgotten through an oversight but because it conflicted too sharply with the legislative rights to which the papacy laid claim; for details see Fasolt, 'A New View', pp. 313–15.

tions, such as the general exemptions granted to the mendicants, posed so great a threat to the stability of the ancient law that they had to be included among the responsibilities of general councils. But on the other hand most dispensations amounted to minor adjustments of the laws, matters of everyday business which general councils could not possibly have supervised without creating a vast bureaucracy of their own – and that was out of the question. Hence such dispensations had to be left to the responsibility of executive councils.

The only hint (though nothing more than a hint) as to how Durant may have thought this ambiguity could be resolved is found at the beginning of the rubric on exemptions. There he required the pope to account for why exemptions had been granted in the past and why they continued to be granted in the present.[90] Since his treatise was written in anticipation of the council of Vienne, that is presumably where he wished such an account to be given, and it would have been logical to make this a regular practice at every general council.[91] Perhaps he thought that the papacy should continue to grant dispensations and exemptions whenever circumstances warranted but that such grants should be subject to review or ratification by general councils.

There is another question about which Durant is not nearly as explicit as one might wish. What if council and pope disagreed? Was the pope required to obtain the council's consent, or was he entitled to proceed alone against conciliar opposition? Thirteenth-century lawyers had regularly considered the distinction between an obligation to consult an advisory body and an obligation to abide by its decision. Their answers had been shaded carefully according to different contexts. No one could have been unaware that it was important to determine whether the pope should or should not be bound by the advice of councils. It was important enough with regard to executive councils, but it was absolutely essential with regard to general councils, for, depending on the

---

[90] See below, p. 172.
[91] It would also have been similar to the contemporary practice of *sindicatio*, in which the councils of city governments reviewed the actions of executive officers upon completion of their term in office, a practice with which Durant must have been familiar from his personal experience. It was also familiar from Aristotle's *Politics*, which gave 'the people the two general functions of electing the magistrates to office and of calling them to account at the end of their tenure of office, but not the right of holding office themselves in their individual capacity'. Aristotle, *Politics* 3.11, 1281b32–4, transl. Barker, p. 125. The difference was, of course, that the pope's tenure of office was not limited in time.

answer, supreme authority in the church would lie either with the pope or with the council.

At first sight Durant does seem to give an answer. He quotes the famous maxim of Roman law that 'what touches all must, according to the rule of both canon law and civil law, be approved by all in common'. This would seem to furnish certain proof that Durant did not intend to let the pope act without express conciliar consent. But on closer inspection this conclusion turns out to be at best uncertain, in part because the principle of approval by all has been the subject of sharply conflicting interpretations. There are those who maintain that it did in fact endow assemblies with an unqualified right to support or oppose a ruler by granting or withholding their consent according to their own free choice.[92] But others argue exactly the opposite: that the principle that 'what touches all must be approved by all' did not give an assembly any right to withhold its consent to the ruler's decision, at least not after he had fulfilled his obligation to seek its advice in good faith. In their opinion, consent was not 'free' but 'procedural', even 'compulsory'.[93] The latter view seems to have both the evidence and a heuristic preference for what one might call the *interpretatio difficilior* on its side. But even if one were willing to admit that such a narrow interpretation is inappropriately legalistic, the mere fact that the principle of approval has been interpreted in opposite ways would make it unwise to rely on it as the sole proof that in cases of a conflict between pope and council Durant wished to prevent the pope from acting without the council's consent.[94]

---

[92] This is how it is interpreted by Marongiu, 'The Theory of Democracy and Consent', pp. 404f., who defines the principle of approval as a 'principle of democracy and consent' and declares that 'the juridical and political principle that this concise maxim so happily expressed was neither a hothouse flower nor a rhetorical flourish nor the far-fetched fantasy of obscure thinkers; it was the successful and realistic expression of a widespread notion of group life and, thus, an expression of the spirit of the age'. Cf. Marongiu, *Il Parlamento*, p. 42; Ullmann, *History*, pp. 12f.; Carlyle, *History*, 5:140.

[93] Thus Post, 'A Romano-Canonical Maxim', p. 251: 'Did Edward I transform *q.o.t.* into a "constitutional principle" and give it a "new and political sense"? Broadly speaking he did; but strictly speaking, in the legal sense his statement of *q.o.t.* was simply an embodiment of a constant medieval theory of consent, without constitutional and political implications . . . In the public as in the private law, therefore, a large measure of compulsory, procedural, judicial consent remained as the real essence of *q.o.t.*' Similarly Morrall, *Political Thought*, p. 65; Congar, 'Quod omnes tangit', pp. 222–31; Oakley, 'Legitimation by Consent', p. 315.

[94] For a detailed analysis of this question see Fasolt, 'Quod omnes tangit: The Words and the Meaning', forthcoming in *In Iure Veritas: Studies in Canon Law in Memory of Schafer Williams*.

There is another, more weighty consideration that points in the same direction. Durant does mention the principle of approval, but he does so in a subordinate clause that contained the reason for his demand. In the main clause, which contained the substance of his demand, he merely required the pope to convoke a general council and said nothing at all about consent. The same is true of every other instance in which he demanded an increased role for general councils.[95] He always asked the pope to convoke a general council when law was to be changed and when matters that concerned all were to be dealt with. He regularly appended the principle of approval in a subordinate clause, but he never asked the pope to obtain the council's consent in so many words. This leaves us with the clear impression that he did not consider the principle of approval strong enough to require more than 'procedural' consent. It also leaves us without so much as a hint at how he meant to proceed in cases where the pope and the council disagreed with each other.

There are two major issues, then, on which Durant's 'further limitation and regulation' of power lacked clarity. Both of them had to do with the line of demarcation between executing laws and instituting laws. The former left some doubt as to whether such a line would fall on this or that side of dispensations, and the latter as to whether the council was or was not entitled to withhold consent from papal legislative measures. They serve as an important reminder that what we have called execution is not as easily distinguished from legislation as the modern familiarity with those terms suggests. Besides, it is important to remember that the pope was a member of the council, and Durant was not about to abolish his role as 'lord and founder' of the canons, as Gratian had described it. But this should not obscure the central issue. While both of the specific difficulties we have considered are ambiguous, the point of principle is not ambiguous at all: new laws should no longer be

---

[95] 'Item quod [Romana ecclesia] nulla iura generalia deinceps conderet nisi *vocato concilio generali.*' TMA 2.96 (3.27), fol. 59ra. My italics. 'Item cum in viii. c. concilii Millevitani sub imperatoribus Arcadio et Honorio celebrati fuerit constitutum quod cause ecclesiastice que communes non sunt toti ecclesie Affricane in suis provinciis iudicentur, et quod illis qui communes sunt *generalis synodus convocetur,* videtur utile quod predictum *concilium per Romanam ecclesiam servaretur* quandocunque iura condenda sunt, cum dicta iura pro tangentibus communem utilitatem sint edenda, iiii. di. §. i. et c. facte et c. erit. Et quod *idem servaretur quandocunque aliquid esset ordinandum de tangentibus communem statum ecclesie vel ius novum condendum,* cum illud quod omnes tangit ab omnibus approbari debeat, lxv. di. c. i., ii. et iii., lxvi. di. c. i.' TMA, 2.41, fol. 34rb. Cf. D.4 a.c.1–2, D.65 c.1–3, D.66 c.1. My italics.

instituted without the participation of a general council. In the past one might have said: 'The pope should not change any laws without a general council, but perhaps he can', as, in fact, Durant himself would put it in dealing with exemptions.[96] But if Durant's proposal had been accepted, that would no longer have been possible. Instead one would have had to say that 'the pope should not and cannot change any laws without a general council'. At least in this respect Durant's proposal did define a sure means 'further to limit and to regulate the exercise of power by those who preside over the monarchy'.

Durant concluded the fourth chapter with a review of his entire argument. It consisted of three simple steps. The first was to recall the sanctity of general law:

As St Augustine says in *De vera religione*, although men make judgments about temporal laws when they enact them, once such laws have been enacted and affirmed no judge may judge about them, but only according to them. Whence Pope Leo writes that general laws which have been ordained for the sake of eternal utility may not be changed in any respect, and neither may laws that have been prescribed for the common good be turned to private advantage. Rather, the laws established by the Fathers shall remain intact, no one shall unjustly usurp what belongs to another, and each shall exercise his charity as he is able by spreading it within proper and lawful limits.[97]

Thus once again Durant insisted on the notion that general laws established for the common good were immutable, and once again he relied on a canon in that twenty-fifth *causa* of Gratian's *Decretum* from which he had so liberally quoted when he had first tried to refute the claim that rulers were exempt from law. In this sense he returned to the beginning of his argument. But now the sense in which no ruler was exempt from any general laws, whether human or divine, could be specified more clearly, because Durant had

---

[96] See below, pp. 173f.
[97] 'Ut enim Augustinus ait in libro de vera religione c. lx., in istis temporalibus legibus, quamquam de his homines iudicent cum eas instituunt, tamen cum fuerint institute et firmate non licebit iudici de ipsis iudicare, sed secundum ipsas, iiii. di. in istis. Unde Leo papa scribit quod illa que ad perpetuam sunt generaliter ordinata utilitatem nulla commutatione varientur, nec ad privatam trahantur commodum que ad bonum sunt commune prefixa, sed manentibus terminis quos constituerunt patres nemo iniuste usurpet alienum; sed intra fines proprios atque legitimos, prout quisque valuerit, in latitudine se exerceat charitatis, xxv. questione i. que ad perpetuam.' *TMA* 1.4, fol. 7va. Cf. D.4 c.3, C.25 q.1 c.3. On C.25 q.1 c.3, *Que ad perpetuam*, see Post, 'Copyists' Errors', pp. 358, 378–81, 391–8; Marrone, 'Ecclesiology', p. 74.

clearly distinguished between the execution and the institution of the laws. In executing laws rulers enjoyed a certain 'prerogative of power' which gave them a certain freedom from the laws; but they were not free at all to change the laws without the assistance of a general council.

Second, Durant announced more clearly than he had done before why legislation must not be left to rulers alone:

For it is certain that those who preside over the spiritual and temporal power are human beings, and hence can stumble easily. This is why Emperor Valentinian addressed a council with the following words: Raise someone to the pontifical see to whom we, too, who govern the empire, can faithfully bow our heads so that whenever we err as human beings we can take his warnings as we take medicine from a doctor, as can be read in the *Historia tripartita*. And as far as the pope is concerned, Pope Symmachus says that the privileges of the papal see do most certainly not include permission to sin, not even for blessed Peter himself. But as Pope Alexander said, the more intimate [those who preside over the spiritual and temporal power] ought to be with the Saviour, the more they are exposed to the attacks of the enemy of the human race, who knows a thousand ways of deceit, as Pope John said, and who has striven from the beginning of his fall to rend the unity of the church, to wound charity, to taint the sweet works of the saints with the bile of envy, and to overturn and agitate the human race in every way. No one has any doubt, moreover, that the more things there are that need to be attended to, the less attention can be paid to each of them. Although the presidents of the spiritual and temporal power excel others by their dignity, it therefore sometimes happens that they do not excel others by the certainty of their actions and judgments, because they are occupied with too much business, as Pope Gregory said in his *Pastoral Rule*.[98]

---

[98] 'Certum namque est quod presidentes spirituali et temporali potestati sunt homines, et ideo tamquam homines de facili possunt labi. Et ideo dicebat Valentinianus imperator alloquens sinodum: talem in pontificali constituite sede cui et nos qui gubernamus imperium sincere nostra capita submittamus, et eius monita, dum tanquam homines delinquimus, necessario veluti curantis medicinam suscipiamus, sicut habetur in historia tripartita, lxiii. di. Valentinianus. De domino autem papa certum est, sicut Symacus papa ait, quod nec ipse nec etiam beatus Petrus cum sedis privilegio licentiam acceperunt peccandi, ut patet xl. di. non nos et c. si papa. Quinimo, sicut Alexander papa ait, quanto familiariores esse debent salvatori, tanto magis impugnantur ab inimico *humani* [M] generis, qui mille habet fallendi modos et qui conatur a principio ruine sue unitatem ecclesie rescindere, caritatem vulnerare, sanctorum operum dulcedinem invidie felle inficere, et omnibus modis humanum genus evertere et perturbare, sicut Joannes papa ait, iii. q. i. nulli, xvi. q. ii. visis. Nulli etiam dubium est quin pluribus intentus minor sit ad singula sensus. Unde, quamquam sint dignitate ceteris altiores, interdum evenit propter *nimiam* [M] preoccupationem negotiorum, sicut Gregorius in Pastorali ait, quod non sunt in agendis et in iudiciis ceteris certiores.' *TMA* 1.4, fol.7va–b. Cf. D.63 c.3, D.40 c.1,

# The assertion of justice

Durant thus finally defined the main weakness of monarchy. That weakness was ignorance. All human beings, including the pope, were fallible. One man should therefore never be allowed to bear the burden of government alone, especially not since his higher dignity made him far more likely to be attacked by the devil, and far less likely to know everything he needed to know in order to fulfil his duty well. Secular government had it perhaps a little easier than spiritual government, since the emperor could receive guidance from the pope. But both 'presidents of the spiritual and temporal power' needed assistance in order to acquire that *scientia* without which law and reason could not be made to match.

Which is why not only the commonwealth but [the administrators of the commonwealth] themselves would profit if, according to the words of the wise man, everything were to be done with counsel and they were not to stray from the path of justice at all, and regret it only afterwards.[99]

### DISPENSATIONS AND EXEMPTIONS

Durant completed his discussion of the principles of reform with a closer look at the reasons why dispensations and exemptions ought to be revoked. Dispensations were one of several means that had been devised to regulate legitimate exceptions from the laws. Indeed, they formed so crucial an ingredient in the papacy's ability to modify the law that by the late thirteenth century they had come to be considered as legislative measures in their own right.[100] They afforded Durant an opportunity to describe the principles that he

---

D.40 c.6, C.3 q.1 c.5, C.16 q.2 c.1, *Regula pastoralis* 1.4, *PL* 77:17. On D.40 c.6 see Tierney, *Foundations*, pp. 56–67, 171–5; Martin, 'Comment s'est formée la doctrine de la supériorité du concile', pp. 124–30; Marrone, 'The Absolute and the Ordained Powers', p. 24. On a parallel use of D.63 c.3 by the secular clergy in 1289 see *Tractatus de usurpata potestate fratrum*, pp. 171f. On a parallel attack on the fallibility of the pope see *Tractatus de usurpata potestate fratrum*, pp. 163, 171.

99 'Propter quod prospiceretur non solum rei publice, sed eisdem quod omnia cum consilio agerentur, iuxta dictum sapientis, et a iuris tramite nequaquam discederent nec postmodum peniterent.' *TMA* 1.4, fol. 7vb. Cf. Proverbs 13:10, 13:16.

100 'La *dispensatio*, però, allarga presto i suoi orizzonti. Almeno dall'epoca di Sicardo da Cremona appare in atto l'esperimento canonistico di riallacciarla all'attività legislativa: e a questo punto la sua convergenza con la *potestas plena* si accelera, perché opera finalmente nell'àmbito più vasto di qualsiasi contegno sovrano affatto libero nei confronti del sistema normativo.' Cortese, *Norma giuridica*, 2:213f. Le Bras et al., *L'Age classique*, pp. 514–32, esp. 531f., is less willing to recognize the legislative quality of dispensations.

168

thought should govern not only dispensations but all other modifications of the law as well. He began with a definition:

If, furthermore, it is alleged that one may dispense from the law, it may be replied that according to the jurists a dispensation is a careful relaxation of common law, based on an evaluation of its utility or necessity and granted according to the forms of canon law by someone with the proper competency, as is gathered from C.1 q.7 p.c.5 and the following canons. Anything else must, according to the jurists, be called not a dispensation but a dissipation because it violates the law.[101]

These technical but well-known formulae limited dispensations in three basic ways. First, dispensations could not be granted unless they were required by utility or necessity. Second, they could only be granted by the proper authorities. And third, they had to be granted according to certain 'forms of canon law'. Durant immediately went on to explain what that meant:

One may not, therefore, proceed to grant such dispensations without careful deliberation, for the Lord, whom the lord Pope represents as his vicar, as Saint Ambrose says in his book on offices, wishes his bounties not to be spent at once but rather to be dispensed with measure, especially because dispensations are granted against the law [*ius*]. But the law is the art of the good and the equitable (which is why someone has called us *sacerdotes*, that is, ministers of sacred precepts) and the good and equitable may not be dispensed with unless there is a great necessity or utility, for what is done according to the law [*ius*] is done with justice [*iustitia*]. And this, as Augustine said to Macedonius, is well said indeed. For these reasons dispensations should be granted only for due and necessary reasons, neither out of pure will nor for the sake of gain, because they pose risks to the state of the church. Those who dispense for undue reasons sin, and even those who obtain the dispensation are perhaps not at all helped, but rather burdened by it.[102]

---

[101] 'Porro, si pretendatur quod licitum est dispensare supra iura, responderi potest quod, cum dispensatio, sicut iuriste tradunt, sit provida iuris communis relaxatio, utilitate seu necessitate pensata per eum ad quem spectat canonice facta, ut colligitur i. q. vii. §. nisi rigor discipline, et c. necessaria cum sequentibus, non est secundum iuristas censenda dispensatio sed dissipatio si aliter fiat, cum ius vulneretur ex ea, xxiii. q. iiii. ipsa pietas circa finem.' *TMA* 1.4 De dispensationibus, fol. 7vb. Cf. C.1 q.7 p.c.5–22, C.23 q.4 c.24. On the standard definition of a dispensation as 'provida iuris communis relaxatio utilitate seu necessitate pensata' see Brys, *De dispensatione*, pp. 163–70.

[102] 'Unde non est ad dictam dispensationem absque deliberatione provida procedendum, extra de transactionibus, c. fi. Dominus enim, cuius est vicarius dominus papa, sicut ait beatus Ambrosius in libro de officiis, non vult simul effundi opes, potius dispensari, lxxxvi. di. non satis, potissime cum ius contra quod fit ipsa dispensatio sit ars boni et equi, cuius merito quis nos sacerdotes, id est sacrorum preceptorum ministros, appellat, ff. de iustitia et iure, l. i. §. ius, ii. di. vii. §. fuerunt, contra quod quidem bonum et equum

These terse words embodied a whole array of legal doctrines and
more than a century of legal analysis. Each clause could give rise to
difficulties and had in fact provided food for searching investigations of canonical theory.[103] But Durant avoided them, just as
he had avoided similar questions when he first mentioned reason,
equity, and justice in the rubric on the 'power of superiors'. The
point to which he wished to draw attention was again as basic as it
was simple: the law had been established for good reasons. In
principle the law embodied justice. That meant that it was sacred.
Indeed, it meant that in a certain sense lawyers were indistinguishable from priests, since both priests and lawyers were givers of a
sacred law – that is, *sacerdotes*, as Durant did not fail to point out
with the help of Ulpian's famous opening words in the *Digesta*.
There had to be excellent reasons indeed in order to justify any
dispensation from the law. Mere assertions that such reasons did
exist were not enough: they had to be substantiated 'by careful
deliberation'. We have already seen that minimally such deliberation required the assistance of cardinals or 'good men', and that in
the case of some dispensations it even required the convocation of
general councils. Moreover, if after deliberation any doubts
remained, it was better not to grant a dispensation but to stay with
the law,

for one condition must always be observed: in matters that are doubtful or
obscure we should never follow any practices that will be found contrary
to the precepts of the Gospels or opposed to the decrees of the holy
fathers.[104]

absque magna necessitate vel utilitate dispensari non debet, cum illud quod iure agitur
iuste agatur. Et bene, sicut Augustinus ad Macedonium ait, xiiii. q. iiii. quid dicam, extra
de verb. signif., ius, dictum est. Igitur dicte dispensationes ex causis debitis et necessariis
non ex voluntate nec acquisitis fieri debent, cum de *decoloratione* [P] status ecclesie
agatur, i. q. vii. et si illa, et c. tali coniugio, extra de elect., innotuit §. multa et §. finali.
Unde si dispensant ex causis indebitis peccant, nec forte illi cum quibus dispensatur
iuvantur sed potius gravantur.' *TMA* 1.4 De dispensationibus, fols. 7vb–8ra. Cf.
X.1.36.11, D.86 c.14, Dig.1.1.1, C.2 q.7 c.2, C.14 q.4 c.11, X.5.40.12, C.1 q.7 c.23, C.1
q.7 c.17, X.1.6.20. The counter-argument of Innocent IV had been that 'in his enim
dispensationibus (in iure nempe positivo) sufficit sola voluntas dispensatoris, etiam sine
causa'. Brys, *De dispensatione*, p. 192 n. 4. On the possibility of dispensations even from
apostolic law see Kuttner, 'Pope Lucius III'.

[103] See the literature cited above, n. 56.

[104] 'Unde prudenter aget dominus papa si in dispensationibus et aliis servet consilium
Leonis pape I. in preallegato c. sicut. Dicit enim quod sicut quedam sunt que nulla
possunt ratione convelli, ita multa sunt que aut pro necessitate temporum aut pro
consideratione etatum oporteat temperari, illa consideratione semper servata ut in his

Once more Durant thus returned to the foundation of his convictions. No one, not even the papacy, was ever at liberty to disregard 'the decrees of the holy fathers'. These decrees afforded a standard over which utility and necessity could not prevail so long as there was any doubt. Durant concluded by declaring that the pope had been too liberal in granting dispensations and advised him to revoke them:

Therefore his holiness the lord pope should ponder whether the sinews of ecclesiastical discipline, to which the holy fathers once attended with due care, have not been torn by indiscriminate grants of dispensations according to the style of the Roman curia, and if, provided the remedy of law suits himself and the universal church, he should not abide by tradition and abstain from dispensations, indulgences, concessions, privileges, and exemptions that go against the common good, which ought to be preferred to the good of individuals. For, as Jerome wrote to Bishop Rusticus of Narbonne, ever since avarice began to grow in the churches, as it had in the Roman empire, the law of priests and the vision of the prophet have perished.[105]

The rubric on exemptions, with which the first part of the treatise concluded, applied these principles to a particular issue. The choice of topic was revealing. The secular clergy regarded general exemptions of monks and friars as one of the most dangerous changes that the papacy had introduced; it was this issue that had provoked them into organized resistance. Durant, too, thought that exemptions were a crucial threat to the 'state of the church'. Aside from his demand for regular general councils this was the only demand for a specific measure of reform that he included in

que vel dubia fuerunt aut obscura id noverimus sequendum quod nec preceptis evangelicis contrarium nec decretis sanctorum patrum inveniatur adversum.' *TMA* 1.4 De dispensationibus, fol. 8ra. Cf. D.14 c.2, and Kuttner, 'Pope Lucius III', p. 441.
[105] 'Penset itaque eiusdem domini pape sanctitas si ex dispensationibus que passim iuxta stilum Romane curie fiunt rumpitur nervus *ecclesiastice discipline qui cum cautela debita fuit a sanctis patribus actenus observatus* [P], l. di. presbyteros, xxxiiii. q. ii. in lectum, xv. q. i. si quis insaniens, xxiii. q. v. excommunicatorum, et, si esset sibi et universali ecclesie de prelibato remedio iuris conveniens, acquiesceret traditionibus et cessaret a dictis dispensationibus, indulgentiis et concessionibus, privilegiis et exemptionibus, que sunt contra bonum commune, quod preferendum est privato, vii. q. i. scias, viii. q. i. in scripturis. Nam sicut scribit Ieronymus ad Rusticum Narbonensem episcopum, ex quo in ecclesiis sicut in Romano imperio crevit avaritia, periit lex de sacerdotibus et visio de propheta, xciii. di. diaconi sunt.' *TMA* 1.4 De dispensationibus, fol. 8ra–b. Cf. D.50 c.32, C.34 q.2 c.6, C.15 q.1 c.12, C.23 q.5 c.47, C.7 q.1 c.35, C.8 q.1 c.9, D.93 c.23 §.5. For a similar reference to 'nervus ecclesiastice discipline' see *Tractatus de usurpata potestate fratrum*, p. 197.

the first part of the treatise. The issue of exemptions thus furnishes
something of a concrete test for his understanding of the reasons
why laws should or should not be changed.

The rubric on exemptions comprises more than half of the entire
first part of the treatise, and it contains an astonishing number of
citations intended to show that no kind of exemption from
episcopal jurisdiction was ever justified. But Durant presented all
of this according to a simple schema. He began with an assertion
that, so to speak, turned the debate about legal change on its head:

His holiness the pope must give a reason why these exemptions have been
granted, why they continue to be granted, and what fruit they are bearing
nowadays. For the church of God must take the following authority
seriously indeed: There are acts by some of our predecessors and ancestors
that may have been irreproachable at the time but that later turned into
error and superstition. Such acts must be immediately and emphatically
rejected by their successors. This is why Ezechias removed the high places
and broke the images and cut down the groves and broke into pieces the
brazen serpent that Moses had made at God's behest, lest the people
should perish by a serpentine death. And Ezechias is praised for destroying
what Moses had made at God's command because it was leading to ruin.
Therefore it must not be judged reprehensible if human statutes are
sometimes changed according to changing times, especially when the
necessity is urgent or an evident utility demands it, since God himself
changed some of the statutes of the Old Testament in the New, as we read
in the [Fourth Lateran] general council. All of which proves that, if the
damage and the inconvenience that arise from dispensations and exemptions are greater than their utility, they must be revoked by provision of
the highest pontiff.[106]

---

[106] 'De exemptionibus autem predictis, ex qua causa concesse fuerint et continuo concedan-
tur et quis fructus modernis temporibus subsequatur ex eis, haberet eiusdem [pape]
sanctitas providere. Magna nanque auctoritas ista in Dei ecclesia est habenda: etsi
nonnulli ex predecessoribus et maioribus nostris fecerunt aliqua que illorum tempore
potuerunt esse sine culpa et postea vertuntur in errorem et superstitionem, ut sine
tarditate aliqua et cum magna auctoritate a posteris destruantur, lxiii. di. §. verum. Unde
Ezechias dissipavit excelsa et contrivit statuas et succidit lucos confregitque serpentem
eneum a Moyse iussu Dei factum ne serpentina morte populus interiret. Et laudatur
dictus Ezechias destruxisse quod tendebat ad perniciem quod iubente Deo fecerat ille,
Num. xxi., iiii. Regum xviii. c. Non enim debet irreprehensibile iudicari si secundum
varietatem temporum statuta quandoque varientur humana, presertim cum urget
necessitas, vel evidens utilitas id exposcit, cum ipse Deus ex his que in veteri testamento
statuerat nonnulla mutaverit in novo, sicut habetur ex concilio generali, extra de
consang. et affin., non debet, xxix. di. c. i. et ii., iiii. di. erit, xxxii. q. iiii. quis ignoret, et
c. obiiciuntur, xxiii. q. viii. occidit, extra de transact. c. fi., de sent. excomm. super eo.

This was an interesting beginning. Durant now insisted on the need not for immutability but for change. Indeed, he invoked a famous canon of Pope Innocent III that had served as a tool to legitimate papal modifications of general law.[107] At first sight this might seem to amount to a surrender to the papacy's assumption of control over all legislation. But in fact it was the opposite: Durant accepted the papal argument for changing law, but only because he recognized that it could be turned against itself. Once it was admitted that general law had to be changed as necessity and utility demanded, it obviously followed that those changes could also be reversed in agreement with necessity and utility.

These ideas determined the strategy Durant employed to prove that exemptions had to be revoked. Three simple questions needed to be answered: first, what was the letter of the law; second, what were the circumstances; and third, did the circumstances require any changes in the law? He began by stating the general law:

First comes the general ordination of the universal church, which proceeds from God and has been approved and observed by the apostles, the holy fathers, the general councils, and the Roman pontiffs. According to this ordination, any aspect of practising the Christian religion and, as a rule, all monasteries, religious places, abbots, abbesses, monks, nuns, religious persons, and ecclesiastical persons are immediately subject to the government and the care of the bishop of their respective city or diocese, who is their superior, a successor to the apostles and their power. Since the lord pope should not, and perhaps cannot, change an observance of such importance, he may not so randomly grant general exemptions, privileges, liberties, and immunities that derogate from, or are prejudicial to, the honour, power, status, ordination and order of the said bishops and ordinaries, contrary to the said general ordination, and perhaps he cannot even do so.[108]

Ex quibus infertur quod si maius damnum et maius inconveniens subsequatur ex dictis dispensationibus et dictis exemptionibus quam utilitas, quod haberent per eiusdem summi pontificis providentiam revocari.' *TMA* 1.4 De exemptionibus, fol. 8rb. Cf. D.63 p.c.28, Numbers 21:8, 2 Kings 18:4, X.4.14.8, D.29 c.1–2, D.4 c.2, C.32 q.4 c.6, C.32 q.4 c.7, C.23 q.8 c.14, X.1.36.11, X.5.39.51. The passage on Ezechias had already been used in the *Tractatus de usurpata potestate fratrum*, p. 200. With the exception of Z, the printed editions and the manuscripts agree on the reading *irreprehensibile*, but that makes no sense and conflicts with the text of the law in X.4.14.8.

[107] X.4.14.8.

[108] 'Primum est generalis ordinatio universalis ecclesie procedens ex Deo, ab apostolis, sanctis patribus, generalibus conciliis, et Romanorum pontificibus comprobata et observata, secundum quam *omnis* [P] religio Christiana et generaliter omnia

That was the law. But since changing circumstances could justify exceptions from the law, Durant could not altogether deny the pope the right to make exemptions: the pope certainly 'should not' change the law (*non debet*), but that he 'could not' change the law had to be qualified with a 'perhaps' (*nec etiam forsitan valeat*).[109] The significance of that 'perhaps' depended on the circumstances. Hence Durant went on to declare that

> second, even supposing that the lord pope can grant the said exemptions, liberties, and immunities, it will still be shown that because of the foul scandals and the waste that are caused by them such concessions are expedient neither for himself nor for the universal church nor for the religious state nor even for the persons of the religious themselves.[110]

There followed a lengthy consideration of the various ways in which exemptions from episcopal oversight contributed to immoral conduct in the monasteries, scandalous disrespect for ecclesiastical jurisdiction, and a general breakdown of order. The conclusion followed as a matter of course:

> Even though some such privileges may in some respects have been appropriate before, they are now inappropriate because the circumstances

---

monasteria et loca religiosa, abbates, abbatisse, monachi, moniales, et omnes alii religiosi et persone ecclesiastice immediate subsunt gubernationi et cure episcoporum in civitatibus et diocesibus eorundem tanquam superiorum suorum, apostolorumque successorum et potestatem habentium. Unde cum dominus papa tantam et talem observationem ★mutare★ [P] non debet nec forte valeat, ergo nec generales exemptiones, privilegia, libertates, et immunitates derogativas et preiudicativas honori, potestati, statui, ordinationi, et ordini dictorum episcoporum et ordinariorum contra predictam generalem ordinationem sic passim concedere non debet, nec etiam forsitan valeat.' *TMA* 1.4 De exemptionibus, fol. 8va.

[109] This was closely parallel to the distinction between a legal obligation and the quasi-legal capacity to go against it which thirteenth-century canonists designated by the difference between *decet* (or *oportet*, or *expedit*) and *licet* and to which Durant himself referred a little later: 'Memor namque esse debet dominus papa verbi apostoli, qui ait i. Cor. vi. c., omnia mihi licent, sed non omnia expediunt.' *TMA* 1.4 De exemptionibus, fol. 11rb. Cf. 1 Corinthians 6:12. Torquebiau, 'Le Gallicanisme', pp. 277–82, has properly insisted on this distinction to demonstrate that Durant did not deny the papacy's ability to change even the most fundamental law of the church. But it should be stressed that the distinction went against the very grain of Durant's thinking and that he never drew attention to it. On the entire topic see Buisson, *Potestas und Caritas*; Marrone, 'The Absolute and the Ordained Powers'; and Oakley, *Omnipotence, Covenant and Order*.

[110] 'Secundo ostenditur quod, supposito quod idem dominus papa supradictas exemptiones, libertates, et immunitates concedere possit, non tamen expedit sibi nec universali ecclesie, nec statui religionis, nec personis religiosorum eas concedi propter plura mala scandala et dispendia que proveniunt ex eisdem.' *TMA* 1.4 De exemptionibus, fol. 11ra.

are different. Since one must take circumstances into consideration they ought to be abolished.[111]

The rubric on exemptions thus amounted to a ringing affirmation of the view that the general law of the church agreed with utility in ruling out exemptions. But the triumphant tone of the conclusion ought not to conceal the tension in which it stood to the beginning of Durant's argument. He had begun by declaring that the road to reform consisted of nothing more than obedience to the law. But he had found that course of argument obstructed because rulers were exempt from law. He had suggested for a moment that conciliar law was divine, but he had not been able to support that point of view to his satisfaction. He had then turned to reason and to the example of antiquity, but had found that by themselves they, too, were insufficient to limit papal power. Hence he had asked for general councils because they had better access to 'the truth'. But in the end his argument had turned out to be about utility and changing circumstances.

In the rubric on exemptions William Durant the Younger thus completed the shift from law to utility that forms the subtext of his argument for general councils. This has important implications. It reveals how keenly he was aware of the significance of changing circumstances and of the fact that change could not be avoided simply by insisting on the immutability of law: here we are on the verge of that new appreciation of history and historical change that would flourish in early modern times. It was this which led Durant to level the finely shaded distinctions between many different kinds of laws that excited the glossators in favour of the single sharp dichotomy between the letter of the law and its utility: here we are close to a rather more modern concept of legislation than can be reconciled with medieval notions of authority. But as a result the road to reform had turned out to be much longer and more treacherous than Durant suggested. It was all very well to argue

---

[111] 'Et licet *forsitan aliqua in aliquibus fuerunt talia* [P] privilegia congrua, nunc tamen ratione diversarum circunstantiarum sunt incongrua, quare tolli deberent ratione circunstantiarum que pensande sunt, xxiii. q. viii. occidit, *lxxxi. di. in omnibus, lxxxvi. di. non satis* [P], de pen. di. ii. §. opponitur, in fine, xxxii. q. iiii. quis ignoret et c. sequenti.' *TMA* 1.4 De exemptionibus, fol. 12vb (*male* 9vb). Cf. C.23 q.8 c.14, D.81 c.26, D.86 c.14, De pen. D.2 p.c.39, C.32 q.4 c.6–7. Durant summed up his case against exemptions by restating its complementary halves with all the legalistic righteousness of which he was capable; *TMA* 1.4 De exemptionibus, fol. 13rb.

that utility supported the existing laws about the order of the church, and that general councils were the proper institution to determine what was useful for the state of the church and what not. But once it had been granted that 'perhaps' the pope could go against general law, who was to say that in such a case the council would be right and the pope wrong? Who was to say that the return to the ancient state of the church so ardently desired by Durant might not come into conflict with utility?

*Chapter 5*

# MAGNUS ORDO DIFFERENTIE

The orders of the church have been divided and ranked for the concord of the human race, as Pope Leo has said, so that no schism would befall the church of God, as Jerome demonstrated to Bishop Evandrus.

William Durant[1]

This, then, was the argument for reforming the church by general councils that William Durant the Younger presented in the first part of his treatise. It pretended to rest on a coherent vision of law and order – but we have already suggested that beneath this placid surface there was a veritable abyss of doubts. The nature of those doubts still needs to be identified, and the broader programme of reform that was contained in the second part of the *Tractatus Maior*, as well as its relationship to the conciliar proposal, still need to be considered. These are the tasks to which the following three chapters are dedicated.[2]

Part of the reason why so much uncertainty has beset the study of Durant's intentions is that he never took the time to specify his purpose in any systematic way. He did say that he aimed at a 'healthy regime for the human race' and that according to St Paul the powers that be are ordained by God and therefore ought to conform to God's commands. He also made numerous suggestions how to improve this or that aspect of the world. But such communications are either much too general to form a detailed picture of the order they were meant to describe, or else they concentrate on specific violations of the law and thus allow us to perceive that order only from a negative perspective. It is as though

---

[1] 'Dicta diversitas ordinum ecclesiasticorum prelationis est propter concordiam humani generis instituta, sicut Leo papa ait, xlv. di. licet ii., et ne schisma fieret in ecclesia Dei, sicut probat Hieronymus ad Evandrum episcopum, xciii. di. legimus.' *TMA* 1.4 De exemptionibus, fol. 8vb. Cf. D.45 c.6, D.93 c.24.

[2] Readers who would like to consult a reasonably detailed paraphrase of the second part of the *Tractatus Maior* in the order in which it appears in the printed editions are referred to Viollet, pp. 85–110.

Durant thought that the order of the church itself was self evident, a given that required neither explanation nor defence.[3] Yet we need just such an explanation to understand precisely what his reform was meant to achieve.

Fortunately Durant could not avoid the question of church order altogether. Some violations went so deep that they required him to elaborate on what he thought they violated. Such was the case with exemptions; his discussion of them constitutes one of the rare occasions on which he offered a positive description of church order and an explanation of why he thought that order was right. The reason hinged upon a canon taken from the writings of Pope Gregory I:

That the general ordination of the universal church proceeds from God and is to be observed can be proven by the authority of Gregory in D.89 c.7 and C.16 q.1 c.63, where it is said that the purpose for which divine providence has distinguished between different ranks and orders is that the minor ones may exhibit their reverence to the powerful and the more powerful bestow their love upon the minor ones, so that true concord may come about, diversity may be turned into connection, and each office may be rightly administered. For if this great order of difference did not conserve the whole, it could not subsist on any other ground. The example of the heavenly armies instructs us, moreover, that the condition in which each creature is governed or lives cannot be the same for all, for there are not only angels but also archangels, and they are manifestly not equal but differ from each other in power and order.[4]

---

[3] It is worth pointing out that 'ecclesiology' strictly speaking was only just about to come into its own, which is why Arquillière referred to James of Viterbo's *De regimine christiano* as 'Le plus ancien traité de l'église'. The lack of a systematic ecclesiology in Durant's treatise is no failure. It is rather evidence for his preoccupation with preventing a political tradition from turning into the subject of theory.

[4] 'Quod autem generalis ordinatio *universalis* [P] ecclesie procedat a Deo et attendenda sit probatur auctoritate Gregorii, lxxxix. di. ad hoc, et xvi. q. i. ad hoc. Nam, ut ibidem dicitur, ad hoc *dispositionis* [P] provisio gradus diversos et ordines disposuit esse distinctos, ut dum reverentiam minores potentibus exhiberent, et potentiores minoribus dilectionem impenderent, vera concordia fieret, et ex diversitate connexio, et recte officiorum gereretur administratio singulorum. Neque enim universitas alia poterat ratione subsistere nisi huiusmodi magnus eam differentie ordo conservaret. Quia vero queque creatura in una eademque qualitate gubernari vel vivere non potest, celestium militiarum exemplar nos instruit, quia dum sunt angeli, sunt archangeli, et liquet quia non sunt equales, sed in potestate et ordine differunt alter ab altero.' *TMA* 1.4 De exemptionibus, fol. 8va–b. Cf. D.89 c.7, C.16 q.1 c.63. A few lines later Durant quoted the text of C.16 q.1 c.63, which agreed with D.89 c.7 in stating that 'ad hoc locorum gradus rationis ordo distinxit et iudicia esse constituit, ut nec prepositi in opprimendo subiectos se frustra valeant occupare, nec subiectis iterum contra suos prepositos effrenata sit resultandi licentia.' *TMA* 1.4 De exemptionibus, fol. 8vb. Cf. C.11 q.3 c.31. On the

This canon is absolutely crucial. Durant used it more than once in the *Tractatus Maior* in order to support his view of the proper extent of government, and he was still insisting on it toward the end of his life when once again he found it necessary to explain the principles of government to the obstreperous noblemen of the Gévaudan.[5] Its general meaning is clear enough. As he put it a few lines later, 'these different ecclesiastical orders of prelacy have been established for the sake of concord among the human race and in order to prevent schism in the church'.[6] But it requires some analysis to determine precisely what he meant when he spoke of concord and of schism.

## CONCORD AND SCHISM

Let us begin by noting that Gregory's words plainly, almost outrageously, ignore distinctions that we regard as fundamental. On the one hand he emphatically uses the language of power and government. Terms like *potentes, potestas, officium, administratio, gubernare*, and especially *militia* should leave no doubt that this power is not purely 'spiritual' – although it is that, too – but real. On the other hand Gregory speaks with no less emphasis of love (*dilectio*), reverence, and true concord. This sounds strange to modern ears: on the whole we do not expect the powerful to love us, and usually we are content if public concord exists in any form from indifference to self-restraint. Far from inviting the powerful into our private lives, we take precautions not to let them learn too much about us without duly executed warrants and we are

close correspondence between Durant's view of order and that of the secular clergy in the 1280s see Congar, 'Aspects', pp. 63–80; Schleyer, *Anfänge*, pp. 77–90; Lagarde, 'La Philosophie sociale'. In general see Schwer, *Stand und Ständeordnung*; Struve, *Entwicklung der organologischen Staatsauffassung*; Michaud-Quantin, *Universitas*.

5  Durant had already referred to D.89 c.7 and C.16 q.1 c.63 in *TMA* 1.3, fol. 5ra, in order to support the principle that the powers that be must conform to God because they are ordained by God. He referred to the same two canons again at *TMA* 2.7, fol. 17rb. In 1328, when a dispute with the de Peyre erupted while Durant happened to be absent from Mende, he wrote to his subordinates with instructions in which he quoted D.89 c.7; Viollet, p. 53. Viollet translated the passage without giving the original Latin and without identifying the source of the quotation, but the text leaves no doubt that what he called a 'préambule philosophique' was identical with D.89 c.7.

6  'Dicta diversitas ordinum ecclesiasticorum prelationis est propter concordiam humani generis instituta, sicut Leo papa ait, xlv. di. licet ii., et ne scisma fieret in ecclesia Dei, sicut probat Hieronymus ad Evandrum episcopum, xcii. di. legimus, et idem probat ad Neopotianum scribens, xcv. di. esto subiectus pontifici tuo.' *TMA* 1.4 De exemptionibus, fol. 8vb. Cf. D.45 c.6, D.93 c.24, D.95 c.7.

certainly not used to mixing love with the exercise of power, as Pope Gregory does, but tend to treat them as incommensurables, relegating the former to the realm of private life and the latter to the realm of politics. Here that is not so: the order in question places love and power in one category.

Gregory's words similarly conflict with modern sensibilities when he compares the relations between angels and archangels to those between human beings. In modern times human beings and angels would be thought to belong to entirely separate spheres of reality – to the extent that angels are still thought to be part of reality at all – so that whatever may apply to angels has little bearing on the rules of human society. But here, human government has to follow the example of angelic government.[7] Both are subject to similar rules and belong to a single order comprising heaven and earth.

Again, Pope Gregory declares that the order of the church consists of 'creatures'. And what do these creatures do? They 'are governed or they live', *gubernari vel vivere*, as though the act of living were something basically comparable to the act of being governed, as though there were no need to refer to the difference between a creature and a citizen by anything more than a simple *vel*. We tend to regard life as something physical and government as something moral, ethical, or political, and we distinguish rather sharply between the two. Life is to be studied by biologists and physicians; government by political scientists, lawyers, perhaps historians. But here no such distinction seems to exist. The physical differences between creatures – indeed, the hierarchical gradations of the universe itself – are considered to have been created for a moral purpose and to form an integral element of governmental order, while good government is predicated on observing physical differences. The order in question thus straddles the border between physics and ethics.

There is one other way in which Gregory ignores distinctions that we consider fundamental, and it is perhaps the most telling. He says that 'the whole could not subsist on any other ground if this great order of difference did not conserve it'. The 'whole' of which

---

7 To put it in different terms, the church militant is patterned on the church triumphant, as Durant pointed out in *TMA* 1.4 De exemptionibus, fol. 9va, with words quoted from St Bernard's *De consideratione*, 3.17–18. The mendicants, on the other hand, disputed that there was an exact correspondence between the church militant and the angelic hierarchy; Congar, 'Aspects', pp. 129–32.

he speaks is *universitas*, a term which in the present context means the whole church but which can also mean the universe – especially since the church itself was 'universal' and proceeded from God. The 'ground' is *ratio*, reason. But we cannot translate it as 'reason' without some explanation because this *ratio* is not merely something by which the universal church is said to be administered, or supervised, or governed in a rational way; it is something without which the universal church cannot 'subsist'. Nor can we simply translate it as 'ground' unless we stress that this 'ground' is not merely physical or existential, but also rational. In other words, the order in question links reason to existence, truth to reality. Beyond a shadow of a doubt this is the most important respect in which Gregory saw things as linked that we regard as separate, indeed, as fundamentally diverse. It is also impossible to render in any modern language, for the simple reason that we no longer consider 'reason' as a ground for anything other than the truth, expressed in rational propositions, but do not see it as a ground of physical existence.[8]

The order of the church was thus universal in a sense that has been virtually lost in modern thought. It overrides distinctions between love and power, heaven and earth, physics and ethics, and truth and existence. It identifies the extent of the church, 'one, holy, catholic, and apostolic', with the universe. It postulates a single entity behind fundamentally different kinds of phenomena: heavenly as well as earthly, natural as well as rational, efficient causes as well as final causes, physical facts as well as moral purposes – and that entity, of course, is God: 'The said order of the church must neither be slighted nor interdicted, because it has God as its author.'[9]

Universal unity, however, is only one of two dimensions that make up the order of which Gregory was speaking. The other consists of the differences between the more and less powerful. This is not an order of equality but of inequality or 'difference', and it should be stressed that the inequalities are explicitly identified with different degrees of power. If there is a corresponding equality,

---

[8] Although it might be argued that there are modern equivalents. The debate over quantum physics versus the theory of relativity is, after all, in part a debate about the extent to which the physical structure of the universe does or does not conform to 'reason'.

[9] 'Non igitur parvipendenda nec interdicenda est dicta ordinatio que Deum habet autorem.' *TMA* 1.4 De exemptionibus, fol. 9va.

then only in the sense that no rank and order is to be disturbed by any other. Power is distributed in parcels of different sizes to different ranks but it does not cross the borders between one rank and another. It is specific to each rank. This is why acts of living can be regarded as identical with acts of government; there is no act of government, that is, no exercise of power, that transgresses the boundaries between the creatures. All creatures are supposed to live in respect of their creator and stay within their ordained limits so that no act of life will violate the harmony of the universe. Conversely, since life is the purpose for which each creature was created each act of life is evidence for its obedience to the creator, and thus an act of being governed, too.

Consequently the distinction between the public and private spheres is virtually the reverse of that which applies in modern thought. Here power is a private matter, a propriety, a property almost like private property, both in the sense of 'something owned' and in the sense of 'quality'. Power, therefore, does not and cannot serve as a means by which to hold the whole together. On the contrary, power is the main criterion of distinction. The means by which the whole is held together rather consists of love from above and reverence from below. Love and reverence do transgress the boundaries that are established by different degrees of power. They are what makes it possible for all hearts to beat in harmony: they bring about that 'true concord' by which all creatures are freely joined together in a single, natural, and moral universe. Love and reverence, in other words, not power, are truly public forces, bonds of the true body politic, and thus the very opposite of personal emotions.

The differences between the orders of the church thus have a twofold function. On the one hand, they divide the whole into parts and limit the exercise of power by one creature over another. In this regard they are like boundaries that cannot be transgressed by power without destroying true concord. Indeed, they are essential for the 'subsistence' of the union between reason and reality and cannot be transgressed without putting the universe itself in jeopardy. On the other hand, these differences make it possible for love and reverence to unite all creatures in a single universe. Without such differences there could be no 'true concord' but only monotony; without those differences there would then be no purpose to the universe. In other words, the differences between the creatures protect the existence and secure the purpose of the universe.

This, then, was how William Durant the Younger pictured the foundations of the order of the church. It does not matter much by which name we choose to refer to them – 'general order of the church', 'hierarchy', and 'great order of difference' are all good candidates. The point is that this order balances two equally important elements, hierarchical subordination and the coincidence of reason with reality, which differ fundamentally from modern views both of the church and of the world. It deviates from stereotypical assumptions about the nature of medieval hierarchical thought, which often equate 'hierarchy' with a sort of pyramidal structure, regular in shape and completely dominated by an apex towering above the whole. To do so, however, is to give pride of place to a secondary quality of hierarchy while omitting its fundamental quality, which is that of a 'holy government' in which there is no conflict between what is and what ought to be. It is legitimate – indeed, it is revealing – to point out that the subordination of the different ranks and orders in the great order of difference resembles a central feature of modern bureaucratic structures and their preoccupation with ruling out any kind of overlapping responsibilities. But to describe both as 'hierarchical' without further comment would be an exercise in equivocation.[10]

Such equivocations are not easy to avoid in the case of an author who uses words that we still use in other ways in order to express ideas that we no longer hold. We can therefore only deal with Durant's ideas about reform by constantly resisting our natural tendency to follow our own conception of the world and reminding ourselves instead of what he meant by true concord and by schism. 'True concord' was a state in which reason coincided with existence, love harmonized with power, and each creature occupied its proper place in the universe. 'Schism', in contrast, severed reason from existence. It resulted if power was allowed to grow

---

[10] The 'pyramidal' notion is integral to Ullmann's characterization of ecclesiastical theories of power as 'descending', but popular far beyond his writings. See, e.g., Beer, 'The Rule of the Wise and the Holy'. For correctives see the writings of Luscombe, especially 'Conceptions of Hierarchy', the investigations into medieval social vocabulary by Michaud-Quantin in *Universitas* and *Etudes sur le vocabulaire philosophique*, and the illuminating essay by Schwer, *Stand und Ständeordnung*. For an anthropological perspective see the fascinating studies of Dumont, *Homo hierarchicus* and *Essays on Individualism*.

beyond its natural limits and, like a cancer, to devour those beneath it, if love and reverence were overridden by a force that transgressed divine distinctions. Whether such power grew from excessive love or from arrogance was immaterial; in either case it was inordinate, out of proportion with the reason of the universe, and had to be resisted, for reason could not be split from existence without threatening the universe with extinction.

### REFORM OF THE MEMBERS

While historians who have dealt with Durant's treatise have often noted with dismay its apparent lack of organization, their complaints are not quite justified. They rest in part on the confusion caused by the faulty transmission of the text but in greater part on their failure to place Durant's ideas against the logic of the background that we have just sketched. True, Durant presented his suggestions in a form that did not express that logic, but to do so was not necessary since his audience's familiarity with hierarchical conceptions would have enabled it to understand the systematic coherence of his ideas without much prompting. That coherence rested on the logic of the 'great order of difference'.

Accordingly there were two basic goals that governed Durant's proposals: to clarify the distinctions between the ranks and orders of the church; and to elaborate the unifying bonds that were the sole means of maintaining true concord. Both were equally important for containing the growth of papal power, and thus for protecting the universe from cataclysm, but the majority of Durant's proposals were meant to confirm distinctions. They eloquently testify to his conviction that such distinctions were like joints without which the church's body would collapse.

These distinctions can be divided into three kinds: distinctions between Christians and non-Christians, between laymen and clerics, and between different kinds of clerics.[11] Given the universal claims of the great order of difference, one might have thought that Durant would spend much energy on the first of these; but whether universality is more relative a term than it appears to be, or whether Durant was more parochial than he imagined, it received

---

[11] On other schemes of dividing society into different orders see Michaud-Quantin, *Etudes*, pp. 163–86.

much less attention than the other two. There are a few injunctions on Christians to stay away from Jews.[12] There is an attempt to sanction King Philip IV's expulsion of the Jews, from which Durant had personally benefited, by lending the authority of Saint Louis to a decree expelling Jews that actually had come from an ancient council of Toledo – with curious consequences for geography and chronology.[13] There are a few attacks on pagan practices and an attempt to strengthen the embargo on trading arms with Saracens because such trade hurt the crusade.[14] But that is about all.

The detail in which Durant delineated distinctions within Christian society is overwhelming by comparison. If we may judge according to the bulk of his suggestions, the most important issue was the boundary between the clergy and the laity. During the later middle ages – in part because of the increase in the power of the state, in part because of the very success with which the church had managed to coopt the laity – the task of distinguishing between the 'two peoples' became increasingly complex.[15] There were too many clerics who led a borderline existence and too many laymen who thought that the temporal world was thoroughly imbued with spiritual blessings – hence the ideals of Gregory VII and his followers became ever harder to maintain.

This posed a crucial threat not merely to the separate existence of

12 Christians who broke bread with Jews were to be excommunicated and princes who employed Jews were to be punished. Jews were to wear distinctive clothing, stay indoors on the days of Christ's passion, and keep their windows shut at Easter. They were not to eat or bathe with Christians, serve as their physicians, keep them as slaves, have sexual intercourse with them, or testify against them. Spain was singled out for special criticism, since the rulers there employed them as servants at their table and appointed them to public office, including offices that should have been reserved to clerics. *TMA* 2.61, fols. 42rb–43ra.

13 *TMA* 2.71, fol. 51rb–va; cf. Viollet, pp. 99f. The canon was VI Toletanum c. 3, the King was Chintila, the date was AD 638. Nevertheless Durant declared that Louis IX had authored the decree.

14 Love-potions, auguries, divinations 'secundum morem gentilium', and any kind of magic were to be punished with five years of penance; *TMA* 2.12, fol. 21ra–b. Traders with the Saracens were to be excommunicated *ipso facto*, kept as slaves by anyone who captured them, their goods to be sold, and absolution not to be granted unless they dedicated their illicit gains to the crusade. The pope was specially criticized for the ease with which he granted indulgences in such cases; *TMA* 2.61, fol. 43ra; cf. *TMA* 2.96 (3.27), fol. 59rb.

15 E.g. Mundy, *Europe*, pp. 30f., 42, 541; Gilles, 'Clergé méridional'; Strayer, *Reign of Philip the Fair*, pp. 193f., 198, 243f. Cf. especially the 'Enquête sur la juridiction en Languedoc (vers 1300),' ed. Boutaric, 'Notices', pp. 132–5.

the clergy but to its perceived superiority over the laity as well. Ecclesiastical supremacy depended on the separate existence of the clergy. Durant therefore devoted much of his energy to driving home means by which the boundaries between clerics and laymen could be protected from erosion. He had experience in trying to coax promises from King Philip IV to respect the rights of borderline clerics.[16] He railed against the rather reasonable compromise of Boniface VIII that allowed married clerics to be taken into temporal courts unless they were tonsured and wore ecclesiastical attire, arguing that this raised the requirements for certified association with the clergy higher than was licit according to the ancient law.[17] In short, he tried to keep the circle describing the limits of the clergy as wide as possible. He was a clerical imperialist.

At the same time he pointed out how much it mattered for the clergy to keep their distance from the laity.[18] He repeated all of the ancient rules about the special conduct of the clergy.[19] Laughter, drink, and spectacles were out; modest gait was in; taverns, fancy clothes, and animals for hunting were forbidden; fasting and reading psalms were encouraged; and times set aside for spiritual matters were not to be disturbed by any type of secular activity.[20] Laymen and women were not to dance in church, sing worldly songs, or disturb the ministers.[21] They were especially not to be allowed to enter the sacrarium, to touch utensils for mass, or to

[16] In 1300 Philip had granted him rather broadly that 'a clericis uxoratis et non uxoratis dicte diocesis clericaliter sine fraude viventibus quinquagesimalis vel quevis alia pro nobis subventio deinceps non levetur'. R-S, no. 11 (24.II.1300), p. 19.

[17] 'Decretalis Bonifaciana de clericis coniugatis, clerici, haberet revocari, cum per ipsam generale privilegium ecclesie quoad personas et res ecclesiasticas coniugatorum ab ipso restringantur. Et hoc a dicto domino Bonifacio factum fuerit absque auctoritate et vocatione concilii generalis, cum tamen secundum decretum Gregorii pape, xxii. di. si qui, tales clerici coniugati stipendia etiam ab ecclesia recipere possent et sub ecclesiastica essent tenendi regula.' *TMA* 2.4, fol. 16ra. Cf. VI.3.2.1, D.32 c.3. This was the only occasion in the treatise on which he stated that a pope ought not to have issued a particular decree without the assistance of a general council. Müller, *Konzil von Vienne*, p. 615, misinterpreted Durant's reason for rejecting Boniface's decretal.

[18] The very first canon of the second part was that 'episcopus at presbyter aut diaconus nequaquam curas seculares assumat sin aliter deiiciatur, ponitur lxxxviii. di. episcopus'. *TMA* 2.1, fol. 14rb. Cf. D.88 c.3.

[19] The main chapters on clerical conduct are *TMA* 2.1, fols. 14rb–15rb, *TMA* 2.32, fols. 28va–29vb, *TMA* 2.38, fols. 31va–33vb (with special attention to bishops), *TMA* 2.53, fols. 37ra–39va (with special attention to monks), and *TMA* 2.92 (3.23), fols. 56vb–57rb (with special attention to abbots). On clothing see also *TMA* 2.79 (3.10), fol. 54rb–va; on dogs and falcons for the hunt: *TMA* 2.51, fols. 36vb–37ra; on fasting: *TMA* 2.56, fols. 40ra–41ra, *TMA* 2.83 (3.13), fol. 54vb.

[20] *TMA* 2.64, fol. 43va.     [21] *TMA* 2.58, fol. 41rb–va.

carry crosses in processions.[22] They were also not to meet in churches or cemeteries for communal eating or any kind of business, especially not judicial business.[23] Nor were they to be buried in churches.[24] Confraternities provoked Durant's particular displeasure. In his opinion they mainly served as an occasion for clerics to fraternize with laymen in order to get drunk and to complain about their superiors.[25] And so the plaints continued.

Three matters received particular attention from Durant because they were particularly dangerous for the distinction between the clergy and the laity: women; money or property; and temporal authority – a familiar list and one well designed to highlight that Durant meant to continue the Gregorian tradition of reform. On all three points his views were thoroughly conventional – with some significant exceptions that will require our attention later on. Concerning women, he insisted ruthlessly on their subjection to men and on enforcing chastity.[26] Clerics were not to meet any women without supervision, not even if they were their relatives, since in the words of Augustine 'not all of those who accompany my sister are themselves my sisters'.[27] Bishops, priests, and ministers who had been 'polluted' by women were to be deposed from office.[28] Laymen were not to attend the masses of

---

[22] *TMA* 2.55, fols. 39vb–40ra.     [23] *TMA* 2.35, fols. 30vb–31ra.

[24] *TMA* 2.80 (3.11), fol. 54va. Men who died in tournaments or duels were to be denied ecclesiastical burial altogether: *TMA* 2.62, fol. 43ra–b.

[25] 'Videretur insuper utile quod confratrie in quibus tam clerici quam laici se ingurgitant et commessationibus et ebrietati et in multis diversis tractatibus contra eorum superiores vacant, reprobarentur.' *TMA* 2.35, fol. 31ra.

[26] Women were not to receive letters from, nor send letters to, other men without their husbands' knowledge: *TMA* 2.63, fol. 43rb. They were not to abuse studying as a pretext to meet with other men, 'quia tam in ecclesiis quam extra ecclesias viri et mulieres extranee ab eorum parentela in diversis ludis se exercitant et tactibus, appetitibus, et applausibus mutuo ad concupiscentiam inflammantur.' *TMA* 2.69, fol. 45va–b. A woman who cut her hair, 'quam Deus ad velamen eius et ad memoriam subiectionis illi dedit, tamquam resolvens ius subiectionis anathema sit.' *TMA* 2.69, fol. 45vb. Adulterers were to be excommunicated and put to public shame: *TMA* 2.59, fols. 41va–42ra.

[27] 'Unde in i. capitulo concilii Taraconensis statutum est quod etiam clerici ad proximas sanguinis sine testimonio non accedant. Nam, ut Augustinus dicit, omnes qui cum sorore mea sunt sorores meae non sunt, lxxxi. di. legitur.' *TMA* 2.10, fol. 18ra. Cf. D.81 c.25ff. Access of women to churches or cemeteries was to be supervised in order to prevent secret misdeeds: *TMA* 2.58, fol. 41rb. Brothels were not to be located near churches, especially not near the papal palace, and the papal marshal was to take no payments from whores and pimps: *TMA* 2.10, fol. 18ra–b.

[28] 'In vii. autem concilio Toletano, quarta disputatione, statuitur quod episcopi qui cum mulieribus polluuntur locis suis, ordine, et dignitate priventur. Et in quinta disputatione dicti concilii de sacerdotibus et ministris statuitur illud idem.' *TMA* 2.59, fols. 41vb–42ra. Cf. *TMA* 2.1, fol. 14va. In Hinschius' edition the Toledan council in question is the 8th.

priests known to keep concubines.²⁹ The children of such unions
were to be reduced to perpetual servitude in their father's church.³⁰
And clerics who had been raised at church expense were to make a
public declaration upon reaching eighteen years of age as to
whether they would enter orders or marry, so that they could be
forced to make restitution if later on they abused their benefices.³¹

Second, concerning money or property, Durant recalled all of
the basic, and many of the more elaborate, rules about simony.
Simony was heresy.³² The sale of clerical offices, of baptism, burial,
penance, the eucharist, or any other sacrament was to be punished
by excommunication, deposition from office, or other penalties,
depending on the nature of the offence and the offender's status.³³
The benefits of ecclesiastical jurisdiction were to be rendered free of
charge.³⁴ The church's property belonged to all in common.³⁵
Clerics who acquired private property deserved excommunica-
tion.³⁶ Clerics were not to engage in any form of secular traffick-
ing.³⁷ The bishops were solely responsible for the administration
of ecclesiastical revenues, which were to be divided into the four
canonical portions for the bishop, the clergy, the poor, and the
repair of the church.³⁸ No gifts were to be accepted from unclean
sources.³⁹ If any monetary penalties were imposed for violations of
ecclesiastical laws (a custom Durant deplored because it made the

²⁹ 'Etiam constitutum fit a Nicolao papa et ab Alexandro ii. et a Leone papa quod nullus
missam audiat presbyteri quem scit concubinam habere indubitanter vel subintroductam
mulierem, xxxii. di. nullus, et c. preter hoc, de coha. muli. et cle. unam, xv. q. viii. fere
per totum.' *TMA* 2.59, fol. 41vb. Cf. D.32 c.5–6, X.3.2.7, C.15 q.8.
³⁰ *TMA* 2.76 (3.7), fol. 54vb.
³¹ *TMA* 2.33, fol. 30ra–b. The proper age for ordination and consecration was to be
observed for every clerical office in order to avoid the peril of fornication: *TMA* 2.13, fol.
21rb.
³² 'Videretur super hoc maxime providendum. Nam hec heresis maxime corrumpit
ecclesiam universalem et universos populos, et provisa iam remedia pro nihilo reputan-
tur.' *TMA* 2.20, fol. 24vb.
³³ *TMA* 2.1, fol. 14vb. *TMA* 2.60, fol. 42ra–b.
³⁴ *TMA* 2.67, fol. 45ra. Judges, advocates, procurators, and notaries were to be appointed
to render their services free of charge to the poor: *TMA* 2.31, fol. 28va.
³⁵ *TMA* 2.2, fol. 15rb–va.
³⁶ *TMA* 2.37, fol. 31rb–va. Bishops were to prepare an inventory of their private
possessions at the time of their promotion: *TMA* 2.1, fol. 15ra.
³⁷ *TMA* 2.8, fol. 17va.
³⁸ *TMA* 2.1, fol. 15rb; *TMA* 2.78 (3.9), fol. 54ra–b. On the need to provide housing and
income for lepers: *TMA* 2.86 (3.17), fol. 56ra. On the need to restore and build new
*xenodochia, orphanotrophia, gerontocomia,* and *brephotrophia:* *TMA* 2.88 (3.19), fol. 56rb.
³⁹ Such as Jews, usurers, oppressors of the poor, thieves, robbers, pimps, and whores: *TMA*
2.10, fol. 18ra–b; *TMA* 2.39, fols. 33vb–34ra; *TMA* 2.67, fol. 45ra.

church susceptible to defamation), they ought at least to be 'converted to pious purposes'.[40] And bishops were to be assisted by clerical economists and advocates in order to free their time for purely spiritual functions.[41] In short, as far as possible the church was not to be infected by mammon, and inasmuch as the church had to have an endowment in order to fulfil its duties, that endowment was to be subjected to controls that prevented any mixing of spiritual with temporal purposes.

Third, concerning temporal power, Durant insisted on the general principle that 'ecclesiastical law ought to be distinguished from temporal law'.[42] He also compiled a list of fifty gravamina by which the temporal authorities were violating that distinction.[43] Attacks on pilgrims, taxes on clerics, interference with appointments to benefices, exacting spoils, disregard for benefit of clergy, disregard for ecclesiastical jurisdiction, and use of force to overturn excommunications were some of them. Plain bad manners in meetings with the clergy were criticized as well.[44] Temporal lords were not to restrict donations to the church.[45] Donations to the

---

[40] 'Item cum propter penam quam ecclesia frequenter recipit ex consuetudine ab his qui excommunicationem sustinent animo indurato et sacrilegis et aliis criminosis pro criminibus ecclesiasticis commissis per eos ipsa ecclesia apud laicos frequenter diffametur, . . . videretur pensandum an expediret ipsam in pios usus esse convertendam.' TMA 2.89 (3.20), fol. 56rb–va.

[41] TMA 2.24, fol. 27ra–b; cf. Tractatus de usurpata potestate fratrum, pp. 194f.

[42] 'Videretur ideo utile . . . quod distinguerentur iura ecclesiastica et secularia, cum hoc videatur consonum iuri, x. di. quoniam, xcvi. di. cum ad verum, et c. duobus.' TMA 2.9, fol. 18ra. Cf. D.10 c.8, D.96 c.6, D.96 c.10. Cf. TMA 2.96 (3.27), fol. 59va: 'Quod primatus dicte Romane ecclesie declararetur, et distingueretur per iura ecclesiastica et secularia.' Henry of Ghent used D.96 c.6 very similarly: Lagarde, 'La philosophie sociale', pp. 124–6.

[43] TMA 2.70, fols. 45vb–49rb. In TMA, 2.100 (3.30), fol. 51vb, Durant declared that he had listed exactly fifty gravamina in TMA 2.70. Both in the printed editions and in the manuscripts TMA 2.70 is subdivided into paragraphs, but the totals are not the same and amount in neither case to fifty.

[44] 'Item multi ex dictis regibus et principibus imitantur errorem imperatoris Constantinopolitani, quia archiepiscopis et episcopis regni eorum et aliorum regnorum ad eos venientibus, sicut deberent, reverenter non assurgunt, nec eis iuxta eos venerabilem sedem assignant. Imo, quod est deterius, vix interdum ingressum possunt habere ad eos et ad cancellarios et consiliarios eorundem, et cum difficultate audientia prestatur eisdem, et dictis regibus et principibus in solio eorum vel lectis sedentibus predicti archiepiscopi, episcopi, abbates, et alii prelati cum laicis et communibus personis in terra vel communibus sedibus sedere coguntur contra honorem et reverentiam totius cleri et ecclesiastice dignitatis, et contra iura de maiorit. et obed. solite, lxiii. di. valentinianus, xcvi. di. duo, xi. q. i. sacerdotibus.' TMA 2.70, fol. 49ra–b. Cf. X.1.33.6, D.63 c.3, D.96 c.10, C.11 q.1 c.41.      [45] TMA 2.5, fol. 16ra–b; TMA 2.47, fols. 35vb–36ra.

church were not be diminished by charges of any kind since in such cases 'infinity is the best measure'.[46] Temporal lords who offended the church in any way, especially by seizing or arresting clerics, were to be punished without hesitation.[47] Indeed, Durant believed that the church might do well to reinstitute the ancient rule by which public officials were excluded from communion during their term of office 'because of the molestations which nowadays officials of the commonwealth inflict upon the church'.[48] And defenders of the church were to be appointed by temporal authorities at every cathedral, 'since by a certain necessity ecclesiastical persons are nowadays compelled to litigate more frequently than others in the courts of princes'.[49]

These were some of Durant's ideas about the ways in which the clergy could be kept at a proper distance from the laity and by which the special dangers posed by women, money, and temporal power were to be resisted.[50] Distinctions between different kinds of clerics were simpler and more schematic, largely because they coincided with the boundaries of the various ecclesiastical administrative districts. Thus the basic rule was quite simply that every cleric ought to stay in the place where his office was while all forms of ecclesiastical vagrancy were condemned.[51] Monks were to stay in their monasteries, without which they were like fish without water.[52] If they wished to leave their monasteries for any length of

---

[46] 'Cuilibet licet res patrimoniales vel partem, sive causa mortis, vel iure institutionis, vel quocunque alio modo relinquere ecclesie, vel inter vivos donare, nec est necesse quod talis donatio actis insinuetur, C. de sacrosanctis ecclesiis, l. illud, nam in donationibus que fiunt ecclesiis optima mensura est immensitas.' *TMA* 2.66, fol. 44rb. Cf. Cod.1.2.19.

[47] *TMA* 2.1, fol. 14rb (*male* 15rb); *TMA* 2.3, fol. 15va–b; *TMA* 2.38, fols. 27vb–28ra; *TMA* 2.70, fols. 46ra–47rb.

[48] 'Videretur pensandum propter molestiam quam officiales rei publice ingerunt hodie ecclesie, si dictum concilium posset vel expediret revocari.' *TMA* 2.42, fol. 34rb, with reference to I Arelatense c.7, Elibertanum c.56.

[49] 'Videretur providendum si esset utile huiusmodi defensores ab universis principibus per ecclesiam postulari, cum persone ecclesiastice ex quadam necessitate habeant hodie plus ceteris in curiis principum litigare.' *TMA* 2.40, fol. 34ra.

[50] It is instructive to compare Durant's complaints with their mirror image in the 'Enquête sur la juridiction en Languedoc (vers 1300)' published by Boutaric, 'Notices', pp. 132–5, which contains detailed complaints about unjustified extensions of ecclesiastical jurisdiction.

[51] 'Et dicta iura et consimilia non serventur, ex quo multe insolentie committuntur, plurima scandala in clero et populo eveniunt, et pericula animarum. Videretur super hoc providendum, cum videantur omnes persone ecclesiastice evagari sicut oves non habentes pastorem.' *TMA* 2.52, fol. 37ra.

[52] *TMA* 2.53, fol. 37rb–va. Cf. C.16 q.1 c.8.

time, they had to get permission from the bishop.[53] Priests were not to be allowed to leave the diocese without episcopal permission either.[54] If they wished to visit the royal court, permission had to come from even higher authorities, namely, the archbishop or the provincial council.[55] Bishops who wished to leave their diocese always had to obtain permission from the archbishop or the provincial council.[56] And no permission was to be given to any cleric to leave his church for longer than three weeks, and never on major holidays, although (or perhaps because) it was precisely on those holidays that kings and popes seemed to require bishops to appear at court with unfortunate persistence.[57] Visits to Rome were to be limited as well, but here was a case in which even Durant accepted that a three-week limit was unrealistic; such visits were allowed to last up to six months.[58]

Preserving the distinctions between Christians and non-Christians, between clerics and laymen, and between different kinds of clerics thus constituted one means of keeping the order of the church intact. The other means was to promote the bonds of union. The central point to be made in this connection was that union had to be achieved by means other than power. Two basic principles of unity can be identified among Durant's suggestions, roughly corresponding to the principles announced in the first and second chapters of the *Tractatus Maior*. We may refer to these as exemplary efficiency and knowledge of the law. The point of exemplary efficiency was this: if someone in a superior order gave his inferiors clear examples of a certain type of conduct, they would adopt it without further prompting. Here we encounter a particularly important difference between our own conceptions and that of the 'great order of difference' – one that we have noted previously but whose significance is better appreciated in the present context. From our point of view, examples, good or bad, can be employed as illustrations to clarify a point of information or even to teach a moral lesson, but hardly to exercise a direct effect, moral or otherwise. Durant, however, clearly regarded examples as different from mere illustrations. Examples could 'compel' a certain kind

---

[53] *TMA* 2.53, fol. 37va.      [54] *TMA* 2.52, fol. 37ra.
[55] *TMA* 2.17, fol. 22va–b. Cf. *TMA* 2.16, fol. 22va.
[56] *TMA* 2.17, fol. 22va–b. Cf. *TMA* 2.16, fol. 22va, *TMA* 2.38, fol. 32rb.
[57] *TMA* 2.1, fol. 14va–vb; *TMA* 2.16, fol. 22va; *TMA* 2.38, fol. 32ra; *TMA* 2.54, fol. 39va–b.      [58] *TMA* 2.96 (3.27), fol. 59rb.

of action by the sheer force of their impression.[59] This helps to explain the anger with which he pointed out that laymen really could not be expected to pay respect to the clergy if the friars gave them a contrary example.[60] It also helps to explain why reform had to begin at the top. If it was true that lower ranks and orders imitated the conduct of their superiors, then it was hopeless to aim at reforming the laity before the clergy had reformed itself. The reform of the laity rather depended on the previous reform of, in descending order, Rome, the prelates, the clergy, the religious, and kings and princes.[61] Durant's reference to Christ's example in the opening words of the *Tractatus Maior* thus was much more than a command to respect the moral reciprocity of the golden rule of natural law. Quite the contrary: the point was the difference between superiors and subordinates, that is, the lack of reciprocity. It was not just unfair for priests with beams in their eyes to remove the motes in the eyes of laymen: it was impossible.[62] Much less could laymen remove such motes on their own. Hence superiors bore the considerable weight of full responsibility for the conduct of their inferiors.[63] That meant that for the same offence prelates were justly subjected to harsher penalties than laymen.[64] It also meant that women who were convicted of adultery were not to be

59 'Predictus dominus papa et reges primo bene et bona facerent et exemplo suo ad idem faciendum alios compellerent.' *TMA* 1.3, fol. 5rb. On the question of examples see Buisson, *Potestas und Caritas*, Bynum, *Docere Verbo et Exemplo*, and Brémond *et al.*, *L'Exemplum*. The evidence presented by Bynum suggests, not surprisingly, a connection between Durant's conception of reform and that of the twelfth-century canons.

60 'Quam reverentiam et obedientiam impendent laici et domini principes temporales dictis episcopis et ordinariis, quibus patenter et notorie et manifeste religiosi de ordine paupertatis et alii frequenter inobedientes et irreverentes existunt? Certe quod ab eis facile agitur trahitur ab aliis in exemplum, de accusat. qualiter et quando.' *TMA* 1.4 De exemptionibus, fol. 12ra (*male* 9ra). Cf. X.5.1.24. Cf. Schleyer, *Anfänge*, p. 138. Out of a similar concern for reverence Henry of Ghent had even insisted that 'legislator non potest concedere privilegium aut condere statutum ad quod sequitur in ecclesia subtractio debite reverentie'. Marrone, 'The Absolute and the Ordained Powers', p. 23.

61 'Ad reformationem autem totius status secularis faceret specialiter reformatio dictorum regum et principum quo ad predicta, et reformatio etiam ecclesie Romane, prelatorum, religiosorum, et totius cleri, quia quod ab eis agitur trahitur ab ipsis laicis in exemplum.' *TMA* 2.100, fol. 51vb. Not in this passage, but everywhere else Durant insisted on placing the religious after the rest of the clergy. It was precisely this mediation of action through the ranks of the hierarchy that was contested by the mendicants; Congar, 'Aspects', pp. 127–9.     62 See above, pp. 129f.

63 'Secundum [Gregorium] tot unusquisque portare onera cogitur quot in hoc mundo principatur, sicut in pastorali ait.' *TMA* 1.3 De limitanda potestate, fol. 7ra.

64 'Nicolaus papa ad Lotharium regem Francie scribit deterius quippe in populis prelati delinquunt, ac per hoc ipsi gravius quam ceteri puniuntur. Tot enim mortibus digni sunt, quot ad subditos suos perditionis exempla transmittunt, xi. q. iii. precipue. Certum est enim quod homo Christianus, sicut Joannes Chrisostomus ait, fortiter cadit in peccatum

punished to the same degree as men, 'because it pertains to the men to conquer women by their virtue and to rule them by their example'.[65]

The second principle of unity was knowledge of the law. Durant's opinion about the effects to be expected from knowledge of the law is just as different from our way of thinking as is his faith in exemplary efficiency. Just as we do not believe that good example are regularly imitated, so we do not think that knowledge of the law is enough to procure obedience to it. We separate knowledge from conduct by a will that is sometimes recalcitrant and does not do what it knows perfectly well to be right. Not so Durant. In his opinion something that agreed with the will of God had to agree with the will of man as well.[66] Like the devoted representative of a medieval version of enlightened political philosophy that he was, Durant was convinced that ignorance, not will, was the mother of all vices.[67] Thus the reason the clergy did not behave appropriately was not that it was ill-intentioned, or that it wilfully resisted reform; the reason was that it was poorly educated and abysmally ignorant. Not even among the literate were there many who knew the faith well enough to escape from ridicule in debates with infidels.[68] Reform of the church therefore required a reform of education. If the contents of the law were made as plain as possible, obedience would follow as a matter of course. Obedience, after all, as is suggested by its etymology, is not

propter duas causas: aut propter magnitudinem peccati, aut propter altitudinem dignitatis, xl. d. homo Christianus.' *TMA* 1.3 De limitanda potestate, fols. 6vb–7ra (*male* 7vb–7ra). Cf. C.11 q.3 c.3, D.40 c.5. It may be worth noting that Pope Urban IV had once reminded William Durant the Elder of the need to pay attention to this very principle; see Urban IV, no. 2,886 (7.11.1262).

[65] '[Adulteri laici] gravius puniendi sunt quam adultere, pro eo quod magis ad eos pertinet et virtute vincere et exemplo regere feminas sicut Augustinus de adulterinis coniugiis attestatur, xxii. q. vi. indignantur et capitulis precedentibus et sequentibus.' *TMA* 2.59, fol. 41vb. Cf. C.32 q.6 c.4.

[66] At the beginning of his treatise Durant thus declared that the reform of the church 'plene videretur esse conforme voluntati divine et *per consequens* humane'. *TMA* 1.1, fol. 4rb–va. My italics.

[67] 'Ignorantia enim mater est cunctorum errorum, et ideo in sacerdotibus Dei, qui in populo docendi susceperunt officium, maxime est vitanda, sicut habetur in tertio concilio Toletano et xxxviii. di. c. i.' *TMA* 2.18, fol. 23va–b. Cf. D.38 c.1. Durant thus displayed an optimism about the relationship between will and reason that seems rather 'enlightened' (if one may substitute plain reason for divine reason) and strikingly remote from Augustine's psychology, but nonetheless characteristically medieval.

[68] 'Paucissimi in his que ad fidem et eius articulos et animarum salutem pertinent etiam literati inveniantur instructi, propter quod risui patent infidelibus quandocunque de fide habetur collatio cum eisdem.' *TMA* 2.73 (3.4), fol. 53ra.

the result of an exercise of force but the result of 'listening'. Hence, 'just as the great have the power to rule and to command, so the small must of necessity obey'.[69]

The reform of education was to consist of several ingredients. At the most general level instruction in the faith ought to be improved.[70] More particularly, times at table – especially the table of the pope – were not to be wasted by listening to entertaining fables but should be devoted to readings from the Bible.[71] But most important, 'since art is long, but life is short, and proof is difficult, but conflicts of interpretation often result in confusion and occasion for lawsuits', committees of university experts were to be established who would purge the books of unnecessary 'similitudes and superfluities'.[72] Only the 'original texts' were to be retained, and any doubts to which they might give rise were to be resolved by the papacy according to the judgment of the experts. In addition these experts were to publish authoritative, comprehensive, and straightforward textbooks for every branch of knowledge containing 'explanations' with the help of which 'scholars, curates, and administrators and rectors of the commonwealth' could inform themselves quickly and precisely about the extent of their duties.[73] Both the original texts and the new textbooks were to be distributed far and wide, and clerics were to be required to own the books appropriate for their office.[74]

[69] 'Sicut in maioribus est regendi et iubendi potestas, ita in minoribus est obsequendi necessitas.' *TMA* prefatio, fol. 4ra.
[70] 'De regulis fidei et doctrine Christiane catholicis exponendis.' *TMA* 2.73 (3.4), fol. 53ra.
[71] *TMA* 2.74 (3.5), fol. 53va.
[72] 'Item cum nimia prolixitas et etiam similitudo confusionem inducant, sicut habetur prohemio decretalium, et ut alibi scribitur: ars longa, vita brevis, et experimentum difficile et diversitas interpretantium frequenter confusionem *et* [P] materiam litium et discordiarum inducunt', videretur utile quod de qualibet facultate sumerentur literati et experti viri et arbitri, ad quorum iudicium per summum pontificem omnes probabiles dubitationes circa quaslibet scientias exorte, resecatis omnibus similibus et superfluis, remanentibus tamen ipsarum scientiarum textibus originalibus, tollerentur.' *TMA* 2.73 (3.4), fol. 53ra–b. This is mainly directed against glosses, as is clear from the parallel in *TMI* 22 (3.45), fol. 68vb, cited above, pp. 126f.
[73] 'Ac etiam alique declarationes compendiose pro sacerdotibus et curatis in omni scientia ederentur, per quas possent in eis scolastici, curati, et rei publice administratores, et rectores brevi tempore informari in omnibus pertinentibus ad officia eorundem, et libri scriberentur in quibus esset videndum, cum propter dictam diversitatem opinionum, dubiorum diffusionem, et confusionem scripturarum, ad quas habendas vix unius scolaris divitis sufficiunt facultates, ab ipsarum scientiarum disquisitione et studio plurimum retrahantur, et ignorantes preficiantur cure animarum que est ars omnium artium, ut de etate et qualitate, cum sit ars.' *TMA* 2.73 (3.4), fol. 53ra–b. Cf. X.1.14.14.
[74] 'Videretur utile quod canones penitentiales, quos secundum Augustinum omnes sacerdotes scire debent, et si ignorent, sacerdotum nomen vix habere non merentur, xxxviii.'

Durant's ideas were not, however, limited to a reform of books. In order to ensure that the contents of those books would be known he insisted that the level of knowledge expected from every ecclesiastical rank should be defined precisely and that the possession of such knowledge was to be supervised by examinations and encouraged through the award of benefices.[75] No cleric was to be promoted without the required knowledge and moral maturity.[76] In order to promote education in every diocese and to assure a steady flow of educated clerics, masters were to be appointed at every cathedral, as was required by existing legislation.[77] But since that legislation had so far proved insufficient Durant added one of his most radical suggestions: one tenth of the revenue of every benefice, both of the regular and of the secular clergy, should be reserved for scholarships to enable poor clerics to study at universities.[78] Finally the education of the laity was not to be neglected. Since the illiterate often learned about Christianity from pictures in church, pictures were an essential instrument of education. Quickly retracing the steps by which doubts about the use of images had been resolved in late antiquity Durant therefore declared that pictures were not to be destroyed, but to be cleansed of all misrepresentations.[79] In addition the clergy was to inform the

---

di. que ipsis sacerdotibus, in unum redigerentur volumen, cuius copia et notitia ex necessitate ab omnibus curatis et aliis confessiones audientibus haberetur et sciretur.' *TMA* 2.36, fol. 31rb. Cf. D.38 c.5. Collections of the ancient conciliar canons were to be made accessible at each episcopal see: *TMA* 2.73 (3.4), fol. 53rb.

[75] Bishops should have had doctorates in law or theology: 'Et declararetur que scientia est in singulis gradibus requirenda, et quod nullus caracteretur episcopus nisi esset doctoratus in theologia vel in iure.' *TMA* 2.18, fol. 24rb (*male* 23rb). Clerics were not to be ordained to the priesthood unless their knowledge of the canon law had been examined: *TMA* 2.30, fol. 28rb. 'Nec aliis provideri posset quandiu doctores remanerent improvisi aliqua civitate vel diocesi.' *TMA* 2.96 (3.27), fol. 58vb.

[76] 'Doctores literati, sufficientes, et idonei ceteris illiteratis, iuvenibus, et insufficientibus preferrentur, affectione contraria non obstante.' *TMA* 2.49, fol. 36rb. Bishops who gave benefices to unqualified relatives were to be excommunicated and deprived of their own benefices: *TMA* 2.18, fol. 24ra (*male* 23ra). On neophytes: *TMA* 2.18, fols. 22vb–23ra. 'Claustrales non ponerentur ad prelationem, cum non habeant experientiam temporalem.' *TMA* 2.18, fol. 24ra (*male* 23ra).

[77] *TMA* 2.38, fol. 32va. Cf. X.5.5.1, X.5.5.4.

[78] 'Videretur utile ampliari [statuta] ut decima pars omnium beneficiorum ecclesiasticorum secularium et regularium assignaretur pauperibus scholaribus in singulis facultatibus studentibus in studio generali, per quos Dei posset illuminari ecclesia, qui in ea, prout Daniel xii. legitur, et eodem titulo, super specula, velut splendor fulgerent firmamenti.' *TMA* 2.38, fol. 32va. Cf. X.5.5.5.

[79] 'Videretur utile quod per ordinarios et rectores locorum omnes imagines deformes et in quibus a veritate rei geste deviatur delerentur, ... cum error cui non resistitur pro veritate reputetur.' *TMA* 2.57, fol. 41ra–b. Cf. Elibertanum c.36, De cons. D.3 c.27–9, D.83 c.3.

laity about the penitential canons that were particularly important
for their conduct, such as prohibitions on intercourse with men-
struating or lactating women, intercourse during times of fasting,
and wet-nursing.[80]

Examples and knowledge of the law thus were the operative
principles of unity. It remained to make sure that they were put
into practice. An essential precondition for this purpose was to
assure a perfect and constant symmetry between hierarchical
offices and worthy clerics. No cleric was to be responsible for more
than a single office, a principle that Durant supported with lengthy
quotations from, not surprisingly, Pope Gregory.[81] Conversely,
no office that existed in the hierarchy was to be left vacant. Seven
deacons were to be appointed in every city.[82] Wherever for some
reason there were no metropolitans or patriarchs, these ought to be
supplied.[83] To shorten vacancies in Rome, the cardinals were to be
forced to make their choice of a new pope within three months or
else surrender their right to elect the pope to the bishops and
archbishops.[84] Finally, every cleric who served at the altar had to
assure himself of qualified representatives in case he were unexpec-
tedly prevented by accident or illness from performing his duties.[85]

The most serious obstacle to these ideals was pluralism.[86] In
order to establish the gravity of this offence Durant departed from
his usual procedure of drily listing appropriate laws and told an
anecdote about a chancellor of the university of Paris whom even
on his deathbed Bishop William of Paris could not convince that

[80] *TMA* 2.73 (3.4), fol. 53rb.
[81] 'Videretur perquam esse utile ecclesie sancte Dei, ut dominus papa et ceteri inferiores et
totum concilium acquiescerent beato Gregorio super hoc scribenti omnibus episcopis in
hunc modum: Singula ecclesiastici iuris officia singulis quibusque personis sigillatim
committi iubemus. Sicut enim in uno corpore multa membra habemus, omnia autem
membra non eundem actum habent, ita et in ecclesie corpore multa membra sunt
secundum veridicam Pauli sentententiam ad Corinthios xii.' *TMA* 2.21, fol. 25va–b. Cf.
D.89 c.1; 1 Corinthians 12:12.
[82] *TMA* 2.14, fol. 21va.
[83] 'Videretur insuper quod essent constituendi metropolitani et patriarche in singulis regnis
ubi non sunt, qui episcopis et archiepiscopis preessent.' *TMA* 2.11, fol. 19rb.
[84] 'Item quod si dicta Romana ecclesia vacaret ultra tres menses, quod ex tunc cardinales
essent eligendi potestate illa vice privati, et quod ad aliquos archiepiscopos et episcopos et
alios de quibus videretur expediens illa vice devolveretur eligendi potestas, vel quod aliud
tale adhiberetur remedium ultra illud quod statutum fuit a Gregorio X. *quod* [P] ex
necessitate cardinales concordare haberent.' *TMA* 2.96 (3.27), fol. 59va. Cf. VI.1.6.3.
[85] *TMA* 2.77 (3.8), fol. 54ra.
[86] 'Et ex hoc paretur generale preiudicium universalis ecclesie, que debitis officiis et
obsequiis, rectoribus, administratoribus et defensoribus defraudatur. Eleemosyne subtra-
huntur, persone ecclesiastice sic ditate in superbiam efferuntur.' *TMA* 2.21, fol. 25va.

pluralism was a mortal sin. The chancellor died. But at his funeral, 'as Bishop William was saying the *De profundis*, the chancellor appeared as a horrifying ghost and said in an audible voice that Bishop William ought not to pray for him because he had been damned for failing to heed William's warning about pluralism'.[87] In order to prevent the recurrence of such lamentable affairs Durant proposed to broaden the scope of a constitution of Boniface VIII by making any cleric who succumbed to the vice of pluralism *ipso facto* lose his benefices.[88]

Once the ecclesiastical hierarchy was properly provided for, it could be put in action in order to confirm the bonds of union. Communion, both in the narrow sense of taking communion at mass and in the wider sense of sharing in the life of the church, was to be intensified. Everybody was to take communion thrice per year – considerably more than the minimum of one communion annually that was required by the Fourth Lateran Council, but less than was required by those ancient canons which had inflicted excommunication on anyone who ever went to church without taking communion.[89] Bishops were to conduct visitations of their dioceses at least once annually, either in person or by representatives.[90] Attendance at mass was to be enforced: laymen were to be punished for going to spectacles instead of mass, or for leaving church before mass was over. Clerics who did not participate in mass were to suffer loss of income – and even if they had been granted leaves of absence they were to receive only a third or a fourth of their ordinary income.[91] On the other hand, certain requirements were to be made less stringent in order to facilitate attendance at mass: weekly masses for the dead were to be said early, so that they would not prevent rural folk from attending to the needs of agriculture;[92] holidays that conflicted with harvest or

---

[87] 'Et cancellarius Parisiensis, qui tunc erat magister in theologia pluribus abundans beneficiis, huic sententie, affectu et non ratione superatus, acquiescere nollet etiam in infirmitate de qua obiit a domino Guilielmo Parisiensi episcopo, magistro in theologia, de hoc admonitus et rogatus, eidem episcopo iuxta eius sepulturam de profundis pro eo dicenti in teterrima umbra dictus cancellarius intelligibili voce dicens apparuit, quod non oraret pro eo, nam damnatus erat pro eo quod non acquieverat eiusdem episcopi monitis et sententie sue.' *TMA* 2.21, fol. 26ra. The chancellor was Philip the Chancellor.

[88] *TMA* 2.21, fol. 26ra. Cf. VI.3.4.32, which applied only to the religious.

[89] *TMA* 2.48, fol. 36ra–b, with reference to De cons. D.2 c.19, De cons. D.1 c.16, De cons. D.2 c.13, and I Toletanum c.13.

[90] *TMA* 2.66, fol. 43vb. Durant was doubly incensed by the 'duplex infamia negligentie et avaricie' of taking procurations in the first place, and then for visitations that were not even executed.     [91] *TMA* 2.50, fol. 36va.     [92] *TMA* 2.19, fol. 24va.

vintage time were to be moved at the discretion of local ordinaries;[93] and boring readings were to be abbreviated.[94] All forms of divine worship were to be purified and different customs of celebrating mass were to be abolished. Such different customs were an especially insidious cause of schism because they scandalized the faithful and undermined church discipline 'more than almost any other plague'.[95] The customs of the metropolitan were to be followed in his entire province, by both the secular and the regular clergy.[96] 'Irreverent songs', 'disorderly motets', and excessive lamentations at funerals were to be banished.[97] Mass was to take place at the right time, the liturgy was to be pronounced slowly and clearly, and Our Fathers and Ave Marias were to be said at every hour.[98]

Councils were of course the most important means of putting ecclesiastical unity into practice. We have already dealt with Durant's demand that general councils ought to meet every ten years or 'whenever there is something to be ordained for the common state of the church'.[99] But this demand should not be seen in isolation as dealing with purely public or governmental matters; it was part of a conciliar system that was designed, not merely to place limits on the papal plenitude of power in a negative sense, but also to increase 'communion' throughout the entire church in a positive sense. At the most basic level Durant required bishops not to be secretive in their private lives but always to surround themselves with monks and clerics in order to inspire as many of their disciples as possible with their good examples.[100] Durant's

---

93 *TMA* 2.81 (3.12), fol. 54va–b.   94 *TMA* 2.19, fol. 24va.
95 'Nulla pene pestis magis discipline mores ab ecclesia Christi depulit quam inordinata diversitas officii, que apud carnales scismatis errorem videtur ostendere et multis est materia scandalorum.' *TMA* 2.68, fol. 45va. Another deplorable consequence of too many different customs was that 'perdunt multi pauperes clerici et presbyteri victum suum, et multi prelati convenientes et idoneos non inveniunt in divino officio servitores.' *TMA* 2.68, fol. 45va.   96 *TMA* 2.68, fol. 45rb.
97 'Nam multe tragedie et moteti et alia, ex quibus auditores non edificantur, non ad devotionem sed potius ad contrarium excitant.' *TMA* 2.68, fol. 45rb. Cf. *TMA* 2.75 (3.6), fol. 53va–b.
98 *TMA* 2.19, fol. 24rb–va; *TMA* 2.19, fol. 24va.   99 See above, pp. 160–6.
100 'Sicut est illud Gregorii in generali sinodo, ii. q. vii. cum pastoris vita in exemplum debeat esse discipulis, plerunque clerici qualis in secreto sit vita sui pontificis nesciunt, quam tamen seculares pueri et servientes sciunt. De qua re presenti decreto constituimus ut quidam ex clericis vel etiam ex monachis electi in ministerio cubiculi pontificali obsequantur, ut is qui in loco regiminis est et tales habeat testes qui veram eius in secreto conversationem videant, et ex sedula visione exemplum profectus sumant.' *TMA* 2.38, fol. 32rb. Cf. C.2 q.7 c.58, which reads 'cubiculi pontificalis'. A passage with interesting implications for competing conceptions of privacy.

insistence on weekly meetings of the parish clergy grew out of a similar concern.[101] But most important for creating conciliar communion were provincial councils, because they provided a crucial link not only between the parish and the universal church but also between the clergy and the laity. Indeed, Durant insisted at much greater length on provincial councils than on general ones, in part because their authority had waned under the impact of papal government.[102] In every province at least one and preferably two councils were to meet each year, and they were to be attended not only by the prelates but also by representatives of the cathedral chapters and the laity.[103] According to the Pseudo-Isidorean *Ordo de celebrando concilio*, from which Durant quoted extensively, the first three days of a provincial council were to be spent listening to the decrees about the Trinity and the order of the church. Time would then be allocated to settle pending issues. The last day was to be devoted to a public reading of newly issued canons.[104] Thus provincial councils would function to stabilize the church by publicizing and confirming law and faith at the crucial intersections between the clergy and the laity and between the universal and the local church.

The natural counterpart to this renewed insistence on the intensity and purity of every form of communion in the body of the church was a renewed emphasis on its complement – that is, on excommunications. Excommunication was the 'bishops' dagger', and it was being blunted if, as Durant believed, it was commonly inflicted 'for sixpence'.[105] Durant could not refrain from pointing out that there was a certain justice in the frequent excommunications that the church of Rome fulminated against prelates, for in

---

[101] *TMA* 2.65, fol. 43va–b.

[102] 'De conciliis provincialibus.' *TMA* 2.11, fols. 18rb–21ra. Cf. Munier, 'L' "Ordo de celebrando concilio" wisigothique'. Fuhrmann, *Einfluss*, 1:58, 182, 2:313f., 458f.

[103] *TMA* 2.11, fol. 18rb–va. On other occasions, however, Durant seems to ask for provincial councils every three years; see below, p. 237 n.55. One of the most important canons supporting Durant's case was IV Toletanum c.3, which did not enter into Gratian's *Decretum*, and from which he quoted extensively at *TMA* 2.11, fols. 18vb–19ra. This particular canon, along with III Carthaginense c.2, was quoted by Pierre d'Ailly, *Tractatus super reformatione ecclesiae*, col. 904, affording conclusive proof that d'Ailly had read Durant's *Tractatus Maior*; see Viollet, p. 126.

[104] *TMA* 2.11, fols. 19va–21ra.

[105] 'Dicta sententia sit mucro episcopalis, qui sepius hebetatur vel frangitur cum de eo passim et indistincte percutitur, xvi. q. ii. visis.' *TMA* 2.38, fol. 33ra. Cf. C.16 q.2 c.1. 'Que tamen male servantur in ecclesia Dei, cum pro sex denariis in multis partibus dicte sententie proferantur.' *TMA* 2.38, fol. 33ra.

this way God justly made the prelates taste their own medicine.[106]
But he was firm on the point of principle: no one ought to be
excommunicated unless he had committed a mortal sin and all
other means of correction had failed.[107]

The papacy posed the central challenge to Durant's ideas for
reform: their implementation would require undoing the transformation of the pope from bishop of Rome, successor of St Peter,
and guarantor of the unity of the Christian faith into the sovereign
lord of Christendom. To do so without violating canonical
tradition required tact and subtlety. The easiest method of attack
was perhaps to put the papacy on the defensive by charging it with
disregard for standards of Christian decency on which all parties
were agreed. Hence Durant enthusiastically launched an indictment of the vices that were commonly believed to have turned the
court of Rome into a den of thieves. The heresy of simony was
practised blatantly in Rome: fees were charged for promotions,
letters, judgments, and so on, and no one was deceived if payment
was required only after the gifts of the Holy Spirit had been
granted.[108] We even get a foretaste of Luther's attack on Tetzel
when Durant expressed his disdain for Roman fiscal agents who
sold indulgences for almost nothing but knew so little of the faith
that they turned Rome into a laughing-stock among the
knowledgeable.[109]

Pluralism was another issue on which it was not hard to score
points against Rome. Durant declared that the cardinals were in

---

[106] 'Quod minime observatur in Romana ecclesia, in qua et a cuius delegatis contra prelatos
et alios pro minimo sententie fulminantur, contra decretalem illam Alexandri iiii. de
officio deleg. quia pontificali, et hoc non iniuste Dei iudicio, ut in quo ipsi prelati et
eorum curie delinquunt et hoc etiam puniantur, xiii. q. i. §. his, i. q. i. §. ex his.' *TMA*
2.38, fol. 33ra. Cf. VI.1.14.2, C.13 q.1 p.c.1, C.1 q.1 p.c.97.

[107] *TMA* 2.38, fol. 33ra, with reference to C.24 q.3 c.17, C.24 q.1 c.21, C.11 q.3 c.41, C.11
q.3 c.8, C.11 q.3 c.42.

[108] 'In curia Romana publice contrarium fiat, ac si non esset peccatum committere
simoniam, vel si dare vel accipere post non esset idem sicut dare vel accipere ante, i. q. i.
eos, et c. si quis prebendas, et c. si quis obiecerit, eadem causa q. iii. salvator.' *TMA* 2.20,
fol. 24vb. Cf. C.1 q.1 c.21, C.1 q.3 c.15, C.1 q.1 q.3 c.7–8. Similarly *TMA* 2.96 (3.27), fols.
58vb–59ra.

[109] 'Item cum in universali ecclesia questores multos errores disseminent, multosque
seducant simplices, et multas abusiones procurent, et vitam gerant enormiter dissolu-
tam, in tantum quod patent risui potestasque clavium ecclesie contemnitur cum pro uno
obolo vel nihilo indulgentia concedatur.' *TMA* 2.84 (3.15), fol. 55ra.

the habit of accumulating benefices worth thousands of florins and extorting pensions from those whom they promoted. Those pensions 'never die'; they were passed on from one cardinal to another, while overburdened clerics were forced to beg in the streets, take on servile labour, and ask for public alms.[110] More recently the cardinals had even taken to acquiring benefices in monastic establishments without considering it necessary to enter into monastic orders.[111] If they continued in this fashion, soon no benefices would be left at all.[112] Nepotism went along with pluralism.[113] And then there was Rome's intolerable arrogance. It was bad enough that the pope permitted cardinals who were mere priests or deacons to take precedence before the bishops, who were successors of the apostles; but it was 'still more indecent' to place vice-chancellors, auditors, referendaries, notaries, and other curial officials ahead of bishops in seating arrangements.[114] Such abuses of papal primacy prompted Durant to issue barely veiled threats:

The people have a proverb: if you want everything, you lose everything. The church of Rome claims everything; hence it is to be feared that it will lose everything. For as Solomon says in Proverbs 30, if you blow your nose too hard, you draw blood, as is confirmed by the example of the Greek church, which is said to have refused obedience for this reason to the church of Rome.[115]

[110] '[Cardinales] in grave animarum ipsorum periculum et universalis ecclesie dispendium multa milia florenorum, librarum, et marcharum sibi et suis pestifera adinventione super ecclesias etiam parochiales et curatas faciunt cumulari, et ecclesias etiam cathedrales et ultramarinas sub diversis coloribus commendari, et certas sibi solvi ab illis qui eorum promoventur auxilio pensiones que nunquam in Romana ecclesia moriuntur, sed ab uno cardinali in alium vel in eius vel domini pape vel propinquum vel nepotulum detinentur. Ex quibus sequitur, cum sibi vendicent universa, infelix quod clericus qui de predictis beneficiis sustentari et eis personaliter deservire debuerat mendicat in plateis et servili operi mancipatus publicam deposcit elemosynam.' *TMA* 2.21, fol. 26ra–b. Cf. *TMA* 2.96 (3.27), fol. 59ra. [111] *TMA* 2.21, fol. 26rb.
[112] 'Quod [cardinales] pluralitatem beneficiorum in animarum suarum et ecclesiarum dispendium et pernitiosum aliorum exemplum nullatenus retinerent, sed quod essent suo cardinalatu contenti, ★ne per tempus, si★ [P] modus per eos assumptus ad posteros dirivaretur, finaliter sibi omnia beneficia et officia ecclesiastica que alicuius ponderis sunt usurpantur, cum multis libris marcarum multi ex eis contenti aliquatenus non existant.' *TMA* 2.1, fol. 15va. [113] *TMA* 2.96 (3.27), fol. 59rb. [114] *TMA* 2.7, fol. 17ra.
[115] 'Proverbium vulgare est: qui totum vult, totum perdit. Ecclesia Romana sibi vendicat universa, xciii. di. diaconi sunt, unde timendum est quod universa perdat. Nam sicut Salomon ait Proverbiis xxx., qui multum emungit, sanguinem elicit, iiii. di. denique. Sicut habetur exemplum de ecclesia Grecorum que ex hoc ab ecclesie Romane obedientia dicitur recessisse.' *TMA* 2.7, fol. 17rb. Cf. D.93 c.23, Proverbs 30:33, D.4 c.6. The image of drawing blood from your nose by blowing it too hard, from Proverbs 30:33, had already been turned against the papacy in the French *gravamina* against Innocent IV of 1247; see Matthew Paris, *Chronica*, 6:110.

Concerning papal titles, there was incontrovertible canonical evidence to prove that titles like 'universal pope', or 'prince of priests', or 'prince of the universal church . . . inflate the truth and wound charity'.[116] Durant could not refrain from listing a whole series of ancient papal letters to prove that the popes of antiquity had addressed bishops as 'brothers and co-disciples', thus displaying more respect for the fundamental equality between the pope and other bishops than popes in the present. As it happens these letters were the forged papal decretals in the Pseudo-Isidorean collection – which reveals Durant to have had a certain capacity for irony (those decretals had, after all, been meant to heighten, not to limit, the role of the papacy) and by implication a remarkable grasp of the history of canon law.[117]

All this was easy. It was much harder to establish that the lower ranks and orders of the church enjoyed inalienable rights that were immune to papal interference. For this purpose, Durant concentrated on the two estates that were most likely to suffer: the bishops and temporal authorities. Concerning bishops, the most important issue was that of exemptions from episcopal jurisdiction. As we have previously noted, Durant attacked exemptions by pointing out that the hierarchical gradation of the church proceeded from God himself: it was established in the Old Testament and confirmed by Christ. Exemptions from the hierarchy opposed an arbitrary power to the 'reasoned' order of the church and thus led to schism.[118] In the same context, Durant addressed another and

---

[116] 'Ut prime sedis episcopus princeps sacerdotum vel universalis ecclesie non appelletur . . . Gregorius, Eulogio patriarche Alexandrino scribens, reprehendat eum quia in literis directis ipsi Gregorio vocaverat eum papam universalem, et prohibebat quod hoc de cetero non fiat, dicens quod prelatis subtrahitur quod eidem pape plusquam non exigit prebetur . . . Quare vult idem papa quod cessent talia verba, ne universalis vocetur, que verba veritatem inflant et caritatem vulnerant, xcix. di. ecce.' *TMA* 2.34, fol. 30rb. Cf. D.99 c.5, *TMA* 2.7, fol. 17rb, *TMA* 2.96 (3.27), fol. 59va. On the history of the papal title see Kuttner, 'Universal Pope'; Maccarrone, *Vicarius Christi*; Stockmeier, 'Die Übernahme des Pontifex-Titels'; Schieffer, 'Der Papst als Pontifex Maximus'.
[117] 'Nam beatus Clemens et alii Romani pontifices etiam hactenus scribendo episcopis preferebant eos.' *TMA* 2.34, fol. 30vb. Durant went on to refer to Pope Clement's formula of address 'dilectissimis fratribus et condiscipulis' as it appeared in C.12 q.1 c.2, and to the letters of Popes Evaristus, Sixtus I, Pius I, Sotherus, Zepherinus, Calixtus I, Fabianus, Cornelius, Lucius I, Stephanus I, Sixtus II, Felix I, Euticianus, Gaius, Marcellinus, Marcellus I, Eusebius, and Melchiades. This was the only occasion in the *Tractatus Maior* on which Durant referred to the forged decretals.
[118] 'Omne regnum in se ipsum divisum non stabit, et omnis scientia et lex adversum se divisa destrueretur . . . Ex quibus patet quod si [papa] concedat [exemptiones], ad eius

much deeper threat of which exemptions were only one consequence – namely, the primacy of Rome. He granted that Christ
had made St Peter the rock of the church and even that the apostles
had wanted Peter to be their 'prince'; but he was totally unwilling
to concede that as a consequence St Peter and his successors had any
power that was not held by every other bishop, too. Insisting on
the same famous Pseudo-Isidorean letter of Pope Anacletus that we
have already encountered in connection with his conciliar proposal, and insisting on a parallel but rather more authentic canon by
'Pope' Cyprian, he pointed out that the apostles received exactly
the same powers from Christ as did St Peter and that they shared
power and honour with him in equal measure.[119] Since the bishops
were descended from the apostles, they enjoyed the same partnership with the pope.[120]

There was no mention here of the papalist position that all
bishops derived all of their powers of jurisdiction from the
pope.[121] Indeed, there was no mention whatsoever of the distinction between the power of jurisdiction and the power of order.

reatum pertinet, nisi causa legitima subsit, et quod non constructor, sed eversor et
divisor est regni ecclesiastici et unitatis ecclesie, que divisionem non capit, xxiiii. q. i.
loquitur, et c. scisma.' *TMA* 1.4 De exemptionibus, fol. 11ra–b. Cf. C.24 q.1 c.18, c.34.

[119] 'Ligandi atque solvendi potestatem tam Petrus quam ceteri apostoli a Christo receper-
unt. Primo tamen Petrus, sicut Anacletus papa ait, hanc ligandi et solvendi supra terram
potestatem accepit a Domino, primusque ad fidem populum virtute sue predicationis
adduxit, Actuum ii., Rom. x. Ceteri vero apostoli cum eodem Petro pari consortio
honorem et potestatem acceperunt a Christo, ipsumque Petrum principem eorum esse
voluerunt.' *TMA* 1.4 De exemptionibus, fols. 8vb–9ra. Cf. D.21 c.2, Acts 2:14–40,
Romans 10:1–5, and above, pp. 159f. 'Hoc erant utique ceteri apostoli quod Petrus
fuerat, pari consortio prediti et honoris et potestatis.' *TMA* 1.4 De exemptionibus, fol.
9ra. Cf. C.24 q.1 c.18. Durant went on to support episcopal rights with the example of
Paul's rebuke of Peter and a variety of canon and civil laws; cf. Dig.8.6.16, Dig.8.1.17,
C.24 q.1 c.6, C.2 q.7 c.33–37, D.22 c.4, D.68 c.6.

[120] 'Ipsis vero apostolis decedentibus in loco eorum successerunt episcopi, quos qui recipit et
verba eorum, Deum recipit, qui autem spernit, Deum, a quo missi sunt et cuius
funguntur legatione, spernit, et ipse indubitanter spernetur a Domino.' *TMA* 1.4 De
exemptionibus, fol. 9ra. Cf. D.21 c.2. 'Patet itaque quod dicta generalis ordinatio
prelationis a Deo in veteri testamento et a Christo in novo processit, et quod inde
episcopi potestatem suam acceperunt quam apostoli habebant, et quod dicta ordinatio
non est contemnenda nec interdicenda probat Augustinus per dicta Basilii, xi. di.
ecclesiasticarum.' *TMA* 1.4 De exemptionibus, fol. 9va. Cf. D.11 c.5.

[121] As supported, for example, by Thomas of York, Bonaventure, and Hervaeus Natalis;
Tierney, *Origins of Papal Infallibility*, pp. 66, 82–6, 160–4; Tierney, *Religion*, p. 61. In
general: Congar, 'Aspects,' and Pennington, *Pope and Bishops*, as well as the extensive
literature on the power of the pope, e.g., Gagnér, *Studien zur Ideengeschichte*, Benson,
'Plenitudo potestatis', Marrone, 'The Absolute and the Ordained Powers', and Oakley,
*Omnipotence, Covenant and Order*.

This was a crucial point, for it had been precisely this distinction, developed in the twelfth century by theologians and adopted by the canonists, which made it possible to assert papal primacy in terms that did not seem to violate the principles of order – and it was a distinction that had been elaborated precisely in order to deal with the letter of Pope Anacletus.[122] If powers of order were limited to purely sacramental functions while powers of jurisdiction were defined as something altogether different, then one could grant that the bishops were the equals of the pope in order but still assert that they were his inferiors in jurisdiction.

There can be little doubt that Durant was more than a little dissatisfied with the effects of this distinction between powers of order and of jurisdiction. He was too cautious to tackle it head on, but he did point out repeatedly how closely jurisdiction and order were related to each other. His favourite weapon consisted of a canon of Pope Gregory I that we have mentioned previously but that deserves to be repeated: 'As Gregory wrote to Romanus, the defender of Sicily, our duty is to protect the order of the church. But if we fail to preserve each bishop in his rights of jurisdiction, what are we doing if not confounding the order of the church?'[123] In Durant's opinion the jurisdiction of a bishop was clearly part of the general order of the church. By implication the legitimacy of separating a bishop's sacramental power of order from his power of jurisdiction was called into question: was not such a distinction rather a dangerous kind of schism that put the overarching order of the church itself in jeopardy?[124]

In order to protect the powers of the bishops from papal interference Durant called for a number of specific limits on papal

---

122 Tierney, *Foundations*, pp. 25–36; Tierney, *Religion*, pp. 30–4; Van de Kerckhove, 'La Notion de juridiction'; Stenger, 'Episcopacy as an Ordo'; Michaud-Quantin, *Etudes*, pp. 85–101. See also above, p. 159 n. 83.

123 'Sicut idem Gregorius Romano defensori Sicilie *scribit* [P], si qua unicuique episcopo iurisditio non servatur, *quid aliud agitur nisi ut per nos per quos ecclesiasticus ille ordo custodiri debuerat, confundatur* [P], xi. q. i. pervenit.' *TMA* 1.3 De limitanda potestate, fol. 6ra. Cf. C.11 q.1 c.39, and above, pp. 145f. On the uses to which the secular clergy had put C.11 q.1 c.39 earlier on see Henry of Ghent, 'Sermo', p. 149; *Tractatus de usurpata potestate fratrum*, p. 157; Schleyer, *Anfänge*, pp. 85 n. 17, 149; Marrone, 'Ecclesiology', p. 147 n. 55.

124 In his debates with William of Plaisians over the rights to the bishopric of Mende Durant argued that prior to the times of the Old Testament royal and priestly powers were always indiscriminately fused and went on to liken his own power as bishop to those of the priest-king Melchisedek; cf. *Mémoire relatif au paréage*, p. 115, with references to Cod.1.3.21, Cod.12.3.1, Nov.23.4, Dig.1.12.1, Cod.1.4.8, and p. 118, with references to Genesis 14:18–20, 1 Samuel 3, 1 Samuel 8, D.10 c.8, D.21 c.1 §.8, Dig.1.1.1.

jurisdiction. Sentiments of local patriotism were easily enlisted for an attack on the supposed papal preference for having foreigners preside over a flock whose language they did not understand.[125] Clerical offices ought rather to be filled by electing candidates of local origin at the local level,[126] and the papacy was asked to refrain from interfering in the affairs of parishes, canonries, priories, abbacies, dioceses, and archdioceses with suits, appeals, provisions, reservations, and exemptions.[127] Papal judges and executors were to refrain from excommunicating prelates and from imposing interdicts without due warning and compelling reasons.[128] In principle, all judicial matters were to be settled by the local ordinaries.[129] If such matters were found to go beyond the ordinary's competence or were appealed, they were not to be sent to Rome but to the provincial council. If they were appealed from there as well, they were still not to be sent to Rome without prior examination of the reasons for the appeal by bishops in neighbouring provinces.[130] Durant did admit, at least by implication, that 'major causes' (*causae maiores*) were reserved to Rome, but he insisted that suits involving bishops, which had traditionally been one of the most important kinds of 'major causes', ought to be excluded from this category; such suits were rather to be heard by

---

125 'Hoc autem non servatur a Romana curia et a presbyteris prelatis, qui curas animarum et prelationis committunt talibus qui nec subditos intelligunt nec intelliguntur ab eis.' *TMA* 2.15, fol. 22rb–va.

126 'De clericis presbyteris alterius regionis linguarum et ecclesie non recipiendis, nec promovendis in alienis regnis et ecclesiis, nisi ibi eligant mansionem, quamdiu alii sufficientes reperiantur in regnis, civitatibus, et ecclesiis propriis.' *TMA* 2.15, fol. 21va. 'Nullus in ecclesia ubi duo vel tres in congregatione fuerint nisi eorum electione canonica presbyter eligatur.' *TMA* 2.15, fol. 22ra–b.

127 *TMA* 2.96 (3.27), fol. 58vb, with an allusion to C.11 q.1 c.39.

128 *TMA* 2.96 (3.27), fol. 59va. Cf. *TMA* 2.94 (3.25), fol. 58rb.

129 'Sicut papa in plenitudinem potestatis, ita et ipsi in partem solicitudinis in decretis provinciis, civitatibus, et diocesibus sunt assumpti, extra de autoritate et usu palii, ad honorem, ii. q. vi. qui se scit, ix. q. iiii. episcopi, cum capitulis precedentibus et sequentibus . . . Dicti episcopi in suis diocesibus sint de iure et esse debeant pre-ordinatores in cunctis, ut ait Isidorus in epistola ad Ludifredum, et xxv. di. perlectis.' *TMA* 2.7, fol. 16va. Cf. X.1.8.4, C.2 q.6 c.12, C.9 q.2 c.8, D.25 c.1.

130 'Quod omnia negotia contingentia statum cleri in regularibus et secularibus personis que coram suis ordinariis non possent accipere finem, vel a quibus esset appellatum, deferrentur ibidem [ad concilia provincialia], et prius ad Romanam curiam devolvi non possent, nisi essent maxime cause secundum tenorem legis canonizate, ii. q. vi. anteriorum §. illud. Et si contingeret appellari ad sedem apostolicam a conciliis, quod prima causa appellationis remitteretur ad examen convicinorum episcoporum secundum providentiam et ordinationem super hoc habitam in Nicena synodo.' *TMA* 2.11, fol. 18rb–va. Cf. C.2 q.6 c.28 and Nicea c.5. On the issue of appeals to Rome see the judicious treatment in Sieben, *Konzilsidee des lateinischen Mittelalters*, pp. 353–5.

provincial councils.[131] Lawsuits against clerics that started in Rome were to be limited as well: no charges were to be heard without an investigation of the plaintiff's character;[132] no cleric was to be called to Rome unless a summary investigation had already been completed;[133] if a trial did result it was not to last beyond three years, and appeals were not to last beyond two, 'for some lawsuits in the Roman courts are almost immortal and are occasionally delayed even longer than in secular courts';[134] and finally Durant reminded Rome that canonical sentences of deposition were not to be issued without the testimony of truly overwhelming numbers of witnesses.[135]

Durant's enthusiasm for defending temporal authorities from Roman interference was noticeably weaker than that with which he defended his own estate, but it was by no means negligible. As with bishops, the case hinged on a distinction, except that in the prior case the novel, anti-hierarchical distinction between powers of order and of jurisdiction had to be suppressed, while here the old, hierarchical distinction between spiritual and temporal power needed to be reaffirmed. Throughout the first part of the treatise Durant paid scrupulous attention to the dualism of temporal and spiritual authorities. As we have seen, his conciliar proposal itself, the centre-piece of his reform, included even-handed references to

[131] "Item cum in vii. c. iii. concilii Carthaginensis fuerit constitutum quod cause episcoporum coram provinciali concilio infra duos menses audiantur, et hoc sit satis conforme aliis conciliis et iuribus, ut iii. q. si quis episcoporum, cum c. sequentibus, et dicta iura et consimilia non serventur quia Romana ecclesia causas episcoporum maioribus annumerans omnia ad se trahit, per illa capitula, ii. q. vi. ad romanum, et capitulis precedentibus et sequentibus, et ix. q. iii. cuncta per mundum, et c. per principalem, videtur utile cogitare an esset aliquod remedium super hoc adhibendum. Et insuper, cum lites non debeant esse immortales, ut extra de dolo et contu. finem, potissime ecclesiastice, que ceteris periculosiores sunt, ut ibidem et de electio. ne pro defectu, quod in eisdem contraheretur eremodicium, sicut secundum leges contrahitur, C. de iudi. properandum §. i. et §. sin autem.' *TMA* 2.32, fol. 28va. Cf. III Carthaginense c.7, C.3 q.6 c.2, C.2 q.6 c.6–8, C.9 q.3 c.17–18, C.9 q.3 c.21, X.2.14.5, X.1.6.41, Cod.3.1.13.1–2. Durant thus directly countered the Pseudo-Isidorean tradition according to which precisely suits involving bishops were to be adjudicated nowhere else than in Rome.

[132] *TMA* 2.23, fols. 26vb–27ra. Cf. *TMA* 2.96 (3.27), fol. 59va.

[133] *TMA* 2.96 (3.27), fol. 59va.

[134] 'Item quod [Romana ecclesia] in iustitia exhibenda tantam et talem diligentiam exhiberet quod nullo modo terminatio alicuius cause principalis ultra triennium, nec appellationes ultra biennium, prorogari valerent, cum in ipsa lites quodammodo immortales existant, et in ea amplius quam in secularibus curiis prorogentur interdum.' *TMA* 2.96 (3.27), fol. 59ra. Cf. *TMA* 2.31, fol. 28va.

[135] Prelates were not to be deposed without seventy-three witnesses, cardinal priests required sixty-four, and deacons twenty-six: *TMA* 2.83 (3.14), fols. 54vb–55ra.

pope and kings.[136] More generally, Durant stressed the divine ordination of royal power. In every church the clergy were to pray for their kings by name.[137] To violate an oath of obedience to a king was not only a sacrilege against the anointed of the Lord but a sign of faithlessness in general, for, as Jerome had asked, 'how can anyone be faithful to God if he cannot even be faithful to his carnal lord?'[138] The councils of Toledo furnished extensive ammunition in the most solemn language to support this point of view by calling once, twice, and thrice for eternal penalties on anyone who dared rebel against a king.[139]

On all these points Durant was on solid ground. But – strange to tell about a man who took such pride in his respect for law – in an attempt to magnify the role of royal power he tampered with the text of the most venerable canon about the relationship between temporal and spiritual power: *Duo sunt* by Pope Gelasius. Where Gelasius had written that 'there are two by which this world is principally ruled, namely the sacred authority of the pontiffs and royal power', Durant wrote that there are 'two powers that rule the human race like servants of God, that is, ecclesiastical authority and royal power'.[140] He thus replaced Gelasius's 'principally' with 'servants of God', and 'sacred authority of the pontiffs' with 'ecclesiastical authority'. The first change gave a divine quality to royal power and the second emphasized the authority of the church, while both reduced the role of the papacy. This implied

---

136 See above, p. 160.

137 *TMA* 2.6, fol. 16rb. Cf. 1 Timothy 2:1–2, De primitiva ecclesia c.12.

138 'Quomodo enim potest esse fidelis in substantiam Dei qui carnali fidem domino exhibere non potuit?' *TMA* 2.71, fol. 49va. Cf. C.23 q.5 c.24. On the king as the anointed of the Lord see *TMA* 2.71, fol. 49rb, with reference to C.22 q.5 c.19.

139 *TMA* 2.71, fols. 49vb–50ra. *TMA* 2.71 is one of the chapters that were mutilated in the printed editions. Its contents are distributed over fols. 49rb–51va, 60va–61rb, and 52rb–vb. Except for the beginning it consists in its entirety of quotations from IV Toletanum c.74, V Toletanum c.2–9, VI Toletanum c.3, c.13, VIII Toletanum c.10, and X Toletanum c.2.

140 Gelasius, as quoted in D.96 c.10, declared that 'duo sunt quippe, inperator auguste, quibus principaliter hic mundus regitur: auctoritas sacra Pontificum, et regalis potestas'. In *TMA* 1.2, fol. 4vb, Durant changed this into 'duo a quibus regitur humanum genus sicut a ministris Dei, videlicet ecclesiastica autoritas et regalis potestas, sicut Gelasius papa scribit Anastasio imperatori, xcvi. di. duo sunt'. It is hard to imagine that the difference could have been an oversight. D.96 c.10 was one of the best-known medieval laws on church and state, familiar to people well outside the circle of professional canon lawyers. Changes were bound to be noticed. Besides, Durant did cite the original version in *TMI* 8 (3.31), fol. 61vb: 'Duo a quibus secundum Gelasium papam principaliter hic mundus regitur, videlicet auctoritas sacra pontificum et regalis potestas . . .'

not merely a contemporary criticism of *Unam sanctam* but also a direct assault on the supremacy of the papacy over the temporal power as it had been asserted in the eleventh century in another and no less significant instance of tampering with the text of Gelasius – that by Pope Gregory VII.[141]

The stringent limitations that Durant intended to place on the papal power of jurisdiction and his willingness to underscore the divine quality of royal power in a manner not unlike that adopted by John of Paris are two particularly striking indications of how serious he was about reforming the head of the church.[142] But we must not exaggerate. He was concerned to limit what he regarded as excrescences of papal supremacy, and he was certain that the pope had gone too far in asserting his domination over kings and bishops – but he was not about to question the supreme role of the papacy as such. He still called the church of Rome 'the mother of the faith, the teacher of the universal church, the head of all other churches, from which they must receive the norm of religion'.[143] He called the pope 'Vicar of Christ' or 'Vicar of the Lord'.[144] Indeed, in spite of his own prohibition on titles exaggerating papal power he once referred without comment to the pope as 'prince of

---

[141] D.96 c.10 was not taken directly from the writings of Gelasius but from Gregory VII's famous letter to Hermann of Metz, in which Gregory had changed the meaning of Gelasius rather sharply by omitting the passages in which Gelasius had admitted to the emperor that bishops had to obey imperial commands 'quantum ad ordinem pertinet publicae disciplinae, cognoscentes imperium tibi superna dispositione collatum'. See Miethke, *Kaiser und Papst*, pp. 20f., 63, for Gregory VII's wording and Carlyle, *History*, 1:191 n. 1, for Gelasius' original. Almost surely unbeknown to himself, Durant's tampering with D.96 c.10 thus merely served to undo the effects of Gregory VII's tampering and may well have approached more closely to Gelasius' original understanding of the relationship between temporal and ecclesiastical power. Simon of Beaulieu had already used D.96 c.10 in a similar manner; Schleyer, *Anfänge*, p. 93.

[142] When John of Paris dealt with *Duo sunt*, he insisted on characterizing the power of the king as that of a minister of God in language similar to Durant's: 'Sic sunt distinctae [spiritualis potestas et secularis] quod una in aliam non reducitur, sed sicut spiritualis immediate a Deo, ita et temporalis . . . Dicit enim Apostolus *Ad Romanos* xiii (4–6) de rege et principe: "Si malefeceris, time! Non enim sine causa gladium portat. Dei enim minister est, vindex malorum in ira" etc. Et infra: "Ideo praestatis tributa. Ministri enim Dei sunt." Non dicit "papae" sed "Dei"!' John Quidort of Paris, *De regia potestate et papali* c. 10, ed. Bleienstein, pp. 110f., 113. But it is impossible to tell if Durant was drawing directly on John of Paris.

[143] 'Romana ecclesia . . . mater est fidei et magistra debet esse universalis ecclesie, et ad quam omnis sancte religionis relatio ⋆sicut ad caput aliarum⋆ [P] debet referri et ab ea normam recipere.' *TMA* 2.96 (3.27), fol. 58va. Cf. D.12 c.2.

[144] *TMA* 1.4 De dispensationibus, fol. 7vb; *TMA* 2.18, fol. 23rb; *TMA* 2.20, fol. 25ra.

all priests and of the entire world'.[145] He was naturally hesitant to say much about papal supremacy over the bishops, but when it came to temporal power he was happy to offer an unqualified endorsement of Giles of Rome's *De ecclesiastica potestate*, surely one of the most remarkable defences of papal supremacy to have appeared in the middle ages.[146] He also quoted the most famous pieces of ecclesiastical legislation in support of papal supremacy.[147] Indeed, he seemed to have no doubt at all that the Donation of Constantine was valid.[148]

---

[145] 'Pontifex qui per tempora ipsius sacrosancte Romane ecclesie extiterit celsior et princeps cunctis sacerdotibus et totius mundi existat.' *TMA* 2.9, fols. 17vb–18ra. These words, however, were not Durant's own, but quoted from D.96 c.14, the Donation of Constantine.

[146] 'De potestate ecclesiastica super temporales dominos et dominia temporalia. Istam rubricam non prosequor nec etiam lxxii. de presenti propter librum quem de contentis in dictis duabus rubricis reverendus in Christo frater Egidius Bituricensis archiepiscopus, in quo profunditas et sublimitas vigent scientie, copiose et utiliter edidit, in quo plenius videri possunt pertinentia ad istas duas rubricas quam posset hic explicari.' *TMA* 2.95 (3.26), fol. 58rb–va. The parallel chapter *TMA* 2.72 (3.3), fols. 52vb–53ra, entitled 'De his que imperatores, reges, principes, et domini temporales intra ecclesiam et in personis ecclesiasticis, rebus, et bonis agere et exercere possunt', repeats these words almost exactly.

[147] In *TMA* 2.9, fol. 18ra, Durant cited Pope Nicholas II's canon *Omnes*, D.22 c.1, which declared that Christ had given St Peter unique control over the keys to the kingdoms of both heaven and earth, Pope Innocent III's famous assertion of papal primacy in *Solite*, X.1.33.6, and Pope Nicholas III's more recent constitution *Fundamenta militantis ecclesie*, VI.1.6.17, which regulated the government of Rome, but at the same time restated the papacy's view of its own dignity. In *TMA* 2.93 (3.24), fols. 57va–58ra, he added a brief exposition on *Novit*, X.2.1.13, that other famous decretal of Innocent III, which gave the church the right to involve itself in temporal affairs *ratione peccati* and led Durant to call broadly for ecclesiastical jurisdiction over such issues as debasement of coinage, unequal weights, fraudulent contracts, scarcity, concealed usury, excessive dowries, enslaving freemen, arbitrary secular jurisdiction and taxation, and to conclude that 'etiam in foro seculari divine leges et iura canonica serventur'. *TMA* 2.93 (3.24), fol. 58ra. This was hardly the language of a man concerned to defend the autonomy of secular power.

[148] 'In eadem synodo Nicena ponatur edictum donationis Constantini imperatoris de qua habetur in illa palea Constantinus, xcvi. di. Et in dicto edicto specialiter contineatur qualiter dictus Constantinus decrevit ut Romana ecclesia principatum teneat tam super quatuor sedes patriarchales, scilicet Alexandrinam, Antiochenam, Hierosolimitanam et Constantinopolitanam, quam etiam in universo orbe super omnes ecclesias; et pontifex, qui per tempora ipsius sacrosancte Romane ecclesie extiterit celsior, et princeps cunctis sacerdotibus et totius mundi existat. Et eidem Romanam urbem et omnis Italie sive omnium occidentalium civitates regionum et provincias reliquerit et imperium occidentale ut ibidem contineatur.' *TMA* 2.9, fols. 17vb–18ra. Cf. D.96 c.13–14. Gérard of Abbeville had similarly insisted on the validity of the Donation of Constantine; Douie, *Conflict*, p. 17; see also Maffei, *La donazione di Costantino* and Pascoe, 'Gerson and the Donation of Constantine'.

# The assertion of justice

In other words, scandals like that between Boniface VIII and Philip IV had to be avoided, and to that end the line between temporal and spiritual jurisdiction was to be clearly specified. But that was not to deny papal supremacy over the temporal power: quite the contrary, the rights of the church over the state were to be 'urged on the ears of princes until they understand that the church does not injure their rights if it interferes in certain secular cases'.[149] If anything, Durant believed that Rome had not been as assertive as it should have been in all respects. We have already mentioned his disdain for Boniface's compromise regarding borderline clerics.[150] He was similarly distressed by the ease with which Rome permitted laymen to arrest clerics – not improbably a reference to the fate of the Templars and Bernard Saisset.[151] He thought that Rome should have been more reticent in granting absolution to enemies of the church.[152] And as to *Clericis laicos*, the bull that had started the escalation of hostilities between Boniface and Philip, Durant considered it an eminently reasonable measure.[153]

---

[149] 'Videretur ideo utile, si absque scandalo fieri posset, hec taliter secularium principum auribus inculcari quod cognoscerent nullam sibi fieri iniuriam cum ecclesia se de aliquibus casibus secularibus intromittat.' *TMA* 2.9, fol. 18ra.

[150] See above, p. 186.

[151] 'Nec videtur quod Romana ac universalis ecclesia deberet pati ut episcopi et cetere persone ecclesiastice a regibus, principibus, atque ceteris dominis temporalibus eorum auctoritate caperentur, sicut cotidie videmus attentari de facto. Nec dicta Romana ecclesia deberet, ut videtur prima facie quod possit, super hoc eis privilegium concedere, sed concessa potius revocare, cum talis concessio tendat ad destructionem universalis ecclesie, xxv. q. i. sunt quidam, et q. ii. si ea destruere, ut in iii. rubrica supra in prima parte posita plenius est probatum, cum hoc sit ius publicum, divinum, et humanum, personaliter et realiter ecclesiis concessum, cui renuntiari non potest, cum sit publicum autoritate et utilitate.' *TMA* 2.3, fol. 15vb. Cf. C.25 q.1 c.6, C.25 q.2 c.4, as well as *TMA* 2.70, fols. 46rb, 47rb, 48ra–b.

[152] 'Item quod in foro penitentiali et penitentiarie eiusdem Romane curie citra transgressores iuris publici, offensores personarum ecclesiasticarum, et alios Dei ecclesiam scandalizantes, facilitas relaxaretur venie.' *TMA* 2.96 (3.27), fol. 59rb.

[153] 'Verum si dicatur iura antiqua hoc [i.e., taxation of the clergy by secular lords] suadere, responderi potest quod talia iura corrigantur per iura canonica de immunitate ecclesiarum, quia nonnulli, et c. clericis lib. vi., et per concilium Lateranense et c. non minus.' *TMA* 2.70, fol. 47vb. Cf. VI.3.23.1, VI.3.23.3, X.3.49.4. VI.3.23.3 is *Clericis laicos*. Cf. *TMA* 2.5, fol. 16ra–b, and *TMA* 2.66, fol. 44ra, which reinforce the point. When Durant declared in a more general way that the church of Rome 'personas ecclesiasticas et ecclesiastica bona in concessionibus decimarum, *annalium* [P] et aliarum subventionum, quas facit regibus et principibus qui oppido infesti sunt, non gravaret, sed contra dictos reges et principes et quoscunque alios per se et generales defensiones in singulis provinciis in iure suo foveat eosdem', *TMA* 2.96 (3.27), fol. 59ra, he evidently had the opening words of *Clericis laicos* in mind as well. Durant repeatedly referred to decretals of Boniface VIII with expressions of regret that they were not being enforced; see *TMA* 2.70, fol. 47ra, for VI.3.23.4; fol. 47va, for VI.5.11.12, VI.3.23.5;

Thus the reform at which Durant was aiming could not possibly have been intended as an exercise of popular resistance or rebellion or an imposition of rules by a sovereign people on an unwilling papacy. There was to be reform, but reform had to proceed from the head. Rome would reform itself in order to establish good examples and would thereby

> become a rule and school of virtue, so that by living well it will conduct itself as a norm of living well for others and will walk on the straight paths of justice . . . and thus, having removed the beams from its eyes, will correct and reform whatever it finds wicked and distorted in its subjects and inferiors, like Christ, who acted first and taught thereafter.[154]

Rome would impose the law on itself.[155] Then it would impose the law on everybody else as well – and it is very much worth stressing that nowhere was this said more clearly than precisely at the point at which Durant raised his demand for decennial general councils:

> Henceforth the church of Rome ought to enact no general laws unless a general council has been convoked, and such a council ought to be convoked every ten years. And just as the church of Rome should in itself observe the good and provident statutes that were established in the past, so it ought to cause them to be observed by everybody else, by imposing the law on patriarchs and primates, who will compel archbishops and metropolitans [to obey] the aforesaid matters without qualification; and [by imposing it] on archbishops and metropolitans, who will compel the

---

and fol. 47va, for VI.2.2.2, VI.2.11.2. On the origins of *Clericis laicos* in C.2 q.7 c.5, and on the enthusiasm with which local councils supported its point of view well before Boniface VIII's pontificate, see Gaudemet, 'Aspects', p. 339. Boniface VIII mitigated its impact in 1297 by publishing *Etsi de statu* and canonizing Louis IX. Clement V revoked *Clericis laicos* in 1306; see Izbicki, '"Clericis Laicos"'; Strayer, *Reign of Philip the Fair*, pp. 254f.; and Clement V, no. 890 (1.II.1306).

154 'Sane quantum ad reformationem Romane ecclesie, videretur quod ipsa Romana ecclesia, que non debet habere maculam neque rugam . . . exhiberet se regulam et scholam virtutum, ut bene vivendo normam aliis bene vivendi et recte per semitas iustitie se ipsam duceret, nec aliquid aborsum traheret, et sic correctione in se ipsa prehabita, in Dei et proximi dilectione, vera humilitate, vite honestate, morum gravitate, divini cultus sedulitate, victus et vestitus parcitate fundata, ornamentorum, aparatuum, et familiarum et pomparum elativa superfluitate restricta, scientie profunditate dotata, trabeque de oculo suo eiecta, quod distortum est pravumque reperiret in subiectis et inferioribus, corrigeret, et etiam reformaret Christi exemplo, qui prius cepit facere quam docere.' *TMA* 2.96 (3.27), fol. 58va.

155 'Item quod legem sibi ipsi imponeret ne transgredetur contenta in divinis et humanis legibus approbatis, quibus genus debet per eam et autoritate imperiali et regali gubernari humanum, sed ea usque ad sanguinem et [animam] observari mandaret.' *TMA* 2.96 (3.27), fol. 58va. The emendation is suggested by C.25 q.1 c.6.

bishops; and [by imposing it] on the bishops, who will compel abbots, chapters, and all secular and regular persons in their cities and dioceses, without contradiction or appeal.[156]

This passage shows with striking clarity that councils were not meant to transform the hierarchy or to conflict with it in any way. Rather, Durant's call for councils was accompanied by an emphatic declaration that the papacy had an exclusive right to enforce the law over anyone and that such enforcement was to proceed from Rome along the ranks of the ecclesiastical hierarchy.

### THE RULE OF UNIVERSAL REASON

The reason why there has been so much uncertainty about Durant's intentions can now be specified more clearly. Modern scholars, like the rest of modern men and women, do not share his view of the world. They believe that good examples are as often disobeyed as they are followed, and they do not consider that reason always coincides with reality. As a result they are uncertain of how to account for his enthusiastic reliance on the laws and on Christ's examples. They turn a sceptical eye on his expectation that the clergy as a whole could be made to follow Christ's example (especially given the size of the beams in Durant's own eyes) and they suspect that whatever good examples the clergy could have given would not in any case have been enough to achieve the reform of the laity. Again, for Durant to insist that laws should be obeyed seems meaningless and tautological unless he was ready to rely on some force apart from the law, such as the conscience of the individual or public institutions, in order to assure obedience to it. After all, the reason reform was needed was that the laws had not been heeded previously.[157] In short, Durant's invocations of law

---

[156] 'Item quod nulla iura generalia deinceps conderet nisi vocato concilio generali, quod de decennio in decennium vocaretur. Et sicut ipsa Romana ecclesia que bene et consulte fuerunt hactenus statuta in se ipsa servaret, ita et ea faceret ab omnibus observari, imponendo legem patriarchis et primatibus per quam archiepiscopos et metropolitanos, et eis per quam episcopos, et episcopis per quam abbates, capitula, et omnes seculares et regulares personas in eorum civitatibus et diocesibus constitutis, omnium contradictione et appellatione cessantibus, necessario compellerent ad predicta.' *TMA* 2.96 (3.27), fol. 59rb.

[157] Kuhn, 'Concepts of Cause', pp. 24f., provides an excellent brief definition of the tautology at issue. His case is that of Aristotelian science, whose statement that heavy bodies fall because it is the nature of heavy bodies to move downwards seems just as tautological to us as Durant's statement that 'the church needs reform because it does not

and good examples are seen as attempts at moral persuasion that were hardly sufficient to effect reform. To account for his evident satisfaction with those attempts it seems necessary to assume that he was either a childlike character, well intentioned but naively unaware that good examples lacked efficacy, or a self-serving cynic whose moralizing must constitute a veneer with which he tried to conceal his actual motives from inspection.

But to accept the need for this alternative is to misconstrue the issue, for it implies a distinction between reason and reality that Durant did not see in this way. Both charitable and cynical interpretations of Durant's intentions add a modern element – of faith and disbelief, respectively – which is not needed to explain the evidence. Conversely, they both suppress a part of the evidence which is indubitably there: namely, the faith that the universe is really governed by God and his laws and that consequently Christ's examples do have a real effect. This faith may well be unfounded, but not to recognize that for Durant it was unquestionably true is to invite misinterpretations. It was this faith that furnished consistency to his ideas about reform and that informed his moral tone. Accordingly, his style of argument may have been sharp throughout, including every now and then a touch of irony and often more than a tinge of bitterness – but it included neither cynicism nor any faith in human goodness. Durant did not pay much attention to the possibility that ordinary human beings, in full and clear knowledge of the law, could wilfully choose to disobey – unless they were in the clutches of the devil. Of course he was aware that often laws were not obeyed – otherwise it would have been superfluous to call for reform. But in his view disobedience arose from ignorance and lack of good examples, which let power grow beyond its proper limits. Thus there was no need for force to control recalcitrant wills, nor was there anything particularly good about people who obeyed the law; they simply functioned normally. Reform could be achieved by publicizing the law and making sure that good examples were provided: if that were done, the rest would follow of its own accord. A clergy well instructed by Rome would furnish good examples to a laity which would obediently imitate the

follow Christ's example'. In both cases the appearance of a tautology is caused by our unfamiliarity with the conceptual framework by which the meaning of those statements was shaped: Aristotelian science in the former case and the 'great order of difference' in the latter.

clergy's conduct, as Durant believed it had been doing all along. To found an entire programme of reform on such beliefs was neither childlike *naïveté* nor a form of ideological deception; it was simply to draw natural conclusions from an accepted view about the operation of the universe.

Durant's ideas about morality thus differ fundamentally from modern views. In his conception moral conduct was founded neither on the inner voice of private conscience nor on submission to the force of public institutions. Rather it was founded on that 'great order of difference' which defined morality in terms of spontaneous imitation and obedience, of 'listening' to the law. This moral sense was similar to conscience in that it had to do with moral conduct, but very unlike conscience in that it did not fall within the limits of individual responsibility to nearly the same degree. Questions of right and wrong were thoroughly unproblematic for Durant because the answers to such questions consisted of objective facts. These could be ignored and might even prove impossible to establish without the help of general councils, but their objective truth was certainly not subject to individual discretion. Moral assent, insofar as assent was a necessary part of moral conduct at all, was not the cause of obedience to law but its consequence.

This moral sense is what Durant had in mind when he spoke of *mores*, a term that is impossible to render in modern terminology. We cannot translate it as 'morals' because it contains no trace of the subjective quality that we associate with moral choice. But neither can we translate it as 'customs', for even though in effect that is precisely what *mores* are, *mores* are binding in an objective sense whereas 'customs' are not. Finally, we cannot translate it as 'laws', because *mores* do not require any formal public sanction to be binding. The fact of the matter simply is that *mores* have disappeared from existence.[158] Hence we have no word for them and are easily misled into regarding any writer who relied on *mores* with undue cynicism or undue benevolence. That is quite unwarranted, for, as Gratian stated at the beginning of the *Decretum* and as Durant repeated, *mores* governed the human race in harmony with

---

[158] I am not sure if it goes without saying that this is neither to condemn modern Europeans for moral inferiority nor to call for a return to medieval morality. It is simply to insist that Durant constructed moral issues in a rather different way from ours and that this needs to be taken into consideration if his ideas are to be understood.

natural law.[159] For Durant, in other words, *mores* were part of the structure of the universe.

The structure of the universe, however, had proved susceptible to disarray – and Durant was very well aware of that. The most important cause that he was able to identify consisted of the papacy's exaggerated use of its plenitude of power. The papacy claimed that it possessed a power of jurisdiction that was not merely different from the powers of order possessed by every bishop but that was universal. That claim created the potential for an arbitrary power, one that was absolute, out of harmony with the reason of the universe. The reason of the universe, however, was not merely an intellectual thing; it was the ground on which the universe subsisted. A power that exceeded reason therefore brought about a schism in the church that threatened the universe with extinction.

The solution was to find a means to keep power infallibly limited by reason. General councils were to be that means. After all, the pope had not gone astray because he practised heresy or consciously desired to overturn the church; had that been the case, he would not have been a proper pope and could have been deposed. The trouble was that the laws were incomplete and furnished insufficient guidance to deal with changing circumstances – hence the pope went astray in spite of the best intentions. Fallible as he was, he misconstrued only too easily the finely articulated distinctions that constituted the order of the church, and in his eagerness to respond to changing circumstances he sometimes applied his extraordinary power with less than the proper discretion. That could be remedied by making sure that whenever he was tempted to exercise his power beyond the proper limits – that is to say, whenever given laws were not enough to decide a given issue – a general council would be consulted to decide what the law ought to say; for councils revealed the truth and thus were able to link reason infallibly to power.

This is the underlying meaning of the words with which Durant began his treatise: 'Counsel is not only considered to support our present life but also enjoys the prospect of eternal remuneration.'[160] Indeed, counsel deserved eternal remuneration, for it bridged the gaps between human fallibility and God, between this

---

[159] See above, p. 132.     [160] See above, pp. 116, 124f.

world and the next, between time and eternity. When Durant proposed that general councils should be convoked whenever laws were to be changed, his intention was thus neither to maintain the interests of his episcopal estate nor to change the constitution of the church from a monarchy into a democracy. It was rather to preserve the 'ground', the *ratio*, on which the church was built and thereby to protect the world from imminent destruction.

*Chapter 6*

# RES PUBLICA

As Pope Gregory points out, subjects must be admonished not to humble themselves excessively, for if they bow to the authority of others more than necessary, they may be forced to venerate their vices.

William Durant[1]

The 'great order of difference' dominates Durant's ideas about reform, but it is insufficient for a complete interpretation of the *Tractatus Maior*. Side by side with exemplary efficiency and obedience to law one finds ideas about the proper way to organize a body politic that no interpretative artifice can fit into the notion of hierarchy and that give a different meaning to Durant's conciliar demand. These ideas are no more systematically elaborated than the great order of difference itself. Sometimes they appear in the form of asides that seem to leap from the page as foreign elements in the surrounding congeries of medieval jurisprudence. At other times they take the form of suggestions which in spite of their apparent harmony with hierarchical assumptions leave the reader with a nagging feeling that they lead in an entirely different direction. Only rarely do they occur as straightforward statements of principle. Fortunately for our purposes those rare occasions leave no doubt that the treatise embodies an idea of political organization which does not merely modulate the themes of hierarchy – it is opposed to them in principle. This idea of order is republican.[2]

---

[1] 'Ad predicta facit quod admonendi sunt subditi ne plusquam expediat sint subiecti, sicut idem Gregorius ait, ne cum student plusquam necesse est hominibus subiici compellantur eorum vitia venerari, ii. q. vii. admonendi.' *TMA* 2.34, fol. 30rb–va. Cf. C.2 q.7 c.57.

[2] 'Republican' is not to be confused with 'democratic'. On hierarchical principles the body politic is seen as grounded in the structure of the universe, whereas on republican principles the body politic is seen as grounded in the common good. It is a 'commonwealth'. That the notion of a commonwealth did not by any means require a preference for democratic government is clearly evidenced by Bodin's famous 'Six Books of the Republic', a work best known for its defence of absolute sovereignty. According to this understanding, the meaning of 'republic' is defined by its opposition to 'hierarchy' and not far removed from 'state'. But 'state' lacks the connotation of 'emancipation from hierarchical subordination', which is a crucial aspect of 'republic'.

## THE COMMONWEALTH OF ROME

The first opportunity for Durant to express his attachment to republican ideas of order occurred in the rubric on the 'need to limit the power of superiors'. It may be worth recalling the points he made in that rubric and exploring their significance. They turned on a quotation from Cicero's *De officiis*:

As Tully says in *De officiis*, Plato had two precepts for those who want to govern well and advance the commonwealth, namely, first, to aim only at civic utility and to be oblivious to their private advantage and, second, not to take care of only a part of the commonwealth but to attend to its whole body, lest they should neglect the other parts.[3]

Cicero thus succinctly enunciated two fundamental ways in which a commonwealth differs from a hierarchy. First he pointed out that to promote the commonwealth meant to promote the 'civic utility'; second, he stressed that the *res publica*, this 'public thing' or 'commonwealth', had to be treated as a whole and that the same attention had to be paid to all of its parts. An implication of these views which is sufficiently important to qualify as a separate, third difference is the sharp distinction between a private realm, on the one hand, in which individuals may be divided from each other by the pursuit of private advantages, and a public realm, on the other, in which those same individuals are united by their shared interest in a common good.

All three of these principles conflict with hierarchy. True, when we suggested that a hierarchy treats power as a private matter and love and reverence as instruments of public union, we allowed for a similar distinction between the private and public realms.[4] But in the present context the contents of public and private are reversed: 'action', not love or reverence – not to mention imitation or obedience – is here the force of public union; love appears, if at all, in the restricted sphere of private advantage, which is to say as love of self. Moreover, in a hierarchy the distinction between private and public, insofar as it exists at all, is overridden by a universal concord which makes it possible for every creature to 'live and be

---

[3] 'Duo etiam fuerunt precepta Platonis, sicut ait Tullius libro primo de officiis, volentibus rem publicam salubriter gubernare et rei publice prodesse, unum, videlicet, ut utilitati civium sic tuerentur ut quecunque agerent ad eam referrent, obliti commodorum suorum, alterum ut totum corpus rei publice curarent ne, dum ad partem aliquam attenderent, reliquam desererent.' *TMA* 1.3 De limitanda potestate, fol. 6rb (*male* 7rb). Cicero, *De officiis* 1.25(85).     [4] See above, p. 182.

governed' well, whereas in the commonwealth the point is precisely that living well in private and being governed well in public are two such different things that they conflict with each other just as the pursuit of private gain does with the common good.

The principle that the commonwealth forms a whole might at first sight appear to conform with hierarchical assumptions as well, for the great order of difference is, of course, also a single body. But not only is it universal, extending beyond citizens to other creatures and to God – it also rests on an essential unity of reason and existence that is incompatible with the sharp distinction between a common and private good. Even though in a republican environment, too, it may be thought that reason is in some sense an 'existential' property which nature has implanted in all individuals, the link between their reason and their existence is seen to be a fragile thing and regularly tested as private interests dictate actions that do not always meet the common good – not to mention the effects of sleep, irritation, or insanity. Hence, from a 'republican' perspective, reason and existence may and regularly do conflict, both within and between individuals. Leaving aside the question of why this is so (God may lack the power, the will, or the understanding to create a perfect world, or maybe all three) a republican idea of order thus presupposes existential conflicts between reason and reality, common good and private interest. The harmony at which it aims is never an essential union but merely a functional equilibrium resting on the assumption that different human beings, in spite of their conflicting interests, have common interests, too. This partial and precarious harmony lets them join in a commonwealth that will, at least up to a point, protect them from the arbitrary use of power for private purposes. But it can never override the fundamental difference between private and public motivations. The commonwealth therefore consists neither of creatures nor of citizens but is an abstract entity, a public understanding that there is a common good in which all citizens have an equal stake and for the sake of which they are united, but which exists apart from them and from which they can even be expelled in ways that they could not possibly be expelled from the universe. Everything else, such as the role and definition of love and reverence, law and utility, progress and reform, is shaped by this effort to establish a functional harmony. There are two factors, then, that guarantee the unity of the great order of difference: it has been made by God and it is aimed at 'true concord'; but there is only one factor that guarantees the unity of the commonwealth: the common good.

Again, utility is not foreign to hierarchy, but there it mainly serves to justify dispensations from the law. It is a secondary consideration, a principle that maintains the consistency of juris-prudential reasoning in the face of changing circumstances. Occasionally it is granted precedence over the law, but law is never robbed of its basic primary identification with justice and equity. Hence, even when utility succeeds in procuring dispensations from the law, it stands in an uneasy relationship to justice and equity.[5] But this is not so in the context of Cicero's quotation. There utility is raised to the level of a principle that rules the common good and to which all rulers must subject themselves; laws are not even mentioned since it is clear that they are but an instrument of utility. Republican utility is no mere tool designed to mediate a circum-stantial conflict between law and equity; it is 'civic', unmediated, and concrete.

Also in the rubric on the 'need to limit the power of superiors' Durant specified two particular respects in which the ancient commonwealth excelled the contemporary church.[6] First, in ancient times wealth had been concentrated in the public treasury, whereas private individuals, even those who held the highest offices of state, were satisfied with a frugal life. Second, public office was occupied only by people who were able to promote the common good. These particulars were undergirded by a keen sense of civic virtue which required every citizen to subordinate his private life entirely to the common good.[7] But as Durant explained by quoting the example of Marcus Curius, if the purpose of these self-denying practices was not to acquire gold for oneself, it was to acquire power over those who possessed the gold.[8] The subordination of personal advantages to the common good was predicated on a powerful drive to participate in the exercise of a public power, an *imperium*, that was beyond the capacities of separate individuals and could not be obtained without coope-ration. Frugality in private life was but the complement of empire

---

[5] See above, pp. 169–71.    [6] See above, pp. 149–51.    [7] See above, p. 148.
[8] 'Unde cum Marco Curio consuli magnum pondus auri oblatum fuisset, ait, ipsum respuens, non aurum preclarum haberi sibi videri, sed eis qui habent aurum imperare.' *TMA* 1.3 De limitanda potestate, fol. 6va (*male* 7va). Cf. Valerius Maximus, *Facta et dicta memorabilia* 4.3(5).

in public. Precisely this understanding of the relationship between
civic virtue, the common good, and public power was nicely
summed up in Cato's explanation of why Rome had become a
great commonwealth, which Durant used to conclude his account
of Roman virtues: 'Your ancestors did not turn a little commonwealth into a great commonwealth by relying only on arms . . .
[but by relying on] industry at home, just empire abroad, and a
spirit that was free to give sound advice and not indebted to the lust
for crime.'[9]

These were the ancient Roman principles according to which
the modern Christian commonwealth was to be governed, too: 'If
the rectors and princes of this world only observed Plato's counsels
and precepts, as well as what we said before, they would govern the
human race and the commonwealth as well as did the ancients.'[10]
To be sure, there were two important differences between the past
and the present: unlike the ancient commonwealth, the modern
one was universal; and it was marked by the distinction between
spiritual and temporal powers. But all the same it was a commonwealth, *res publica*; it rested on the same conviction that the
common good is no one's property but something that exists apart
from all citizens, a separate entity that is entrusted to the care of
public officers by whom it is 'administered', a term denoting
service, not possession, because in fact the common good is not a
property at all that could be owned by them or anybody else.
Hence it was necessary to remind the cardinals that 'in the primitive
church everything was owned in common';[11] and to remind the
kings that on their death they were obliged to leave to the kingdom
whatever they might have acquired during their reign, because
'what makes a king a king is not his person, but eternal laws'.[12]

---

[9] See above, p. 153. The opposite vices were defined as luxury, avarice, public poverty,
private opulence, sloth, and ambition.

[10] 'Si itaque mundi huius rectores et principes observarent ista concilia et precepta Platonis
et ea que supra premissa sunt, humanum genus et rem publicam salubriter gubernarent,
sicut et fecerunt antiqui.' *TMA* 1.3 De limitanda potestate, fol. 6rb (*male* 7rb).

[11] 'Qualiter in primitiva ecclesia erant omnia communia, et quod deliberetur si esset utile
quod adhuc idem in dominis cardinalibus et in collegiis et aliis servaretur.' *TMA* 2.2, fol.
15rb.

[12] 'Regem eterna iura faciunt, non persona, quia non constat sui mediocritate, sed
sublimitatis honore. Que ergo honori debeant, honori deserviant, et que reges accumu-
lant regno relinquant, ut quia eos regni gloria decorat, ipsi quoque regni gloriam non
extenuent sed exornent.' *TMA* 2.71 (3.1), fol. 52rb. The text is taken from the *decretum
universalis concilii editum in nomine principis* appended to the canons of VIII Toletanum; *PL*
130:517.

Indeed, as if to stress that the distinction between temporal and spiritual power did nothing to throw doubt upon the unity of the modern commonwealth or on the ministerial quality of modern public power, Durant referred to kings and popes not merely as the 'presidents of the spiritual and temporal power', which emphasized the separability of the presiding person from the power over which he was presiding, but also as the 'presidents of the monarchy', which emphasized the unity of the commonwealth.[13] In all of these regards the ancient and the modern commonwealths were virtually the same. Accordingly Durant saw nothing difficult at all in calling both ancient Rome and the modern combination of church and state a commonwealth, and both ancient and modern rulers the 'administrators' of that commonwealth.[14]

The frankness with which William Durant the Younger spoke of the contemporary church and state in such terms is surely remarkable. It allows us to assert that he conceived of kings and popes as public officers who were essentially no different from the officers of the Roman Republic, even if the comparison served mainly to contrast the vices of the former with the virtues of the latter. It gives us some insight into his understanding of republican government in general and tells us something of the reasons why he was attracted to that kind of government. But all of this is abstract: it does not tell us precisely how he thought a Christian common-wealth should have looked in the early fourteenth century, or what he had in mind when he spoke of 'industry', 'just empire', and 'the common good', or of the 'reason' by which the 'presidents of the monarchy' ought to be governed. This is something we cannot learn by looking at his praise of ancient Rome but only by taking another look at the second part of his treatise, where Roman republican ideas took on a rather more contemporary shape.

---

[13] '. . . de limitando et regulando exercitio potestatis dictorum presidentium monarchie'. *TMA* 1.4, fol. 7ra. This is the only time that Durant spoke of 'monarchy' in this fashion, but it should be noted that he did so at a particularly prominent place: the heading of the chapter in which he made his conciliar proposal. At *TMA* 1.3, fol. 5ra, and *TMA* 1.4, fol. 7va, Durant spoke of 'presidentes spirituali et temporali potestati'.

[14] E.g., *TMA* 1.3 De limitanda potestate, fol. 6vb (*male* 7vb): '. . . in rectoribus et in administratoribus rei publice qui legis divine notitiam non habebant . . . moderni administratores rei publice qui fide illuminati sunt'; *TMA* 1.4, fol. 7rb: '. . . consilium pro re publica et pro dictis administratoribus rei publice'. On 'administration' in an ecclesiastical context see Tierney, *Foundations*, pp. 118–27.

## TRUTH AND UTILITY

One of the more important occasions for Durant to consider the principles that underlay his vision of how a contemporary Christian commonwealth ought to be constructed occurred in the preface to the second part of the *Tractatus Maior*. The reader may recall that this preface began with a technical explanation of the rationale Durant had adopted in order to present the ancient conciliar laws to the council of Vienne. But once he had finished setting forth the external particulars of his procedure he went on to elaborate several fundamental issues. He began by distinguishing sharply between truth and custom:

For the Lord said in the Gospel of John c. 14: 'I am the truth.' He did not say: 'I am custom.' When truth is manifest custom must therefore yield to truth. For Peter, too, who practised circumcision, yielded to Paul, who preached the truth, as is written in Galatians c. 2 and C.2 q.7 c.40. Since Christ, the head and spouse of the universal church, is the truth and the way by which we come to life, we ought to follow the truth rather than wicked customs or the abuses practised by the church. For reason and truth always exclude mere custom.[15]

This distinction had profound implications for the conception of reform. In the great order of difference reform was to be achieved by obedience to law and by following the example of superiors; but the distinction between truth and custom threw a fundamental doubt upon all laws and all examples. For every law imposed from on high and for every example given by a superior it raised the question of whether that law or that example conformed to the truth or to a 'wicked custom'. That question was impossible to answer by mere reliance on the text of the law itself or by obedience of any kind. It required an entirely different approach: unquestioning subjection to the laws must give way to indepen-

---

15 'Nam Dominus in evangelio ait Joan. xiiii.: Ego sum veritas, et non dicit: Ego sum consuetudo, ut veritate manifesta veritati cedat consuetudo. Nam et Petrus, qui circumcidebat, cessit Paulo veritatem predicanti, sicut habetur ad Galat. ii. et ii. q. vii. Petrus. Unde cum Christus caput et sponsus universalis ecclesie sit veritas et via per quam venitur ad vitam, magis veritatem quam pravam ecclesie consuetudinem seu abusum sequi debemus, quia consuetudinem ratio et veritas semper excludit.' *TMA* 2.prefatio, fol. 13va. Cf. John 14:6, Galatians 2:11–14, C.2 q.7 c.40, as well as D.8 c.4–9. The distinction between truth and custom was of course not new. On the crucial role of Ivo of Chartres and Gregory VII in making it widely kown see Ladner, 'Two Gregorian Letters'.

dent judgments about the legitimacy of those laws; conformity must be replaced with the capacity to legislate; and obedience must yield to liberty.

An immediate consequence of the distinction between truth and custom, therefore, was a marked shift in emphasis from hierarchical subordination to equality. If the truth was neither identical with law nor the sole prerogative of superiors, then inferiors who knew the truth could stand up against their superiors. Regardless of their hierarchical position, they had a right not only to express their views but also to have their views considered seriously:

For, as Augustine says in his *Confessions*, it is true that in human society greater powers are placed above smaller ones in order to be obeyed, but God is placed above all of them. No one, however eminent in terms of learning, may therefore refuse to listen to the reasons which his inferiors have to offer, and the apostle Paul has said accordingly: 'If something has been revealed to someone who is seated', that is, to someone inferior, 'his superior ought to be silent'.[16]

The formulation may have been meek, but the principle was radical and it spurred Durant on occasion to utter rather ominous threats of disobedience if the pope did not see fit to treat his subjects with the respect that was their due:

Why should I treat you as a prince if you do not treat me as a senator? Those who despise others are despised themselves; bad faith is sometimes requited with bad faith; those who do not pay their debts seek in vain to recover their loans; and promises are sometimes not kept with those who do not keep their promises themselves. There must be some reciprocity between the eminence of the church of Rome and its acknowledgment.[17]

Durant thus countered the hierarchical fear of 'setting one's mouth against the heavens' to which he himself had paid tribute in

[16] 'Nempe prout predictus Augustinus in libro confessionum ait, sicut enim in potestatibus societatis humane maior potestas minori ad obediendum preponitur, ita Deus omnibus, viii. di. que contra, cum capitulis sequentibus. Nemo itaque dedignetur, quantumcumque preeminentie literature existat, audire si qua minoribus rationabiliter proferantur. Nam et Paulus apostolus ait: Si aliquid sedenti, id est, minori, fuerit revelatum, prior taceat, i. Cor. xiiii., xcv. di. esto subiectus, et concor. C. de offi. rec. pro. l. potiores.' *TMA* 2.prefatio, fol. 13vb. Cf. D.8 c.2, Augustine, *Confessions* 3.8, 1 Corinthians 14:30, D.95 c.7, Cod.1.40.5. Cf. the use of 1 Corinthians 14:30 by Luther, *An den christlichen Adel*, 6:411.

[17] 'Cur te habeam ut principem, cum me non habeas ut senatorem, xcv. di. esto subiectus? Nam qui contemnit contemnitur, et dolus interdum cum dolo compensatur, et frustra petit debitum qui quod debet non impendit, et non servanti fidem fides interdum non servatur eidem. Debet itaque *reciprocari* [P] Romane ecclesie altitudo et cognitio.' *TMA* 2.7, fol. 17rb. Cf. D.95 c.7. This important text is directly followed by a reference to D.89 c.7 and the 'great order of difference'.

the opening chapter of his treatise, and he replaced it with the bold assertion of an equality that guaranteed the rights of hierarchical inferiors. Because the pope could not expect his subjects to meet their promises to him if he did not keep his to them, there was a sense in which his power depended directly on his subjects' recognition. Indeed, there was a sense in which his subjects were entitled to withhold their recognition. To compare relations between the pope and the members of the church in such a way to the reciprocal obligations between contracting parties – between a debtor and a creditor – was to inject an element into the great order of difference that changed its very essence.

At the same time Durant adopted a markedly different attitude toward law:

If some of the cases specified [among the conciliar canons that will introduce every chapter in the second part of this treatise] are found to be useful to the universal church, the holy council should deliberate whether they ought to be observed, revoked, altered, or reinterpreted, provided that appears to be expedient.[18]

In spite of their brevity, the significance of these words – like Cicero's similarly brief definition of the virtues required from rulers of a commonwealth – cannot be overrated. Durant distinguished between four different kinds of action that could be taken with regard to law. Obedience (*observatio*), of course, was one of them. But obedience was now accompanied by three other possibilities: revocation (*revocatio*), change (*immutatio*), and reinterpretation (*declaratio*). There can be a legitimate degree of doubt as to whether the terms 'revocation', 'change', and 'reinterpretation' can accurately render Durant's technical meaning, especially since *immutatio*, 'change', is a doubtful reading: most manuscripts have *immitatio*, 'imitation'. But since these actions ranged from wholesale observation at one extreme to wholesale revocation at the other, they entailed *a fortiori* the possibility of changing law, regardless of whether *immutatio* or *immitatio* is the proper reading.[19] Moreover, the possibility of changes extended to precisely those conciliar laws to which in the first part of the treatise Durant

---

[18] 'Si aliqua in dicta specificatione casuum [canonum?] reperiantur utilia et universali ecclesie proficua, quod sacri provisione concilii super eorum observantia vel revocatione aut \*immutatione\* [P; alias: immitatione] vel declaratione deliberatio, si visum fuerit expediens, habeatur.' *TMA* 2.prefatio, fol. 13va.

[19] That *revocatio* indubitably means 'revocation', and not 'calling back into use', has been shown above, p. 119 n. 11.

had appeared to ask the same unqualified obedience that was owed to divine law. It thus seems reasonable to suppose that with these terms he meant to describe exhaustively the range of potential actions with regard to law which he envisioned for the council. It was, in other words, not just superiors who had to respect the truth in the mouth of 'someone seated', and it was not just superiors who needed to have their power recognized by their inferiors: the laws did, too. Obedience to law was overridden by a decided turn toward legislation.

In the passage just quoted, Durant specified the principle that was to underlie such legislation: a determination of what was 'useful to the universal church'. Under the pressure of the conflict between truth and custom, utility had thus been changed from a secondary means of justifying exceptions from the law under certain pressing circumstances into a primary principle of legislation. Considerations of utility decided whether a given law, including the most solemn conciliar law, was to be kept, changed, or abolished altogether. This kind of utility – the kind which Cicero had called the utility of citizens – could hardly be determined by studying the law and noticing conflicting circumstances only as they occurred by chance and in isolation from each other. It required a systematic grasp of social order as a whole in order to foresee which laws would achieve the common good. As Durant declared in connection with one of his bolder suggestions to adjust the law to utility, 'we have to weigh the ills that were committed in the past in order to avoid ills in the future; we must encounter future dangers in a timely fashion and provide for the ecclesiastical estate so that – God forbid – these ills will not recur'.[20] In short, defining utility for purposes of legislation required empirical analysis and accurate prognostication of the real needs of the commonwealth.

It is therefore no accident that in the final section of the preface to the second part of the *Tractatus Maior* Durant described the Christian commonwealth no longer in terms of hierarchy but in those of utility. St Bernard had pointed out that every reward for every order in society was balanced by an equal burden. But what,

---

[20] 'Preterita mala pensanda sunt ut futura caute caveantur, xxxi. di. ante triennium, et futuris sit periculis proinde occurrendum et ecclesiastico statui providendum ne recidiva, quod absit, mala prevaleant, xxiii. di. c. i. prope principium, et xxviii. di. de syracusane.' *TMA* 2.46, fol. 35va–b. Cf. D.31 c.1, D.23 c.1, D.28 c.13. The context was Durant's suggestion to do away with celibacy, on which see below, p. 238.

he had asked, were the burdens of the clergy? Like knights they searched for glory, but unlike knights they avoided the weight of knightly armour and sleepless nights in castles. Like women they enjoyed baths and handsome dress, but they showed no trace of female shame or discipline – not to mention female labour. Peasants were sweating, vintners were digging, and merchants were travelling overseas at danger to their lives; but the clergy were content to have their granaries filled with corn at harvest time, their cellars stocked with wine, and their tables loaded with imported delicacies.[21]

Where do you think this breed will find a place when every human being is resurrected in his proper order? If they should turn to the knights, they will be turned away because they did not bear with them the burdens and dangers of military service; likewise the peasants, the merchants, and every other order will expel them because they did not participate in the labour of human beings. What else will be left to them if not that they whom every order has rejected will be cast down on earth to a place where there exists no order, but only eternal error?[22]

With this ominous prophecy Durant concluded his preface to the second part. The point here is not simply his apocalyptic tone,

[21] 'Habent quoque genera hominum labores et voluptates. Et advertenda est aliquorum prudentia miranda, non imitanda, qui quodam artificio miro decernentes et sequestrantes totum quod delectat carnem eligunt et amplectantur, quod autem molestum est fugiunt et declinant. Cum militibus capiunt quod habere volunt, superbie fastum, amplam familiam, nobiles apparatus, equorum phaleras, accipitres, aleas, et eorum similia. Frequentant thalamos et balnea, et molliciem omnem et vestium gloriam a mulieribus mutuantur. Cavent autem lorice pondus et insomnes in castris noctes, et discrimina preliorum, muliebrem quoque verecundiam et disciplinam, et si quid sexus ille laboris habere cernitur, declinantes. Sudant agricole; putant et fodiunt vineatores. Sed hi inter hoc torpent otio. Sed accedente fructuum tempore innovari sibi orrea iubent et promptuaria eorum vino et tritico. Bibunt vinum meracissimum. Uve sanguine inebriantur, impinguantur et dilatantur ex adipe frumenti herbarum succis, peregrinis mutant vini saporem, et additur oleum camino. Similiter negotiatores circumierunt mare et aridam in labore corporis et periculo vite perituras sibi divitias congregantes. Prudentes autem nostri dulces in terra somnos capiunt et cibos et potus percipiunt delicatos.' *TMA* 2.prefatio, fol. 14ra–b (*male* 15ra–b). Cf. 1 Corinthians 15:23. The entire passage is quoted from Saint Bernard's *Declamationes de colloquio Simonis cum Jesu, PL* 184:435–76, here 443. On the text and authorship of this work, which is commonly attributed to Geoffrey of Auxerre, see Leclercq, 'Les Ecrits de Geoffroy d'Auxerre', and Leclercq, 'Saint Bernard et ses secrétaires', pp. 221–4.

[22] 'Cum autem resurgent homines unusquisque in suo ordine, ubi putas generatio ista locabitur? Si ad milites deverterint, exsufflabunt eos quia non secum labores militie et pericula tolerarint. Sic agricole, sic negotiatores, et singuli quique ordines hos a suis arcebunt finibus utpote qui in labore hominum non sunt. Quid ergo restat nisi ut quos omnis ordo repellit subiiciantur in terra in locum ubi nullus ordo set sempiternus error habitat?' *TMA* 2.prefatio, fol. 14rb (*male* 15rb). Still quoted from Bernard's *Declamationes de colloquio Simonis cum Jesu, PL* 184:444.

his dire warning that unless the clergy changed their ways they would be sent to hell; he had condemned the clergy long before. The point is that he framed the condemnation in terms of useful labour. He represented society as a single, functional whole, all of whose members had an equal obligation to 'participate in the labour of human beings'; the clergy, too, like every other order, must make a useful contribution to the common good. The difference between the clergy and the laity was not, of course, abolished, but its difference from the other orders, and their differences from each other, was levelled by the emphasis on the mutual dependence of all orders. The clergy were condemned not because they failed to go ahead with good examples, but because they were a leisure class of drones who consumed without producing. Hence they could lose their right to membership in society and could even be expelled from it on the day of the last judgment. In other words, just as the truth had been divorced from custom, so utility had been divorced from social rank; just as all laws must be suspected of sanctioning wicked customs, so hierarchical eminence must be suspected as a pretext to legitimate the lives of social parasites.

That changed the nature of reform. In order to appreciate the change, it is instructive to compare the contents of the preface to the second part of the treatise with the two chapters at the beginning of part I. In both instances Durant was dealing with two main instruments of reform, and in a general sense those instruments remained the same: the clergy and the law. In a sense, therefore, the preface to the second part simply resumed the themes stated in the opening two chapters. But the resumption differed in crucial ways from the original: Durant had first stressed the clergy's duty to set a good example, but now he stressed its duty to make a useful contribution to society; before he had stressed its duty to abide by law, but now he emphasized the need to change the law by reference to utility. In both cases the difference turned on a distinction: in the first case that between the place the clergy occupied in the hierarchy and the function which it exercised in society; and in the second case that between custom and truth.

The effect of these distinctions was reflected in Durant's decision to reverse the sequence in which he dealt with the clergy and the law. In the first part of the treatise he had begun with the clergy and only then had turned to law; now he began with law and only then turned to the clergy. This reversal may appear to be a minor change of purely formal consequence, but in fact it signifies a profound reorientation in the conception of reform. In the beginning of the treatise Durant had placed his hopes primarily on that coincidence of truth with reality, of excellence of conduct with hierarchical position which informed the idea of the 'great order of difference'; it was this which had enabled him to describe the divine law of nature and human *mores* as constituting a single short road to reform. That road was now obstructed by the discrepancy between truth and custom, between the law of God and the law of man. *Mores* no longer yielded a proper standard for reform; at best they had become mere custom, at worst the wicked custom of the church. That precluded any hope of basing reform on the hierarchical principles of imitation and obedience, and hence of beginning reform with the clergy – but by no means did it preclude reform altogether. Reformers simply had to proceed along a different 'road to reform': instead of placing their hopes on the clergy and its ability to give good examples, they had to place their hopes on laws that conformed to social utility. Such laws would be able to transform society, including the clergy, into a proper commonwealth each of whose members contributed the share they owed to the common good. By reversing the sequence in which he dealt with the clergy and the law Durant thus signalled a completely new approach to reform: good examples were not to result in establishing obedience to law, but the reverse; establishing good laws would result in good examples.

The preface to the second part of the *Tractatus Maior* thus announced a rather modern vision of reform consisting of two elements: social utility and legislation. The prominence Durant gave to legislation suggests not only that the pace of social change was quickening but also that the clergy were beginning to emancipate themselves from the respect with which for centuries they had looked upon an ancient heritage that often could not be made to exhibit an intelligible meaning for the contemporary medieval world without impressive feats of intellectual acrobatics. Similarly, the value Durant placed on social utility may suggest that the ambivalent position of the secular clergy between the monasteries of the early middle ages and the workshops of early modern times, between prayer and industry (an ambivalence inherent in the very notion of a 'secular clergy'), could not be maintained forever. His charge that the clergy were a useless blight on the body of society contains the seeds of the attack on the monastic ethic that reached maturity in the Reformation and that bore its ripest fruit in the derision with which, in the eighteenth century, enlightened philosophers drew the distorted but effective image of the clergy as a bunch of gloomy ascetics whose function in the world was to spoil the fun for everybody else.


### MONEY, WORK, AND FORCE

Truth and utility thus were the principles Durant placed at the head of reform in the preface to the second part of his treatise. In the body of the second part these principles recurred in the shape of concrete suggestions for reform. Many of them furnish no better than equivocal evidence for the particular conception of society that is under consideration at the moment, and we have therefore dealt with them in the preceding chapter.[23] However, some of them – those concerning money, work, and force – are more appropriately treated in the present context.

To begin with money, Durant did not restrict himself to admonishing the clergy to keep their hands as far as possible off filthy mammon and to spend their revenues on charitable purposes. He also displayed a keen awareness of the essential role that money, along with weights and measures, played as a medium of exchange in society, and consequently he launched a sharp attack on those who tampered with the coinage:

The emperors, kings, princes, prelates, and other temporal lords who since antiquity have had the right of minting coins are in all sorts of ways at variance with the commonwealth if, in violation of the law and the commendable practices of their ancestors, they debilitate the coinage and defraud the commonwealth of legitimate weights and standards. By so doing they cause and encourage a universal rise in prices and similar kinds of fraud, endangering their souls and the souls of others. This is why there exist unequal weights, coins that are not worth their value, all sorts of sophisticated and fraudulent practices in every business and trade, high prices for everything, covert and surreptitious contracts for usury, and

---

[23] Perhaps it should be stressed at this point that *all* of Durant's suggestions can be interpreted from *both* of the perspectives that are the subject of this and the preceding chapter. How they are related to each other will be considered in the following chapter.

[this is] why all subjects, the great, the middling, and the small, are being plundered.[24]

In order to improve this sad state of affairs Durant, with noteworthy sympathy for the needs of a stable market, demanded that all weights and measures be standardized and that the value of money not be manipulated:

Coins should be prevented from being altered to the prejudice of anyone, ought everywhere to be accepted at their true value, and should never be the cause of any scarcity in silver, gold, or any other thing; in any given kingdom the same measures and weights ought to be valid everywhere.[25]

Turning to work, that issue is best approached by looking at Durant's ideas on begging. A beggar's very manner of existence conflicted with the notion that every member of society ought to make a useful contribution; hence it is hardly a surprise that Durant launched an attack on begging. He described it as an 'iniquity' that was tantamount to 'sinning'; it was also an 'injustice' and an 'error' that bespoke the presence of a 'wicked will'.[26] To correct that wicked will strong measures were required. Durant did not shrink from a certain degree of severity in stating that 'it is more useful to take bread away from someone who is hungry . . . than to break it with him and thus let him go on indulging his injustice'. Indeed, begging prompted a rare display of cynicism: Durant agreed that beggars needed alms – but not the alms they wanted. The alms they

[24] 'Multipliciter abhorreatur contra rem publicam ab imperatore, regibus, principibus, prelatis, et aliis dominis temporalibus ius cudendi monetam ab antiquo habentibus, quia contra ius et ea que fuerunt hactenus laudabiliter ab eorum maioribus observata monetam debilitant et rem publicam legitimo pondere et valore illegitime defraudant, caristie universalis et consimilis defraudationis materiam exhibentes et occasionem prestantes in periculum animarum suarum et etiam aliorum, et ex hoc sequantur pondera inequalia, statere dolose, sophisticationes et falsitates omnium negotiationum et mercationum ac rerum universalis caristia, et palliati et simulati contractus usurarum, et depredatio subditorum, maiorum, mediocrium, et minorum.' *TMA* 2.93 (3.24), fol. 57va.

[25] 'Quod dicte monete mutari non possent in preiudiciis aliorum, et quod pro valore suo ubique currerent, nec efficeretur propter eas argenti vel auri vel aliarum rerum carista, et quod intra idem regnum eedem essent mensure et pondera.' *TMA* 2.93 (3.24), fol. 57vb.

[26] 'Item cum scribat Augustinus in vii. epistola ad Marcellinum ultra medium, et in sermone de puero centurionis, xxiii. q. i. paratus, quod cui licentia iniquitatis eripitur utilius vincitur, quoniam nihil est infelicius felicitate peccantium, qua penalis nutritur impunitas et mala voluntas velut hostis interior roboratur, utilius esurienti panis tollitur, si de cibo securus iustitiam negligat *quam* [P] eidem frangitur ut seductus iniustitie acquiescat.' *TMA* 2.87 (3.18), fol. 56ra. Cf. C.23 q.1 c.1. Durant means all of this to be applied to beggars.

231

needed was a general ban on begging for all healthy beggars, for 'many good things can be bestowed on the unwilling if we take their utility to heart, not their desire . . . It is in fact a kind of alms to lead the wayward back to truth.'[27] Those who begged because they were invalids, lepers, orphans, or simply 'miserable persons whom some debility prevents from working with their hands' were to be taken into the care of cities and dioceses.[28] Here we can begin to sense the atmosphere of those poor-houses whose main reason for existence was the belief that the poor must be forced to make themselves useful to society because their poverty was in some way their own fault – houses whose last surviving specimens Charles Dickens castigated.

Durant's attack on begging had obvious implications for those members of the church who thought that begging was a particularly virtuous Christian way of life: the friars mendicant. To be sure, Durant did not condemn the friars out of hand. He respected them for their 'exemplary honesty, austerity, and singular manner of life, their knowledge and their preaching', and he conceded that they were a 'bulwark of the faith' for many Christians who were despairing of their priests.[29] There were also many reasons to criticize the mendicants that had nothing to do with mendicancy: they were vainglorious;[30] they bragged about the nobility, wealth, and power of their relatives and let their personal affections destroy the unity of the church;[31] they believed they were better candi-

---

[27] 'Multaque bona prestantur invitis quando eorum utilitati, licet non voluntati, consulitur, sicut idem Augustinus in Enchiridion lxxi. c. ait, xlv. di. et que emendat, et secundum Albinum unum sit genus eleemosyne errantes in viam reducere veritatis, eadem di. tria, et c. due. Videretur providendum quod omnes mendicantes validi, contra quos leges seculares etiam invehunt, cohiberentur ab eleemosynis recipiendis.' *TMA* 2.87 (3.18), fol. 56ra–b. Cf. D.45 c.11–13.

[28] 'Leprosi et alie persone miserabiles qui debilitate faciente suis manibus laborare non possunt victum et vestitum inquantum possibile est episcoporum largitione assequi debeant.' *TMA* 2.86 (3.17), fol. 56ra. 'Quod provideretur mendicis invalidis per singulas civitates et dioceses.' *TMA* 2.87 (3.18), fol. 56rb. 'Fuerit ab antiquo ordinatum quod in re publica habeant xenodoches monasteria, ptochotrophia, orphanotrophia, gerontocomia, et brephotrophia et loca similia in quibus pauperes peregrini recipiantur, senes, parentibus orbati infantes, et miserabiles persone alantur.' *TMA* 2.88 (3.19), fol. 56rb.

[29] 'Propter honestatis, austeritatis, et singularis vite eorum exemplum, scientie et predicationis documentum, confessionum audiendarum consolamentum, defendende fidei et expugnationis infidelium pugnaculum populorum de vita et scientia propriorum sacerdotum plerumque diffidentium, magnum in ecclesia Dei hactenus retulerint et adhuc referant fructum.' *TMA* 2.85 (3.16), fol. 55rb.

[30] 'Putantes quod eorum auxilio plurimum indigerent et quod sine eis factum esset nihil.' *TMA* 2.85 (3.16), fol. 55va.

[31] 'In dictis religionibus de nobilitate, divitiis, et potentiis parentum intumescant, et ex hoc et secundum regna, provincias, et dioceses et secundum proprias affectiones in unitate

dates for any benefice than other clerics;[32] they despised prelates and simple priests;[33] they undermined ecclesiastical jurisdiction by consorting with excommunicates;[34] and they endangered many souls by their refusal to inform parish priests in writing about which members of the parish flock had confessed to them.[35] But the centre-piece of Durant's treatment of the friars was a frontal assault on the belief that begging was an honourable way of life because it granted freedom from the cares of wealth and property. That belief was simply false. To the contrary, at best begging placed additional burdens on a society whose hard-earned livelihood should not go to support the idle; at worst it meant dependence on the wealthy – as was demonstrated by the frequency with which the mendicants attended funerals of usurers.[36] If it was argued that begging was the apostolic way of life, Durant could counter that the apostles had not begged; they worked.[37] Far from being a virtue it was 'nothing special for those who sow spiritual things to reap temporal things'.[38] Therefore the friars were to make themselves useful to society. Those among them who had the necessary qualifications were to be integrated with the parish

---

religionis, que scissuram recipere non debet, sicut ait Pelagius papa, xxiiii. q. i. scisma, *partes et divisiones faciant* [P].' *TMA* 2.85 (3.16) fol. 55vb. Cf. C.24 q.1 c.34.

[32] 'Non solum abbates et priores guardiani et alii in statu alicuius administrationis et prelationis existentes, verum etiam minores fratres et persone dictarum religionum putant frequenter episcopis, archiepiscopis, et aliis prelatis se quodammodo fore equales, et debere quibuscunque aliis personis ecclesiasticis ecclesiastica beneficia obtinentibus anteferri.' *TMA* 1.4 De exemptionibus, fol. 13ra.

[33] 'Ratione eminentie vite et scientie, que inflat in superbiam, efferuntur et prelatos et alios quibus dicunt se non esse subiectos contemnunt, et simplices sacerdotes et curatos cum barbarismis *et solecismis* [P] Deum, licet ex devotione innocentes, despiciunt.' *TMA* 2.85 (3.16), fol. 55va.

[34] 'Et hoc non servetur a fratribus predicatoribus et minoribus et aliis religiosis exemptis, nec ad hoc refrenandum prosint antiqua nec nova remedia, et propter hoc excommunicatio contemnatur et sic mortalis efficiatur.' *TMA* 2.28, fols. 27vb–28ra. Cf. *TMA* 2.85 (3.26), fol. 55vb.

[35] 'Et ex predictis multa subsequantur pericula animarum, potissime cum rectoribus qui habent administrare ecclesiastica sacramenta non constet de illis qui confitentur eisdem, nec eorum nomina ipsis rectoribus per dictos religiosos reddantur in scriptis.' *TMA* 2.85 (3.16), fols. 55vb–56ra.

[36] 'Videretur esse super hoc providendum verissime, potissime cum a religiosis de ordine paupertatis frequenter usurariorum funera pre ceteris honorentur.' *TMA* 2.39, fol. 34ra.

[37] Durant's scriptural foundation was Acts 20:34–5, where Paul declared that 'ad ea quae mihi opus erant, et his qui mecum sunt, ministraverunt manus istae. Omnia ostendi vobis, quoniam sic laborantes, oportet suscipere infirmos ac meminisse verbi Domini Iesu, quoniam ipse dixit: Beatius est magis dare, quam accipere.'

[38] 'Nam et secundum apostolum qui seminant spiritualia, non est magnum si temporalia metant, i. Cor. ix., de prebendis, cum secundum, et xii. q. i. ex his.' *TMA* 2.85 (3.16), fol. 55rb. Cf. 1 Corinthians 9:11, X.3.5.16, C.12 q.1 c.22.

clergy and to exercise the care of souls under episcopal super-vision;[39] the church was to supply them with benefices which they should own in common and from which they could draw a livelihood, like the rest of the clergy; and if those benefices proved to be insufficient, the friars were to 'provide for themselves by their own hands, as the apostles did in order not to be a burden unto others'.[40] In short, Durant wished to abolish the peculiarly mendi-cant way of life.

Durant's attack on begging had consequences for the secular clergy, too, for even though secular clerics did not practise begging as a virtue, some of them were forced to beg of necessity.[41] Indeed, 'in Sicily and elsewhere the bishops are so poor that they can barely afford a horse and a servant, so that they lose the respect of the people'.[42] While such begging did not provoke the wrath with which Durant inveighed against begging by choice, nonetheless the honour of the church was incompatible with indigence, for, even if it did not lead clerics into simony or other vices, indigence was in and of itself enough to cause disrespect. Hence begging from necessity could not be tolerated either.

Part of the solution was to increase the church's revenues by levying the tithe on revenues that custom had exempted, such as proceeds of commerce, crafts, science, military service, and hunt-ing.[43] One could also use existing revenues more economically by combining several poor bishoprics into one 'so that they will not be

---

[39] 'Videretur pensandum an expediret quod illi qui probati essent in dictis religionibus per episcopos dispensatione assumi possent ad curam et regimen animarum.' *TMA* 2.85 (3.16), fol. 55va.

[40] 'Videretur quod per universalem esset ecclesiam eorum inopie providendum, . . . ita quod in communi haberent de bonis prelatorum religiosorum et aliorum qui super-abundant, unde possent sibi in ecclesiis, sed non in superfluis ornamentis ecclesiarum et edificiis et aliis superstitiosis, convenienter providere, vel quod manibus propriis sibi providerent, sicut faciebant apostoli ne essent aliis onerosi, de censib. cum apostolus, in principio, xxviii. q. i. iam nunc, in fine, xxi. q. i. c. i.' *TMA* 2.85 (3.16), fol. 55rb. Cf. X.3.39.6, C.28 q.1 c.8, C.21 q.1 c.1. Durant was particularly insistent that mendicant houses ought never to accept any more members than they could support, and no one at all against the will of their parents: *TMA* 2.85 (3.16), fol. 55va. Similar precautions were separately stated for nuns and especially Beguines: *TMA* 2.25, fol. 27rb–va.

[41] 'Pensari posset an esset super premissis aliquid innovandum, cum in aliquibus partibus episcopi quasi per totum et in aliis ita modicum obtineant, et in aliis capitula et clerus tanta paupertate laborent quod mendicari coguntur.' *TMA* 2.78 (3.9), fol. 54ra–b.

[42] 'Verum cum in regno Sicilie et in multis aliis mundi partibus sint episcopi adeo pauperes quod vix unum equum et unum servitorem secum tenere possint, et ex hoc vilescat apud vulgus conditio eorundem, videretur super hoc providendum.' *TMA* 2.38, fol. 33va.

[43] *TMA* 2.90 (3.21), fol. 56va.

held in contempt'.[44] The same procedure was advisable for poor
conventual priories and impoverished parish churches in the
presentation of exempt monasteries.[45] But it was especially
important to assure that every ordinary cleric would be self
sufficient in the face of adversity: 'If the church cannot support
them, they should procure what they need by a craft of their own
or by agriculture, following the example of the apostles who lived
by the labour of their hands.'[46] Indeed, 'every cleric, regardless of
how well educated in the word of God he may be, ought to gain his
food and clothing by exercising some craft or engage in agriculture, provided he does not detract from his duties, and every cleric
who can work ought to learn some kind of craft or work'.[47] In
order to enforce this requirement no one henceforth ought to be
admitted to the clergy unless he could demonstrate that he was
wealthy, that he had a sufficient benefice, or that he could earn an
honest living by a craft or by writing.[48] In sum, begging in all of its
manifestations was to be banned, punished, and prevented, regardless of whether the cause was idleness, mistaken notions of the
apostolic way of life, or sheer necessity.

The third and final topic in the present context consists of
Durant's ideas about enforcement. From the perspective of the
great order of difference, enforcement was an issue that took care of
itself as soon as the laws were properly understood and good
examples accordingly given to the faithful. Not so from the
perspective of the commonwealth. In the absence of a reason that

---

[44] 'Quod illis qui non habent unde vivant assignaretur de beneficiis diocesis unde
convenienter vivere possent, vel quod plures episcopatus unirentur in unum ne
contemptui haberentur.' *TMA* 2.7, fol. 17va.
[45] On priories: *TMA* 2.53, fol. 39rb. On parish churches: *TMA* 2.91 (3.22), fol. 56va–b.
[46] 'Quod clerici turpi lucro vel inhonesto negotio sibi victum querere prohibentur. De
oblationibus ecclesie stipendia consequantur. Quod si eis ecclesia sufficere non posset,
proprio artificio vel agricultura, exemplo apostolorum, qui de labore manuum vivebant,
sibi necessaria invenirent.' *TMA* 2.8, fol. 17vb, with reference to Acts 20:34 and D.91.
[47] 'Quod quilibet clericus quantumcunque verbo Dei eruditus artificiolo victum et
vestitum sibi acquirat, vel quod agriculturam absque officii sui dumtaxat detrimento
preparet, et quod omnes clerici qui ad operandum validi sunt artificiola et operas
addiscant.' *TMA* 2.32, fol. 29va, quoted from IV Carthaginense c.51–3.
[48] 'Item quod nullus de clero mendicaret, sed omnes priusquam admitterentur ad clerum
haberent unde viverent, vel artem scribendi seu aliam honestam artem de qua vivere
possent, vel quod de bonis ecclesie assignarentur redditus illis qui perpetuo vellent clerici
esse et clericaliter vivere, et quod aliter non admitterentur ad clerum.' *TMA* 2.98 (3.29),
fol. 60ra. Note that in this passage Durant does not mention agriculture among potential
clerical occupations, as he had done in *TMA* 2.8, fol. 17vb.

coincided with the foundation of the universe, neither examples nor laws by themselves could function as an effective means of social union; they had become mere illustrations of morality (or immorality, as the case might be) which did not of their own accord procure imitation. Hence new ways had to be found to deal with violations of laws. The most obvious solution was to secure more effective means of enforcement. Given his professed faith in what we have called exemplary efficiency, the persistence and particularity with which Durant aimed to increase the likelihood and intensity of punishment 'so that the laws will not be violated with impunity' is decidedly remarkable.[49] The tone was set by his observation that 'there is no point in making laws that no one will protect and execute',[50] and by a general demand that 'those whom the fear of the Lord does not recall from evil should be coerced by the fear of ecclesiastical discipline'.[51] In order to instil such fear he was sometimes content with broad injunctions, as for example in demanding that clerics, monks, and laymen who conspired against their bishops ought to be deposed from office, publicly censured, and punished, any privileges to the contrary notwithstanding.[52] On other occasions his thoughts crystallized in specific propositions to improve the efficiency of existing disciplinary mechanisms.[53] But above all he called for the establishment of a new kind of ecclesiastical police that was to be appointed and held accountable by councils and would be responsible for enforcing the law. This force would operate on two levels. Provincial councils were to appoint 'visitators and correctors' who would cooperate with episcopal officials at the provincial level to enforce the statutes of the provincial council and to report infractions.[54] General

---

[49] 'Et provideretur ne in contrarium [contra legem, evangelium, concilia, et alias humanas et comprobatas leges et iura] impune attemptaretur.' *TMA* 1.2, fol. 5ra.

[50] 'Parum prosit condere iura nisi sit qui ea tueatur et exequatur, de electione, ubi periculum, de statu regularium, periculoso c. quoniam, in lib. vi'. *TMA* 2.11, fol. 19rb. Cf. VI.1.6.3, VI.3.16.1.4.

[51] 'Videretur utile quod [iura] servari mandarentur, ut quos divinus timor a malo non revocat, coherceret timor ecclesiastice discipline, extra de heretic. vergentis, de elec. cum in cunctis, lxxxii. di. plurimos, in fine, l. di. constitueretur, C. de emenda. propin. l. una.' *TMA* 2.27, fol. 27vb. Cf. X.5.7.10, X.1.6.7, D.82 c.3, D.50, Cod.9.15.1.

[52] *TMA* 2.22, fol. 26va–b.

[53] A good example is his demand that the correctors of the monastic orders ought not to be responsible for monasteries in more than a single province, since they would not be able to supervise the discipline of monasteries in distant provinces: *TMA* 2.53, fol. 39va. Cf. X.3.35.7.

[54] 'Visitatores deputarentur in [conciliis provincialibus] per quos una cum officialibus episcoporum executioni mandarentur quae fuerunt constituta.' *TMA* 2.11, fol. 18rb.

councils, in turn (or so it would appear), were to appoint executors at higher levels, each of whom would be responsible for an entire kingdom and would coordinate the efforts of the provincial councils by participating in each of them at least once every three years.[55]

At the same time Durant was very well aware that enforcement had its limitations. Some infractions of the laws proceeded from motives so powerful or so ubiquitous that the force that would have been required to achieve compliance was impossible to muster. In such cases he could be just as willing to step back from the letter of the law as he was in other cases to insist upon enforcement. Fasting on Saturdays, for example, was not to be made obligatory 'because that would cause many, indeed, an infinite number of mortal sins'.[56] Admittedly, such fasting had not much more than ceremonial significance. Nevertheless, it formed a part of the fabric of the great order of difference, and if we

---

'Videtur utile quod in singulis conciliis provincialibus ordinarentur certi visitatores et correctores, sicut statuitur in regularibus, de statu monachorum, in singulis, qui statuta facerent observari, vel saltem in ★casibus★ [P] provincialibus omnia facta promant que correctione et reformatione indigent referrentur, corrigerentur, et reformarentur ibidem singulis annis.' TMA 2.11, fol. 19rb. Cf. X.3.35.7. It may be that Durant wanted special agents to be established with the assistance of temporal princes in order to compel temporal judges and other laymen to appear before metropolitan synods: 'Pro compellendis iudicibus vel secularibus viris ad synodum metropolitani studio quidam executor a principe postuletur.' TMA 2.11, fol. 18va. But since this is quoted from IV Toletanum c.3, it seems more likely that it is simply a different formulation for the 'visitators' of whom Durant had spoken in the heading of this chapter, along the lines of X.3.35.7.

55 '. . . certis aliis nihilominus super hoc executoribus et visitatoribus deputatis in singulis regnis qui de triennio in triennium omnibus causis provincialibus interessent et unum concilium post alium facerent celebrari'. TMA 2.96(3.27), fol. 59rb. The grammar does not make it clear whether these 'executors and visitators' were to participate once every three years in the councils of a given province, regardless of how often those councils were meeting, or whether those councils themselves were to be convened once every three years. Durant had previously endorsed the more stringent ancient demands for two, or at the very least one, provincial councils per year; see above, p. 199. But X.3.35.7, on which Durant had relied at that point, required the regular clergy to follow the Cistercian model of provincial or national councils once every three years, which makes it likely that Durant, too, was really thinking of provincial or national councils once every three years. It is also worth noting that Pierre d'Ailly, Tractatus super reformatione ecclesiae, col. 904, in a passage evidently borrowed from Durant, endorsed the same three-year period for provincial councils, and that Martin V did the same in his constitution of 13.IV.1425; see Viollet, p. 127; Valois, La Crise, 1:81. Durant does not say by whom these executors were to be appointed. But because his demand is appended to the proposal that general councils ought to meet every ten years, and because of the evident parallel to the 'visitators' that were to be appointed by provincial councils, it seems rather likely that he meant them to be appointed by the general council.

56 'Nullo modo expedit quod contenta in hoc capitulo sub precepto ponantur, multa enim, immo infinita peccata mortalia sequerentur.' TMA 2.56, fol. 40va. See De cons. D.3 c.13.

remember how ardently Durant had attacked other violations of purely ceremonial laws (as, for example, those prohibiting laymen from touching sacred vessels), his leniency with regard to fasting on Saturdays may be seen as a sign of some weakening in his hierarchical resolve. Moreover, there was at least one case in which that weakening went far beyond mere ceremony and led him to attack what has to be considered a cardinal ingredient in the medieval Latin clergy's definition of the great order of difference: clerical celibacy. In his opinion all attempts to enforce this cherished centre-piece of ecclesiastical reform had failed in the past and would continue to fail in the future 'because the road to lust slopes downward and nature imitates the vices'.[57] As a result untold miseries had been inflicted, not only on the sinners them- selves but also on their innocent offspring.[58] The harm resulting from such an inflexible insistence on the law was evidently out of proportion with whatever good it achieved. Hence Durant advised that 'the Western church ought to observe the custom of the Eastern church about the vows of chastity, especially since that custom used to be observed at the time of the apostles'.[59] In this fashion Durant abandoned one of the most important lines of demarcation by which the great order of difference divided the clergy from the laity. At the same time he took a turn toward that more favourable view of marriage that came to the fore in the Reformation. It was a great step away from the ideals of an ascetic world toward those of a society inhabited by married, working citizens.

Establishing new agents of enforcement, on the one hand, and abolishing unenforceable laws, on the other, went a long way toward achieving that equilibrium of force and reason based on

[57] 'Sicut dicitur in vii. concilio Toletano, proclivus sit cursus ad voluptatem, et natura sit imitatrix vitiorum, xx. q. iii. proclivus. Et sicut in eodem concilio Toletano dicitur, omnis aetas ab adolescentia in malum prona sit, xii. q. i. omnis aetas.' *TMA* 2.46, fol. 35va. Cf. C.20 q.3 c.2, C.12 q.1 c.1.

[58] 'Nullatenus ipsorum [clericorum] reformari quiverit correctio morum. Usque adeo sententiam iudicantium protraxerunt commissa culparum, ut non tantum inferretur ultio in actores scelerum, verum etiam in progeniem damnatorum, sicut dicitur in ix. concilio Toletano, xv. q. ultima c. ii.' *TMA* 2.46, fol. 35va. Cf. C.15 q.8 c.3.

[59] 'Videretur pensandum an expediret et posset provideri quod in ecclesia occidentali quantum ad votum continentie servaretur consuetudo ecclesie orientalis quantum ad promovendos secundum dictum capitulum Nicena xxxi. di. cum capitulis sequentibus, potissime cum tempore apostolorum consuetudo ecclesie orientalis servaretur, sicut in i. rubrica huius secunde partis est prolatum.' *TMA* 2.46, fol. 35vb. Cf. D.31 c.12. In *TMA* 2.1, fol. 15ra, Durant had quoted *Canones apostolorum* c.40, which dealt with wives and sons as heirs of bishops.

social utility at which Durant was aiming. But it did not go far enough. There were some violations of the law that were both impossible to suppress by force and much too dangerous to be treated with leniency. This was the case above all with the violence done to the church by the nobility. It posed a mortal threat to episcopal autonomy and yet could not simply be policed, in part because the nobility itself controlled the local agents of enforcement. Durant devised an extremely interesting means of dealing with this predicament: he suggested integrating the interests of the nobility with those of the church in such a way that the nobility could be relied upon to police itself. We have already mentioned how Durant planned to achieve this goal: by making the access of noblemen to canonries in their diocese dependent on abstention from violence against that church.[60] What we have not yet pointed out is how fundamentally the logic of this measure differs from that of hierarchy. Its basis was neither law nor force, neither good examples nor obedience, but Durant's discovery of a structure of conditional reciprocity that could be mobilized in order to achieve noble obedience to the church. Noblemen were inclined to attack the church because they wished to control the disposal of its wealth. Hence the wealth of the church could be used to secure peace, not by refusing noble appointments to canonries, but by making them dependent on noble obedience to law. If the nobility observed the peace, it could count on canonries; conversely, if the bishop gave canonries to local noblemen, he could count on their obedience to the law.

The unconditional obedience to law that is required if the law is 'true' was thus replaced with a conditional obedience that depended on noble interest in canonries. The kind of rationality embodied in this measure has nothing to do with that reason which functions as the foundation on which alone the great order of difference can subsist. Rather, it has to do with the ability to ascertain a given interest, to place a comparable value on goods as different as canonries and peace, to weigh the consequences of anticipated actions, and to link them to certain conditions – in

---

[60] Concerning the statute to that effect which Durant established in Mende, see above, p. 76 n. 17. He repeated the idea in *TMA* 2.94 (3.25), fol. 58ra–b: 'Quod ad canonicatus, prebendas, personatus, dignitates, et alia ecclesiastica beneficia et officia nulli reciperentur, obtentu quarumcunque literarum apostolicarum vel aliarum, per quos vel per quorum parentes usque ad tertium gradum iniuriaretur ecclesiis in quibus mandaretur provisio fieri vel illis ad quorum presentationem, collationem, provisionem, vel dispositionem pertinerent nisi esset prius integraliter satisfactum.'

short, the ability to invest the theory of justice with a utilitarian calculus of pains and pleasures that results in a kind of 'social contract', an exchange of mutual benefit that rewards good conduct and punishes bad conduct by granting or withholding the goods over which a commonwealth disposes: public office and public wealth. In this fashion love from above, reverence from below, and the communion of all members of the church were replaced by interests as the central bonds of social union. Interest may have lacked the beauty of universal concord as a social ideal, but at least it could be expected to place a more effective limit on noble violence than the pure faith in justice that exhausted itself in impotent reminders of the law.

Obviously Durant never sang the praises of money, work, or force, and certainly not those of marriage; he merely dealt with limits that were not to be transgressed. However, his definition of those limits entailed a shift away from the logic of the great order of difference. It is of course no coincidence that his 'republican' inclinations showed themselves particularly clearly in these areas. Productive work, commercial exchange, and the resolution of conflicts between private and public interests by force or compromise are, after all, in many ways constitutive of a society in which different individuals contribute in different ways to a common good – hence these were topics on which Durant moved farther away from the conception of that other kind of society founded on the immutable reason of the universe and more intent on preserving differences than on facilitating exchange. In so doing he gave a more specific meaning to the virtues Cato had extolled as 'industry at home, just empire abroad, and a spirit that is free to give sound advice and not indebted to the lust for crime'.[61] At least in part these virtues were translated into honesty in trade, dedication to work, and the proper use of public force.

A corollary of this shift was that it led Durant to treat three particular kinds of outsiders from the commonwealth in a new way: those who interfered with the mechanisms of exchange by deception; those who did not work; and those who sought to usurp the fruits of social labour by force. All three were sinners – and all three were also criminals. Criminalization was the logical complement to Durant's recognition of interest as the fabric of society. For a society in which communion was replaced with social utility as

---

[61] See above, pp. 221f.

the principle of inclusion also had to transform the principle of exclusion from excommunication into the imprisonment or exile of criminals, defined as those who refused to obey the rules of social utility. Hence one of Durant's more revealing suggestions consisted of a restriction he wished to place on that right of ecclesiastical sanctuary by which the wicked sometimes tried to escape from secular justice: sanctuary was to be denied, by force if necessary, not just to those who had intentionally murdered anyone or had committed an 'enormous' crime but also to clerics who had committed crimes for which they ought to be degraded and to debtors who were trying to avoid their creditors.[62]

### THE RULE OF THE COMMON GOOD

These, then, were some of the more revealing ways in which Durant elaborated on his vision of the commonwealth. The question that remains for us to consider is how he meant to guarantee that truth and utility would be coordinated with money, work, and force to serve the common good. Part of the answer can be found in his ideas about the reform of education.[63] For, in suggesting that university professors together with the papacy ought to revise the books that formed the basis of all 'sciences', Durant distinguished between two very different kinds of action: the expert judgment of the university professors and the enactment of their judgment by the papacy. This is an excellent illustration of that functional cooperation of different sectors in society characteristic of Durant's notion of a commonwealth. Here the coincidence of truth and power is no longer thought to occur by imitation but rather is to be produced by the cooperation of different social agents. One of them, the university professors, specializes in truth, *scientia*; the other, the papacy, specializes in exercising power. Together they promote the common good.

The difficulty in this conception was that by themselves neither experts in truth nor experts in government had any definite interest in the common good. Their function guarantied that truth and

---

[62] 'De immunitate ecclesiarum subtrahenda his qui ad eas confugiunt si homicide voluntarii fuerint, vel pro debitis fugerint, vel in tali casu in quo degradati tradi curie seculari deberent, et quod persone ecclesiastice per iudicium, industriam, et insidias homicidium committentes degradentur.' *TMA* 2.45, fols. 34vb–35rb. In this respect Durant was in complete agreement with a complaint raised by the Languedocian nobility against the clergy; 'Enquête sur la juridiction', ed. Boutaric, 'Notices', p. 134.

[63] See above, pp. 194–6.

force as such would be looked after and perfected, but not that they would be linked to the interests of society at large. How was such a link to be achieved? It was precisely in response to this question that Durant made two truly revolutionary suggestions that constitute the capstone of his notion of the commonwealth. Both of them, characteristically, occur neither in the first nor in the second part of the *Tractatus Maior*, where Durant assembled the available legal evidence, but in the concluding section, where he summed up his case – a clear indication that he himself was very well aware of how far they went beyond what the laws recommended.

The first suggestion was, of course, that 'henceforth the church of Rome ought to enact no general laws unless a general council has been convoked, and such a council ought to be convoked every ten years'.[64] What made this revolutionary was that it added an entire new dimension to the demand for general councils. The argument by which Durant had previously justified his call for general councils was limited to the need to make justice manifest. In formulating his demand in the first part of the treatise Durant observed this limitation with precision: general councils were to be convoked if and only if there was any doubt about the validity of law. To add that general councils ought to meet every ten years exploded the limits of the argument with a completely different proposition. It redefined the reason for convoking general councils in terms of mere time, devoid of any meaning other than that of cyclical recurrence. In place of an obligation to discern and abide by eternal justice it put an obligation to repeat general councils at predetermined intervals, regardless of whether or not there were any doubts about the law. This was not merely simpler – it also implied that the law was always full of doubt. It changed the function of general councils from a means of communication with God's eternal reason to a means of communication among the members of the commonwealth about their own concerns in order to secure a proper understanding of the common good. Thus it amounted to a shift away from jurisprudence toward the concrete and constantly changing needs of society as the fundamental matrix of political thought.

Adopting an obligatory ten-year period would have made the convocation of general councils independent of the preferences of

---

[64] 'Item quod nulla iura generalia deinceps conderet nisi vocato concilio generali, quod de decennio in decennium vocaretur.' *TMA* 2.96 (3.27), fol. 59rb.

the papacy and it would also have increased their frequency. To be sure, six general councils had met during the previous 200 years or so, at an average of one council every thirty years, which compares rather favourably with the four or five or six – depending on one's willingness to include councils of debated universality – that met during the following two-and-a-half centuries at an average of only one every forty to sixty years.[65] Nevertheless, at the rate of one council every thirty years councils could hardly have developed an institutional memory; most prelates could have attended only one, a few might have attended two, and hardly anyone could have attended three. One council every ten years, on the other hand, would have allowed participants to devise a stable conciliar agenda by taking up the unfinished business of previous councils. There can be no doubt at all that the adoption of a ten-year period alone, quite apart from questions of constitutional authority, would have greatly enhanced the ability of general councils to control papal government.

Durant's second revolutionary suggestion was designed to enhance this ability still more effectively. It consisted of a two-part plan to revise papal finances. First, it would equip the church of Rome with a sufficient source of revenues:

The surplus possessions of the clergy ought to be used to provide for the aforesaid church of Rome so that it and its members, both as a community and as individuals, can live honourably and fulfil the responsibilities of the church of Rome without having to incur the blame and infamy arising from taxation . . .[66]

To endorse the fiscal needs of the papacy as legitimate was a concession of considerable significance for a man who otherwise did whatever he could to control the power of the papacy. The papacy had, after all, tried to improve its finances ever since the beginning of the thirteenth century. Innocent III had liked the idea of a general ecclesiastical tax, and Honorius III had actually tried to persuade the clergy to surrender two benefices at each cathedral to

---

[65] Even the relatively liberal *Conciliorum Oecumenicorum Decreta* excludes the councils of Pisa and Pavia; Alberigo, 'Il movimento conciliare', p. 914 n. 5.

[66] 'Item quod de bonis ecclesiasticarum personarum superabundantibus talis provisio fieret supradicte Romane ecclesie quod absque omni taxationis nota et infamia posset communiter et divisim honorabiliter vivere *et* [M] onera incumbentia supportare . . .' *TMA* 2.96 (3.27), fol. 59rb. There are two parallel statements which deal more specifically with the cardinals: *TMA* 2.2, fol. 15va; *TMA* 2.20, fol. 25rb.

the permanent use of the church of Rome.[67] Similar proposals had been aired time and again, and they were clearly on the mind of Clement V when he convoked the council of Vienne.[68] But such propositions invariably failed due to the protests of those from whose purses the money would have come. John of Viktring, for example, did not shrink from charging that the council of Vienne had been convoked for no other purpose than 'extorting money'.[69] This, on the face of it, might seem just the attitude to be expected from Durant, but in fact it was far from it. In keeping with his republican conviction that private wealth ought to be slender and the treasury full, and looking askance at the clergy's preoccupation with protecting their own revenues, he broke with the obstructive attitude traditionally favoured by the clergy. He agreed with the papacy that for the commonwealth to prosper ecclesiastical revenues had to be diverted to strengthen the two foundations of the commonwealth: truth and force. Hence there were two, and only two, objectives for which he envisioned something approaching general taxation: education and papal government.[70]

At the same time Durant was not about to drop his mistrust of papal government. In order to assure that the papacy would not abuse its increased revenues he added, as the second ingredient of his proposal to reform papal finances, a truly remarkable condition:

... provided that without a general council the church of Rome will not give rein to its plenitude of power against divine and human law, above

[67] Congar, 'Quod omnes tangit', p. 218; Kay, 'An Eye-Witness Account of the 1225 Council of Bourges'; Hall, 'King Henry III', p. 128; with references to Walter of Coventry's *Memoriale*, 2:274–6, Matthew Paris, *Chronica*, 3:106f., and Mansi, *Collectio*, 22:1,217–20.

[68] Clement V planned to introduce a general ecclesiastical tax, and at the council of Vienne tried to assure to the cardinals the use of one prebend at each cathedral; Müller, *Konzil von Vienne*, pp. 67f., 629–31.

[69] 'Pro extorquenda pecunia' were his words; see Müller, *Konzil von Vienne*, p. 6 n. 23, citing Baluze, *Vitae paparum*, 1:19.

[70] It may be worth pointing out that Durant was not recommending a system of ecclesiastical taxation strictly speaking, by which a certain percentage of ecclesiastical revenues would have been regularly collected in Rome. He rather defined his purpose as avoiding 'the infamy arising from taxation' by a permanent redistribution of ecclesiastical property so that the church of Rome would be relieved of any need to raise taxes. The effect, of course, was pretty much the same. Besides, his proposal to dedicate one tenth of all ecclesiastical benefices to the finance of education can hardly be called anything other than a tax; see above, p. 195.

and beyond what has been said before and may seem reasonable to the council.[71]

There can be little doubt that this amounts to a rudimentary formulation of the budgetary process which even today still constitutes one of the most important tools in the hands of representative institutions to control the power of the executive. The papacy was to obtain its money only on condition that the papal plenitude of power would be subjected to the council's view of what was 'reasonable'. Here, finally, Durant addressed not just the papacy's 'prerogative of power' or its right to issue general laws, which he had attempted to limit by his conciliar proposal, but dealt directly and explicitly with the papal plenitude of power itself. The logic of his proposal was precisely the same as that with which he hoped to contain the nobility: it mobilized the papacy's own interest in securing revenues with which to perfect its government as a means of subjecting its power to law. In just the same way it replaced the logic of unconditional, but unenforceable, insistence on obedience to the law with the conditional obedience that proceeded from a contractual exchange. That was hardly an accident. In Durant's opinion the papacy and the nobility were, after all, the two most dangerous threats to the order of the church. Hence a new approach was required to ensure their obedience to law. The difference was that while the measure to control the nobility had local significance, to link the revenues of the papacy to its acceptance of general councils amounted to a kind of social contract in the broadest sense. This contract really did replace the 'reason' on which the universe subsisted with the very different kind of reason that was required for the subsistence of a commonwealth; in the place of law it put the common good as defined by a general council.

It deserves to be stressed that neither the condition on which Durant made the reform of papal revenues dependent nor the adoption of a ten-year period would have given the council any legal authority over the pope. The papal plenitude of power remained the pope's sole and uncontested prerogative; not even here did Durant assert that the council had any legal right to impose

---

[71] '. . . proviso tamen quod ultra et contra predicta et alia que concilio rationabilia viderentur contra divinas et humanas leges non posset absque generali concilio habenas extendere plenitudinis potestatis.' *TMA* 2.96 (3.27), fol. 59rb.

its will upon the pope. In this sense he never solved the question raised by his failure to consider the locus of supreme authority in the church – but in another sense he surely solved that question in an incisive way. He recognized that the council, quite apart from the authority to which it was entitled by the law, had the ability to withhold from the papacy what the papacy urgently needed, and consequently that it had a means by which to subject the head of the commonwealth to reason – except that this reason was not the eternal reason of the law but the utility of citizens.

In this fashion Durant replaced the idea of the great order of difference with the idea of a commonwealth. *Ordo* became *res publica*. Where before there had been eternity, now there was time; where there had been the categorical commands of law, there were conditional obligations; where there had been the linear subordination of unequals, there was the contractual reciprocity of equals; where there had been imitation, there was scientific thought, on the one hand, and public action, on the other. Love from above had turned into the judicious use of force; reverence from below had turned into paying taxes; interest had taken the place of difference in the fabric of society; and concord had given way to compromise. All of the elements of which the great order of difference was composed – the ranks and orders of the church, the differences, the bonds of union – were still there, but in the face of the discrepancy between truth and custom, in the awareness of an irrational reality that did not simply yield to truth, and in the absence of a reason that functioned as the ground of the universe, they had been thoroughly transformed.

Therefore we must vindicate the liberal interpretation of Durant's ideas from the opprobrium to which we may have seemed to sentence it in the preceding chapter. There we declared that the purpose of Durant's conciliar proposal was to forestall the end of the world by reviving the reason on which the universe subsisted. But now it is clear that Durant was just as much a republican as a hierocrat, and his conciliar proposal may therefore just as properly be interpreted as an attempt to secure the common good by institutionalizing representative assemblies in order to subject the power of government to the will of the people.

## Chapter 7

# THE PERVERSION OF ORDER

Jerome said that when he looked through the books of history he could not find anyone who had introduced schisms into the church of God and led the people away from the house of the Lord except for those whom God had set up to be priests and prophets.                    William Durant[1]

The two preceding chapters have served two different purposes, one relatively modest, the other more ambitious: first, to give a reasonably full description of the programme to reform the church that William Durant the Younger presented in the second part of his *Tractatus Maior*; and second, to offer an analysis of this programme according to two different ideas of order, namely, *magnus ordo differentie* and *res publica*. This analysis is not yet complete. We have distinguished between ideas of hierarchy and commonwealth and have identified some of the many ways in which they shaped the *Tractatus Maior*. We have accordingly distinguished two meanings of Durant's conciliar proposal: one was to protect the hierarchical articulation of the church from the power of the papacy by assuring a steady link between the divine reason of the universe and the government of the church; the other was to mediate between the conflicting interests of functionally differentiated sectors of society in order to assure the harmonious cooperation of all for the common good. But we have not yet studied how these conceptions were related to each other.

### MEMORY AND 'MORES'

William Durant the Younger firmly believed that *magnus ordo differentie* and *res publica* were fundamentally identical. As far as we

---

[1] 'Nam sicut Hieronymus ait, xxiiii. q. iii. transferunt, veteres scrutans historias invenire non potuit aliquos alios scidisse ecclesiam Dei, et de domo Domini populum seduxisse, preter eos qui sacerdotes a Deo positi fuerant et prophete.' *TMA* 1.1, fol. 4va. Cf. C.24 q.3 c.33.

can tell, he saw no contradiction between the conception of the council as an instrument to bring the true, just, and immutable reason of God to bear on human affairs 'whenever new laws are to be enacted' and that of the council as an instrument to reconcile the highly mutable and often selfish interests of different social agents in order to establish a public consensus that could be brought to bear on government 'every ten years'. In his opinion, any kind of order that deserved to be called a 'healthy regime for the human race' had to encompass both. In one grand sweep, sustained by the ardent faith that the church could never be a true commonwealth unless it followed the example of both Jesus Christ and Scipio, he sought to demonstrate the fundamental harmony of council and hierarchy. Thus the message he carried to the council of Vienne was not that a choice had to be made between two mutually exclusive alternatives but that there was one sole objective: to reform the church by returning to the example of antiquity.

There is a sense in which Durant was profoundly justified. Deeply embedded in the foundations of political thought there is a pattern of contradictory relationships that cannot be expressed much better than by pairing Scipio with Jesus Christ. Political thought has to explain why certain actions are right for a community of people while others have to be condemned as wrong. At first sight it may appear as though this task could be completed in a single step: distinguishing right from wrong. But right and wrong are, first and foremost, normative concepts of the human mind that differ not only from each other but also, and more deeply, from the actions they are meant to regulate. Political thought must thus contend with not just one but two pairs of opposites. One pair consists of the conceptual dichotomy of right and wrong which constitutes a realm of thought whose extent is fully measured by the golden rule of natural law that you should never treat someone else as you do not wish to be treated. The force of this rule derives from the fact that it refrains from advising specific actions of any kind, but lets you do what you like so long as you permit everyone else to do the same. It is abstract. Political thought, however, cannot afford to be abstract; it has to judge specific actions, or at the very least has to show how such a judgment can be made. Hence it has to contend with a second opposition: that between the dichotomy of right and wrong in its entirety, on the one hand, and the seamless reality in which actions take place, on the other. This opposition is completely different from the former because here

248

the dichotomy of right and wrong recurs as only one of two elements in a relation that opposes logic to reality. These elements are so unlike each other that their relation is impossible to understand in terms of logic strictly speaking – if only for the simple reason that logic is a part of it: the relation between a logical opposition and reality cannot itself be understood as a logical opposition without an infinite regress.

The function of political thought, considered from an abstract point of view, is to reconcile these different but overlapping pairs of opposites by aligning them within a single matrix in order to be able to judge specific actions as right or wrong. The question of how such a matrix is to be constructed evidently cannot be answered simply in terms of matching the eternal logic of the golden rule of natural law directly to reality. Applying the golden rule requires, at the very least, that two actions be compared. But no action is ever quite the same as any other action, if only because it differs in space and time. It may or may not conflict with the golden rule of natural law, but it inevitably differs from the past. Every new action to be judged therefore demands not just an exercise of imagination (to be able to reflect on its conformity with the golden rule of natural law) but also an exercise of memory (to incorporate the difference between the action that is being judged and the remembered actions to which it is compared), not only an account of its logical consistency with concepts of right and wrong but also a chrono-logical account of its relation to the past. Political thought thus is historical by definition; unless it relies on memory it cannot bridge the gap between thought and action, and unless it constantly readjusts memory in order to incorporate the experience of change its judgment will be faulty.[2] If it succeeds it takes concrete shape in *mores*, for *mores* are quite unlike the mere custom of thoughtlessly repeated ancient practices; rather, they represent the eminently thoughtful integration of all three elements that make it possible for a society to maintain a shared understanding of right and wrong: justice, memory, and action.

Both *magnus ordo differentie* and *res publica* are conceptual tools designed precisely to make such a shared understanding intelligible. Both of them deal directly with the fundamental task of aligning thought and action in a single matrix, and both of them

---

[2] 'We study change *because* we are changeable. This gives us a direct experience of change: what we call memory.' Momigliano, 'Historicism Revisited', p.368.

are meant to secure the stability of *mores*, although in different ways. Hierarchy tries to transcend partisanship by interpreting social reality exhaustively in terms of logical dichotomies. It also subdivides society into sequentially ordered parcels, but even though this is its most obvious characteristic, it is merely a consequence of its underlying purpose: such parcels appear to be more amenable to the dichotomous classification that is required by conceptual thought. The different ranks and orders by which hierarchical society is articulated thus are like cybernetic furrows that logic draws on the face of society, like echoes of the voice of abstract reason reverberating in the hollows between thought and reality. They are a secondary matter, an elaborate mirage reflecting the interminable efforts of human beings to make their lives conform to logic. 'Commonwealths', on the other hand, satisfy the desire for logic in politics by dividing social reality into 'private' and 'public' interests and corresponding parties. In hierarchy there can be parties, too, but they are parties only of a sort; they involve particular estates more than the whole of society, and they appreciate partisanship only insofar as it promises to put an end to the need for any parties. Parties in a commonwealth are more consciously constructed on the principle that the common good can never be defined except by reconciling two fundamentally different approaches through debate. One party, more often than not, argues in terms of the opposition between right and wrong, the other in terms of the opposition between ideas and facts (with the concurrent danger that they speak at cross-purposes when one says 'wrong' and the other 'fact', one 'right' and the other 'mere ideal'). Perhaps the simplicity of this bipartite structure reflects a better appreciation of the circle that politics aims to square than does the proliferating logic of hierarchical distinctions: indeed, it may help separate the circle from the square and, in the opening between the two, make room for the expression of real social interests, private as well as public. But both hierarchy and commonwealth proceed from the same desire to reconcile logic with reality – which gives us reason to believe that future political theorists will look on 'commonwealths' in which private and public interests are opposed with the same lack of sympathy with which we look at 'hierarchies' in which the holy live at the expense of the poor.

*Magnus ordo differentie* and *res publica* are therefore thoroughly misunderstood if they are considered to be opposite extremes.

Both of them stretch across the logical abyss – not the contradiction – that lies between the realm of conceptual dichotomies and that of action. Both aim to transcend party spirit by means of a true understanding of the common good; both aim at the kind of total union that is conceivable only in logic and cannot be imposed on society without practising subordination and exclusion. This is of course not to deny that there are fundamental differences between *magnus ordo differentie* and *res publica*: there are, and they constitute the substance of politics. But differences do not have to be exclusive in order to be fundamental. In many ways the differences in this case are no greater than those between two different virtues: *magnus ordo differentie* favours humility, while *res publica* favours courage. But courage and humility – different and, indeed, conflicting though they may be – are not exclusive of each other. In the same way 'hierarchy' and 'commonwealth' are not exclusive, but contiguous and interpenetrating, reflecting different preferences for different virtues, perhaps according to the different needs of societies in stagnation or expansion. Their nature can very well be understood in the terms that Aristotle used to speak of virtue itself. For just as Aristotle thought that every virtue consists of a 'golden mediocrity' somewhere between two opposing vices, so *magnus ordo differentie* defines a public space for humility somewhere between pride and servility (between subjecting the ranks and orders of the church without distinction to a single overweening power and dividing all of them completely from each other), while *res publica* defines a public space for courage somewhere between foolhardiness and cowardice (between subjecting the citizens to the state and subjecting the common good to private interests). But both seek to protect society from the opposing vices of abstract justice and brute force.

Thus *magnus ordo differentie* and *res publica* are intimately linked to each other: *magnus ordo differentie* is just as inconceivable without a republican component, and *res publica* without some form of hierarchical subordination, as courage is without humility. Hence it is no accident that Pope Gregory I supplied Durant not only with the concept of the great order of difference but also with an admonition to subjects not to be too submissive to their rulers (used as the epigraph for the preceding chapter). The same Pope Gregory identified universal consent as the reason he revered the four great ecumenical councils as much as the four Gospels; they were like a 'four-cornered stone' supporting both 'the structure of the faith' and 'the norms for any common life or action' – a bipartite formulation mirroring perfectly the distinction between hierarchy and commonwealth.[3] The converse that *res publica* includes a hierarchical dimension is equally true. It says a lot that Durant believed Seneca to have coined the pithy statement that 'examples move more effectively than words', whereas, in fact, St Gregory is its more likely author.[4] More to the point, the basic principles of republican order which Durant quoted from Cicero's *De officiis* were, as he himself pointed out, taken from Plato;[5] and while the title of the book in question is commonly rendered as *The Republic*, few books in the tradition of the West have a better claim to embodying hierarchical ideas. Again, in Durant's opinion the greatest glory of the ancient rulers of the commonwealth was that they excelled in precisely those two respects we have described as consummately hierarchical: exemplary efficiency and obedience to law.[6]

This fusion of 'hierarchy' with 'commonwealth' is particularly evident in the uses to which Durant put St Augustine's *City of God*. The reader may have regarded it as curious that the *City of God* supplied him with most of his illustrations of proper civic virtue in ancient Rome: after all, St Augustine had suggested that ancient Rome was a den of pagan iniquity in which no true justice could flourish, but only a kind of 'painted' justice, and Durant himself introduced his account of ancient virtues by quoting St Augustine's declaration that kingdoms without true – that is, without Christian – justice are nothing but great bands of robbers.[7] That he could nonetheless conclude from the *City of God* that ancient pagans were better governors than modern Christians might seem to amount to a complete misunderstanding. However, St Augustine did not reject the classical political tradition out of hand but adopted it and turned it into a Christian political philosophy incorporating both the ideas of hierarchy and commonwealth. To be sure, he gave

---

[3] 'Idem [Gregorius] etiam scribit quod sicut sancti evangelii quatuor libros, sic quatuor concilia se suscipere et venerari fatetur, scilicet Nicenum, Constantinopolitanum, Ephesinum, et Calcedonense, subiiciens: hec tota devotione complector, integerrima custodie approbatione, quia in his velut in quadrato lapide sancte fidei structura consurgit et cuiuslibet vite communis atque actionis norma consistit.' *TMA* 1.3, fol. 5va. Cf. D.15 c.2.

[4] See above, pp. 136f. n. 39.    [5] See above, p. 149.    [6] See above, p. 148.

[7] *De civitate Dei*, books 1–10. For the 'painted justice' of the Romans see *De civitate Dei* 2.21 and the resumption of the same theme in 19.21. For the 'great band of robbers' see *De civitate Dei* 4.4.

pride of place to hierarchy – but he believed as well that 'a happy city and a happy man have the same origin, since a city is nothing else than a harmonious [*concors*] multitude of men'.[8] In both the title and the substance of the *City of God* he preserved the political tradition of the ancient city-states, and he could do so only because classical thought itself embodied hierarchical principles amenable to being translated into the language of Christianity.[9]

Any attempt to oppose Durant's 'conciliarism' to the supposed 'papalism' of his opponents without stressing the degree to which both were shaped by a single frame of reference is therefore bound to result in one-sided interpretations. To be sure, there is a sense in which it is appropriate to distinguish between 'papalists' like Giles of Rome or William Durant the Elder and 'conciliarists' like William Durant the Younger – but one must keep in mind how much they were agreed on basic principles. Given the regularity with which Giles, the man who was responsible for *Unam sanctam*, is perceived as an extremist member of the 'papalist' party of Boniface VIII, his proximity to the 'conciliarist' William Durant the Younger is well worth underlining. Giles was Durant's archbishop; they were two of only three bishops from the province of Bourges to attend the council of Vienne, and there can be no doubt that they cooperated there.[10] We have already seen how enthusiastically Durant endorsed Giles' *De ecclesiastica potestate* on two separate occasions.[11] Apparently he did not share the belief of modern historians that the conciliar order he envisioned for the church conflicted in any serious way with Giles' famous study of papal supremacy. Giles, for his part, agreed completely with Durant's attack on exemptions. He had opposed exemptions as early as the 1280s, when he had sided publicly with the secular clergy, and he was still actively doing so at the council of Vienne.[12]

---

[8] 'Neque enim aliunde beata civitas, aliunde homo, cum aliud civitas non sit quam concors hominum multitudo.' *De civitate Dei* 1.15. Augustine says so in his commentary on the death of Marcus Regulus from which Durant quoted in *TMA* 1.3 De limitanda potestate, fol. 6ra (*male* 7ra). See also *De civitate Dei* 19.24 for Augustine's more modest definition of a 'people'.

[9] For a brief but incisive critique of the assumption that the political thought of classical antiquity was 'secular' see Oakley, 'Celestial Hierarchies Revisited', pp. 46f.

[10] The bishop of Limoges was the third. The bishop of Le Puy was exempt. See Müller, *Konzil von Vienne*, p. 664.      [11] See above, p. 209.

[12] Giles believed that the pope could grant special exemptions, but that a general exemption of an entire order of mendicants unduly overturned the ordinary jurisdiction of the prelates; Congar, 'Aspects', pp. 141f.; cf. Douie, *Conflict*, p. 28 and n. 3; Gratien, *Histoire*, p. 349. His contribution to the debates about *Ad fructus uberes* in the assembly of Paris,

It was a point of principle with Giles to stress the importance of those same 'middling powers' in the great hierarchy of the universe whom Durant was so concerned to protect from papal arrogance.[13] There is thus little reason to place Durant and Giles in hostile camps: Giles stressed papal power in the battle with the state, whereas Durant, in the battle for reform of the church, stressed the limits on that power; but both did what they could to maintain an idea of a divinely instituted order that justified the supremacy of the clergy over the laity. There is still less reason to believe that fundamental disagreements existed between Durant and his uncle, the Speculator, who after all helped him to get started in his ecclesiastical career. Quite the contrary: they shared principles and differed primarily on points of emphasis and nuance.[14] Only in hindsight is it clear that those nuances could eventually grow to the size of such mutually exclusive views of order as 'papalism' and 'conciliarism' – if, indeed, they ever did – and that had certainly not yet happened in the early fourteenth

December 1286, was described in glowing terms by, most probably, one of the greatest defenders of the secular clergy, namely, Geoffrey of Fontaines: 'Super his postea disputatum fuerat a magistro Egidio de Ordine Augustini, qui modo melior de tota villa in omnibus reputatur, et determinatum fuit ab eodem, quod episcopi essent in parte longius saniori.' *Chartularium Universitatis Parisiensis*, 2:10, no. 539. At the council of Vienne Giles restated his position in a treatise against exemptions arguing that 'Summus Pontifex intelligitur ordinarius ubique et posse ad se reservare ordinariam et immediatam cognitionem cujuslibet Ecclesiae. Hoc tamen non obstante quilibet praelatus in dioecesi habet cognoscere causas illius dioecesis, et est ordinarius in tota sua dioecesi: quod ideo contingit quia praelati sunt assumpti in partem sollicitudinis; sed Summus Pontifex assumptus est in totalem plenitudinem potestatis. Et quia totum stat simul cum parte, ideo simul stat immediata jurisdictio, etiam ordinaria, Summi Pontificis, cum ordinaria jurisdictione cujuscumque praelati. Et quia exemptio hoc tollit, et privat jurisdictionem mediam praelatorum, ideo quaedam inordinatio dici potest: quia facit de jure praelatorum non jus.' Cited by Congar, 'Aspects', 142 n. 358, from Giles' *Tractatus contra exemptos* c. 3, fol. 23v. Durant would hardly have disagreed.

13 'Hoc ergo requirit ordo universi, ut infima in suprema per media reducantur.' *De ecclesiastica potestate* 1.4, p. 12. 'Concludamus quod homines reducantur in Deum per angelos spiritus, et per angelos praelatos vel pontifices vel episcopos.' *Tractatus contra exemptos* c. 10, fol. 7r, cited by Congar, 'Aspects', p. 141 n. 356. '[Praelati] quodam ordine reducuntur in Summum Pontificem ut episcopi per archiepiscopos per primates et patriarcas.' *Tractatus contra exemptos* c. 8, fol. 5v, cited by Congar, 'Aspects', p. 141 n. 356. Compare this with Durant's formulation in *TMA* 2.96 (3.27), quoted above, pp. 211f. John Quidort of Paris, *De regia potestate* c. 18, ed. Bleienstein, p. 165, declares that 'infimi non reducuntur ad supremos nisi per medios nec supremi perficiunt hierarchiae infimos immediate sed mediantibus mediis. Igitur summus pontifex non habet potestatem generalem et mediatam super laicos nisi quam habent medii de hierarchia immediatam et magis contractam, ut episcopi vel abbates.'

14 For evidence see the passages quoted above, pp. 66f. nn. 41–4, 78f. nn. 24–5, to reflect both 'papalist' and 'conciliarist' elements in the *Speculum iudiciale*.

century. Hence that anonymous biographer who credited the Speculator with authoring the *Tractatus Maior* turns out to have been better justified than at first appears.[15]

Thus it is misleading to characterize Durant as a reformer who failed to resolve the tension between hierarchical and republican ideas of order because he lacked a proper theory of the church; or who failed to subject the papacy to conciliar authority; or who, on the contrary, did subject the papacy to conciliar authority and thus became one of the first conciliarists. His conciliar proposal was designed to accomplish none of these objectives but rather to regain the common ground by which all the participants in the movement to reform the church – the pope, the bishops, the clergy, the religious, and the laity – had once been united but which had lately been disturbed by dissension between the papacy and the episcopate, not to mention between state and church. In the face of these dissensions Durant hoped to restore the church to the true authority with which it had been endowed by his ancestors in the eleventh century, not, as Macaulay said in a comparable situation, 'by superstitiously adhering to what they, in other circumstances, did, but by doing what they, in our circumstances, would have done'.[16] *Res publica* and *magnus ordo differentie* were equally integral to the success of this endeavour, for both were firmly rooted in a tradition that stretched from the middle ages back to St Augustine's successful integration of classical with Biblical ideas. That the *Tractatus Maior* embodied both was therefore not a sign of weakness but a source of strength that allowed Durant to reach back and rearticulate the fundamental principles that were shared by both the papacy and the bishops.[17] Hence it is meaningless to debate whether Durant was a conciliarist or a papalist; he was both and neither. In that sense our own distinction between *magnus ordo differentie* and *res publica* is arbitrary. His real achievement was to demonstrate that papal primacy and conciliar representation were not mutually exclusive but could both be encompassed in a single programme of political reform. As a result he broke the limits of partisanship, spoke to every party, and defined the agenda for an entire age of ecclesiastical history: reform in head and members. That was his original intention and made his programme great.

---

[15] See above, p. 9 n. 35.    [16] Macaulay, 'Speech on Parliamentary Reform', p. 47.
[17] Tierney, *Foundations*, p. 196.

# The assertion of justice

At the same time Durant was not content to pursue a vision of Christian politics that squared hierarchical with republican convictions – as if that would not have been sufficiently ambitious. His intention was to reform the church by making it conform not merely to the golden rule of natural law but also to the conciliar legislation of late Roman antiquity. When he spoke of *mores*, he did not allow for the possibility that memory and justice might have to be reconciled with action in some way yet to be determined. Rather, he was convinced that *mores* had already been defined once and for all in 'the councils approved by the inspiration of the Holy Spirit and other approved human laws and rights' and he set out to restore obedience to these laws.[18]

This is the point at which Durant's thought began to lose its footing. Justice, memory, and action cannot be linked in judgment except through a constant process of infinite approximation whose success is never better than temporary and precarious. As soon as the golden rule is applied to life, there is room for dispute. This is true even of such basic laws as those of the decalogue. Easy as it may be to obtain agreement that murder, theft, and lies are wrong, it can be just as difficult to determine whether an act of killing is murder rather than a judicial execution; an act of taking, theft rather than taxation; and an act of stating an untruth, a lie rather than the result of ignorance. Sometimes this happens because the action is so unprecedented that memory fails to supply anything to compare, but just as often it happens because memory is so strong that it prevents an understanding of the difference between present experience and remembered past. Once *mores* are defined in a particular way, especially if they are written down, the constant reflective innovation needed to incorporate the experience of change may prove too difficult – particularly for a society that may be occupied in other ways or overburdened by respect for antiquity.

---

[18] See above, pp. 132–4. In principle Durant's identification of natural law with the Law of the Old Testament and the Gospel raises even greater problems than his identification of *mores* with the ancient conciliar canons, but we do not need to deal with them separately, if only because they are identical in structure; because a determined interpretative effort had already been made to subsume no more than a few rather general prescriptions of the Old Testament under the rubric of natural law; and because the New Testament did not contain much by way of legislation anyway.

When memory is fixed without remaining open to present experience it is transformed into history. At best it then serves the scientific investigation of a past whose links to the present can be dispassionately studied, but not felt; at worst, it results either in the transfixed admiration of a past golden age or in the compassionate contemplation of a past state of misery, neither of which existed in reality and both of which bear no relation to the present. In no case can such history furnish the kind of memory that enters into deliberations about the common good; it merely seeks to understand the past, not judge it, and much less to furnish grounds for judgment of the present – or so at least it would appear.[19] As a result, precisely to the same degree that memory is absorbed by history, the moral application of principles of right and wrong is blocked. Instead, the golden rule of natural law is turned into the tautological assertion of right as right and wrong as wrong that remains when it is robbed of the temporal referents which alone make it possible to ascertain the reciprocity that it commands. Indeed, with memory pre-empted by history, justice is changed in its very nature: it is transformed into the prerogative of sovereignty – regardless of whether the sovereignty is that of conscience, by which each private individual claims a right to legislate morality for the universe, or that of a public person whom in the absence of a shared understanding of morality the community entitles to enforce their commands for the sake of preserving a modicum of peace.[20] Conscience and sovereignty are structurally identical; they know no other limits to their sway than those imposed by brute fact. Without the aid of memory neither maintains the reciprocity commanded by natural law. Hence action loses moral intelligibility, comes to be indistinguishable from natural events, and in the end escapes from judgment altogether.[21]

Whoever reads the *Tractatus Maior* expecting that it will say anything about the common good or the 'utility of citizens' in

---

[19] Momigliano, 'Historicism Revisited', p. 370, disputes that such moral abstemiousness is possible: 'What history-writing without moral judgements would be is difficult for me to envisage, because I have not yet seen it.'

[20] These are among the reasons why Bodin believed that even tyrants who violate the natural law retain their sovereignty; why Rousseau denied that the sovereign can be bound by any law; and why Kant believed that every individual moral judgment amounts to legislation for the universe.

[21] The result is an attitude like Luther's, who states in his 'Letter to Pope Leo X', p. 327, that 'I have no quarrel with any man concerning his morality, but only concerning the Word of truth.'

medieval Europe is therefore bound to be disappointed: it does nothing of the kind. It does not even offer a description of the ways in which the laity, the clergy, and the papacy behaved, much less the reasons why their conduct had or had not come into conflict with the ancient laws. What it does offer in prolific, luxuriant, and maddening detail are the old laws of the church. Relentlessly Durant instructs his readers in the laws that are being violated day in and day out, but hardly ever does he specify exactly what it is that any violator does beyond making the obvious point that it does not agree with the law. Exceedingly rare are the occasions on which he condescends to tell us something tangible – as, for example, that Sicilian bishops cannot afford more than one horse, or that the mendicants are particularly fond of attending funerals of usurers, or that Pope Boniface VIII issued his constitution concerning married clerics without conciliar consent – scarcely enough to preserve the reader's imagination from being stupefied by the sheer weight of law.[22]

Vast areas of political and social life and facts of great importance for our understanding of medieval history can therefore be perceived only obliquely or not at all in the pages of the *Tractatus Maior*. What, for example, are we to make of the statement that 'it would be useful for the church to request *defensores* from all princes, since ecclesiastical persons are forced by a certain necessity to sue more frequently than others in the law courts of princes nowadays'.[23] The laws and canons cited by Durant give us to understand that a council of Carthage had demanded defenders of churches to be provided by the emperor on the grounds that the defence of the poor was the church's special duty.[24] But if we turn from the reasons why those laws had been enacted many hundred years ago to the reasons why they should be restored in Durant's own time, we are offered nothing more specific than 'a certain necessity'. One does not know whether to laugh or cry. Was 'a certain necessity' all that Durant could say to describe the real and growing interpenetration of secular and ecclesiastical justice, the growth of secular

---

[22] See above, pp. 186, 233, 234.

[23] 'Videretur providendum si esset utile huiusmodi defensores ab universis principibus per ecclesiam postulari, cum persone ecclesiastice ex quadam necessitate habeant hodie plus ceteris in curiis principum litigare.' *TMA* 2.40, fol. 34ra.

[24] He cites V Carthaginense c.9, Milevitanum c.16, D.10 c.7, C.23 q.5 c.20, 23, 26, and C.23 q.4 c.37. He did not cite the underlying imperial law, Cod.1.55, which established 'defenders of the city' to whom the lower orders of society were to turn for help against oppressive landlords.

bureaucracies employing law on the curial model, and the centralizing force of government that constituted some of the most important elements in medieval constitutional change and that forced him to spend as much time in Paris as in Mende? Was it enough to evoke the reasons that led him to conclude a *paréage* with the king of France, not to mention any of its specific provisions? Far from it. No one who has read only the *Tractatus Maior* would so much as suspect the possibility that its author, who complained so harshly about the vices of the temporal lords and wished them to bow to the interference of the church in temporal affairs, had not only actively pursued negotiations with the most powerful temporal lord in Europe but even managed to come to an agreement that was highly beneficial to himself and that determined the history of the Gévaudan for centuries to come. So much the less can one rely on the *Tractatus Maior* as evidence for the social and political experience of other clerics – not to mention of the aristocracy and ordinary people.

It would of course be quite misguided to chide Durant for failing to provide us with a social and political history of his times. Much as modern historians may regret it, that was not what he set out to do. Nor is it quite impossible to see the links between what we know about his life and what he tells us in the language of the ancient laws. The point is that in stubbornly insisting on the identity of ancient laws with *mores* he held his own society to an unreasonable standard. Those laws had been formulated up to a thousand years ago to deal with specific circumstances completely different from those of the high middle ages. They reflected the situation of the church in the late ancient Mediterranean world, whose basic elements were the city, the office, and the emperor. They gave much prominence to bishops, and they reflected the presence of an empire in which 'ecumenical' or 'world-wide' councils were still feasible. Without a radical reinterpretation such laws were hardly suitable to the world of the high medieval European continent in which the city had yielded to the manor, the castle, and the monastery, the officer to the knight or monk, and the emperor to the pope. Indeed, a radical reinterpretation would have been particularly necessary in the age of William Durant, when it was just beginning to appear that the dominant political institution in the future would be the state.

But in spite of his close cooperation with a king who is reputed to have been one of the greatest medieval champions of the state,

such was not William Durant the Younger's point of view. He
rather liked the ancient laws just as they were, in part out of
conventional respect for their antiquity, in part because they
helped to buttress his independence from papal government. Of
course he recognized that there was room for change – indeed, he
advocated change with passion – but only on the premise that
change would consist of a return to the ancient conciliar canons
concerning the state of the church. His strongest words in support
of change were thus reserved for asking the papacy to revoke
exemptions and to return the dioceses to the complete control the
bishops had exercised (or, seemed to have exercised) before the
monastic orders had multiplied and the papacy had risen to lead the
Latin church.[25] Precisely there where he appeared to be at his most
innovative, he really meant to engineer a return to the state of
affairs depicted in the ancient conciliar canons. Like Emperor
Justinian, he was convinced that 'the novel circumstances of this life
should not lead us to neglect what antiquity once decreed with
foresight and deliberation';[26] and like Pope Zosimus he was
determined that 'not even the authority of the apostolic see can
enact decrees or make any changes in conflict with the statutes of
the Fathers. The past shall remain alive with us and its roots shall
not be torn out, because the Fathers decreed that it must be treated
with reverence.'[27]

The ancient laws thus served Durant as the lens through which
he inspected his society, or as the net with which he gathered his
experience. Perhaps some such lens or net is necessary; but in this
case the focus of the lens was much too wide, the meshes of the net
too tight. The ancient laws allowed him to determine where
present conduct conflicted with the past – indeed, they allowed that
determination only too well – but they did not allow him to
discriminate reliably between contemporary 'abuses' that really
were abuses and those that were the figment of an imagination in
servitude to ancient laws. Much less did they permit him to
discriminate between 'necessities' that deserved to be endorsed
because, in fact, they corresponded to the legitimate needs of the
present and other 'necessities' that could not be tolerated because
they conflicted not just with ancient law but with contemporary
*mores* as well, perhaps even with natural law.

With his attention preoccupied by ancient laws Durant's ability

[25] See above, pp. 171–5.  [26] See above, pp. 134f.  [27] See above, p. 138.

260

to diagnose the state of his society was impaired. If it was true that *mores* were identical with ancient laws, then any differences between the ancient laws and present practice – especially all those 'dispensations, privileges, liberties, and exemptions that contradict the abovementioned divine and human general and approved laws' – could not be understood in any terms other than those of a 'certain necessity' or of outright 'abuses' that 'ought to be abolished'.[28] This was indeed the conclusion at which Durant arrived, like countless other late medieval moralists. But neither the language of 'necessity' nor that of 'abuse' allowed him to come to reasonable terms with the ways in which the *mores* of antiquity had justifiably been overtaken by the customs of the present.[29] Indeed, it precluded him from recognizing the extent to which his own experience was happier than that of his predecessors, not only in an institutional sense (because with royal help he finally managed to assert episcopal control over the Gévaudan) but also in a personal sense (because with papal help he managed to secure the benefits of wealth and power for his family). If anything, his career furnished eloquent testimony to the success of the reform of the church. But since he took ancient laws as the basic standard of morality, he deprived himself of a reliable criterion of moral judgment and thus prepared the way for the modern habits of either refraining from judgment in the face of historical relativity (on the fallacious grounds that no customs can be binding because all customs change) or of legitimating unjust actions by reference to necessity and reason of state (on the fallacious grounds that no necessities of state can be denied because some are legitimate).

[28] See above, pp. 134f.
[29] This is the reason why no attempt to explain late medieval and early modern movements of reform can succeed so long as it is based on the objectively verifiable condition of whatever was to be reformed. It seems not at all impossible that, objectively speaking, the late medieval church was better governed than ever before. As early as 1903 Johannes Haller, in his moving preface to *Papsttum und Kirchenreform*, pp. viif., suggested that the documents might not support the contention that the papacy was to blame for the decline of medieval ecclesiastical institutions, and in 1935 Geoffrey Barraclough, *Papal Provisions*, furnished a classic illustration of the care with which the papacy exercised its power. Indeed, Moeller, 'Piety in Germany', p. 52, has rightly insisted 'that there has hardly been an age in the second millennium of Church history which offered less resistance to the dogmatic absolutism of the Catholic Church' than the fifty years just prior to the explosion of Luther's Reformation, a time when no heresies seemed to be left and when popular piety appears to have reached unprecedented heights. But the demand for reform was fuelled by the perception of abuse, not its reality – and that perception became more acute precisely to the same degree that reform succeeded in imbuing the clergy and the laity with its ideals. It was the success of the medieval movement of reform, not its failure, that proved to be its undoing.

The story of this breakdown in the temporal logic of *mores* leads far beyond William Durant the Younger and his treatise to the development of sovereignty, science, and history in modern times. There is no doubt at all that this development is not what he intended. To the contrary, he meant to revive the authority of the 'original texts'. But, his intention notwithstanding, his own attempt to restore *mores* by reference to ancient laws produced a gap that divorced the present from the past and robbed actual conduct of moral intelligibility. It left him not with one 'short road' to reform but with two complementary options: either he could continue to concentrate on the ancient laws in the hope that increased familiarity would breed increased respect; or he could call on the assistance of an extraneous force in order to suppress abuses. But while the former option was designed to turn the ancient laws into objects of pure historical curiosity without obligatory force, the latter transformed their obligatory force into that of norms of pure reason, and both options would complete the disjunction of ancient law from *mores*.

In this way Durant himself contributed to the elaboration of history and sovereignty. Indeed, his contribution can be identified in the *Tractatus Maior*. It is well worth remembering how little medieval people really knew about the past. Even as great a scholar as Joannes Andreae was convinced that at the beginning of the church the pope appointed bishops, and that episcopal elections were the result of subsequent innovations.[30] This was precisely the sort of reconstruction of the past that was only natural for those whose faith that the law did coincide with *mores* had not been shaken by historical investigations. Durant, by comparison, showed a keen appreciation of the historicity of law. The very premise of his treatise that ancient conciliar law had been forgotten and conflicted with present practice deserves to be termed a historical discovery on the basis of empirical research into ancient canon law. He read the Pseudo-Isidorean collection not merely as a source of law but also as a source of information about the history of law. The structure of the treatise reflected a similar appreciation of the distance between the present and the past. For even though

---

[30] See Joannes Andreae's gloss *ad* VI.1.6.18: 'Ut igitur huius iuris originem scias, veritatem scire debes, scilicet, de antiquo iure et dispositione ecclesiae potestas conferendi episcopatus, ad papam pertinere ... Sed haec regula fallit in casibus qui postmodum a iure fuerint expressi. Voluerunt enim iura, quod in cathedralibus sibi eligerent canonici ...' Cited by Ganzer, *Papsttum*, p. 26 n. 12.

that structure resembled that of the Pseudo-Isidorean collection, its meaning under the circumstances was completely different. The Pseudo-Isidorean collection reflected, roughly speaking, the order in which its contents had been published because at the time its contents were still well enough remembered to require little or no analysis; by contrast, Durant's decision to adopt that order in the high middle ages reflected a departure from the more recent methods of classifying law that had come to supplant the Pseudo-Isidorean procedure during the classical period of canon law. It expressed a respect for the 'original texts' and a critical attitude toward contemporary law that were equally historical in inspiration. Indeed, the emphasis which he placed on the structure of the Pseudo-Isidorean collection was designed as a piece of evidence to corroborate his attack on papal law by exposing it as a historical innovation. What he may not have recognized was that to demonstrate the historicity of present law was implicitly as well to demonstrate the historicity of past law.

At the same time Durant proceeded to transform *mores* from binding expressions of social practice into pure norms of reason with an unconditional authority requiring both scientific analysis and sovereignty to be of any social use. There is a sense in which his entire treatise, with its relentless recitation of the ancient laws and its refusal (with rare exceptions) to engage in discussing reasons for or against those laws, is testimony to his tendency to treat the ancient laws as though the mere fact of their being laws was enough to sustain their obligatory force beyond any reasonable doubt. But there are two points at which his love of the law for its own sake and his transformation of its character from *mores* into norms with an unconditionally obligatory force emerge particularly clearly. One consists of his telling gloss on Gratian's opening words in the *Decretum*: where Gratian had simply said that 'the human race is governed by two laws: natural law and *mores*', Durant felt compelled to add: 'that is, it ought to be governed by these laws'.[31] This, of course, does not mean that Gratian had been unaware that there can be a difference between what is and what ought to be: some recognition of this difference is the starting point of all moral thought. But it does signify that in Durant's opinion natural law

---

[31] 'Sane videretur ad correctionem et reformationem ecclesie et ad salubre regimen humani generis posse perveniri hac brevi via: scriptum namque est in principio decretorum quod regitur genus humanum duobus, id est, regi debet, videlicet iure naturali ★et moribus★ [P].' *TMA* 1.2, fol. 4vb.

and *mores*, on the one hand, stood at a greater distance from reality than Gratian thought and did not govern the human race quite as effectively as he seemed to have believed and, on the other hand, that nevertheless they did not lose any of their ability to command obedience.

The other point at which this transformation can be perceived particularly clearly consists of Durant's proposal to abolish the 'superfluities and similitudes' by which he thought the legal literature to be overburdened and to replace the subtleties of scholarly classification with a radical dichotomy between the 'original texts' and their publicly sanctioned meaning. To be sure, he used many different terms to refer to different types of law (canons, decrees, statutes, divine law, *mores*, constitutions), different types of modifications of the law (exemptions, dispensations, concessions, privileges, indulgences), and different principles underlying law (justice, *ius*, the common good, equity, reason, utility). However, he did not pay much attention to the precise significance of any of these terms; instead he regularly lumped them all together.[32] If the glossators were convinced that the meaning of the laws could be derived from patient analysis of the texts themselves, Durant was equally convinced that laws were meaningless unless they were interpreted and enforced with a sovereign freedom from the text that could only be obtained by the cooperation of university professors with the papal plenitude of power.

In short, Durant was well on the road toward transforming jurisprudence into legal history and jurisdiction into sovereignty. Precisely to the same degree that he succeeded in reminding his audience of what the ancient laws demanded, he proved that there existed arbitrary forces in the world exceeding the bounds of reason and morality; precisely to the same degree that he insisted on the ancient laws he undermined their authority; and precisely to the same degree that he insisted on respect for the 'original texts' he demonstrated the need for a sovereign authority to put an end to any doubts about their meaning. There can therefore be little doubt that there exists a direct conceptual link between his own attention to the Pseudo-Isidorean collection and Valla's proof that this collection was a forgery, between his own considered point of view that ignorance was the mother of all vices and the early

---

[32] See above, pp. 134, 146, 170, 194, 225f., 228f. Cf. Alberigo, *Chiesa conciliare*, p. 175, on the parallel with *Haec sancta*.

modern combination of science with sovereignty that came to fruition in the works of Bodin and Hobbes.

The manner in which this conceptual link was forged by Durant himself is nowhere seen more clearly than in the rubric on the 'need to limit the power of superiors'.[33] This is no accident. In the preceding chapter Durant had just confronted the central question of whether or not government could be exempt from law and had protested with great vehemence that there could be no exemption from ancient conciliar law. This, therefore, was the point in the logic of his argument at which the problem of preserving the integrity of *mores* in the face of the competing claims of memory and action was most acutely posed. In an attempt to resolve the question once and for all in favour of constraining action by ancient law, Durant used the beginning of the rubric to push his claims to their logical and chronological extreme: he invoked the underlying principles of justice and the exemplary moral conduct of Christ and ancient pagans. Indeed, in his opening statement he quoted Gregory I to the effect that reason itself commanded respect for 'the constitutions that were instituted and handed on down by superiors and predecessors', as if reason could never give rise to any doubts about ancient practices.[34] But in so doing he merely managed to exacerbate the contrast between the present and the past to such an intensity that he was forced to formulate his most radical conclusion: the Christian rulers of the present failed to live up to the standards of pagan antiquity.

In a single agonizing instant the past was divorced from the present by a gap that no experience could bridge. The pain that Durant expressed on this occasion is more than a rhetorical device. It has a theoretical significance: the violent disintegration of the moral universe on which his ideas were predicated. It marks the point at which the image of republican Rome was turned into a mere historical ideal and hierarchy transformed into the unconditional assertion of a power that was no longer bounded by reason. Thereafter it became impossible to reconcile council with hierarchy. Instead the man who meant to keep *mores* intact found himself reduced to lamenting the passing of an apparently more moral age and to suspecting illicit motivations on the part of rulers whose reasons were beyond his ken and whose power he lacked the means to control – in fact, he had become a humanist. It is therefore

---

[33] See above, pp. 144–56.    [34] See above, p. 145.

fitting that this was the first and the most pronounced occasion on which Durant turned to the canonical exemption of the papacy from human judgment, and that he went on to invoke the wrath of God upon 'the judges of the ends of the earth who have not judged aright' and concluded by appealing to the conscience of the pope to abide by law. He was merely drawing the conclusions that followed with a certain kind of inevitability from his own stubborn faith in ancient laws, a faith that made it impossible for him to see the differences between the present and the past as anything other than the result of a deplorable decline and thus left him no choice but to subject the present to the combined demands of a conscience that lacked power and a power that was absolute.

All of this was quickly passed over, as it were. For a brief moment Durant had come face to face with the consequences of his insistence on the ancient laws – consequences that he could have avoided only by reconsidering the principles to which his programme to reform the church was dedicated. Had he been willing to relent in his devotion to antiquity he might have recognized that in and of itself the papacy's failure to conform to the standards of antiquity was no disgrace at all but held the promise of a reasonable way to govern medieval Europe, and thus he might perhaps have managed to avoid the pain to which he condemned himself by his denial of legitimacy to the present. Instead, at the conclusion of the rubric on the 'need to limit the power of superiors', he reasserted the principles with which he had begun and in the following chapter expanded them to call for a 'further limitation and regulation of the power of the presidents of the monarchy'. That 'further limitation' was going to postpone the crisis, but only for a while and ultimately at the cost of deepening the gulf that separates morality from history and sovereignty.

This makes it possible for us to give another meaning to Durant's conciliar proposal. It was an attempt to conceal the fact that the foundations of his thought were split by a schism of power from reason, to palliate the painful disintegration of his trust in *mores*, and to reassure the devotees of authority that their obedience to law would be rewarded. But the apparent confidence with which he promised that a 'healthy regime of the human race' could still be managed if only general councils would regularly be consulted was deceptive. Once the potential of power to escape from law had been revealed, once the pain had been felt that followed from condemning the Christian present in the light of the pagan past, Durant had made an experience that could not be undone. The path on which he steadfastly tried to continue had been obstructed. Sooner or later he as well as those who agreed with him were to be stopped in their advance by an encounter with a kind of power from which Durant had almost immediately averted his eyes but that was going to assert itself with a force so much the less to be denied because he himself had helped to reveal its necessity. At that point the historical momentum that had driven the medieval movement of reform would be transferred to humanists and princes. It was no inherent conflict between *magnus ordo differentie* and *res publica* that endangered the success of his endeavour; it was his insistence on the ancient law.

### ORIGINS OF CONCILIARISM

Durant's conciliar proposal was thus ambivalently placed over a chasm between the competing claims of liberty and obedience, designed to enhance the authority of the traditions of the past on the left and to condemn them to impotence on the right. Some of the reasons for this ambivalence were specific to his person, time, and circumstances. The tone of the *Tractatus Maior* reflects the kind of law-and-order mentality that relishes the authority of law for its own sake without regard to reason. His treatment of the de Peyre even suggests that he derived a certain satisfaction from breaches in the law because they could serve as a pretext for unbounded wrath in the name of righteousness – the kind of wrath that Luther had in store for the rebellious peasants of Germany. The station he held in society was that of a commoner from a town in southern France whom fate had cast into dangerous vicinity with the lords of the Gévaudan. The pope promoted him to high ecclesiastical office and the king helped him to ride rough-shod over the jealously guarded liberties of the local nobility, but he desired nonetheless to garner for himself the rights of an ecclesiastical aristocrat secure and independent from pope and king. His diocese was situated on the border between the mercantile south and the chivalrous north, between the councils and communes of Italy and the lords and manors of France. And then, of course, he lived in a period of rapid change and witnessed a moment of supreme ambivalence when in the name of the Christian faith the king of France staged a violent

assault on the pope while simultaneously appealing for judgment
to the true pope-to-be. Durant thus found himself straddling more
than one of the many boundaries by which his times were divided.
That certainly helped to exacerbate the tensions inherent in his
thought.

From a more universal point of view, Durant's condition was
the same as that of any prophet – whether he be Cato or Isaiah –
who ever in the name of a violated law called fire and brimstone
down on a wicked present from which he set himself apart, but
which he nonetheless hoped to encourage by his prophecies to
return to the straight path of justice. But if we wish to identify the
point at which the universal intersected with the particular in such a
way as to lay the real historical foundations for the uncertainties
with which Durant was struggling, we can do no better than to
turn to the beginning of the movement to reform the church under
the leadership of the papacy in the eleventh and twelfth centuries. It
was at that time that in a moment of lasting significance for
European history an attempt on the grand scale was launched to
reduce an entire age, an entire continent, indeed, the world to the
commands of ancient law. It was Pope Gregory VII who asserted
the claims of truth over the claims of custom, identified the truth
with the decrees of the Fathers, and steered the church onto its
course of recovering the ancient law of the church from the
oblivion to which it seemed to have been condemned by unclean
temporal powers.[35] It was in this environment that the ambivalent
relationship of government to *mores* was first established. Hence it
was there as well that we encounter all of the trappings of that
relationship for the first time and in their basic shape. If we consider
Peter Damian, we find ready made the belief in the legitimacy of a
power that exceeds all understanding;[36] if we consider Gregory
VII himself, we find the origin of temporal power attributed
directly to the devil;[37] if we look at the gloss on Gregory I's
definition of the great order of difference, we find that it ruptures
the continuum between the church in heaven and the church on
earth by insisting that government by prelates is but a temporal

[35] Ladner, 'Two Gregorian Letters'.
[36] Oakley, *Omnipotence, Covenant and Order*, pp. 42–4.
[37] 'Quis nesciat reges et duces ab his habuisse principium, qui Deum ignorantes, superbia,
rapinis, perfidia, homicidiis, postremo universis paene sceleribus, mundi principe
videlicet diabolo agitante, super pares, scilicet homines, dominari caeca cupidine et
intolerabili praesumptione affectaverunt?' *Quellen zur Geschichte Kaiser Heinrichs IV.*, p.
302.

necessity that will pass away when God is all in all;[38] if we look at law, we find the first suggestions of purely positive law;[39] and finally we find the first expressions of the same sense of loss that was to be more highly cultivated by early modern humanists.[40]

In short, what we find is that the reform of the church was from the beginning caught between conflicting claims of tradition and innovation that could not be reconciled without devices striking a permanent link between the liberty of the church and the sovereignty of the papacy and in the long run threatening to undermine the moral intelligibility of action. Schism did not arise apart from reform: reform itself gave rise to schism because it was inseparably wedded to an assertion of the unconditional authority of ancient law that served to undermine the ability to integrate the experience of change in a shared understanding of morality and thus helped to prepare the split of authority into sovereignty and history. Hence it is that the cardinals opposing Pope Gregory VII were already insisting that papal measures taken without consent are illegitimate;[41] hence it is that at the very height of reform St Bernard was concerned to protect the rights of the middling powers from papal arrogance;[42] and hence it is, too, that he charged the papacy with having followed Emperor Constantine rather than the Apostle

---

[38] 'In quo quidem capitulo dicit glossa lxxxix. di. quod dicta prelatio durabit usque in diem iudicii, quod probat auctoritate apostoli dicentis prime Corinth. xv.: dum mundus iste durabit homines presunt hominibus, demones demonibus, angeli angelis. Cum autem Deus erit omnia in omnibus, cessabit dicta prelatio, non tamen ordo vel maioritas, de pen. di. iiii. in domo.' TMA 1.4 De exemptionibus, fol. 8vb. Cf. the gloss ad D.89 c.7, 1 Corinthians 15:25–8, De pen. D.4 c.11.

[39] Kuttner, 'Sur les origines'.

[40] 'Sane cum Alexandro papa recolentes quomodo hec sancta plantatio ecclesie Dei fuerit instituta, dolentes dicere possumus cum eodem quod, etsi non ab omnibus, neque in omnibus, *a* [P] plerisque tamen et in pluribus ab illa sancta institutione primitive ecclesie sanctorum patrum, conciliorum, et decretorum Romanorum pontificum in tantum videatur esse declinatum ut aliqui ex nobis prime institutionis videantur obliti, extra de statu monacho., recolentes.' TMA 2.prefatio, fol. 14ra. Cf. X.3.35.3.

[41] Gesta Romanae aecclesiae contra Hildebrandum, pp. 369–422, esp. pp. 369f., 409f., 418–21.

[42] 'Erras si, ut summam, ita et solam institutam a Deo vestram apostolicam potestatem existimas. Si hoc sentis, dissentis ab eo qui ait: "Non est potestas nisi a Deo." Proinde quod sequitur: "Qui potestati resistit, Dei ordinationi resistit," etsi principaliter pro te facit, non tamen singulariter. Denique enim ait: "Omnis anima potestatibus sublimioribus subdita sit." Non ait, "sublimiori", tamquam in uno, sed "sublimioribus", tamquam in multis. Non tua ergo sola potestas a Domino; sunt et mediocres, sunt et inferiores.' Bernard of Clairvaux, De consideratione 3.4.16–17, Opera 3:444, with references to 1 Corinthians 6:12, Ins.1.1.1, and Romans 13:1–2. Bernard's use of Romans 13 to prevent the pope from interfering with the 'middling powers' and his identification of 'justice' with a hierarchical order are quite like Durant's.

Peter and exclaimed in dismay: 'There is peace with pagans and peace with heretics but certainly no peace with our sons.'[43]

The permutations in moral thought to which the programme of reform thus gave rise as soon as it had been announced are nowhere seen more clearly than in that masterpiece of law by which it was given authoritative shape: Gratian's *Decretum*.[44] The very opening words of the *Decretum* announced the cardinal distinction on which reform was based and that would jeopardize its viability, namely, between natural law and *mores*. We hardly need to wait for Durant to encounter a historical attitude to law: Gratian's *Decretum* itself was an historical attempt to recover the meaning of the 'old law', as it came to be known precisely at that time, that is, a law whose meaning had slipped so deeply into the past that it was difficult to understand without a conscious effort of collecting, surveying, and systematically interpreting the ancient texts. It is with Gratian that the transformation of jurisprudence into legal history began, and with Gratian, too, that jurisdiction began to be transformed into the unconditional commands of sovereignty, namely, when he declared the pope to be the lord and founder of the decrees.[45] Indeed, it is with Gratian that the foundations were prepared for the specific meaning of the conciliar theory that we have just identified in the *Tractatus Maior*, that is, to prevent the split of *mores* into the unconditional commands of sovereignty, and the abstention of history from commanding anything at all.

This meaning is inscribed in the most important canon from the *Decretum* on which Durant relied in order to validate his demand for general councils, namely, D.20 c.3. D.20 c.3 occurred at the very end of the twentieth distinction of the first part of the *Decretum*. This is significant because the twentieth distinction marked the boundary between the two main sections into which the first part of the *Decretum* was divided. The first of these sections dealt with the principles of law, explaining how the heterogeneous mass of canons, letters, and opinions that had been handed down from the past were to be turned into a harmonious body of legal doctrine; in many ways it was not merely the beginning, but the

---

[43] 'Pax a paganis, pax ab haereticis, sed non profecto a filiis.' Bernard of Clairvaux, *Super cantica canticorum*, Sermo 33.15, *Opera* 1:244. For the charge that the pope was imitating Emperor Constantine rather than Peter see Bernard, *De consideratione* 4.3.6, *Opera* 3:453, with reference to John 21:15.

[44] In general: Kuttner, *Harmony from Dissonance*; Chodorow, *Christian Political Theory*; Le Bras *et al.*, *L'Age classique*, pp. 52–129.     [45] See above, pp. 151f.

core of a work also known as the *Concordia discordantium canonum*. The second section dealt with the ministers of the ecclesiastical hierarchy who were going to put those canons into effect. Just like the rubric on the 'need to limit the power of superiors', the twentieth distinction thus marked a point of transition from law to action where the competing claims of memory and action were most acutely posed; just like Durant's conciliar proposal, D.20 c.3 was Gratian's final answer to the question how the authority of ancient law was to be kept intact; and just as Durant went on to turn his attention from law to the proper order of the church, so Gratian, too, went on to discuss the ecclesiastical hierarchy, went on, indeed, to supply Durant in the immediately following distinction, in D.21 c.2, with his cardinal piece of canonical support for deriving the general order of the church from God and for denouncing exemptions from episcopal jurisdiction.[46]

D.20 c.3, however, did not merely parallel Durant's conciliar proposal in that it came at the end of a discussion of the principles of law. It also responded to a similar difficulty that had appeared in the course of that discussion. The question that Gratian meant to settle in the twentieth distinction was this: does a pope have to obey the decisions of the Fathers of the church? This was but one specific aspect of the general question whether or not the pope was bound to obey the laws of the ancient church. In the immediately preceding distinction Gratian had dealt with another aspect of that question, namely whether papal letters possessed the same authority as conciliar canons even if they were not included in the ancient canonical collections. There his answer had been an unequivocal yes.[47] His first words in the twentieth distinction, however, suggested that papal letters might not equal the authority of the writings of the Fathers:

The more clearly anyone is supported by reason [*ratio*], the more authority [*auctoritas*] would seem to inhere in his words. Now, as most of the ancient exegetes surpass other men because they are fuller of the grace of the Holy Ghost and excel by their deeper knowledge [*scientia*], they

---

[46] Gratian himself articulated the transition as follows: 'Decretis ergo Romanorum Pontificum et sacris canonibus conciliorum ecclesiastica negotia, et supra monstratum est, terminantur. Ministri vero sacrorum canonum et decretorum Pontificum sunt summi Pontifices et infra presules atque reliqui sacerdotes, quorum institutio in veteri testamento est inchoata, et in novo plenius consummata.' D.21 a.c.1. The gloss points to a link between D.20 c.3 and D.21 c.2, for which see below, p. 274 n. 52.

[47] Nevertheless the decretists had ranked conciliar canons consistently above papal decretals; Tierney, 'Pope and Council', p. 201 n. 22.

obviously adhere more closely to reason. Hence the sayings of Augustine, Jerome, and other exegetes would appear to be preferable to the constitutions of quite a few popes.[48]

With these words Gratian seemed to ascribe to the sayings of the Fathers a true and immutable authority that rested neither on power nor on office but on the divine reason of the Holy Ghost. If this had been all, there would have been no way for the papacy to justify any actions that conflicted with the writings of the Fathers. But indefatigable champion of reform that he was, Gratian was unwilling to restrict papal activity to such a narrow circle. Therefore he went on to make a cardinal distinction:

But there is a difference between settling cases and interpreting the meaning of Scripture. For when there are affairs to be settled, knowledge [*scientia*] is not the only thing that is required; power [*potestas*] is, too. Just before Christ said to Peter: 'Whatsoever you shall bind on earth, shall be bound in heaven', and so on, he gave him two keys to the kingdom of heaven: one for the knowledge to distinguish between different kinds of leprosy, the other for the power to expel anyone from the church or to admit him into the church. Therefore, when any kind of affair is to be settled – whether the innocent are to be absolved or the guilty to be condemned – both absolution and condemnation require not only knowledge but also the power of presidency. Hence the exegetes of Sacred Scriptures may exceed the pontiffs in knowledge and are to be preferred insofar as the question is about the meaning of Scripture. But if the question is about settling cases they deserve second place, since they have not attained to the apex of pontifical dignity.[49]

In other words: the Fathers might have been right insofar as the meaning of Scriptures was concerned, but they had not been

---

48 'Quo enim quisque magis ratione nititur, eo maioris auctoritatis eius verba esse videntur. Plurimi autem tractatorum, sicut pleniori gratia Spiritus sancti, ita ampliori scientia aliis precellentes, rationi magis adhesisse probantur. Unde nonnullorum Pontificum constitutis Augustini, Ieronimi atque aliorum tractatorum dicta eis videntur esse preferenda.' D.20 a.c.1.

49 'Sed aliud est causis terminum imponere aliud scripturas sacras diligenter exponere. Negotiis diffiniendis non solum est necessaria scientia, sed etiam potestas. Unde Christus dicturus Petro: "Quodcumque ligaveris super terram, erit ligatum et in celis, etc." prius dedit sibi claves regni celorum: in altera dans ei scientiam discernendi inter lepram et lepram, in altera dans sibi potestatem eiciendi aliquos ab ecclesia, vel recipiendi. Cum ergo quelibet negotia finem accipiant, vel in absolutione innocentium vel in condempnatione delinquentium, absolutio vero vel condempnatio non scientiam tantum sed etiam potestatem presidentium desiderant: aparet, quod divinarum scripturarum tractatores, etsi scientia Pontificibus premineant, tamen, quia dignitatis eorum apicem non sunt adepti, in sacrarum scripturarum expositionibus eis preponuntur, in causis vero diffiniendis secundum post eos locum merentur.' D.20 a.c.1.

writing to settle legal cases. To take that kind of action required more than knowledge (*scientia*), of which the Fathers had enough; it also required power (*potestas*), which they lacked. Therefore the decisions of the papacy took precedence over the writings of the Fathers. By dividing the immutable authority of divine reason into two elements, knowledge and power, Gratian had thus emancipated the papacy from the past.

This distinction implicitly raised the possibility that the papacy might be emancipated too completely; once power had been given independent rights from knowledge, there was the danger that the harmonious conjunction of knowledge with power on which the preservation of authority depended might be disrupted by a power outside of any limits defined by mere knowledge. It was precisely this possibility to which the final canon of the twentieth distinction put a stop. The question raised at that point was this: what if there were no laws at all to guide the pope's decision? What if no councils, no papal letters, and no writings of the Fathers could be found to solve a pending legal issue? What if, in other words, knowledge failed entirely to resolve the issue – or more precisely, what if knowledge lacked the support of authoritative writings of any kind? One might have thought that in such cases the pope should have been allowed to decide on his own. But such was not Gratian's view:

When all of these texts have been inspected and it is still impossible to determine the nature of the issue lucidly, assemble the elders of the province and question them. For answers are found more easily when they are sought from many elders. For the Lord, who is our true surety, said: If two or three of you on earth shall gather together in my name, anything that they shall ask shall be done for them of my Father.[50]

Thus the function of Gratian's distinction between power and knowledge was evidently not to assert that power could ever be legitimately exercised apart from knowledge. Its function rather was to supply a hermeneutical criterion in order to determine the

---

[50] 'Quod si in his omnibus inspectis huius questionis qualitas non lucide investigatur, seniores provinciae congrega et eos interroga. Facilius namque invenitur, quod a pluribus senioribus queritur. Verus etiam repromissor Dominus ait: "Si duo ex vobis vel tres conveniunt super terram in nomine meo, de omni re, quamcunque petierint, fiet illis a patre meo."' D.20 c.3. The scriptural quotation is slightly different from its source in Matthew 18:19–20. The original has 'agree', *consenserint*, instead of 'gather', *conveniunt*, hardly an insignificant variant, but then of course the original goes on to promise Christ's presence to any two or three individuals 'assembled', *congregati*, in his name.

sequence in which canonical texts were to be consulted: it secured a place ahead of patristic treatises to papal letters.[51] But it also presupposed that there were laws and letters to be interpreted and it did not support the exercise of a power that was absolute. Hence, when the laws fell silent, the pope was not to use his keys without deliberation; rather he was to hold a council, for Christ had unconditionally promised that councils would be able to ascertain the truth even if the laws fell silent.[52]

If we reflect on the logic underlying the twentieth distinction, we can identify a sequence of coordinated steps by which Gratian meant to strike a balance between the respect owed to the writings of antiquity and the need of the papacy to exercise its power freely for the sake of reform. First, he asserted authority; next, he distinguished power from knowledge in order to increase the papacy's freedom; and finally he defined the outermost boundaries of that freedom by requiring the papacy to consult the members of the ecclesiastical hierarchy whenever no writings were available to furnish certain guidance. In this fashion Gratian attempted to secure an idea of authority that rested on investing power with truths derived from the writings of antiquity.

This structure is the same as that which informs the first part of the *Tractatus Maior*.[53] To be sure, the differences are not to be belittled. Gratian's distinction of power from knowledge served as a hermeneutical principle to guide the interpretation of different kinds of canonical texts; in the case of Durant the power of the papacy had grown to a size that threatened both in theory and practice to exceed the limits not merely of the exegetical writings of the Fathers but of the ancient conciliar law itself. Gratian made

---

[51] D.20 c.1 and D.20 c.3 are by no means unambiguous in their determination of this sequence. The ordinary gloss *ad* D.20 c.3 *s.v. De quibus* makes it clear that medieval canonists themselves had trouble deciding whether or not these canons required Greek writings to be consulted after the Bible but before conciliar canons and papal letters, or after all of these.

[52] It might be added that the ordinary gloss *ad* D.20 c.3 identifies *seniores* with *sapientes* and refers for further elucidation to D.84 c.6. D.84 c.6, in turn, identifies both *seniores* and *sapientes* with priests. Since D.84 c.6 is an excerpt from the same letter of Pope Anacletus that was quoted in D.21 c.2, the gloss strikes a direct link between the two canons in the *Decretum* that furnished the primary canonical justification for Durant's conception of church government, D.20 c.3 and D.21 c.2, and thus confirms that combination of wisdom with hierarchical standing that suffused Durant's conception of authority and formed the premise of his conciliar proposal.

[53] Indeed, the similarities are substantial enough to suggest the possibility that the bipartite structure of Durant's treatise reflects the bipartite structure of the first part of the *Decretum*.

his distinction in order to enable the papacy to exercise its authority with greater freedom; Durant tried as best he could to reduce the effects of the distinction by subjecting the papacy to conciliar reason; and while in Gratian's case D.20 c.3 was a concluding observation on which he did not spend much attention, in Durant's it served as the cornerstone for a concerted effort to limit papal government. But these differences can be explained as the result of different interests and experiences. They led to major shifts in emphasis but they did nothing to dislodge the fundamental structure. In both cases the issue was how to preserve authority in the face of the need for action, and in both the answer consisted of the faith that councils would reveal the truth.

The several different meanings of Durant's conciliar proposal that we have previously distinguished can thus be brought into an intelligible relationship. *Magnus ordo differentie* and *res publica* signify, respectively, the claims of truth and action. Durant's demand for general councils was designed to harmonize these two and thereby to secure the continued progress of reform without endangering authority. But the cohesion of his plan was undermined by his decided preference for ancient laws. In principle there was nothing new about these ideas. They were firmly anchored in the logic that had governed the movement to reform the church ever since the eleventh century. There is an identifiable sense, therefore, in which Gratian himself anticipated Durant's conciliar agenda. New, however, were the circumstances of the early fourteenth century, which raised the tension between ancient law and present practice to an intolerable level. Durant's painful susceptibility to that excruciating tension, combined with his powerful intellect and with what appears to have been his constitutional incapacity for living with half-truths – those are the traits that make his thought unique. Relentlessly demanding obedience to ancient laws in ways that were fundamentally at odds with his passionate championship of the right of general councils to act for the common good, he stretched the limits of memory and *mores* to extremes. The tension broke in the rubric on the 'need to limit the power of superiors'. There the effort to keep *magnus ordo differentie* and *res publica* united, the effort to preserve a common understanding of *mores*, encountered unsurmountable obstacles. There the logic of reform was turned inside out and gave way to the admission of a moral past that was irrecoverably lost and of an extra-moral power that escaped from law.

Durant's political thought thus culminates not in his conciliar
proposal, but in the rubric on the 'need to limit the power of
superiors', a piece of text whose effect on the surrounding chapters
was thoroughly unsettling in terms of both style and substance.
Like a vector pointing beyond itself it pointed to the profoundly
different future that would arrive with the Renaissance and
Reformation, when the past would become the province not of
reformers but of historians, when reformers would insist on the
omnipotence of God and deny the ability of human beings to
govern their fate themselves, and when rulers would be endowed
with the sovereign right to command obedience without contradiction. There he proceeded further than anywhere else on the road
out of the quandary into which he was led by his respect for
antiquity. There he prepared the way for a new reading of Romans
13: whereas in the preceding chapter he had insisted that this
passage commanded the powers that be to conform their government to law, now it appeared that there could be no other limits to
their power than those imposed by themselves and by the wrath of
God. There he extolled the exemplary morality of Scipio and
Marcus Regulus. There he laid the foundations for the dual
transformation that was to be completed in early modern times by
an alliance of humanists with princes: on the one hand, the
transformation of *res publica* into a 'republic of letters' that would
be populated by philologists and historians with an idea of liberty
that was not to be located anywhere except in the distant past, in
scholarship, and in the utopian imagination of a Thomas More,
and, on the other hand, the transformation of *magnus ordo differentie*
into the skeletal structure of a bureaucracy at the service of a
sovereign – whether that sovereign be the prince, the people, or the
nation – who could command unconditional obedience and whose
reforms would no longer be designed to restore the past but to
advance more rapidly into the future.[54] There, in short, the vision
of an integral commonwealth that was both *res publica* and *magnus
ordo differentie* was undone.

[54] I am indebted to Marc Fumaroli for having shared with me his discovery that the concept
of the 'republic of letters' can first be identified at the council of Constance.

# RESULTS: LIBERTY AND LAW

In Durant's opinion the central obstacle to the reform of the church was the conflict between law and government. In itself, of course, this opinion was by no means new. Ever since the papacy had risen to lead the medieval church there had been doubts about the legitimacy of its policies. One need not turn to the party of the emperor and his Ghibelline supporters or to Cathar heretics to demonstrate the depth of such doubts; St Bernard could not have put it more soberly when he announced that the papal plenitude of power was not the same as a plenitude of justice.[1] Hence thinkers of unquestionably orthodox intentions, with deep roots in the ancient traditions of the church, had attempted to limit papal government long before the days of William Durant. Canonists, not heretics, were responsible for showing that, above and beyond the articles of faith, there was a 'state of the church' which the pope was not at liberty to change; canonists, not heretics, taught that a pope who fell into heresy or committed outrageous crimes could be deposed from office; canonists, not heretics, declared that councils were greater than popes.

While there were precedents for Durant's desire to establish legal limits on papal power, however, the depth and extent of his concern were new. The canonists before his time were worried about papal heresy and crime – threats that were serious but remote. They never doubted that a pope who was not a heretic was 'lord and founder of the decrees', and they were accordingly unanimous in their opinion that no law or council was valid unless it had received the pope's approval. Durant, on the other hand, was not particularly worried about papal heresy. His fears concerned ordinary faithful popes going about their ordinary daily business. The threat they posed was not as monumental as that of heresy, but it was omnipresent and therefore more corrosive of the authority

---

[1] 'Sic factitando probatis vos habere plenitudinem potestatis, sed iustitie forte non ita.' Bernard of Clairvaux, *De consideratione* 3.4.14, *Opera*, 3:442.

of the church. Unlike his canonistic predecessors Durant declared outright that the papacy could not be trusted to preside over reform – not because it was neglectful of its duties, but because those duties surpassed the capacity of any single human being. He insisted that ancient laws defined the agenda of reform more reliably than could the papacy and that, in case those laws were insufficient, the proper procedure was not for the pope to make a decision by himself, nor even only on the advice of the cardinals, but for him to rely on general councils because they enjoyed the assistance that Christ had promised to assemblies of his followers. In a sense Durant's entire case can be summed up in his decision not to mention Gratian's view that the pope, like Christ, was 'lord and founder of the decrees' and to replace it with the demand that henceforth no law ought to be valid unless it had received the approval, not of the pope, but of the council.[2]

These ideas amounted to a fundamental realignment of the relationship between pope, law, and councils on which the movement for reform had been founded thus far.[3] Pope, law, and councils had been the main ingredients of church reform ever since it had gotten under way in the eleventh century. To confirm that point one need only look at the *Dictatus Papae*, list the canonical collections produced in the twelfth and thirteenth centuries, and count the councils over which the papacy presided since 1049. But whereas previously pope, law, and councils had been linked together in a single structure of which the pope, so long as his faith was not in doubt, was the undisputed head, by the early fourteenth century reform had fallen on hard times, its goals had become uncertain, and papal leadership had raised suspicions that could no longer be allayed by demonstrations of compliance with the faith.

---

[2] See above, pp. 151–3.

[3] Sieben, *Konzilsidee des lateinischen Mittelalters*, pp. 232–76, 352–7, shows well how radically Durant broke with the decretists, who had on the whole made the council dependent on the pope, and even more so the decretalists, who had shown very little interest in general councils at all. A similar case can be made for Durant's use of his favourite source of laws, the Pseudo-Isidorean collection. The authors of Pseudo-Isidore had invented unprecedented powers for the papacy, including exclusive control over councils and conciliar legislation, in order to protect the Frankish bishops from the laity. Durant tried to recover the purpose at which the forgers had once aimed – but at his time that was no longer possible without attacking the very prerogatives with which Pseudo-Isidore had endowed the papacy. Hence, in stark contrast to the forgers and the Gregorian reformers, Durant did not emphasize the forged papal decretals but the conciliar sections in Pseudo-Isidore. Sieben, *Konzilsidee des lateinischen Mittelalters*, pp. 61–74, 113–52, 188–231, sums up the literature on Pseudo-Isidore and the uses to which he was put in the eleventh and twelfth centuries.

Just when heresy had been decisively defeated a more insidious threat to the foundations of reform materialized in the form of human fallibility. Durant therefore set out to restructure the mechanisms of reform in ways that he hoped would prove impervious to fallibility. He severed law and councils from the papacy, changing them from instruments of papal government into agencies of reform that were not merely independent of the papacy but that also could and ought to be used in opposition to the papacy. The union of pope, law, and councils that had been part and parcel of the doctrine of the 'state of the church' was thus undone. The pope was transformed from head of that state into its most eminent administrator, and the movement for reform was turned into a search for infallibility.[4]

Two different ideas of order dominated that search. One identified the common good by means of normative writings that were regarded as inviolate, such as the Bible and ancient conciliar canons. From that perspective politics was subordinate to law; no one had any right to tamper with the law, and the basic function of government was jurisprudential, that is, to assure correct interpretations of the writings in which the common good had been defined. The other defined the common good in terms of 'the utility of citizens'. From that perspective law was subordinate to politics; no expert probing of the meaning of the law was sufficient to identify the common good and the basic function of government was to identify the common good by studying the 'utility of citizens' in its concrete empirical manifestations.

This distinction manifests itself in several ways. On the one hand, the laws inclined Durant to insist on hierarchical gradation, to ask for general councils 'whenever new laws are to be made', to insist on the superiority of spiritual over temporal powers, and to rely on good examples as a cardinal instrument of reform. On the other hand, the common good encouraged him to call for councils 'every ten years', to regard the clergy as but one part of a society consisting of many functionally differentiated orders united by cooperative labour, and to exploit the interest of the papacy in revenues as a means by which to subject its plenitude of power to conciliar control. The same distinction manifests itself in Durant's

---

[4] The same search manifested itself in the changing role of 'conscience' and of papal sovereignty. In this sense Tierney is certainly right to stress that in the late thirteenth century papal infallibility acquired a quality which it had never had before. For references to the literature see above, pp. 1, 3, 146.

reliance on two different textual traditions. One was juridical and ecclesiological. It was squarely founded on the *Decretum* and the decretist doctrine of the 'state of the church' as it had been applied by the partisans of the secular clergy in the theory and practice of the 1280s, and as it had been redefined by Durant's own recovery of Pseudo-Isidore. It was primarily represented by a few crucial canons from Gratian's *Decretum*: the canons contained in the first *quaestio* of the twenty-fifth *causa*, including especially the famous *Sunt quidam* (C.25 q.1 c.6) which prohibited the papacy from altering the fundamental law of the church; *In novo testamento* (D.21 c.2) which defined the hierarchical order of the church; and *De quibus causis* (D.20 c.3) which declared that councils must be convoked whenever legal issues could not be settled by means of existing writings. The other textual tradition was republican. It was more limited in terms of bulk, but it was just as prominent in terms of conceptual significance. It was primarily represented by excerpts from Valerius Maximus and parts of the *City of God* that praised ancient Rome, then by a crucial quotation from Cicero's *De officiis* (1.25(85)) about the proper way to treat the common good, and above all by the principle that 'what touches all must be approved by all' that had only recently been included in Boniface VIII's *Liber Sextus* (VI.5.12 De reg. iuris 29).

But most importantly the distinction between two different ideas of order informed the very substance of the argument Durant developed in the first part of the *Tractatus Maior* to support his call for general councils. Its starting point was his conviction, as testified by Romans 13, that kings and popes had been ordained by God, so that 'there can be no better order in their rule than if they conform as much as possible to God, from whom their power proceeds and to whose rule the rule of the world must conform'.[5] Hence kings and popes were called upon to 'govern themselves and the human race according to the contents of the Law, the Gospel, the councils approved by the inspiration of the Holy Spirit, and other approved human laws and rights'.[6] The trouble was that sometimes it was necessary to change old laws or make new laws in order to take changing circumstances into consideration. To leave such changes entirely in the hands of kings or popes was much too dangerous because they lacked the certainty of judgment by which alone it could be guarantied that changes in the law would

---

[5] See above, p. 136.    [6] See above, p. 133.

infallibly serve to maintain the order of the church. This was the problem which Durant's conciliar proposal was designed to solve specifically on the grounds that general councils were able to reveal the truth and thus to supply kings and popes with the knowledge that they needed in order to govern well. The foundation of this proposal consisted of Christ's promise in Matthew 18:19–20 as it had been incorporated into D.20 c.3: 'If two or three of you on earth shall gather together in my name, any thing that they shall ask shall be done for them of my father.'

Durant's conciliar proposal was therefore not in any way founded on the corporation theory which the decretalists developed on Roman legal principles and which has come to occupy a prominent position in standard accounts of the origins of the conciliar theory.[7] The basic point of corporation theory is that the members of a corporation have a right to participate in the decisions of the head. Durant's proposal, however, was not founded on any assertion of rights; it was founded on the necessity of determining the truth in matters of common concern. Nevertheless it would be utterly misleading to conclude that Durant's proposal had nothing to do with corporation theory at all. For, after all, he did conclude by quoting the central principle of corporative thought: 'what touches all must be approved by all'; he hoped that the council would be able to exploit the papacy's fiscal needs as a tool with which to ensure that the papal plenitude of power would be exercised in conformity with the council's will; he spoke in glowing terms of the Roman republic, called church and state a 'commonwealth', and referred to popes and kings as the 'administrators' of the commonwealth. Clearly he thought of church and state as a single body politic, a universal corporation, regarded popes and kings as officers of that corporation who were obliged to govern for the common good, and thought of councils as instruments by which to hold these officers accountable. The meaning of his conciliar proposal, therefore, can certainly not be confined to the narrow limits of a case about the proper procedure to be followed in making and interpreting the law. There is no doubt that it was meant to require the papacy to obtain conciliar consent to every measure of general concern and thus to transfer the fundamental authority in the church to general councils.

Durant's conciliar proposal thus combined a jurisprudential

---

[7] The classic exposition in Tierney, *Foundations*, pp. 96–105, 132–53.

argument from law for truth with a political argument from the common good for consent. In order to explicate the relation of these arguments it may be useful to employ the distinction between locutionary meanings and illocutionary acts that has been given prominence by Quentin Skinner.[8] In terms of locutionary meaning Durant's case was strictly limited to the argument for truth. It endowed the council with no other right than that to be heard 'whenever new laws are to be made'. In this regard the role of the principle that 'what touches all must be approved by all' was subsidiary. More technically speaking, its role was that of a rule of law that could be used in order to clarify the meaning of other canons, such as D.20 c.3, but lacked prescriptive force. Since it was placed immediately after the demand for general councils it helped to support that demand, but did not extend its reach beyond the boundaries of the argument for truth and did not endow the council with any independent rights. But if we seek to understand the illocutionary act Durant performed in saying that 'what touches all must be approved by all' – to understand, that is to say, what he was doing in saying what he did; if we step back from considering the locutionary limits of his canonical deduction and look at the illocutionary thrust of his case instead, then it becomes immediately apparent that he was doing something more than merely adducing a rule of canon law: by placing the principle that 'what touches all must be approved by all' at the end of his conciliar proposal he transformed it into the culmination of his argument, the point at which the jurisprudential view of order was superseded by a triumphant assertion of the right of a political community to have its say in all matters of general concern.

Durant's outstanding achievement thus was to have forged an argument of remarkable simplicity combining two different ideas of order into a single syllogism with a meaning that never ventured beyond what was possible in terms of law and yet communicated an intention to transform the church into a political community that would be governed by representative assemblies of its members. The question was, of course, whether or not the syllogism worked – whether or not the link between the meaning and the intention would stand up to scrutiny. The answer to that question is suggested by the fact that Durant never asked the pope

---

[8] Skinner, 'Meaning and Understanding', and now especially Skinner, 'A Reply to My Critics'.

directly to obtain the consent of the council. His conciliar proposal included a quotation of the principle that 'what touches all must be approved by all', but the substance of that principle was never carried over into the formulation of Durant's demand: he always asked the pope to convoke general councils, but never to obtain their consent. There is no doubt that he would have liked to subject the pope to conciliar consent but neither is there any doubt that this is not what he did. This was evidently not the result of an oversight. The difference between consultation and consent was perfectly familiar.[9] The reason therefore must have been that syllogistic reasoning on jurisprudential grounds alone was capable of taking him exactly to the point at which he could demand that general councils had to be convoked whenever laws were to be made – not one step further. As a result the cogency of his argument was undermined by an unacknowledged discrepancy between what he demanded (consultation) and the reason he offered for his demand (what touches all must be approved by all), a discrepancy between locutionary meaning and illocutionary act that threw a fundamental doubt on his intention.

This is not to deny the magnitude of his achievement, and neither is it to belittle the courage it must have taken him to ask Clement V to his face for unprecedented limitations on the papal plenitude of power. Indeed, in one respect Durant's uncanny ability to convey a revolutionary intention (the pope should be subjected to the authority of councils) by restating conventional wisdom (the pope should consult with councils on matters of common concern) was a considerable asset: it made it virtually impossible to prove that his intention did in fact transgress the limits of convention – which may explain the rage with which John XXII would remember his activities in Vienne. But there was an element of bluffing in this defensive cleverness, for there inevitably comes a point at which the question 'what do you really mean?' is raised, a point, in other words, at which illocutionary acts themselves become the subject of debate. It seems doubtful that at that point Durant would have confessed the revolutionary nature

---

[9] See, e.g., Post, *Studies*, pp. 110–27, 160–2; Langmuir, 'Per commune consilium'; Congar, 'Quod omnes tangit'; Watt, 'The Constitutional Law of the College of Cardinals'; Tierney, *Foundations*, pp. 109–17; Tierney, 'Hostiensis and Collegiality'; Brown, 'Cessante causa'. On the other hand 'concilium' was often confused with 'consilium', and Durant used the terms almost interchangeably; see Michaud-Quantin, *Universitas*, pp. 135–41; Congar, 'Quod omnes tangit', pp. 229, 245.

of his intentions. As early as in the general preface of his treatise he declared that 'obedience is better than sacrifice, because sacrifice is performed with the flesh of another, whereas obedience is a sacrifice of ourselves'.[10] Obedience, however, turned out to be a sacrifice of himself in ways that he did not intend. It split the foundations of his programme to reform the church. The weakness was unspoken but very real and it had consequences far beyond the point at which it can be clearly identified. His fundamental goal remained conformity with the law because he was convinced that the law expressed the will of God. Hence, in spite of his conviction that the papacy fell short of pagan standards of morality, he had no means by which to challenge papal supremacy. He failed to ask directly for conciliar consent as a condition for papal government, not because he was afraid of retribution from the pope, but because his own attachment to the law deprived him of a basis on which to ask for such consent – and hence he was afraid of retribution from the pope.

It would therefore be rash to dismiss the disagreements among Durant's interpreters as entirely unfounded or motivated purely by subjective reasons.[11] His ideas themselves invite contradictory assessments. In his desire not to speak with any other voice than that of the authorities he deprived himself of a means by which to state his intentions clearly, indeed, deprived himself of a means by which to keep a firm grasp on his intention. No wonder that the personal preferences of modern historians were able to assert themselves so freely: they simply occupied an interpretative space that was left open by Durant himself – the space between locutionary meaning and illocutionary act. Therefore it is meaningless to try and reduce his views to systematic clarity, whether it is in terms of 'papalism' or 'conciliarism' or others that have yet to be invented. The point is the ambivalence itself. It helps to explain not only Durant's failure at the council of Vienne but also the failure of the conciliar movement. Perhaps it even helps to explain the difficulties repeatedly encountered by modern liberals in their attempts to withstand the appeal of demands for unconditional obedience.

[10] 'Secundum prophetam Samuelem melior est enim obedientia quam victima . . . quia . . . in obedientia propria, in victima aliena caro mactatur.' *TMA* prefatio, fol. 4ra. For the complete text see above, pp. 116f.
[11] See above, pp. 12–16.

# PART III

# THE INCIDENCE OF POWER

The church of Rome and its presidents aim to usurp what belongs to the minor and the middling ranks. The words of Christ are fulfilled in them: 'And I, if I be lifted up from earth, will draw all unto me.' Therefore the entire world is in disarray, the church is wounded and oppressed and, in the words of Gregory, the order of the church has been uprooted.

William Durant, *Tractatus Minor* 8

*Chapter 8*

# THE SUBLIMATION OF REFORM

On 27 April 1311, Pope Clement V forgave King Philip of France in a public consistory in Avignon for everything that he had done against the memory of Pope Boniface VIII, and in his excuse declared that the king had acted out of good intentions, in good faith, and with good zeal.[1]

Continuator of Martinus Polonus[1]

When Durant arrived in Vienne he may have thought that the chances of restoring true concord in the church were still good. The papacy had not yet completely recovered from the defeat it had suffered at Anagni, and Pope Clement V seemed weak. Philip IV, meanwhile, had kept the promise of the *paréage*, and the nobility of the Gévaudan was losing its independence. Assured of royal friendship, convinced of papal weakness, and ready to address a European audience, Durant set out to promote a lasting constitutional rearrangement of the church which he hoped would arrest the deterioration of the world, restore the bishops' honour, and realize the common good.

He was to be disappointed. If Anagni had demonstrated anything at all, it was that the pope had little hope of conducting any stable policy, much less an independent one, if he continued to be locked in battle with the most powerful monarchy in Europe. Friendly relations with the king of France had to be restored. Clement therefore either struck the most offensive bulls of Boniface VIII from the papal registers or reinterpreted their meaning to suit the king and announced that Philip had been moved to his attacks on Boniface VIII by nothing but the best intentions. He consented to an investigation of the Templars and gave no sign

---

[1] 'Anno Domini 1311, quarto die exitus mensis Aprilis, scilicet 5. Kalendas Maii, in Avinione per Clementem papam fuit in consistorio publico excusatus Philippus, rex Franciae, de his quae egerat contra memoriam Bonifacii quondam papae, et pronuntiatum ad excusationem regis quod egerat ea in bona intentione, et bono animo, ac zelo.' Dupuy, *Histoire*, p. 614.

that he wished to prosecute Philip for having arrested the members of the order – a violation of ecclesiastical liberty that was much worse than the arrest of Bishop Bernard Saisset, which had provoked the final conflict with Boniface VIII. He granted tenths to Philip in 1310 and 1312 and a six-year tenth in 1313.[2] Finally, he organized the last of the great medieval papal councils and supervised the last major additions to the body of classical canon law. Thus Clement V removed the most significant impediments to restoring the papal plenitude of power and laid the foundations for Avignon.[3]

Clement's policies came to fruition at the council of Vienne. True, in spite of Philip's support he failed to persuade the council to condemn the Templars in a formal trial, which cast lasting doubt on his treatment of the order and made him 'furiously angry with the prelates'.[4] But that did not prevent him from abolishing the order anyway, 'not by way of a definitive sentence, but by way of apostolic provision or ordination'.[5] And when the prelates objected to his plans to transfer the Templars' properties to the Hospitallers, he let them know in no uncertain terms that, 'if they should advise him to transfer the properties to the Hospitallers, he would be pleased to do so with their consent. But if not, he would most certainly do so anyway, whether they liked it or not.'[6] And so he did. The crowning moment came when he presided with Philip IV over the council's second solemn session, at which the order of

[2] His predecessor Benedict XI had already granted a two-year tenth in 1304, which put an end to the bargaining between the French clergy and the King that had resulted in such important privileges for the clergy; Strayer, *Reign of Philip the Fair*, p. 257.

[3] The most familiar image of Clement still is that of an extravagant nepotist who capitulated abjectly before the temporal authority of France; see, e.g., Oakley, *Western Church*, pp. 38, 43; Haller, *Das Papsttum*, 5:166. Perhaps. But instead of deploring Clement's weakness and his losses we might do better to ask what he could have done differently and to recognize how successfully he prepared the ground for John XXII; see for example Southern's dispassionate statement, *Western Society*, p. 133, that 'in 1309 Clement V moved to Avignon. In most ways it was a very good thing.'

[4] 'Papa movetur ob hoc vehementer contra prelatos.' Müller, *Konzil von Vienne*, pp. 133–45, here p. 135 n. 79.

[5] 'Non per modum definitivae sententiae, sed per modum provisionis seu ordinationis apostolicae.' Müller, *Konzil von Vienne*, pp. 196–200, here p. 198 n. 8. It has been suggested that William Durant the Younger had a hand in formulating this solution; see Naz, *DDC*, 5:1014. But there appears to be no concrete evidence to support such a contention.

[6] 'Finalment dix lo papa als prelats, que, si ells conseylaven, que faes la dita applicatio al Espital, a ell plauria, que ho pogues fer de conseyl dells. Si no que ell ho faria e ho entenia a fer, volguessen ells o no!' Finke, *Papsttum und Untergang*, 2:299; Müller, *Konzil von Vienne*, pp. 219–35, here p. 222. The report comes from the usually well informed Aragonese observers.

the Templars was formally suppressed and plans were promulgated for a new crusade. That was the point at which the rift
between the temporal and the spiritual monarchy was finally,
officially, and publicly healed, the moment when the church of
Avignon was founded. The losers were prelates such as Durant
who had dreamed of an autonomous episcopate.

Under these circumstances the tension between hierarchical and
republican ideas of order with which Durant himself had struggled
in the *Tractatus Maior* was bound to be laid bare and deepened to a
point at which the grand conciliar vision of the Christian commonwealth could no longer be sustained. As a result Durant himself
revised his programme of reform; conceding papal claims on
supremacy, concentrating on improving the education of the
clergy, and replacing recitations of the law with moral criticisms,
he backed away from his attack on the 'presidents of the
monarchy', abandoned the constitutional reform of the church,
and made his peace with the emergence of absolute papal government. He probably disliked the direction in which he was thus
forced to move, but there can be little doubt that in a fundamental
way it was consistent with the ambiguous logic of his own ideas,
indeed, with the ambiguous logic of medieval ecclesiastical reform.

The contents of this and the following chapter are therefore
something in the nature of an epilogue to a case that has been stated
on the preceding pages. They are meant to illustrate the manner in
which Durant performed a change of course that was rooted
neither in Pope Clement V's resistance to his ideas at the council of
Vienne nor in Pope John XXII's outright hostility, but in his own
failure to choose decisively between obedience to ancient law and
constitutional government. As early as the eleventh century Pope
Gregory VII had made it clear that obedience to ancient law was
unthinkable unless there were a single institution with ultimate and
undivided responsibility for the state of the church: the papacy.
Durant's retreat from constitutional reform was simply an admission that Gregory VII had been right. If that admission amounted
to defeat, and if in his later age Durant declined from prominence,
this decline and that defeat were not effected by any ruthless
exercise of force on the part of the papacy, but by Durant's own
secret sympathy for absolute government. Hence his decline was
nothing like a noble battle to assert the principles of liberty against
an overweening tyranny; on the contrary, its most striking feature
was its unceremonious banality – worlds apart from the dramatic

end of Pope Boniface VIII, who paid with his life for his dignity, or of Pope Gregory VII, who died in exile because he had loved justice.

William Durant the Younger's fate at the council of Vienne and in his later years may therefore help to explain, not only why no general councils ever met in Avignon, but also why the great conciliar movement of the fifteenth century, after a glorious beginning, suffered an ignominious and similarly undramatic defeat. When great conciliarists like Cesarini, Piccolomini, and Nicholas of Cusa abandoned the council of Basle and made their peace with the papacy, they, too, did not simply succumb to the superior force of circumstance. Rather, they, too, were confessing what Durant had confessed more than a hundred years before: that there exists an essential link between the unconditional authority of law and absolute sovereignty.

### RECEPTION OF THE 'TRACTATUS MAIOR' IN VIENNE

Ever since Ewald Müller published his monumental study of the council's history it has been well established that the suggestions for reform submitted by the clergy came first to the attention of a committee of five cardinals that had been especially appointed to digest them for presentation to the council.[7] But no one so far seems to have noticed that William Durant the Younger's *Tractatus Maior*, too, was studied by the cardinals' committee. For, among the surviving fragments of the committee's records is a report to the pope about objections the province of Bourges had raised concerning inroads made by temporal rulers on ecclesiastical liberties.[8] The first part of this report referred to 'certain general matters which have been set forth in a booklet of remedies and which it would take too much space to list here in detail. They do not relate to the individual headings that we have distinguished

---

[7] Müller, *Konzil von Vienne*, pp. 117f.

[8] The grievances of Bourges are printed as part of the 'Vorschläge des leitenden Comités zur Erledigung der von den Prälaten eingereichten Beschwerden' in Ehrle, 'Ein Bruchstück', pp. 399–417, here pp. 415–17; cf. Müller, *Konzil von Vienne*, pp. 471–3. Bourges was one province among many that had raised objections about temporal inroads. But whereas the cardinals rearranged the submissions from other churches according to topic headings of their own devising, those of Bourges were left intact and described separately at the very end of the report.

above, but rather consist of certain general provisions about the reform of the universe.'[9] 'General provisions about the reform of the universe' would surely fit the ideas Durant developed in the *Tractatus Maior*. That the *Tractatus Maior* was in fact the text involved is borne out by the second part of the report, which lists a number of specific remedies for the temporal lords' oppression of the church, all of which are familiar from the *Tractatus Maior*.[10] Some of the phraseology is the same as well.[11] And there is one particularly striking similarity: the report combines two subjects that are not intrinsically related (the penalties to be imposed on the offspring of violators of ecclesiastical liberties and the proper terms to be observed in passing excommunications) in the same way Durant did in *Tractatus Maior* 2.94. There can thus be no doubt at all that the cardinals' report refers directly to the *Tractatus Maior*.[12] Unfortunately we cannot tell precisely which aspects of the *Tractatus Maior* the cardinal who drafted the report had in mind when he characterized them as 'general provisions about the reform of the universe'. But we do know that he did not like them:

[9] 'Adduntur tamen aliqua generalia, que longum esset omnia particulariter hic ponere et sunt distincte in quaterno remediorum; nec faciunt ad articulos singulariter supra distinctos; sed sunt quedam provisiones generales ad reformationem universi ... Si tamen mandet vestra sanctitas poni de verbo ad verbum in hoc quaterno, ponentur, quia alias non possunt sub singularibus articulis comprehendi.' Ehrle, 'Ein Bruchstück', p. 415:13–20; cf. Müller, *Konzil von Vienne*, p. 471. Müller believed that Clement did in fact order the committee to write those general provisions down and that they are identical with the measures listed in the second part of the report. But that is unlikely. The measures in the second half could easily have been included in the preceding sections of the report and they were certainly nothing like 'general provisions about the reform of the universe'.
[10] 'Provincia Bituricensis ponit remedia generaliter contra omnia gravamina, que per dominos temporales ecclesiis, personis ac bonis ecclesiasticis inferuntur.' Ehrle, 'Ein Bruchstück', pp. 415:21–417:12, here 415:21–3. The most important points were these: the reach of Boniface VIII's constitution *Quoniam* (VI.5.11.19) was to be specified more clearly; cf. *TMA* 2.70, fol. 47ra. Temporal lords who were excommunicated for infringing upon ecclesiastical rights, as well as their offspring down to the second, third, and fourth degree, were to be prevented from obtaining ecclesiastical benefices; cf. *TMA* 2.94 (3.25), fol. 58ra–b. Excommunications and interdicts were to take effect only after thirty days had passed; cf. *TMA* 2.94 (3.25), fol. 58rb. And lay defenders of the church were to be established by temporal powers, as was demanded by existing conciliar legislation; cf. *TMA* 2.40, fol. 34ra.
[11] Compare the use of *mucro episcopalis* and *mortalis* to describe excommunications in Ehrle, 'Ein Bruchstück', p. 416:36–8, with *TMA* 2.38, fol. 33ra, and *TMA* 2.28, fol. 28ra.
[12] It seems even conceivable that Durant served as an official spokesman for his province. There is no evidence for any other suggestions from Bourges, and the only other bishops from the province of Bourges to attend the council were the archbishop, Giles of Rome, and the bishop of Limoges, not counting the exempt bishop of Le Puy; Müller, *Konzil von Vienne*, p. 664. On Durant's excellent relations with Giles of Rome see above, pp. 253f.

'In my judgment these provisions for the reform of the universe are not just difficult in several respects, but impossible.'[13]

The reaction of the cardinals' committee was hardly an auspicious beginning, and more serious troubles were to follow. We hear about them in two letters that Pope John XXII wrote to the king and queen of France much later and under very different circumstances – in April 1319, seven years after the council had been concluded.[14] As it happened, John XXII had been a member of the cardinals' committee and was therefore well placed to judge Durant's activity at the council of Vienne; perhaps the critical opinion just quoted came from his own pen. He told the king what he remembered about William Durant the Younger's conduct at the council:

He complains of being treated unjustly. But perhaps he intends something other than he pretends, namely to place a schism between yourself and this see – Lord forbid – just as he studiously laboured at the council of Vienne to place a schism between the prelates and Pope Clement V of happy memory.[15]

We are fortunate to have an assessment of Durant's ideas by as astute a witness as Pope John XXII. His words may be the single most important contemporary clue to the role Durant has played in history, and they confirm our basic interpretation of what he attempted to achieve in the *Tractatus Maior*. Of course, Durant would have put it differently: he would have said that his purpose was not to produce a schism but to confirm the proper relations between the ranks and orders of the hierarchy. Indeed, he would have reversed the charge of schism and pinned it on the pope. But shorn of its censorious quality Pope John's judgment is entirely appropriate: Durant wished to protect the limits of the diocese from papal interference and to increase the distance between the temporal and spiritual powers; from the perspective of a pope who

---

[13] 'Meo iudicio [in: add. Ehrle] aliquibus non solum continent difficultatem sed et impossibilitatem.' Ehrle, 'Ein Bruchstück', p. 415:17–18. Müller, *Konzil von Vienne*, p. 471, on the other hand, rejoiced over the broad view taken by the grievances of Bourges: 'So werden hier endlich einmal grundsätzliche Erwägungen angestellt, die uns natürlich einen ganz anderen Einblick in die hier umstrittenen Probleme geben als jenes Gewirre von Einzelbeschwerden und Remedia.'

[14] We shall consider the circumstances below, pp. 309–11.

[15] 'Sed ipse intendens aliud forsitan quam pretendat, videlicet scisma, quod absit, inter te et Sedem istam ponere sicut et in Viennensi consilio inter felicis recordationis Clementem papam quintum et prelatos studiose ponere laboravit, injuste conqueritur secum agi.' John XXII, *LS* no. 850 (10.IV.1319).

insisted on subordinating the bishops to his power and on close cooperation with the king of France that was the same as promoting schism. Two rather different conceptions of schism thus clashed at Vienne. One defined unity in terms of a universal concord, the other in terms of the pope's *potestas iurisdictionis* and his ability to cooperate with the temporal monarchy of France.

In writing to the queen of France Pope John added some interesting details:

At the council of Vienne William Durant tried to create a schism from our predecessor, Pope Clement V of blessed memory, to whom the ties of fealty were binding him: he fabricated a book against him and this see, as is known to our brothers and to many others who were present at the time. But when this came to our predecessor's notice, he sought his forgiveness and dedicated the book to him with what appeared to be the greatest humility, as those know who procured their reconciliation.[16]

A lot is left unsaid in this account. It is likely, but not certain, that the book in question was the *Tractatus Maior*; it is unclear whether Durant was actually engaged in secret agitation or merely charged with doing so, perhaps because he failed to clear his book with Clement before distributing it to others; and it is not certain if the book he dedicated to the pope was quite the same as the one that had provoked the incident. Unless new evidence comes to light, we shall never know precisely how and why Durant provoked the displeasure of the pope at the council of Vienne.[17] But we do learn two important things: Durant got into trouble with the pope because of what he wrote, and his trouble ended in submission.

[16] 'In consilio siquidem Viennensi, contra felicis recordationis Clementem papam quintum, predecessorem nostrum, cui ipsum fidelitatis vinculum astringebat, scisma suscitare voluit et temptavit librum contra ipsum et Sedem hujusmodi, sicut notum est fratribus nostris qui tunc aderant et multis aliis, fabricando, et demum cum hec ad prefati predecessoris nostri notitiam pervenissent, librum ipsum cum humilitate apparenti maxima eidem predecessori nostro, petita venia, assignavit sicut sciunt qui reconciliationem hujusmodi procurarunt.' John XXII, *LS* no. 849 (10.IV.1319).

[17] It has been suggested that Durant revised his book as a result of the clash with Clement V. Haller, *Papsttum und Kirchenreform*, pp. 58–60, believed that the whole treatise must have been revised; Müller, *Konzil von Vienne*, pp. 593, 595, believed that Durant added the preface after the clash with Clement, but did not otherwise revise the text; Posch, 'Reformvorschläge', p. 289, believed that the third part of the treatise in the printed editions did not belong to the original version. Most of those suspicions are founded on the confusion in the printed editions. There is a possibility that a few chapters may have been omitted from the *Tractatus Minor*; see below, p. 295 n. 20. But the evidence for that is inconclusive and there is no other evidence for revisions at all.

'TRACTATUS MINOR'

While the council of Vienne was in session, William Durant the
Younger wrote a second book on the reform of the church, which
we have called *Tractatus Minor*.[18] The differences between this
book and the *Tractatus Maior* provide invaluable evidence for the
effect of Durant's experiences at the council of Vienne on his
conception of reform. These differences are considerable. The
*Minor* is only about a quarter of the length of the *Maior* and has an
entirely different structure.[19] Formally, it consists of a single series
of thirty-four chapters; there are no parts or sections. Three parts
can nevertheless be distinguished substantively: the first is devoted
to the principles on which reform should rest; the second to the ills
that ought to be reformed; and the third to specific remedies. The
*Minor* thus substitutes a simple, topical arrangement for the
complicated mixture of systematic analysis with chronological
procedure that is characteristic of the *Maior*. It also has a very
different way of dealing with the legal sources. As in the *Maior*
Durant regularly quotes conciliar and papal laws, but he does not
quote them quite as frequently, and he does not refer the reader to
the source of the quotation in the canonical collections. Most
commonly he merely mentions the name of the author and
continues with a direct quotation. While this makes it difficult and
time consuming to identify the law at issue, it also frees the text
from the relentless alternation of intelligible sentences with legal
ciphers that is so typical of the *Tractatus Maior*.

Thus the appearance of the *Minor* is different indeed. Instead of
forcing the reader to shift his attention to another topic with almost

[18] The *Tractatus Minor* regularly speaks of the council as present, whereas the *Tractatus Maior* speaks of it as future. Compare especially *TMI* 9 (3.32), fol. 62vb, 'presenti sacro concilio', with *TMA* prefatio, fol. 4ra, 'futurum concilium'. The colophon of the *Minor* declares outright that 'ista dictata fuerunt in concilio generali Vienne celebrato per reverendum patrem dominum Guillelmum Dei gratia episcopum Mimatensem'. *TMI* colophon, fol. 74vb. Unaware of the distinction between *Maior* and *Minor*, Müller, *Konzil von Vienne*, p. 593 n. 28, and Göller, 'Zur Geschichte', p. 16 n. 2, misinterpreted this evidence. Müller, ibid., also interpreted *dictata* as referring to some form of public agitation, but that is impossible to maintain on the basis of a single word with an ambiguous meaning that may well signify nothing more dramatic than 'compose'. We know that the *Minor* was written at Vienne, but we have no information about its specific function at the council at all.
[19] The *Minor* consists of 34 chapters, as compared to the *Maior*'s 104, and none of them is longer than about a folio in the *editio princeps*, while many fill no more than just one column. The whole amounts to roughly fourteen folios, compared to fifty-seven for the *Maior*.

every chapter, Durant now offers a single line of argument that
smoothly integrates quotations from the laws into the text and
suppresses technical references. The *Minor* is legato compared to
the staccato of the *Maior*. The law no longer occupies centre stage
and Durant pays more attention to rhetorical devices – impas-
sioned speech, apostrophe, and similes – that serve to capture the
reader's imagination. On every count, the *Minor* is more personal
and easier to read. Conversely, however, it does not have the
manifest authority that the presence of the law gave the *Maior*. The
*Maior* was a monument; the *Minor* is an essay.

These are the formal differences. The differences in substance are
best approached by a description of the contents of the *Tractatus
Minor*. The first three chapters deal with what Durant referred to as
three general methods of reform, beginning with the church of
Rome:[20]

Concerning the question of how the universal church can be usefully,
permanently, and effectively reformed, it appears that the guiding reason
must be provided by the head, the sacrosanct church of Rome, which is

[20] In the manuscripts these three chapters are curiously numbered 1, 8, and 9. (Hence the
final chapter of the *Tractatus Minor* is numbered 40, although the sum of all chapters is
only thirty-four.) I used to believe that the six 'missing' chapters 2 to 7 did originally
exist, but were lost, perhaps because Durant excised them in order to placate Pope
Clement; see Fasolt, 'A New View', pp. 309f. But now this seems more than unlikely to
me, and for two reasons. First, the first two chapters of the *Minor*, numbered 1 and 8, are a
composite of quotations taken verbatim or with minor changes from *TMA* 1.1–3 and
*TMA* 2.96: compare the beginning of *TMI* 1 (3.1), fol. 52ra–b, with *TMA* 2.96 (3.27),
fol. 58va, and the rest of *TMI* 1 (3.1) and all of *TMI* 8 (3.31) with *TMA* 1.1–3. Since there
is no evidence at all that anything is missing from *TMA* 1.1–3, and since the parallel
between *TMI* 1–8 and *TMA* 1.1–3 is very close indeed, it is difficult to imagine what
could possibly have been the purpose of six entire chapters between *TMI* 1 and *TMI* 8;
the first two chapters of the *Tractatus Minor* are a perfectly smooth and natural echo of the
argument Durant unfolded in the first three chapters of the *Tractatus Maior*. Second, the
first three chapters of the *Minor, TMI* 1, 8, and 9, deal with three parallel methods of
reform, which are defined as such by the author. That, too, suggests that there is nothing
missing from the text. It thus seems probable that the three opening chapters of the
*Tractatus Minor* were consecutively written, but at a later point erroneously numbered 1,
8, 9. This conclusion is complicated, but not altered, by the numbering of the 'methods of
reform' in the chapter headings. P, fols. 93r, 94v, entitles the third extant chapter (*TMI* 9
(3.32)) 'de tercio modo reformationis ecclesie'. M, fol. 58vb, and the printed editions,
however, entitle the same chapter 'de secundo modo reformationis ecclesie'. But
'secundo' is certainly wrong, for, at a later point, namely *TMI* 26 (3.49), fol. 70ra–b,
Durant referred the reader back to the third chapter, and on this occasion P, fol. 106rb,
M, fol. 65vb, and the printed editions all agree on referring to it as 'de tercio modo
reformationis ecclesie'. A copyist, who was followed by M and the printed editions, must
thus have changed 'tercio' in the heading of the third chapter into 'secundo' – perhaps
because the second extant chapter (*TMI* 8 (3.31)) is introduced with an ambiguous
'porro' – but forgot to make the same change at the point of the cross-reference in *TMI*
26 (3.49).

the head of all other churches . . . For, as testifies Isaiah, when the head languishes, all the body's members suffer; and when those who march in front in order to bear the burdens of sin give way, those who follow behind will only too easily retreat; and if prelates act perversely, their subjects follow their example readily, for, as Seneca says, if words are contradicted by deeds, deeds move more strongly than words.[21]

Emphasizing both hierarchical subordination and papal primacy, Durant thus leaves no doubt that the church of Rome is fully responsible for reform. A few lines later he declares even more directly that

the church of Rome is the mistress and judge of all others, and its catholic rector must not be judged by anyone because his see was given a singular power over all other churches, first, by the merits of Apostle Peter and, second, by the authority of councils according to the Lord's command.[22]

To be sure, the concluding reference to the authority of councils balanced the overriding stress on the papal plenitude of power and on its derivation from St Peter. Moreover, Durant went on to launch a blistering attack on clerical misconduct, including the conduct of the papacy.[23] But first of all he failed to elaborate on the potentially explosive notion that papal primacy was partially

---

[21] 'De reformatione ecclesie universalis, et quod in ea est *primo a capite, scilicet Romana ecclesia, ★ [P] prelatis, et aliis superioribus inchoandum. Sane quantum ad reformationem universalis ecclesie utiliter et perseverabiliter ac efficaciter faciendum, videtur quod a capite ratio sit edenda, videlicet a sacrosancta Romana ecclesia, que caput est omnium aliarum . . . Capite namque languescente omnia corporis membra dolent testimonio Esaye, et cum incurvantur hi qui preeunt ad ferenda onera peccatorum, facile inclinantur sequentes, et si quid perverse agitur a prelatis, cum facta verbis contraria plus quam ipsa verba secundum Senecam moveant, trahitur a subditis de facili in exemplum.' *TMI* 1 (3.1), fol. 52ra. Cf. *TMA* 2.96 (3.27), fol. 58va, and Isaiah 1:5. For parallel uses of the same passage from Isaiah in a secular context see Digard, *Philippe le Bel*, 2:265, and Boutaric, 'Notices', p. 200.

[22] 'Ut psalmista ait, oculi servorum, id est subditorum et laicorum, sunt in manibus et operationibus dominorum suorum, id est prelatorum superiorum, et oculi ancille, id est universalis ecclesie, in manibus domine sue, hoc est Romane ecclesie, que domina ac iudex est aliarum, cuius rector catholicus non iudicatur a quoquam, cum eius sedi primum Petri apostoli meritum, deinde secura iussione Domini conciliorum autoritas singularem in ecclesiis tradiderit potestatem, sicut scribitur in decretis.' *TMI* 1 (3.1), fol. 52rb. Cf. Psalm 122:2, D.17 p.c.6.

[23] The pertinent passages in *TMI* 1 (3.1), fol. 52ra–b, consisting of references to the golden rule of natural law, to Augustine's conception of priests as doctors who must first heal themselves, to Balaam, whose madness was exposed by an animal, to Jews and pagans who reproach the clergy, and so on, were compiled in their entirety from *TMA* 1.1, fol. 4rb–vb. They recur in an almost identical sequence and they culminate in the same conclusion 'quod beatus Petrus considerans ait tempus esse ut iudicium incipiat a domo Dei'. *TMI* 1 (3.1), fol. 61va.

derived from conciliar authority – not to mention that this was not by any means his own idea but quoted word for word from Gratian's *Decretum*[24] – and, second, he concluded the first chapter of the *Minor* by repeating that the pope was entirely exempt from human judgment (unless he fell into heresy), and that the church of Rome was solely responsible for demonstrating 'how to conduct oneself in the house of the Lord'.[25] The first chapter of the *Minor* may thus be characterized as a revision of the first chapter of the *Maior* that places far greater stress on papal primacy, the self-reform of Rome, and the responsibility of Rome for the rest of the church.[26] It is, therefore, no accident that those interpreters who were inclined to argue for Durant's adhesion to the papacy and against his radical intentions have often taken their cues from the *Tractatus Minor*, without being aware, of course, that it was written under very different circumstances from the *Maior*.[27]

The second chapter of the *Minor* may similarly be described as a revision of the *Maior*.[28] It takes up the ideas about the law that Durant had expressed in the second and third chapters of the earlier work. Durant begins with familiar observations about the two kinds of law, natural and human, and the two powers, spiritual and temporal, that ought to enforce those laws without exception; he continues with a few quotations from the rubrics on the 'power of superiors', on dispensations, and on exemptions; and he concludes

---

24 It may well be that Durant's quotation of D.17 p.c.6 ought to be considered as evidence for his continued desire to derive papal primacy from conciliar authority, as does Scholz, *Publizistik*, p. 221, but it is surely misleading not to add that the formulation was Gratian's.

25 'Et quia aliqua culpa vel negligentia aut remissio, si qua reperiretur in eo, ad mancipium gehenne innumerabiles populos trahit, nec huiusmodi culpas istic redarguere mortalium ullus presumit, quia cunctos ipse iudicaturus a nemine est iudicandus, nisi a fide deprehendatur devius, sicut Bonifacius papa et martyr scribit, habet secundum Nicolaum papam et sanctam sinodum sacrosancta ecclesia Romana in sinu suo colligere causam suam et in se ipsa ostendere qualiter alios in domo Dei oporteat conversari.' *TMI* 1 (3.1), fol. 61va–b. Cf. D.40 c.1, D.40 c.6, D.21 c.7.

26 The same tendency is evident in the body of the *Minor*. If Durant had once insisted on the equality of all apostles in order to defend the independence of the bishops from the pope, he now finds nothing wrong with admitting that 'in omnem Italiam et Galliam et Ispaniam et Affricam atque Siciliam et insulas interiacentes nullum instituisse ecclesias nisi eos quos venerabilis apostolus Petrus aut successores eius constituerunt sacerdotes, nec in predictis provinciis alius apostolus invenitur aut legitur docuisse'. *TMI* 32 (3.45), fol. 72ra.

27 See for example Viollet, p. 118, Posch, 'Die Reformvorschläge', p. 290, Müller, *Konzil von Vienne*, p. 593 n. 27, and Torquebiau, 'Le Gallicanisme', pp. 286f.

28 'De modo generali per quem universalis ecclesia deberet reformari, scilicet ut servarentur iura, et revocarentur in contrarium attentata.' *TMI* 8 (3.31), fol. 61vb.

with a concise restatement of the principle that rulers, even if they can change the law, are not exempt from reason.[29] But in the middle of the chapter Durant adds a new perspective:

Although the authority of age should be revered, our time of novelty has wickedly neglected what was well established in antiquity. The spiritual and temporal magistrates were set in order and distinguished from each other so that there would be some ranks that are major, some middling, and some minor. Each of these ranks was meant to have control over its proper office; each was meant to exercise the appurtenances of its office according to its rank; and what was delegated to one office was not in any way to be disturbed by another. But our times are times of novelty and restlessness because we have abandoned rank and order. According to St Augustine, whatever is less ordered is not at rest, but what is ordered is at rest. The church of Rome and its presidents, however, neither preserve the ancient order of ruling the world and the church, nor do they leave to each his jurisdiction. They rather aim to usurp what belongs to the minor and the middling ranks so that the words are fulfilled in them: 'And I, if I be lifted up from earth, will draw all unto me.' Therefore the entire world is in disarray, the church is wounded and oppressed and, in the words of Gregory, the order of the church has been uprooted.[30]

This is a better, and gloomier, summary of Durant's basic convictions than can be found anywhere in the *Tractatus Maior*. Insisting on the authority of ancient law, condemning the 'novelty' of the present, recalling the principles of the great order of difference, and quoting Augustine and Gregory, he drew a firm conclusion: the arrogance of Rome had thrown the entire world in turmoil. That was the stark and hopeless diagnosis of his times to which Durant was driven by his insistence on the laws, and it

---

[29] 'Consideranda est itaque ratio equitatis, ut sacrosancta Romana ecclesia, que iustitie mater est, in nullo ab ea dissentire videatur.' *TMI* 8 (3.31), fol. 62rb.

[30] 'Nam quod antiquitas bene statuit, novitas nostri temporis, licet veneranda esset vetustatis auctoritas, male neglexit. Et cum magistratus spirituales et temporales digesti fuerint et distincti ut alii maiores, alii medii, et alii minores existerint, et ad quosque eorum que ipsorum officiis appropriata fuerant pertinerent, et gradatim ad eorum officia pertinentia exercerent, et que uni officio deputata fuerant nequaquam ab alio turbarentur, novitas nostri temporis sub inquietudine degit, quia dictum gradum et ordinem derelinquit. Secundum namque Augustinum minus ordinata inquieta sunt, ordinata vero quiescunt, et ideo, quia antiqua ordinatio de regimine mundi et ecclesie et sua unicuique jurisdictio a Romana ecclesia et presidentibus non servatur [et ordo . . . attestatur: *om*. P], sed ad se que ad minores et medios pertinent trahere volunt, ut in eis verificetur illud: "Cum exaltatus fuero a terra omnia traham ad meipsum", mundus turbatur universalis, ecclesia leditur et gravatur, et ordo ecclesiasticus confunditur, sicut Gregorius attestatur.' *TMI* 8 (3.31), fols. 61vb–62ra. Cf. John 12:32, C.11 q.1 c.39.

instilled in him the fear of doom. The words that were fulfilled in the papacy were after all the words with which upon his final entry to Jerusalem Christ had announced the judgment of the world: 'Now is the judgment of this world: now shall the prince of this world be cast out. And I, if I be lifted up from the earth, will draw all unto me.'[31]

At this point, as if to confirm that this conclusion left no hope of constitutional reform, the *Minor* ceases to parallel the *Maior*. In the third chapter, instead of turning his attention to general councils, Durant insists on the need to counter bad examples:

Third, the universal church could be reformed if the church of Rome were to remove, first from itself and then successively from prelates and the rest, the bad examples that are a scandal to the people, by which they are infected, so to speak, so that the rulers of the people, according to Isaiah, cause the name of the Lord to be blasphemed. For according to Augustine there is nothing that more effectively confounds and harms the church of God than to have to admit that clerics are worse than laymen.[32]

This is immediately followed by a passage in which Durant recited a vision of Isaiah about the desolation of Babylon and applied it to the present, creating a powerful image of the contemporary church as a deserted city with streets and mansions roamed by seven soulless creatures, which he identified with the seven mortal sins.[33] Perhaps this helped to introduce the notion of the 'Babylonian captivity'. It certainly afforded Durant an occasion to warn of the impending dangers for the church and to impress upon the

---

[31] 'Nunc iudicium est mundi: nunc princeps huius mundi eiicietur foras. Et ego si exaltatus fuero a terra, omnia traham ad me ipsum.' John 12:31–2. The Speculator had already used the same source to express his criticism of Roman centralization: 'Ecclesia tamen Romana, que tanquam domina omnia ad se trahit . . .' *Speculum iudiciale* 1.1, De dispensationibus 5.7, fol. 30v.

[32] '*Tertio* [P] posset universalis ecclesia reformari, si Romana ecclesia a se primo et gradatim a prelatis et aliis mala exempla tolleret, ex quibus scandalizatur et quasi inficitur populus universalis et nomen Domini dominatores populi secundum Esaiam ex hoc *faciunt* [P] blasphemari. Nam secundum Augustinum nihil magis confundit ecclesiam Dei vel ei officit quam dicere peiores sunt clerici quam laici.' *TMI* 9 (3.32), fol. 62va.

[33] 'Proh dolor quia videtur in ipsa ecclesia verificari dictum Esaie xxxiiii. in figuram Babylonice civitatis, gloriose in regnis et inclite in superbia Caldeorum, de qua dicitur: erit cubile draconum et pascua struthionum [et occurrent demonia: *om.* P]. Onocentaurus et pilosus clamabit alter ad alterum. Ibi *cubabit* [P] lamia et *inveniet* [P] sibi requiem. Ibi *habebit* [P] foveam ericius, et *enutriet* [P] catulos. Illic *congregabuntur* [P] milvi alter ad alterum.' *TMI* 9 (3.32), fol. 62va. Isaiah, 34:13–15, was actually speaking of Edom, not Babylon. The printed editions revised Durant's words according to the Vulgate, changing not only the future tense to the past, but also destroying the parallelism of seven animals with seven mortal sins.

pope, the cardinals, and the council that action could no longer be postponed:

If this holy council does not provide for suitable remedies against the aforesaid ills, which are manifestly and notoriously being committed in the church of God, the faith, which is dead without works according to St James, will be considered by believers and unbelievers alike to have perished through the fault of the prelates and the clergy . . . Events incomparably worse than those of the past will follow, and all of them will be blamed upon our lord the highest pontiff, his venerable college of cardinals, and this sacred council, who can and who must correct and withstand the aforementioned ills.[34]

In the next seven chapters Durant offers a quick review of the bad examples by which the church infected the world.[35] He arranges his charges according to the seven creatures of Isaiah's vision as symbols of the seven mortal sins.[36] Chapter by chapter, sin by sin, he relentlessly accumulates the evidence to show how the clergy has fallen prey to avarice, pride, lust, gluttony, envy, hate, and sloth – in short, to every conceivable vice. The substance of these charges is not unfamiliar from the *Maior*, but the impression they make on the reader is different indeed. By relying on the systematic framework of the seven mortal sins and illustrating each of them in some detail Durant not only manages to suggest that the corruption of the clergy exhausts the realm of possibilities completely, but also gives a new, more intimate, more strictly 'moral' quality to his case and fills his reader's mind with an overwhelming sense that the clergy are personally and individually responsible for inundating the world with a flood of nothing but ignorance, vice, and decay.

The remaining twenty-four chapters, the bulk of the *Tractatus Minor*, are smoothly linked to the final chapter of the preceding

---

[34] 'Et nisi in hoc sacro concilio provideatur de competenti remedio in premissis, que quasi manifeste et notorie in Dei ecclesia committuntur, fides, que secundum Jacobum sine operibus mortua est, dicetur per fideles et infideles in prelatis et personis ecclesiasticis . . . periisse . . . *Incomparabiliter* [P] peiora prioribus subsequentur, et omnia imputabuntur domino nostro summo pontifici eiusque venerabili collegio et huic sacro concilio, qui possunt et debent corrigere supradicta et obviare eisdem.' *TMI* 9 (3.32), fol. 62va–b. Cf. James 2:17.     [35] *TMI* 10–16 (3.33–39), fols. 63ra–66vb.

[36] *TMI* 10 (3.33), fol. 63ra–va, deals with avarice and ambition (*ericius*). *TMI* 11 (3.34), fols. 63va–64ra, deals with pride (*draco*). *TMI* 12 (3.35), fols. 64ra–65ra, deals with lust (*pilosus*). *TMI* 13 (3.36), fol. 65ra–vb, deals with gluttony and inebriation (*milvus*). *TMI* 14 (3.37), fols. 65vb–66ra, deals with envy (*lamia*). *TMI* 15 (3.38), fol. 66ra–va, deals with hate and anger (*onocentaurus*). And *TMI* 16 (3.39), fol. 66va–b, deals with sloth, negligence, and ignorance (*struthio*).

section, which deals with negligence.[37] In fact, they can be read as an extended list of remedies for three different kinds of negligence. The first is negligence of education.[38] Dealing in turn with prelates, curates, and other clerics, Durant suggests several ways to improve the education of the clergy, all of which are familiar from the *Tractatus Maior*.[39] The second kind of negligence concerns the care of souls: clerics are asked to reside in their churches; pluralism, which goes hand in hand with absenteeism, is to be ruled out; and Rome is not to keep churches vacant by interfering in elections.[40] In addition clerics should not let themselves be moved by unjustifiable mercy but must punish all notorious sinners with the necessary firmness.[41] The third kind of negligence concerns divine worship, which gives Durant another opportunity to rail against lascivious songs and irreverent motets.[42] The last four chapters of the *Minor* deal with the obligation of the clergy to take proper care of their buildings, vestments, and utensils, and to spend their revenues on charitable purposes.[43]

In many ways the *Tractatus Minor* resembles the *Tractatus Maior* very closely; it offers similar suggestions for reform, it proceeds from similar principles, and it does so in words that are sometimes directly quoted from the *Tractatus Maior*. But the similarities are balanced by differences that are at least as striking. Some merely reflect Durant's desire to soften the impact of a particular sugges-

---

[37] *TMI* 17–40 (3.40–63), fols. 66vb–75vb.

[38] This is considered in *TMI* 17–22, (3.40–5), fols. 66vb–69ra.

[39] *TMI* 17 (3.40), fols. 66vb–67ra, specifies qualifications for promotions to the prelacy. *TMI* 18 (3.41), fol. 67ra–b, deals with manuals of penance and confession. *TMI* 19 (3.42), fol. 67rb–va, deals with schools and curricula. *TMI* 20 (3.43), fols. 67vb–68rb, suggests ways of paying for the education of the clergy. *TMI* 21 (3.44), fol. 68rb–va, requires clerics to be able to earn a living. And *TMI* 22 (3.45), fols. 68va–69ra, demands that specific kinds of knowledge ought to be required from each rank of the hierarchy, and that glosses ought to be reduced to a 'compendium veritatis' to be approved by Rome.

[40] *TMI* 23–4 (3.46–7), fol. 69ra–b.     [41] *TMI* 25–6 (3.48–9), fols. 69va–70rb.

[42] *TMI* 27 (3.50), fol. 70rb–vb, insists on clerical attendance at mass. *TMI* 28 (3.51), fols. 70vb–71ra, condemns clerical preoccupation with collecting fees for attending mass. *TMI* 29 (3.52), fol. 71ra–b, condemns the laity's lax attitude to mass. *TMI* 30–2 (3.53–5), fols. 71rb–72ra, requires strict observance of holidays, communion three times a year, and the Roman order of the mass. *TMI* 33–4 (3.56–7), fol. 72ra–vb, calls for standardizing provincial and national liturgical customs, but allows exceptions for the regular clergy. *TMI* 35–6 (3.58–9), fols. 72vb–73rb, insists on keeping the laity from touching any of the holy objects used in mass.

[43] *TMI* 37 (3.60), fol. 73rb–va, asks that churches ought to be kept in good repair. *TMI* 38 (3.61), fol. 73va–b, insists on protecting ecclesiastical rights from temporal attacks. *TMI* 39 (3.62), fols. 73vb–74rb, calls on the clergy to share their income properly and bestow one part of it upon the poor. *TMI* 40 (3.63), fol. 74rb–vb, condemns the waste of ecclesiastical money on clothes, ornaments, food, drink, and relatives.

tion while keeping its substance intact. A good example is Durant's revision of his ideas about financing clerical education: in the *Tractatus Maior* he had asked for one-tenth of all ecclesiastical benefices to pay for the education of poor students, but in the *Tractatus Minor* the money was to come from pluralists, wealthy clerics, and 'certain parish churches which are so fat and so abundant that, even when an appropriate sum is reserved for their perpetual vicar, they can still pay for educating many students'.[44] That was bound to be more popular than taking 10 per cent from the revenues of every cleric with a benefice – but it would also embroil the reform of education in endless legal proceedings to determine who was a pluralist and which parish churches were unconscionably fat. Where the *Maior* placed the need to obtain a reliable source of income first, the *Minor* thus bowed to vested interests.

The most remarkable differences between the *Minor* and the *Maior*, however, consist of the omissions. Gone is the attack upon exemptions; gone is most of the struggle between bishops, monks, and friars; gone are the long disquisitions on the proper relationship between state and church, kings, noblemen, and clerics; gone is the idea that provincial councils ought to assume the role of an intermediary between the bishops and the church of Rome that would effectively enforce provincial laws and reduce appeals to papal courts; gone are the attack on begging, the call for new agents of enforcement, and the suggestion to do away with celibacy; gone, too, is the plan to give the church of Rome a stable source of income; and gone, of course, is the 'further limitation' of governmental power by general councils – the culmination of Durant's ideas about reform in the *Tractatus Maior*. The beginning of the *Tractatus Minor* contains the closest parallels to the *Tractatus Maior*, but precisely at the point where in the *Maior* Durant had turned from criticizing the 'power of superiors' to offering a proposal for major constitutional reform, the parallels come to a sudden end. Instead we find the meek suggestion that the church of Rome ought to remove bad examples successively from itself and its inferiors. Papal exemption from the law no longer seems to be an issue. In short, the *Tractatus Minor* lacks virtually all of what we have called the republican dimension of Durant's ideas.

---

[44] 'Posset etiam provideri predictis de aliquibus parochialibus ecclesiis que ita pingues sunt et abundantes quod, relicta congrua portione vicario perpetuo, possent de eis multi scholares in studio sustentari.' *TMI* 20 (3.43), fol. 68ra. Cf. the provisions of the *Maior*, above, p. 195.

These changes may surely be attributed to Durant's recognition that the resumption of friendly relations between Clement V and Philip IV placed unsurmountable obstacles in the way of constitutional reform. Nevertheless, it would be wrong to regard the *Tractatus Minor* as nothing but the result of a retreat. The *Minor* also signals an advance in a new direction, a further step in the internal transformation of the logic of reform that was foreshadowed by the *Maior*. There was nothing that Durant now saw more clearly than the 'abuses' practised by the church of Rome.[45] That made it possible for him to formulate his criticisms more acutely than before. But on the other hand he found himself condemned to the posture of a moralist without the means to control the exercise of power. As a result the field of action for reform was shifted away from politics and legislative change and sublimated to the higher plane of education, worship, and the care of souls. Durant himself thus distilled a concentrate from the *Tractatus Maior* that looks like a blueprint for the measures that were eventually taken by the council of Trent.[46]

There is therefore no contradiction between the *Tractatus Maior* and the *Tractatus Minor*; rather, there is a change of heart. Under the pressure of a power that had escaped from ancient law, the combination of the great order of difference with the commonwealth was transformed from a principle of action into a theoretical and ceremonial ideal. Henceforth the law was going to be separated from morality; henceforth reason of state was going to be left to its own mysterious devices. This is not to say that Durant's ideas had no effect on the decisions of the council of Vienne. Contrary to what Döllinger and Haller used to think, Ewald Müller has established that Durant inspired a good deal of the legislation of Vienne.[47] To give a few examples, the council agreed

[45] It is instructive to notice Durant's pronounced shift from insisting on the need for good examples in the *Tractatus Maior* to denouncing bad examples in the *Tractatus Minor*.

[46] Bellone, 'Cultura e studi', pp. 72–5, has highlighted the significance of Durant for the educational reforms of Trent.

[47] Döllinger, *Der Papst und das Concil*, pp. 241–3, Haller, *Papsttum und Kirchenreform*, pp. 65f., Müller, *Konzil von Vienne*, pp. 594f.; see also Viollet, pp. 120–3. Given the complex history behind the publication of the Clementine decrees, on which see Müller, *Konzil von Vienne*, pp. 387–422, 649–54, Müller found it difficult to establish which among those decrees could safely be considered the result of conciliar deliberations, and he repeatedly relied on parallels to the *Tractatus Maior* in order to establish the conciliar origin of specific decrees. His index, p. 755 *s.v. Wilhelm Duranti*, provides excellent guidance to those parallels. With a single exception all of these parallels are found in the *Maior* – and even the exception, namely Durant's demand at *TMI* 19 (3.42), fol. 67va, to revoke

with him that anyone who attacked a bishop should lose all fiefs, offices, and benefices in that bishop's diocese, and that his children and grandchildren ought to be declared ineligible to receive benefices in that diocese as well;[48] it acted on his desire to expedite the proceedings of the courts of Rome by adopting a summary procedure for suits regarding episcopal elections, postulations, provisions, or appointments to benefices of any kind;[49] it strengthened the control of bishops over exempt abbots;[50] and in a particularly poignant scene it prevailed upon a recalcitrant Clement V to restore the relationship between the friars and the bishops that Boniface VIII had enacted in *Super cathedram*.[51] But the significance of all of this was limited. No system of conciliar representation was adopted, no general councils met for more than one hundred years, and even as Durant attempted to separate the spiritual from the temporal power, Clement V and Philip IV conducted secret negotiations pointing the way to Avignon. The grand vision of a reform of the church 'in head and members', the vision of a true Christian commonwealth that would keep politics and morals united under justice, reason, and the utility of citizens – this vision that Durant had brought to the council of Vienne had thus been laid to rest.

Boniface VIII's decretal *Clerici qui cum unicis* (VI.3.2.1), would have been much better documented by *TMA* 2.4, fol. 16ra; Müller, *Konzil von Vienne*, p. 615 n. 14. Since Müller was completely unaware of the distinction between the *Maior* and the *Minor* his results suggest so much the more strongly that the *Minor* had no effect on the council's official actions at all.

[48] Clem.5.8.1; Müller, *Konzil von Vienne*, pp. 475–9. Durant had asked more broadly to exclude the relatives of anyone who had 'injured' a church or cleric from obtaining benefices there: *TMA* 2.94 (3.25), fol. 58ra–b.

[49] Clem.2.1.2. Cf. *TMA* 2.31, fol. 28va; *TMA* 2.96(3.27), fol. 59ra; Müller, *Konzil von Vienne*, pp. 490f.

[50] Clem.1.5.1. Cf. *TMA* 2.92 (3.23), fol. 57ra–b; Müller, *Konzil von Vienne*, pp. 539f.

[51] Clem.3.7.2. Cf. *TMA* 2.85 (3.16), fol. 55vb. On *Super cathedram* see Schleyer, *Anfänge*, pp. 107–11, Gratien, *Histoire*, pp. 354–9, Marrone, 'Ecclesiology', pp. 189–200, and Müller, *Konzil von Vienne*, pp. 547–52. At Vienne the French prelates, William Durant foremost among them, mounted a major offensive to reinstitute *Super cathedram*, which Benedict XI had overturned in 1304, and to abolish exemptions of the religious orders altogether. They failed with exemptions, but they succeeded with *Super cathedram*: 'Rogavit tamen [Clemens V] prelatos ter diversis vicibus in eadem tertia sessione, quod aliquid benignitatis ostenderent religiosis, ultra quam dicatur in illa *super cathedram*, maxime circa quartam; nam non possent alias vivere. Nichilominus tamen, si non consentirent prelati in aliqua mutatione illius *super cathedram*, ipse papa sequebatur voluntatem ipsorum et ipsam, ut predictum est, renovabit.' Müller, *Konzil von Vienne*, pp. 678f. Hence Clem.3.7.2 was said to have been enacted 'sacro instante et approbante concilio', a formula with a special emphasis on the will of the council that Clement used on no other occasion, as is pointed out by Müller, *Konzil von Vienne*, p. 548.

## Chapter 9

# THE ADVENT OF THE PRINCE

It is not unheard of that bishops and even more exalted dignitaries are sometimes reported to the Apostolic See and their deeds subjected to its judgment.                                                                John XXII[1]

When the council of Vienne was over William Durant the Younger found himself in a precarious position. He had launched an attack on papal government whose viability depended upon a fortuitous combination of circumstances beyond his control that had quickly passed away. Whereas Pope Clement V had regained a position from which the plenitude of power could be exercised with confidence, his own project of restoring hierarchy through councils had miscarried. The justice on which, as he believed, it had been founded was now a justice without weight.

In this way the seeds of William Durant the Younger's decline were sown. But that did not become apparent until some years thereafter. The disagreement with Clement may have been deep in principle – and we can only guess how deep – but it was manifested only briefly. Soon after the council was over Clement granted Durant a number of favours.[2] While this was only a common courtesy which was also bestowed on other participants in the council, it does indicate that their relationship had not been disturbed in any lasting way.[3] These were also the years when his local opponents were finally and decisively subjected to his control, while his association with the monarchy was blossoming. He was invited to Paris in January 1313 in order to participate in an assembly for the crusade, and it was almost certainly on this occasion that he composed a memorandum about the best way to

---

[1] 'Non sit novum episcopos et alios etiam superiori dignitate fulgentes Sedi apostolice quandoque defferri ejusque subire judicium super commissis ab eis.' John XXII, *LS* no. 775 (13.XII.1319), a letter to King Philip V explaining the papal proceedings against Durant.

[2] Clement V, nos. 8,719–23 (23.VI.1312).          [3] Müller, *Konzil von Vienne*, p. 593.

defeat the infidels.[4] A little later, in August 1314, he responded with alacrity to a royal summons for help with the campaign in Flanders and ordered his vassals to carry the banner of Mende to Arras, where he joined them in the following year.[5] It was this campaign that provoked organized resistance to Philip IV from a sizeable number of French lords in a kind of secular 'conciliar movement' that cast a cloud over the final months of Philip's life. There is no evidence that Durant took any part in it.

Neither the death of Philip IV nor that of Clement V had an adverse effect on Durant's affairs. On the contrary: two troubled years during which the papacy was vacant after Clement's death prevented his eventual successor, John XXII, from exercising the firm control over the bishoprics of France for which he later came to be known. As for the monarchy, Philip IV's successor, Louis X, confirmed the *paréage* of 1307 and the privilege of 1303, and in addition granted two new charters of liberties to Mende.[6]

The sudden death of Louis X in 1316 helped to improve Durant's affairs still further. His firm support of Philip V's rights to the throne earned him the king's lasting gratitude and resulted in his rise to national prominence.[7] During the years from 1316 to 1319 he made more frequent and more prominent appearances on the political scene than at any previous or later time. He sat in Parlement, became a member of the royal council, and served on royal committees to correct misconduct by royal officials. On other occasions he acted as a diplomat, both at home and abroad. He was asked by the king to draft a treaty with Castile, and for some months he negotiated on the king's behalf with the nobility of Artois and Picardy. In 1318 he participated in the conference of Royallieu to negotiate a peace treaty with Flanders, and in 1319 he presided over a conference at Compiègne that concluded an accord between Philip V and the nobles of Vermandois. During the same years Durant was increasingly asked to help resolve local disputes in various parts of France, which testifies to his growing reputation

---

[4] Viollet, pp. 31, 129–34.    [5] Viollet, pp. 27 n. 4, 32.

[6] Viollet, pp. 26f.; *Ordonnances* 1:354, 11:439f. The charters were modelled on the charter to the Burgundians resulting from the leagues of 1314.

[7] In 1317 he served as a member of a commission that Philip established in order to confirm his right to the succession against Louis X's daughter Jeanne. In that same year he witnessed the treaty of Poissy and participated prominently in an embassy that Philip sent to Avignon in order to achieve an understanding with John XXII. For the details of Durant's ascendancy under Philip V see Viollet, pp. 32–9, 55–7. In general see Lehugeur, *Philippe le Long*, pp. 28–105.

for legal expertise and skill in arbitration.[8] He even enjoyed the favour of John XXII, who appointed him in 1316 to a commission charged with investigating the bishop of Chalons.[9] The reward, as usual, consisted of liberal grants of benefices to his friends and relatives.[10]

## THE TURNING POINT

Just at this point, however, things began to change. It is perhaps not without irony that the beginning of Durant's troubles almost exactly coincided with a successful mission to secure Philip V's succession to the throne. The political details need not concern us here. What does concern us is that Philip V's succession depended on a marriage between the daughter of Louis X and the son of the count of Evreux that would have violated natural law – the spouses were related to each other and Princess Jeanne had not yet even reached seven years of age – and that Philip V sent William Durant the Younger on an embassy to Avignon in order to procure the necessary dispensation from the pope. Here, in other words, Durant was faced with a conflict between political necessities and natural law that subjected his faith in the law to a crucial test.

In his desire to accommodate the king Pope John XXII consulted with six cardinals, all professors of theology or law and all, as

[8] In 1317 he was involved in settling a bitter conflict over market rights that divided Bernard VI of Armagnac and the town (*bourg*) of Rodez, on the one hand, from the bishop, chapter, and city of Rodez, on the other. The result consisted of a *paréage* which did, however, not achieve a lasting peace. As late as 1325 he was asked to involve himself again, with not much more success; Viollet, p. 35. In April 1318 he was engaged in settling a disagreement about the viscounty of Limoges that divided the duchess of Brittany from her brother-in-law Gui; Viollet, p. 37.

[9] The commission was created in order to expedite proceedings which had previously been entrusted to the archbishop of Reims and his provincial council; John XXII, *LC* no. 1,457 (14.x.1316); cf. John XXII, *LS* no. 410 (14.x.1316–17). Viollet, p. 36, may well have been correct in his opinion that at the time Durant was too preoccupied with royal business to spend much of his energy on this investigation, which did in fact take several more years to complete. Nevertheless, when John decided in March 1318 to change the members of the commission, William Durant the Younger was the only member to be reappointed; John XXII, *LS* no. 516 (21.iii.1318).

[10] Five of Durant's favourites, with at least three of whom he was related, received substantial benefits: John XXII, *LC* nos. 1,566–9, 1,571 (all dated 20.x.1316). During the week immediately preceding his reappointment in 1318, no less than ten papal grants were made out to seven recipients in Mende, with six of whom Durant seems to have been related: John XXII, *LC* nos. 6,524–5, 6,529–31, 6,539, 6,603, 6,612–13, 6,615 (all dated 10–17.iii.1318). For the privileges given to Durant himself see John XXII, *LC* nos. 6,532–6 (all dated 10.iii.1318).

he took care to point out, well disposed toward the king. But they declared unanimously that a dispensation for marriage at such an early age 'was unheard of, quite unparalleled, and in a fashion contrary to natural law'. That put the pope on the spot. He could not very well ignore the considered advice of six experts without seeming 'to stretch the plenitude of power beyond its due and customary limits', as he put it to the king. But neither could he afford to alienate Philip and endanger the peace of France. He devised a solution that was ingenious indeed. He granted two different dispensations: both dispensed the spouses from their blood relationship, but only one explicitly required them to wait until they were old enough to marry according to natural law, whereas the other tactfully neglected to make any mention of the issue. The decision as to which of the two dispensations ought to be applied was left to Philip and his ecclesiastical advisers, 'provided they believe that it is licit and fitting for ourselves, and that it is expedient for you, for your affairs, and for your realm'.[11] In June 1318 the wedding was celebrated.

[11] The pertinent passages of the extraordinary letter in which John XXII informed Philip V of his decision are worth quoting in full: 'Ecce, fili carissime, petitionibus tuis super quibusdam dispensationibus matrimonialibus nobis recenter oblatis, statim, nullo deliberationis interjecto preambulo, litteras dispensationum super gradibus mandavimus expediri. Quia vero petitio dispensationis super etate nedum difficilis, ymmo prorsus inexaudibilis videbatur, sex ex fratribus nostris, tuorum honoris et comodi fervidos zelatores, ad nostram fecimus vocari presentiam, ut super dispensatione jam dicta plenioris deliberationis consilium haberemus, . . . quorum duo theologie facultatis, et reliqui aut legum, aut canonum professores existunt, qui omnes post habite invicem diligentis collationis indaginem, quasi uno ore concorditer responderunt quod dispensare super matrimoniis in etate inaudito erat, et prorsus insolitum, ac quodam modo juri naturali repugnans, quodque non decebat, imo non licebat nobis aliquatenus super hoc dispensare, nec expediebat tibi vel illis pro quibus dispensatio petebatur. Rem ergo sic insolitam, sic inauditam et juri naturali contrariam, ut prefertur, noluimus agredi, ne plenitudinem potestatis extendere ultra debitum vel solitum videremur; fecimus ergo quod licuit et decuit in hac parte; dispensavimus etenim circa matrimonium in tempus pubertatis debite contrahendum, factis super hoc litteris apostolicis oportunis quas pro partis utriusque cautela fecimus duplicari, set et alias fieri fecimus similiter duplicatas in quibus, nulla de etate habita mentione, super expressis consanguinitatis vel affinitatis gradibus, duximus generaliter dispensandum. Ut etiam tibi apertius liqueat quod in hiis tuis in quantum possumus satisfacere desideriis affectamus, per speciales committimus litteras venerabilibus fratribus nostris Egidio, Rothomagensi archiepiscopo et R.[adulpho], Laudunensi ac G.[uillelmo], Mimatensi episcopis, tuis consiliariis, ut ipsi vel duo ex eis super impedimentis omnibus propter quod inter personas pro quibus supplicare curasti matrimonia contrahi prohibentur, si nobis id licere nostreque convenire decentie ac tibi tuisque ac regnorum tuorum negotiis viderint expedire, auctoritate dispensent. Poteris autem illis uti litteris de quibus expedientius judicabis, et hec quidem tue debent celsitudini ex ratione sufficere, cum nec potuerimus, nec debuerimus aliud circa illa licenter aut decenter egisse.' John XXII, *LS* no. 579 (5.v.1318). John XXII, *LS* no. 576

For our purposes this incident has two very different meanings. On the one hand, it confirmed the hopes that William Durant the Younger had long placed on his cooperation with the temporal monarchy. Here he had been entrusted with negotiating a decision that was not only crucial for the success of Philip V but that also could have embroiled the pope in an embarrassment of serious proportions. From this perspective the trajectory of his career had reached its apogee. He acted no longer as bishop of Mende but as a man of state who represented the interests of the king of France, who negotiated with the pope, and whose diplomatic tact was valued by both sides. But on the other hand his willingness to execute the mandate of the pope conflicted with the principles that he had advocated in Vienne. There he had maintained that there was no alternative to law. Peace, law, and order were identical, 'for what is ordered is at rest'.[12] But now, instead of fighting for that Augustinian view of justice in which hierarchy and peace were indistinguishable, he endorsed the very disrespect for law that he had condemned at Vienne. He thus cooperated in overturning the authority of law and through his own acts revealed that the great order of difference had become a mere ideal.[13]

Thus the ambiguities that had permitted William Durant the Younger to plead the cause of episcopal autonomy ever since Boniface VIII had clashed with Philip IV were removed and the pattern that had informed the life of William Durant the Older was put back in place, except that it had been adapted to the requirements of national politics. Soon there arrived an occasion to extend the defeat of Durant's ideas from the area of national politics to his own career. Pope John XXII may well have been waiting for such an occasion. As we have pointed out before, his assessment of Durant's conduct at the council of Vienne was less than friendly.[14] Perhaps he had a personal grudge as well: just prior to the council of Vienne Durant had been involved in a bitter dispute with his

---

(5.v.1318), contains the dispensation that requires the spouses to have reached a legitimate age. John XXII, *LS* no. 577 (5.v.1318), gives the same dispensation without mentioning the question of age. John XXII, *LS* no. 575 (2.v.1318), authorizes the archbishop of Rouen, the bishop of Laon, and William Durant the Younger to issue the required dispensation. [12] See above, p. 298.

[13] I agree with Viollet, pp. 38f., that this event reveals a sharp conflict between Durant's ideas and his conduct, but not that it furnishes evidence for duplicity and moral failure. Even if Durant's respect for the law had been unimpeachable, the point is that he could not act for the sake of peace without violating the law if he believed, as he had good reason to, that Philip's marriage plans were essential for the common good.

[14] See above, pp. 292f.

The incidence of power

nephew, Jacques de la Rue.[15] At any rate, when in 1318 Durant was denounced to the papal see on charges of an undetermined nature, and in spite of vigorous protestations by King Philip and Queen Jeanne that their councillor was being made the victim of a personal vendetta, Pope John XXII immediately ordered a full-blown investigation of William Durant the Younger's conduct.[16] At first he proceeded with restraint. He tried to mollify the king and promised that Durant would be given every chance to clear himself. By April 1319, however, when Philip and the queen had once again sent letters in favour of Durant, he dropped his diplomatic reservation and clearly stated his opinion:

Truly, my son, if it is not the spirit of arrogance we do not know what has moved William Durant these many years to belittle this See and its honour without interruption, never ceasing to bark against it. This Holy See did not raise him out of the dust and place him among the bishops because of any merits of his own, but because of the merits of his predecessor. We understand that even now he does not cease from such conduct, but damnably insists on it and strives to kick against the spur and to deflect yourself and others from their devotion to this See.[17]

Contending that Durant was undermining the alliance between the spiritual and the temporal monarchy, the pope thus confronted Philip with a choice between the friendship of the pope and the friendship of Durant. That was an effective argument. As a result

---

[15] In 1310 Clement V had asked François André to surrender the archdeaconry of Mende to Jacques de la Rue. In compensation he was to become archdeacon of Fréjus. William Durant and his chapter protested that according to a long-standing custom only canons of Mende could become archdeacons, but Clement V undercut their complaint by adding a canonry to the benefices for Jacques de la Rue: Clement V, nos. 6,144 (4.IX.1310), 6,726 (23.III.1311). When Jacques de la Rue died in 1317 John XXII made sure of protecting the presence of his family in Mende by transferring the archdeaconry to Jacques' brother: see John XXII, LS nos. 267 (2.VII.1317), 279 (2.VII.1317), 302 (10.VII.1317), 337, 340, 342, 344 (all 1.VIII.1317).

[16] John XXII, LS nos. 762 (10.XI.1318), 775 (13.XII.1318), 778 (19.XII.1318); Viollet, pp. 39–44. We do not know precisely what Durant was said to have been guilty of or by whom he was denounced. Perhaps it was Béraud de Mercoeur, one of Durant's latent enemies who had not forgotten the defeat he had suffered in connection with the paréage, and whose name was mentioned several times. Perhaps it was also the bishop of Rodez, who was displeased with the results of Durant's arbitration of 1317.

[17] 'Vere, fili, nescimus quo ductus nisi superbie spiritu, jam plures anni sunt quod Sedi isti et ejus honori detrahere non cessavit, contra ipsum latrare non desiit, licet hec Sancta Sedes non suis sed alienis potius meritis, videlicet predecessoris sui, ipsum elevarit de pulvere et inter presules collocarit, nec adhuc, sicut fertur, cessat a talibus, sed in ipsis insistens dampnabiliter, contra stimulum calcitrare nititur ac te et alios a devotione Sedis hujusmodi deviare.' John XXII, LS no. 850 (10.IV.1319); cf. John XXII, LS no. 849 (10.IV.1319).

Durant never quite managed to recover from John XXII's blunt and cruel condemnation.[18]

## THE DENOUEMENT

To be sure, the impact of this affair should not be overestimated. After the initial flurry of excitement it gradually faded from attention and its outcome is unknown.[19] Besides, Durant's career was far from coming to a grinding halt. From 1320 to 1321 he went to England once again, this time in order to negotiate a peace between England and Scotland, which earned him a favourable letter from King Edward II to the pope; in 1321 he presented the royal point of view about the coinage to an assembly of town representatives in Paris; and in 1323 he witnessed a marriage contract between Charles of Calabria and Marie of Valois.[20] His rule over the diocese of Mende does not appear to have been weakened either.[21] Quite the contrary, he successfully pursued the vengeance that he had sworn to the de Peyre in 1304.[22] As late as 1328, in a confrontation with Richard de Peyre which prompted him once more to invoke the 'great order of difference', he gained a noteworthy victory.[23] And even his relationship with John XXII

---

[18] Essentially the same argument was to prove crucial for the defeat of the conciliar movement in the fifteenth century when Pope Eugenius IV deprived the men in Basle of the support of temporal monarchies by pointing out that the crowned heads of Europe could not very well support conciliarists without digging their own graves: Mundy, 'The Conciliar Movement', pp. 18–20; Stieber, *Pope Eugenius IV*. In this regard, too, the fate of William Durant the Younger may be seen as foreshadowing that of the conciliar movement as a whole.

[19] See John XXII, *LS* nos. 878 (April–May 1319), 914–15 (4.VIII.1319). The last time we hear about the affair is in 1324, when it had still not been settled: John XXII, *LS* nos. 2,090–1 (10.VI.1324).

[20] For the following details see Viollet, pp. 56f.

[21] In 1323, however, John XXII appointed three *judices conservatores* to the chapter of Mende: John XXII, *LC* no. 17,700 (13.VI.1323). Such judges were commonly appointed in order to defend a church from diminutions in its rights, which does not reflect well on Durant's ability to govern Mende at the time.

[22] Astorg de Peyre lost several villages and castles and was fined 10,500 marks to be divided by Durant and Philip V. He appealed to Parlement to overturn his sentence, but Durant protested to King Charles, who overruled the Parlement and let the bishop keep most of the goods of the de Peyre; Viollet, pp. 46–8.

[23] Richard de Peyre tried to alienate his shares of the joint-lordship over La Garde-Guérin to Guibert de Peyre without giving Durant the right of first purchase. That violated a statute which Durant had issued in 1313. Durant wrote to his subordinates in Mende with instructions to resolve the issue and in 1329 his representatives did in fact purchase the shares in question from Guibert de Peyre for 260 pounds; Viollet, pp. 50–5. For Durant's reference to D.89 c.7 on this occasion see above, p. 179.

# The incidence of power

was not all bad: the pope sometimes employed his services for certain minor duties and showed him certain kindnesses.[24]

All this is evidence that Durant did not completely fall from grace. Nevertheless, as soon as he had been indicted in the papal courts his fortunes changed promptly and markedly for the worse. During the early 1320s his public role in France was waning; by 1325 it had virtually ceased and his name vanished completely from John XXII's secret letters. That was surely not for lack of opportunities. Pope John could easily have taken advantage of Durant's familiarity with Italy in battling against the spiritual Franciscans and Emperor Louis the Bavarian. But instead the main effect of those struggles on the church of Mende was that the pope used it as a base for his tax collectors.[25] And above all Pope John was granting benefices in Durant's collation with increasing frequency to clerics with whom Durant had no connections, while grants to his friends and relatives abruptly stopped in 1318.[26]

There was one role, however, in which Durant did not lose prominence, namely, the role of a crusader. We have already mentioned that in 1313 Philip IV called him to Paris in order to participate in an assembly for the crusade.[27] In 1317 he presented Philip V's views on the crusade to John XXII.[28] In 1318 he even

[24] In February 1324 John XXII asked him to provide for eight royal nominees in four cathedrals and four collegiate churches; John XXII, LC no. 18,984 (6.II.1324). Soon thereafter he granted him the right to have a representative to rededicate desecrated churches and cemeteries in his diocese; John XXII, LC no. 19,160 (19.III.1324). In the following year he granted him the right to have his sins remitted by his confessor in mortis articulo; John XXII, LC no. 22,467 (1.VI.1325). See also John XXII, LC nos. 15,803 (15.VI.1322), 17,409 (24.V.1323), 22,406 (21.V.1325), 44,572 (1.III.1329).

[25] Two names stand out from John XXII's secret letters: William Rufus, hebdomadarius of Mende and canon of Le Puy, and Hugo de Mirabello, provost of Mende and later papal chaplain, both of whom served John in a variety of fiscal functions throughout the 1320s, and neither one of whom appears to have belonged to the circle of William Durant the Younger's friends; on William Rufus see John XXII, LS nos. 1,071 (1.VI.1320), 1,352 (8.I.1322), 1,361 (30.I.1322), 1,664 (28.IV.1323), 2,914 (23.VII.1326), 3,138 (11.II.1327), 3,141 (13.II.1327). On Hugo de Mirabello see John XXII, LS nos. 2,324–5 (19.XII.1324), 2,354 (5.I.1325), 2,377 (1.II.1325), 2,439 (25.III.1325), 3,260 (28.V.1327), 3,854 (22.V.1329), 3,855 (22.V.1329), 4,085–6 (21.I.1330), 4,102 (22.II.1330), 4,391 (23.XII.1330). On two less prominent figures see John XXII, LS nos. 3,199 (7.IV.1327), 3,239 (9.V.1327), 3,308 (28.VII.1327), 3,331 (26.VIII.1327), 3,394 (1.XI.1327), 3,406 (16.XI.1327), 3,539 (4.IV.1328), 3,612 (15.VI.1328).

[26] See John XXII, LC nos. 15,562 (12.VI.1322), 16,988 (28.II.1323), 17,766 (3.VII.1323), 24,314 (26.I.1326), 26,229 (13.VIII.1326), 26,350 (27.VIII.1326), 28,235 (20.III.1327), 28,961 (15.VI.1327), 29,053 (29.VI.1327), 41,188 (14.V.1328), 42,825 (16.IX.1328), 44,453 (21.II.1329), 50,997 (28.IX.1330), 51,984 (14.XII.1330).

[27] See above, p. 305.     [28] Viollet, pp. 36f.

seems to have hoped that John would make him patriarch of
Jerusalem. But that, of course, was just when the proceedings
against him were getting under way at Avignon. John would have
none of Durant's plans and denied that he had ever even contem-
plated the possibility of giving him the patriarchate.[29] Thus what
was perhaps William Durant the Younger's fondest wish failed to
come true; but his crusading ardour did not subside. In 1323 King
Charles IV appointed him and others to collect a subsidy for a
crusade to help the kingdoms of Cyprus and Armenia;[30] and in
1326 Marino Sanudo, the Venetian promoter of crusades, wrote
letters to Durant that indicate that he enjoyed a European reputation for his attachment to the conquest of the Holy Land.[31]

Finally, in 1329, there was an opportunity to go beyond mere
planning. A marriage was projected between Marie of Bourbon
and Gui of Lusignan, and an escort was required to conduct the
princess to Cyprus. Pope John XXII and Philip VI appointed
Durant and Pierre de la Palu, the man who had in fact become
patriarch of Jerusalem, to sail to Cyprus in order to celebrate the
wedding.[32] From Cyprus they were to continue into Egypt in
order to negotiate with the sultan for his neutrality or even his
assistance in the crusade. On this occasion John XXII did what he
could to help Durant: he authorized him to be accompanied by a
train of his familiars and thirty other people into the Holy Land; he
granted him the right to be absolved of all his sins by his confessor
*in articulo mortis*; he issued an indulgence and permitted him, in case
he died abroad, to have his bones collected and taken to a
predetermined burial place; and he was most particularly helpful
with the finances of the journey.[33]

Late in 1329 Durant thus departed with Pierre de la Palu and
Princess Marie in a convoy of four galleys; and in January 1330 the
wedding took place in Nicosia. As planned, Durant and Pierre de la
Palu continued into Egypt, but the results of their diplomatic
efforts are uncertain. When they returned to Cyprus William

[29] John XXII, *LS* no. 762 (10.XI.1318).
[30] John XXII, *LS* no. 1,683 (7.II.1323); Viollet, pp. 56–7.     [31] Viollet, p. 57.
[32] Viollet, pp. 58f.; cf. John XXII, *LC* nos. 45,027 (24.IV.1329), 45,977 (10.VIII.1329).
[33] Durant's debts needed to be settled before he went on a voyage from which it was
    possible that he might not return. His creditors insisted on cash, but his cash was
    insufficient to pay both for his debts and for the expenses of his journey. John XXII
    helped out by asking his creditors to take the arrears that were owed to Durant as their
    security; John XXII, *LC* no. 45,978 (10.VIII.1329).

Durant fell ill and died, and he was buried in Nicosia in July.[34]
Soon afterwards Pope John XXII put an end to the ascendancy of
the Durants over the Gévaudan by appointing Jean d'Arcy, canon
of Langres, as bishop of Mende.[35]

[34] Viollet, pp. 60f. In spite of direct inquiries in Nicosia I have not been able to verify
Viollet's statement that Durant was buried in the Cistercian church of Ste Marie de
Beaulieu, which was later apparently known as San Giovanni in Monte.
[35] John XXII, *LS* nos. 4,367–8 (6.XII.1330), 4,380 (15.XII.1330), 4,385 (16.XII.1330).

# CONCLUSION

Mein Freund, die Zeiten der Vergangenheit
Sind uns ein Buch mit sieben Siegeln.
Was Ihr den Geist der Zeiten heißt,
Das ist im Grund der Herren eigener Geist,
In dem die Zeiten sich bespiegeln.

Goethe, Faust I, lines 575–9

William Durant the Younger was the author of two equally remarkable documents for the history of political thought: the *paréage* of Mende and the *Tractatus Maior*. But whereas he succeeded in putting into effect the ideas that he articulated in the former – succeeded, indeed, in laying down a constitutional regime that would survive intact for almost half a thousand years – he failed completely with the latter. What explains this spectacular success and this no less spectacular defeat? It is not that in the *paréage* he opted for princely sovereignty whereas in the *Tractatus Maior* he opted for republican government. Nor is it that the *paréage* dealt with a local territory whereas the *Tractatus Maior* dealt with the universal church. It is not even that the circumstances favoured his attempt to subject the nobility of the Gévaudan to his control, but did not favour his attempt to subject the papacy to the will of general councils. It is that he insisted on the authority of law.

There is a sense in which the authority of law is inseparably wedded to republican government, namely, the sense in which the law defines the common good and curbs the capricious will of arbitrary rulers. It was Durant's profound understanding of this meaning of the law that enabled him to formulate a grand and unprecedented plan to change the church into a commonwealth in which the papal plenitude of power was to be subjected to the supreme authority of representative assemblies meeting every ten years in order to express the will of the community. But in another sense the authority of law is hostile to republican government, namely, the sense in which the law commands what is right and

315

prohibits what is wrong. In that sense the law requires absolute obedience to a supreme administrator, as Gregory VII asserted with uncanny clarity in the *Dictatus Papae*. Durant fought hard to reconcile the claims of the community with the competing claims of right and wrong, and there is no inherent reason why he should have failed. For right and wrong are absolutes that override the will of the community only because their meaning is entirely abstract. What may be right and wrong in the concrete can never be defined except by reference to the context in which right should be done and wrong avoided, and there is no one better qualified to say what that context is than an assembly representing the community. But Durant could never bring himself to admit that the meaning of the law might be entirely dependent on circumstance. Like Gregory VII he was convinced that there had to be some standard of right and wrong that was concrete and that still governed absolutely. That conviction sapped the strength of his republican ideals and launched him on a pursuit of the true meaning of the law that could not end except by changing him into an historian and a reluctant champion of sovereignty. For history is the pursuit of meaning for no other sake than that of meaning, and sovereignty the rule of law for the sake of nothing but the law.

The difference between the *paréage* of Mende and the *Tractatus Maior* is therefore mainly one of time and circumstance. William Durant the Younger's interests inclined him to participate in the elaboration of sovereignty in the Gévaudan while trying to resist it in the universal church. But interests notwithstanding, the logic of the *paréage* of Mende was fundamentally the same as that of the *Tractatus Maior*. Both of them placed the authority of law above the common good and both of them tended toward sovereignty. That is the reason why Durant succeeded with the *paréage* and failed with the *Tractatus Maior*. That is the reason, too, why both maintained their hold on the imagination for centuries to come: the one because it defined a constitutional reality, the other because it expressed the countervailing constitutional ideal.

This makes it possible to resolve the dilemmas confronting previous interpreters of the *Tractatus Maior*. Misled by categorical distinctions between conciliarists and papalists they misconstrued the issue with which Durant was struggling and failed to capture the meaning of his ideas. The object of his treatise was neither to assert the authority of general councils nor to propose a theory of government but to achieve a reform of the church in head and members by restoring the authority of ancient law. General councils were the most important means in order to secure that end. But the apparent simplicity of that objective concealed a fundamental inconsistency between two very different ideas of law: law as an expression of the common good (the means) and law as a standard of right and wrong (the end). Hence those who insist that Durant was a conciliarist are obviously right. There cannot have been many men who sought more fervently than he to subject the papal plenitude of power to the authority of general councils. But those who insist that he maintained papal supremacy are right as well because his attachment to republican government never went far enough to overturn the papal plenitude of power by an unqualified assertion of the right of the community to act as the final arbiter of right and wrong. It is the same with different assessments of Durant's sincerity. Insofar as it is possible to read the mind of anyone at all, there is no doubt that he was perfectly sincere. But neither is there any doubt that he was very much inclined to act on his own interests and that his conception of the common good entitled him to do just that. The truth of the matter simply is that previous interpreters have sought to find a kind of consistency in the *Tractatus Maior* that is not there and that ought not to be expected.

In closing it may be pertinent to state the implications of these results for matters of more general concern. First, they suggest that the history of the conciliar theory has a more ambivalent complexion than is sometimes recognized. On the one hand, they confirm Brian Tierney's judgment that 'the roots of the conciliar tradition lie deeper in the past than has usually been supposed'.[1] There could hardly be more telling evidence for this contention than the fact that William Durant the Younger's conciliar proposal was in essence nothing more than a reprise – albeit a reprise vastly extended and with a very different emphasis – of a conclusion which Gratian had already formulated in the twentieth distinction of his *Decretum*. But, on the other hand, the case of the *Tractatus Maior* suggests that the roots of sovereignty lie just as deeply in the past as those of its apparent opposite and, what is more, in the same soil. The very twentieth distinction from which Durant derived his single most important canonical justification for conciliar representation furnished an equally important argument for sovereignty by placing the power of the pope above the knowledge of the interpreters of Scripture. That is no coincidence, and neither is

---

[1] Tierney, *Foundations*, p. 245.

# Conclusion

it coincidental that both of these arguments arose in the context of Gratian's effort to reconcile the freedom of the papacy to act on behalf of the church with the authority of ancient law. It would appear that both the conciliar theory and the theory of papal sovereignty are rooted in the same attempt to base the reform of the church on the authority of ancient law. Durant's ambivalence about the role of general councils thus has a historical significance extending far beyond the narrow limits of his life and thought. It helps to understand the ease with which conciliarists like Nicholas of Cusa managed to switch their allegiance from the council of Basle to the papacy – a switch that it would be presumptuous to explain in terms of political expediency alone – and thus to explain the failure of the whole conciliar movement.[2]

Second, with regard to current debates about the proper methods for intellectual history, this interpretation of the *Tractatus Maior* may serve as a case in point for Quentin Skinner's judgment that it is fundamentally misguided to write intellectual history in terms of the history of doctrines.[3] The conceptual distinction between conciliar and papal theories of government is a useful heuristic tool to select and arrange the evidence for the history of medieval political thought, but it is not appropriate to capture that history itself. To put it bluntly, there can be no history of the conciliar theory, and therefore no foundations of the conciliar theory, because no such thing as the conciliar theory was ever a historical reality – except, as Giuseppe Alberigo has pointed out, as a polemical device designed to taint defenders of conciliar authority with heresy.[4] Sometimes it is not even possible to understand the views of a single author in terms of a 'theory' – and it may very well be true that it is never possible if by 'understanding' we mean 'understanding thoroughly'. As I have tried to show above,

---

[2] I thus find myself in basic agreement with Giuseppe Alberigo, *Chiesa conciliare*, especially pp. 225–7, 237–9, who attributes the failure of the conciliar movement to a disparity between conciliar ecclesiology and the historical conjuncture that permitted the resolution of the schism. Hence conciliar ecclesiology proved inadequate to the challenge of church reform in the crucial year 1417 and thereafter.

[3] The classic statement remains Skinner, 'Meaning and Understanding', to be read in conjunction with his recent 'Reply to My Critics'. An outstanding presentation of the opposing point of view can be found in Oakley, *Omnipotence, Covenant and Order*, pp. 15–40.

[4] 'A questo punto occorre andare molto più in là dell'ammissione di una molteplicità di significanti del termine conciliarismo, per accettare che si tratta di una denominazione controversistica, inadeguata a esprimere ciò che è accaduto nella cristianità occidentale durante lo scisma d'occidente.' Alberigo, *Chiesa conciliare*, p. 17.

William Durant the Younger's conciliar proposal had at least three different meanings: to found the order of the church on the divine reason of the universe; to create an institution with the right to define the common good; and to delay the inexorable progress of the logic that led from asserting the authority of law to sovereignty. Hence it is hard to see how Durant could be said to have had a conciliar theory. Hence Tierney's attempt to write the history of medieval political thought in terms of *Religion, Law and the Growth of Constitutional Thought* is no less problematic than Ullmann's attempt to write the same history in terms of *The Growth of Papal Government*. The truth of the matter rather seems to be that both the growth of papal government and that of constitutional thought are different aspects of a single history.

In one significant respect, however, this interpretation of the *Tractatus Maior* expands on Skinner's argument. It is not just historians, after all, who are sometimes seduced by the 'mythology of doctrines'; agents of history themselves are, too. Again William Durant the Younger may serve as a case in point. To the extent that he believed the law to have a meaning that was separable from the context in which the law was framed he, too, fell victim to the mythology of doctrines and, more important, to the extent that he endeavoured to impose that mythology on the contemporary church he transformed it from an interpretative fallacy into a real historical force. His treatise cannot only be misinterpreted in anachronistic terms – it was itself one vast anachronism. His conciliar proposal does not only lend itself to a proleptic misinterpretation – it was itself an act of prolepsis that really did anticipate the decrees of Constance. Indeed, the failure of historians to understand Durant's intentions has its real counterpart in history: with his attention divided between meaning and circumstance, Durant deprived himself of the ability to focus his intention on the common good. Instead he brought the question 'council or pope?' to a head and thus endowed the mythology of coherence with a monstrous capacity to devour all intentions other than those obeying the alternative between 'papalism' and 'conciliarism'. In short, Skinner's critique of the ways in which intellectual history is written deserves to be applied to the ways in which that history is made.

Third, and finally, these observations suggest a definite perspective on the history of Europe. Ever since the papacy in the eleventh century proclaimed the authority of ancient texts to be inviolate –

precisely at the point at which Europe had just begun to organize itself in ways that differed fundamentally from those of antiquity – the inhabitants of Europe have yoked their understanding of the common good to the interpretation of ancient texts. That is the distinguishing characteristic of European history. To be sure, the framework that was thus put into place allowed for great variety. The texts have changed from Roman and canon law to the Gospel, the constitution, and the book of nature. The English have always reserved the right to act with a certain freedom from antiquity. Hence they have not only created their own law but also been enormously successful in the joint pursuit of liberty at home and empire abroad. By contrast, the Germans have been particularly enamoured with antiquity, have proved inept at formulating a coherent political intention, and have specialized in elaborating the logic of history and sovereignty.[5] But notwithstanding such variety, to the extent that the medieval church imposed the logic of interpretation on European politics, the history of Europe was transformed into a counterfeit history of ideas. That is the reason why the history of Europe abounds both in anachronisms (Renaissance and Reformation) and in prolepses (progress, the rise of the bourgeoisie, the rise of the state); why the moments when Europeans focused their intentions clearly on a present common good have been so rare and so explosive (the Investiture Controversy, the Reformation, the French Revolution); and why as soon as sufficient time has passed for the mythology of coherence to wreak its destructive work such moments are regularly followed by the irrational oscillation between mutually exclusive isms (conciliarism, papalism, constitutionalism, absolutism, liberalism, communism, individualism, nationalism). As a result Europeans have never really managed to steer their understanding of morality safely out of the straits between the Scylla and Charybdis of history's moral diffidence and sovereignty's command of absolute obedience.

---

[5] Hence the passage of historical time in England is marked by less violent interruptions than it is in Germany; hence the conciliar tradition merged smoothly into the political thought of seventeenth-century England whereas in Germany it was abruptly cancelled by the Reformation; hence Anglophone historians from Stubbs via Maitland to Tierney and Oakley prefer to write the history of liberty whereas German historians from Ranke via Meinecke to Ullmann prefer to write the history of sovereignty. To pit one tradition against the other as if only one of them could be right seems misguided.

# APPENDIX: A NOTE ON TEXTS AND CITATIONS

There are several early modern printed editions of the lengthy treatise which William Durant the Younger wrote some time between August 1308 and the beginning of the council of Vienne in October 1311, but none of them are critical and all of them suffer from a variety of flaws. The most important is that they conflate the treatise with another, much shorter work written by Durant while the council was in session, in which he repeated some, but by no means all, of the proposals he had made in the longer work, and modified others in response to events that were taking place at the council. I refer to the first as *Tractatus Maior* and the second as *Tractatus Minor*. The title *Tractatus de modo generalis concilii celebrandi*, which appears in all of the printed editions and many manuscripts, is not authentic, but was coined by a fifteenth-century copyist. It is also misleading; Durant was not writing about 'the manner of holding a general council' but about the reform of the church in head and members – a reform which it was his outstanding achievement to link to a particular variety of the conciliar theory. The structural differences between the printed *Tractatus de modo generalis concilii celebrandi* and the two treatises originally written by Durant are graphically represented on figure 2 on p. 325. For more details concerning the distinction between *Tractatus Maior* and *Tractatus Minor* see Fasolt, 'A New View'.

In order to be able to quote Durant accurately I have collated the extant medieval manuscripts both with each other and with the printed editions. But there was no point in burdening the footnotes of this book with the apparatus that would be proper in a critical edition. I have therefore presented the text in a form as close to that of the available editions as the manuscript evidence allows: whenever possible I have quoted the *editio princeps* published by Jean Crespin in Lyons 1531; whenever necessary I have emended it with the help of the manuscripts. Such emendations are enclosed in

321

asterisks and followed by square brackets containing the siglum of the most important manuscript on which they are based, usually P or M. This procedure has seemed the more justifiable because, apart from its conflation of the *Tractatus Maior* with the *Tractatus Minor*, which changes the sequence but not the substance of the text, the *editio princeps* is a better witness for Durant's original text than all surviving manuscripts except P and M. Readers who are interested in a stemma of the manuscripts, a detailed discussion of the transmission of the text, and the principles which I have used to establish reliable readings are referred to chapter 2 of my dissertation 'William Durant the Younger's "Tractatus de modo generalis concilii celebrandi"', pp. 54–100.

On the whole I have preserved Crespin's orthography, which corresponds roughly to the orthography of the most important manuscripts. I have changed his capitalization consistently: only proper names, references to God, and the titles of books have been capitalized. I have also changed Crespin's punctuation and his paragraph divisions in order to achieve what I hope is greater readability throughout and what I believe is sometimes a clearer presentation of Durant's meaning.

References to the *Tractatus Maior* consist of the abbreviation *TMA* followed by the part and chapter of the treatise in Durant's own numbering, e.g., *TMA* 2.42. References to the *Tractatus Minor* consist of *TMI* followed by the number of the chapter, e.g., *TMI* 31. Where Durant's numbering of parts and chapters differs from that of the editions – as is the case for the last thirty chapters of the *Maior* and for all the chapters of the *Minor* – the numbering of the editions has been added in parentheses, e.g., *TMA* 2.96 (3.27), *TMI* 31 (3.54). All references are accompanied by an indication of the corresponding folio (recto or verso) and column (a or b) in Crespin's edition. Some folios are misnumbered in Crespin's edition. In such cases the correct folio has been given first, followed by parentheses including a '*male*' and the number of the folio as it was actually printed. Since the *editio princeps* is relatively rare, concordances to the edition in the *Tractatus universi iuris* (Venice, 1584) and the edition by François Clousier (Paris, 1671) are included at the end of this book. Both editions are inferior to Crespin's, but they are more easily available, especially since the edition by Clousier has been photographically reproduced by the Gregg Press (London, 1963 (?)).

In the footnotes Durant's technical references to the canon law and other sources have been preserved in their original form. Modernized versions of the same references have been appended to each quotation in the order in which Durant mentioned them. For the method used in referring to canonical sources see Kuttner, 'Notes on the Presentation of Text and Apparatus'. References to the Pseudo-Isidorean collection consist of the Latin name of the respective council or text as it appears in Hinschius' edition followed by the number of the canon and, if necessary, preceded by the number of the council, e.g. Agathense c.16, or III Arelatense c.1. The books, titles, laws, and paragraphs of Roman law have been cited according to the principle *de maiore ad minorem*. For an explanation of abbreviations see the list of abbreviations above, pp. xviif.

References to papal letters consist of the name of the pope, the number of the letter in the published edition of his register, and the date of the letter, e.g., Clement V, no. 1246 (4.III.1306). The bibliography contains bibliographical details on the editions I have used. In the case of the letters of Pope John XXII, '*LC*' and '*LS*' have been added to distinguish between his 'common' letters (*LC*) and his 'secret' letters (*LS*), e.g., John XXII, *LC* no. 6,524 (10.III.1318). The letters of Philip IV regarding the Gévaudan, edited by Jean Roucaute and Marc Saché and referred to as 'R-S', have been treated similarly, e.g., R-S, no. 84 (22.III.1314). The reader should be warned, however, that the printers misnumbered a good many of those letters. Page numbers have therefore always been included. If the letter is misnumbered, the number that is actually printed has been given first and is followed by parentheses including a '*melius*' and the correct number of the letter, e.g., R-S, no. 56 (*melius* 61, 31.VIII.1310), p. 121.

In the body of the text I have consistently translated quotations from Durant's treatises or other documents in foreign languages into English. Where the translation is not my own, I have acknowledged its author. The sole exception is the Authorized Version of the Bible on whose solemn language I have occasionally drawn without acknowledgment. For the sake of the reader's convenience Durant's references to his sources have been omitted from the English translations unless they are the object of direct attention, in which case they have been given in the modernized version. I have systematically avoided the use of quotation marks. Separating Durant's own words from the sources he so regularly quotes is not always possible in practise because the borderline between quotation and text is fluid. It also does violence to Durant's purpose. His quotations are neither embellishments nor evidence adduced to substantiate a point: they are the substance of his argument.

As every translator knows, the names of medieval persons cannot be treated consistently without an element of artificiality. Some names are better given in English, some in modern French, and some in Latin. On the whole I have favoured English versions, but the reader should not expect any more consistency than the basic rule that the same person is always referred to in the same way. Concerning William Durant the Younger himself, I have felt free to choose 'William', even though this is hardly what his parents called him, instead of 'Guilielmus', which they hardly called him either. I also share the preference of Paul Viollet, Durant's biographer, for 'Durant', in spite of the fact that Heckel, 'Eine Kanzleianweisung', p. 110 n. 4, makes an excellent case for 'Duranti' as historically correct, a fact of which Viollet, p. 2 n. 2, himself seems to have been aware. But the reader should be cautioned that in the secondary literature William Durant is variously referred to as Guilielmus, Guillaume, Guglielmo, or Wilhelm, and as Durandus, Durantis, Duranti, Durant, or Durand.

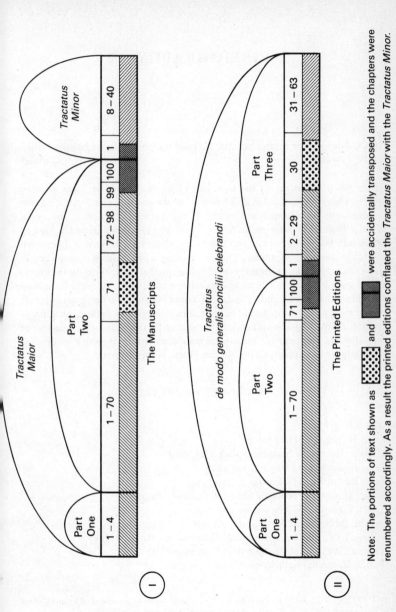

The Manuscripts

The Printed Editions

Note: The portions of text shown as ▒▒▒ and ▓▓▓ were accidentally transposed and the chapters were renumbered accordingly. As a result the printed editions conflated the *Tractatus Maior* with the *Tractatus Minor*.

Figure 2  The manuscripts compared with the printed editions

# BIBLIOGRAPHY

Don Quijote went insane because he read too much. That happens only
rarely nowadays.
                                                    Ernst Robert Curtius[1]

I have taken advantage of the footnotes to quote extensively from primary
sources. I have felt justified in doing so because the primary sources are, first, the
foundation of my argument and, second, not always readily available. The text of
William Durant the Younger's treatises in particular can only be found in editions
whose treachery increases in direct proportion to their availability. Besides, even
where the text is sound, reading Durant's writing is like walking through brush:
readers may appreciate a collection of the blossoms that spares them the thorns. As
a consequence I have not been able to refer as completely as might have been
desirable to the primary and secondary literature that, without being immediately
related to my argument, furnishes its historical, legal, and philosophical background. The bibliography is intended to make up for that. It includes a number of
titles that are indispensable because of their distinctive perspective or detailed
information even though I have not cited them in the footnotes.

## PRIMARY SOURCES

MANUSCRIPTS
Kues, St. Nikolaus Hospital, ms. 168
Munich, Bayerische Staatsbibliothek, clm. 6605
Paris, Bibliothèque Mazarine, ms. 1687
Paris, Bibliothèque Nationale, ms. lat. 1443
Rome, Biblioteca Nazionale Centrale, Fondo Varia, ms. 1
Tours, Bibliothèque Municipale, ms. 237
Troyes, Bibliothèque Municipale, ms. 786
Vatican City, Biblioteca Apostolica Vaticana, ms. Barb. lat. 1487
Vatican City, Biblioteca Apostolica Vaticana, ms. Ottob. lat. 823
Zurich, Zentralbibliothek, ms. S 2040

---

[1] 'Don Quijote ist durch zu vieles Lesen in Geistesverwirrung geraten. Das kommt heute
kaum noch vor.' E. R. Curtius, 'Meisterworte' (typescript, n.p., n.d.), p.6.

# Bibliography

PUBLISHED SOURCES

*Acta Sanctorum* (Antwerp, 1643– )

d'Ailly, Pierre. *Tractatus super reformatione ecclesiae.* In J. Gerson, *Opera omnia.* Ed. L. E. du Pin (Antwerp, 1706), 2:903–16

*Tractatus de ecclesiastica potestate.* In J. Gerson, *Opera omnia.* Ed. L. E. du Pin (Antwerp, 1706), 2:925–60

Alexander IV. *Les Registres d'Alexandre IV.* Eds. C. Bourel de la Roncière, J. de Loye, and A. Coulon. 3 vols. (Paris, 1895–1959)

Aristotle. *The Politics of Aristotle.* Trans. E. Barker (Oxford, 1946)

Augustine. *De civitate Dei libri XXII.* Ed. E. Hoffmann. 2 vols. (Vienna, 1899–1900)

Baluze, E. *Vitae paparum Avenionensium.* Ed. G. Mollat. 4 vols. (Paris, 1914–27)

*Miscellanea novo ordine digesta.* Ed. J. D. Mansi. 4 vols. (Lucca, 1761–4)

Barbiche, B., ed. *Les Actes pontificaux originaux des Archives Nationales de Paris.* 2 vols. (Vatican City, 1975–8)

Benedict XI. *Les Registres de Benoît XI.* Ed. C. Grandjean (Paris, 1883–1905)

Bernard Gui. *De fundatione et prioribus conventuum provinciarum Tolosanae et Provinciae ordinis praedicatorum.* Ed. P. A. Amargier (Rome, 1961)

Bernard of Clairvaux. *Opera.* Eds. J. Leclercq, C. H. Talbot, and H. M. Rochais. 8 vols. (Rome, 1957–77)

*De consideratione ad Eugenium Papam.* In *Opera,* 3:379–493

Bessin, G., ed. *Concilia Rotomagensis provinciae* (Rouen, 1717)

Boniface VIII. *Les Registres de Boniface VIII.* Eds. G. Digard, M. Faucon, and A. Thomas. 4 vols. (Paris, 1884–1939)

*Liber Sextus Decretalium d. Bonifacii papae VIII.* In *Corpus Iuris Canonici.* Ed. E. Friedberg (Leipzig, 1879–81), 2:929–1,124

*Unam sanctam.* In P. Dupuy, *Histoire du différend d'entre le pape Boniface VIII. et Philippes le Bel* (Paris, 1655), pp. 182–6

Bossuet, J. B. *Oeuvres de Bossuet, évêque de Meaux.* 43 vols. (Versailles, 1815–19)

Bourgeois du Chastenet, L. *Nouvelle histoire du concile de Constance* (Paris, 1718)

Boutaric, E. 'Notices et extraits de documents inédits relatifs à l'histoire de France sous Philippe le Bel', *Notices et extraits des manuscrits de la Bibliothèque Nationale et autres bibliothèques,* 20/2 (Paris, 1862), pp. 83–237

Brandmüller, W. *Das Konzil von Pavia-Siena, 1423–1424.* 2 vols. (Münster, 1968–74)

Brunel, C., ed. *Les Miracles de Saint Privat, suivis des opuscules d'Aldebert III, évêque de Mende* (Paris, 1912)

Bruno of Olmütz. *Relatio de statu ecclesiae in regno Alemanniae.* Ed. J. Schwalm, *MGH, Leges* 4/3 (Hanover, 1904–6), pp. 589–94

Burdin, G. de, ed. *Documents historiques sur la province de Gévaudan.* 2 vols. (Toulouse, 1846–7)

Calixtus II. *Bullaire du pape Calixte II.* Ed. U. Robert (Paris, 1891 = Hildesheim, 1979)

*Chartularium Universitatis Parisiensis.* Eds. H. Denifle and E. Chatelain. 4 vols. (Paris, 1889–97)

*Chronica monasterii S. Albani.* Ed. H. T. Riley. 7 vols. (London, 1863–76)

# Bibliography

*Chronicon breve de gestis Aldeberti.* In C. Brunel, ed., *Les miracles de Saint Privat* (Paris, 1912), pp. 124–34

Cicero. *De officiis.* Loeb Classical Library (London, 1921)

Clement IV. *Les Registres de Clément IV.* Ed. E. Jordan. 2 vols. (Paris, 1893–1945)

Clement V. *Clementinae: Clementis papae V. constitutiones.* In *Corpus Iuris Canonici.* Ed. E. Friedberg (Leipzig, 1879–81), 2:1,125–1,200

*Regestum Clementis papae V.* 9 vols. (Rome, 1885–8)

*Tables des registres de Clément V.* Eds. Y. Lanhers and C. Vogel (Paris, 1948–57)

*Codex Iustinianus.* In *Corpus Iuris Civilis,* 2. Ed. and rev. P. Krüger. 9th edn. (1915 = Zurich, 1967)

*Conciliorum Oecumenicorum Decreta.* Eds. J. Alberigo *et al.* 3rd edn. (Bologna, 1973)

*Concilium Bituricense a Simone de Belloloco archiepiscopo cum suffraganeis celebratum, XV. Kal. Octobr. ann. MCCLXXXVI.* In J. D. Mansi, ed., *Sanctorum conciliorum nova et amplissima collectio,* 24:625–48

*Concilium Florentinum: Documenta et scriptores.* Ed. G. Hofmann (Rome, 1940– )

Conring, H. *Opera.* 7 vols. Ed. J. W. Göbel (Brunswick, 1730)

*Corpus Iuris Canonici.* Ed. E. Friedberg. 2 vols. (Leipzig, 1879–81)

*Corpus Iuris Civilis.* Eds. T. Mommsen, P. Krueger, R. Schoell, and W. Kroll. 3 vols. (Berlin, 1872–95)

Crowder, C. M. D. *Unity, Heresy, and Reform, 1378–1460: The Conciliar Response to the Great Schism* (New York, 1977)

Davidsohn, R., ed. 'Bericht der päpstlichen Legaten, Guillielmus (Duranti) . . . und Pilifortis abbas Lumberiensis . . . an den Papst Clemens V., von Ende 1305.' In R. Davidsohn, *Forschungen zur Geschichte von Florenz: Dritter Teil, 13. und 14. Jahrhundert* (Berlin, 1901), pp. 287–321

Denifle, H., ed. 'Die Denkschriften der Colonna gegen Bonifaz VIII. und der Cardinäle gegen die Colonna', *Archiv für Literatur- und Kirchengeschichte des Mittelalters,* 5 (1889), pp. 493–529

ed. 'Die Statuten der Juristen-Universität Bologna vom Jahre 1317–1347', *Archiv für Literatur- und Kirchengeschichte des Mittelalters,* 3 (1887), pp. 196–408

*Digesta: Iustiniani Digesta.* In *Corpus Iuris Civilis,* 1. Ed. T. Mommsen, rev. P. Krüger. 11th edn. (1908 = Zurich, 1973)

Dionysius Areopagita. *Dionysiaca. Recueil donnant l'ensemble des traductions latines des ouvrages attribués au Denys de l'Aréopage.* Eds. P. Chevailler *et al.* 2 vols. (Paris and Bruges, 1937–49)

Diplovatatius, T. *De praestantia doctorum.* Ed. G. Pescatore (Berlin, 1890)

*De claris iuris consultis. Pars prior.* Eds. H. Kantorowicz and F. Schulz (Berlin, 1919)

*Liber de claris iuris consultis. Pars posterior.* Eds. F. Schulz, H. Kantorowicz, and G. Rabotti. *Studia Gratiana,* 10 (Bologna, 1968)

*Disputatio inter clericum et militem.* Ed. and trans. N. N. Erickson. *Proceedings of the American Philosophical Society,* 111 (1967), pp. 288–309

Du Boulay, C. E. *Historia Universitatis Parisiensis.* 6 vols. (Paris, 1665–73)

Duchesne, A. *Historiae Francorum scriptores.* 5 vols. (Paris, 1636–49)

Dupuy, P. *Histoire du différend d'entre le pape Boniface VIII. et Philippes le Bel* (Paris, 1655)

Ehrle, F. 'Zur Vorgeschichte des Concils von Vienne', *Archiv für Literatur- und*

# Bibliography

*Kirchengeschichte des Mittelalters*, 2 (1886), pp. 353–416; 3 (1887), pp. 1–195
'Ein Bruchstück der Acten des Concils von Vienne', *Archiv für Literatur- und Kirchengeschichte des Mittelalters*, 4 (1888), pp. 361–470
'Zur Geschichte des päpstlichen Hofceremoniells im 14. Jahrhundert', *Archiv für Literatur- und Kirchengeschichte des Mittelalters*, 5 (1889), pp. 565–602
*Historia bibliothecae Romanorum pontificum tum Bonifatianae tum Avenionensis* (Rome, 1890)
'Enquête sur la juridiction en Languedoc (vers 1300).' Ed. E. Boutaric. *Notices et extraits des manuscrits de la Bibliothèque Nationale*, 20/2 (Paris, 1862), pp. 132–5
Finke, H., ed. *Acta concilii Constanciensis*. 4 vols. (Münster, 1896–1928)
  *Aus den Tagen Bonifaz VIII.: Funde und Forschungen* (Münster, 1902)
  ed. 'Bericht über das Pariser Nationalkonzil von 1290 und das Auftreten des Kardinals Benedikt Gaëtani auf demselben.' In *Aus den Tagen Bonifaz VIII.* (Münster, 1902), part 'Quellen', pp. iii–vii
Fournier, M., ed. *Les Statuts et privilèges des universités françaises depuis leur fondation jusq' en 1789*. 4 vols. (Paris, 1890–4)
*Gallia Christiana*. 16 vols. (Paris, 1715–85, 1856–65)
García y García, A., ed. *Constitutiones concilii quarti Lateranensis una cum commentariis glossatorum* (Vatican City, 1981)
Gerson, J. *Opera omnia*. Ed. L. E. du Pin. 5 vols. (Antwerp, 1706)
  *Œuvres complètes*. Ed. P. Glorieux. 10 vols. (Paris, 1960–73)
*Gesta Romanae aecclesiae contra Hildebrandum*. Ed. K. Francke, in *MGH, Libelli de lite* (Hanover, 1892), 2:366–422
Gilbert of Tournai. *Collectio de scandalis ecclesiae*. Ed. A. Stroick. *Archivum franciscanum historicum*, 24 (1931), pp. 33–62
Giles of Rome. *De ecclesiastica potestate*. Ed. R. Scholz (Weimar, 1929)
  *De regimine principum* (Venice, 1498)
  *Tractatus contra exemptos* (Rome, 1555)
Gratian. *Decretum Magistri Gratiani*. In *Corpus Iuris Canonici*, vol. 1. Ed. E. Friedberg (Leipzig, 1879)
*Gravamina ecclesiae Gallicanae*. In Matthew Paris, *Chronica majora* (London, 1872–83), 6:99–112
Gregory VII. *Dictatus Papae*. In J. Miethke and A. Bühler, eds. *Kaiser und Papst im Konflikt* (Düsseldorf, 1988), pp. 61f. Trans. by B. Tierney, *The Crisis of Church and State* (Englewood Cliffs, 1964), pp. 49f.
Gregory IX. *Liber Extra = Decretalium d. Gregorii papae IX. compilatio*. In *Corpus Iuris Canonici*. Ed. E. Friedberg (Leipzig, 1879–81), 2:1–928
  *Les Registres de Grégoire IX*. Ed. L. Auvray. 4 vols. (Paris, 1896–1955)
Gregory X. *Les Registres de Grégoire X*. Ed. J. Guiraud (Paris, 1892–1906)
Haller, J., ed. *Concilium Basiliense*. 8 vols. (Basle, 1896–1936)
Hardt, H. von der. *Magnum oecumenicum Constantiense concilium*. 6 vols. (Frankfurt and Leipzig, 1697–1700)
Henry of Ghent. 'Sermo magistri Henrici de Gandavo . . . factus in synodo anno Domini M°CC°LXXXVII°.' Ed. K. Schleyer, *Anfänge des Gallikanismus* (Berlin, 1937), pp. 141–50
Hieronymus. *Die Chronik des Hieronymus: Hieronymi Chronicon*. Ed. R. Helm (Leipzig, 1913)

# Bibliography

Hoberg, H., ed. *Taxae pro communibus servitiis ex libris obligatorum ab anno 1295 usque ad annum 1445 confectis* (Vatican City, 1949)

Honorius III. *Regesta Honorii Papae III*. Ed. P. Pressuti. 2 vols. (Rome, 1888–95)

Honorius IV. *Les Registres d'Honorius IV*. Ed. M. Prou (Paris, 1886–8)

Humbert of Romans. *Liber de tractandis in concilio Lugdunensi 1274 celebrando*. In E. Martène and U. Durand, *Veterum scriptorum . . . amplissima collectio* (Paris, 1724–33), 7:174–98

Innocent IV. *Les Registres d'Innocent IV*. Ed. E. Berger. 4 vols. (Paris, 1884–1920)

*Institutiones: Iustiniani Institutiones*. In *Corpus Iuris Civilis*, 1. Ed. P. Krüger. 11th edn. (1908 = Zurich, 1973)

James of Viterbo. *De regimine christiano*. Ed. H.-X. Arquillière, in *Le plus ancien traité de l'église* (Paris, 1926), pp. 85–310

Johannes Teutonicus. *Glossa ordinaria*. In *Decretum Gratiani emendatum* (Lyons, 1606)

John XXI. *Le Registre de Jean XXI*. Ed. E. Cadier (Paris, 1898)

John XXII. *Lettres communes*. Ed. G. Mollat. 17 vols. (Paris, 1904–59)
    *Lettres secrètes et curiales relatives à la France*. Eds. A. Coulon and S. Clémencet. 3 vols. (Paris, 1900–72)

John of Salisbury. *Policraticus*. Ed. C. C. I. Webb. 2 vols. (Oxford, 1909)

John Quidort of Paris. *Über königliche und päpstliche Gewalt. De regia potestate et papali*. Ed. F. Bleienstein (Stuttgart, 1969)

Jordanes. *Romana et Getica*. Ed. T. Mommsen, *MGH, Auctores antiquissimi* 5/1 (Berlin, 1882)

Latini, Brunetto. *Li livres dou tresor*. Ed. F. J. Carmody (Berkeley, 1948)

Luther, Martin. *An den christlichen Adel deutscher Nation*. In *Kritische Gesamtausgabe*, 1. Abteilung (Weimar and Graz, 1883–1982), 6:404–69
    'Letter to Pope Leo X.' In *The Renaissance*. Eds. E. Cochrane and J. Kirshner (Chicago, 1986), pp. 325–33

Mansi, J. D., ed. *Sacrorum conciliorum nova et amplissima collectio*. 50 vols. (Florence, 1759–98; Paris, 1901–62)

Marca, Pierre de. *De concordia sacerdotii et imperii* (Paris, 1704)

Martène, E. and U. Durand. *Thesaurus novus anecdotorum*. 5 vols. (Paris, 1717)
    *Veterum scriptorum et monumentorum historicorum, dogmaticorum, moralium amplissima collectio*. 9 vols. (Paris, 1724–33)

Martin IV. *Les Registres de Martin IV*. Ed. F. Olivier-Martin (Paris, 1901–35)

Martin of Braga. *Formula vitae honestae*. In *Opera omnia*. Ed. C. W. Barlow (New Haven, 1950), pp. 236–50

Matthew Paris. *Chronica majora*. Ed. H. R. Luard. 7 vols. (London, 1872–83)

*Mémoire relatif au paréage de 1307 conclu entre l'évêque Guillaume Durand II et le roi Philippe-le-Bel*. Ed. A. Maisonobe. Published by the S. d. L. (Mende, 1896). In *Bulletin de la S. d. L.*, 49 (Mende, 1897)

*Monumenta conciliorum generalium seculi decimi quinti*. Ed. Caesarea Academia Scientiarum Vindobonensis. 4 vols. (Vienna, 1857–1935)

Nicholas III. *Les Registres de Nicolas III*. Ed. J. Gay (Paris, 1898–1938)

Nicholas IV. *Les Registres de Nicolas IV*. Ed. E. Langlois. 2 vols. (Paris, 1886–93)

Nicholas of Clémanges. *Le Traité de la ruine de l'église de Nicolas de Clamanges*. Ed. A. Coville (Paris, 1936)

# Bibliography

Nicholas of Cusa. *Opera omnia*. Heidelberg Academy of Letters (Leipzig and Hamburg, 1932–   )

*De concordantia catholica*. Ed. G. Kallen. *Opera omnia*, 14 (Hamburg, 1939–68).

Nicholas of Lisieux. *Liber de antichristo et ejusdem ministris*. In E. Martène and U. Durand, *Veterum scriptorum . . . amplissima collectio* (Paris, 1724–33), 9:1,273–1,446

Niem, Dietrich von. *Dialog über Union und Reform der Kirche, mit einer zweiten Fassung aus dem Jahre 1415*. Ed. H. Heimpel (Leipzig and Berlin, 1933)

*Novellae: Iustiniani Novellae*. In *Corpus Iuris Civilis*, 3. Eds. R. Schoell and W. Kroll (1895 = Zurich, 1972)

*Ordonnances des roys de France de la troisième race*. Eds. E.-J. de Laurière *et al.* 22 vols. (Paris, 1723–1849)

Panzirolus, G. *De claris legum interpretibus libri quatuor* (Leipzig, 1721)

*Paréage of Mende*. In *Ordonnances des roys de France de la troisième race*, eds. E.-J. de Laurière *et al.*, 22 vols. (Paris, 1723–1849), 11:369–403. Also in G. de Burdin, ed., *Documents historiques sur la province de Gévaudan*, 2 vols. (Toulouse, 1846–7), 1:359–76, and in J. Roucaute and M. Saché, eds., *Lettres de Philippe-le-Bel relatives au pays de Gévaudan* (Mende, 1896), appendix 1, pp. 173–95

*Patrologia Latina: Patrologiae cursus completus*. Ed. J. P. Migne. 221 vols. (Paris, 1844–64)

Piccolomini, Aeneas Silvius (Pius II). *Opera inedita*. Ed. G. Cugnoni, in *Atti della R. Accademia dei Lincei*, 3rd series, 8 (Rome, 1883), pp. 319–686

Picot, G., ed. *Documents relatifs aux états généraux et assemblées réunis sous Philippe le Bel* (Paris, 1901)

Probus, P., ed. *Pragmatica sanctio, cum glossis . . . Cosmae Guimier . . . opera aut labore D. Philippi Propi Biturici, officialis Ambian. et d. nostri papae cappellani . . . secunda editio quoad additiones*. 2 vols. (Paris, 1555)

Pseudo-Isidore. *Decretales Pseudo-Isidorianae et Capitula Angilramni*. Ed. P. Hinschius (Leipzig, 1863)

*Isidori Mercatoris Decretalium collectio*. Ed. J. Merlin (Paris, 1530 = *PL*, 130)

*Quellen zur Geschichte Kaiser Heinrichs IV*. Ed. F.-J. Schmale (Darmstadt, 1968)

Roucaute, J. and M. Saché, eds. *Lettres de Philippe-le-Bel relatives au pays de Gévaudan* (Mende, 1896)

Sarti, M. *De claris archigymnasii Bononiensis professoribus* (Bologna, 1769)

Schütte, L., ed. *Vatikanische Aktenstücke zur italienischen Legation des Duranti und Pilifort d. J. 1305–1306*. Beilage zum Osterprogramm 1909 des Königl. kath. Gymnasiums zu Leobschütz (Leobschütz, 1909)

*Tractatus de usurpata potestate fratrum contra praelatos et rectores parrochialium ecclesiarum*. Ed. K. Schleyer, *Anfänge des Gallikanismus* (Berlin, 1937), pp. 151–200

*Tractatus ex variis iuris interpretibus collecti*. 18 vols. (Lyons, 1549)

*Tractatus universi iuris, duce et auspice Gregorio XIII . . . in unum congesti*. 22 vols. (Venice, 1584–6)

Urban IV. *Les Registres d'Urbain IV*. Ed. J. Guiraud. 4 vols. (Paris, 1901–58)

Valerius Maximus. *Factorum et dictorum memorabilium libri novem*. Ed. C. Kempf (Leipzig, 1888)

Valls-Taberner, F. 'Une Lettre de Guillaume Durand le Jeune à Jacques II

# Bibliography

d'Aragon', *Le Moyen Age*, 28 (1915), pp. 347–55

*Vindiciae contra tyrannos* (n. p., 1589)

Walter of Coventry. *Memoriale*. Ed. W. Stubbs. 2 vols. (London, 1872–3)

Walter of Hemingburgh. *Chronicon*. Ed. H. C. Hamilton. 2 vols. (London, 1848–9)

Walther, H., ed. *Proverbia sententiaeque Latinitatis medii aevi*. 5 vols. (Göttingen, 1963–7)

William of Conches. *Das Moralium Dogma Philosophorum des Guillaume de Conches*. Ed. J. Holmberg (Uppsala, 1929)

William Durant the Elder. *Les Instructions et constitutions de Guillaume Durand le Spéculateur publiés d'après le manuscrit de Cessenon*. Eds. J. Berthelé, M. Valmary. *Mémoires de la section des lettres de l'Académie des sciences et lettres de Montpellier*, 2nd series, 3 (Montpellier, 1900–7), pp. 1–148

    *Rationale divinorum officiorum* (Lyons, 1539)

    *Speculum iudiciale*. 3 vols. (Lyons, 1547)

William Durant the Younger. *De modo generalis concilii celebrandi tractatus*. Ed. J. Crespin (Lyons, 1531)

    *Tractatus de modo generalis concilii celebrandi*. Ed. P. Probus (Paris, 1545)

    *Tractatus de modo generalis concilii celebrandi*. In *Secundum volumen tractatuum ex variis iuris interpretibus collectorum* (Lyons, 1549), fols. 88v–117v

    *Tractatus de modo generalis concilii celebrandi*. Ed. Michele Tramezino (Venice, 1562)

    *Tractatus de modo generalis concilii celebrandi*. In *Tractatus universi iuris*, 13/1: *De potestate ecclesiastica* (Venice, 1584), fols. 154–82v

    *Tractatus de modo generalis concilii celebrandi*. Ed. F. Clousier (Paris, 1671; rpt. London: Gregg Press, n.d. (1963?))

William Le Maire. *Liber Guillelmi Majoris*. Ed. C. Port (Paris, 1877)


## SECONDARY LITERATURE

Alberigo, G. *Cardinalato e collegialità: Studi sull'ecclesiologia tra l'XI e il XIV secolo* (Florence, 1969)

    'Il movimento conciliare (XIV–XV sec.) nella ricerca storica recente', *Studi medievali*, 19/2 (1978), pp. 913–50

    *Chiesa conciliare: Identità e significato del conciliarismo* (Brescia, 1981)

André, F. 'Les Evêques de Mende pendant le XIVᵉ siècle', *Bulletin de la S. d. L.*, 22/2 (1871), pp. 29–45

    *Inventaire sommaire des archives communales antérieures à 1790, séries AA–II* (Mende, 1885)

André, F., M. Saché, A. Maisonobe, C. Porée, and A. Philippe. *Inventaire sommaire des archives départementales antérieures à 1790, Lozère, archives ecclésiastiques, séries G–H*. 3 vols. (Mende, 1882–1904)

Andresen, C. 'Geschichte der abendländischen Konzile des Mittelalters.' In *Die ökumenischen Konzile der Christenheit*. Ed. H. J. Margull (Stuttgart, 1961), pp. 75–200

Andrieu, M. *Le Pontifical Romain au Moyen Age*. 4 vols. (Vatican City, 1938–41)

*Antiqui und Moderni: Traditionsbewusstsein und Fortschrittsbewusstsein im späten*

# Bibliography

*Mittelalter.* Ed. A. Zimmermann. *Miscellanea Mediaevalia*, 9 (Berlin, 1974)

Arquillière, H.-X. 'L'Origine des théories conciliaires', *Séances et travaux de l'Académie des Sciences Morales et Politiques*, 175 (Paris, 1911), pp. 573–86

'L'Appel au concile sous Philippe le Bel et la genèse des théories conciliaires', *Revue des questions historiques*, 89 (1911), pp. 23–55

*L'Augustinisme politique: Essai sur la formation des théories politiques du Moyen Age.* 2nd edn. (Paris, 1955)

Artonne, A. *Le Mouvement de 1314 et les chartes provinciales de 1315* (Paris, 1912)

*Die Auseinandersetzungen an der Pariser Universität im XIII. Jahrhundert.* Ed. A. Zimmermann. *Miscellanea Mediaevalia*, 10 (Berlin, 1976)

*Authority and Power: Studies on Medieval Law and Government presented to Walter Ullmann on his Seventieth Birthday.* Eds. B. Tierney and P. Linehan (Cambridge, 1980)

Baldwin, J. W. *Masters, Princes, and Merchants: The Social Views of Peter the Chanter and his Circle.* 2 vols. (Princeton, 1970)

Balmelle, M. *Bibliographie du Gévaudan.* 3 vols. (Mende, 1942–53)

Balmelle, M. and S. Pouget. *Histoire de Mende* (Mende, 1947)

Balon, J. 'La "ratio" fondement et justification du droit avant Gratien', *Studia Gratiana*, 9 (1966), pp. 11–25

Baratier, E. 'Nominations et origines des évêques des provinces d'Aix et Arles.' In *Les Evêques, les clercs, et le roi* (Toulouse, 1972), pp. 115–45

Barker, E. *The Dominican Order and Convocation: A Study of the Growth of Representation in the Church during the Thirteenth Century* (Oxford, 1913)

Baron, H. 'Cicero and the Roman Civic Spirit in the Middle Ages and Early Renaissance', *Bulletin of the John Rylands Library*, 22 (1938), pp. 72–97

Barraclough, G. *Papal Provisions: Aspects of Church History, Constitutional, Legal, and Administrative in the Later Middle Ages* (Oxford, 1935)

*The Medieval Papacy* (London, 1968)

Barroux, R., M. Daucet, H. Bouillier de Branche, and G. Dumas. *Archives départementales de la Lozère, série E: Minutes des notaires, répertoire numérique.* 2 vols. (Mende, 1931–57)

Baudrier, H. L. *Bibliographie lyonnaise.* 12 vols. (Lyons, 1895–1921)

Bäumer, R. 'Die Interpretation und Verbindlichkeit der Konstanzer Dekrete', *Theologisch-praktische Quartalsschrift*, 116 (1968), pp. 44–53

'Die Reformkonzilien des 15. Jahrhunderts in der neueren Forschung', *Annuarium historiae conciliorum*, 1 (1969), pp. 153–64

*Nachwirkungen des konziliaren Gedankens in der Theologie und Kanonistik des frühen 16. Jahrhunderts* (Münster, 1971)

'Die Konstanzer Dekrete "Haec sancta" und "Frequens" im Urteil katholischer Kontroverstheologen des 16. Jahrhunderts.' In *Von Konstanz nach Trient* (Munich and Paderborn, 1972), pp. 547–74

'Die Bedeutung des Konstanzer Konzils für die Geschichte der Kirche', *Annuarium historiae conciliorum*, 4 (1972), pp. 26–45

'Um die Anfänge der päpstlichen Unfehlbarkeitslehre', *Theologische Revue*, 69 (1973), pp. 441–50

'Antwort an Tierney', *Theologische Revue*, 70 (1974), pp. 193–4

ed. *Die Entwicklung des Konziliarismus* (Darmstadt, 1976)

# Bibliography

'Die Erforschung des Konziliarismus.' In *Die Entwicklung des Konziliarismus* (Darmstadt, 1976), pp. 3–56

Bautier, R.-H. 'Le Jubilé de 1300 et l'alliance franco-pontificale au temps de Philippe le Bel et de Boniface VIII', *Le Moyen Age*, 86 (1980), pp. 189–216

Bayer, H. 'Zur Soziologie des mittelalterlichen Individualisierungsprozesses: Ein Beitrag zu einer wirklichkeitsbezogenen Geistesgeschichte', *Archiv für Kulturgeschichte*, 58 (1976), pp. 115–53

Becker, H.-J. '"Protestatio", "Protest": Funktion und Funktionswandel eines rechtlichen Instruments', *Zeitschrift für historische Forschung*, 5 (1978), pp. 385–412

*Die Appellation vom Papst an ein Allgemeines Konzil: Historische Entwicklung und kanonistische Diskussion im späten Mittelalter und in der frühen Neuzeit* (Cologne and Vienna, 1988)

Beer, S. 'The Rule of the Wise and the Holy: Hierarchy in the Thomistic System', *Political Theory*, 14 (1986), pp. 391–422

*Der Begriff der Repraesentatio im Mittelalter: Stellvertretung, Symbol, Zeichen, Bild.* Ed. A. Zimmermann. *Miscellanea Mediaevalia*, 8 (Berlin, 1971)

*Beiträge zum Berufsbewusstsein des mittelalterlichen Menschen.* Ed. P. Wilpert. *Miscellanea Mediaevalia*, 3 (Berlin, 1964)

Bellone, E. 'Cultura e studi nei progetti di reforma presentati al concilio di Vienne, 1311–1312', *Annuarium historiae conciliorum*, 9 (1977), pp. 67–111

Below, G. v. *Der deutsche Staat des Mittelalters: Ein Grundriss der deutschen Verfassungsgeschichte* (Leipzig, 1914)

Bendix, R. *Kings or People: Power and the Mandate to Rule* (Berkeley, 1978)

Benson, R. L. 'Plenitudo potestatis: Evolution of a Formula from Gregory IV to Gratian', *Studia Gratiana*, 14 (1967), pp. 193–217

*The Bishop-Elect: A Study in Medieval Ecclesiastical Office* (Princeton, 1968)

'Political "Renovatio": Two Models from Roman Antiquity.' In *Renaissance and Renewal in the Twelfth Century* (Cambridge/Mass., 1982), pp. 339–86

Benz, E. *Ecclesia spiritualis: Kirchenidee und Geschichtstheologie der franziskanischen Reformation* (Stuttgart, 1934)

Benzinger, J. *Invectiva in Romam: Romkritik im Mittelalter vom 9. bis zum 12. Jahrhundert* (Lübeck, 1968)

Berger, A. *Encyclopedic Dictionary of Roman Law* (Philadelphia, 1953)

Berges, W. *Die Fürstenspiegel des hohen und späten Mittelalters* (Leipzig, 1938)

Berman, H. J. *Law and Revolution: The Formation of the Western Legal Tradition* (Cambridge/Mass., 1983)

Bernheim, E. *Mittelalterliche Zeitanschauungen in ihrem Einfluss auf Politik und Geschichtsschreibung* (Tübingen, 1918)

Bernstein, A. *Pierre d'Ailly and the Blanchard Affair: University and Chancellor of Paris at the Beginning of the Great Schism* (Leiden, 1978)

Besse, J.-M. *Abbayes et prieurés de l'ancienne France, 4: Provinces ecclésiastiques d'Alby, de Narbonne et de Toulouse* (Ligugé and Paris, 1911)

Beumann, H. 'Zur Entwicklung transpersonaler Staatsvorstellungen.' In *Das Königtum: Seine geistigen und rechtlichen Grundlagen. Vorträge und Forschungen*, 3 (Lindau, 1956), pp. 185–224

'Die Bedeutung des Kaisertums für die Entstehung der deutschen Nation im

# Bibliography

Spiegel der Bezeichnungen von Reich und Herrscher', *Nationes*, 1 (1978), pp. 317–66

Bezold, F. v. 'Die Lehre von der Volkssouveränetät während des Mittelalters', *Historische Zeitschrift*, 36 (1876), pp. 313–67

Biechler, J. E. 'Nicholas of Cusa and the End of the Conciliar Movement: A Humanist Crisis of Identity', *Church History*, 44 (1975), pp. 5–21

Bisson, T. N. *Assemblies and Representation in Languedoc in the Thirteenth Century* (Princeton, 1964)

'Consultative Functions of the King's Parliaments, 1250–1314', *Speculum*, 44 (1969), pp. 353–73

'The General Assemblies of Philip the Fair: Their Character Reconsidered', *Studia Gratiana*, 15 (1972), pp. 537–64

'The Problem of Feudal Monarchy: Aragon, Catalonia, and France', *Speculum*, 53 (1978), pp. 460–78

Black, A. 'The Political Ideas of Conciliarism and Papalism, 1430–1450', *Journal of Ecclesiastical History*, 20 (1969), pp. 45–66

*Monarchy and Community: Political Ideas in the Later Conciliar Controversy, 1430–1450* (Cambridge, 1970)

'The Council of Basle and the Vatican Council.' In *Councils and Assemblies* (Cambridge, 1971), pp. 229–34

*Council and Commune: The Conciliar Movement and the Fifteenth-Century Heritage* (London, 1979)

'What Was Conciliarism? Conciliar Theory in Historical Perspective.' In *Authority and Power* (Cambridge, 1980), pp. 213–24.

'The Conciliar Movement.' In *Cambridge History of Medieval Political Thought*. Ed. J. H. Burns (Cambridge, 1988), pp. 573–87

'The Individual and Society.' In *Cambridge History of Medieval Political Thought*. Ed. J. H. Burns (Cambridge, 1988), pp. 588–606

Bliemetzrieder, F. P. *Das Generalkonzil im grossen abendländischen Schisma* (Paderborn, 1904)

Bloch, M. *La Société féodale* (Paris, 1939)

*Feudal Society*. Trans. L. A. Manyon (Chicago, 1961)

*Les Rois thaumaturges: Etude sur le caractère surnaturel attribué à la puissance royale, particulièrement en France et en Angleterre*. Rev. ed. (Paris, 1983)

Bloomfield, M. W. *The Seven Deadly Sins* (Michigan, 1952)

Blumenthal, U.-R. *Der Investiturstreit* (Stuttgart, 1982)

*The Investiture Controversy: Church and Monarchy from the Ninth to the Twelfth Century* (Philadelphia, 1988)

Boase, T. S. R. *Boniface VIII* (London, 1933)

Bock, F. 'Kaisertum, Kurie und Nationalstaat im Beginn des 14. Jahrhunderts', *Römische Quartalsschrift*, 44 (1936), pp. 105–22, 169–220

'Nationalstaatliche Regungen in Italien bei den guelfisch-ghibellinischen Auseinandersetzungen von Innozenz III. bis Johann XXII.', *Quellen und Forschungen aus italienischen Archiven und Bibliotheken*, 33 (1944), pp. 1–48

Boisset, L. *Un Concile provincial au treizième siècle, Vienne 1289: Eglise locale et société* (Paris, 1973)

Boockmann, H. 'Zur politischen Geschichte des Konstanzer Konzils', *Zeitschrift*

335

*für Kirchengeschichte*, 85 (1974), pp. 45–63

Bories, M. 'Les Origines de l'université de Montpellier.' In *Les Universités du Languedoc* (Toulouse, 1970), pp. 92–107

Bosse, L. 'Notes pour servir à l'histoire de Marvejols, XIIIᵉ–XVIIIᵉ s.,' *Bulletin de la S. d. L.*, 18 (1867), pp. 152–214

Bossy, J. 'The Mass as a Social Institution, 1200–1700', *Past and Present*, 100 (1983), pp. 29–61

*Christianity in the West, 1400–1700* (Oxford, 1985)

Boudet, M. 'Les Derniers Mercoeurs: Béraud VII de Mercoeur, Connétable de Champagne, 1272–1321', *Revue d'Auvergne*, 21 (1904), pp. 1–20, 93–127, 241–66, 373–96, 453–60; 22 (1905), pp. 47–63, 97–123, 161–78

'Les Derniers Mercoeurs: Les Mercoeurs seigneurs de Gerzat, leurs auteurs et leur fin', *Revue d'Auvergne*, 22 (1905), pp. 179–92, 244–72, 333–46, 373–89

*Les Derniers Mercoeurs* (Paris, 1906)

Boutaric, E. *La France sous Philippe le Bel: Etude sur les institutions politiques et administratives du Moyen Age* (Paris, 1861)

Boyle, L. 'The Date of the Commentary of William Duranti on the Constitutions of the Second Council of Lyons', *Bulletin of Medieval Canon Law*, 4 (1974), pp. 39–47

Brandmüller, W. 'Besitzt das Konstanzer Dekret "Haec sancta" dogmatische Verbindlichkeit?', *Annuarium historiae conciliorum*, 1 (1969), pp. 96–113

*Ignaz v. Döllinger am Vorabend des I. Vatikanums* (St Ottilien, 1977)

Brémond, C., J. Le Goff, and J. C. Schmitt. *L'Exemplum* (Turnhout, 1982)

Brentano, R. *Two Churches: England and Italy in the Thirteenth Century* (Princeton, 1968)

Brett, E. T. *Humbert of Romans: His Life and Views of Thirteenth-Century Society* (Toronto, 1984)

Brooke, R. B. *The Coming of the Friars* (London, 1975)

Brown, D. C. *Pastor and Laity in the Theology of Jean Gerson* (Cambridge, 1987)

Brown, E. A. R. 'Cessante causa and the Taxes of the Last Capetians: The Political Application of a Philosophical Maxim', *Studia Gratiana*, 15 (1972), pp. 565–87

'Representation and Agency Law in the Later Middle Ages: The Theoretical Foundations and the Evolution of Practice in the Thirteenth- and Fourteenth-Century Midi', *Viator*, 3 (1972), pp. 329–64

'Taxation and Morality in the Thirteenth and Fourteenth Centuries', *French Historical Studies*, 8 (1973), pp. 1–28

'The Tyranny of a Construct: Feudalism and Historians of Medieval Europe', *American Historical Review*, 79 (1974), pp. 1,063–88

'Reform and Resistance to Royal Authority in Fourteenth-Century France: The Leagues of 1314–1315', *Parliaments, Estates & Representation*, 1 (1981), pp. 109–37

Brunel, C. 'Les Juges de la paix en Gévaudan au milieu du XIᵉ siècle', *Bibliothèque de l'Ecole des Chartes*, 109 (1951), pp. 32–41

Brunner, O. *Land und Herrschaft: Grundfragen der territorialen Verfassungsgeschichte Österreichs im Mittelalter*. 5th edn. (Vienna, 1965)

Brys, J. *De dispensatione in iure canonico praesertim apud Decretistas et Decretalistas usque ad medium saeculum decimum quartum* (Bruges, 1925)

Buisson, L. *Potestas und Caritas: Die päpstliche Gewalt im Spätmittelalter.* 2nd edn. (Cologne, 1982)

Burdach, K. *Reformation, Renaissance, Humanismus: Zwei Abhandlungen über die Grundlage moderner Bildung und Sprachkunst.* 2nd edn. (Berlin, 1926)

Bynum, C. *Docere Verbo et Exemplo: An Aspect of Twelfth-Century Spirituality* (Missoula, 1979)
  'Did the Twelfth Century Discover the Individual?', *Journal of Ecclesiastical History*, 31 (1980), pp. 1–17

Caillet, L. *La Papauté d'Avignon et l'église de France* (Paris, 1975)

Calasso, F. *I glossatori e la teoria della sovranità.* 3rd edn. (Milan, 1957)

Cam, H. M., A. Marongiu, and G. Stökl. 'Recent Work and Present Views on the Origins and Development of the Representative Assemblies', *Relazioni del X Congresso Internazionale di Scienze Storiche* (Florence, 1955), pp. 3–101

*Cambridge History of Medieval Political Thought, c. 350 – c. 1450.* Ed. J. H. Burns (Cambridge, 1988)

Campbell, G. J. 'The Protest of Saint Louis', *Traditio*, 15 (1959), pp. 405–18
  'The Attitude of the Monarchy toward the Use of Ecclesiastical Censures in the Reign of Saint Louis', *Speculum*, 35 (1960), pp. 535–55

Canning, J. P. 'The Corporation in the Political Thought of the Jurists of the Thirteenth and Fourteenth Centuries', *History of Political Thought*, 1 (1980), pp. 9–32
  'Introduction: Politics, Institutions and Ideas.' In *Cambridge History of Medieval Political Thought*, ed. J. H. Burns (Cambridge, 1988), pp. 341–66
  'Law, Sovereignty, and Corporation Theory, 1300–1450.' In *Cambridge History of Medieval Political Thought*, ed. J. H. Burns (Cambridge, 1988), pp. 454–76

Carlyle, R. W. and A. J. Carlyle. *A History of Mediaeval Political Theory in the West.* 6 vols. (Edinburgh and London, 1903–36)

Caron, P. G. *Aequitas romana, misericordia patristica ed epicheia aristotelica nella dottrina dell'aequitas canonica* (Milan, 1971)
  '"Aequitas et interpretatio" dans la doctrine canonique aux XIIIᵉ et XIVᵉ siècles', *Proceedings of the Third International Congress of Medieval Canon Law* (Vatican City, 1971), pp. 131–41

Carreyre, J. 'Pithou', *Dictionnaire de théologie catholique*, 12/2 (1935), cols. 2,233–8

Castaing-Sicard, M. *Monnaies féodales et circulation monétaire en Languedoc, Xᵉ– XIIIᵉ siècles* (Toulouse, 1961)

Chazaud, A. 'L'Evêque de Mende et les seigneurs du Tournel', *Bibliothèque de l'Ecole des Chartes*, 16 (1855), pp. 309–21

Cheney, C. R. *From Becket to Langton: English Church Government, 1170–1213* (Manchester, 1956)

Chenu, M. D. *Nature, Man, and Society in the Twelfth Century: Essays on New Theological Perspectives in the Latin West.* Trans. J. Taylor and L. K. Little (Chicago, 1968)

Chevailler, L. 'Observations sur le "Speculum legatorum" de Guillaume Durand.' In *Mélanges offerts au Professeur Louis Falletti. Annales de la faculté de droit de Lyon*, 2 (1971), pp. 85–98

Cheyette, F. 'La Justice et le pouvoir royal à la fin du Moyen Age français', *Revue historique de droit français et étranger*, 40 (1962), pp. 373–94

ed. *Lordship and Community in Medieval Europe* (New York, 1968)

'"Suum cuique tribuere"', *French Historical Studies*, 6 (1970), pp. 287–99

Chiffoleau, J. *Les Justices du pape: Délinquance et criminalité dans la région d'Avignon au quatorzième siècle* (Paris, 1984)

Chodorow, S. *Christian Political Theory and Church Politics in the Mid-Twelfth Century: The Ecclesiology of Gratian's Decretum* (Berkeley, 1972)

Christianson, G. *Cesarini, the Conciliar Cardinal: The Basel Years, 1431–1438* (St Ottilien, 1979)

Chroust, A.-H. 'The Corporate Idea and the Body Politic in the Middle Ages', *Review of Politics*, 9 (1947), pp. 423–52

*Church and Government in the Middle Ages: Essays presented to C. R. Cheney on his Seventieth Birthday*. Ed. C. N. L. Brooke, D. Luscombe, G. H. Martin, and Dorothy Owen (Cambridge, 1976)

Clanchy, M. T. 'Remembering the Past and the Good Old Law', *History*, 55 (1970), pp. 165–76

*From Memory to Written Record: England 1066–1307* (London, 1979)

Clarke, M. V. *Medieval Representation and Consent* (London, 1936)

Classen, P. 'Die hohen Schulen und die Gesellschaft im 12. Jahrhundert', *Archiv für Kulturgeschichte*, 48 (1966), pp. 155–80

Coing, H., ed. *Handbuch der Quellen und Literatur der neueren europäischen Privatrechtsgeschichte, 1: Mittelalter, 1100–1500: Die gelehrten Rechte und die Gesetzgebung* (Munich, 1973)

Coleman, J. 'Medieval Discussions of Property: "Ratio" and "Dominium" According to John of Paris and Marsilius of Padua', *History of Political Thought*, 4 (1983), pp. 209–28

'"Dominium" in Thirteenth and Fourteenth-Century Political Thought and its Seventeenth-Century Heirs: John of Paris and Locke', *Political Studies*, 33 (1985), pp. 73–100

'The Two Jurisdictions: Theological and Legal Justifications of Church Property in the Thirteenth Century', *Studies in Church History*, 24 (1987), pp. 75–110

'Property and Poverty.' In *Cambridge History of Medieval Political Thought*. Ed. J. H. Burns (Cambridge, 1988), pp. 607–48

Congar, Y. M.-J. 'Quod omnes tangit, ab omnibus tractari et approbari debet', *Revue historique de droit français et étranger*, 36 (1958), pp. 210–59

'Aspects ecclésiologiques de la querelle entre mendiants et séculiers dans la seconde moitié du XIIIᵉ siècle et le début du XIVᵉ', *Archives d'histoire doctrinale et littéraire du Moyen Age*, 36 (1961), pp. 35–151

*Vraie et fausse réforme dans l'église*. 2nd edn. (Paris, 1968)

*L'Eglise de Saint Augustin à l'époque moderne* (Paris, 1970)

'Status ecclesiae', *Studia Gratiana*, 15 (1972), pp. 1–31

*Droit ancien et structures ecclésiales* (London, 1982)

*Etudes d'ecclésiologie médiévale* (London, 1983)

Constable, G. 'Renewal and Reform in Religious Life: Concepts and Realities.' In *Renaissance and Renewal in the Twelfth Century* (Cambridge/Mass., 1982), pp. 37–67

# Bibliography

Cortese, E. *La norma giuridica: Spunti teorici nel diritto comune classico*. 2 vols. (Milan, 1962–4)

Costa, P. *Iurisdictio: Semantica del potere politico nella pubblicistica medievale, 1100–1433* (Milan, 1969)

Cottineau, L. H. *Répertoire topo-bibliographique des abbayes et prieurés*. 2 vols. (Mâcon, 1935–7)

*Councils and Assemblies*. Eds. G. J. Cuming and D. Baker (Cambridge, 1971)

Cowdrey, H. E. J. 'The Peace and the Truce of God in the Eleventh Century', *Past and Present*, 46 (1970), pp. 42–67

Crowder, C. M. D. *Unity, Heresy, and Reform, 1378–1460: The Conciliar Response to the Great Schism* (New York, 1977)

D'Agostino, F. *La tradizione dell'epieikeia nel medioevo latino: Un contributo alla storia dell'idea di equità* (Milan, 1976)

Damiata, M. *Guglielmo d'Ockham: Povertà e potere* (Florence, 1979)

Daunou, P.-C.-F. 'Adelbert de Tournel', *Histoire littéraire de la France*, 14 (1869), p. 623

Dauzat, A. *Dictionnaire étymologique des noms de famille et prénoms de France*. 2nd edn. (Paris, 1955)

David, M. *La Souveraineté et les limites juridiques du pouvoir monarchique du IX$^e$ au XV$^e$ siècle* (Paris, 1954)

D'Avray, D. L. 'A Letter of Innocent III and the Idea of Infallibility', *Catholic Historical Review*, 66 (1980), pp. 417–21

'Origins of the Idea of Infallibility: A Rejoinder to Professor Tierney', *Catholic Historical Review*, 67 (1981), pp. 60–4

Dawson, J. D. 'William of Saint-Amour and the Apostolic Tradition', *Mediaeval Studies*, 40 (1978), pp. 223–38

Deane, H. A. *The Political and Social Ideas of St. Augustine* (New York, 1963)

Décarreaux, J. *Les Grecs au concile de l'union Ferrare-Florence, 1438–1439* (Paris, 1970)

Delaruelle, E., E.-R. Labande, and P. Ourliac. *L'Eglise au temps du grand schisme et de la crise conciliaire, 1378–1449* (Paris, 1962)

'L'Université de Toulouse à la fin du XIII$^e$ siècle.' In *Les Universités du Languedoc* (Toulouse, 1970), pp. 108–15

Delcambre, E. 'Le Paréage du Puy', *Bibliothèque de l'Ecole des Chartes*, 92 (1931), pp. 121–69, 285–344

Dempf, A. *Sacrum Imperium: Geschichts- und Staatsphilosophie des Mittelalters und der politischen Renaissance* (Munich, 1929)

Denisy, L. 'Notice historique sur la ville de Marvejols', *Bulletin de la S. d. L.*, 24 (1873), pp. 57–277

*Notice topographique et historique sur le canton de Marvejols*. 2 vols. (Issoire, 1876)

Denton, J. H. *Robert Winchelsey and the Crown, 1294–1313: A Study in the Defense of Ecclesiastical Liberty* (Cambridge, 1980)

Devic, C. and J.-J. Vaissete. *Histoire générale de Languedoc avec des notes et les pièces justificatives*. Rev. edn. by A. Molinier *et al.* 16 vols. (Toulouse, 1872–1904)

*Dictionnaire de droit canonique*. Ed. R. Naz. 7 vols. (Paris, 1935–65)

*Dictionnaire d'histoire et de géographie ecclésiastiques*. Eds. A. Baudrillart, A. Vogt, U. de Rouziès, A. de Meyer, and E. van Cauwenbergh. (Paris, 1909–   )

# Bibliography

*Dictionnaire de théologie catholique.* Ed. A. Vacant, E. Mangenot, and E. Amann. 15 vols. (Paris, 1903–50)

Digard, G. A. L. *Philippe le Bel et le Saint-Siège de 1285 à 1304.* 2 vols. (Paris, 1936)

Ditsche, M. 'Die ecclesia primitiva im Kirchenbild des hohen und späten Mittelalters.' Phil. Diss. (Bonn, 1958)

  'Zur Studienförderung im Mittelalter', *Rheinische Vierteljahrsblätter*, 41 (1977), pp. 53–62

Döllinger, J. J. I. von. *Der Papst und das Concil* (Leipzig, 1869)

Dollinger, P. and P. Wolff, eds. *Bibliographie de l'histoire des villes de France* (Paris, 1967)

Dondaine, A. 'Documents pour servir à l'histoire de la province de France: L'appel au concile, 1303', *Archivum fratrum praedicatorum*, 22 (1952), pp. 381–439

Dortel-Claudot, M. 'Origine du terme "clercs réguliers".' In *Ius populi Dei: Miscellanea in honorem Raymundi Bidagor* (Rome, 1972), 2:307–26

Dossat, Y. 'Opposition des anciens ordres à l'installation des mendiants.' In *Les Mendiants en pays d'Oc* (Toulouse, 1973), pp. 263–306

  *Eglise et hérésie en France au XIII^e siècle* (London, 1982)

Douie, D. *The Conflict between the Seculars and the Mendicants at the University of Paris in the Thirteenth Century* (London, 1954)

Dubois, J. 'La Carte des diocèses de France avant la Révolution', *Annales*, 20 (1965), pp. 680–91

Duchon, R. 'De Bossuet à Febronius', *Revue d'histoire ecclésiastique*, 65 (1970), pp. 375–422

Dufeil, M.-M. *Guillaume de Saint-Amour et la polémique universitaire parisienne, 1250–1259* (Paris, 1972)

  'Gulielmus de Sancto Amore: Opera omnia, 1252–1270.' In *Die Auseinandersetzungen an der Pariser Universität* (Berlin, 1976), pp. 213–20

  'HIERARCHIA: Un concept dans la polémique universitaire parisienne du XIII^e siècle.' In *Soziale Ordnungen im Selbstverständnis des Mittelalters* (Berlin, 1979–80), pp. 56–83

Dumont, L. *Homo hierarchicus: The Caste System and its Implications.* Rev. edn. (Chicago, 1980)

  *Essays on Individualism: Modern Ideology in Anthropological Perspective* (Chicago, 1986)

Dunbabin, J. *France in the Making, 843–1180* (Oxford, 1985)

  'Government.' In *Cambridge History of Medieval Political Thought.* Ed. J. H. Burns (Cambridge, 1988), pp. 477–519

Dupont, A. 'Evolution des institutions municipales de Beaucaire, du début du XIII^e siècle à la fin du XV^e siècle', *Annales du Midi*, 77 (1965), pp. 257–74

Dupré Theseider, E. 'Bonifacio VIII, papa', *Dizionario biografico degli Italiani*, 12 (1970), pp. 146–70

Durieux, F.-R. 'Approches de l'histoire Franciscaine du Languedoc au XIII^e siècle.' In *Les Mendiants en pays d'Oc* (Toulouse, 1973), pp. 79–100

Dykmans, M. 'Notes autobiographiques de Guillaume Durand le Spéculateur.' In *Ius populi Dei: Miscellanea in honorem Raymundi Bidagor* (Rome, 1972), 1:119–42

*Le Cérémonial papal de la fin du Moyen Age à la Renaissance.* 3 vols. (Brussels and Rome, 1977–85)

'A propos de synodes languedociens: Auger de Montfaucon ou Durand le Spéculateur', *Bulletin de littérature ecclésiastique*, 82 (1981), pp. 5–24

Ebeneter, A. 'Luther und das Konzil', *Zeitschrift für katholische Theologie*, 84 (1962), pp. 1–48

Eckermann, K. *Studien zur Geschichte des monarchischen Gedankens im 15. Jahrhundert* (Berlin, 1933)

Edwards, K. *The English Secular Cathedrals in the Middle Ages* (Manchester, 1949)

Ehler, S. Z. 'On Applying the Modern Term "State" to the Middle Ages.' In *Medieval Studies Presented to Aubrey Gwynn* (Dublin, 1961), pp. 492–501

Ehlers, J. 'Karolingische Tradition und frühes Nationalbewusstsein in Frankreich', *Francia*, 4 (1976), pp. 213–35

Ehrle, F. *Historia bibliothecae Romanorum pontificum* (Rome, 1890)

Elias, N. *The Civilizing Process*. Trans. E. Jephcott. 2 vols. (New York, 1978–81)

Elze, R. *Päpste, Kaiser, Könige und die mittelalterliche Herrschaftssymbolik* (London, 1982)

Emerton, E. 'The First European Congress', *Harvard Theological Review*, 12 (1919), pp. 275–93

Emery, R. W. *The Friars in Medieval France: A Catalogue of French Mendicant Convents, 1200–1550* (New York, 1961)

*Die Entwicklung des Konziliarismus: Werden und Nachwirken der konziliaren Idee.* Ed. R. Bäumer (Darmstadt, 1976)

Ercole, F. *Dal commune al principato* (Florence, 1929)

Erdmann, C. *Die Entstehung des Kreuzzugsgedankens* (Stuttgart, 1935)

*The Origin of the Idea of Crusade*. Trans. M. W. Baldwin and W. Goffart (Princeton, 1977)

Eubel, C. *Hierarchia catholica medii aevi*. 2 vols. (Münster, 1913–23)

Evans, G. R. *The Mind of St Bernard of Clairvaux* (New York, 1983)

*Les Evêques, les clercs, et le roi, 1250–1300*. Cahiers de Fanjeaux, 7 (Toulouse, 1972)

Falletti, L. 'Guillaume Durand', *Dictionnaire de droit canonique*, 5 (1953), cols. 1,014–75

'Les "Instructions et Constitutions" de Guillaume Durand comme source du concile provincial de Trèves de 1310.' In *Etudes historiques à la mémoire de Noël Didier* (Paris, 1960), pp. 95–110

Fasolt, C. 'The Manuscripts and Editions of William Durant the Younger's "Tractatus de modo generalis concilii celebrandi"', *Annuarium historiae conciliorum*, 10 (1978), pp. 290–309

'Die Erforschung von Wilhelm Durants d. J. "Tractatus de modo generalis concilii celebrandi": Eine kritische Übersicht', *Annuarium historiae conciliorum*, 12 (1980), pp. 205–28

'A New View of William Durant the Younger's "Tractatus de modo generalis concilii celebrandi"', *Traditio*, 37 (1981), pp. 291–324

'William Durant the Younger's "Tractatus de modo generalis concilii celebrandi": An Early 14th-Century Conciliar Theory.' Ph.D. thesis (Columbia University, 1981)

'At the Crossroads of Law and Politics: William Durant the Younger's

# Bibliography

"Treatise" on Councils', *Bulletin of Medieval Canon Law*, n. s. 18 (1988), pp. 43–53

'Quod omnes tangit ab omnibus approbari debet: The Words and the Meaning.' In *In Iure Veritas: Studies in Canon Law in Memory of Schafer Williams*. Eds. Steven Bowman and Blanche Cody (Cincinnati, in press), pp. 21–55

'Die Rezeption der Traktate Wilhelm Durantis d. J. im späten Mittelalter und der frühen Neuzeit.' Forthcoming in *Das Publikum politischer Theorie im 14. Jahrhundert: Zu den Rezeptionsbedingungen politischer Philosophie im späteren Mittelalter*. Ed. J. Miethke. Schriften des Historischen Kollegs, Munich

Favier, J. *Philippe le Bel* (Paris, 1978)

Feine, H. E. *Kirchliche Rechtsgeschichte: Die katholische Kirche*. 5th edn. (Cologne, 1972)

Fichtenau, H. 'Askese und Laster in der Anschauung des Mittelalters.' In H. Fichtenau, *Beiträge zur Mediävistik: Ausgewählte Aufsätze* (Stuttgart, 1975), I:24–107

Figgis, J. N. *The Divine Right of Kings*. 2nd edn. (Cambridge, 1914)

*Studies of Political Thought from Gerson to Grotius, 1414–1625*. 2nd edn. (Cambridge, 1916)

Fink, K. A. 'Die konziliare Idee im späten Mittelalter.' In *Die Welt zur Zeit des Konstanzer Konzils* (Konstanz, 1965), pp. 119–34

*Papsttum und Kirche im abendländischen Mittelalter* (Munich, 1981)

Finke, H. *Aus den Tagen Bonifaz VIII.: Funde und Forschungen* (Münster, 1902)

*Papsttum und Untergang des Templerordens*. 2 vols. (Münster, 1907)

'Die Nation in den spätmittelalterlichen allgemeinen Konzilien', *Historisches Jahrbuch*, 57 (1937), pp. 323–38

Fliche, A. *La Réforme Grégorienne*. 3 vols. (Paris, 1924–37)

Folz, R. *L'Idée d'empire en Occident du Vᵉ au XIVᵉ siècle* (Paris, 1953)

*The Concept of Empire in Western Europe from the Fifth to the Fourteenth Century* (London, 1969)

Forest, A., F. van Steenberghen, and M. de Gandillac. *Le Mouvement doctrinale du IXᵉ au XIVᵉ siècle* (Paris, 1951)

Foreville, R. *Latran I, II, III et Latran IV* (Paris, 1965)

Fournier, M. *Histoire de la science du droit en France* (Paris, 1892)

Fournier, P. and G. Le Bras. *Histoire des collections canoniques en Occident depuis les Fausses Décrétales jusq'au Décret de Gratien*. 2 vols. (Paris, 1931–2)

Fransen, G. *Les Décrétales et les collections de décrétales* (Turnhout, 1972)

*Les Collections canoniques* (Turnhout, 1973)

'Les Gloses des canonistes et des civilistes.' In *Les Genres littéraires* (Louvain-la-Neuve, 1982), pp. 133–49

Franzen, A. and W. Müller, eds. *Das Konzil von Konstanz* (Freiburg, 1964)

'Das Konstanzer Konzil: Probleme, Aufgaben und Stand der Konzilsforschung', *Concilium*, 1 (1965), pp. 555–74

'The Council of Constance: Present State of the Problem', *Concilium: Theology in an Age of Renewal*, 7 (1965), pp. 29–68

Fried, J. *Die Entstehung des Juristenstandes im 12. Jahrhundert* (Cologne, 1974)

# Bibliography

Friedlander, A. 'Les Sergents royaux du Languedoc sous Philippe le Bel', *Annales du Midi*, 96 (1984), pp. 235–51

Frowein, P. 'Der Episkopat auf dem 2. Konzil von Lyon, 1274', *Annuarium historiae conciliorum*, 6 (1974), pp. 307–31

Fryde, E. B. and E. Miller, eds. *Historical Studies of the English Parliament*, 1: *Origins to 1399* (Cambridge, 1970)

Fuhrmann, H. 'Das ökumenische Konzil und seine historischen Grundlagen', *Geschichte in Wissenschaft und Unterricht*, 12 (1961), pp. 672–95

*Einfluss und Verbreitung der pseudoisidorischen Fälschungen.* 3 vols. (Stuttgart, 1972–4)

'Das Reformpapsttum und die Rechtswissenschaft.' In *Investiturstreit und Reichsverfassung.* Ed. J. Fleckenstein. *Vorträge und Forschungen*, 17 (Sigmaringen, 1973), pp. 175–203

'Gregor VII., "Gregorianische Reform" und Investiturstreit.' In *Gestalten der Kirchengeschichte*, 11. Ed. M. Greschat (Stuttgart, 1985), pp. 155–75

Fumaroli, M. *L'Age de l'éloquence: Rhétorique et "res literaria" de la renaissance au seuil de l'époque classique* (Geneva, 1980)

Gagnér, S. *Studien zur Ideengeschichte der Gesetzgebung* (Uppsala, 1960)

Gallagher, C. *Canon Law and the Christian Community: The Role of Law in the Church according to the 'Summa aurea' of Cardinal Hostiensis* (Rome, 1978)

*Gallia Christiana.* 16 vols. (Paris, 1715–85, 1856–65)

Gams, P. B. *Series episcoporum ecclesiae catholicae.* 2 vols. (Regensburg, 1873–86)

Ganzer, K. *Papsttum und Bistumsbesetzungen in der Zeit von Gregor IX. bis Bonifaz VIII.: Ein Beitrag zur Geschichte der päpstlichen Reservationen* (Cologne and Graz, 1968)

'Päpstliche Gesetzgebungsgewalt und kirchlicher Konsens: Zur Verwendung eines Dictum Gratians in der Concordantia Catholica des Nikolaus von Kues.' In *Von Konstanz nach Trient* (Munich and Paderborn, 1972), pp. 171–88

Gaudemet, J. '"Ius" et "Leges"', *Iura*, 1 (1950), pp. 223–52

'Aspects de la législation conciliaire française au XIIIᵉ siècle', *Revue de droit canonique*, 9 (1959), pp. 319–40

'Recherches sur l'épiscopat médiéval en France', *Proceedings of the Second International Congress of Medieval Canon Law* (Vatican City, 1965), pp. 139–54

*Le Gouvernement de l'église à l'époque classique*, 2: *Le gouvernement local* (Paris, 1979)

*La Société ecclésiastique dans l'Occident médiéval* (London, 1980)

*La Formation du droit canonique médiéval* (London, 1980)

*Eglise et société en Occident au Moyen Age* (London, 1984)

*Genèse et débuts du grand schisme d'Occident.* Colloques internationaux du CNRS, 586 (Paris, 1980)

Généstal, R. *Le privilegium fori en France du Décret de Gratien à la fin du XIVᵉ siècle.* 2 vols. (Paris, 1921–4)

*Les Genres littéraires dans les sources théologiques et philosophiques médiévales: Définition, critique et exploitation* (Louvain-la-Neuve, 1982)

*Geschichtliche Grundbegriffe: Historisches Lexikon zur politisch-sozialen Sprache in*

*Deutschland.* Eds. O. Brunner, W. Conze, and R. Koselleck (Stuttgart, 1972– )

Gibbs, M. and J. Lang. *Bishops and Reform, 1215–1272, with Special Reference to the Lateran Council of 1215* (London, 1934)

Gierke, O. *Das Deutsche Genossenschaftsrecht.* 4 vols. (Berlin, 1868–1913)
  *Political Theories of the Middle Age.* Trans. F. W. Maitland (Cambridge, 1900)

Giesey, R. E. *If Not, Not: The Oath of the Aragonese and the Legendary Laws of Sobrarbe* (Princeton, 1968)
  '"Quod omnes tangit" – A post scriptum', *Studia Gratiana,* 15 (1972), pp. 319–32

Gilby, T. *The Political Thought of Thomas Aquinas* (Chicago, 1958)

Gilchrist, J. T. 'Gregory VII and the Juristic Sources of his Ideology', *Studia Gratiana,* 12 (1967), pp. 1–37

Gill, J. *The Council of Florence* (Cambridge, 1959)
  *Personalities of the Council of Florence* (Oxford, 1964)
  'The Fifth Session of the Council of Constance', *The Heythrop Journal,* 5 (1964), pp. 131–43
  *Constance et Bâle-Florence* (Paris, 1965)
  'Il decreto "Haec sancta synodus" del concilio di Costanza', *Rivista di storia della chiesa in Italia,* 21 (1967), pp. 123–30

Gilles, H. 'L'Enseignement du droit en Languedoc au XIIIᵉ siècle.' In *Les Universités du Languedoc* (Toulouse, 1970), pp. 204–29
  'Le Clergé méridional entre le roi et l'église', In *Les Évêques, les clercs, et le roi* (Toulouse, 1972), pp. 393–417

Gillmann, F. 'Romanus pontifex iura omnia in scrinio pectoris sui censetur habere', *Archiv für katholisches Kirchenrecht,* 92 (1912), pp. 3–17

Gilmont, J.-F. *Jean Crespin: Un éditeur réformé du XVIᵉ siècle* (Geneva, 1981)

Gilmore, M. P. *Argument from Roman Law in Political Thought, 1200–1600* (Cambridge, 1941)

Glorieux, P. 'Prélats français contre religieux mendiants: Autour de la bulle "Ad fructus uberes", 1281–1290', *Revue d'histoire de l'église de France,* 11 (1925), pp. 309–31, 471–95
  *Le Concile de Constance au jour le jour* (Tournai, 1964)

Göller, E. 'Die Gravamina auf dem Konzil von Vienne und ihre literarische Überlieferung.' In *Festgabe für H. Finke* (Münster, 1904), pp. 195–221
  'Zur Geschichte der italienischen Legation Durantis des Jüngeren von Mende', *Römische Quartalsschrift für christliche Altertumskunde und für Kirchengeschichte,* 19 (1905), part 'Kirchengeschichte', pp. 14–24
  *Die Einnahmen der apostolischen Kammer unter Johann XXII.* (Paderborn, 1910)

Gottlob, A. *Die Servitientaxe im 13. Jahrhundert* (Stuttgart, 1903)

Gouron, A. 'La Diffusion des consulats méridionaux et l'expansion du droit romain au XIIᵉ et XIIIᵉ siècles', *Bibliothèque de l'Ecole des Chartes,* 121 (1963), pp. 26–76
  'The Training of Southern French Lawyers during the Thirteenth and Fourteenth Centuries', *Studia Gratiana,* 15 (1972), pp. 217–27
  *La Science du droit dans le midi de la France au Moyen Age* (London, 1984)

Grabmann, M. *Studien über den Einfluss der aristotelischen Philosophie auf die*

# Bibliography

*mittelalterlichen Theorien über das Verhältnis von Kirche und Staat* (Munich, 1934)

Gratien. 'Ordres mendiants et clergé séculiers à la fin du XIII<sup>e</sup> siècle', *Etudes franciscaines*, 36 (1924), pp. 499–518

*Histoire de la fondation et de l'évolution de l'ordre des frères mineurs au XIII<sup>e</sup> siècle* (Paris, 1928)

Grundmann, H. *Religiöse Bewegungen im Mittelalter.* 2nd edn. (Hildesheim, 1961)

Guenée, B. *Entre l'église et l'état: Quatre vies de prélats français à la fin du Moyen Age, XII<sup>e</sup> – XV<sup>e</sup> siècle* (Paris, 1987)

Guillemain, B. *La Cour pontificale d'Avignon, 1309–1376: Etude d'une société* (Paris, 1962)

'Les Elections épiscopales de la province de Narbonne entre 1249 et 1317.' In *Les Evêques, les clercs, et le roi* (Toulouse, 1972), pp. 107–13

'Origines sociales, intellectuelles et ecclésiastiques des évêques de la province de Narbonne entre 1249 et 1317.' In *Les Evêques, les clercs, et le roi* (Toulouse, 1972), pp. 91–106

*Les Recettes et les dépenses de la chambre apostolique pour la quatrième année du pontificat de Clément V, 1308–1309* (Rome, 1978)

Guizard, L. *L'Œuvre canonique de Guillaume Durand* (Montpellier, 1956)

Gwynn, A. *The English Austin Friars* (Oxford, 1940)

Hackett, J. H. 'State of the Church: A Concept of the Medieval Canonists', *The Jurist*, 23 (1963), pp. 259–90

Haines, R. M. *The Church and Politics in Fourteenth-Century England: The Career of Adam Orleton, 1275–1345* (Cambridge, 1978)

*Archbishop John Stratford: Political Revolutionary and Champion of the Liberties of the English Church, ca. 1275/80–1348* (Toronto, 1986)

Hall, E. 'King Henry III and the English Reception of the Roman Law Maxim Quod omnes tangit', *Studia Gratiana*, 15 (1972), pp. 125–45

Hallam, E. M. *Capetian France, 987–1328* (London, 1980)

Haller, J. *Papsttum und Kirchenreform: Vier Kapitel zur Geschichte des ausgehenden Mittelalters* (Berlin, 1903)

Review of R. Scholz, *Die Publizistik zur Zeit Philipps des Schönen und Bonifaz' VIII.* In *Historische Zeitschrift*, 99 (1907), pp. 366–80

*Das Papsttum: Idee und Wirklichkeit.* 5 vols. (Hamburg, 1965)

Hashagen, J. *Staat und Kirche vor der Reformation: Eine Untersuchung der vorreformatorischen Bedeutung der Laieneinflüsse in der Kirche* (Essen, 1931)

Hauck, A. *Der Gedanke der päpstlichen Weltherrschaft bis auf Bonifaz VIII.* (Leipzig, 1904)

'Die Rezeption und Umbildung der allgemeinen Synode im Mittelalter', *Historische Vierteljahrsschrift*, 10 (1907), pp. 465–82

Heber, M. *Gutachten und Reformvorschläge für das Wiener Generalconcil, 1311–1312* (Leipzig, 1896)

Heckel, R. v. 'Eine Kanzleianweisung über die schriftmässige Ausstattung der Papsturkunden aus dem 13. Jahrhundert in Durantis speculum iudiciale.' In *Festschrift für Georg Leidinger* (Munich, 1930), pp. 109–18

Hefele, K. J. *Conciliengeschichte.* 2nd edn. 9 vols. (Freiburg, 1869–90)

*Histoire des conciles.* Trans. H. Leclercq. 11 vols. (Paris, 1907–52)

# Bibliography

Heiler, F. *Altkirchliche Autonomie und päpstlicher Zentralismus* (Munich, 1941)

Heimpel, H. *Dietrich von Niem* (Münster, 1932)

*Die Vener von Gmünd und Strassburg, 1162–1447: Studien und Texte zur Geschichte einer Familie sowie des gelehrten Beamtentums in der Zeit der abendländischen Kirchenspaltung und der Konzilien von Pisa, Konstanz und Basel.* 3 vols. (Göttingen, 1982)

Helmrath, J. *Das Basler Konzil, 1431–1449* (Cologne, 1987)

Hendrix, S. 'In Quest of the Vera Ecclesia: The Crises of Late Medieval Ecclesiology', *Viator*, 7 (1976), pp. 347–78

Henneman, J. B. 'Taxation of Italians by the French Crown, 1311–1363', *Mediaeval Studies*, 31 (1969), pp. 15–43

*Royal Taxation in Fourteenth-Century France: The Development of War Financing, 1322–1356* (Princeton, 1971)

Herde, P. *Beiträge zum päpstlichen Kanzlei- und Urkundenwesen im dreizehnten Jahrhundert.* 2nd edn. (Munich, 1967)

*Audientia Litterarum Contradictarum: Untersuchungen über die päpstlichen Justizbriefe und die päpstliche Delegationsgerichtsbarkeit vom 13. bis zum Beginn des 16. Jahrhunderts.* 2 vols. (Tübingen, 1970)

Heumann, H. G. *Handlexikon zu den Quellen des römischen Rechts.* 9th edn. by E. Seckel (Jena, 1914)

Heydte, F. A. von. *Die Geburtsstunde des souveränen Staates* (Regensburg, 1952)

Hinsley, F. H. *Sovereignty.* 2nd edn. (Cambridge, 1986)

Hintze, O. 'Weltgeschichtliche Bedingungen der Repräsentativverfassung', *Historische Zeitschrift*, 143 (1930), pp. 1–47

Hirsch, K. *Die Ausbildung der konziliaren Theorie im XIV. Jahrhundert* (Vienna, 1903)

*Histoire des conciles oecuméniques.* Ed. G. Dumeige (Paris, 1962– )

*Histoire du Languedoc.* Ed. P. Wolff (Toulouse, 1967)

*Histoire littéraire de la France.* Ed. Académie des Inscriptions et Belles Lettres (Paris, 1733– )

Hoeflich, M. 'The Concept of Utilitas Populi in Early Ecclesiastical Law and Government', *Zeitschrift der Savigny-Stiftung für Rechtsgeschichte*, Canon law section, 67 (1981), pp. 36–74

Hoffmann, H. 'Der Kirchenstaat im hohen Mittelalter', *Quellen und Forschungen aus italienischen Archiven und Bibliotheken*, 57 (1977), pp. 1–45

Hofmann, H. *Kardinalat und kuriale Politik in der ersten Hälfte des 14. Jahrhunderts* (Leipzig, 1935)

Hofmann, Hasso. *Repräsentation: Studien zur Wort- und Begriffsgeschichte von der Antike bis ins 19. Jahrhundert* (Berlin, 1974)

Hollnsteiner, J. *Die Kirche im Ringen um die christliche Gemeinschaft vom Anfang des 13. Jahrhunderts bis zur Mitte des 15. Jahrhunderts* (Freiburg, 1940)

Holt, J. C. *Magna Carta* (Cambridge, 1969)

Horn, N. 'Die legistische Literatur der Kommentatoren und der Ausbreitung des gelehrten Rechts.' In H. Coing, ed. *Handbuch der Quellen und Literatur der neueren europäischen Privatrechtsgeschichte*, 1 (Munich, 1973), pp. 261–364

Hourlier, J. *L'Age classique, 1140–1378: Les religieux* (Paris, 1971)

Housley, N. *The Italian Crusades: The Papal–Angevin Alliance and the Crusades*

# Bibliography

against *Christian Lay Powers, 1254–1343* (Oxford, 1982)

*The Avignon Papacy and the Crusades, 1305–1378* (Oxford, 1986)

Howe, J. 'The Nobility's Reform of the Medieval Church', *American Historical Review*, 93 (1988), pp. 317–39

Hübinger, P. E. *Die letzten Worte Papst Gregors VII.* (Opladen, 1973)

Hübler, B. *Die Constanzer Reformation und die Concordate von 1418* (Leipzig, 1867)

Imkamp, W. *Das Kirchenbild Innocenz' III., 1198–1216* (Stuttgart, 1983)

*Indices canonum, titulorum et capitulorum Corporis Iuris Canonici.* Eds. X. Ochoa and A. Diez (Rome, 1964)

*Indices Corporis Iuris Civilis iuxta vetustiores editiones cum criticis collatas.* Eds. H. Nicolini and F. S. D'Amico. 5 vols. (Milan, 1964–70)

Izbicki, T. M. *Protector of the Faith: Cardinal Johannes de Turrecremata and the Defense of the Institutional Church* (Washington, 1981)

'"Clericis Laicos" and the Canonists.' In *Popes, Teachers, and Canon Law* (Ithaca, 1989), pp. 179–90

Jacob, E. F. *Essays in the Conciliar Epoch.* 3rd edn. (Manchester, 1963)

'The Conciliar Movement in Recent Study.' In E. F. Jacob, *Essays in Later Medieval History* (Manchester, 1968), pp. 98–123

Jaeger, S. *The Origins of Courtliness: Civilizing Trends and the Formation of Courtly Ideals, 939–1210* (Philadelphia, 1985)

Jedin, H. *Geschichte des Konzils von Trient,* 1: *Der Kampf um das Konzil.* 2nd edn. (Freiburg, 1951)

*Bischöfliches Konzil oder Kirchenparlament?* (Stuttgart and Basle, 1963)

*Kleine Konziliengeschichte.* 7th edn. (Freiburg, 1969)

Jones, W. R. 'Bishops, Politics, and the Two Laws: The "Gravamina" of the English Clergy, 1237–1399', *Speculum*, 41 (1966), pp. 209–45

'Relations of the Two Jurisdictions: Conflict and Cooperation in England during the Thirteenth and Fourteenth Centuries', *Studies in Medieval and Renaissance History*, 7 (1970), pp. 77–210

Jordan, W. C. *Louis IX and the Challenge of the Crusade: A Study in Rulership* (Princeton, 1979)

Kahl, H. D. '"Natio" im mittelalterlichen Latein', *Nationes*, 1 (1978), pp. 63–108

Kaminsky, H. *A History of the Hussite Revolution* (Berkeley, 1967)

*Simon de Cramaud and the Great Schism* (New Brunswick, 1983)

Kämpf, H., ed. *Herrschaft und Staat im Mittelalter* (Darmstadt, 1956)

Kantorowicz, E. *The King's Two Bodies: A Study in Mediaeval Political Theology* (Princeton, 1957)

Kay, R. 'An Eye-Witness Account of the 1225 Council of Bourges', *Studia Gratiana*, 12 (1968), pp. 61–79

'"Ad nostram praesentiam evocamus": Boniface VIII and the Roman Convocation of 1302', *Proceedings of the Third International Congress of Medieval Canon Law* (Vatican City, 1971), pp. 165–89

'Dante's Razor and Gratian's D.XV', *Dante Studies*, 97 (1979), pp. 65–95

Kempf, F. 'Die päpstliche Gewalt in der mittelalterlichen Welt: Eine Auseinandersetzung mit Walter Ullmann', *Miscellanea historiae pontificiae*, 21 (1959), pp. 117–69

'Die Absetzung Kaiser Friedrichs II. im Lichte der Kanonistik.' In *Probleme um*

# Bibliography

*Friedrich II*. Ed. J. Fleckenstein. *Vorträge und Forschungen*, 16 (Sigmaringen, 1974), pp. 345–60

Kern, F. *Gottesgnadentum und Widerstandsrecht im früheren Mittelalter: Zur Entwicklungsgeschichte der Monarchie* (Leipzig, 1914)

'Recht und Verfassung im Mittelalter', *Historische Zeitschrift*, 120 (1919), pp. 1–79

*Kingship and Law in the Middle Ages*. Trans. S. B. Chrimes (Oxford, 1948)

Kibre, P. *The Nations in the Mediaeval Universities* (Cambridge/Mass., 1948)

King, P. D. 'The Barbarian Kingdoms.' In *Cambridge History of Medieval Political Thought*. Ed. J. H. Burns (Cambridge, 1988), pp. 123–53

Kirsch, J. P. *Die Finanzverwaltung des Kardinalkollegiums im XIII. und XIV. Jahrhundert* (Münster, 1895)

Kisch, G. *Erasmus und die Jurisprudenz seiner Zeit: Studien zum humanistischen Rechtsdenken* (Basle, 1960)

Klinkenberg, H. M. 'Die Theorie der Veränderbarkeit des Rechtes im frühen und hohen Mittelalter.' In *Lex et Sacramentum im Mittelalter* (Berlin, 1969), pp. 157–88

Kneer, A. *Kardinal Zabarella: Ein Beitrag zur Geschichte des grossen abendländischen Schismas* (Münster, 1891)

*Die Entstehung der konziliaren Theorie* (Rome, 1893)

Koch, J. 'Der Prozess gegen den Magister Johannes de Polliaco und seine Vorgeschichte, 1312–1321', *Recherches de théologie ancienne et médiévale*, 5 (1933), pp. 391–422

Koeniger, A. M. 'Prima sedes a nemine iudicatur.' In *Beiträge zur Geschichte des christlichen Altertums und der byzantinischen Literatur: Festgabe Albert Ehrhard zum 60. Geburtstag* (Bonn and Leipzig, 1922), pp. 273–300

Kölmel, W. *Regimen Christianum: Weg und Ergebnisse des Gewaltenverhältnisses, 8. bis 14. Jahrhundert* (Berlin, 1970)

*Das Konstanzer Konzil*. Ed. R. Bäumer (Darmstadt, 1977)

Koschaker, P. *Europa und das römische Recht*. 2nd edn. (Munich, 1953)

Koselleck, R. *Futures Past: On the Semantics of Historical Time*. Transl. K. Tribe (Cambridge/Mass., 1985)

Krämer, W. *Konsens und Rezeption: Verfassungsprinzipien der Kirche im Basler Konziliarismus* (Münster, 1980)

Krause, H. 'Dauer und Vergänglichkeit im mittelalterlichen Recht', *Zeitschrift der Savigny-Stiftung für Rechtsgeschichte*, Germanic law section, 75 (1958), pp. 206–51

Krieger, L. *The German Idea of Freedom: History of a Political Tradition* (Chicago, 1957)

Kuhn, T. 'Concepts of Cause in the Development of Physics.' In T. Kuhn, *The Essential Tension: Selected Studies in Scientific Tradition and Change* (Chicago, 1977), pp. 21–30

Küng, H. *Strukturen der Kirche* (Freiburg, 1962)

Kurz, H. *Volkssouveränität und Volksrepräsentation* (Cologne, 1965)

Kuttner, S. 'Sur les origines du terme "droit positif"', *Revue historique de droit français et étranger*, 15 (1936), pp. 728–40

'Wer war der Dekretalist "Abbas antiquus"?', *Zeitschrift der Savigny-Stiftung für*

*Rechtsgeschichte*, Canon law section, 57 (1937), pp. 471–89

*Repertorium der Kanonistik, 1140–1234: Prodromus corporis glossarum* (Vatican City, 1937)

'The Father of the Science of Canon Law', *The Jurist*, 1 (1941), pp. 2–19

'Bernardus Compostellanus Antiquus', *Traditio*, 1 (1943), pp. 277–340

'Cardinalis: The History of a Canonical Concept', *Traditio*, 3 (1945), pp. 129–214

'Quelques observations sur l'autorité des collections canoniques dans le droit classique de l'église', *Actes du congrès de droit canonique* (Paris, 1950), pp. 303–12

'Notes on the Presentation of Text and Apparatus in Editing the Works of the Decretists and Decretalists', *Traditio*, 15 (1959), pp. 452–64

*Harmony from Dissonance: An Interpretation of Medieval Canon Law* (Latrobe, 1960)

'Pope Lucius III and the Bigamous Archbishop of Palermo.' In *Medieval Studies presented to Aubrey Gwynn* (Dublin, 1961), pp. 409–53

'Joannes Andreae and His "Novella" on the Decretals of Gregory IX', *The Jurist*, 24 (1964), pp. 393–408

'Urban II and the Doctrine of Interpretation: A Turning Point?', *Studia Gratiana*, 15 (1972), pp. 53–85

*Medieval Councils, Decretals and Collections of Canon Law* (London, 1980)

*The History of Ideas and Doctrines of Canon Law in the Middle Ages* (London, 1980)

'Universal Pope or Servant of God's Servants: The Canonists, Papal Titles, and Innocent III', *Revue de droit canonique*, 32 (1981), pp. 109–49

'On "Auctoritas" in the Writing of Medieval Canonists: The Vocabulary of Gratian.' In *La Notion d'autorité au Moyen Age* (Paris, 1982), pp. 69–81

'The Revival of Jurisprudence.' In *Renaissance and Renewal in the Twelfth Century* (Cambridge/Mass., 1982), pp. 299–323

Kuttner, S. and A. García y García. 'A New Eyewitness Account of the Fourth Lateran Council', *Traditio*, 20 (1964), pp. 115–78

Kyer, C. I. 'The Legation of Cardinal Latinus and William Duranti's "Speculum legatorum"', *Bulletin of Medieval Canon Law*, 10 (1980), pp. 56–62

La Brosse, O. de. *Le Pape et le concile: La comparaison de leurs pouvoirs à la veille de la Réforme* (Paris, 1965)

Ladner, G. B. 'Aspects of Mediaeval Thought on Church and State', *Review of Politics*, 9 (1947), pp. 403–22

'The Concepts of "Ecclesia" and "Christianitas" and their Relation to the Idea of Papal "Plenitudo Potestatis" from Gregory VII to Boniface VIII.' In *Sacerdozio e regno da Gregorio VII a Bonifacio VIII* (Rome, 1954), pp. 49–77

'Two Gregorian Letters: On the Sources and Nature of Gregory VII's Reform Ideology', *Studi Gregoriani*, 5 (1956), pp. 221–42

*The Idea of Reform: Its Impact on Christian Thought and Action in the Age of the Fathers.* Rev. edn. (New York, 1967)

'Justinian's Theory of Law and the Renewal Ideology of the "Leges Barbarorum"', *Proceedings of the American Philosophical Society*, 119 (1975), pp. 191–200

'Terms and Ideas of Renewal.' In *Renaissance and Renewal in the Twelfth Century*

(Cambridge/Mass., 1982), pp. 1–33

Lagarde, G. de. 'La Philosophie sociale d'Henri de Gand et Godefroid de Fontaines', *Archives d'histoire doctrinale et littéraire du Moyen Age*, 14 (1943–5), pp. 73–142
   *La Naissance de l'esprit laïque au déclin du Moyen Age*. 3rd edn. 5 vols. (Louvain, 1956–1970)

Lambert, M. D. *Franciscan Poverty: The Doctrine of the Absolute Poverty of Christ and the Apostles in the Franciscan Order, 1210–1323* (London, 1961)

Langlois, Ch.-V. *Saint Louis, Philippe le Bel, les derniers Capétiens directs, 1226–1328* (Paris, 1901)

Langmuir, G. 'Concilia and Capetian Assemblies', *Studies presented to the International Commission for the History of Representative and Parliamentary Institutions*, 24 (1961), pp. 29–63
   'Politics and Parliaments in the Early Thirteenth Century.' In *Etudes sur l'histoire des assemblées d'états. Travaux et recherches de la Faculté de Droit et des Sciences Economiques de Paris*, 8 (1966), pp. 47–62
   'Per commune consilium regni in Magna Carta', *Studia Gratiana*, 15 (1972), pp. 465–85

Laski, H. J. 'Political Theory in the Later Middle Ages.' In *Cambridge Medieval History*, 8 (1936), pp. 620–45

Laudage, J. *Priesterbild und Reformpapsttum im 11. Jahrhundert* (Cologne, 1984)

*Law, Church, and Society: Essays in Honor of Stephan Kuttner*. Eds. K. Pennington and R. Somerville (Philadelphia, 1977)

Le Bras, G. 'Boniface VIII, symphoniste et modérateur', *Mélanges d'histoire du Moyen Age, dédiés à la mémoire de Louis Halphen* (Paris, 1951), pp. 383–94
   *Les Institutions ecclésiastiques de la Chrétienté médiévale*. 2 vols. (Paris, 1959–64)

Le Bras, G., Ch. Lefebvre, and J. Rambaud. *L'Age classique, 1140–1378: Sources et théorie du droit* (Paris, 1965)

Lecler, J. 'La Réforme de l'église au temps de Philippe le Bel: A propos du concile de Vienne, 1311–1312', *Etudes*, 224 (1935), pp. 5–21
   'Les Théories démocratiques au Moyen Age', *Etudes*, 225 (1935), pp. 5–26, 168–92
   *Vienne* (Paris, 1964)
   *Le Pape ou le concile? Une interrogation de l'église médiévale* (Le Chalet, 1973)

Le Clerc, V. 'Guillaume Duranti', *Histoire littéraire de la France*, 20 (1842), pp. 411–97

Leclercq, J. *Jean de Paris et l'ecclésiologie du XIIIᵉ siècle* (Paris, 1942)
   'Saint Bernard et ses secrétaires', *Revue bénédictine*, 61 (1951), pp. 208–29
   'Les Ecrits de Geoffroy d'Auxerre', *Revue bénédictine*, 62 (1952), pp. 274–91

Leclerq, J., F. Vandenbroucke, and L. Bouyer. *The Spirituality of the Middle Ages* (New York, 1982)

Lefebvre, C. *Les Pouvoirs du juge en droit canonique* (Paris, 1938)

Leff, G. 'The Apostolic Ideal in Later Medieval Ecclesiology', *Journal of Theological Studies*, 18 (1967), pp. 58–82
   *The Dissolution of the Medieval Outlook: An Essay on the Intellectual and Spiritual Change in the Fourteenth Century* (New York, 1976)

Le Goff, J. 'Les Universités du Languedoc dans le mouvement universitaire

# Bibliography

Européen au XIII⁰ siècle.' In *Les Universités du Languedoc* (Toulouse, 1970), pp. 316–28

*Time, Work and Culture in the Middle Ages* (Chicago, 1980)

Lehmann, P. *Erforschung des Mittelalters.* 5 vols. (Stuttgart, 1941–62)

'Konstanz und Basel als Büchermärkte während der grossen Kirchenversammlungen.' In P. Lehmann, *Erforschung des Mittelalters*, 1:253–80

Lehugeur, P. *Histoire de Philippe le Long, roi de France, 1316–1322* (Paris, 1897)

Lemaître, H. 'Géographie historique des établissements de l'ordre de saint François en Aquitaine du XIII⁰ au XIX⁰ siècle', *Revue d'histoire franciscaine*, 3 (1926), pp. 510–74

Lenfant, J. *Histoire du concile de Constance.* Rev. edn. 2 vols. (Amsterdam, 1727)

Lerner, R. *The Powers of Prophecy: The Cedar of Lebanon Vision from the Mongol Onslaught to the Dawn of the Enlightenment* (Berkeley, 1983)

Le Roy Ladurie, E. *Histoire du Languedoc* (Paris, 1962)

Lewis, A. R. *The Development of Southern French and Catalan Society, 718–1050* (Austin, 1965)

*Medieval Society in Southern France and Catalonia* (London, 1984)

Lewis, E. 'Organic Tendencies in Medieval Political Thought', *American Political Science Review*, 32 (1938), pp. 849–76

'Natural Law and Expediency in Medieval Political Theory', *Ethics*, 50 (1939–40), pp. 144–63

*Medieval Political Ideas.* 2 vols. (New York, 1954)

*Lex et Sacramentum im Mittelalter.* Ed. P. Wilpert. *Miscellanea Mediaevalia*, 6 (Berlin, 1969)

Lizerand, G. *Clément V et Philippe IV le Bel* (Paris, 1910)

Longnon, A. H. *Atlas historique de la France* (Paris, 1885–9)

Loomis, L. R. 'Nationality at the Council of Constance', *American Historical Review*, 44 (1939), pp. 508–27

Lot, F. and R. Fawtier. *Histoire des institutions françaises au Moyen Age.* 3 vols. (Paris, 1957–62)

Lovejoy, A. O. *The Great Chain of Being: A Study of the History of an Idea* (Cambridge/Mass., 1936)

Lucas, R. H. 'Ennoblement in Late Medieval France', *Mediaeval Studies*, 39 (1977), pp. 239–60

Lunt, W. *Papal Revenues in the Middle Ages.* 2 vols. (New York, 1934)

*Financial Relations of the Papacy with England, 1327–1534* (Cambridge/Mass., 1962)

Luscombe, D. E. 'The "Lex divinitatis" of the Bull "Unam Sanctam" of Pope Boniface VIII.' In *Church and Government in the Middle Ages: Essays presented to C. R. Cheney on his Seventieth Birthday.* Eds. C. N. L. Brooke, D. Luscombe, G. H. Martin, and Dorothy Owen (London, 1976), pp. 205–21

'Some Examples of the Use Made of the Works of Pseudo-Dionysius by University Teachers in the Later Middle Ages.' In *The Universities in the Late Middle Ages* (Louvain-la-Neuve, 1978), pp. 228–41

'Conceptions of Hierarchy before the Thirteenth Century.' In *Soziale Ordnungen im Selbstverständnis des Mittelalters* (Berlin, 1979–80), pp. 1–19

'Introduction: The Formation of Political Thought in the West.' In *Cambridge*

# Bibliography

*History of Medieval Political Thought.* Ed. J. H. Burns (Cambridge, 1988), pp. 157–73

'Thomas Aquinas and Conceptions of Hierarchy in the Thirteenth Century.' In *Thomas von Aquin* (Berlin, 1988), pp. 261–77

Luscombe, D. E. and G. R. Evans. 'The Twelfth-Century Renaissance.' In *Cambridge History of Medieval Political Thought.* Ed. J. H. Burns (Cambridge, 1988), pp. 306–38

Lytle, G. F., ed. *Reform and Authority in the Medieval and Reformation Church* (Washington, 1981)

Macaulay, T. B. 'Speech on Parliamentary Reform, 2 March 1831.' In *Nineteenth-Century Europe: Liberalism and Its Critics.* Eds. J. Goldstein and J. Boyer (Chicago, 1988), pp. 41–54

Maccarrone, M. *Chiesa e stato nella dottrina di papa Innocenzo III* (Rome, 1940)
*Vicarius Christi: Storia del titolo papale* (Rome, 1952)

McCready, W. 'Papal "Plenitudo potestatis" and the Source of Temporal Authority in Late Medieval Papal Hierocratic Theory', *Speculum*, 48 (1973), pp. 654–74

'Papalists and Antipapalists: Aspects of the Church/State Controversy in the Later Middle Ages', *Viator*, 6 (1975), pp. 241–73

'The Papal Sovereign in the Ecclesiology of Augustinus Triumphus', *Mediaeval Studies*, 39 (1977), pp. 177–205

*The Theory of Papal Monarchy in the Fourteenth Century* (Toronto, 1982)

McGrade, A. S. *The Political Thought of William of Ockham: Personal and Institutional Principles* (Cambridge, 1974)

McIlwain, C. H. *The Growth of Political Thought in the West, from the Greeks to the End of the Middle Ages* (New York, 1932)
'Medieval Estates.' In *Cambridge Medieval History*, 7 (1932), pp. 664–715
*Constitutionalism, Ancient and Modern* (Ithaca, 1940)

McKitterick, R. *The Carolingians and the Written Word* (Cambridge, 1989)

McNamara, J. A. 'Simon de Beaulieu and "Clericis Laicos"', *Traditio*, 25 (1969), pp. 155–70

McNeill, J. T. 'The Emergence of Conciliarism.' In *Medieval and Historiographical Essays in Honor of J. W. Thompson.* Eds. J. L. Cate and E. N. Anderson (Chicago, 1938), pp. 269–301
'The Relevance of Conciliarism', *The Jurist*, 31 (1971), pp. 81–112

Maffei, D. *Gli inizi dell'umanesimo giuridico* (Milan, 1956).
*La donazione di Costantino nei giuristi medievali* (Milan, 1964)

Mager, W. *Zur Entstehung des modernen Staatsbegriffs* (Mainz, 1968)
'Republik.' In *Geschichtliche Grundbegriffe*, 5 (1984), pp. 549–651

Magnou-Nortier, E. *La Société laïque et l'église dans la province ecclésiastique de Narbonne (zone cispyrénéenne) de la fin du VIII<sup>e</sup> à la fin du XI<sup>e</sup> siècle* (Toulouse, 1974)

Maier, A. *Ausgehendes Mittelalter: Gesammelte Aufsätze zur Geistesgeschichte des 14. Jahrhunderts.* 3 vols. (Rome, 1964–77)
'Internationale Beziehungen an spätmittelalterlichen Universitäten.' In A. Maier, *Ausgehendes Mittelalter*, 2:317–334
'Die "Bibliotheca Minor" Benedikts XIII. (Petrus' de Luna).' In: A. Maier,

# Bibliography

*Ausgehendes Mittelalter*, 3:1–53

Manzke, F. W. *Die konziliaren Theorien des Mittelalters und die Anschauung Luthers vom Konzil* (Kiel, 1965)

Marchetto, A. *Episcopato e primato pontificio nelle decretali pseudo-Isidoriane: Ricerca storico-giuridica* (Rome, 1971)

Markus, R. A. *Saeculum: History and Society in the Theology of St Augustine* (Cambridge, 1970)

Marongiu, A. 'Il principio della democrazia e del consenso (quod omnes tangit, ab omnibus approbari debet) nel XIV secolo', *Studia Gratiana*, 8 (1962), pp. 553–75

*Il parlamento in Italia nel medio evo e nell'età moderna: Contributo alla storia delle istituzioni parlamentari dell'Europa occidentale* (Milan, 1962)

*Medieval Parliaments: A Comparative Study*. Trans. and adapted by S. J. Woolf (London, 1968)

'The Theory of Democracy and Consent in the Fourteenth Century.' In *Lordship and Community in Medieval Europe*. Ed. F. L. Cheyette (New York, 1968), pp. 404–21

*Dottrine e istituzioni politiche medievali e moderne: Raccolta* (Milan, 1979)

Marrone, J. 'The Ecclesiology of the Parisian Secular Masters, 1250–1320.' Ph.D. thesis (Cornell University, 1972)

'The Absolute and the Ordained Powers of the Pope: An Unedited Text of Henry of Ghent', *Mediaeval Studies*, 36 (1974), pp. 7–27

Marrone, J. and C. Zuckerman. 'Cardinal Simon of Beaulieu and Relations between Philip the Fair and Boniface VIII', *Traditio*, 31 (1975), pp. 195–222

Martin, A. *Notice historique sur la ville de Mende* (Marvéjols, 1894)

Martin, V. 'Comment s'est formée la doctrine de la supériorité du concile sur le pape', *Revue des sciences religieuses*, 17 (1937), pp. 121–43, 261–89, 405–27

*Les Origines du Gallicanisme*. 2 vols. (Paris, 1939)

Maurel, J. *Histoire de la commune de Puimisson et de la commanderie des chevaliers de Malte* (Paris, 1897)

*Meaning and Context: Quentin Skinner and his Critics*. Ed. J. Tully (Princeton, 1988)

*Medieval Studies presented to Aubrey Gwynn, S. J.* Eds. J. A. Watt, J. B. Morrall and F. X. Martin (Dublin, 1961)

Meijers, E. M. *Etudes d'histoire du droit*. 4 vols. (Leiden, 1956–73)

'L'Université d'Orléans au XIII^e siècle.' In E. M. Meijers, *Etudes d'histoire du droit*, 3:3–148

'La Première Epoque d'épanouissement de l'enseignement de droit à l'université de Toulouse, 1280–1330.' In E. M. Meijers, *Etudes d'histoire du droit*, 3:167–208

'Le Conflit entre l'équité et la loi chez les premiers glossateurs.' In E. M. Meijers, *Etudes d'histoire du droit*, 4:142–56

Meinecke, F. *Die Idee der Staatsräson in der neueren Geschichte* (Munich, 1924)

*Die Entstehung des Historismus*. 2 vols. (Berlin, 1936)

*Les Mendiants en pays d'Oc au XIII^e siècle*. Cahiers de Fanjeaux, 8 (Toulouse, 1973)

*Mentalitäten im Mittelalter: Methodische und inhaltliche Probleme*. Ed. F. Graus. Vorträge und Forschungen, 35 (Sigmaringen, 1987)

Merzbacher, F. 'Wandlungen des Kirchenbegriffs im Spätmittelalter: Grundzüge der Ekklesiologie des ausgehenden 13., des 14. und 15. Jahrhunderts', *Zeitschrift der Savigny-Stiftung für Rechtsgeschichte*, Canon law section, 39 (1953), pp. 274–361

Meuthen, E. *Nikolaus von Kues, 1401–1464: Skizze einer Biographie* (Münster, 1964)

Miccoli, G. *Chiesa Gregoriana: Ricerche sulla riforma del secolo XI* (Florence, 1966)

Michaud-Quantin, P. 'Le Droit universitaire dans le conflit parisien de 1252–1257', *Studia Gratiana*, 8 (1962), pp. 577–99

'La Conscience d'être membre d'une universitas.' In *Beiträge zum Berufsbewusstsein des mittelalterlichen Menschen* (Berlin, 1964), pp. 1–14

'Aspects de la vie sociale chez les moralistes.' In *Beiträge zum Berufsbewusstsein des mittelalterlichen Menschen* (Berlin, 1964), pp. 30–43

*Universitas: Expressions du mouvement communautaire dans le Moyen Age latin* (Paris, 1970)

*Etudes sur le vocabulaire philosophique du Moyen Age* (Rome, 1970)

Michel, R. *L'Administration royale dans la sénéchaussée de Beaucaire au temps de Saint Louis* (Paris, 1910)

Miethke, J. *Ockhams Weg zur Sozialphilosophie* (Berlin, 1969)

'Repräsentation und Delegation in den politischen Schriften Wilhelms von Ockham.' In *Der Begriff der Repraesentatio* (Berlin, 1971), pp. 163–85

'Zeitbezug und Gegenwartsbewusstsein in der politischen Theorie der ersten Hälfte des 14. Jhds.' In *Antiqui und Moderni* (Berlin, 1974), pp. 262–92

'Papst, Ortsbischof und Universität in den Pariser Theologenprozessen des 13. Jahrhunderts.' In *Die Auseinandersetzungen an der Pariser Universität* (Berlin, 1976), pp. 52–94

'Geschichtsprozess und zeitgenössisches Bewusstsein: Die Theorie des monarchischen Papats im hohen und späteren Mittelalter,' *Historische Zeitschrift*, 226 (1978), pp. 564–99

'Zur Bedeutung der Ekklesiologie für die politische Theorie im späteren Mittelalter.' In *Soziale Ordnungen im Selbstverständnis des Mittelalters* (Berlin, 1979–80), pp. 369–88

'Die Rolle der Bettelorden im Umbruch der politischen Theorie an der Wende zum 14. Jahrhundert.' In *Stellung und Wirksamkeit der Bettelorden in der städtischen Gesellschaft* (Berlin, 1981), pp. 119–53

'Die Konzilien als Forum der öffentlichen Meinung im 15. Jahrhundert', *Deutsches Archiv*, 37 (1981), pp. 736–73

'Die Traktate "De potestate papae": Ein Typus politiktheoretischer Literatur im späten Mittelalter.' In *Les Genres littéraires* (Louvain-la-Neuve, 1982), pp. 193–211

'Die Kirche und die Universitäten im 13. Jahrhundert.' In *Schulen und Studium im sozialen Wandel des hohen und späten Mittelalters*. Ed. J. Fried. *Vorträge und Forschungen*, 30 (Sigmaringen, 1986), pp. 285–320

'Politische Theorie und die "Mentalität" der Bettelorden.' In *Mentalitäten im Mittelalter: Methodische und inhaltliche Probleme*. Ed. F. Graus. *Vorträge und Forschungen*, 35 (Sigmaringen, 1987), pp. 157–76

Miethke, J. and A. Bühler. *Kaiser und Papst im Konflikt: Zum Verhältnis von Staat und Kirche im späten Mittelalter* (Düsseldorf, 1988)

Mill, J. S. *On Liberty*. Ed. G. Himmelfarb (Harmondsworth, 1974)

# Bibliography

Millet, H. *Les Chanoines du chapitre cathédral de Laon, 1272–1412* (Rome, 1982)

Mitteis, H. *Lehnrecht und Staatsgewalt: Untersuchungen zur mittelalterlichen Verfassungsgeschichte* (Weimar, 1933)

    *Der Staat des hohen Mittelalters: Grundlinien einer vergleichenden Verfassungsgeschichte des Lehnszeitalters.* 3rd edn. (Weimar, 1948)

Mochi Onory, S. *Fonti canonistiche dell'idea moderna dello stato* (Milan, 1951)

Moeller, B. 'Piety in Germany around 1500.' In *The Reformation in Medieval Perspective.* Ed. S. E. Ozment (Chicago, 1971), pp. 50–75

Molinier, A. 'Sur la géographie de la province de Languedoc au Moyen Age.' In C. Devic and J.-J. Vaissete, *Histoire générale de Languedoc*, 12 (Toulouse, 1889), pp. 130–355

Mollat, G. 'Les Doléances du clergé de la province de Sens au concile de Vienne', *Revue d'histoire ecclésiastique*, 6/1 (1905), pp. 319–26

    *La Collation des bénéfices ecclésiastiques sous les papes d'Avignon, 1305–1378* (Paris, 1921)

    'Le Roi de France et la collation plénière (pleno jure) des bénéfices ecclésiastiques', *Académie des Inscriptions et Belles Lettres: Mémoires présentés par divers savants*, 1st series, 14/2 (Paris, 1951), pp. 107–286

    *Les Papes d'Avignon, 1305–1378.* 10th edn. (Paris, 1965)

Momigliano, A. *Essays in Ancient and Modern Historiography* (Middletown, 1977)

    'Historicism Revisited.' In A. Momigliano, *Essays in Ancient and Modern Historiography*, pp. 365–73

    'The Fault of the Greeks.' In A. Momigliano, *Essays in Ancient and Modern Historiography*, pp. 9–23

Moore, R. I. *The Origins of European Dissent* (London, 1977)

    *The Formation of a Persecuting Society: Power and Deviance in Western Europe, 950–1250* (Oxford, 1987)

Moorman, J. *A History of the Franciscan Order from its Origins to the Year 1517* (Oxford, 1968)

Morrall, J. B. *Political Thought in Medieval Times* (London, 1958)

    *Gerson and the Great Schism* (Manchester, 1960)

    'Ockham and Ecclesiology.' In *Medieval Studies presented to Aubrey Gwynn* (Dublin, 1961), pp. 481–91

Morris, C. *The Discovery of the Individual, 1050–1200* (New York, 1972)

    *The Papal Monarchy: The Western Church from 1050 to 1250* (Oxford, 1989)

Morrison, K. F. *Tradition and Authority in the Western Church, 300–1140* (Princeton, 1969)

    *The Mimetic Tradition of Reform in the West* (Princeton, 1982)

Morrissey, T. E. 'Franciscus de Zabarellis (1360–1417) and the Conciliarist Tradition.' Ph.D. thesis (Cornell University, 1973)

    'The Decree "Haec Sancta" and Cardinal Zabarella', *Annuarium historiae conciliorum*, 10 (1978), pp. 145–76

Moynihan, J. M. *Papal Immunity and Liability in the Writings of the Medieval Canonists* (Rome, 1961)

Mühlmann, S. 'Luther und das Corpus Iuris Canonici bis zum Jahre 1530: Ein forschungsgeschichtlicher Überblick', *Zeitschrift der Savigny-Stiftung für Rechtsgeschichte*, Canon law section, 58 (1972), pp. 235–305

# Bibliography

Muldoon, J. 'Extra ecclesiam non est imperium: The Canonists and the Legitimacy of Secular Power', *Studia Gratiana*, 9 (1966), pp. 551–80

'Boniface VIII's Forty Years Experience in the Law', *The Jurist*, 31 (1971), pp. 449–77

Müllejans, H. *Publicus und privatus im römischen Recht und im älteren kanonischen Recht unter besonderer Berücksichtigung der Unterscheidung ius publicum et ius privatum* (Munich, 1961)

Müller, E. *Das Konzil von Vienne, 1311–1312: Seine Quellen und seine Geschichte* (Münster, 1934)

Müller, F. W. 'Zur Geschichte des Wortes und Begriffes "nation" im französischen Schrifttum des Mittelalters bis zur Mitte des 15. Jahrhunderts', *Romanische Forschungen*, 58–9 (1947), pp. 247–321

Muller, J. *Dictionnaire abrégé des imprimeurs-éditeurs français du seizième siècle* (Baden-Baden, 1970)

Mundy, J. H. 'The Conciliar Movement and the Council of Constance.' In L. R. Loomis, *The Council of Constance*. Eds. J. H. Mundy and K. M. Woody (New York, 1962), pp. 3–65

*Europe in the High Middle Ages, 1150–1309* (New York, 1973)

'In Praise of Italy: The Italian Republics', *Speculum*, 64 (1989), pp. 815–34

Munier, C. 'L'"Ordo de celebrando concilio" wisigothique: ses remaniements jusqu'au X$^e$ siècle', *Revue des sciences religieuses*, 37 (1963), pp. 250–71

Murray, A. *Reason and Society in the Middle Ages* (Oxford, 1978)

Neiske, F. 'Reform oder Kodifizierung? Päpstliche Statuten für Cluny im 13. Jahrhundert', *Archivum historiae pontificiae*, 26 (1988), pp. 72–118

Nelli, R. *Histoire du Languedoc* (Paris, 1974)

Nelson, J. 'Kingship and Empire.' In *Cambridge History of Medieval Political Thought*. Ed. J. H. Burns (Cambridge, 1988), pp. 211–51

Nonn, U. 'Heiliges Römisches Reich deutscher Nation: Zum Nationen-Begriff im 15. Jahrhundert', *Zeitschrift für historische Forschung*, 9 (1982), pp. 129–42

Nörr, K. W. *Kirche und Konzil bei Nicolaus de Tudeschis* (Cologne, 1964)

*La Notion d'autorité au Moyen Age: Islam, Byzance, Occident.* Colloques Internationaux de la Napoule, 1978 (Paris, 1982)

Oakley, F. 'On the Road from Constance to 1688: The Political Thought of John Major and George Buchanan', *Journal of British Studies*, 2 (1962), pp. 1–31

*The Political Thought of Pierre d'Ailly: The Voluntarist Tradition* (New Haven, 1964)

'Almain and Major: Conciliar Theory on the Eve of the Reformation', *American Historical Review*, 70 (1965), pp. 673–90

*Council over Pope?* (New York, 1969)

'Figgis, Constance, and the Divines of Paris', *American Historical Review*, 75 (1969), pp. 368–86

'The "New Conciliarism" and its Implications: A Problem in History and Hermeneutics', *Journal of Ecumenical Studies*, 8/4 (1971), pp. 815–40

'Celestial Hierarchies Revisited: Walter Ullmann's Vision of Medieval Politics', *Past and Present*, 60 (1973), pp. 3–48

'Conciliarism in the Sixteenth Century: Jacques Almain Again', *Archiv für Reformationsgeschichte*, 68 (1977), pp. 111–32

# Bibliography

*The Western Church in the Later Middle Ages* (Ithaca, 1979)

'Natural Law, the "Corpus Mysticum", and Consent in Conciliar Thought from John of Paris to Matthias Ugonius', *Speculum*, 56 (1981), pp. 786–810

'Legitimation by Consent: The Question of the Medieval Roots', *Viator*, 14 (1983), pp. 303–35

'Conciliar Theory.' In *Dictionary of the Middle Ages*, 3 (1983), pp. 510–23

*Natural Law, Conciliarism, and Consent in the Late Middle Ages* (London, 1984)

*Omnipotence, Covenant and Order: An Excursion in the History of Ideas from Abelard to Leibniz* (Ithaca, 1984)

Oberman, H. *The Harvest of Medieval Theology: Gabriel Biel and Late Medieval Nominalism* (Cambridge/Mass., 1963)

Olsen, B. M. 'Les florilèges d'auteurs classiques.' In *Les Genres littéraires* (Louvain-la-Neuve, 1982), pp. 151–64

Olsen, G. 'The Idea of the "Ecclesia Primitiva" in the Writings of the Twelfth-Century Canonists', *Traditio*, 25 (1969), pp. 61–86

Ourliac, P. *Etudes d'histoire du droit médiéval* (Paris, 1979)

Panofsky, E. *Renaissance and Renascences in Western Art* (Stockholm, 1960)

Pantin, W. A. *The English Church in the Fourteenth Century* (Cambridge, 1955)

Parker, T. M. 'The Conciliar Movement.' In *Trends in Medieval Political Thought.* Ed. B. Smalley (Oxford, 1965), pp. 127–39

Partner, P. *The Lands of St Peter: The Papal State in the Middle Ages and the Early Renaissance* (London, 1972)

Pascoe, L. B. *Jean Gerson: Principles of Church Reform* (Leiden, 1973)

'Jean Gerson: The "Ecclesia Primitiva" and Reform', *Traditio*, 30 (1974), pp. 379–409

'Jean Gerson: Mysticism, Conciliarism, and Reform', *Annuarium historiae conciliorum*, 6 (1974), pp. 135–53

'Gerson and the Donation of Constantine: Growth and Development within the Church', *Viator*, 5 (1974), pp. 469–85

Passerin d'Entreves, A. *The Medieval Contribution to Political Thought* (Oxford, 1939)

Pater, J. *Die bischöfliche Visitatio liminum ss. Apostolorum: Eine historisch-kanonistische Studie* (Paderborn, 1914)

Paulus, C. *Welt- und Ordensklerus beim Ausgange des XIII. Jahrhunderts im Kampf um die Pfarrechte* (Essen, 1900)

Pegis, A. C. 'Henry of Ghent and the New Way to God', *Mediaeval Studies*, 30 (1968), pp. 226–47; 31 (1969), pp. 93–116; 33 (1971), pp. 158–79

Pennington, K. 'The Legal Education of Pope Innocent III', *Bulletin of Medieval Canon Law*, 4 (1974), pp. 70–7

'The Canonists and Pluralism in the Thirteenth Century', *Speculum*, 51 (1976), pp. 35–48

'Pope Innocent III's Views on Church and State: A Gloss to "Per Venerabilem".' In *Law, Church, and Society* (Philadelphia, 1977), pp. 49–67

'Pro peccatis patrum puniri: A Moral and Legal Problem of the Inquisition', *Church History*, 47 (1978), pp. 137–54

*Pope and Bishops: The Papal Monarchy in the Twelfth and Thirteenth Centuries* (Philadelphia, 1984)

# Bibliography

'Law, Legislative Authority, and Theories of Government, 1150–1300.' In *Cambridge History of Medieval Political Thought*. Ed. J. H. Burns (Cambridge, 1988), pp. 424–53

Peterson, D. S. 'Conciliarism, Republicanism and Corporatism: The 1415–1420 Constitution of the Florentine Clergy', *Renaissance Quarterly*, 42 (1989), pp. 183–226

Pfaff, V. 'Der Widerstand der Bischöfe gegen den päpstlichen Zentralismus um 1200', *Zeitschrift der Savigny-Stiftung für Rechtsgeschichte*, Canon law section, 66 (1980), pp. 459–65

Philippe, A. *La Baronnie du Tournel et ses seigneurs du début du XIII<sup>e</sup> siècle à la fin du XV<sup>e</sup> siècle: Documents publiés avec une introduction et des notes* (Mende, 1903–6)

Piaia, G. *Marsiglio da Padova nella riforma e nella controriforma: Fortuna ed interpretazione* (Padua, 1977)

'La fondazione filosofica della teoria conciliare in Francesco Zabarella.' In *Scienza e filosofia all'università di Padova nel quattrocento*. Ed. A. Poppi (Trieste and Padua, 1983), pp. 431–61

Pichler, I. H. *Die Verbindlichkeit der Konstanzer Dekrete: Untersuchungen zur Frage der Interpretation und Verbindlichkeit der Superioritätsdekrete 'Haec sancta' und 'Frequens'* (Vienna, 1967)

Plique, G. 'Etude sur le chapitre cathédral de Mende de 1123 à 1516', *S. d. L., Chroniques et mélanges*, 5 (1930–9), pp. 1–229

Podlech, A. 'Repräsentation', *Geschichtliche Grundbegriffe*, 5 (1984), pp. 509–47

Pontal, O. 'Le Role du synode diocésain et des statuts synodaux dans la formation du clergé.' In *Les Evêques, les clercs, et le roi* (Toulouse, 1972), pp. 337–59

*Popes, Teachers, and Canon Law in the Middle Ages.* Eds. J. R. Sweeney and S. Chodorow (Ithaca, 1989)

Poquet du Haut-Jussé, B. A. 'Le Second Différend entre Boniface VIII et Philippe le Bel.' In *Mélanges Albert Dufourcq* (Paris, 1932), pp. 73–168

Porée, C. *Le Consulat et l'administration municipale de Mende* (Paris, 1902)

*Etudes historiques sur le Gévaudan* (Paris, 1919)

'La Domination Aragonaise en Gévaudan, 1172–1258.' In C. Porée, *Etudes historiques sur le Gévaudan*, pp. 195–266

'Le Procès du paréage de 1307 et le fonds de ce procès aux archives de la Lozère.' In C. Porée, *Etudes historiques sur le Gévaudan*, pp. 281–331

'Les Evêques-comtes de Gévaudan: Etude sur le pouvoir temporel des évêques de Mende aux XII<sup>e</sup> et XIII<sup>e</sup> siècles.' In C. Porée, *Etudes historiques sur le Gévaudan*, pp. 347–509

Posch, A. 'Die Reformvorschläge des Wilhelm Durandus jun. auf dem Konzil von Vienne', *Mitteilungen des österreichischen Instituts für Geschichtsforschung*, Ergänzungsband 11 (1929), pp. 288–303

*Die 'Concordantia Catholica' des Nikolaus von Cusa* (Paderborn, 1930)

Post, G. '"Plena Potestas" and Consent in Medieval Assemblies: A Study in Romano-Canonical Procedure and the Rise of Representation, 1150–1325', *Traditio*, 1 (1943), pp. 355–408

'A Romano-Canonical Maxim, "quod omnes tangit", in Bracton', *Traditio*, 4 (1946), pp. 197–251

'"Ratio publicae utilitatis", "ratio status", and "Reason of State", 1100–1300', *Die Welt als Geschichte*, 21 (1961), pp. 8–28, 71–99

*Studies in Medieval Legal Thought: Public Law and the State, 1100–1322* (Princeton, 1964)

'Copyists' Errors and the Problem of Papal Dispensations "contra statutum generale Ecclesiae" or "contra statum generalem Ecclesiae" according to the Decretists and Decretalists, *ca.* 1150–1234', *Studia Gratiana*, 9 (1966), pp. 357–405

'Vincentius Hispanus, "pro ratione voluntas", and Medieval and Early Modern Theories of Sovereignty', *Traditio*, 28 (1972), pp. 159–84

Posthumus Meyjes, G. H. M. *Jean Gerson: Zijn kerkpolitiek en ecclesiologie* ('s-Gravenhage, 1963)

*Proceedings of the Second International Congress of Medieval Canon Law*. Ed. S. Kuttner (Vatican City, 1965)

*Proceedings of the Third International Congress of Medieval Canon Law*. Ed. S. Kuttner (Vatican City, 1971)

*Proceedings of the Fourth International Congress of Medieval Canon Law*. Ed. S. Kuttner (Vatican City, 1976)

Prodi, P. *The Papal Prince*. Trans. S. Haskins (Cambridge, 1987)

Prunières, B. 'L'Ancienne Baronnie de Peyre d'après des documents originaux et inédits', *Bulletin de la S. d. L.*, 17/2 (1866), pp. 159–361

Pycke, J. *Le Chapitre Cathédral Notre-Dame de Tournai de la fin du XI<sup>e</sup> à la fin du XIII<sup>e</sup> siècle: Son organisation, sa vie, ses membres* (Nauwelaerts and Brussels, 1986)

Quillet, J. 'Community, Counsel, and Representation.' In *Cambridge History of Medieval Political Thought*. Ed. J. H. Burns (Cambridge, 1988), pp. 520–72

Rashdall, H. *The Universities of Europe in the Middle Ages*. 3rd edn. 3 vols. (Oxford, 1936)

Ratzinger, J. 'Der Einfluss des Bettelordensstreites auf die Entwicklung der Lehre vom päpstlichen Universalprimat unter besonderer Berücksichtigung des heiligen Bonaventura.' In *Theologie in Geschichte und Gegenwart: Festgabe M. Schmaus*. Eds. J. Auer and H. Volk (Munich, 1957), 2:697–724

Reinhard, W. 'Nepotismus: Der Funktionswandel einer papstgeschichtlichen Konstanten', *Zeitschrift für Kirchengeschichte*, 86 (1975), pp. 145–85

*Renaissance and Renewal in the Twelfth Century*. Eds. R. L. Benson and G. Constable (Cambridge/Mass., 1982)

Renardy, C. *Le Monde des maîtres universitaires du diocèse de Liège, 1140–1350* (Paris, 1979)

Renaudet, A. *Préréforme et humanisme à Paris pendant les premières guerres d'Italie, 1494–1517*. 2nd edn. (Paris, 1953)

Renouard, P. *Répertoire des imprimeurs parisiens* (Paris, 1965)

Renouard, Y. *The Avignon Papacy, 1305–1403* (Hamden, 1970)

*Republiken und Republikanismus im Europa der frühen Neuzeit*. Ed. H. G. Koenigsberger (Munich, 1988)

Reynolds, S. *Kingdoms and Communities in Western Europe, 900–1300* (Oxford, 1984)

Ribaucourt, C. 'Les Mendiants du Midi d'apres la cartographie de l'enquête.' In *Les Mendiants en pays d'Oc* (Toulouse, 1973), pp. 25–33

Richard, J. *Saint Louis: Roi d'une France féodale, soutien de la Terre Sainte* (Paris, 1983)

Richardson, H. G. and G. O. Sayles. *The Governance of Mediaeval England from the*

# Bibliography

*Conquest to Magna Carta* (Edinburgh, 1963)

Richter, J. 'Stufen pseudoisidorischer Verfälschung: Untersuchungen zum Konzilsteil der pseudoisidorischen Dekretalen', *Zeitschrift der Savigny-Stiftung für Rechtsgeschichte*, Canon Law Section, 64 (1978), pp. 1–72

Riesenberg, P. *Inalienability of Sovereignty in Medieval Political Thought* (New York, 1956)

Rivière, J. 'In partem sollicitudinis: Evolution d'une formule pontificale', *Revue des sciences religieuses*, 5 (1925), pp. 210–31

*Le Problème de l'église et de l'état au temps de Philippe le Bel* (Louvain, 1926)

Roberg, B. 'Subsidium Terrae Sanctae: Kreuzzug, Konzil und Steuern', *Annuarium historiae conciliorum*, 15 (1983), pp. 96–139

Robinson, I. S. 'Gregory VII and the Soldiers of Christ', *History*, 58 (1973), pp. 169–92

'"Periculosus homo": Pope Gregory VII and Episcopal Authority', *Viator*, 9 (1978), pp. 103–31

'Church and Papacy.' In *Cambridge History of Medieval Political Thought*. Ed. J. H. Burns (Cambridge, 1988), pp. 252–305

Rogozinski, J. 'The Counsellors of the Seneschal of Beaucaire and Nîmes, 1250–1350', *Speculum*, 44 (1969), pp. 421–39

*Power, Caste, and Law: Social Conflict in Fourteenth-Century Montpellier* (Cambridge/Mass., 1982)

Roucaute, J. *La Formation territoriale du domaine royal en Gévaudan, 1161–1307, avec la carte des terres propres au roi au temps de Philippe le Bel* (Paris, 1901)

Royer, J.-P. *L'Eglise et le royaume de France au XIVᵉ siècle d'après le 'Songe du vergier' et la jurisprudence du Parlement* (Paris, 1969)

Ruiz, T. 'Reaction to Anagni', *Catholic Historical Review*, 65 (1979), pp. 385–401

*Sacerdozio e regno da Gregorio VII a Bonifacio VIII: Studi presentati alla sezione storica del Congresso della Pontificia Università Gregoriana* (Rome, 1954)

Samaran, C. and G. Mollat. *La fiscalité pontificale en France au XIVᵉ siècle* (Paris, 1905)

Sauer, J. *Symbolik des Kirchengebäudes und seiner Ausstattung in der Auffassung des Mittelalters. Mit Berücksichtigung von Honorius Augustodunensis und Durandus* (Freiburg, 1902)

Schieffer, R. 'Der Papst als "Pontifex Maximus": Bemerkungen zur Geschichte eines päpstlichen Ehrentitels', *Zeitschrift der Savigny-Stiftung für Rechtsgeschichte*, Canon law section, 57 (1971), pp. 300–9

Schleyer, K. *Anfänge des Gallikanismus im 13. Jahrhundert* (Berlin, 1937)

Schmale, F.-J. 'Systematisches zu den Konzilien des Reformpapsttums im 12. Jahrhundert', *Annuarium historiae conciliorum*, 6 (1974), pp. 21–39

Schmitt, J.-C. *Mort d'une hérésie: L'église et les clercs face aux béguines et aux béghards du Rhin supérieur du XIVᵉ au XVᵉ siècles* (Paris, 1978)

Schmugge, L. 'Über "nationale" Vorurteile im Mittelalter', *Deutsches Archiv*, 38 (1982), pp. 439–59

Schneider, H. *Der Konziliarismus als Problem der neueren katholischen Theologie: Die Geschichte der Auslegung der Konstanzer Dekrete von Febronius bis zur Gegenwart* (Berlin, 1976)

Schnürer, G. *Kirche und Kultur im Mittelalter*. 3 vols. (Paderborn, 1924–30)

# Bibliography

Scholz, R. *Die Publizistik zur Zeit Philipps des Schönen und Bonifaz' VIII.* (Stuttgart, 1903)

*Wilhelm von Ockham als politischer Denker* (Leipzig, 1944)

Schramm, P. E. *Kaiser, Rom und Renovatio: Studien zur Geschichte des römischen Erneuerungsgedankens vom Ende des karolingischen Reiches bis zum Investiturstreit* (Leipzig, 1929)

*Herrschaftszeichen und Staatssymbolik.* 3 vols. (Stuttgart, 1954–6)

*Der König von Frankreich.* 2nd edn. (Weimar, 1960)

Schulte, A. *Der Adel und die deutsche Kirche im Mittelalter: Studien zur Sozialrechts- und Kirchengeschichte* (Stuttgart, 1910)

Schulte, J. F. von. *Die Stellung der Concilien, Päpste und Bischöfe vom historischen und canonistischen Standpunkte* (Prague, 1871)

*Die Geschichte der Quellen und Literatur des canonischen Rechts.* 3 vols. (Stuttgart, 1875–80)

Schüppert, H. *Kirchenkritik in der lateinischen Lyrik des 12. und 13. Jahrhunderts* (Munich, 1972)

Schüssler, H. *Der Primat der Heiligen Schrift als theologisches und kanonistisches Problem im Spätmittelalter* (Wiesbaden, 1977)

Schwaiger, G. 'Der päpstliche Primat in der Geschichte der Kirche', *Zeitschrift für Kirchengeschichte*, 82 (1971), pp. 1–15

Schwer, W. *Stand und Ständeordnung im Weltbild des Mittelalters: Die geistes- und gesellschaftsgeschichtlichen Grundlagen der berufsständischen Idee.* 2nd edn. (Paderborn, 1952)

Seidlmayer, M. *Die Anfänge des grossen abendländischen Schismas* (Münster, 1940)

Review of B. Tierney, *Foundations of the Conciliar Theory.* In *Die Entwicklung des Konziliarismus* (Darmstadt, 1976), pp. 156–73

Seckel, E. *Beiträge zur Geschichte beider Rechte im Mittelalter, 1: Zur Geschichte der populären Literatur des römisch-canonischen Rechts* (Tübingen, 1898)

Sieben, H. J. *Die Konzilsidee der alten Kirche* (Paderborn, 1979)

*Traktate und Theorien zum Konzil: Vom Beginn des grossen Schismas bis zum Vorabend der Reformation, 1378–1521* (Frankfurt, 1983)

*Die Konzilsidee des lateinischen Mittelalters, 847–1378* (Paderborn, 1984)

Sigmund, P. E. *Nicholas of Cusa and Medieval Political Thought* (Cambridge/Mass., 1963)

Sikes, J. G. 'John de Pouilli and Peter de la Palu', *English Historical Review*, 49 (1934), pp. 219–40

Sivéry, G. *Saint Louis et son siècle* (Paris, 1983)

Skinner, Q. 'Meaning and Understanding in the History of Ideas', *History and Theory*, 8 (1969), pp. 3–53

'Motives, Intentions and the Interpretation of Texts', *New Literary History*, 3 (1972), pp. 393–408

'Some Problems in the Analysis of Political Thought and Action', *Political Theory*, 2 (1974), pp. 277–303

*The Foundations of Modern Political Thought.* 2 vols. (Cambridge, 1978)

'A Reply to My Critics.' In *Meaning and Context.* Ed. J. Tully (Princeton, 1988), pp. 231–341

Smalley, B. 'Ecclesiastical Attitudes to Novelty, c. 1100–c. 1250.' In *Church,*

# Bibliography

Society, and Politics. Ed. D. Baker (Oxford, 1975), pp. 113–31
Solanet, A. 'Instructions et Constitutions synodales de Guillaume Durand dit le
   Spéculateur pour le clergé et les fidèles du diocèse de Mende', *Bulletin de la S.
   d. L.*, 49 (1897), pp. 141–9
Southern, R. *The Making of the Middle Ages* (New Haven, 1953)
   *Western Society and the Church in the Middle Ages* (Harmondsworth, 1970)
   *Robert Grosseteste: The Growth of an English Mind in Medieval Europe* (Oxford,
   1986)
*Soziale Ordnungen im Selbstverständnis des Mittelalters.* Ed. A. Zimmermann.
   *Miscellanea Mediaevalia*, 12/1–2 (Berlin, 1979–80)
*Stellung und Wirksamkeit der Bettelorden in der städtischen Gesellschaft.* Ed. K. Elm
   (Berlin, 1981)
Stenger, R. P. 'The Episcopacy as an Ordo according to the Medieval Canonists',
   *Mediaeval Studies*, 29 (1967), pp. 67–112
Stickler, A. M. *Historia iuris canonici latini*, 1: *Historia fontium* (Rome, 1950)
   'Concerning the Political Theories of the Medieval Canonists', *Traditio*, 7
   (1949–51), pp. 450–63
   'Sacerdotium et regnum nei decretisti e primi decretalisti', *Salesianum*, 15
   (1953), pp. 575–612
   'Ordines judiciarii', *Dictionnaire de droit canonique*, 6 (1957), cols. 1,132–43
   'La "Sollicitudo omnium ecclesiarum" nella canonistica classica', *Communio*, 13
   (1972), pp. 547–86
   'Papal Infallibility – a Thirteenth-Century Invention? Reflections on a Recent
   Book', *Catholic Historical Review*, 60 (1974), pp. 427–41
   'Rejoinder to Professor Tierney', *Catholic Historical Review*, 61 (1975), pp.
   274–9
Stieber, J. *Pope Eugenius IV, the Council of Basel, and the Secular and Ecclesiastical
   Authorities in the Empire* (Leiden, 1978)
Stock, B. *The Implications of Literacy: Written Language and Models of Interpretation
   in the Eleventh and Twelfth Centuries* (Princeton, 1983)
Stockmeier, P. 'Die Alte Kirche – Leitbild der Erneuerung', *Tübinger theologische
   Quartalschrift*, 146 (1966), pp. 385–480
   'Causa reformationis und Alte Kirche: Zum Geschichtsverständnis der
   Reformbewegungen.' In *Von Konstanz nach Trient* (Munich and Paderborn,
   1972), pp. 1–13
   'Die Übernahme des Pontifex-Titels im spätantiken Christentum.' In *Konzil
   und Papst: Festgabe H. Tüchle* (Munich, 1975), pp. 75–84
Strayer, J. R. 'The Laicization of French and English Society in the Thirteenth
   Century', *Speculum*, 15 (1940), pp. 76–86
   'Philip the Fair – A "Constitutional" King', *American Historical Review*, 62
   (1956–7), pp. 18–32
   'La Noblesse du Gévaudan et le paréage de 1307', *Revue du Gévaudan*, n. s. 13
   (1967), pp. 66–72
   'France: The Holy Land, the Chosen People, and the Most Christian King.' In
   *Essays in Memory of E. H. Harbison* (Princeton, 1969), pp. 3–19
   *Les Gens de justice du Languedoc sous Philippe le Bel* (Toulouse, 1970)
   *On the Medieval Origins of the Modern State* (Princeton, 1970)

362

# Bibliography

*Medieval Statecraft and the Perspectives of History: Essays by Joseph R. Strayer*. Eds.
    J. F. Benton and T. N. Bisson (Princeton, 1971)
*The Reign of Philip the Fair* (Princeton, 1980)
Strayer, J. R. and C. H. Taylor. *Studies in Early French Taxation* (Cambridge/
    Mass., 1939)
Struve, T. *Die Entwicklung der organologischen Staatsauffassung im Mittelalter*
    (Stuttgart, 1978)
Stump, P. 'Reform in Head and Members: The Reform Ideas of the Council of
    Constance.' Ph.D. thesis (University of California, 1978)
    'The Reform of Papal Taxation at the Council of Constance, 1414–1418',
    *Speculum*, 64 (1989), pp. 69–105
Stutz, U. *Die Eigenkirche als Element des mittelalterlich-germanischen Kirchenrechtes*
    (Berlin, 1895)
Sullivan, R. E. 'The Carolingian Age: Reflections on its Place in the History of the
    Middle Ages', *Speculum*, 64 (1989), pp. 267–306
Swanson, R. N. *Universities, Academics, and the Great Schism* (Cambridge, 1979)
Szabó-Bechstein, B. *Libertas ecclesiae: Ein Schlüsselbegriff des Investiturstreits und
    seine Vorgeschichte, 4. – 11. Jahrhundert* (Rome, 1985)
Tangl, G. *Die Teilnehmer an den allgemeinen Konzilien des Mittelalters* (Weimar,
    1922)
Taylor, C. H. 'The Composition of Baronial Assemblies in France, 1315–1320',
    *Speculum;* 29 (1954), pp. 433–59
Tecklenburg-Johns, C. *Luthers Konzilsidee in ihrer historischen Bedingtheit und ihrem
    reformatorischen Neuansatz* (Berlin, 1966)
Tellenbach, G. *Libertas: Kirche und Weltordnung im Zeitalter des Investiturstreites*
    (Stuttgart, 1936)
    *Church, State and Christian Society at the Time of the Investiture Contest*. Trans. R.
    F. Bennett (Oxford, 1959)
*Thomas von Aquin*. Ed. A. Zimmermann. *Miscellanea Mediaevalia*, 19 (Berlin,
    1988)
Thomson, W. R. *Friars in the Cathedral: The First Franciscan Bishops, 1226–1261*
    (Toronto, 1975)
Tierney, B. 'Ockham, the Conciliar Theory, and the Canonists', *Journal of the
    History of Ideas*, 15 (1954), pp. 40–70
    'Some Recent Works on the Political Theories of the Medieval Canonists',
    *Traditio*, 10 (1954), pp. 594–625
    *Foundations of the Conciliar Theory: The Contribution of the Medieval Canonists
    from Gratian to the Great Schism* (Cambridge, 1955)
    'Grosseteste and the Theory of Papal Sovereignty', *Journal of Ecclesiastical
    History*, 6 (1955), pp. 1–17
    'Pope and Council: Some New Decretist Texts', *Mediaeval Studies*, 19 (1957),
    pp. 157–218
    '"The Prince is not Bound by the Laws": Accursius and the Origins of the
    Modern State', *Comparative Studies in Society and History*, 5/4 (1963), pp.
    378–400
    *The Crisis of Church and State, 1050–1300* (Englewood Cliffs, 1964)
    'The Continuity of Papal Political Theory in the Thirteenth Century: Some

# Bibliography

Methodological Considerations', *Mediaeval Studies*, 27 (1965), pp. 227–45

'Medieval Canon Law and Western Constitutionalism', *Catholic Historical Review*, 52 (1966), pp. 1–17

'"Sola Scriptura" and the Canonists', *Studia Gratiana*, 11 (1967), pp. 347–66

'Hermeneutics and History: The Problem of "Haec Sancta".' In *Essays in Medieval History presented to Bertie Wilkinson* (Toronto, 1969), pp. 354–70

*Origins of Papal Infallibility, 1150–1350: A Study on the Concepts of Infallibility, Sovereignty and Tradition in the Middle Ages* (Leiden, 1972)

'From Thomas of York to William Ockham: The Franciscans and the Papal Sollicitudo omnium ecclesiarum, 1250–1350', *Communio*, 13 (1972), pp. 607–58

'On the History of Papal Infallibility: A Discussion with Remigius Bäumer', *Theologische Revue*, 70 (1974), pp. 185–94

'Divided Sovereignty at Constance: A Problem of Medieval and Early Modern Political Theory', *Annuarium historiae conciliorum*, 7 (1975), pp. 238–56

'Infallibility and the Medieval Canonists: A Discussion with Alfons Stickler', *Catholic Historical Review*, 61 (1975), pp. 265–73

'Hostiensis and Collegiality', *Proceedings of the Fourth International Congress of Medieval Canon Law* (Vatican City, 1976), pp. 401–9

'"Only the Truth has Authority": The Problem of "Reception" in the Decretists and in Johannes de Turrecremata.' In *Law, Church, and Society* (Philadelphia, 1977), pp. 69–96

*Church, Law, and Constitutional Thought in the Middle Ages* (London, 1979)

'Public Expediency and Natural Law: A Fourteenth-Century Discussion on the Origins of Government and Property.' In *Authority and Power* (Cambridge, 1980), pp. 167–82

*Religion, Law, and the Growth of Constitutional Thought, 1150–1650* (Cambridge, 1982)

'Hierarchy, Consent, and the "Western Tradition"', *Political Theory*, 15 (1987), pp. 646–52

Torquebiau, P. 'Le Gallicanisme de Durand de Mende le Jeune.' In *Acta congressus iuridici internationalis*, 3 (Rome, 1936), pp. 269–89

*Trends in Medieval Political Thought*. Ed. B. Smalley (Oxford, 1965)

Trinkaus, C. '*In Our Image and Likeness*': Humanity and Divinity in Italian Humanist Thought. 2 vols. (London, 1970)

Tschackert, P. *Peter von Ailli* (Gotha, 1877)

Tuck, R. *Natural Rights Theories: Their Origin and Development* (Cambridge, 1979)

Tyerman, C. J. 'Philip V of France, the Assemblies of 1319–1320 and the Crusade', *Bulletin of the Institute of Historical Research*, 57 (1984), pp. 15–34

Ullmann, W. *The Origins of the Great Schism* (London, 1948)

'The Development of the Medieval Idea of Sovereignty', *English Historical Review*, 64 (1949), pp. 1–33

*Medieval Papalism: The Political Theories of the Medieval Canonists* (London, 1949)

*Principles of Government and Politics in the Middle Ages* (London, 1961)

*The Relevance of Medieval Ecclesiastical History* (Cambridge, 1966)

*The Individual and Society in the Middle Ages* (Baltimore, 1966)

# Bibliography

'Juristic Obstacles to the Emergence of the Concept of the State in the Middle Ages', *Annali di storia del diritto*, 13 (1969), pp. 43–64

*The Growth of Papal Government in the Middle Ages: A Study in the Ideological Relation of Clerical to Lay Power.* 3rd edn. (London, 1970)

*A History of Political Thought: The Middle Ages.* Rev. edn. (Harmondsworth, 1970)

*Law and Politics in the Middle Ages: An Introduction to the Sources of Medieval Political Ideas* (Ithaca, 1975)

*The Papacy and Political Ideas in the Middle Ages* (London, 1976)

*Jurisprudence in the Middle Ages* (London, 1980)

*Les Universités du Languedoc au XIIIᵉ siècle.* Cahiers de Fanjeaux, 5 (Toulouse, 1970)

*The Universities in the Late Middle Ages.* Eds. J. Ijsewijn and J. Pacquet (Louvain-la-Neuve, 1978)

Valois, N. *La France et le grand schisme d'Occident.* 4 vols. (Paris, 1896–1902)

*Histoire de la Pragmatique Sanction de Bourges sous Charles VII* (Paris, 1906)

*La Crise religieuse du XVᵉ siècle: Le pape et le concile.* 2 vols. (Paris, 1909)

'Jean de Pouilli, théologien', *Histoire littéraire de la France*, 34 (1914), pp. 220–81

'Jacques Duèse, pape sous le nom de Jean XXII', *Histoire littéraire de la France*, 34 (1914), pp. 391–630

Van de Kerckhove, M. 'La Notion de juridiction chez les décrétistes et les premiers décrétalistes, 1140–1250', *Etudes franciscaines*, 49 (1937), pp. 420–55

*La Notion de juridiction dans la doctrine des décrétistes et des premiers décrétalistes* (Assisi, 1937)

Van Engen, J. 'The Christian Middle Ages as an Historiographical Problem', *American Historical Review*, 91 (1986), pp. 519–52

Vansteenberghe, E. *Le Cardinal Nicolas de Cues, 1401–1464: L'action – la pensée* (Paris, 1920)

Vereecke, L. 'La Réforme de l'église au concile de Vienne, 1311–1312', *Studia moralia*, 14 (1976), pp. 283–335

Vicaire, M.-H. 'Le Developpement de la province dominicaine de Provence, 1215–1295', *Les Mendiants en pays d'Oc* (Toulouse, 1973), pp. 35–77

Vinogradoff, P. *Roman Law in Medieval Europe.* 2nd edn. by F. de Zulueta (Oxford, 1929)

Viollet, P. 'Guillaume Durant le Jeune, évêque de Mende', *Histoire littéraire de la France*, 35 (1921), pp. 1–139

*Von Konstanz nach Trient: Beiträge zur Geschichte der Kirche von den Reformkonzilien bis zum Tridentinum.* Ed. R. Bäumer (Munich and Paderborn, 1972)

Vooght, P. de. *Les Pouvoirs du concile et l'autorité du pape au concile de Constance* (Paris, 1965)

'Les Controverses sur les pouvoirs du concile et l'autorité du pape au concile de Constance', *Revue théologique de Louvain*, 1 (1970), pp. 45–75

Wakefield, W. L. *Heresy, Crusade, and Inquisition in Southern France, 1100–1250* (Berkeley, 1974)

Walsh, K. *A Fourteenth-Century Scholar and Primate: Richard Fitz-Ralph in Oxford, Avignon and Armagh* (Oxford, 1981)

Walther, H. G. *Imperiales Königtum, Konziliarismus und Volkssouveränität: Studien zu den Grenzen des mittelalterlichen Souveränitätsgedankens* (Munich, 1976)

# Bibliography

Watt, J. A. 'The Early Medieval Canonists and the Formation of the Conciliar Theory', *Irish Theological Quarterly*, 24 (1957), pp. 13–31

'The Theory of Papal Monarchy in the Thirteenth Century: The Contribution of the Canonists', *Traditio*, 20 (1964), pp. 179–317

*The Theory of Papal Monarchy in the Thirteenth Century* (New York, 1965)

'The Use of the Term "Plenitudo Potestatis" by Hostiensis', *Proceedings of the Second International Congress of Medieval Canon Law* (Vatican City, 1965), pp. 161–87

'The Constitutional Law of the College of Cardinals: Hostiensis to Joannes Andreae', *Mediaeval Studies*, 33 (1971), pp. 127–57

'Hostiensis on "Per Venerabilem": The Role of the College of Cardinals.' In *Authority and Power* (Cambridge, 1980), pp. 99–113

'Spiritual and Temporal Powers.' In *Cambridge History of Medieval Political Thought*. Ed. J. H. Burns (Cambridge, 1988), pp. 367–423

Weakland, J. E. 'Administrative and Fiscal Centralization under Pope John XXII, 1316–1334', *Catholic Historical Review*, 54 (1968), pp. 39–54, 285–310

Weigand, R. *Die Naturrechtslehre der Legisten und Dekretisten von Irnerius bis Accursius und von Gratian bis Johannes Teutonicus* (Munich, 1967)

*Die Welt zur Zeit des Konstanzer Konzils. Vorträge und Forschungen*, 9 (Konstanz, 1965)

Welter, J.-Th. *L'Exemplum dans la littérature religieuse et didactique du Moyen Age* (Paris, 1927)

Werner, K. F. 'Les Nations et le sentiment national dans l'Europe médiévale', *Revue historique*, 244 (1970), pp. 285–304

Wieruszowski, H. *Vom Imperium zum nationalen Königtum* (Munich, 1933)

Wilkinson, B. *Studies in the Constitutional History of the Thirteenth and Fourteenth Centuries* (Manchester, 1937)

Wilks, M. *The Problem of Sovereignty in the Later Middle Ages: The Papal Monarchy with Augustinus Triumphus and the Publicists* (Cambridge, 1963)

Williams, S. *Codices Pseudo-Isidoriani: A Palaeographico-Historical Study* (New York, 1971)

Wohlhaupter, E. *Aequitas canonica: Eine Studie aus dem kanonischen Recht* (Paderborn, 1931)

Wolff, P., ed. *Histoire du Languedoc* (Toulouse, 1967)

Wolgast, E. 'Reform, Reformation', *Geschichtliche Grundbegriffe*, 5 (1984), pp. 313–60

Wolter, H. *Lyon I et Lyon II* (Paris, 1966)

Zeyen, R. *Die theologische Disputation des Johannes de Polliaco zur kirchlichen Verfassung* (Frankfurt, 1976)

Zimmermann, H. *Papstabsetzungen des Mittelalters* (Graz, 1968)

Zuckerman, C. 'Dominican Theories of the Papal Primacy, 1250–1320', Ph.D. thesis (Cornell University, 1971)

'The Relationship of Theories of Universals to Theories of Church Government in the Middle Ages: A Critique of Previous Views', *Journal of the History of Ideas*, 36 (1975), pp. 579–94

'The Ending of French Interference in the Papal Financial System in 1297: A Neglected Episode', *Viator*, 11 (1980), pp. 261–88

# CONCORDANCE

The concordance is meant to make it easier for the reader to check references to the *editio princeps* of Durant's treatise (Lyons, 1531) in one of the more easily obtainable texts, namely Venice 1584 or Paris 1671. The editions of 1531 and 1584 are numbered by folios. r and v stand for the recto and verso, and a and b stand for the first and second column. Because the columns in the edition of 1584 are very large, I have added A, B, C, and D to stand respectively for the top, higher middle, lower middle, and bottom sections of each column. The edition of 1671 is numbered by pages.

| Lyons 1531 | Venice 1584 | Paris 1671 |
|---|---|---|
| 3ra | — | ciiv–ciiir |
| 3rb | — | ciiir–ciiiv |
| 3va | — | ciiiv |
| 3vb | — | ciiiv |
| 4ra | 154raA–B | ciiiir–ciiiiv |
| 4rb | 154raC–D | ciiiiv–2 |
| 4va | 154rbA–B | 2–3 |
| 4vb | 154rbB–D | 3–5 |
| 5ra | 154rbD–154vaB | 5–6 |
| 5rb | 154vaB–D | 6–7 |
| 5va | 154vaD–154vbA | 7–8 |
| 5vb | 154vbA–B | 8–9 |
| 6(*male* 7)ra | 154vbB–D | 9–11 |
| 6(*male* 7)rb | 154vbD–155raB | 11–12 |
| 6(*male* 7)va | 155raB–C | 12–13 |
| 6(*male* 7)vb | 155raC–D | 13–14 |
| 7ra | 155raD–155vaA | 14–16 |
| 7rb | 155vaA–B | 16–17 |
| 7va | 155vaC–D | 17–18 |
| 7vb | 155vaD–155vbA | 18–19 |

| Lyons 1531 | Venice 1584 | Paris 1671 |
|---|---|---|
| 8ra | 155vbB–C | 19–20 |
| 8rb | 155vbC–D | 20–2 |
| 8va | 155vbD–156raA | 22–3 |
| 8vb | 156raB–C | 23–4 |
| | | |
| 9ra | 156raC–D | 24–5 |
| 9rb | 156raD–156rbB | 25–6 |
| 9va | 156rbB–C | 26–8 |
| 9vb | 156rbC–D | 28–9 |
| | | |
| 10ra | 156rbD–156vaB | 29–31 |
| 10rb | 156vaB–C | 31–2 |
| 10va | 156vaD–156vbA | 32–3 |
| 10vb | 156vbA–B | 33–4 |
| | | |
| 11ra | 156vbB–C | 34–5 |
| 11rb | 156vbD–157raA | 35–7 |
| 11va | 157raA–B | 37–8 |
| 11vb | 157raB–D | 38–9 |
| | | |
| 12(*male* 9)ra | 157raD–157rbB | 39–40 |
| 12(*male* 9)rb | 157rbB–C | 40–1 |
| 12(*male* 9)va | 157rbC–D | 41–2 |
| 12(*male* 9)vb | 157rbD–157vaA | 42–4 |
| | | |
| 13ra | 157vaA–C | 44–5 |
| 13rb | 157vaC–157vbA | 45–7 |
| 13va | 157vbA–B | 47–9 |
| 13vb | 157vbC–D | 49–50 |
| | | |
| 14(*male* 15)ra | 157vbD–158raB | 50–2 |
| 14(*male* 15)rb | 158raB–D | 52–4 |
| 14(*male* 15)va | 158raD–158rbA | 54–5 |
| 14(*male* 15)vb | 158rbA–C | 55–6 |
| | | |
| 15ra | 158rbC–D | 56–7 |
| 15rb | 158rbD–158vaB | 57–9 |
| 15va | 158vaB–D | 59–60 |
| 15vb | 158vaD–158vbA | 60–1 |
| | | |
| 16ra | 158vbA–C | 62–3 |
| 16rb | 158vbC–D | 63–4 |
| 16va | 158vbD–159raB | 64–6 |
| 16vb | 159raB–D | 66–7 |

# Concordance

| Lyons 1531 | Venice 1584 | Paris 1671 |
|---|---|---|
| 17ra | 159raD–159rbA | 67–8 |
| 17rb | 159rbA–C | 68–9 |
| 17va | 159rbC–D | 69–71 |
| 17vb | 159rbD–159vaB | 71–2 |
| 18ra | 159vaB–C | 72–3 |
| 18rb | 159vaC–159vbB | 73–5 |
| 18va | 159vbB–C | 75–6 |
| 18vb | 159vbC–D | 76–7 |
| 19ra | 159vbD–160raB | 77–8 |
| 19rb | 160raB–C | 78–9 |
| 19va | 160raD–160rbA | 80 |
| 19vb | 160rbA–B | 80–1 |
| 20ra | 160rbB–C | 81–2 |
| 20rb | 160rbC–D | 82–3 |
| 20va | 160vaA–B | 83–4 |
| 20vb | 160vaB–C | 84–5 |
| 21ra | 160vaC–160vbA | 85–7 |
| 21rb | 160vbA–C | 87–8 |
| 21va | 160vbC–D | 88–9 |
| 21vb | 160vbD–161raA | 89–90 |
| 22ra | 161raB–C | 90–1 |
| 22rb | 161raC–D | 91–2 |
| 22va | 161raD–161rbB | 92–4 |
| 22vb | 161rbB–161vaA | 94–5 |
| 23ra | 161vaA–B | 95–6 |
| 23rb | 161vaB–C | 96–7 |
| 23va | 161vaC–161vbA | 97–8 |
| 23vb | 161vbA–B | 98–9 |
| 24(male 23)ra | 161vbB–C | 99–101 |
| 24(male 23)rb | 161vbD–162raA | 101–2 |
| 24(male 23)va | 162raA–B | 102–3 |
| 24(male 23)vb | 162raC–D | 103–4 |
| 25ra | 162rbA–B | 104–5 |
| 25rb | 162rbB–D | 105–7 |
| 25va | 162rbD–162vaB | 107–8 |
| 25vb | 162vaB–C | 108–9 |

| Lyons 1531 | Venice 1584 | Paris 1671 |
|:---:|:---:|:---:|
| 26ra | 162vaC–D | 109–10 |
| 26rb | 162vaD–162vbA | 110–11 |
| 26va | 162vbB–C | 111–13 |
| 26vb | 162vbC–163raA | 113–14 |
| | | |
| 27ra | 163raA–B | 114–15 |
| 27rb | 163raB–D | 115–16 |
| 27va | 163raD–163rbB | 116–18 |
| 27vb | 163rbB–C | 118–19 |
| | | |
| 28ra | 163rbD–163vaA | 119–20 |
| 28rb | 163vaA–C | 120–2 |
| 28va | 163vaC–163vbA | 122–3 |
| 28vb | 163vbA–B | 123–4 |
| | | |
| 29ra | 163vbB–C | 124–5 |
| 29rb | 163vbD–164raA | 125–6 |
| 29va | 164raA–B | 126–7 |
| 29vb | 164raB–C | 127–9 |
| | | |
| 30ra | 164raD–164rbA | 129–30 |
| 30rb | 164rbA–B | 130–1 |
| 30va | 164rbC–D | 131–2 |
| 30vb | 164rbD–164vaA | 132–3 |
| | | |
| 31ra | 164vaA–C | 133–5 |
| 31rb | 164vaC–164vbA | 135–6 |
| 31va | 164vbA–D | 136–7 |
| 31vb | 164vbD–165raB | 137–8 |
| | | |
| 32ra | 165raB–C | 138–9 |
| 32rb | 165raC–D | 139–40 |
| 32va | 165raD–165rbA | 140–2 |
| 32vb | 165rbA–B | 142–3 |
| | | |
| 33ra | 165rbC–D | 143–4 |
| 33rb | 165rbD–165vaB | 144–5 |
| 33va | 165vaB–C | 145–6 |
| 33vb | 165vaC–D | 146–50 |
| | | |
| 34ra | 165vbA–B | 150–1 |
| 34rb | 165vbC–D | 151–2 |
| 34va | 165vbD–166raB | 152–3 |
| 34vb | 166raB–D | 154–5 |

| Lyons 1531 | Venice 1584 | Paris 1671 |
|---|---|---|
| 35ra | 166raD–166rbA | 155–6 |
| 35rb | 166rbA–C | 156–7 |
| 35va | 166rbC–D | 157–8 |
| 35vb | 166rbD–166vaB | 158–60 |
| 36ra | 166vaC–D | 160–1 |
| 36rb | 166vaD–166vbB | 161–2 |
| 36va | 166vbB–C | 162–4 |
| 36vb | 166vbD–167raA | 164–5 |
| 37ra | 167raA–D | 165–6 |
| 37rb | 167raD–167rbB | 166–8 |
| 37va | 167rbB–C | 168–9 |
| 37vb | 167rbD–167vaA | 169–70 |
| 38ra | 167vaA–B | 170–1 |
| 38rb | 167vaC–D | 171–2 |
| 38va | 167vaD–167vbA | 172–3 |
| 38vb | 167vbA–B | 173–4 |
| 39ra | 167vbB–D | 174–6 |
| 39rb | 167vbD–168raA | 176–7 |
| 39va | 168raA–C | 177–8 |
| 39vb | 168raC–D | 178–9 |
| 40ra | 168raD–168rbC | 179–80 |
| 40rb | 168rbC–D | 180–2 |
| 40va | 168rbD–168vaB | 182–3 |
| 40vb | 168vaB–C | 183–4 |
| 41ra | 168vaD–168vbA | 184–5 |
| 41rb | 168vbA–C | 185–7 |
| 41va | 168vbC–D | 187–8 |
| 41vb | 168vbD–169raB | 188–9 |
| 42ra | 169raB–C | 189–91 |
| 42rb | 169raD–169rbA | 191–2 |
| 42va | 169rbA–C | 192–3 |
| 42vb | 169rbC–D | 193–4 |
| 43ra | 169rbD–169vaB | 194–5 |
| 43rb | 169vaC–D | 195–7 |
| 43va | 169vaD–169vbB | 197–8 |
| 43vb | 169vbB–C | 198–9 |

| Lyons 1531 | Venice 1584 | Paris 1671 |
|---|---|---|
| 44ra | 169vbD–170raA | 199–201 |
| 44rb | 170raB–C | 201–2 |
| 44va | 170raC–D | 202–3 |
| 44vb | 170rbA–C | 203–4 |
| 45ra | 170rbC–D | 204–5 |
| 45rb | 170rbD–170vaB | 205–6 |
| 45va | 170vaB–C | 206–8 |
| 45vb | 170vaD–170vbD | 208–9 |
| 46ra | 170vbD–171raA | 209–10 |
| 46rb | 171raA–C | 210–11 |
| 46va | 171raC–D | 211–12 |
| 46vb | 171raD–171rbA | 212–14 |
| 47ra | 171rbA–C | 214–15 |
| 47rb | 171rbC–171vaA | 215–16 |
| 47va | 171vaA–B | 216–17 |
| 47vb | 171vaB–D | 217–19 |
| 48ra | 171vaD–171vbA | 219–20 |
| 48rb | 171vbA–C | 220–1 |
| 48va | 171vbC–D | 221–2 |
| 48vb | 172raA–B | 222–3 |
| 49ra | 172raC–D | 223–5 |
| 49rb | 172raD–172rbA | 225–6 |
| 49va | 172rbA–C | 226–7 |
| 49vb | 172rbC–D | 227–8 |
| 50ra | 172rbD–172vaB | 228–30 |
| 50rb | 172vaB–D | 230–1 |
| 50va | 172vaD–172vbA | 231–2 |
| 50vb | 172vbA–C | 232–4 |
| 51ra | 172vbC–D | 234–5 |
| 51rb | 173raA–B | 235–6 |
| 51va | 173raB–D | 236–8 |
| 51vb | 173raD–173rbA | 238–9 |
| 52ra | 173rbB–C | 240–1 |
| 52rb | 173rbC–173vaA | 241–2 |
| 52va | 173vaA–C | 242–4 |
| 52vb | 173vaC–D | 244–5 |

| Lyons 1531 | Venice 1584 | Paris 1671 |
|------------|-------------|------------|
| 53ra | 173vbA–B | 245–7 |
| 53rb | 173vbC–D | 247–8 |
| 53va | 173vbD–174raB | 248–50 |
| 53vb | 174raB–D | 250–1 |
| | | |
| 54ra | 174raD–174rbB | 251–3 |
| 54rb | 174rbB–D | 253–4 |
| 54va | 174rbD–174vaB | 254–6 |
| 54vb | 174vaC–D | 256–7 |
| | | |
| 55ra | 174vaD–174vbA | 257–8 |
| 55rb | 174vbB–D | 259–60 |
| 55va | 174vbD–175raA | 260–1 |
| 55vb | 175raB–C | 261–2 |
| | | |
| 56ra | 175raC–175rbA | 263–4 |
| 56rb | 175rbA–C | 264–6 |
| 56va | 175rbC–D | 266–8 |
| 56vb | 175vaA–B | 268–9 |
| | | |
| 57ra | 175vaC–D | 269–70 |
| 57rb | 175vaD–175vbB | 270–2 |
| 57va | 175vbB–C | 272–3 |
| 57vb | 175vbC–D | 273–4 |
| | | |
| 58ra | 176raA–B | 274–5 |
| 58rb | 176raC–D | 276–7 |
| 58va | 176raD–176rbC | 277–8 |
| 58vb | 176rbC–176vaA | 278–80 |
| | | |
| 59ra | 176vaA–B | 280–1 |
| 59rb | 176vaC–D | 281–2 |
| 59va | 176vaD–176vbA | 282–3 |
| 59vb | 176vbB–C | 283–4 |
| | | |
| 60ra | 176vbC–D | 285–6 |
| 60rb | 176vbD–177raB | 286–7 |
| 60va | 177raB–D | 287–8 |
| 60vb | 177raD–177rbA | 288–9 |
| | | |
| 61ra | 177rbA–B | 289–90 |
| 61rb | 177rbC–D | 290–2 |
| 61va | 177rbD–177vaA | 292–3 |
| 61vb | 177vaA–C | 293–4 |

| Lyons 1531 | Venice 1584 | Paris 1671 |
|:---:|:---:|:---:|
| 62ra | 177vaD–177vbA | 294–5 |
| 62rb | 177vbA–B | 295–6 |
| 62va | 177vbC–D | 296–7 |
| 62vb | 177vbD–178raB | 297–8 |
| 63ra | 178raC–D | 299–300 |
| 63rb | 178raD–178rbB | 300–1 |
| 63va | 178rbB–D | 301–2 |
| 63vb | 178rbD–178vaA | 302–4 |
| 64ra | 178vaA–C | 304–5 |
| 64rb | 178vaC–D | 305–6 |
| 64va | 178vbA–B | 306–7 |
| 64vb | 178vbC–D | 307–8 |
| 65ra | 178vbD–179raB | 308–9 |
| 65rb | 179raB–C | 310–11 |
| 65va | 179raD–179rbA | 311–12 |
| 65vb | 179rbA–B | 312–13 |
| 66ra | 179rbC–179vaA | 313–14 |
| 66rb | 179vaA–B | 314–15 |
| 66va | 179vaC–D | 315–17 |
| 66vb | 179vaD–179vbB | 317–18 |
| 67ra | 179vbB–C | 318–19 |
| 67rb | 179vbD–180raA | 319–20 |
| 67va | 180raA–B | 320–1 |
| 67vb | 180raC–D | 321–2 |
| 68ra | 180raD–180rbA | 323–4 |
| 68rb | 180rbB–C | 324–5 |
| 68va | 180rbD–180vaA | 325–6 |
| 68vb | 180vaA–C | 326–7 |
| 69ra | 180vaC–D | 327–9 |
| 69rb | 180vaD–180vbB | 329–30 |
| 69va | 180vbC–D | 330–1 |
| 69vb | 180vbD–181raB | 331–3 |
| 70ra | 181raB–C | 333–4 |
| 70rb | 181raD–181rbA | 334–5 |
| 70va | 181rbA–C | 335–6 |
| 70vb | 181rbC–D | 336–7 |

| Lyons 1531 | Venice 1584 | Paris 1671 |
|:---:|:---:|:---:|
| 71ra | 181rbD–181vaA | 337–9 |
| 71rb | 181vaB–C | 339–40 |
| 71va | 181vaD–181vbA | 340–1 |
| 71vb | 181vbA–C | 341–2 |
| | | |
| 72ra | 181vbC–D | 342–3 |
| 72rb | 181vbD–182raA | 343–4 |
| 72va | 182raB–C | 345–6 |
| 72vb | 182raC–D | 346–7 |
| | | |
| 73ra | 182rbA–B | 347–8 |
| 73rb | 182rbB–D | 348–9 |
| 73va | 182rbD–182vaA | 349–50 |
| 73vb | 182vaA–C | 350–1 |
| | | |
| 74ra | 182vaC–D | 351–2 |
| 74rb | 182vbA–B | 352–3 |
| 74va | 182vbB–C | 354 |
| 74vb | 182vbC | 354 |

# INDEX

The index is divided into two parts. The first part refers to citations or discussions of primary sources, including not only Durant's own writings and the sources on which he drew but also related texts such as Pierre d'Ailly's *Tractatus super reformatione ecclesiae*, the golden bull of Mende, the *paréage* of Mende, and papal and royal letters. The second part refers to persons, places, and subjects. There are no cross-references from the first part to the second or vice versa, but most authors and a few texts, notably the Bible, appear in both parts. Footnotes are indexed only where there is no entry for the main text or where an entry may be difficult to identify in a note.

## I. TEXTS

# Index of texts

Denifle, H., ed. (*cont.*)
  gegen Bonifaz VIII. und der
  Cardinäle gegen die Colonna', 115
  n.2, 119 n.11
'Die Statuten der Juristen-
  Universität Bologna vom Jahre
  1317–1347', 67 n.45, 70 n.56
*Digesta, see Corpus Iuris Civilis*
*Digna vox, see Codex Iustinianus*
  1.14.4
*Donation of Constantine, see*
  Pseudo-Isidore
Du Boulay, César Egasse, *Historia
  Universitatis Parisiensis*, 8 n.32
Duchesne, André, *Historiae Francorum
  scriptores*, 42 n.42, 45 n.55
*Duo sunt, see* D.96 c.10
Dupuy, Pierre, *Histoire du différend
  d'entre le pape Boniface VIII. et
  Philippes le Bel*, 55 n.1, 56 n.6, 85
  n.35, 287 n.1

Ehrle, F., ed. 'Ein Bruchstück der
  Acten des Concils von Vienne', 115
  n.2, 116 n.5, 290–2 and nn.8–13'

Finke, H., ed. 'Bericht über das
  Pariser Nationalkonzil von 1290 und
  das Auftreten des Kardinals
  Benedikt Gaëtani auf demselben',
  61–2
*Frequens*, 5
*Fundamenta militantis ecclesiae, see*
  VI.1.6.17

*Gallia Christiana*, 37 n.22, 40 n.34, 44
  n.50, 45 n.54, 46 n.58, 69 n.53, 73
  n.6, 75 n.14, 76 n.15, 78 n.23, 84
  n.34, 104 n.1
Gelasius I, *Duo sunt, see* D.96 c.10
*Gesta Romanae aecclesiae contra
  Hildebrandum*, 269 n.41
Gilbert of Tournai, *Collectio de
  scandalis ecclesiae*, 58 nn.12 and 14
Giles of Rome
  *De ecclesiastica potestate*, 121 n.14,
    209, 253
  1.4, 254 n.13
  *De regimine principum*, 121 n.14

*Tractatus contra exemptos*
  3, 254 n.12
  8, 254 n.13
  10, 254 n.13
*Glossa ordinaria* on the Bible, 159 n.83
*Golden bull of Mende*, 22–3, 39–43, 45,
  49, 54, 63–4, 68, 72, 85, 102
  confirmations, 39 n.33, 50–1 and
    n.78
  enforcement and litigation, 47, 51–2,
    71, 76 n.18, 85, 99
  and the *Paréage of Mende*, 87–9, 94,
    108
Gospel, *see* Bible
Gratian, *Decretum, see Corpus Iuris
  Canonici*
*Gravamina ecclesiae Gallicanae*, 57, 146
  n.55, 201 n.115
*Gravamina* of the province of
  Bourges, *see* Ehrle
Gregory I
  *Moralia*, 116–17, 129–30, 155
  *Regula pastoralis*, 155, 167–8 and
    n.98
Gregory VII, *Dictatus Papae*, 278, 289,
  315–16
Gregory IX
  *Liber Extra, see Corpus Iuris Canonici*
  *Registres*
    nos. 902–6, 46 n.60
    no. 1,472, 46 n.59
    no. 1,474, 46 n.59
    no. 1,477, 46 n.59
    no. 1,615, 38 n.25
    no. 3,926, 46 n.60
    no. 4,347, 46 n.59
    no. 4,857, 46 n.60
    no. 4,859, 46 n.60
    no. 5,282, 46 n.60
    no. 5,310, 46 n.60
Gregory X
  *Constitutions*, 70
  *Registres* no. 1,160, 116 n.3

*Haec sancta*, 5, 9, 264 n.32
Henry of Ghent, 'Sermo . . . factus in
  synodo anno Domini
  MᶜCCᶜLXXXVIIᵒ', 158 n.81, 204
  n.123

# Index of texts

## 2. PERSONS, PLACES, AND SUBJECTS

Subjects are identified by small capitals. Secondary authorities are only indexed
in cases bearing directly on the argument of this study and are identified by
italics. To avoid confusion, foreign words appearing as main headings in the
index are not italicized, even though they appear in italics in the text.

# Index of persons, places, and subjects

# Index of persons, places, and subjects

BALAAM OF BOZOR, 131, 296 n.23
Baluze, Etienne, 6, 9 n.34
BAPTISM, 188
BARCELONA, COUNTS OF, 35, 37 n.20, 42
*Barraclough*, G., 1 n.2, 55 n.2, 76 n.18, 261 n.29
BASLE, COUNCIL OF (1431–49), 25, 290, 311 n.18, 318
BASLE COUNCIL OF (1482), 7
*Bäumer*, R., 19 n.75
BAYLE, *see* Marvéjols
Beaucaire, 77 n.20
BEAUCAIRE, SENESCHAL OF, 32 n.2, 47–8, 49 n.71, 51–2, 71–2, 76 n.16, 84 n.34, 85 n.36, 88–9, 91 n.56, 92 n.62, 96, 97–8, 109; *see also* Arnoul de Courfraud, Guy de Rochefort, Gévaudan, JURISDICTION
Beauvais, 67
Bede, 159 n.83
BEGGING, 231–5
BEGUINES, 234 n.40
*Bellone*, E., 10 n.38, 115 n.2, 303 n.46
Benedict XI, pope, 77 n.21, 84 n.33, 140 n.46, 288 n.2, 304 n.51
Benedict XIII, pope, 6, 7 n.20
BENEFICES, 38, 75, 188, 189, 195, 197, 200–1, 233, 234, 235, 239–40, 243–4 and n.70, 291 n.10, 302, 303–4, 312; *see also* ECCLESIASTICAL FINANCES, NEPOTISM, PLURALISM, PROVISIONS
BENEFIT OF CLERGY, 186, 189, 210; *see also* CHURCH AND STATE
Benevent, 99 n.83
*Benson*, R., 1 n.2, 203 n.121
Béraud V de Mercoeur, 47
Béraud VI de Mercoeur, 53 n.90
Béraud VII de Mercoeur, 97 n.74, 310 n.16
Berengar Frédol the Elder, cardinal, 104 n.3
Bernard d'Apcher, dean of Le Puy, 50 nn.73–4 and 76
Bernard VI of Armagnac, 307 n.8
Bernard of Clairvaux, 180 n.7, 226, 227 n.21, 269, 270 n.43, 277
Bernard Durant, canon of Mende and

Agde, 98 n.83
Bernard Gui, 52 n.89
Bernard of Parma, 65
Bernard Saisset, 210, 288
Bernard of Spain the Younger, 53 n.93
Bertrand des Bordes, cardinal, 104–5 nn.3–4
Béziers, 64, 98 n.83
Béziers, bishop of, 53 n.93
BÉZIERS, COUNCIL OF (1255), 57 n.10
BÉZIERS, SCHOOL OF, 65 n.36, 74 n.7
BIBLE, 127, 159, 194, 272, 274 n.51, 279; *see also* OLD TESTAMENT, NEW TESTAMENT, DIVINE LAW
BISHOPS, 55–63, 64 n.34, 77 n.20, 83–5, 115–16, 186 n.19, 187, 188–9, 191, 195 n.75, 196, 197, 198, 234, 236, 288–9
their struggle with the mendicants, 3, 57–63, 84 n.32, 140, 171, 178–9 n.4, 253, 304
*see also* Mende, William Durant the Younger, GALLICANISM, JURISDICTION, ORDER OF THE CHURCH
*Black*, A., 19 n.74
Blanche of Castile, 51 n.81
BLASPHEMY, 138
*Bliemetzrieder*, F. P., 19 n.75
Bodin, Jean, 217 n.2, 257 n.20, 265
BOLOGNA, UNIVERSITY OF, 65, 67 n.45, 74
Bonaventure, 203 n.121
Boniface VIII, pope, 3, 56, 61–3, 73, 78, 79, 80–1, 83–5, 99 n.84, 102, 103, 110–11, 115, 186, 197, 210, 253, 280, 287–8, 290, 304, 309; *see also* William Durant the Younger, CHURCH AND STATE
BOOKS, 186, 194–5, 301 n.39; *see also* EDUCATION
Bordeaux, archbishop of, 84 n.34; *see also* Clement V
Bossuet, Jacques Bénigne, bishop of Meaux, 9, 10 n.36
Bourges, 8
BOURGES, ARCHBISHOP OF, 46, 69 n.53, 291 n.12; *see also* Giles of Rome,

394

# Index of persons, places, and subjects

Simon of Beaulieu
BOURGES, COUNCIL OF (1225), 57 n.8
BOURGES, COUNCIL OF (1276), 66, 76 n.17
BOURGES, COUNCIL OF (1286), 63 n.32
BOURGES, COUNCIL OF (1304), 84 n.34
BOURGES, DEAN OF, 50 n.74
BOURGES, PROVINCE OF, 76–7 n.18, 253, 290–1
BREPHOTROPHIA, 188 n.38, 232 n.28
Brice, Jordan, 6 n.19
Briçonnet, Guillaume, bishop of Meaux, 7
Brioude, 45, 53 n.90; see also Stephen of Brioude
Brittany, 34
Brittany, duchess of, 307 n.8
Brown, E. A. R., 106 n.7, 146 n.56, 283 n.9
Bruno of Olmütz, 58
Brys, J., 134 n.33, 142 n.50, 146 n.56, 152 n.69, 169 n.101, 170 n.102
Buisson, L., 3 n.7, 62 n.30, 146 n.56, 174 n.109, 192 n.59
Burdach, K., 1 n.2
BUREAUCRACY, 68–9, 82, 163, 183, 258–9, 276; see also CENTRALIZATION
BURGUNDIAN LEAGUE, 106 n.7
BURIAL, 58, 187, 188, 198, 258
Buxo (Mende), 75
Bynum, C., 192 n.59

CAESAR, 150
Cahors, 46 n.60
CAHORS, BISHOP OF, 86 n.41
Caillet, L., 10 n.37
Calixtus I, pope, 202 n.117
Calixtus II, pope, 38, 70 n.54
Cambridge History of Medieval Political Thought, 10 n.37
Canilhac, marquis of, 97 n.74
CANILHAC, LORDS OF, 36, 48, 52 n.89, 84 n.33, 97 n.74; see also LOCAL NOBILITY
Canning, J. P., 19 n.74
CANON LAW, 2, 16, 21, 65, 74 n.9, 98 n.83, 120, 122, 135, 142, 151, 160, 164, 169, 189, 195 n.75, 202, 203 n.119, 262–3, 278, 288, 320, 322–3;

see also DIVINE LAW, CONCILIAR CANONS
CANONISTS, 2, 4, 17, 21–2, 39, 126, 204, 277; see also EDUCATION
CANONS, 38, 76 n.17, 85 n.35, 192 n.59, 205, 239–40, 245, 303–4; see also Mende, William Durant the Younger, CATHEDRAL CHAPTERS, ORDER OF THE CHURCH
CAPETIANS, 33, 43; see also KING OF FRANCE
Capranica, cardinal, 6 n.19
CARDINALS, 33 n.4, 104 n.3, 122, 160–1, 170, 196, 200–1, 206 n.135, 221, 243 n.66, 244 n.68, 269, 290–2, 300, 307–8; see also CHURCH OF ROME
CARE OF SOULS, 58, 301, 303; see also REFORM OF THE CHURCH
Carlyle, R. W. and A. J., 10 n.37, 68 n.49, 164 n.92, 208 n.141
CAROLINGIAN EMPIRE, 35
Caron, P. G., 146 n.56
CARTHAGINIANS, 148
Castile, 306
Castrum Durantis, 66
CATHARS, 32 n.2, 43–4, 277; see also HERESY
CATHEDRAL CHAPTERS, 4, 59, 199, 212, 307 n.8; see also CANONS
CATO, 153, 221, 240, 268
'CAUSAE MAIORES', 205–6; see also JURISDICTION
Causse de Sauveterre, 36
Celestine III, pope, 158 n.80
CELIBACY, 187–8, 238, 302; see also CLERGY
CEMETERIES, 187, 312, n.24; see also BURIAL
Cénaret, castle of, 39
CÉNARET, LORDS OF, 39, 76 n.16, 96, 97 n.74; see also Gui de Cénaret, LOCAL NOBILITY
CENTRALIZATION, 23–4, 34, 55–7, 63–4, 80–3, 101–11; see also CHURCH AND STATE, JURISDICTION, BUREAUCRACY
Cesarini, Giuliano, 290
Cévennes, 36, 51, 97 n.75
Chadenet (Mende), 99 n.83

COUNCILS (*cont.*)
  convocation of, 165, 186 n.17, 242,
    282–3
  frequency of, 3, 122, 198–9, 237,
    242–3
  general, 1–4, 115, 117, 119, 125, 157,
    160, 161–3, 170, 186 n.17, 198,
    211–12, 215–16, 236–7, 242–6, 290,
    304; *see also* Basle, Constance,
    Lateran, Lyons, Pavia, Pisa, Trent,
    Vatican, Vienne
  provincial, 3, 59, 117, 119, 134 n.33,
    191, 198–9, 205–6, 236–7, 302; *see
    also* Béziers, Bourges, Orléans,
    Paris, Reims, Rome, Ste
    Geneviève, Toledo
  ecumenical, 259
  papal, 288
  national, 3, 59, 61, 237 n.55
  executive, 106 n.7, 161, 162–3
  legislative, 161, 162–3
  *see also* Vienne, CONCILIAR CANONS,
    CONCILIAR THEORY
COUNSEL, 116, 124–5, 157–61, 163–5,
  168, 170, 215–16, 274, 283, 307–8;
  *see also* CONSENT, DELIBERATION,
  'GOOD MEN', ELDERS, SENATE
COURAGE, 251
COURTRAI, BATTLE OF, 84
CRAFTS, *see* WORK
Crespin, Jean, printer of Lyons, 6, 7–
  8, 9 n.35, 11, 321, 322
Crespin, Jean, martyrologist of
  Geneva, 7, 8 n.27
CRIME, 93, 240–1; *see also*
  ENFORCEMENT
CRISIS, 20, 80–3, 103, 156, 266; *see also*
  DUALISM
CRUSADES, 24, 43–4, 45 n.53, 80–1,
  185, 289, 305–6, 312–14
CULT OF SAINTS, 43
CURIA, *see* CHURCH OF ROME
CURIUS, MARCUS DENTATUS, 220
CUSTOM, 69 n.54, 76 n.17, 135, 155,
  198, 214, 223–4, 229, 246, 249, 261,
  268; *see also* MORES, LAW, ABUSE
CYNICISM, 15, 213–14, 231
Cyprian, 203
Cyprus, 24, 313

Damasus, pope, 138
DANCING, 186; *see also* MANNERS
Dante, 82
DEACONS, 196, 201, 206 n.135
DECREES, 76 n.17, 138–9, 142, 151–2,
  170–1, 185, 260, 264, 268, 270, 277,
  303 n.47; *see also* LAW
DECRETALISTS, 19, 75, 127, 278 n.3,
  281; *see also* EDUCATION
DECRETALS, 120, 122, 142, 158, 186
  n.17, 202, 210 n.153, 271–5; *see also*
  LAW
DECRETISTS, 13 n.46, 19, 75, 127, 159
  n.83, 271 n.47, 278 n.3, 280; *see also*
  EDUCATION
DEFENDERS OF THE CHURCH, 190, 258,
  291 n.10; *see also* CHURCH AND
  STATE
DELIBERATION, 108, 117, 135, 169–70,
  225, 260, 274, 303 n.47; *see also*
  COUNSEL
DEMOCRACY, 13 n.47, 164 n.92, 216,
  217 n.2, 246; *see also* RES PUBLICA
*Dempf, A.*, 10 n.37
DEPOSITION, 61, 141, 187, 188, 206,
  236, 277; *see also* ENFORCEMENT
Descartes, René, 125
*Devic, C. and J.-J. Vaissete*, 32 n.2, 35
  n.11, 36 nn.18–19, 37–8 nn.22–4,
  39 n.33, 40 n.35, 42 n.42, 43–4
  nn.48–9, 50 n.78, 51 n.83, 54 n.94,
  86 n.42
DEVIL, 167–8, 213, 268, 299
DIALECTIC, 74, 127; *see also*
  UNIVERSITIES
DIFFERENCE, 178, 180–3, 184–91, 192,
  206, 226–30, 237–8; *see also*
  HIERARCHY
DIOCESES, *see* BISHOPS
DISCIPLES, 158, 159; *see also* APOSTOLIC
  SUCCESSION
DISPENSATIONS, 2, 56, 67, 135, 157,
  160, 161–3, 165, 168–71, 220, 261,
  264, 297, 307–9
  and the bishop of Mende, 45, 46
    n.58, 52 n.90, 70 n.54, 73 n.6, 77,
    78–9 nn.24–5, 98–9 n.83
  *see also* EXEMPTIONS, IMMUNITIES,
    PRIVILEGES, LIBERTIES, INDULGENCES,

# Index of persons, places, and subjects

# Index of persons, places, and subjects

# Index of persons, places, and subjects

Le Puy, department of, 109 n.15
LE PUY, BISHOP OF, 86 n.41, 253 n.10, 291 n.12
LE PUY, CHURCH OF, 46 n.60, 50 n.73, 77 n.18, 312 n.25
LE PUY, PARÉAGE OF, 86 n.41
LEAGUES OF 1314, 106 n.7, 306
*Lecler, J.*, 1 n.2, 10 n.37, 14, 115 n.2
Lefèvre d'Etaples, Jacques, 7
*Leff, G.*, 1 n.2
LEGISLATION, 119–20, 135–6, 151–2, 160–3, 165–6, 172–5, 194, 211–12, 215–16, 223–4, 225–6, 228–30, 260, 264; *see also* COUNCILS, JURISDICTION, LAW, SOVEREIGNTY
Leo I, pope, 139 n.42, 156, 166
Leo IX, pope, 36
LEPERS, 188 n.38, 232
LERIDA, UNIVERSITY OF, 99 n.83
LÈSE MAJESTÉ, 23, 92
LIBERTIES, 9, 40, 43, 50, 76 n.17, 135, 173, 174, 261, 306; *see also* JURISDICTION, LAW
LIBERTY, 22, 40, 42, 102, 105, 111, 269, 276, 289, 320; *see also* EQUALITY, RES PUBLICA
LIMOGES, BISHOP OF, 86 n.41, 253 n.10, 291 n.12
LIMOGES, VISCOUNTY OF, 307 n.8
LITURGY, 70, 197–8, 301 and n.42; *see also* MASS
LOCAL NOBILITY, 23–4, 33, 36–9, 42–3, 47–8, 53 n.91, 71, 76, 83–4, 95–8, 101, 105, 241 n.62, 306, 311; *see also* William Durant the Younger, Mende, Gévaudan, Anduze, Apcher, Canilhac, Cénaret, Chirac, Florac, Lordet, Mercoeur, Mostuéjols, Peyre, Randon, Servissac, Tournel, CHURCH AND STATE
LOCAL PATRIOTISM, 33–4, 42, 47 and n.63, 48, 49–50, 72, 96 n.73, 109 n.15; *see also* Gévaudan, CENTRALIZATION
LORDET, LORDS OF, 34, 47 n.63; *see also* Albert de Lordet
Lot, 31–2

Louis the Bavarian, emperor, 312
Louis VII, king of France, 22, 39, 41, 42, 45 n.55, 88 n.45, 101, 104
Louis VIII, king of France, 47
Louis IX, king of France, 39 n.33, 49, 50, 51, 60, 185, 211 n.153
Louis X, king of France, 85 n.36, 306, 307
Louis XI, king of France, 39 n.33
Louis XIV, king of France, 8, 82
Louis XV, king of France, 109
LOVE, 150, 178, 179–80, 181, 182–3, 184, 218, 219–20, 240, 246; *see also* HIERARCHY, PUBLIC AND PRIVATE
LOVE-POTIONS, 185 n.14
Lozère, department of, 109 n.15; *see also* Gévaudan
LUCIUS I, POPE, 202 n.117
*Luscombe, D. E.*, 183 n.10
LUST, 238, 300
Luther, Martin, 128, 200, 224 n.16, 257 n.21, 261 n.29, 267; *see also* PROTESTANT REFORMATION
LUXURY, 153, 221 n.9
Lyons, 8, 39 n.33, 50 n.74, 74 n.7
LYONS, SECOND COUNCIL OF (1274), 56, 58, 66

Macaulay, T. B., 255
MACEDONIUS, 169
*McIlwain, C. H.*, 10 n.37, 68 n.49
*McNeill, J. T.*, 1 n.2, 11 n.40
MAGIC, 185 n.14; *see also* LAITY
Maguelonne, bishop of, 86
*Maier, A.*, 6–7 n.20
*Maitland, F. W.*, 320 n.5
MANNERS, 185 n.12, 186–7, 189, 201; *see also* EATING, DRINKING, CLOTHING, DANCING, SINGING, MUSIC, TAVERNS, HUNTING, DUELS, TOURNAMENTS, LAITY, CLERGY, REFORM OF THE CHURCH
Marca, Pierre de, 8 n.32
MARCELLINUS, POPE, 154, 202 n.117
Marcellus I, pope, 202 n.117
Marie of Bourbon, 313
Marie of Valois, 311
Marino Sanudo, 313

# Index of persons, places, and subjects

Marongiu, A., 13, 164 n.92
MARRIED CLERICS, 85 n.36, 185, 186,
187–8, 210, 238, 240, 258; see also
CHURCH AND STATE, REFORM OF THE
CHURCH
Marrone, J., 58 n.13, 60 n.19, 80 n.26,
140 nn.44 and 46, 158 n.80, 159
n.83, 174 n.109, 192 n.60, 203
n.121, 304 n.51
Marsiglio of Padua, 14 n.53, 82
Martin IV, pope, 54 n.95, 58, 66, 69
n.53
Martin V, pope, 237 n.55
Martin, V., 10 n.37, 154 n.72, 168
n.98
Marvéjols, 32 n.2, 35 n.11, 48, 51
n.81, 52 n.89, 53 n.91, 77 n.21, 84
n.33, 90, 96 n.73
MARVÉJOLS, BAYLE OF, 71 n.59, 90, 96
n.73
MARVÉJOLS, COURT OF, 84 n.33, 97
n.74
MARVÉJOLS, JUDGE OF, 90
MASS, 70, 186, 187, 197–8, 301, 303;
see also LITURGY
Massif Central, 31
Matthew Orsini, cardinal, 104 n.3
MAURICE, EMPEROR, 145
MEASURES, 230–1
MEAUX, BISHOP OF, 7, 9
MEAUX, REFORM CIRCLE OF, 7
Mediterranean, 47, 64
Meinecke, F., 320 n.5
MELCHIADES, POPE, 202 n.117
MELCHISEDEK, 204 n.124; see also
KINGSHIP
MEMORY, 25, 81, 249 and n.2, 256–7,
265–7, 275; see also HISTORY, TIME
MEN, 192–3; see also LAITY
Mende, 31–3, 35, 37, 39, 42, 49, 52
n.89, 53 n.91, 70 n.54, 73, 75, 90,
104 n.3, 259; see also Gévaudan
Mende, cathedral of, 36, 39, 40 n.35,
95
Mende, College of All Souls of, 97
n.76
Mende, synagogue of, 97 n.76
MENDE, BISHOP OF, 23–4, 31–54, 69–
72, 101–10

his jurisdiction, 22–3, 35–6, 38, 40–
5, 48, 50, 52 nn.84–5, 63, 71–2, 87,
92, 105
his vassals, 36, 39, 41, 44, 47, 50, 54
n.95, 70 n.54, 76 n.16, 92, 306
his lands and possessions, 23, 31 n.2,
36, 43, 51, 85 n.36, 91–5, 104
his finances, 38, 39, 44–6, 47, 49, 51,
76–7, 99 n.84, 312
and the city of Mende, 35, 43 and
n.46, 49, 51 nn.79–80, 54 n.95
and the papacy, 33, 38, 45, 46, 50
52–3, 70 n.54, 75–7, 84, 101–4
and the king of France, 22, 33–4,
39–42, 43, 45, 47–9, 51–2, 63–4,
71–2, 77, 84, 101–10
and the local nobility, 23–4, 35–9,
42–3, 45–6, 47, 49, 50, 71, 72
and the mendicants, 52–3, 63, 69
n.53, 77
see also Aldebert de Peyre, Odilo de
Mercoeur, Stephen of Brioude,
William Durant the Elder, William
Durant the Younger, William de
Peyre, Beaucaire, Gévaudan, KING
OF FRANCE, PAPACY, BISHOPS,
JURISDICTION, ORDER OF THE
CHURCH
MENDE, CHURCH OF, 36–7, 39, 40, 45,
54, 86, 89, 104, 306, 312
diocese, 23, 31, 35 n.11, 36, 38 n.24,
46, 50, 51 n.80, 55, 69, 70, 72, 75,
89, 99, 311, 312 n.24
canons, 37–8, 43, 46, 49–50, 52–3
n.90, 69, 75, 76 n.17, 85 n.35, 86,
95, 98–9 and n.83, 310 n.15, 311
n.21
vicar general, 63 n.32
archdeacon, 36, 75, 310 n.15
provost, 36, 63 n.32, 158 n.79, 312
n.25
officialis, 105 n.4
hebdomadarius, 312 n.25
sacristan, 41 n.36, 52 n.88
MENDE, CITIZENS OF, 34, 43, 49, 51, 54
n.95
MENDE, NOTARIES OF, 70 n.54
MENDE, SYNDICS OF, 51 n.79
MENDICANTS, 3, 52–3, 57–63, 77, 84

# Index of persons, places, and subjects

n.32, 121, 127, 140, 141, 171,
180 n.7, 192, 232–4, 253 n.12, 302,
304; *see also* RELIGIOUS ORDERS,
BISHOPS
Mercadier, bailli of Gévaudan, 48, 49
n.71
MERCOEUR, LORDS OF, 24, 32 n.2, 36,
37, 44, 47, 53 n.90, 96, 97 n.74, 310
n.16; *see also* Béraud de Mercoeur,
Odilo de Mercoeur, LOCAL
NOBILITY
*Merzbacher, F.*, 10 n.37
METROPOLITANS, 196, 198, 211; *see also*
ORDER OF THE CHURCH
MEYRUEIS, VIGUIER OF, 71 n.59, 90
*Michaud-Quantin, P.*, 58 n.12, 60 n.19,
179 n.4, 183–4 nn.10–11, 204
n.122, 283 n.9
MIDDLING POWERS, 63, 82, 231, 254,
269; *see also* BISHOPS
*Miethke, J.*, 58 n.12, 60 n.19, 80 n.26,
208 n.141
MILLAU, VISCOUNTY OF, 43 n.47, 45
n.53
'MILVUS', 300 n.36
Mirepoix, 98 n.83
*Mitteis, H.*, 55 n.2
MODERNISM CRISIS, 16
*Moeller, B.*, 261 n.29
*Mollat, G.*, 55 n.2, 56 n.3, 115 n.2,
116 n.5
*Momigliano, A.*, 249 n.2, 257 n.19
MONARCHY, 56, 82, 157, 168, 216, 222;
*see also* CHURCH AND STATE
MONASTERIES, 173, 174, 190–1, 201,
232 n.28, 235, 236 n.53; *see also*
MONKS AND MONASTICISM
MONEY, 44, 46 n.60, 52 n.84, 81, 85
n.36, 92 n.61, 107 n.10, 121, 187,
188–9, 209 n.147, 230–1, 240, 311;
*see also* UTILITY, ECCLESIASTICAL
FINANCES
MONKS AND MONASTICISM, 1 n.2, 121
n.16, 173–4, 186 n.19, 190–1, 198,
201, 229–30, 234 n.40, 260, 302; *see
also* ABBOTS AND ABBESSES,
MONASTERIES, PRIORIES, EXEMPTIONS,
RELIGIOUS ORDERS
Mont Lozère, 32

Montagnes de la Margeride, 32
Montfort, count of, 46 n.60
MONTPELLIER, UNIVERSITY OF, 65 n.36,
74 n.7
Monts d'Aubrac, 32
*Moore, R. I.*, 55 n.2
MORALITY, 15, 130, 231, 236, 269, 300,
303–4, 320; *see also* MORES
MORES, 132–3, 213–15, 228–9, 248–9,
256–7, 260–7, 268, 270, 275; *see also*
HIERARCHY, CONSCIENCE,
INTENTION, TIME, CUSTOM, LAW
*Morrall, J. B.*, 18 n.74, 164 n.93
MORTAL SINS, 197, 200, 237, 299–300;
*see also* CORRUPTION OF THE
CHURCH, AMBITION, AVARICE, ENVY,
GLUTTONY, HATE, LUST, LUXURY,
NEGLIGENCE, PRIDE, SLOTH
MOSES, 158, 159, 172; *see also*
EXAMPLES
MOSTUÉJOLS, LORDS OF, 37; *see also*
LOCAL NOBILITY
MOTETS, 198, 301
*Müller, E.*, 10 n.38, 11 n.40, 14, 15,
16, 115–16 nn.2–6, 121 n.14, 186
n.17, 288–94 nn. *passim*, 303–4 and
nn.47–51
*Mundy, J. H.*, 39 n.33, 185 n.15, 311
n.18
*Murray, A.*, 1 n.2, 57 n.7
MUSIC, 118, 186, 198, 301

Napoleon Orsini, cardinal, 104 n.3
Narbonne, 69 n.53
NARBONNE, CHURCH OF, 67, 85 n.36
NARBONNE, VISCOUNTS OF, 37 n.20
*National Union Catalog*, 9 n.35
NATURAL LAW, 130, 132–3, 134, 192,
229, 248–9, 256–7, 260, 263–4, 270,
296 n.23, 297, 307–9; *see also* DIVINE
LAW
NATURE, 180, 181, 182, 219, 238, 320;
*see also* HIERARCHY
NAVARRE, COLLEGE OF, 7
NECESSITY, 20, 83, 110, 111, 169, 171,
173, 190, 234, 235, 258–9, 260–1,
267, 307; *see also* UTILITY
NEGLIGENCE, 300 n.36, 301
*Neiske, F.*, 1 n.2

# Index of persons, places, and subjects

PISA, COUNCIL OF (1409), 243 n.65
Pithou, Pierre, 7
Pius I, pope, 202 n.117
Plaisians, *see* Jacques of Plaisians,
    William of Plaisians
Plato, 149, 218, 221, 252
PLURALISM, 196–7, 200–1, 301, 302
  and the bishop of Mende, 52 n.90,
    67, 70 n.54, 75, 77, 98–9 n.83, 104–
    5 nn.4–5
  *see also* CORRUPTION OF THE CHURCH
POISSY, TREATY OF, 306 n.7
POITIERS, CHURCH OF, 60
POLICE, 236–7, 239; *see also*
    ENFORCEMENT
POLITICAL AUGUSTINIANISM, 81
Pompidou, 71 n.57
Poncet le Preux, printer of Paris, 8
    n.28
Pons Durant, canon of Mende and
    Mirepoix, 98 n.83
THE POOR, 188, 301 n.43
*Porée, C.*, 31–54 nn. *passim*, 85–6
    nn.38–41, 87 n.45
*Posch, A.*, 10 n.38, 11 n.40, 13–14, 15
    nn.59 and 62, 16, 121 n.14, 293
    n.17, 297 n.27
POSITIVE LAW, 269
POSSESSION, *see* PROPERTY
*Post, G.*, 3 n.7, 18 n.74, 67 n.44, 119
    n.11, 139 n.42, 146 n.56, 164 n.93,
    283 n.9
POSTULATIONS, 304
POTESTAS ABSOLUTA, 62–3; *see also*
    ABSOLUTE POWER, SOVEREIGNTY
POTESTAS IURISDICTIONIS, 159 n.83,
    203–4, 215, 293; *see also*
    JURISDICTION
POTESTAS ORDINATA, 62–3; *see also*
    ORDER OF THE CHURCH,
    JURISDICTION
POTESTAS ORDINIS, 159 n.83, 203–4,
    215; *see also* HIERARCHY
POVERTY, *see* APOSTOLIC WAY OF LIFE,
    MENDICANTS
POWER, *see* HIERARCHY, JURISDICTION,
    ABSOLUTE POWER, SOVEREIGNTY
POWERS THAT BE, *see* RESISTANCE,
    CHURCH AND STATE

PRELATES, 121 n.16, 122, 192, 206
    n.135, 300; *see also* BISHOPS
PREROGATIVE OF POWER, 160, 161, 167,
    245; *see also* EXECUTIVE
'PRESIDENTS OF THE MONARCHY', 157,
    166, 222
'PRESIDENTS OF THE SPIRITUAL AND
    TEMPORAL POWER', 167, 168, 222
PRIDE, 156, 300
PRIESTS, 58, 130, 131, 159–60, 169,
    170, 187, 191, 201, 232, 233, 274
    n.52, 296 n.23; *see also* ORDER OF
    THE CHURCH
PRIMATES, 211; *see also* ORDER OF THE
    CHURCH
PRIMITIVE CHURCH, 159, 221; *see also*
    APOSTOLIC SUCCESSION
PRIORIES, 205, 235
  in the Gévaudan, 33, 37, 38 n.27, 53
    n.93, 70 n.54, 84 n.33, 95–6, 105
    n.5
  *see also* MONKS AND MONASTICISM
PRISON, 90, 96 and n.73, 240–1; *see
    also* ENFORCEMENT
PRIVATE, *see* PUBLIC AND PRIVATE
PRIVILEGES, 2, 3, 42, 61–2, 135, 151,
    157, 167, 171, 173, 174, 236, 261,
    264, 288 n.2; *see also* LAW
'PROBI HOMINES', *see* 'GOOD MEN'
PROCEDURE, 65, 68, 206, 304
PROCESSIONS, 187
PROCURATIONS 78 n.24, 197 n.90; *see
    also* ECCLESIASTICAL FINANCES
PROCURATORS, 188 n.34
*Prodi, P.*, 149 n.63
PROGRESS, 320; *see also* TIME
PROMOTIONS, 150, 188 n.31, 195 and
    n.75, 200, 301 n.39; *see also*
    BENEFICES, EDUCATION
PROPAGANDA, 59
PROPERTY, 35, 40–1, 91–5, 105, 106–7,
    182, 187, 188–9, 221; *see also* PUBLIC
    AND PRIVATE
PROPHETS, 133, 138, 268
PROPRIETARY CHURCH, 36–7
PROSTITUTION, 187 n.27, 188 n.39
PROTESTANT REFORMATION, 7, 8, 16, 18,
    128, 137, 200, 230, 238, 261 n.29,
    276, 320

# Index of persons, places, and subjects

# Index of persons, places, and subjects

# Index of persons, places, and subjects

Tierney, B., 3, 4 n.12, 10 n.38, 11
n.40, 13, 15, 16, 17, 18–20, 60 n.19,
62 n.30, 75 n.10, 108 n.12, 123, 141
n.47, 142 n.50, 144 n.54, 159 n.83,
161 n.86, 168 n.98, 203–4 nn.121–
2, 222 n.14, 279 n.4, 281 n.7, 283
n.9, 317, 319, 320 n.5
TIME, 81–3, 103, 106–10, 124–5, 215–
16, 226, 242–3, 246, 249, 276, 319–
20; see also HISTORY, MEMORY,
ANACHRONISM, NOVELTY,
ANTIQUITY, MORES, END OF THE
WORLD
TITHE, 234; see also ECCLESIASTICAL
FINANCES
TOLEDO, COUNCILS OF, 116, 125, 185,
207
TONSURE, 186
Torquebiau, P., 10 n.38, 11 n.40, 13,
15, 16, 174 n.109, 297 n.27
TOULOUSE, COUNTS OF, 43–4, 45 n.53,
47, 48
TOULOUSE, UNIVERSITY OF, 65 n.36, 74
n.9, 98 n.83
TOURNAMENTS, 187 n.24; see also
MANNERS
TOURNEL, LORDS OF, 32 n.2, 36, 37, 38
n.27, 42, 44, 46, 47, 48, 49, 50, 54
n.95, 76 n.16; see also Aldebert de
Tournel, Heracle de Tournel,
Odilo de Tournel, LOCAL NOBILITY
Tramezino, Michele, printer of
Venice, 8
TRANSLATION, 181, 183, 214–15, 323–4
TREASON, 92
TRENT, COUNCIL OF (1545–63), 7, 8,
128, 303
TRINITY, 199
TRUTH, 61, 110, 124–8, 157–8, 175,
214, 223–30, 232, 241, 246, 268,
275, 280–3; see also REASON, CHRIST
Tulle, abbot of, 54 n.95

Ullmann, W., 10 n.37, 17–18, 62 n.30,
164 n.92, 183 n.10, 319, 320 n.5
ULPIAN, 170
ULTRAMONTANISM, 16
UNITY, see CONCORD
'UNIVERSITAS', 181

UNIVERSITIES, 59, 61–2, 127, 194–5,
241, 301 n.39; see also Avignon,
Bologna, Lerida, Montpellier,
Orange, Orléans, Paris, Toulouse,
EDUCATION, REASON,
SCHOLASTICISM, THEOLOGY,
PHILOSOPHY, DIALECTIC,
JURISPRUDENCE
URBAN, POPE, 138
Urban II, pope, 37 n.22, 56 n.3
Urban IV, pope, 52 n.88, 53, 104 n.2,
193 n.64
Urban V, pope, 33
Urban VIII, pope, 66
Urbania, 66
USURY, 188 n.39, 209 n.147, 230, 233,
258; see also MONEY
UTILITY, and law, 165 n.95, 166, 169,
171, 172, 173, 175–6, 264, 279; see
also DISPENSATIONS, NECESSITY
and society, 108–10, 149, 218, 220–
1, 226–30, 231–2; see also WORK, RES
PUBLICA
Uzès, bishop of, 77 n.21
UZÈS, VIGUIER OF, 71 n.59, 90

VACANCIES, 69 n.53, 122, 196, 301,
306; see also ORDER OF THE CHURCH
Vaissete, J.-J., see Devic
VALENCE, CHURCH OF, 46 n.60
VALENTINIAN, EMPEROR, 167
Valerius Maximus, 123, 148, 150
n.66, 280
Valla, Lorenzo, 264
VALUE, 230–1, 239–40
VATICAN COUNCIL, FIRST (1869–70),
10, 16
VATICAN LIBRARY, 7
Velay, 32 n.2
VELAY, BAILLI OF, 96
Venice, 8 nn.30–1
Vereecke, L., 10 n.38, 13, 115 n.2
Vermandois, 306
VICAR OF CHRIST, 80, 208
VIENNE, COUNCIL OF (1311–12), 1–2, 3,
4–5, 81, 83, 111, 115–16, 159 n.83,
163, 244, 287–93, 299–300, 303–4,
305; see also William Durant the
Younger, Clement V, COUNCILS

414

# Index of persons, places, and subjects

William Durant the Younger (*cont.*)
his style of argument, 20, 117–19,
122–8, 139–40, 142–3, 144, 177–8,
217, 228–9, 241–2, 257–61, 265,
283–4, 323–4
his demand for general councils, 1–
2, 4, 10, 24, 25, 118–19, 122, 125,
135, 160–6, 171, 198, 203, 206–7,
211–12, 215–16, 217, 242–3, 246,
247, 255, 266–7, 271, 274 n.52,
275–6, 279, 280–4, 302, 315, 317,
318–19
his demand to reform papal
finances, 2, 122, 243–6, 279, 281,
302
his demand to reform canonries, 38,
76 n.17, 85 n.35, 239–40, 245, 291,
303–4
his intention, 4, 20, 117, 212–16,
246, 253–5, 275–6, 281–4, 292–3,
303–4, 309, 316–17
his influence, 4–10, 12 n.42, 199
n.103, 237 n.55, 290–3, 303–4
interpretations of his thought, 10–
16, 20–2, 73 n.5, 123, 144, 177, 184,
212–13, 246, 253–5, 284, 290, 297,
303–4, 316–17, 319
*see also* Mende, CONCILIAR THEORY,
HIERARCHY, RES PUBLICA,
CORRUPTION OF THE CHURCH, ORDER
OF THE CHURCH, REFORM OF THE
CHURCH, LAW, JURISDICTION,
CHURCH AND STATE
William Durant of Cessone, canon of
Mende, rector of the university of
Toulouse, 98–9 n.83
William Durant, canon of St Mary of
Cassan, 98 n.83

William of Mâcon, bishop of
Amiens, 159 n.83
William le Maire, bishop of Angers,
116
William of Nogaret, 76 n.16, 96 n.71,
104 n.3
William III de Peyre, bishop of
Mende (*c.* 1109–51), 36 n.18, 38
n.24
William IV de Peyre, bishop of
Mende (*c.* 1187–1222), 36 n.18, 43–
4, 45, 46 n.58
William de Peyre (*c.* 1308), 97 n.74
William of Plaisians, 34, 41, 85, 86
n.40, 87, 97 n.75, 104 n.3, 105, 204
n.124
William Randon of Châteauneuf, 77
nn.20–1, 97 n.74
William Rufus, hebdomadarius of
Mende, 312 n.25
William of St Amour, 159 n.83
WITNESSES, 206
WOMEN, 186, 187–8, 190, 192–3, 196,
209 n.147, 227; *see also* LAITY
WORK, 153, 197–8, 221, 227–8, 231–4,
235, 240, 301 n.39; *see also* UTILITY
WORLD, *see* HIERARCHY, END OF THE
WORLD

XENODOCHIA, 188 n.38

Zamometic, Andrea, 7
Zepherinus, pope, 202 n.117
Zosimus, pope, 138, 260
*Zuckerman*, C., 18 n.73, 60 n.19, 80
n.26
Zurich, 7
Zwingli, Huldrych, 7

# Cambridge studies in medieval life and thought
## Fourth series

**DATE DUE**

| | | | |
|---|---|---|---|
| | | | |
| | | | |
| | | | |
| | | | |
| | | | |
| | | | |
| | | | |
| | | | |
| | | | |
| | | | |
| | | | |
| | | | |
| | | | |
| | | | |
| | | | |
| | | | |
| | | | |
| | | | |

HIGHSMITH 45-220